CONTROLLING IMMIGRATION

CONTROLLING IMMIGRATION

A Comparative Perspective

Fourth Edition

Edited by
James F. Hollifield
Philip L. Martin
Pia M. Orrenius
François Héran

Stanford University Press
Stanford, California

Stanford University Press
Stanford, California

Printed in the United States of America on acid-free, archival-quality paper

Library of Congress Cataloging-in-Publication Data

Names: Hollifield, James Frank, 1954– editor. | Martin, Philip L., 1949– editor. | Orrenius, Pia M., editor. | Héran Haen, François, editor.
Title: Controlling immigration : a comparative perspective / edited by James F. Hollifield, Philip L. Martin, Pia M. Orrenius, and François Héran.
Description: Fourth edition. | Stanford, California : Stanford University Press, 2022. | Includes bibliographical references and index.
Identifiers: LCCN 2021054182 (print) | LCCN 2021054183 (ebook) | ISBN 9781503631380 (cloth) | ISBN 9781503631663 (paperback) | ISBN 9781503631670 (ebook)
Subjects: LCSH: Emigration and immigration—Government policy—Cross-cultural studies. | Immigrants—Government policy—Cross-cultural studies. | Human rights—Cross-cultural studies.
Classification: LCC JV6271 .C66 2022 (print) | LCC JV6271 (ebook) | DDC 325/.1—dc23/ eng/20220327
LC record available at https://lccn.loc.gov/2021054182
LC ebook record available at https://lccn.loc.gov/2021054183

Cover photo: US-Mexico international border, Border Field State Park, San Diego, California. Tony Webster | Flickr. CC BY 2.0 License
Typeset by Newgen in Minion 10/14

Contents

Preface

This book was launched in 1990 at the Center for US-Mexican Studies at the University of California at San Diego (UCSD) as part of a National Science Foundation research project, under the direction of Wayne A. Cornelius, Philip L. Martin, and James F. Hollifield, comparing national efforts to manage migration. National studies of migration data and control systems that grew out of the NSF project were first published in 1994 by Stanford University Press; a second edition of the book appeared in 2004, and a third in 2014. This fourth edition continues the effort to use systematic, cross-national research to examine the gap between the goals and outcomes of immigration policies in major immigrant-receiving countries. A generation of scholars and students has wrestled with this question, which continues to drive research agendas in the multidisciplinary field of migration studies. We hope that the fourth edition will shed new light on the dilemmas of immigration control and help to advance the comparative study of immigration policy.

The fourth edition is divided into five parts, including (1) an introduction that gives an overview of the dilemmas of immigration control, followed by studies of (2) nations of immigrants in which immigration is part of the founding national ideal, (3) countries of immigration where immigration plays an important role in social and economic development but was not part of the process of nation-building, (4) latecomers to immigration—countries that once sent migrants abroad but in the past few decades made the transition from sending to receiving societies—including a new chapter on Greece and Turkey, and (5) the European Union and regional migration governance. Each country study is followed by one or more commentaries by scholars and policymakers who offer a critique and, in some cases, an alternative interpretation of policy developments.

Our work has benefited from the input of migration scholars and students from around the globe. The workshop for the second edition was hosted by the Center for Comparative Immigration Studies at UCSD. The third conference was organized by the John Goodwin Tower Center for Political Studies at Southern Methodist University (SMU) in conjunction with the Federal Reserve Bank of Dallas. The fourth conference, the basis for this edition, was again organized by the Tower Center at SMU, co-sponsored by the Institut Convergences Migrations, and hosted by the Collège de France. We are grateful to all who participated in this conference and to the staff of the Tower Center and the Collège de France for their invaluable administrative support. The project was underwritten by the Marian Tower International Conference Fund of the Tower Center at SMU, by grants from the Institut Convergences Migrations, and by the Collège de France. The editors and contributing authors are solely responsible for the information and views presented in this book, which do not necessarily represent those of the underwriters.

Special thanks go to Nicole Rafidi, assistant to the Director of the Tower Center, for her tireless work on the project, and to Alan Harvey, Director of Stanford University Press, and his colleagues. Without their extraordinary patience, skill, and support, the fourth edition might never have seen the light of day. To them we are deeply grateful.

James F. Hollifield, Philip L. Martin,
Pia M. Orrenius, and *François Héran,*
January 2022

Contributors

Fiona B. Adamson is a professor of international relations at SOAS, University of London. Her published work has appeared in leading journals in international relations as well as in a number of edited volumes. She is a co-investigator in the European Union Horizon 2020 research project Migration Governance and Asylum Crises (MAGYC) and is a co-convenor of the London Migration Research Group (LMRG). She holds a BA from Stanford University and an MA, MPhil, and PhD from Columbia University. She has held research fellowships at Harvard and Stanford Universities as well as at Humboldt University, Berlin, and the University of Basel, Switzerland.

Jean Beaman is an associate professor of sociology at the University of California, Santa Barbara, and associate editor of the journal *Identities: Global Studies in Culture and Power*. She is author of *Citizen Outsider: Children of North African Immigrants in France* (University of California Press, 2017), as well as numerous articles and book chapters. Her current research is on suspect citizenship and belonging, anti-racist mobilization, and activism against police violence in France. She received her PhD in sociology from Northwestern University. Her Twitter handle is @jean23bean.

Rut Bermejo Casado is a lecturer in politics at Rey Juan Carlos University in Madrid. Her publications on border controls and immigration policies include "Política migratoria y fronteras: La gestión de la inmigración mediante agencias," in *Fronteras en movimiento: Migraciones en el contexto del euromediterráneo* (2012); "El proceso de institucionalización de la cooperación en la gestión operativa de las fronteras externas de la UE," in *Revista CIDOB d'Afers Internacionals* (2010); and "Migration and Security in the EU: Back to Fortress Europe?," in the *Journal of Contemporary European Research* (2009). Her current research deals with immigration politics and policy design in Spain and the European Union.

Grete Brochmann is a professor of sociology and head of the Department of Sociology and Human Geography at the University of Oslo. She has published many books and articles on international migration, sending- and receiving-country perspectives, EU policies, and welfare state dilemmas, as well as historical studies on immigration. She has been a visiting scholar in Brussels, Berkeley, and Boston. In 2002, she held the Willy Brandt Visiting Professorship in Malmö, Sweden, and she was recently head of a governmental commission on international migration and the Norwegian welfare model.

Erin Aeran Chung is the Charles D. Miller Associate Professor of East Asian Politics in the Department of Political Science at the Johns Hopkins University. She has been a Mansfield Foundation US-Japan Network for the Future Program Scholar, an SSRC Abe Fellow at the University of Tokyo and Korea University, an advanced research fellow at Harvard University's Weatherhead Center for International Affairs Program on US-Japan Relations, and a Japan Foundation fellow at Saitama University. She is the author of *Immigration and Citizenship in Japan* (Cambridge University Press, 2010; Japanese translation, Akashi Shoten, 2012) and *Immigrant Incorporation in East Asian Democracies* (Cambridge University Press, 2020). Most recently, she was awarded a five-year grant from the Academy of Korean Studies to support the completion of her third book project, on citizenship, social capital, and racial politics in the Korean diaspora.

Gianni D'Amato is a professor at the University of Neuchâtel and the director of the Swiss Forum for Migration and Population Studies. He is also the director of the National Center of Competence in Research for Migration and Mobility Studies and a member of the Expert Council on Integration and Migration for the government of the Federal Republic of Germany. His research interests are focused on citizenship, human mobility, populism, and the history of migration. His publications include a co-edited volume titled *Critical Mobilities* (Routledge, 2013) and "Monitoring Immigrant Integration in Switzerland" (with Christian Suter) in *Monitoring Integration in Europe* (Netherlands Institute for Social Research/SCP, 2012).

Antje Ellermann is a professor of political science and the founding director of the Centre for Migration Studies at the University of British Columbia, Vancouver. Her research focuses on the politics of migration and citizenship in liberal democracies. She is the author of *The Comparative Politics of Immigration: Policy Choices in Germany, Canada, Switzerland, and the United States* (Cambridge University Press, 2021) and *States Against Migrants: Deportation in Germany and the United States* (Cambridge University Press, 2009). She serves on the editorial board of the *Journal of Ethnic and Migration Studies*.

Alan Gamlen is a professor in the School of Regulation and Global Governance and the College of Asia and the Pacific at The Australian National University, a research affiliate at Oxford University, and a high-level adviser to the International Organization for Migration, part of the United Nations system. He has co-edited several books, including *Migration and Global Governance* and *Diasporas Reimagined*, as well as special issues of journals. He is the founding editor-in-chief of the journal *Migration Studies*, published by Oxford University Press, and co-editor of the Bristol University Press book series Global Migration and Social Change (with Nando Sigona). His book *Human Geopolitics: States, Emigrants, and the Rise of Diaspora Institutions* (Oxford University Press, 2019), won the Distinguished Book Award for Best Book on Ethnicity, Nationalism and Migration from the International Studies Association.

Blanca Garcés-Mascareñas is a senior research fellow and research coordinator at CIDOB (Barcelona Centre for International Affairs). She received a PhD cum laude in social sciences from the University of Amsterdam and a BA in history and anthropology from the University of Barcelona. In her book *Markets, Citizenship and Rights* (2012), she analyzed the extent to which different political contexts (Spain and Malaysia) lead to different immigration policies. In the book *Integration Processes and Policies in Europe* (2014), written with Rinus Penninx, she proposes a heuristic model to study integration processes and policies. She is a member of the European network IMISCOE and of the editorial board of the *Migration Politics Journal*.

Andrew Geddes is a professor of migration studies and the director of the Migration Policy Centre at the European University Institute (EUI). Recent publications include *The Politics of Migration and Immigration in Europe*, co-authored with Peter Scholten (Sage, 2016); *The Dynamics of Regional Migration Governance*, co-edited with Marcia Vera Espinoza, Leila Hadj-Abdou, and Leiza Brumat (Edward Elgar, 2019); "A Rising Tide? The Salience of Immigration and the Rise of Anti-Immigration Political Parties in Western Europe," with James Dennison (*Political Quarterly*, Jan.-Mar. 2019); and *Governing Migration Beyond the State* (Oxford University Press, 2021). Prior to joining EUI he was a professor of politics at the University of Sheffield, where he served as head of department.

Matthew J. Gibney is Elizabeth Colson Professor of Politics and Forced Migration, Fellow of Linacre College, University of Oxford, and Director of the Refugee Studies Centre at Oxford. He has written widely on issues relating to refugees, migration control and citizenship from the perspectives of normative political theory and comparative politics, including many articles and chapters on asylum and immigration and their relationship to issues of ethics, security and the liberal democratic state. His work has been published in the American Political Science Review, the Georgetown Immigration Law Journal, Forced Migration Review, Government and Opposition, and a range of other journals. His books include *Globalizing Rights: The Oxford Amnesty Lectures* (Oxford University Press 2003), which has been translated into Spanish and Italian; *The Ethics and Politics of Asylum: Liberal Democracy and the Response to Refugees* (Cambridge University Press 2004); and (with Randall Hansen) a three-volume encyclopedia entitled *Immigration and Asylum From 1900 to the Present* (ABC-Clio 2005).

Virginie Guiraudon holds a PhD in government from Harvard and is director of research at the CNRS and the Centre for European Studies at Sciences Po, Paris. She has been a Marie Curie Chair Professor at the European University Institute, a visiting fellow at the Center for International Studies at Princeton University, and a visiting professor at the UCLA Sociology Department and the Madrid Center for Political and Constitutional Studies. She is a recipient of the Descartes-Huygens Prize, whose tenure she spent at the University of Nijmegen. She is the author of *Les politiques d'immigration en Europe* (L'Harmattan, 2000). She has co-edited *Controlling a New Migration World* (Routledge, 2001), *Immigration Politics in Europe: The Politics of Control* (Taylor and Francis, 2006), *Politiques publiques*, volume 1 and 2 (Presses de Sciences Po, 2008 and 2010), and *The Sociology of European Union* (Palgrave, 2010).

Leila Hadj-Abdou is a lecturer in politics at the University of Vienna and a part-time assistant professor at the Migration Policy Center at the Robert Schuman Centre for Advanced Studies of the European University Institute. She specializes in migration governance, European Union politics, immigration and immigrant integration policies, and the populist radical right.

Randall Hansen is director of the Munk School's Centre for European, Russian, and Eurasian Studies as well as the Global Migration Lab, full professor in the Department of Political Science at the University of Toronto, and Canada Research Chair in Global Migration. He served as interim director of the Munk School from 2017 to 2020. His books include *Disobeying Hitler: German Resistance After Operation Valkyrie* (Oxford University Press, 2014), *Sterilized by the State: Eugenics, Race and the*

Population Scare in 20th Century North America (Cambridge University Press, 2014), *Fire and Fury: The Allied Bombing of Germany* (Penguin, 2009), and *Citizenship and Immigration in Post-War Britain* (Oxford University Press, 2000). He has co-edited numerous books, including *Immigration and Public Opinion in Liberal Democracies* (Routledge, 2012), *Migration States and International Cooperation* (Routledge, 2011), and *Towards a European Nationality* (Palgrave, 2001).

Miryam Hazán is a migration specialist at the Organization of American States, currently at the Inter-American Commission on Human Rights. Previously, she was a senior consultant with the Inter-American Development Bank, where she led a major research project on international migration in Central America, Mexico, Haiti, and the Dominican Republic. She is also a senior fellow with the Tower Center for Public Policy and International Affairs at Southern Methodist University. Dr. Hazán holds a PhD in government from the University of Texas, Austin, an MA from Georgetown University, and a BA from the Autonomous University of Mexico. She is the author of numerous policy reports, journal articles, book chapters, and blogs on topics related to international migration and refugees in the Americas and Europe, with a focus on Spain, migration and development, immigrant integration in the United States, Latino politics, and US-Mexico relations.

Friedrich Heckmann is professor emeritus of sociology and director of the European Forum for Migration Studies at the University of Bamberg. Previously he was a professor of sociology at the Hamburg School of Economics, and since 1992 he has been a professor at the University of Bamberg. He has served as a policy advisor and expert consultant on migration and integration for the European Union, the German parliament and federal government, state and city governments, and non-governmental organizations. His most recent book is *Integration von Migranten. Einwanderung und neue Nationenbildung* (Springer Verlag, 2015).

François Héran earned a PhD from EHESS (Paris) and a *doctorat d'État* in anthropology from Paris-Descartes University. After four years of fieldwork in Spain and Bolivia in the 1970s, in 1980 he joined the French National Institute for Demographic Research (INED) and the National Institute of Statistics (INSEE) to conduct surveys on sociability, education, family structures, language transmission, and migration. Head of the Population Surveys Branch at INSEE from 1993 to 1998, he was director of INED from 1999 to 2009. He was president of the European Association for Population Studies between 2008 and 2012. In 2017 he was elected professor at the Collège de France (Paris), occupying the Migrations and Societies Chair. In the same year, his project for a migration institute was selected by the program Investing for the Future, leading to the creation of the Institut Convergences Migrations (icmigrations.cnrs.fr), which now supports 620 fellows studying migration in a broad spectrum of disciplines across France. He is the author of many books and scientific articles, most recently *Avec l'immigration: Mesurer, débattre, agir* (2017) and *Lettre aux professeurs sur la liberté d'expression* (2021), both published by La Découverte; as well as *Parlons immigration en 30 questions* (La Documentation française 2021).

James F. Hollifield is Ora Nixon Arnold Chair in International Political Economy, professor in the Department of Political Science, and director of the Tower Center at SMU. He is a global fellow at the Woodrow Wilson International Center and a fellow at the Institut zur Zukunft der Arbeit (IZA) at the University of Bonn. Before joining the faculty at SMU, Hollifield taught at Brandeis and Auburn, was a research fellow at Harvard's Center for European Studies, and was associate director of research at the French CNRS. In addition to many scientific articles and reports, his recent works include *Migration Theory*, 4th edition (Routledge), *Understanding Global Migration* (Stanford University Press), and *International Political Economy: History, Theory and Policy* (Cambridge University Press, forthcoming). Hollifield has served as an advisor for governments around the world and for many international organizations on matters of migration and human and economic development. In 2021–2022 he was named as a fellow of the French Institute for Advanced Study in Paris.

Christian Joppke received a PhD from the University of California at Berkeley (1989) and currently holds a chair in sociology at the University of Bern. Previous appointments include the University of Southern California, European University Institute, University of British Columbia, International University Bremen, and the American University of Paris. He has written extensively on immigration, citizenship, and multiculturalism. His most recent book is *Neoliberal Nationalism: Immigration and the Rise of the Populist Right* (Cambridge University Press, 2021).

Riva Kastoryano is an emeritus research director at the National Center for Scientific Research (CNRS) at the Center for International Studies (CERI), Sciences Po. Her books include *Negotiating Identities: States and Immigrants in France and Germany* (Princeton University Press, 2002). She also edited *Quelle identité pour l'Europe? Le multiculturalisme à l'épreuve* (second edition, Presses de Sciences Po, 2005, with English, Portuguese, and Turkish translations); *Nationalismes en mutation en Méditerranée Orientale*, with A. Dieckhoff (Éditions du CNRS, 2002); *Les codes de la différence. Religion, origine, race en France, Allemagne et Etats-Unis* (Presses de Sciences Po, 2005); *Turkey Between Nationalism and Globalization* (Routledge, 2013); and

Burying Jihadis: Bodies Between Territory and Identity (Hurst and Oxford University Press, 2018).

Desmond King is the Andrew W. Mellon Professor of Government at the University of Oxford. He is the author of many books, including *Making Americans: Immigration, Race and the Origins of the Diverse Democracy* (Harvard University Press, 2000), *The Liberty of Strangers: Making the American Nation* (Oxford University Press, 2005), *Still a House Divided: Race and Politics in the Obama Era*, with Rogers M. Smith (Princeton University Press, 2011), and *Phantoms of a Beleaguered Republic: The Deep State and the Unitary Executive*, with Stephen Skowronek and John Dearborn (Oxford University Press, 2021). His articles have appeared in such leading journals as the *American Political Science Review, British Journal of Political Science, Journal of Politics, Past and Present*, and *World Politics*. King has been a fellow of the British Academy since 2003, and is also a foreign member of several national academies, including the American Academy of Arts and Sciences, the Academia Europaea, the Royal Irish Academy, and the National Academy of Social Insurance. He holds a DLitt from the University of Oxford.

Leo Lucassen is professor of global labor and migration history and director of the International Institute of Social History (IISH) at the University of Leiden. He is the editor or author of numerous books, including *Globalising Migration History: The Eurasian Experience (16th–21st Centuries*, co-edited with Jan Lucassen (Brill, 2014); *Migration and Membership Regimes in Global and Historical Perspective*, co-edited with Ulbe Bosma and Gijs Kessler (Brill, 2013); *Living in the City: Urban Institutions in the Low Countries, 1200–2010*, co-edited with Wim Willems (Routledge, 2012); *The Encyclopedia of Migration and Minorities in Europe: From the 17th Century to the Present*, co-edited with Klaus J. Bade, P. C. Emmer, and Jochen Oltmer (Cambridge University Press, 2011); *Migration History in World History: Multidisciplinary Approaches*, co-edited with Jan Lucassen and Patrick Manning (Brill, 2010); and *The Immigrant Threat: The Integration of Old and New Migrants in Western Europe Since 1850* (University of Illinois Press, 2005).

Willem Maas holds the Jean Monnet Chair and is an associate professor at Glendon College, York University, in Toronto. He is the author of *Creating European Citizens* (2007) and *Historical Dictionary of the European Union* (2014), the editor of *Multilevel Citizenship* (2013) and *Democratic Citizenship and the Free Movement of People* (2013), and the co-editor of *Sixty Years of European Governance* (2014). Currently he is writing about the future of citizenship, politics in the Netherlands, and federalism. He co-founded the Migration and Citizenship section of the American Political Science Association.

Philip L. Martin is professor emeritus of agricultural and resource economics at the University of California at Davis. His research focuses on international labor migration, farm labor, and economic development. Martin is editor of the quarterly *Rural Migration News.* His recent books include *Merchants of Labor: Recruiters and International Labor Migration* (Oxford University Press, 2017). Martin has earned a reputation as an effective analyst who can develop practical solutions to complex and controversial migration and labor issues. He served on the Commission on Agricultural Workers to assess the effects of the Immigration Reform and Control Act of 1986 and evaluated the prospects for Turkish migration to European Union between 1987 and 1990 and the effects of immigration on Malaysia's economy and labor markets in 1994–1995. He was a member of the Binational Study of Migration between 1995 and 1997.

Midori Okabe is an associate professor of international relations in the Faculty of Law at Sophia University in Tokyo. She is a former visiting scholar at the Centre of International Studies, University of Cambridge (2006–2007); academic program associate at the United Nations University in Tokyo (2004–2006); and special advisor to the Japanese Ministry of Foreign Affairs (2000–2002). Her recent work includes *The "Outside-In": An Overview of Japanese Immigration Policy from the Perspective of International Relations* (2011) and *Labor Migration Control over Five Continents* (2010).

Pia M. Orrenius is a vice president and senior economist at the Federal Reserve Bank of Dallas, where she is a regional economist working on economic growth and demographic change, while her academic research focuses on the labor market impacts of immigration, unauthorized immigration, and US immigration policy. She is coauthor with Madeline Zavodny of the book *Beside the Golden Door: U.S. Immigration Reform in a New Era of Globalization* (2010).

Ted Perlmutter is an adjunct professor at Columbia University as well as a technology consultant and information systems architect. His research includes work with Suzette Brooks Masters on a Ford Foundation project, "Networking the Networks: Improving Information Flow in the Immigration Field." He has published numerous articles and book chapters on immigration, refugees, political parties, and civil society, and he has taught in the New York University Political Science Department as a lecturer and assistant professor (1987–1992).

Jeffrey G. Reitz is a professor in the Department of Sociology and the director of Ethnic, Immigration, and Pluralism Studies in the Munk School of Global Affairs at the University of Toronto. He is the author of *Multiculturalism and Social Cohesion: Potentials and Challenges of Diversity* (2009). His articles include "Race, Religion, and the Social Integration of Canada's New Immigrant Minorities" (2009); "Comparisons of the Success of Racial Minority Immigrant Offspring in the United States, Canada and Australia" (2011); "The Distinctiveness of Canadian Immigration Experience" (2012); and "Immigrant Skill Utilization: Trends and Policy Issues" (2013). He was a Marie Curie International Fellow at the École des Hautes Études en Sciences Sociales in Paris.

Camille Schmoll is a social geographer, professor, and director of studies at the École des Hautes Études en Sciences Sociales. She has published widely on international migration issues with a focus on the Mediterranean littoral and Italy in particular. Her recent publications include *Migration, Urbanity and Cosmopolitanism in a Globalized World* (Springer, 2021); *Atlas historique des migrations en Méditerranée. De l'antiquite à nos jours* (Actes Sud, 2021); and *Les damnées de la mer. Femmes et frontières en Méditerranée* (La Découverte, 2020).

Giuseppe Sciortino is professor of sociology at the Università di Trento in Italy. Among his recent works are *Great Minds: Encounter with Social Theory*, with Gianfranco Poggi (2011) and *Foggy Social Structures: Irregular Migration, Informal Economy and Welfare Regimes*, co-edited with Michael Bommes (2011).

Michael Orlando Sharpe is an associate professor of political science at York College of the City University of New York and an adjunct research scholar at Columbia University's Weatherhead East Asian Institute. His first book, *Postcolonial Citizens and Ethnic Migration: The Netherlands and Japan in the Age of Globalization*, was published by Palgrave Macmillan in 2014. He has been a visiting fellow or visiting scholar at the Royal Netherlands Institute of Southeast Asian and Caribbean Studies (KITLV), Leiden University, the University of Amsterdam, the University of Aruba, Sophia University, and Keio University. He has been a Mansfield Foundation and Japan Foundation Center for Global Partnership US-Japan Network for the Future Program Scholar. He is currently completing his second book, *The Politics of Racism and Antiracism in Japan*.

Henry Sherrell is an independent migration researcher, consultant, and policy advisor. In the past, he has worked for the Australian Department of Immigration and Citizenship, for a Federal Member of Parliament, and for the Federal Parliamentary

Library. As a researcher, he has worked for the Development Policy Centre at the Australian National University and the Migration Council Australia.

Kristof Tamas is senior advisor at the Ministry of Justice, Sweden, in charge of the implementation of the Global Compact for Migration in Sweden. He also works with international cooperation within the Global Forum on Migration and Development (GFMD) and on the links between migration, climate change, and the environment. During 2014–2020 he was the director and head of secretariat of DELMI, the Migration Studies Delegation, based in Stockholm. He was previously senior advisor in the secretariat for the Swedish chairmanship of the Global Forum on Migration and Development, a Swedish national expert at the EU Commission, and a special advisor and later deputy director at the Swedish Ministry for Foreign Affairs and Ministry of Justice. He also has worked for the Political Science Department of Stockholm University and as a senior research consultant for the Institute for Futures Studies in Stockholm and as a consultant for, inter alia, IOM, the European Commission, ICMPD, IGC, the World Bank, and the Swedish International Development Cooperation Agency.

Hélène Thiollet is a CNRS permanent researcher at CERI Sciences Po. She teaches international relations, comparative politics, and migration studies at Sciences Po and EHESS. Her research deals with the politics of migration and asylum in the Global South, and she focuses her empirical work on the Middle East and Sub-Saharan Africa. She also works on crises and political transformations linked to migration and asylum. She was awarded several National and European research grants to investigate migration governance and migration crises in Europe and beyond. Her recent publications in 2021 include *Migration, Urbanity and Cosmopolitanism in a Globalized World*, co-edited with Catherine Lejeune, Delphine Pagès-El Karoui, Camille Schmoll (Springer-IMISCOE Research Series), and "Migrants and Monarchs: Regime Survival, State Transformation and Migration Politics in Saudi Arabia" in *Third World Quarterly*.

Dietrich Thränhardt is a professor emeritus and former director of the Institute of Political Science at Universität Münster. He has been a guest professor at the International Christian University in Tokyo and a fellow at both the Netherlands Institute for Advanced Study and the Transatlantic Academy of the German Marshall Fund. Currently, he edits the journal *Studies in Migration and Minorities*. He is the author or co-author of 40 books and 170 articles in German and in English, and his work has been translated into French, Japanese, Dutch, Italian, and Catalan. His present research interests include the relationship of migration and development, the contradictory processes of opening the world with globalization, and the buildup of security walls and fences. He has consulted for the Organisation for Economic Co-operation and Development, for state and local governments and foundations in Germany, and for science organizations in Austria, Belgium, Luxembourg, the Netherlands, and Switzerland, and he has lectured in several American universities.

Daniel J. Tichenor is the Philip H. Knight Chair of Social Science and director of the Program on Democratic Governance of the Wayne Morse Center for Law and Politics at the University of Oregon. He has published seven scholarly books and volumes. His most recent book (with Sidney Milkis) is *Rivalry and Reform: Presidents, Social Movements, and the Transformation of American Politics* (University of Chicago Press, 2018). *The Politics of International Migration* (Oxford University Press), with Marc Rosenblum, has recently been published in paperback. His book, *Dividing Lines: The Politics of Immigration Control* (Princeton University Press), won the American Political Science Association's Gladys Kammerer Award for the best book on US public policy. He has been a research fellow in governmental studies at the Brookings Institution, a visiting scholar at the Center for the Study of Democratic Politics at Princeton University, a faculty scholar at the Eagleton Institute of Politics at Rutgers University, and the Abba P. Schwartz Fellow of Immigration and Refugee Policy at the John F. Kennedy Presidential Library.

Lars Trägårdh is a historian who lived mostly in the United States beginning in 1970, while maintaining his personal and professional ties to Sweden. After many years as an entrepreneur and businessperson, he returned to academic studies in 1986. He received his PhD in history from the University of California at Berkeley in 1993 after living and carrying out research for several years in both Germany and Sweden. He taught modern European history at Barnard College and Columbia University in New York City, where he remained for ten years. He now serves as professor of history and civil society studies at Ersta Sköndal Bräcke University College, where he has focused on projects concerning state/civil society relations, individual right, judicial politics, the Nordic model, and the Swedish social contract, and a comparative project on children's rights regimes in Sweden, France, and the United States. Aside from his academic research and writing, he is a public commentator on Swedish and American politics and society, publishing regularly in Swedish print media and appearing frequently on Swedish radio and TV.

Gerasimos Tsourapas is a senior lecturer in international relations at the School of Social and Political Sciences, University of Glasgow. He is the author of *The Politics of Migration in Modern Egypt: Strategies for Regime Survival in Autocracies* (Cambridge

University Press, 2018) and *Migration Diplomacy in the Middle East and North Africa: Power, Mobility, and the State* (Manchester University Press, 2021). His work has also appeared in the *International Studies Quarterly, European Journal of International Relations, International Migration Review, International Political Science Review, Journal of Ethnic and Migration Studies,* and other leading journals. *The Politics of Migration in Modern Egypt* was awarded the 2020 ENMISA Distinguished Book Award by the International Studies Association and was shortlisted for the British International Studies Association's L. H. M. Ling Outstanding First Book Prize. He was a fellow at the Center for European Studies, Harvard University (2019–2020) and at the American University in Cairo (2013–2014). He received a BA in economics and political science from Yale University (2006), an MSc in international political economy from the London School of Economics and Political Science (2007), and a PhD in politics from SOAS, University of London (2016).

Ingrid Tucci is a sociologist, a CNRS researcher at the Institute for Labour Economics and Industrial Sociology at Aix-Marseille University, and a research fellow of the Institut Convergences Migrations. She is interested in ethno-racial inequality in schools and on the labor market, discrimination, and international comparisons on those issues, with a focus on France and Germany. Her current research focuses on the life courses of migrants' descendants in France and Germany using mixed-methods approaches based on large representative surveys and qualitative interviews.

Catherine Wihtol de Wenden is the director of research emeritus at CNRS and Sciences Po (CERI). She has written about international migration from a political science and public law perspective for over forty years. She studied at Sciences Po, Paris and at the University of Paris I (Panthéon-Sorbonne) and received her PhD in political science in 1986. She has authored or co-authored 20 books and approximately 150 articles. She teaches at Sciences Po, Paris, and at the University La Sapienza in an EU Socrates program. Her publications include *Les immigrés et la politique* (1988), *Le défi migratoire* with Bertrand Badie (1995), *L'immigration en Europe. La documentation française* (1999), *Faut-il ouvrir les frontières* (1999), *La citoyenneté européenne* (1997), *Atlas mondial des migrations,* 3rd ed. (2012), *Sortir des banlieues* with Sophie Body-Gendrot (2007), *La globalisation humaine* (2009), *La question migratoire au XXIᵉ siècle*, 2nd ed. (2013), and *Les nouvelles migrations* (2013).

CONTROLLING IMMIGRATION

1 INTRODUCTION

1 The Dilemmas of Immigration Control in Liberal Democracies

James F. Hollifield, Philip L. Martin,
Pia M. Orrenius, and François Héran

All countries face the challenge of controlling migration. The dilemmas of control are especially acute in liberal democracies. Economic pressures encourage governments to be open to migration, while political, legal, and security concerns argue for closure and control—a liberal paradox (Hollifield 1992). How can countries be simultaneously open to immigration for economic and demographic reasons and closed to immigration to protect sovereignty, ensure security, and enhance the social contract?

This book explores the liberal paradox by comparing immigration trends and policies of major OECD countries. Two leitmotifs are convergence and gaps. The *convergence hypothesis* argues that governments that face similar problems adopt similar solutions, including (1) the policy instruments they choose to control immigration and (2) integration and naturalization policies that generate similar public reactions. The *gap hypothesis* argues that the gap between the goals or outputs of immigration policy (laws, regulations, executive actions, and court rulings) and the results or outcomes of those policies in terms of unauthorized and unwanted migration is growing wider, contributing to public hostility toward immigrants (regardless of their legal status) and putting pressure on political leaders and governments to adopt more restrictive policies (Hollifield 1986; cf. Czaika and De Haas 2013 and Ellermann 2021).

Beyond testing these two hypotheses against the evidence gathered in the countries and regions represented in the book, we seek to explain the efficacy of immigration control measures in an era of globalization that rivals that of the eighteenth and nineteenth centuries. In each of the country and regional profiles, the authors explain the evolution of immigration and immigrant policy and why some policies succeeded in achieving their objectives while others failed. Each country chapter is followed by commentaries that critique the author's principal findings, supplementing them and, in some cases, offering an alternative interpretation.

International migration and mobility have been steadily increasing in the post–World War II era. According to UN data, in 2020 approximately 281 million people—3.6 percent of the world's 7.8 billion people—resided outside of their country of birth for one year or more.[1] Until the global pandemic of 2020, tens of millions of people crossed borders on a daily basis, which added up to roughly 3 billion border crossings per year. Human mobility was part of a broader trend of globalization, which includes more trade in goods and services, increased capital flows, greater ease of travel, and a veritable explosion of readily accessible information.

Migration is a defining feature of the contemporary world (De Haas, Miller, and Castles 2020). It is connected to trade and investment (Peters 2017), but it is also profoundly different. People are not shirts, which is another way of saying that labor is not a pure commodity. Unlike goods and capital, individuals can become actors on the international stage (they have agency), whether through peaceful transnational communities or through violent terrorist/criminal networks. In the rare instances when migrants commit terrorist acts, migration and mobility can be a threat to the security of states.

Many studies highlight the economic benefits of immigration (for example, Orrenius and Zavodny 2010; Martin 2022), such as new sources of human capital and workers, more entrepreneurial activity, more innovation, fewer labor market bottlenecks, and lower levels of inflation in periods of high growth. However, these benefits of migration come with some costs, including the short-term fiscal burdens of concentrated low-wage immigrant populations in certain regions and localities, the long-term challenges of social and economic integration, and, in an age of drug cartels and domestic and international terrorism, security costs—not to mention concerns for public health in times of pandemic. Liberal states also must contend with the issue of the rights (legal status) of migrants, including legalization, naturalization, and citizenship, or risk undermining the social contract. Hence economic needs for openness are pitted against political and legal pressures for closure—the liberal paradox. In liberal democracies, immigrants are typically granted a basic package of (human and civil) rights that enables them to remain, settle, become productive members of society, and (depending on the country) become naturalized citizens. Conversely, they may return to their countries of origin and affect economic and political development there. Migration has important costs (brain drain) and benefits (remittances and brain gain) for less-developed countries in the Southern Hemisphere (Hollifield, Orrenius, and Osang 2006; Hollifield and Foley 2021; Martin 2022).

Of course, not all migration is voluntary—in any given year, tens of millions of people move to escape wars, political violence, hunger, deprivation, and the vagaries of climate change, becoming refugees, asylum seekers, or internally displaced persons. At the end of 2020, the United Nations High Commissioner for Refugees (UNHCR) estimated the number of "persons of concern" at 82.4 million (1 percent of the world's population), including 26.4 million refugees, 4.1 million asylum seekers, 48 million internally displaced people, and a relatively new category, 5.4 million Venezuelans forced to flee their country, a number that continues to rise (Hollifield 2021b; Hazán 2021). Wars in the Middle East (especially Syria and Iraq), East Africa, and West Africa and instability in South Asia (Afghanistan and Pakistan), Central America (the Northern Triangle), South America (Venezuela), and Europe (Ukraine) continue to feed a growing population of forced migrants. Two weeks after the Russian invasion of Ukraine, which occurred on February 23, 2022, more than two million people fled to escape the bombing. At the onset of the war, Ukraine had 44 million inhabitants, twice as many as Syria. If a quarter of the population were to leave Ukraine—a plausible estimate—this would be more than ten million exiles. According to UNHCR, 80 percent of the world's exiles come from just nine countries, each responsible for the flight of at least half a million people. These are, in order of importance, Syria, Venezuela, Ukraine, Afghanistan, South Sudan, Myanmar, Somalia, the Democratic Republic of Congo, and Eritrea. The countries of the European Union, Germany in particular, struggle to cope with waves of forced migration—almost 1 million asylum seekers arrived in Germany in 2015 alone. In 2018–2019 and again in 2021, tens of thousands of Central Americans fled the Northern Triangle countries (El Salvador, Guatemala, and Honduras), most heading north through Mexico to seek asylum in the United States.

Because it is so complex and multifaceted, migration of all types poses a challenge for individual states, for regions such as the European Union (EU) and North America, and for the international community. Eighty-six percent of forced migrants, almost 70 million people, are hosted in countries in the Southern Hemisphere, where the ability of many states to host asylum seekers and refugees is limited. Forced displacement feeds the narrative of a global migration crisis that is destabilizing countries and entire regions (Weiner 1995; cf. Hollifield and Foley 2021). Certainly, understanding the dynamics of forced migration, displacement, and development in the global South is essential for explaining the dilemmas of immigration control in the global North.

Until the election of Donald Trump in the United States in 2016 and the global pandemic of 2020, international migration was generally on the rise. Despite the 9/11 terrorist attack on the United States and the great recession of 2007–2009, followed by the sovereign debt crisis in Europe, liberal democracies remained relatively open to immigration—the United States was admitting over 1 million immigrants annually until 2019, and in 2015 roughly 2.4 million people arrived in the EU from non-EU countries. The pandemic of 2020 led to new restrictions on human mobility, a sharp drop in border crossings, and a general decline in immigration. Legal permanent US immigration dropped by 30 percent between FY 2019 and FY 2020, from 1,031,765 to 707,362. Other forms of immigration to the United States had started falling several years prior due to Trump administration policies regarding Muslim immigrants, foreign students, and asylum seekers (Martin and Orrenius in this volume).

Global economic inequality and demographic differences mean that supply/push forces remain strong while demand/pull forces persist (Martin 2022). During the pandemic, exceptions were made for "essential workers" to continue to enter and work in many OECD countries. Growing demand for low-skilled workers and competition for the highly skilled, coupled with stable or shrinking workforces, have created more economic opportunities for migrant workers. Transnational networks (family and kinship ties) are as dense and efficient as ever, linking sending and receiving societies. Networks help to reduce risk and lower the transaction costs of migration, making it easier for people to cross borders and stay abroad. Moreover, when legal migration is not an option, migrants (especially asylum seekers) have turned to professional smugglers, and a global industry of smuggling has flourished, at times with dire consequences for migrants. In 2016, more than 5,000 migrants perished at sea while trying to enter the EU to seek asylum.

The Unwieldy Politics of Immigration Control

Migration, like any type of transnational activity, does not take place in a legal or institutional void. Governments are deeply involved in organizing and regulating migration (Waldinger and Fitzgerald 2004). The accrual of rights for non-nationals has been an extremely important part of the story of immigration control. For the most part, rights that accrue to migrants come from the legal and constitutional protections guaranteed to all members of a society (Joppke 2001). Thus, if an individual migrant is able to establish some claim to residence on the territory of a liberal state, his or her chances of being able to remain and settle will increase. Deportation or repatriation typically is difficult (Ellermann 2009; Wong 2015). At the same time, developments in international human rights law have helped to solidify the position of the individual vis-à-vis the nation-state, to the point that individuals (and certain groups) have acquired a type of international legal personality (Soysal 1994; Jacobson 1996). Once extended, rights have a very long half-life, and it is hard to roll them back. Regulating international migration requires liberal states to be attentive to the (human or civil) rights of the individual—if rights are ignored, the liberal state risks undermining its own legitimacy and raison d'être.

Four factors undergird immigration policymaking: security, cultural and ideational concerns, economic interests, and rights. National security (the institutions of sovereignty and border control), economics (markets), and rights are all part of a multidimensional game in migration policymaking. In normal times, the debate about immigration revolves around two poles: markets (numbers) and rights (status), or how many immigrants to admit, with what skills, and with what status. Should migrants be temporary (guest) workers or allowed to settle, bring their families, and get on a path to citizenship? Is there a trade-off between rights and numbers, as Martin Ruhs and others (Ruhs 2013; Ruhs and Martin 2008) suggest? These are all good questions. But cultural concerns—which regions of the globe immigrants should come from, which ethnic characteristics they should have, and issues of integration—are often politically more salient than markets and rights, and the trade-offs are more intense in some periods and in some countries than in others.

With the September 11, 2001, terrorist attacks in the United States followed by a series of bloody attacks in Europe in the 2000s and 2010s, policymaking regarding immigration and refugees shifted to a national security dynamic (with fear of Islam a deep cultural subtext) and the concern that liberal migration policies pose a threat to the nation and to civil society (Adamson 2006; Lucassen 2005). In times of war and pandemics, the dynamic of markets and rights gives way to a dynamic of culture, security, and public health, and finding equilibrium (compromise) in the policy game is even more complicated and the liberal paradox more acute. Yet as we can see with the conflict in Ukraine, the national security imperative cuts both ways when states suddenly are confronted with a humanitarian emergency and compelled to open their borders for geopolitical reasons. Making these trade-offs in times of great uncertainty is the policy dilemma facing governments in every immigration country.

The four-sided game (see Figure 1.1) is difficult at the national, state, and local levels, and it is made more complex because migration control has important foreign policy implications. The movement of people affects international relations and security in myriad ways (Adamson 2006; Hollifield 2012; Adamson and Tsourapas 2018). Hence, political leaders are always engaged in a two- or even three-level game (Putnam 1988), seeking to build local and domestic coalitions to maximize support for immigration policy but with an eye on the foreign policy consequences. It is virtually impossible for a state to manage international migration unilaterally, simply by sealing or closing its border—North Korea and other totalitarian states in autarky are a partial exception.

The country studies in this book highlight the administrative, political, legal, and economic difficulties of immigration enforcement in relatively open, liberal, and pluralistic societies. Executive and bureaucratic power in these countries is open to

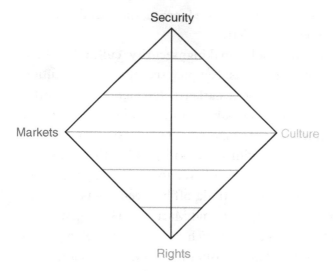

FIGURE 1.1. The Dilemmas of Migration Governance

contestation by a variety of social and economic groups, and reducing the demand/ pull factors that attract migrants is extremely difficult. Competing interests in liberal societies often lead to policymaking gridlock that, in the face of strong economic incentives, permits immigration to continue in one form or another (Freeman 1995; Martin 2022). Such policy paralysis sends mixed signals to prospective emigrants, incentivizing them to overcome obstacles placed in their path at borders (walls, fences, and other external controls) or in the workplace (internal controls). Amnesties for unauthorized migrants create a potential moral hazard, encouraging more irregular migration while fueling the smuggling trade and enlarging illicit economies and black markets. As levels of irregular migration increase along with asylum seeking, public opinion may shift in a xenophobic and nativist direction, spurred on by radical right-wing politicians, and immigration and refugee policies become more populist and symbolic, detached from the reality of migrant flows and stocks (Norris and Inglehart 2019; Joppke 2021; see also various chapters in this volume).

Immigration countries cannot in the short term hope to reduce supply/push pressures in the sending societies—rapid population growth combines with low rates of economic growth to contribute to depressed wages and underemployment in those countries, especially among the young. Past migration, often driven by colonial ties, has created links between sending and receiving areas that are hard to break for cultural, legal, and humanitarian reasons. This is especially true in Europe, where many countries have deep historical ties with sending countries that were former colonies (Kastoryano 1997; Bosma, Lucassen, and Oostendie 2012; Lucassen 2021). Demand/

pull and supply/push forces and networks that link sending and receiving societies are the necessary conditions for emigration to occur, but granting legal status (rights) to foreigners is the sufficient condition for immigration. Migrant rights most often derive from domestic sources of law, especially constitutions, but increasingly they are protected by international law and human rights conventions, particularly in Europe (Joppke 2001; Geddes and Hadj-Abdou in this volume). Despite the rise of rights-based politics (Hollifield 1992; Hollifield and Wilson 2012; also discussed later in this introduction) and regimes, which inhibit the action of states trying to control migration, policies increasingly seek to control immigration by targeting migrants' civil, social, and political rights (Hollifield 2021a).

Legal and constitutional constraints notwithstanding, fixing immigration control systems that are buckling under the pressure of new waves of asylum seekers and economic migrants has become a political imperative in most of the countries included in this volume. The principal exceptions are Japan and South Korea, where the numbers of immigrants are growing but remain relatively small, and Canada, Australia, and New Zealand, where public hostility to immigration remains relatively low. The Great Recession of 2007–2009 led to a decline of flows, especially to the United States, where despite the moderation in the pace of immigration, the politics of immigration shifted more toward control (enforcement) and away from concerns about the integration of a large immigrant population, many of whom are undocumented (Hollifield 2010; Passel, Cohn, and Gonzalez-Barrera 2012). Meanwhile, integration dilemmas are acute in Canada, Australia, and New Zealand—nations of immigrants—where sources of immigration have become much more diverse (Favell 1998; Bloemraad 2006; Schain 2012; Reitz in this volume; Gamlen and Sherrell in this volume). The global pandemic of 2020 has further complicated immigration control policies, adding a security and public health dimension to the politics of migration and mobility.

As a result, immigration is highly contested in the de facto countries of immigration—such as France, Germany, the Netherlands, Switzerland, Britain, and the Scandinavian countries—where immigration is not part of the founding ideal, as in the nations of immigrants. Publics in numerous countries are uneasy about the long-term implications of immigration for the maintenance of national cultures, languages, and identities (see Figure 1.1), and public opinion often is hostile to immigration and asylum seeking (cf. Geddes 2021; Geddes and Hadj-Abdou in this volume). Debates over Muslim immigration in largely Christian societies have been especially vociferous and divisive in Europe (Kastoryano 1997; Kepel 2012; Norris and Inglehart 2019; various chapters in this volume). Even when foreign workers and their dependents are legal residents—there are millions of settled, legally admitted foreign workers, family members, and free movers in European countries (nationals of most

EU member states have the right to move within the EU to search for employment, although free movement for some of the newer member states required a waiting period after accession)—they are often unwanted as a permanent component of the population for non-economic reasons, including low tolerance for cultural, racial, and ethnic diversity; fear of crime and terrorism; and overcrowding in major urban areas (Money 1999; Fetzer 2000; Sides and Citrin 2007; Brader, Valentino, and Suhay 2008; Hopkins 2010).

Public hostility generates strong incentives for officials in liberal democracies to redouble their efforts at immigration control by fine-tuning existing control measures such as employer sanctions (internal control), investing more heavily in border enforcement (external control), and pursuing new experiments to restore at least the appearance of control (such as so-called immigrant trainee programs in Japan and South Korea; see Chung in this volume). For this reason, the politics of immigration in many receiving countries has a strong symbolic dimension (Rudolph 2006; Hollifield 2021a), and wide gaps exist between policy outputs and outcomes and between public opinion—which in most countries wants immigration reduced—and liberal admissions policies (Hollifield 1986; Freeman 1995; Sides and Citrin 2007; cf. Czaika and De Haas 2013; Lutz 2019). Nativist and xenophobic reactions against immigration reached a fever pitch in the United Kingdom in 2016, when Britain voted to leave the European Union (Brexit), and in the United States in the same year with the election of Donald Trump to the presidency.

Immigration is a central issue of politics and public policy in the liberal democracies (Messina 2007; Schain 2012; Norris and Inglehart 2019). Especially in Europe, immigration is a driving factor in electoral politics (Givens 2005; Eatwell and Goodwin 2018; Joppke 2021), and it is a potent electoral issue in the United States (see Wong 2016; Tichenor 2021; Martin and Orrenius in this volume). In the early decades of the postwar era many countries had guest worker policies that sought to rotate foreigners into and out of the labor force (for example, the *braceros* in the United States during the 1940s and 1950s and *Gastarbeiter* in Germany in the 1960s and 1970s), but many of the "guests" stayed—some, in the United States in particular, without authorization. These nations were confronted with the challenge of assimilating large numbers of culturally different migrants and their descendants, many in the second and third generations. In Japan and South Korea, the influx of foreign workers eagerly sought by labor-hungry, small and medium-sized employers into racially and culturally homogeneous societies with a large and growing demographic deficit is a contentious issue of national policy (see Chung 2010, 2020, and her chapter in this volume; cf. Hollifield and Sharpe 2017). In the United States, the fourth wave of largely Hispanic and Asian immigrants provoked a nativist backlash with the election of Donald Trump (Ramakrishnan 2005; Hollifield 2010 2021; McCann and Jones-Correa 2020; Joppke 2021).

Immigration, Foreign Policy, and International Relations

Increasing international mobility of migrant workers and their dependents has had a dramatic effect on international relations throughout the OECD world (Hollifield 2012). Sovereign states must cooperate with each other and coordinate policies for controlling migration, especially refugee flows (Hollifield 2000; Betts 2011). This relatively new dynamic in international relations is particularly evident in Europe (witness the deal struck between the EU and Turkey to stop the influx of asylum seekers in 2015–2016) and in North America (the Obama, Trump, and Biden administrations pressured Mexico to stop Central American asylum seekers from transiting to the US southern border). The relaxation of internal borders in Europe (associated with free movement, the Schengen process, and the drive for greater economic integration) and the refugee "crisis" of 2015–2016 pushed European states to seek common visa and asylum policies and created a crisis of governance in the EU (see the chapter by Geddes and Hadj-Abdou in this volume and Thielemann 2003).

The end of the Cold War contributed to this sea change in international relations by increasing the movement of populations from east to west, but without slowing or stopping south-to-north migration flows. As a policy issue, international migration moved from the realm of "low politics" (problems of domestic governance, especially labor market and demographic policies) to the realm of "high politics" (problems affecting relations between states, including questions of war and peace), inserting itself into foreign policy decision-making. Haiti and the former Yugoslavia provide early examples of this shift. However, in the first decades of the twenty-first century, political instability—associated with wars in South Asia (Afghanistan and Pakistan), the Middle East (Iraq, Syria, and Yemen), East Africa (Sudan, Somalia, Ethiopia, and Eritrea), North Africa, and West Africa, and with conditions in the Northern Triangle in Central America and Venezuela—has increased the propensity for migration from south to north. Refugee migrations again became a major strategic issue with the end of the Cold War and the concomitant rise of terrorism (Greenhill 2010; Betts 2011; Tsourapas 2019) and the war between Russia and Ukraine, which has provoked the largest refugee crisis in Europe since World War II, with millions driven out of the conflict zone. Governments recast migration control as a problem of national security, and international organizations, such as the United Nations High Commission for Refugees, the European Union, and the Organization of American States, came under intense pressure to help states manage forced migrations (Rudolph 2006; Adamson 2006; Hollifield 2012; Adamson and Tsourapas 2018; various chapters in this volume).

Should we therefore conclude that increased movements of people across national borders are primarily a function of conflict and changes in the international system? Clearly, there is a connection between structural changes in the international system, migration interdependence (Hollifield and Foley 2021), and the increasing mobility of people (Hollifield 2000, 2004, 2012; Koslowski 2011), but endogenous factors often are the key determinants of migration. The principal immigrant-receiving countries may ignore the structural economic factors (demand/pull and supply/push) that drive international migration, but they must recognize that the "crisis" of immigration control derives in large part from changes in the international political economy, especially the growing divide between the wealthy states of the global North and the poor states of the global South (Collier 2007, 2013; Hollifield and Foley 2021). Competition for the highly skilled (human capital) is fierce in a global labor marketplace (Chiswick 2011; Orrenius and Zavodny 2010) and the imbalance in global population growth is rising, especially as African and South Asian populations grow while populations in richer countries shrink (Héran 2017).

On the economic and demographic side, neoclassical push-pull arguments provide a simple—some might say simplistic—and straightforward explanation for increases in immigration (Martin 2022). Demand/pull in the United States and European economies during the 1950s and 1960s was sufficient to stimulate large-scale migrations from the poorer economies of the periphery (Mexico, Turkey, and the Maghreb). These labor migrations were initiated and legitimized by the receiving states in western Europe through the so-called guest worker (*Gastarbeiter*) programs, and in the United States through the 1942–1964 Bracero Program of contract labor importation (Tichenor 2002, 2021). However, what started as a market-driven movement of labor from south to north became, in the 1970s and 1980s, a sociopolitical liability as economic growth in western Europe and North America slowed in the aftermath of 1970s recessions (Hollifield 1992; Martin, Abella, and Kuptsch 2006; Héran 2017).

Stopping immigration, even during periods of sharp economic contraction, proved difficult, in part because of migrant networks and powerful, underlying supply/push factors. Demand/pull migration had initiated processes that continued to have unanticipated consequences, from the micro level (employers wanting to retain their guest workers indefinitely) to the macro level (the increasingly large role of immigration in host-country population and labor force growth, and the dependence of sending-country economies on migrant remittances) (see Hollifield, Orrenius and Osang 2006; Martin, Abella, and Kuptsch 2006; Héran 2017; Hollifield and Foley 2021). Moreover, supply/push migration increased as the populations of peripheral countries such as Turkey, Mexico, and Algeria grew at a rapid pace, even as their economies slowed due to the global recession. Migration networks that developed during the years of expansionary immigration policies in the 1950s and 1960s (the so-called Trente Glorieuses) helped to spread information about job opportunities and modes of entry and residence in the receiving countries (Massey et al. 1987). In the 1980s and 1990s, these transnational social networks, perhaps more than any other factor, helped to sustain migration—especially family reunification in Europe and irregular migration from Mexico and Central America to the United States—during periods of high uncertainty regarding employment prospects in the sending countries. In the last decades of the twentieth century, the composition of immigration flows shifted from workers to families and refugees (humanitarian migrants), and family reunification and asylum seeking became the principal avenues of immigration in Europe in the first decades of the twenty-first century. Only in the traditional nations of immigrants did labor migration (skilled and unskilled) retain its prominence, with the notable exception of the United States, which has given priority to family immigration since the 1965 Hart-Celler Immigration Act that abolished the system of national origins quotas (Martin and Orrenius in this volume; see Figure 1.2).

Push-pull forces and the imbalances between economies of the global North and global South (as well as between west and east within Europe, which resulted in a surge in free movers in the first decades of the twenty-first century) provide necessary but not sufficient conditions for immigration, especially on the scale experienced in recent decades. To explain what Myron Weiner (1995) called the "global migration crisis," we must look beyond macro- and microeconomics, and even social networks, to changes in world politics and trends in the political development of the major sending and receiving countries.

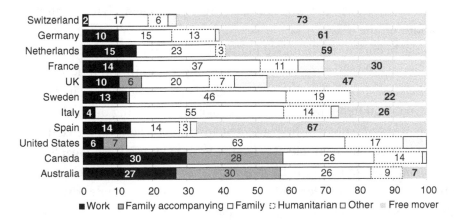

FIGURE 1.2. Composition of Migrant Flows in 2018
Based on OECD Migration Outlook 2020, supplementary tables and figures.

The Liberal Paradox and the Rise of Rights-Based Politics

Immigration control is closely linked to the rise of rights-based politics (see Hollifield 1992, 1999, 2021; Hollifield and Wilson 2012). Rights-based politics are especially evident in debates over immigration, naturalization, and asylum policies in all receiving countries, which must grapple with the fundamental issue of how many immigrants to accept, from which countries, and with what rights (status). Rights-based policies help emigrants to get in, to remain, and to settle. At the same time, human rights and refugee conventions underscore the rights of asylum seekers, migrant workers, and their families. In sum, both political and economic changes within states and internationally explain national immigration policies and their contradictions.

The extension of rights to minorities and foreigners in the decades following World War II is one of the most salient aspects of political development in the liberal democracies. Dudziak (2000) calls them "cold war civil rights." The creation of new legal spaces for marginal groups, including foreigners, in societies as different as Germany, the United States, and Japan (Hollifield and Sharpe 2017; Chung and other chapters in this volume) is linked to a much broader change in international and liberal democratic politics, beginning with the adoption in 1948 of the Universal Declaration of Human Rights and continuing with the civil rights struggles of the 1950s and 1960s in the United States. A new type of rights-based politics has taken shape at many levels of the democratic polity and in the international system itself: in legislative acts, in partisan and interest group (especially ethnic) politics, and in judicial rulings (Schuck 1998; Joppke 2001). Judicial activism has gained many supporters and detractors, and has helped to spawn a plethora of advocacy groups, ranging from social movements and political parties of the extreme right to new civil and human rights organizations on the left.

Even though the history of rights-based politics in the United States is quite different from the comparable history in Europe, the impact on immigration policy has been much the same: expanded rights for marginal and ethnic groups, including foreigners. These political developments have provoked a rethinking of classical liberal theory in the works of scholars who place civil and human rights at the center of a new social contract (see, for example, Rawls 1971; Walzer 1983; Hirsch 1992; Soysal 1994; Bauböck 1994; Jacobson 1996; Benhabib 2004; Carens 2013; Hollifield 2021a). Redefining the relationship between individuals, groups, and the state, through a process of political struggle, has had a great impact on the capacity of democratic states to control immigration and has given rise to a new multiculturalism that has in many ways redefined the social contract (Kymlicka 1995; Joppke 2017). Legislation and judicial rulings have whittled away at some of the rights and protections accorded to immigrants. However, the legal and political legacy of the Cold War era continues to constrain the executive authorities of democratic states in their attempts to achieve territorial closure and to exclude certain individuals and groups from membership in society (Schuck 1998; Benhabib 2004; Hollifield 2004, 2021a).

It is the confluence of markets (the push-pull factors described previously) and rights that explains the challenge of immigration control, highlighting what Hollifield (1992) has called "the liberal paradox." How can a society be simultaneously open for economic reasons while maintaining a degree of political and legal closure, in order to protect the social contract? This political-economic dynamic has weakened the historically close linkage between business cycles and "admissionist" or "restrictionist" immigration policies, creating strange-bedfellows coalitions (Hollifield, Hunt, and Tichenor 2008; Hollifield and Wilson 2011).

Efforts by states to regain control of their borders have led in many cases to a rollback of civil and human rights for non-citizens (Canada and to some extent Australia and New Zealand are notable exceptions; see Reitz in this volume, and Gamlen and Sherrell in this volume). Examples of the rolling back of immigrant rights include the 1996 Illegal Immigration Reform and Immigrant Responsibility Act, which tightened restrictions on legal as well as unauthorized immigrants, and a raft of anti-immigrant measures pursued by the Trump administration in the United States (Tichenor 2021; Martin and Orrenius in this volume); the German decision in 1993 to amend Article 16 of the Basic Law to restrict the blanket right to asylum; the Pasqua and Debré Laws in France in the 1990s; the new and often sweeping powers granted to police and intelligence services in the aftermath of the terrorist attacks of the 2000s to carry out surveillance and identity checks and to detain individuals without charge for extended periods; and of course the vote by Britain in 2016 to leave the EU, driven in large measure by opposition to immigration (Eatwell and Goodwin 2018). Martin Ruhs (2013) argues that there is a trade-off between numbers and rights: states with more temporary foreign workers accord them fewer rights, while those with fewer foreign workers give them more rights. According to Ruhs, no state has both high numbers of guest workers (open labor markets) and extensive rights for those workers. The question is whether this argument is generalizable to the liberal democracies, since it relies so heavily on evidence from Arab Gulf countries (members of the Gulf Cooperation Council). Sweden is a notable exception (see Brochmann in this volume; see also Bevelander and Hollifield 2021).

The postwar development of rights-based politics has not prevented nationalist and nativist backlashes against immigration. The French National Front (renamed in 2018 the Rassemblement National) is one of the oldest and most widely known anti-immigrant political parties, but others have emerged in almost every liberal democracy that has experienced large-scale immigration in recent decades (Kitschelt 1995; Money 1999; Norris 2005; Mudde 2007; Norris and Inglehart 2019) and in some (such as Hungary) that have not. The backlash is nationalist, nativist, and exclusionary in character. Immigrants are the principal targets, and criticisms are leveled at liberal parties and politicians (of the center right and center left) who support the expansion or preservation of civil and political rights for immigrants and ethnic minorities (Wong 2016; Lutz 2019). What has been labeled national or authoritarian populism is widespread in Europe and America, and the passage of Brexit and the election of Donald Trump in 2016 can be attributed in part to voters' opposition to liberal immigration and refugee policies (Eatwell and Goodwin 2018; Norris and Inglehart 2019; Joppke 2021). The growth of extreme-right anti-immigrant political parties places politicians of the center right and left under tremendous electoral pressures (Thränhardt 1996; Perlmutter 1996; Arzheimer, Kai, and Carter 2006; Lutz 2019), and liberalism itself, as a political and economic doctrine, has come under fire (Hollifield 2021a; Joppke 2021).

How can a liberal society tolerate the presence of individuals who are members but not citizens of that society? Should not all individuals who are members (more or less permanent residents) of a liberal society be accorded the full panoply of rights (social and political as well as civil) enjoyed by those who are citizens (Joppke 2010; Carens 2013; Wong 2016)? This is the paradox or dilemma that liberals must face, and it is particularly acute in countries with large, multigenerational resident alien populations that remain just outside the confines of the social contract—see, for example, the DACA (and DAPA) debates in the United States (Martin and Orrenius in this volume). In sum, immigration in most of the countries represented in this book can no longer be debated strictly in economic or demographic terms; the terms of citizenship, membership in national and local communities, and basic human rights must also be addressed (Brubaker 1989; Carens 2000; Hollifield 2021a).

Nations of Immigrants

In settler nations such as the United States, Canada, and Australia, immigration is part of the founding ideal (or myth). But like all immigrant-receiving countries, these states must address key issues, such as how many foreigners to admit, from where, and with what status. We define *nations of immigrants* as those that were founded, populated, and built by immigrants in modern times. They are settler societies created by European conquest and colonization and by the destruction of indigenous societies and cultures. As a result, immigration is a fundamental part of the founding myth, historical consciousness, and national identity of these countries, and they anticipate and welcome large numbers of immigrants, with periodic bouts of nativism and xenophobia. In the first two decades of the twenty-first century, the United States admitted on average slightly more than 1 million legal immigrants per annum. This does not mean, however, that such countries have always been open to immigrants—far from it—nor that immigration is not currently a source of social tension and political conflict there (see, for example, Schlesinger 1992; Smith 1997; Huntington 2004; King 2000; Foley 2021; Martin and Orrenius in this volume). Indeed, during the last twenty years the United States and Australia have been nearly as prone as the reluctant labor importers discussed later to adopt restrictive measures that roll back immigrant rights and indulge anti-immigrant public opinion.

Of all the countries included in this study, the United States has by far the largest gap between the stated goal of controlling immigration and the actual results of policy: with more than 1 million immigrants a year, the United States currently has levels of immigration as high as at any time in history, plus, until the 2007–2009 recession, a large and growing population of unauthorized immigrants. Recent efforts to reduce the influx of unauthorized migrants entering via Mexico through concentrated border enforcement operations, deportation, and other control measures have helped to reduce the stock of such immigrants in the United States; other factors that helped slow the growth of the undocumented population included high US unemployment after the Great Recession and, until the COVID-19 pandemic, improved economic conditions in Mexico. It is important to note that in 2017 visa overstayers accounted for roughly 62 percent of the undocumented population. In the first two decades of the twenty-first century, unauthorized immigrants constituted roughly 5 percent of the US workforce and half of all farm workers (Martin and Orrenius in this volume).

The US stalemate over how to change ineffective immigration control policies could raise the question of whether the efforts being made are genuine or are primarily an attempt to manage public opinion by creating the illusion that illegal immigration is under control (Rudolph 2006; Czaika and De Haas 2013). Although workplace enforcement is potentially a much more effective means of immigration control than border enforcement, employer sanctions and other mechanisms for internal immigration control (enforcement) have been largely ineffective because of the widespread availability of fraudulent documents among unauthorized immigrant workers and little enforcement of the law.

The political debate over immigration in the United States is fueled not only by the large numbers of unauthorized immigrants who find their way into the country—whether crossing the border illegally or overstaying a visa—but also by the perceived impacts of immigration in general on the life chances of native-born workers and by the alleged failure of recent immigrants (especially Mexicans and Central Americans) to assimilate into US society (Huntington 2004). The general public continues to assume that immigrants depress wages, compete unfairly (and effectively) for jobs that would otherwise be taken by native workers, and become a large drain on public services. Martin and Orrenius (in this volume) note that most empirical research does not support such assumptions (see also Orrenius and Zavodny 2010).

Martin and Orrenius describe the debate between integrationists (assimilationists) and pluralists (multiculturalists) over the extent and pace of immigrant incorporation into US society. Earlier attempts to incorporate immigrants through harsh assimilation have been replaced by a greater tolerance for multiculturalism that enables immigrants to retain some aspects of their culture as they integrate into the US economy and society. Although the United States does not have an official immigrant integration policy, immigrants' access to rights, benefits, and social services depends in part on their legal status (King 2000; Tichenor 2002, 2021).

Martin and Orrenius observe that US immigration policy has long followed a zig-zag pattern, with expansionary periods followed by restrictionist ones. With the terrorist attacks of September 11, 2001, and again with the global pandemic of 2020, the United States entered new restrictionist phases, as immigration control was justified on grounds of protecting national security and public health (see Figure 1.1). Tightened border controls, much closer monitoring of foreign students, and ethnic/religious profiling to identify and detain potential terrorists became accepted practices in the post-9/11 era, along with stopping asylum seekers at the US-Mexico border and separating children from their parents, a harsh deterrence policy pursued briefly in 2018 by the Trump administration.

Among the countries represented in this book, Canada is the most comfortable with its immigration policy. As Jeffrey Reitz's chapter makes clear, Canada has a consensual and relatively open (multicultural) approach to immigration, geared more toward nation-building and national economic development than is the case in the United States. As a result, Canada has maintained an expansionary, skills-based immigration policy that admits three times the number of immigrants per capita than the United States. Despite such high immigration levels, the Canadian public is supportive of immigration and tolerant of the increasing diversity that it entails. Reitz attributes this Canadian exceptionalism to various factors, including the "good fortune" of geography and history, as well as economic structures, cultural factors, and institutional arrangements in Canada. Canadian policy aims to admit each year a number of immigrants equal to 1 percent of its population (about 300,000 immigrants per annum), regardless of short-run economic conditions. The Liberal government headed by Justin Trudeau planned to expand immigration, and hoped to admit 340,000 immigrants in 2020, but because of the pandemic and related travel restrictions the actual number (180,000) was far less. Unlike the United States, whose immigration system is based primarily on family ties, Canada has a carefully managed points system that selects immigrants according to their education, skills, and linguistic abilities in an effort to meet the country's long-term labor market needs. In recent years there has been more emphasis in the selection process on language proficiency (in English and/or French) and links to specific employment opportunities. Non-economic immigrants admitted through family reunification or as refugees are kept proportionately lower, although Canada has a relatively liberal policy toward asylum seekers.

Given such clear policy objectives, it is relatively simple to measure gaps between policies and actual outcomes in the Canadian case. In terms of the number of immigrants actually admitted, Canada comes close to hitting its 1-percent-of-population target, which, as Reitz notes, is quite interesting since most countries reluctantly receive more immigrants than desired. It is more difficult to assess whether Canadian immigration policy has been effective in providing the country with enough highly skilled and economically successful immigrants. The educational levels of immigrants were higher than those of native Canadians in the past, but the difference has narrowed and virtually disappears when immigrants are compared to young native-born urban workers today.

The Canadian case is also distinguished by a relatively high level of public support for immigration, compared to the United States and Australia or even New Zealand, the latter two being the other former British dominions represented in this volume. Majorities of Canadians have consistently favored maintaining or increasing current immigration levels. Canadian political discourse on immigration has remained positive, with all major political parties officially supporting immigration. Reitz suggests that support for large-scale immigration in Canada has both economic and cultural roots. The public perception that immigrants are making a positive contribution to the economy is reinforced both by Canada's policy of selecting immigrants according to skills and other qualifications to meet labor market needs and by the small population of unauthorized immigrants. Moreover, the positive association of immigration with nation-building and population maintenance, the emergence of multiculturalism as part of the national identity, and simple cultural tolerance also play a role.

Canada gives immigrants immediate access to various social services, settlement programs, and a relatively easy naturalization process. The country's official immigrant integration ideology seems to have followed a course somewhat similar to that of the United States: an earlier harsh assimilationist paradigm and racist focus on admitting only white Europeans has been replaced by a multicultural approach. Unlike the United States, Canada has an explicit and official multiculturalism policy, which has become a centerpiece of Canadian national identity (see also Kymlicka 1995). The greater feeling of social acceptance this policy generates among immigrants may be one reason rates of naturalization are higher in Canada than in the United States.

Canada is something of a deviant case among the countries considered in this book because of its continued commitment to liberal immigration and refugee policies. The September 11 terrorist attacks on the United States did not provoke a restrictive turn in Canadian immigration policy, despite increased cooperation with the United States on border security. Nor did the global pandemic lead Canada to stop accepting refugees, as was the case in the United States during the Trump administration. Reitz suggests that the difficulties immigrants encounter in securing recognition of their qualifications, the decline in the economic fortunes of successive cohorts of newly arriving immigrants, the administration of temporary immigration to ensure compliance with regulations, and issues of visa compliance and border control could erode the currently positive economic perception of immigrants in Canada. Moreover, there is ongoing concern about the spatial distribution of immigrants, as more than 80 percent of new arrivals head for only three cities: Toronto, Montreal, and Vancouver. Despite these challenges and some gaps between immigration policy outputs and outcomes related to the points system, support for immigration and multiculturalism remains strong.

As Gamlen and Sherrell show, the immigration histories of Australia, New Zealand, and Canada have a number of important similarities. All three countries, like the United States, originated as British colonies and pursued racist (whites-only) immigration policies in the past, designed to keep their countries white and European, but they eventually abandoned such discriminatory policies in favor of a skills-selection (points) system and multicultural policies toward immigrant integration. The three countries regard immigration as a means of economic development and nation-building, and they all have a foreign-born percentage of the total population in the 20–30 percent range, much higher than even the United States or Germany. Australia became more ambivalent about high levels of immigration and especially refugees and asylum seekers, and unlike Canada it saw the rise of a serious anti-immigration political movement in the late 1990s, while New Zealand struggled to balance multiculturalism with British-versus-indigenous "biculturalism." All three of the former British dominions have had difficulties coming to terms with the status of aboriginal peoples who were dispossessed by British and European colonists, further complicating immigration and citizenship policies.

Still, there has been a lot of policy learning among the three, as Australia and New Zealand fashioned carefully managed immigration programs modeled on the Canadian system, admitting skilled immigrants based on a points test but with smaller shares of family-based and humanitarian immigrants (refugees and asylum seekers). Australia and New Zealand have significant temporary foreign worker programs for highly skilled immigrants, "circulating migrants" (workers from countries with high employment migrating to countries with seasonal labor shortages), and international students. The gap between immigration policy outputs and outcomes is similar to that in other high-immigration countries, with politicians vowing to halt immigration even as flows remain high. The points system has been relatively effective in attracting the desired type of skilled, economically successful immigrants in both countries. Indeed, the average skill level of recent immigrants is higher than that of native-born workers, and both first- and second-generation immigrants have experienced substantial occupational mobility. The unauthorized immigrant population is small, partly a consequence of geographical isolation from poorer, developing countries. In terms of immigrant integration, Australia and New Zealand have followed the American and Canadian trajectory: an earlier, harsh assimilationist policy has given way to a multiculturalist stance that recognizes the nation's cultural diversity and improves immigrant rights and access to social services and institutions. As in the United States, there is not a large difference in the rights of citizens and those of permanent residents, and the requirements for naturalization are minimal.

Governments in both countries, again much like Canada, have done an effective job of convincing the public that their countries primarily admit skilled immigrants who contribute to the economy. However, with the rise in humanitarian migration and asylum seeking, plus greater economic uncertainty as a result of recession and pandemic, there is growing public ambivalence toward immigration, seen in the emergence of the anti-immigrant One Nation Party in Australia. Globalization and regional integration—which have increased the number of countries sending immigrants to Australia and New Zealand, especially from Asia—and the surge of asylum seekers who arrive on boats from Indonesia have contributed to a sense that the tightly controlled immigration systems are under threat. In response to the anti-immigrant backlash in Australia, migration and refugee policies have taken a restrictive turn, marked by a draconian tightening of refugee and asylum policy and stronger border controls. As a result, Australia's multiculturalism program has been challenged, especially at the federal level, but is still resilient at the state level. At the same time, pro-immigrant movements are emerging, led by unions and NGOs. Governments in both countries regularly consult with interest and advocacy groups, demonstrating a responsiveness to public pressures, similar in this regard to the United States and Canada.

Countries of Immigration

Immigration has long been a fact of life in Europe, but it is not part of the founding ideal (or myth) of any European country. Germans, for example, emigrated across the globe as early as the seventeenth century, but in the last decades of the twentieth century, Germany became a country of immigration, facing the same issues as traditional settler nations. The liberal paradox was and is especially acute in Germany. We consider *countries of immigration* to be those that have a history of immigration, but officially they have hesitated to define themselves as countries of immigration, and many have only recently acknowledged that they are. Immigration has not been a fundamental part of their national identity or their past nation-building process—they were not settler societies, but many were imperial powers. In countries of immigration, the attitudes of political elites and the general public toward immigration generally have been more negative than in the classic nations of immigrants. During the high-growth decades after World War II (the so-called *Trente Glorieuses*) many of these countries recruited migrants temporarily (that is, as guest workers) rather than as permanent additions to the labor force, and in this sense they are "reluctant lands of immigration," to use a phrase coined by Philip Martin in an earlier edition of this book. France, as we shall see, is a partial exception because of its revolutionary history, republican tradition, and early demographic transition.

James Hollifield and François Héran argue that France has had relatively liberal immigration policies because of the strength of the political ideology of republicanism—initially a form of left-wing, rights-based politics, with a progressive populist undertone—buttressed by the labor requirements of French capitalism and the policy preferences of government economic planners in the post–World War II era. Liberal immigration and naturalization policies also derived from the early establishment, in the nineteenth century, of a pattern whereby immigrant labor was recruited privately by French industry, often with government sanction but with very little state control. The organization of foreign labor importation by the private sector in the interwar period and again in the 1960s largely bypassed the official institutions that were created to manage immigration. The historical pattern has been for immigration to accelerate to the point where the state is compelled, for political reasons, to try to regain control. But the general ineffectiveness of France's immigration control policies has led to a substantial gap between stated policy objectives, often quite restrictive, and actual liberal outcomes (Hollifield 1990).

Consistent with its republican tradition, France has been willing to accept immigrants and incorporate them into the French nation under a generous naturalization policy and with no significant exclusions from the country's welfare state. However, since World War II there have been repeated efforts to curtail immigrant rights, including limiting family reunification, encouraging repatriation, restricting labor permits and employment opportunities, toughening the asylum adjudication process, and expanding the powers of police to detain and deport unauthorized immigrants. Some of these measures were part of a "grand bargain" struck by left-wing governments that tightened control over new immigration flows and accelerated efforts to integrate immigrants already settled in France, through programs of legalization and the granting of citizenship rights. More conservative-minded governments have attempted to make France's citizenship and naturalization laws more exclusionary and limit the civil and social rights of immigrants, partly in an effort to placate the anti-immigrant National Front party and win back its supporters. The center of gravity in the French party system shifted noticeably to the right on immigration issues beginning in the 1990s.

The negative policy stance on immigration led to strong pro-immigrant reactions from civil society, despite public anxiety about the increasing number of Muslim immigrants (France has the largest Muslim population in western Europe) and terrorist attacks by Islamic radicals. The governments of Jacques Chirac and Nicolas Sarkozy secured the enactment of a national ban on the wearing of Muslim head scarves and other religious symbols in public schools. While the legislation was justified as necessary to protect France's strict doctrine of the separation of church/religion and state (*laïcité*), it was also a clear response to public concerns about immigration and the fact that roughly one in five French voters supported the National Front in the first round of the last four presidential elections (and in 2002 in the second round). Part of the public backlash against Muslim immigrants is a concern that they cannot be assimilated in accordance with the republican model.

While republican ideology has not been the sole determinant of French immigration policy, it has acted as a guide and touchstone for government actions. For example, French courts have ruled repeatedly that laws seen to violate the civil liberties of immigrants were unconstitutional on the grounds that they were inconsistent with the country's republican values, derived from universal human rights. The government's anti-immigrant measures have also aroused large-scale public protests. As Hollifield and Héran argue, France and other liberal democratic states have certain built-in constraints that prevent them from crossing a line that infringes basic civil liberties of citizens and denizens in violation of the Republic's founding principles.

In the second half of Emmanuel Macron's five-year term (2019–2021), a harsher version of republican ideology developed in France as a direct reaction to jihadist attacks. This version of republicanism is promoted by hard-liners such as Jean-Pierre Chevènement, who was minister of the interior and minister of national education during the presidency of François Mitterrand, and a leader of his own ultra-republican group (CERES) within the Socialist Party. Chevènement's republican campaign has been supported by Manuel Valls (former prime minister under François Hollande, for whom the unity of the nation is the supreme value) and more recently by Jean-Michel Blanquer (the ambitious minister of national education in the government of Emmanuel Macron). Blanquer sees himself as the great defender of the Republic, and he has been a key player in the so-called Republican Spring movement, which promotes a "militant secularism" and denounces multicultural ideologies, such as postcolonial and critical race studies, "imported from American university campuses" (Traisnel 2021).

While the values of the French Republic helped inspire the 1950 European Convention on Human Rights, the current trend places the Republic in opposition to democracy, republican values in opposition to human rights, and the sovereignty of the nation in opposition to Europe. From this harsh republican perspective, the main objective of immigration policy should be to defend the Republic against its external and internal enemies: radical Islam is perceived as an existential threat to the "French way of life," and Muslims are denounced as a "third column." Those who oppose racial discrimination are seen to be complicit in a campaign to undermine the Republic, and they are denounced as *islamo-gauchistes*. This rhetoric has opened deep divides in the intellectual and political classes, turning erstwhile allies into bitter enemies.

Emmanuel Macron, who is up for reelection in April 2022, is likely to face Marine Le Pen, the leader of the far-right Rassemblement National, in the second-round runoff. President Macron vacillates in his policies and rhetoric between neo-republicanism and a more liberal vision of France grounded in the EU. His hesitation reflects his political predicament and the profound uncertainties of the French public, who are concerned about the assimilation of Muslim immigrants and the fate of the Republic. In this respect, President Macron is the embodiment of a peculiarly French version of the liberal paradox. The patient reader may find the solution to the republican riddle in a future edition of this book.

For much of the postwar period Britain was *not* a country of immigration in the sense that flows remained relatively modest compared with other labor-importing countries. Britain succeeded in controlling immigration, matching outputs to outcomes where others had failed. For this reason, Gary Freeman in earlier editions of this book referred to Britain as "the deviant case." Nevertheless, despite having a "zero-immigration" policy from the 1970s to the 1990s, levels of immigration in Britain rose significantly during that time. Randall Hansen sees this policy shift as a conscious choice made by New Labour governments, led by Prime Minister Tony Blair and Chancellor of the Exchequer Gordon Brown, in the late 1990s and 2000s.

Britain after 1997 reversed a trend toward increasingly restrictive immigration policies that began in 1962, when the country started to impose stringent controls on immigration from its colonies and the British Commonwealth. In the early 1970s the government created a work permit system that generally did not allow family reunification or permanent residence. Additional restrictions, as well as a crackdown on visa overstayers, were implemented by the conservative governments of the 1970s and early 1980s. Unlike many other states in western Europe that granted free movement across borders to EU nationals under the Schengen group protocols, Britain retained intra-EU border controls. However, in 2004, Britain was one of only three EU member states to grant free movement immediately to the formerly communist states of east-central Europe when they acceded to EU membership, with the result that large numbers of workers from these states, especially Poland, came to Britain in search of work. The influx of workers from newly acceded EU states in eastern Europe would be a major issue in the vote by Britain in 2016 to leave the EU (Brexit).

The Conservatives, reelected in 2010, took steps to reduce immigration. They announced an unachievable goal of fewer than 100,000 net migrants per year, and in their zeal to achieve it they promoted a hostile environment for undocumented migrants. When the policy interacted with British nationality law, which successive home secretaries have failed to understand fully, the result for many Black Britons who had been in the country since they were children was the loss of their driver's licenses, flats, and jobs, leading to deportation and even death. These Conservative policies were in effect the most racist immigration policy decisions since the 1960s, and they flowed from a toxic combination of ignorance and anti-immigration fanaticism, spurred on by the UK Independence Party and the Brexit debate.

While historically Britain has had much more restrictive immigration policies than other countries of immigration, the gap between policy outputs and outcomes is no less prominent. As Hansen argued in an earlier edition of this book, neither the British public nor the British state wanted non-white migration, and yet Britain has one of the largest ethnic minority populations in western Europe. Not surprisingly, Britain's reluctance to fully accept its status as a major country of immigration has made it less willing to adopt a proactive and coherent integration policy, which has forced local governments to bear most of the burden of providing basic human services to immigrants and asylum seekers. Brexit gave the British government the veneer of sovereignty and the capacity to control European immigration, but in a fetishization of high-skilled immigration it used that sovereignty to shut out the low-skilled immigration on which the UK economy is wholly dependent. As the COVID-19 pandemic ends, the gaps between outputs and outcomes will only become wider.

The Federal Republic of Germany, formerly the *Gastarbeiter* or guest worker country par excellence, experienced a wave of immigration following the collapse of Communism in eastern Europe in 1989. The arrival in Germany of a million foreigners in 1990—including ethnic Germans relocating from the former Soviet Union and its satellites, relatives of immigrants already settled in Germany, applicants for political asylum, and legal and unauthorized foreign workers—turned Germany into one of the leading recipients of immigrants among OECD countries, even while German leaders continued to insist that their country "is not, nor shall it become, a country of immigration" (*Deutschland ist kein Einwanderungsland*). But by 2000 under a left-wing, Red-Green government, Germany had relaxed its *jus sanguinis* (blood) citizenship law to allow longtime resident foreigners and those born on German soil to naturalize, and in January 2005 Germany enacted its first comprehensive immigration law, which anticipated the arrival and settlement of foreigners and established procedures to foster their integration.

In previous decades, as the chapter by Philip Martin and Dietrich Thränhardt makes clear, Germany had implemented a series of ad hoc immigration control policies that had many unintended consequences. In fact, the history of post–World War II immigration to Germany is one of huge gaps between migration policy goals and outcomes. This is best illustrated by the country's guest worker programs, begun in the 1950s and intended to have foreign workers rotate between jobs in Germany and their homes in Turkey and other southern European countries.

There was no numerical quota on foreign worker recruitment, and an economic boom led to a larger number of guest workers than expected, including a third who settled. Employers wanted experienced guest workers to stay, the workers wanted to prolong their stays, and many stayed long enough to unify their families in Germany. Germany's asylum policy follows a similar story line. Despite a generous and open-ended commitment to provide asylum to those fleeing political persecution—a legacy of World War II—the government did not expect the huge flood of asylum applicants that it received beginning in the late 1980s. The volume of unauthorized immigration also was quite large; estimates of the stock of unauthorized workers varied widely, between 150,000 and 1.5 million.

The government's attempts to assert control over immigration met with limited success. While West Germany was able to stop additional guest worker recruitment in the early 1970s—owing mainly to the deep recession caused by high oil prices—subsequent attempts to reduce the foreign worker population failed. The government respected Article 16 of the Basic Law, which states, "Persons persecuted for political reasons shall enjoy the right of asylum," but starting in 1993 it made it more difficult for foreigners to get to now-unified Germany to seek asylum. Attempts to control unauthorized immigration ran up against the same obstacles as in other countries, including insufficient resources for border control and internal enforcement, lack of political will to deal with employers and pro-immigrant NGOs, and concerns that stringent migration controls would be economically harmful for Germany as well as for immigrant-sending countries.

Germany was ambivalent about integrating Turks and other guest workers and their families during the 1980s and 1990s, hoping that they would return to their countries of origin. When it became apparent that most foreigners were in Germany to stay, and more were going to arrive, the government developed an integration policy that relied on carrots and sticks to encourage foreigners to learn the German language and German culture and to assimilate. The government changed its naturalization policies, transforming Germany from one of the most restrictive to one of the most liberal countries in terms of allowing foreigners to naturalize.

Large gaps between policy goals and outcomes created a perception that the government had lost control over immigration, encouraging a public backlash led by nationalist politicians. Anti-immigrant reactions (including violent attacks on foreigners, accompanied by cries of "Foreigners out" [*Ausländer raus*]) mushroomed in the 1990s, when the surge of asylum seekers was seen as an unacceptable economic burden in a context of high structural unemployment, especially in the former East Germany. The labor force participation rate among immigrants was low, and their unemployment rate was twice that of the native-born, reinforcing the public perception that foreigners, especially refugees, are an economic burden.

The government learned from its mistakes in migration management. Germany's new guest worker programs were more carefully managed. The "green card" program, launched in 2000 to attract highly skilled information technology professionals, was modified and enhanced to develop a "welcome culture" (*Willkommenskultur*) for skilled foreigners seeking to immigrate, in order to better compete with the United States and other English-speaking countries that offer higher salaries and lower taxes. A debate is ongoing over how to welcome skilled foreigners and manage low-skilled migrant workers, but the major challenge today is integrating the asylum seekers who arrived in the 2010s into the labor market, and the vast number of refugees from the conflict in Ukraine, many of whom will be granted temporary protected status in EU countries, especially in Germany and neighboring Poland. The government elected to invest in these newcomers, teaching them German and work skills, so that they could get the "good" (high-paying) jobs available in Germany rather than allow the low-wage and informal labor market to expand.

Another major country of immigration, the Netherlands, became a significant labor importer decades ago. But it is only in recent times that some government officials have begun to acknowledge that the Netherlands is indeed a country of immigration, and this notion remains highly controversial. As a result, the Netherlands does not have a comprehensive policy based on an overall vision of itself as a country of immigration; rather, it has a series of ad hoc policies formulated in response to changing economic and social conditions.

Nevertheless, as Willem Maas argues, migration has been a central feature of Dutch political development going back to the founding of the Dutch state itself, and Dutch society has been defined by core liberal values of pragmatism, tolerance, and humanism. These national values have prevented the government from veering too far toward a restrictionist immigration policy. Dutch policy has been a constant search for balance between pragmatic economic interests and humanitarian concerns. Responding to the economy's need for foreign labor, the Netherlands operated a German-style guest worker program from the early 1960s to the mid-1970s. At the same time, because of its strong humanitarianism, the Netherlands maintained a liberal asylum system, similar to Germany's pre-1993 regime, despite the importance of postcolonial migrations—in this respect the Netherlands is more similar to Britain, Belgium, or France than to Germany.

Immigration policymaking in the Netherlands has been a story of emerging gaps between policy outputs and outcomes, followed by attempts to close the gaps by tightening immigration controls. Virtually all of the country's immigration policies have produced serious unintended consequences. The guest worker program of the 1960s and early 1970s brought more foreign workers to the Netherlands than initially anticipated, and they did not repatriate as expected. After the guest worker program was suspended in 1974, recruitment of foreign workers was allowed to continue, albeit on a smaller scale. In the ensuing decades, the generous Dutch asylum system was quickly overwhelmed as the Netherlands became one of the most attractive destinations for asylum seekers. The Dutch have been more lenient than the Germans and the British in allowing family reunification for asylum seekers, guest workers, and postcolonial migrants, which gave employers back-door access to foreign-born labor. Like other countries of immigration, the Netherlands began to recruit temporary, highly skilled workers from abroad to meet the needs of its increasingly important knowledge-based industries. The Dutch immigration system became a *gedoogbeleid* (a policy that unofficially tolerates what is formally not allowed), and the most densely populated major country in western Europe experienced a large influx of immigrants, especially Muslims from predominantly Islamic countries.

The initial lightning rod for anti-immigrant sentiment was Pim Fortuyn, a former Marxist academic turned populist-conservative who came close to being prime minister in 2002. Fortuyn argued that the Netherlands was "full up" and called Islam a "backward religion." But he was assassinated a few days before the election, and his makeshift political party (List Pim Fortuyn) faded. Nevertheless, he succeeded in turning immigration and asylum seeking into issues that divided the mainstream Dutch parties. The context of immigration politics in the Netherlands was further inflamed with the assassination late in 2004 of the controversial filmmaker Theo van Gogh, who was killed by a Muslim extremist. The mantle of anti-immigrant politics subsequently was taken up by Geert Wilders, leading the right-wing populist Party for Freedom (Partij voor Vrijheid, PVV), which had a minor role in government following parliamentary elections in 2010. As Maas illustrates, the rise of anti-immigrant politics has had a profound effect on Dutch policies with respect to immigration, integration, and citizenship.

Attempts to narrow the gaps between immigration control policies and outcomes have included repeated attempts to limit family reunification immigration, which proved ineffective, as well as a series of measures to discourage asylum seekers, none of which changed the Netherlands' image as a welcoming destination. In February 2004, the Dutch parliament voted to round up and expel up to 26,000 failed asylum seekers who had arrived in the Netherlands before April 2001—a harsher remedy than has been applied to asylum seekers in any other EU country. Legalization programs and stronger controls against irregular migration also have been tried, but the latter mainly had the effect of increasing migrants' reliance on professional people-smugglers. Meanwhile, Dutch integration policies remain generous and inclusive. Paradoxically, these policies are justified as efforts to prevent the establishment of "ethnic minorities" while allowing immigrants to maintain their cultural identities, in line with the Dutch consociational model of democracy. Despite heated political battles, the system has been successful in terms of housing, education, and legal rights for immigrants and has produced high rates of naturalization, but it has been less successful in promoting economic incorporation (cf. Bevelander and Hollifield 2021).

Grete Brochmann writes about the Scandinavian countries of Denmark, Norway, and Sweden, which since the 1960s have become countries of immigration. The Scandinavian case, she argues, differs from others because of the "Nordic model," whereby the social contract is ensured by a comprehensive (cradle-to-grave) universal

welfare state. Guaranteeing basic welfare of all citizens and legal residents is fundamental to the Nordic model of government, and for this reason it is difficult to talk
about immigrant policies outside of the context of the welfare state. And immigration poses an acute dilemma for Scandinavia to the extent that it might weaken social solidarity and undermine the welfare state (Freeman 1986; Crepaz 2008; Bevelander and Hollifield 2021), a dilemma that is similar but not identical to the liberal
paradox described earlier.

Scandinavian countries have had fairly generous admission policies, especially
for refugees and asylum seekers, but as Brochmann notes, the emphasis on social
solidarity and tight regulation of labor markets has made it more difficult for immigrants to integrate into the economy and society. Sweden has a longer history of
immigration than Denmark or Norway, and the politics of immigration in Sweden
have been more liberal (open and tolerant), similar in some respects to Canada with
its multicultural model, whereas Denmark has had the most restrictionist and some
would say xenophobic politics, strongly influenced by the Danish People's Party, with
Norway somewhere in the middle. Since the turn of the century, the immigration,
refugee, and integration policies in the three states have diverged more. Sweden has
been the great magnet in the region, and Swedish governments have pursued a rather
open immigration policy, generally speaking. The large inflow of refugees and migrants in 2015 triggered a change, however, leading Sweden to introduce markedly
more restrictive control and integration policies. Norway and particularly Denmark
reinforced an already more restrictive policy as a consequence of the 2015–2016 "crisis." Despite these differences, Brochmann argues that there are still similarities in
the Nordic approach to immigration policies, characterized by careful admission
policies and integration of immigrants via the welfare state (cf. Bevelander and Hollifield 2021). The Scandinavian welfare state has served paradoxically as a mechanism
for a trade-off between (intentionally) strict control of immigrant admissions and
the rapid integration of landed immigrants—what some have referred to as a grand
bargain, closing side and back doors in order to keep the front door partially open.

Switzerland is a rather unique case with a long and detailed history of immigration, similar to that of France, dating back to the period of industrialization in the
late nineteenth century. As Gianni D'Amato points out, Switzerland is a federal state
with a multicultural society, located in the heart of Europe, and always fearful of
Überfremdung (over-foreignization) and of being overrun by more powerful neighbors. Yet despite the country's relative isolation, the delicate nature of the Swiss constitution and society, and strict adherence to a policy of neutrality and independence
in its foreign policy, Switzerland has relied heavily on foreign labor to fuel economic
growth. During the period of economic reconstruction in Europe after World War II,

the size of the foreign population in Switzerland increased steadily, but Switzerland maintained a strict guest worker or rotation policy that forced many foreign workers to return home following the economic downturns of the 1970s. D'Amato argues that the politics of immigration shifted in the 1980s and 1990s in favor of a more rights-based and integrationist policy that allowed foreigners to settle and acquire citizenship, even though the process of naturalization remains highly decentralized and depends almost entirely on the consent of the commune for accepting and naturalizing foreigners.

The federal and consociational nature of the Swiss political system has made immigration policymaking difficult, with multiple actors and veto points, leading to frequent referenda on immigration, usually framed in terms of *Überfremdung*. As in other small European democracies (the Netherlands, Austria, and Denmark are good examples), the rise of right-wing populist parties has upset the delicate balance between the need for foreign/immigrant labor, the need for maintaining social solidarity based on a highly developed welfare state, and the need to protect citizenship in increasingly multicultural societies. Like Germany, the liberal paradox is much in evidence. However, D'Amato argues that Switzerland is unlikely to embrace more liberal approaches to immigration and citizenship, characteristic of Germany and other EU countries, and that Switzerland will remain more parochial in its approach to migration management.

Latecomers to Immigration

With rapid industrialization, economic growth, and democratization in southern Europe and East Asia, a new group of nations became destinations for immigrants. How have these latecomers managed the relatively quick transition from origin countries to transit countries to destination countries, and are they as welcoming of newcomers as more well-established migration states? Latecomers to immigration are those countries that did not have notable immigration in the early decades of the post–World War II era (1950s–1970s) because labor demands were met in part by internal migration from poorer regions (Italy is a good example), increased utilization of previously untapped labor sources (especially women in Japan and South Korea), and/or mechanization and rationalization of production. Roughly since the 1980s, however, these countries have begun to accept large numbers of immigrants because of demographic trends (their fertility rates are among the world's lowest) and insider-outsider labor markets that increase the demand for workers in the informal sector, especially in Italy, Spain, and Greece. However, the percentage of foreign-born residents remains relatively low—with the notable exceptions of Italy and Spain, where the foreign-born constitute about 12 and 15 percent of the population, respectively—and these latecomers generally do not officially consider themselves to be countries of immigration, much less nations of immigrants. Historically, southern European countries along with South Korea, Taiwan, and (if we go back far enough in time) Japan were prominent *exporters* of labor, countries of emigration, when they were less industrialized than other countries and going through a process of rapid economic, social, and political change with a concomitant rural exodus. As a result, they made a transition from countries of emigration to countries of net immigration beginning roughly in the 1980s.

Among the latecomer immigration countries in southern Europe, Spain has surpassed Italy with the largest population of recently arrived non-citizen residents, the vast majority of whom originated in North Africa, sub-Saharan Africa, or Asia. Italy was a classic country of emigration for most of its history, but this trend was reversed in the early 1980s. While Italy (like Spain) was initially a way station for immigrants and asylum seekers attempting to get to other European destinations through the back door, it is now one of the major countries of immigration in western Europe. Ted Perlmutter shows that Italy faces the same dilemmas of immigration control and integration (the liberal paradox) as more advanced immigration countries. Italian governments, often in rapid succession, have attempted to maintain a balance between strong demand for foreign labor, especially in the large informal sector of the Italian economy, and the need to maintain at least the appearance of immigration control. The need for control became more acute when Italy joined the Schengen group in the 1990s, requiring various Italian governments to hastily construct immigration and refugee policy in a highly ad hoc manner—what Giuseppe Sciortino (1999) called "planning in the dark"—in part to satisfy EU requirements for joining the border-free area.

The reasons Italy became dependent on foreign workers are common to most of today's major labor-importing countries. However, the demographic implosion—declining birth rates and aging populations—is more pronounced in Italy, as it is in Spain. Continued strong demand for foreign labor also reflects a social welfare state that encourages underemployment and early retirement among native workers, as in Greece. And labor unions—which enforce heavy-handed regulation of labor markets—increase the attractiveness of cheap, undocumented foreign labor in non-union firms. As has been the case throughout its history, Italy has maintained a dual labor market, with a highly regulated formal sector (mostly in the north) and a largely unregulated informal, secondary labor market (most pronounced in the south).

Perlmutter argues that government interventions to control immigration to Italy were overwhelmed by powerful market forces and by the extreme volatility of Italian politics, which saw fifteen different governments in the twenty-year period from 1990 to 2010 before stabilizing somewhat in the 2010s. Mainstream political parties are whipsawed between xenophobic and nationalist forces of the Northern League and the Five-Star Movement on the one hand and fragile coalition politics on the other, making it extremely difficult to find consensus on the contentious issue of immigration control. Italian politicians find themselves making promises to the public about controlling immigration that they cannot keep, enacting many laws and creating a tangled and ineffective system of control. Substantial gaps between policy outputs and outcomes are virtually guaranteed by quotas that are set too low and become de facto legalization programs for unauthorized immigrants already in the country; by employer sanctions that are not enforced because of legal challenges by the courts and so lead to confusion and division within the government over policy implementation; by the high percentage of unauthorized immigrants working in the underground economy; and by amnesty programs that fail because of the fiscal burdens that they impose on employers (a newer program based on legalization, initiated by the immigrants themselves, has been more successful). Meanwhile, the stock of unauthorized immigrants in Italy has continued to rise, and pressure continues to mount from other EU member states to improve Italy's external border controls in order to reduce the influx of unauthorized migrants and waves of asylum seekers, especially from Africa and the Middle East. This pressure from its neighbors to control its porous sea border became even more acute in the aftermath of the Arab Spring, the Syrian civil war, and the collapse of authoritarian regimes in Africa and the Middle East, especially in Libya, which under Muammar Gaddafi acted as a gatekeeper or buffer state for Italy and the EU, preventing migrants from West Africa from transiting across the Mediterranean, but at a price (see Greenhill 2010; Tsourapas 2019).

Italy's recent record on immigrant integration is mixed. Immigration law affirms labor rights for immigrants and provides access to basic human services. However, some of these provisions have been obstructed by local officials fearing a community backlash. Naturalization remains difficult, and multiculturalism has not been pursued as a social integration policy because of the widespread belief that the cultures of African immigrants—Muslims in particular—threaten Italy's social cohesion and national identity.

Public opinion on immigration is highly polarized in Italy. Italy was once quite tolerant of diversity (in the 1990s and 2000s), but there is growing antagonism toward immigrants and asylum seekers based on the commonly held belief that they threaten public safety, especially with the horrific terrorist attacks in neighboring France and elsewhere in western Europe. Right-wing political parties have made considerable headway in some parts of the country using anti-immigrant and xenophobic appeals. But anti-immigration political forces have been counterbalanced by a powerful coalition of pro-immigrant groups (employers, labor unions, NGOs, and religious groups, including the Vatican) that presses the government for more open policies and measures to reduce the illegality and marginality of foreign workers and asylum seekers. Italian labor unions, well entrenched in the formal economy and thus largely insulated from foreign-worker competition, have been particularly strong supporters of rights for undocumented immigrants, and powerful NGOs work to protect the rights of refugees and asylum seekers. As Perlmutter notes, however, the hallmark of Italian immigration policy is extreme politicization and polarization, which make it difficult for Italy to settle on a coherent policy.

Like Italy, Spain's experience with immigration is historically limited. Only since the mid-1980s have migrant workers, mostly from North and West Africa, replaced "sunbird" northern Europeans as the largest category of foreigners in Spain. The foreign-born population grew rapidly in the 2000s, surpassing 7 million in 2020 (15.2 percent of the total population), most of them from non-EU countries. Spain has become an important destination country for unauthorized migrants from Africa, Latin America, and East Asia. As Miryam Hazán and Rut Bermejo Casado note at the beginning of their chapter, however, the economic collapse that began in 2008 and the resulting high levels of unemployment throughout the Spanish economy stopped immigration in its tracks and shifted the dilemma of control to one of integration of a large, settled foreign population.

Until the recession of 2008, Spain was fairly typical of the latecomers to immigration, grappling with the rising share of foreign workers in the booming construction sector while struggling to control unauthorized immigration. As in Italy, most unauthorized immigrants in Spain worked in service industries, such as construction, home (or domestic) work, restaurants and hotels, health care, and agriculture, which were until 2008 the most dynamic sectors of the economy. As in Italy, the country's vast underground economy absorbed much of this foreign labor. With one of Europe's best-performing economies until 2008, a native-born workforce no longer willing to migrate internally for employment or to do low-wage manual jobs, and a demographic profile (rock-bottom fertility rates, rapid population aging) that cried out for an expansionary immigration policy, Spain was destined to be a large-scale importer of foreign workers in the twenty-first century.

Gaps between Spanish immigration control policies and their outcomes were and are quite large and growing. Five different legalization programs (amnesties) implemented since 1986 have not reduced the stock of unauthorized immigrants, and a dysfunctional system of interlinked work and residence permits turned once-legal foreign workers into *irregulares* with dismaying regularity. A quota system enabling employers to import foreign workers, mostly on short-term visas, fell far short of meeting the demand for such workers. Moreover, it was limited to nationals of five countries with which Spain had signed bilateral migrant labor agreements. Employer sanctions were inhibited by the high percentage of unauthorized immigrants employed in the underground economy and by the closeness of the ties between government and business.

As in Italy, the high demand for foreign labor and the large informal economy combined to create high levels of irregular migration, leading governments of the right and the left to pursue policies of amnesty, regularization, and legalization. Hazán and Bermejo explain that from the Plan Greco, enacted by the right-of-center Aznar government in 2000, through the 2005 legalization put in place by the left-of-center socialist government under Zapatero, the emphasis of Spanish immigration policy was on quick and generous legalization of the large foreign workforce to allow the foreign population to integrate as rapidly as possible. This approach to migration management, combined with a fairly decentralized policymaking process that relies on the autonomous regional governments to implement immigration policy, has stymied xenophobic and populist parties. But, like Italy, Spain has been under pressure from the EU to control its borders and prevent African and Latin American migrants from transiting Spanish territory on their way to other EU destinations. Beginning in the 2000s, Morocco and Spain cooperated to stem the flow of migrants across the western route of the Mediterranean; however, the decision by the Moroccan government in 2021 to allow thousands of migrants to enter Ceuta (a free port city on the coast of Morocco that is part of Spanish territory) showed that Morocco can use migration to put pressure on Spain and the EU to recognize Morocco's claim on the Western Sahara, more evidence of how migrants are used by states as pawns in geopolitics (Greenhill 2010; Hollifield 2012; Adamson and Tsourapas 2018). Hazán and Bermejo conclude by pointing out that the severe economic crisis of the late 2000s has put pressure on native Spanish youth to emigrate in search of gainful employment, bringing Spain full circle from a sending country to a receiving country and back to a sending country.

Greece and Turkey, two of the most recent latecomers to immigration, have a shared history and a common border, and they have faced similar dynamics with regard to cross-border migration movements. Yet, as Adamson and Tsourapas note, there are also some striking differences between the two states, including their internal political trajectories and their relationship to the EU and other external actors. The authors delve into the evolution of migration management regimes in these two latecomers to immigration, from bilateral cooperation over population exchanges in the 1920s through their participation in European guest worker programs in the 1960s and 1970s to the management of regional refugee crises in the 2010s. They argue that shifts in migration management regimes in the two states are linked to changes in the broader geopolitical context, as well as larger state interests of nation-building, economic development, and the maintenance of national sovereignty. By employing a *longue durée* perspective on cross-border mobility in the two countries, they demonstrate the complexities of emigration, immigration, transit, and the management of forced migration on Europe's southeastern border, a flashpoint in the politics of international migration. Greece and Turkey are at the crossroads of the Middle East, South Asia, the "stans" (particularly Afghanistan), Africa, and Europe, and as a result they have been forced to deal with millions of (mostly forced) migrants seeking passage to the EU. Again, geopolitics drives migration control policies in these two states, and each is compelled to play two-level games; for Turkey, this involves balancing between the EU and the Middle East, and for Greece, it involves desperately seeking to externalize control and abide by its treaty commitments, respecting the refugee convention, while seeking help from the EU and the international community to shelter and care for hundreds of thousands of forced migrants.

Although past Japanese and Korean emigration was never on the scale of that seen from Italy, Spain, Turkey, or even Greece (in proportional terms), hundreds of thousands of Japanese did emigrate to the Americas from the late nineteenth century to the mid-twentieth century, creating large communities of Japanese descendants in the United States, Brazil, and elsewhere in South America. Koreans also emigrated in large numbers to Japan, especially during the colonial period, and many went to the United States, China, and the former Soviet Union. The economic and demographic factors that turned Japan and Korea into countries of immigration are similar to those operating in Italy and Spain. However, unlike Italy and Spain, until recently Japan has insisted on a closed-door immigration policy that prohibited the importation and settlement of unskilled migrant workers and permitted only the admission of highly skilled and professional workers. Korea, on the other hand, has taken a somewhat more liberal approach to immigrant settlement.

Both the Japanese and South Korean governments maintained a restrictive stance toward immigration through the high-growth periods of the 1960s to 1980s. Both countries wanted to maintain their ethnic homogeneity and feared that large numbers of racially and culturally different immigrants would provoke social unrest. Japan's bureaucratic and centralized immigration policymaking regime shielded the state from lobbying by small and medium-sized employers and other pro-immigration groups. However, demographic decline has placed great pressure on Japan to open its economy and society to higher levels of immigration, despite the so-called lost decades of slow economic growth in the 1990s and 2000s. The Japanese population has ceased to grow and is projected to decline by 22 million during the next fifty years, assuming current levels of fertility and immigration. A similar though less acute demographic dynamic is at work in Korea, which has been much more economically dynamic than Japan.

As a result, the gaps between immigration policy and actual outcomes in Japan and South Korea are substantial. Despite attempts to exclude the importation of unskilled foreign workers, Japan and South Korea have become countries of immigration. Large economic disparities exist between Japan and South Korea, on the one hand, and South and Southeast Asia, on the other, and with high levels of growth in the 1980s in Japan and in South Korea over the last twenty years, foreign workers from the global South have found their way into both societies. As Chung argues, they have found ways to settle and integrate into both societies, although the mechanisms of settlement and the acquisition of rights have been quite different.

Some immigrants to Japan were smuggled in clandestinely—most notoriously in the construction sector during the boom years of the 1980s and more recently in the home care sector and in the sex and marriage industry—and many immigrants entered Japan and South Korea on short-term visas and simply overstayed. Even after the bubble burst in the construction and housing sectors, and after the financial collapse of the 1990s in Japan and the Asian financial crises of 1997–1998 that led to a sharp economic downturn in South Korea, neither state was able to crack down on illegal immigration, because key sectors in both economies already were dependent on foreign labor, and rights were accruing to foreigners in both societies. The Japanese and Korean governments seemed to recognize that employers were dependent on foreign labor and that a crackdown would further depress the economy. Meanwhile, both governments undermined otherwise restrictive policies by enabling large numbers of unskilled foreign workers to be imported through various side-door mechanisms, as company trainees, students, entertainers, and, in the case of Japan, ethnic Japanese return migrants from Brazil, the so-called *dekasegi*.

Japan's insistence on treating all foreign workers, except for ethnic Japanese returnees, as short-term "guests"—not potential permanent settlers—delayed the formulation of explicit, national-level policies and programs to facilitate the social integration of settled immigrants. But as Chung demonstrates in her chapter, local governments, NGOs, and other actors in civil society provided basic social services and protections to foreign residents, creating a mechanism for integration of foreigners, allowing them to acquire rights, and in the process helping transform Japanese politics and society.

Thus far, the Japanese public—well known for its ethnic insularity—has showed surprising tolerance toward the immigrants who have arrived over the past decades, despite the long-running recession that followed the collapse of the bubble economy of the late 1980s. This relative tolerance is partly a function of the widely shared belief that foreign workers are alleviating Japan's labor shortage and thus contributing to the economy. But it also is indicative of the weakening of traditional conceptions of citizenship and nationhood, as Chung illustrates in her chapter (see also Chung 2010).

Like Japan, Korea historically was a labor-exporting country that did not begin importing immigrants until the late 1980s. And as in Japan, foreign workers constitute only a small segment of the population. They are concentrated in the manufacturing and construction sectors, with a growing presence in service industries. Like Japan, Korea has traditionally denied that it is a country of immigration, officially forbidding the entry of unskilled immigrant labor and rejecting asylum seekers. But, as Chung shows, a powerful labor movement succeeded in legalizing the status of foreign workers through the establishment of a formal guest worker program in 2004. The Korean state also has taken an accommodating approach to integrating the foreign population.

Policy convergence between Korea and Japan, according to Chung, is partly the result of the strength of local institutions and the willingness of civil society to incorporate de facto immigrants. Like Japan, Korea traditionally has a monocultural approach to citizenship, even though Korea is more ethnically homogeneous than Japan. Both states still reject large-scale, permanent immigration. Nevertheless, the demand for immigrant labor in Korea has acquired a structural character because high levels of economic growth have been coupled with low fertility and population aging, a wealthy and highly educated native workforce that shuns unskilled jobs, and limited alternative sources of labor. In addition, Korea has a Japanese-style, bureaucracy-dominated immigration policymaking system that has responded in similar fashion to the contradictory pressures of keeping the country immigrant-free and meeting domestic labor shortages. As a former Japanese colony, Korea inherited Japanese laws and subsequently imported many of its policies from Japan. The Korean government copied wholesale several Japanese immigration control policies and programs. Nonetheless, as long as Korean and Japanese civil societies remain relatively tolerant, these latecomers to immigration may converge toward the more liberal immigration policies of Euro-American countries, even though citizenship remains out of reach for most foreigners.

The Future of Immigration Control

The country cases in this volume provide ample evidence that most of the OECD countries, until the pandemic of 2020, were highly integrated into a global market for labor and their economies were heavily dependent on foreign labor. The rise of reactive, right-wing populism combined with the global pandemic has made migration and mobility even more explosive political issues, and it remains to be seen whether the global economy will return to the same levels of migration and mobility that existed before the pandemic. We must ask whether the international political economy will revert to a multilateral, rules-based order—a regime that was already weak with respect to migration and asylum seeking (Hollifield 2000, 2012, 2021b)—or if we are witnessing the "end of liberalism" (Hollifield 2021a; Joppke 2021). Virtually all of the countries in this book, including many of the nations of immigrants (Canada remains the exception), prefer to classify themselves as reluctant or unwilling countries of immigration—recall the German refrain *Deutschland ist kein Einwanderungsland* or the elusive search in western Europe for "zero immigration."

Across the OECD world, we can observe four trends:

1. Demand/pull forces remain strong—the great recession of 2008–2009 and the global pandemic notwithstanding—due to demographic stagnation and aging, near full employment (before the pandemic), and dynamic economies that need foreign workers at the low- and high-skill ends of the labor market, especially with renewed demand as the global economy recovers from the pandemic.

2. Supply/push forces remain strong because of global inequalities, even though some major sending countries, such as Mexico, Turkey, and Morocco, have gone through demographic transitions of their own and net migration from these countries recently turned negative (since 2007, more Mexicans are returning home than moving to the United States). These and other sending countries are now countries of transit and destination (Hollifield and Foley 2021).

3. Conflict and political instability along with climate change are forcing more people to move within countries and internationally. The number of forced migrants, especially internally displaced people, has soared. While the majority of forced migrants (87 percent) are in the Southern Hemisphere, the potential for new waves of asylum seekers moving into Europe and North America remains high. The ongoing war in Ukraine has the potential to transform immigration policy and politics in Western Europe.

4. A nativist, populist, and right-wing backlash against immigration has led governments in the United States and Europe to roll back the rights of im-

migrants and asylum seekers, and Britain has left the EU, ending freedom of movement for EU nationals into and out of the United Kingdom.

The confluence of economic, security (health, war, and civil strife), and political trends produces deep ambivalence about immigration, coupled with a keen sensitivity to the challenge of integrating ethnically and culturally diverse populations (Bevelander and Hollifield 2021).

The cases that we have examined illustrate vividly the difficulties of intervening in the migration process to stop so-called chain migration, break up migration networks, and roll back the rights of migrants, their families, asylum seekers, and refugees. Governments are increasingly prone to pursue symbolic policies such as building more walls and fences—interventions that appear to work at first, but which have little staying power, much like the Maginot Line between France and Germany or the Great Wall of China—and these policies result in long-term unintended consequences that are often the opposite of the initial, intended effects. The hardening of the US southern border had the effect of stopping circular migration and freezing a large undocumented population in place (Massey, Durand, and Malone 2002; Massey 2020; Schain 2019).

Immigration control measures are driven increasingly by an electoral dynamic, and governments of the left and the right have sought to demonstrate that they are tough, especially on irregular immigration (Lutz 2019). Parties and party systems have been disrupted by a new national populism, leading to dealignment (Perlmutter 1996; Arzheimer, Kai, and Carter 2006; Eatwell and Goodwin 2018; Norris and Inglehart 2019). Governments of widely varying ideological bent fine-tune their immigration policies and devise new ones because these measures are seen as useful in convincing the general public that governments have not lost control of immigration. This political calculus has caused even liberal and moderate governments to crack down on irregular migration (in his two terms Barack Obama deported more migrants than all previous US presidents combined) and toughen the political asylum process (Donald Trump banned migrants and refugees from some Muslim-majority countries and struck a deal with Mexico to block Central American asylum seekers from crossing the US southern border, forcing them to remain in dangerous camps). In Europe, as the chapter by Geddes and Hadj-Abdou in this volume illustrates, some member states, such as Germany and Sweden, lend their support to regional efforts to "harmonize" immigration and asylum policies, while others, especially Brexit Britain, seek to restrict labor mobility within an enlarged European Union, forge new repatriation agreements with African and Asian sending countries, and limit asylum seeking. The so-called Visegrad Group of countries in eastern

Europe adamantly refused to accept large numbers of asylum seekers during the refugee "crisis" of 2015–2016. Meaningful, supranational migration controls remain elusive, even in Europe, where these policies are the most advanced, and global governance of migration is weak, even as the UN moves to implement global compacts for migration and refugees.

Nation-states retain a capacity to control immigration, but that capacity is limited by client politics (in particular, the privileged position of business) and by rights-based politics both at the domestic level (constitutional protections for migrants still are strong in many of the countries under study here, especially those with active judiciaries, and in the EU) and at the international level (the refugee and human rights conventions provide a measure of safety and protection). As a result, large gaps persist between policy outputs and outcomes because the number of domestic stakeholders in an expansionary (de facto) immigration policy is significant and likely to increase as demand/pull and supply/push factors intensify in the twenty-first century. Ineffective and symbolic immigration control measures (building walls and closing borders) are thus perpetuated because they give the appearance of control (Schain 2019).

One major question remains the extent to which future governments in the liberal democracies will succeed in rolling back the legal, political, and social rights of migrants and limiting mobility in the wake of the pandemic (Bevelander and Hollifield 2021). Curtailing the rights of immigrants and asylum seekers is a tempting course for governments seeking to deal with basic market and demographic forces—in both sending and receiving countries—that drive migration. This approach may mitigate some of the diplomatic costs associated with stringent border enforcement or imposing tough new visa restrictions on the nationals of high-emigration countries. However, such measures are unlikely to stem the flow of new migrants, since the availability of social services or entitlements is not a powerful magnet for would-be unauthorized entrants, compared with other demand/pull factors. Moreover, once migrant rights have been extended, they have a very long half-life, and it is exceedingly difficult for governments that operate under liberal constitutions with active judiciaries simply to roll back the civil rights of immigrants (Hollifield 1999). Cracking down on migrant rights, if carried to the extreme, also can undermine the raison d'être and raison d'état of liberal states (Gibney 1999; Hollifield 1992, 2004, 2021a).

At what point in the future will the politics of appeasing anti-immigrant public opinion collide with the national interests of the receiving countries, defined in terms of economic growth, global competitiveness, and the interest of individual citizens in maintaining lifestyles often made possible by immigrant service providers and producers of low-cost goods? When that point is reached, the goals of national immigration policy may have to be redefined in order to reduce the large and constantly widening gap between policy goals and outcomes. Redefining the goals of national immigration policies will compel reluctant countries of immigration, such as Japan and Korea, to confront rather than ignore or downplay the trade-offs between more effective immigration control and other societal goals and principles (Chung in this volume; Hollifield and Sharpe 2017). What basic values, what civil liberties, how much in tax revenues, and how much in future economic growth are to be sacrificed in order to gain greater control over immigration and reduce the size of foreign-born populations? The outcomes of ongoing debates over these questions will determine whether persistently high levels of immigration—in whatever form—will be tolerated in the long term. Meanwhile, market forces and demography, along with transnational social networks, remain powerful drivers of international migration in the twenty-first century—like an engine pulling a train down the tracks. However, to use a Weberian metaphor, the switches on the track are controlled by states. The switches will determine the direction of the speeding train, whether it continues along a safe course or hurtles off a cliff (Hollifield and Wong 2022).

Some governments, as well as international organizations, continue to hope for market-based/economic solutions to the problem of regulating international migration. Trade and foreign investment—bringing capital and jobs to people, either through private investment or via official development assistance—will substitute for migration, it is hoped, alleviating both supply/push and demand/pull factors (Martin 2022). Even though trade can lead to factor-price equalization in the long term, as we have seen in the case of the EU, in the short and medium terms exposing developing countries to strong market forces results in increased (rather than decreased) migration, as was evident with NAFTA (Martin 2022; Hollifield, Orrenius, and Osang 2006). Likewise, trade in services can stimulate more "high-skill" migration, because these types of products cannot be produced or sold without the movement of the individuals who make and market them (Ghosh 1997).

In short, the global integration of markets for goods, services, and capital entails higher levels of international migration. Therefore, if states want to promote freer trade and investment, they must be prepared to manage higher levels of migration (Bhagwati 1998; Hollifield 2012). Many states (such as Canada, Australia, and even Germany) are willing, if not eager, to sponsor high-skill migration, because the numbers are manageable, and there is likely to be less political resistance to the importation of highly skilled individuals (Hainmueller and Hiscox 2010; Chiswick 2011). However, mass migration of unskilled and less educated workers is likely to meet with greater political resistance, even in situations and in sectors, such as construction, food service, and health care, where there is high demand for this type of labor. In these instances, the tendency is for governments to go back to the old guest worker models, in hopes of bringing in just enough temporary workers to fill gaps in the labor market, but with strict contracts between foreign workers and their employers that limit the length of stay and prohibit settlement or family reunification (see the chapter by Chung in this volume). The alternative is irregular immigration and a growing black market for labor—a Hobson's choice, which is the dilemma facing all of the OECD countries as they search for grand bargains that will allow comprehensive immigration reform (Martin and Orrenius in this volume; Orrenius and Zavodny 2010; Hollifield 2010).

Conclusion: Solving the Immigration Control Dilemma

The nineteenth and twentieth centuries saw the rise of what Richard Rosecrance (1986) has labeled the *trading state*. The latter half of the twentieth century has given rise to what Hollifield (2004) calls the *migration state*. From strategic, economic, and demographic standpoints, trade and migration go hand in hand, because the wealth, power, and stability of the state are heavily dependent on its willingness to risk both trade and migration. As they have done in the areas of trade and finance, states must find ways to cooperate and to manage migration for strategic gains (Hollifield 2004, 2012). Likewise, international security and stability are dependent on the capacity of states to manage migration. It is extremely difficult, if not impossible, for states to manage or control migration unilaterally or bilaterally. Some type of global migration governance (Hollifield 2000; Betts 2011) is required, similar to what the EU has achieved at the regional level for nationals of its member states. The EU model, as described by Geddes and Hadj-Abdou in this volume, points the way to future migration control regimes, because it is not based purely on *homo economicus* but incorporates rights for individual migrants and European citizenship (which continues to evolve). The problem, of course, in this type of regional migration regime is how to deal with third-country nationals (TCNs). The issue of TCNs, asylum seekers, and immigrant integration is ever more pressing in Europe. In the end, the EU, by creating a regional migration regime and a kind of supranational authority to deal with migration and refugee issues, allows member states to finesse, if not escape, some of the dilemmas of immigration control described earlier, if not to solve the liberal paradox itself. The price, as with many EU policies, is loss of sovereignty and the ability to set rules of entry and exit (Joppke 1998; Guiraudon and Lahav 2000). The vote by Britain to leave the EU was driven largely by concerns over immigration (Norris and Inglehart 2019).

Regional integration reinforces the trading state and acts as a midwife for the migration state (Hollifield 2004). As Geddes and Hadj-Abdou point out, in the EU migrants are gradually acquiring the rights they need in order to live and work on the territory of the member states. Regional integration blurs the lines of territoriality but feeds a cultural backlash. The fact that there is an increasing disjuncture between people and place has provoked a crisis of national identity, leading to the rise of anti-immigration and anti-system political parties, and it has undermined the legitimacy of the nation-state. Protests against globalization and nativist or xenophobic reactions against immigration have become commonplace throughout the OECD world. Nonetheless, regional integration—especially when it has a long history and is deeply institutionalized, as it is in Europe—makes it easier for states to open their economies and societies to immigration and trade, and for governments to construct the kinds of political coalitions that will be necessary to support and institutionalize greater openness, Brexit and reactive populism notwithstanding.

By contrast, the United States has pulled back from globalization and regional integration, preferring instead to create new temporary or guest worker programs, or to continue with the current immigration system, which limits the number of visas (and green cards) while tolerating high levels of unauthorized migration. Clearly, however, North America is the region that is closest to taking steps toward an EU-style regional migration regime; meanwhile, the United States is facing the prospect of another legalization program, similar to the Immigration Reform and Control Act of 1986, especially for those immigrants brought to the United States as children. In the long run it is difficult for liberal states, such as the United States, to sustain a large, irregular population, as it undermines rule of law and the social contract. For this reason, amnesties, legalizations, or regularizations—policies like DACA—have become a common feature of immigration policy throughout the OECD world.

Even though there are large numbers of economic migrants in Asia, this region remains divided into relatively closed and often authoritarian societies, with limited prospects of granting rights to migrants and guest workers. The more liberal and democratic states, such as Japan, Taiwan, and South Korea, are the exceptions (Chung 2020), but as Chung points out in this volume, they have only just begun to grapple with the problem of immigration control and immigrant integration. In Africa and the Middle East, which have high numbers of foreign workers and refugees, there is a great deal of political and social instability, and many states are fluid or failed, with little institutional or legal capacity for dealing with international migration (Hollifield and Foley 2021).

In conclusion, we can see that migration is both a cause and a consequence of political and economic change. It is endogenous. International migration, like trade and foreign direct investment, is a fundamental feature of the interdependent world in which we live. As states and societies become more liberal, more open, and more democratic, migration will increase. Will the increase be a virtuous or vicious cycle? Will it be destabilizing, leading the international system into greater anarchy, disorder, and war, or will it lead to greater openness, wealth, and human development? Much will depend on how migration is managed by powerful liberal states, because they will set the trend for the rest of the globe. To avoid a domestic political backlash against immigration, the rights of migrants must be respected, and states must find ways to manage migration for strategic gains. As states strive to master this extraordinarily complex phenomenon, it may be possible to construct a truly international migration regime under the auspices of the United Nations. But we are not sanguine about this possibility, because the asymmetry of interests between the North and the South is too great. Even as states become more interdependent in an era of globalization, they are likely to remain trapped in a liberal paradox for decades to come.

Note

1. The average number of international migrants is low in part because of seven "demographic giants" (China, India, Pakistan, Indonesia, Brazil, Nigeria, and the United States), which together have 52 percent of the world population but account for very few emigrants, since in many of them internal migration replaces emigration. The rest of the planet has 223 million emigrants out of 3.7 billion inhabitants, a rate of 6.1 percent. Moreover, these emigrants tend to concentrate in rich countries: the migrant stock makes up 12.8 percent of the total population in high-income countries (11.9 percent in the euro zone, 14.9 percent in North America [the United States and Canada]).

References

Adamson, Fiona. 2006. "Crossing Borders: International Migration and National Security." *International Security* 31, no. 1: 165–199.

Adamson, Fiona B., and Gerasimos Tsourapas. 2018. "Migration Diplomacy in World Politics." *International Studies Perspectives* 20, no. 2: 123–128.

Arzheimer, Kai, and Elisabeth Carter. 2006. "Political Opportunity Structures and Right-Wing Extremist Party Success." *European Journal of Political Research* 45, no. 3: 419–443.

Bauböck, Rainer. 1994. *Transnational Citizenship: Membership and Rights in International Migration*. Aldershot, UK: Edward Elgar.

Benhabib, Seyla. 2004. *The Rights of Others: Aliens, Residents and Citizens*. Cambridge: Cambridge University Press.

Betts, Alexander. 2011. *Global Migration Governance*. Oxford: Oxford University Press.

Bevelander, Pieter, and James F. Hollifield. 2021. "Managing Migration in Modern Welfare States." In *Handbook on Migration and Welfare*, edited by Markus M. L. Crepaz, 13–44. London: Edward Elgar.

Bhagwati, Jagdish. 1998. *A Stream of Windows: Unsettling Reflections on Trade, Immigration, and Democracy.* Cambridge, MA: MIT Press.

Bloemraad, Irene. 2006. *Becoming a Citizen: Incorporating Immigrants and Refugees in the United States and Canada.* Berkeley: University of California Press.

Bosma, Ulbe, Jan Lucassen, and Gert Oostindie, eds. 2012. *Postcolonial Migrants and Identity Politics.* Oxford: Berghahn.

Brader, Ted, Nicholas A. Valentino, and Elizabeth Suhay. 2008. "What Triggers Public Opposition to Immigration? Anxiety, Group Cues, and Immigration Threat." *American Journal of Political Science* 52, no. 4: 959–978.

Brubaker, Rogers, ed. 1989. *Immigration and the Politics of Citizenship in Europe and North America.* Lanham, MD: University Press of America.

Carens, Joseph. 2000. *Culture, Citizenship, and Community: A Contextual Exploration of Justice as Evenhandedness.* New York: Oxford University Press.

Carens, Joseph. 2013. *The Ethics of Immigration.* New York: Oxford University Press.

Chiswick, Barry R., ed. 2011. *High-Skilled Immigration in a Global Labor Market.* Washington, DC: AEI Press.

Chung, Erin. 2010. *Immigration and Citizenship in Japan.* New York: Cambridge University Press.

Chung, Erin. 2020. *Immigrant Incorporation in East Asian Democracies.* New York: Cambridge University Press.

Collier, Paul. 2007. *The Bottom Billion.* Oxford: Oxford University Press.

Collier, Paul. 2013. *Exodus: How Migration Is Changing the World.* Oxford: Oxford University Press.

Crepaz, Markus. 2008. *Trust Beyond Borders: Immigration, the Welfare State, and Identity in Modern Societies.* Ann Arbor: University of Michigan Press.

Czaika, M., and H. De Haas. 2013. "The Effectiveness of Immigration Policies." *Population and Development Review* 39, no. 3: 487–508.

De Haas, Hein, Mark J. Miller, and Stephen Castles. 2020. *The Age of Migration: International Population Movements in the Modern World.* New York: Guilford Press.

Dudziak, Mary. 2011. *Cold War Civil Rights: Race and the Image of American Democracy.* Princeton, NJ: Princeton University Press.

Eatwell, Roger, and Matthew Goodwin. 2018. *National Populism: The Revolt Against Liberal Democracy.* London: Pelican/Penguin Books.

Ellermann, Antje. 2009. *States Against Migrants: Deportation in Germany and the United States.* Cambridge: Cambridge University Press.

Ellermann, Antje. 2021. *The Comparative Politics of Immigration: Policy Choices in Germany, Canada, Switzerland, and the United States.* New York: Cambridge University Press.

Favell, Adrian. 1998. *Philosophies of Integration: Immigration and the Idea of Citizenship in France and Britain.* New York: St. Martin's Press.

Fetzer, Joel. 2000. *Public Attitudes Toward Immigration in the United States, France, and Germany.* Cambridge: Cambridge University Press.

Foley, Neil. 2021. "Who Belongs? Politics of Immigration, Nativism, and Illiberal Democracy in the United States." In *Understanding Global Migration*, edited by James F. Hollifield and Neil Foley, 234–268. Stanford, CA: Stanford University Press.

Freeman, Gary P. 1986. "Migration and the Political Economy of the Welfare State." *Annals* 485 (May): 51–63.

Freeman, Gary P. 1995. "Modes of Immigration Politics in Liberal Democratic States." *International Migration Review* 29, no. 4: 881–902.

Geddes, Andrew. 2021. *Governing Migration Beyond the State: Europe, North America, South America, and Southeast Asia in a Global Context*. Oxford: Oxford University Press.

Ghosh, Bimal. 1997. *Gains from Global Linkages: Trade in Services and Movement of Persons*. London: Macmillan.

Gibney, Matthew J. 1999. "Liberal Democratic States and Responsibilities to Refugees." *American Political Science Review* 93, no. 1: 169–181.

Givens, Terri E. 2005. *Voting Radical Right in Western Europe*. Cambridge: Cambridge University Press.

Greenhill, Kelly M. 2010. *Weapons of Mass Migration: Forced Displacement, Coercion, and Foreign Policy*. Ithaca, NY: Cornell University Press.

Guiraudon, Virginie, and Gallya Lahav. 2000. "The State Sovereignty Debate Revisited: The Case of Immigration Control." *Comparative Political Studies* 33, no. 2: 163–195.

Hainmueller, Jens, and Michael J. Hiscox. 2010. "Attitudes Toward Highly Skilled and Low-Skilled Immigration: Evidence from a Survey Experiment." *American Political Science Review* 104: 61–84.

Hazán, Miryam. 2021. "International Migration and Refugee Movements in Latin America." In *Understanding Global Migration*, edited by James F. Hollifield and Neil Foley, 310–341. Stanford, CA: Stanford University Press.

Héran, François. 2017. *Avec l'immigration: Mesurer, débattre, agir*. Paris: La Découverte.

Hirsch, Harry N. 1992. *A Theory of Liberty: The Constitution and Minorities*. New York: Routledge.

Hollifield, James F. 1986. "Immigration Policy in France and Germany: Outputs vs. Outcomes." *Annals* 485 (May): 113–128.

Hollifield, James F. 1990. "Immigration and the French State." *Comparative Political Studies* 23, no. 1: 56–79.

Hollifield, James F. 1992. *Immigrants, Markets and States: The Political Economy of Postwar Europe*. Cambridge, MA: Harvard University Press.

Hollifield, James F. 1999. "Ideas, Institutions and Civil Society: On the Limits of Immigration Control in Liberal Democracies." *IMIS-Beiträge* 10 (January): 57–90.

Hollifield, James F. 2000. "Migration and the 'New' International Order: The Missing Regime." In *Managing Migration: The Need for a New International Regime*, edited by Bimal Ghosh, 75–109. Oxford: Oxford University Press.

Hollifield, James F. 2004. "The Emerging Migration State." *International Migration Review* 38: 885–912.

Hollifield, James F. 2010. "American Immigration Policy and Politics: An Enduring Controversy." In *Developments in American Politics 6*, edited by Gillian Peele et al., 271–296. New York: Palgrave Macmillan.

Hollifield, James F. 2012. "Migration and International Relations." In *The Oxford Handbook of the Politics of International Migration*, edited by Marc R. Rosenblum and Daniel J. Tichenor, 345–379. Oxford: Oxford University Press.

Hollifield, James F. 2021a. "General Perspectives on Membership: Citizenship, Migration, and the End of Liberalism?" In *Handbook of Citizenship and Migration*, edited by Marco Giugni and Maria Grasso, 101–117. London: Edward Elgar.

Hollifield, James F. 2021b. "Driven Out." *The Wilson Quarterly,* fall (online).

Hollifield, James F., Valerie F. Hunt, and Daniel J. Tichenor. 2008. "Immigrants, Markets, and Rights: The United States as an 'Emerging Migration State.'" *Washington University Journal of Law and Policy* 27: 7–44.

Hollifield, James F., Pia M. Orrenius, and Thomas Osang. 2006. *Migration, Trade and Development.* Dallas, TX: Federal Reserve Bank of Dallas.

Hollifield, James F., and Michael Orlando Sharpe. 2017. "Japan as an 'Emerging Migration State.'" *International Relations of the Asia Pacific* 17, no. 3: 371–400.

Hollifield, James F., and Carole J. Wilson. 2011. "Rights-Based Politics, Immigration, and the Business Cycle: 1890–2008." In *High-Skilled Immigration in a Global Labor Market*, edited by Barry R. Chiswick, 50–80. Washington, DC: AEI Press.

Hollifield, James F., and Tom K. Wong. 2022 "The Politics of International Migration: How Can We 'Bring the State Back In'?" In *Migration Theory: Talking Across Disciplines*, 4th ed., edited by Caroline B. Brettell and James F. Hollifield. New York: Routledge.

Hopkins, Daniel J. 2010. "Politicized Places: Explaining Where and When Immigrants Provoke Local Opposition." *American Political Science Review* 104: 40–60.

Huntington, Samuel P. 2004. *Who Are We? The Challenges to America's Identity.* New York: Simon & Schuster.

Jacobson, David. 1996. *Rights Across Borders: Immigration and the Decline of Citizenship.* Baltimore, MD: Johns Hopkins University Press.

Joppke, Christian, ed. 1998. *Challenge to the Nation-State: Immigration in Western Europe and the United States.* Oxford: Oxford University Press.

Joppke, Christian. 2001. "The Legal-Domestic Sources of Immigrant Rights: The United States, Germany and the European Union." *Comparative Political Studies* 34, no. 4: 339–366.

Joppke, Christian. 2010. *Citizenship and Immigration.* Cambridge: Polity Press.

Joppke, Christian. 2017. *Is Multiculturalism Dead? Crisis and Persistence in the Constitutional State.* Cambridge: Polity Press.

Joppke, Christian. 2021. *Neoliberal Nationalism: Immigration and the Rise of the Populist Right.* Cambridge: Cambridge University Press.

Kastoryano, Riva. 1997. *La France, l'Allemagne et leurs immigrés: Négocier l'identité.* Paris: Armand Colin.

Kepel, Gilles. 2012. *Banlieues de la République.* Paris: Gallimard.

King, Desmond. 2000. *Making Americans: Immigration, Race and the Diverse Democracy.* Cambridge, MA: Harvard University Press.

Kitschelt, Herbert. 1995. *The Radical Right in Western Europe.* Ann Arbor: University of Michigan Press.

Koslowski, Rey, ed. 2011. *Global Mobility Regimes*. New York: Palgrave Macmillan.

Kymlicka, Will. 1995. *Multicultural Citizenship*. Oxford: Clarendon Press.

Lucassen. Leo. 2005. *The Immigrant Threat: The Integration of Old and New Migrants in Western Europe Since 1850*. Urbana: University of Illinois Press.

Lucassen, Leo. 2021. "Beyond the Migration State: Western Europe Since World War II." In *Understanding Global Migration*, edited by James F. Hollifield and Neil Foley, 385–412. Stanford, CA: Stanford University Press.

Lutz, Philipp. 2019. "Reassessing the Gap-Hypothesis: Tough Talk and Weak Action in Migration Policy?" *Party Politics* 20, no. 10: 1–13.

Martin, Philip L. 2022. "Economic Aspects of Migration." In *Migration Theory: Talking Across Disciplines*, edited by Caroline B. Brettell and James F. Hollifield. New York: Routledge.

Martin, Philip L., Manolo Abella, and Christiane Kuptsch. 2006. *Managing Labor Migration in the Twenty-First Century*. New Haven, CT: Yale University Press.

Massey, Douglas. 2020. "Immigration Policy Mismatches and Counterproductive Outcomes: Unauthorized Migration to the U.S. in Two Eras." *Comparative Migration Studies* 8, no. 21 (online).

Massey, Douglas S., et al. 1987. *Return to Aztlan: The Social Processes of International Migration from Western Mexico*. Berkeley: University of California Press.

Massey, Douglas S., Jorge Durand, and Nolan J. Malone. 2002. *Beyond Smoke and Mirrors: Mexican Immigration in an Era of Economic Integration*. New York: Russell Sage Foundation.

McCann, James A., and Michael Jones-Correa. 2020. *Holding Fast: Resilience and Civic Engagement Among Latino Immigrants*. New York: Russell Sage.

Messina, Anthony. 2007. *The Logic and Politics of Post-WWII Migration to Western Europe*. New York: Cambridge University Press.

Money, Jeannette. 1999. *Fences and Neighbors: The Geography of Immigration Control*. Ithaca, NY: Cornell University Press.

Mudde, Cas. 2007. *Populist Radical Right Parties in Europe*. Cambridge: Cambridge University Press.

Norris, Pippa. 2005. *Radical Right: Voters and Parties in the Electoral Market*. Cambridge: Cambridge University Press.

Norris, Pippa, and Ronald Inglehart. 2019. *Cultural Backlash: Trump, Brexit, and Authoritarian Populism*. Cambridge: Cambridge University Press.

Orrenius, Pia M., and Madeline Zavodny. 2010. *Beside the Golden Door: US Immigration Reform in a New Era of Globalization*. Washington, DC: AEI Press.

Passel, Jeffrey, D'Vera Cohn, and Ana Gonzalez-Barrera. 2012. "Net Migration from Mexico Falls to Zero—and Perhaps Less." Pew Hispanic Center, Washington, DC.

Perlmutter, Ted. 1996. "Bringing Parties Back In: Comments on 'Modes of Immigration Politics in Liberal Democratic Societies.'" *International Migration Review* 30: 375–388.

Peters, Margaret. 2017. *Trading Barriers: Immigration and the Remaking of Globalization*. Princeton, NJ: Princeton University Press.

Putnam, Robert. 1988. "Diplomacy and Domestic Politics: The Logic of Two-level Games." *International Organization*. 42: 427–460.

Ramakrishnan, Karthick. 2005. *Democracy in Immigrant America: Changing Demographics and Political Participation*. Stanford, CA: Stanford University Press.

Rawls, John. 1971. *A Theory of Justice*. Cambridge, MA: Harvard University Press.

Rosecrance, Richard. 1986. *The Rise of the Trading State*. New York: Basic Books.

Rudolph, Christopher. 2006. *National Security and Immigration: Policy Development in the United States and Western Europe Since 1945*. Stanford, CA: Stanford University Press.

Ruhs, Martin. 2013. *The Price of Rights: Regulating International Labor Migration*. Princeton, NJ: Princeton University Press.

Ruhs, Martin, and Philip L. Martin. 2008. "Numbers vs. Rights: Trade-Offs and Guest Worker Programs." *International Migration Review* 42: 249–265.

Schain, Martin. 2012. *The Politics of Immigration in France, Britain, and the United States: A Comparative Study*, 2nd ed. New York: Palgrave Macmillan.

Schain, Martin. 2019. *The Border Policy and Politics in Europe and the United States*. Oxford: Oxford University Press.

Schlesinger, Arthur, Jr. 1992. *The Disuniting of America*. New York: W. W. Norton.

Schuck, Peter H. 1998. *Citizens, Strangers and In-Betweens: Essays on Immigration and Citizenship*. Boulder, CO: Westview.

Sciortino, Giuseppe. 1999. "Planning in the Dark: The Evolution of Italian Immigration Control." In *Mechanisms of Immigration Control: A Comparative Analysis of European Regulation Policies*, edited by Grete Brochmann and Tomas Hammar, 233–260. Oxford: Berg.

Sides, John, and Jack Citrin. 2007. "European Opinion About Immigration: The Role of Identities, Interests and Information." *British Journal of Political Science* 37, no. 3: 477.

Smith, Rogers. 1997. *Civic Ideals: Conflicting Visions of Citizenship in U.S. History*. New Haven, CT: Yale University Press.

Soysal, Yasemin N. 1994. *Limits of Citizenship: Migrants and Postnational Membership in Europe*. Chicago: University of Chicago Press.

Thielemann, Eiko. 2003. "European Burden-Sharing and Forced Migration." *Journal of Refugee Studies* 16, no. 3: 223–235.

Thränhardt, Dietrich, ed. 1996. *Europe: A New Immigration Continent*. Münster: Lit Verlag.

Tichenor, Daniel J. 2002. *The Politics of Immigration Control in America*. Princeton, NJ: Princeton University Press.

Tichenor, Daniel J. 2021. "The Development of the U.S. Migration State: Nativism, Liberalism, and Durable Structures of Exclusion." In *Understanding Global Migration*, edited by James F. Hollifield and Neil Foley, 203–232. Stanford, CA: Stanford University Press.

Tsourapas, Gerasimos. 2019. *The Politics of Migration in Modern Egypt: Strategies for Regime Survival in Autocracies*. Cambridge: Cambridge University Press.

Traisnel, Antoine. 2021. "No, American Academe Is Not Corrupting France." *Chronicle of Higher Education*, April 1, 2021.

Waldinger, Roger, and David Fitzgerald. 2004. "Transnationalism in Question." *American Journal of Sociology* 109, no. 5: 1177–1195.

Walzer, Michael. 1983. *Spheres of Justice: A Defense of Pluralism and Equality*. New York: Basic Books.

Weiner, Myron. 1995. *The Global Migration Crisis: Challenge to States and to Human Rights*. New York: HarperCollins.

Wong, Tom K. 2015. *Rights, Deportation, and Detention in the Age of Immigration Control*. Stanford, CA: Stanford University Press.

Wong, Tom K. 2016. *The Politics of Immigration: Partisanship, Demographic Change, and American National Identity*. New York: Oxford University Press.

History Matters

Leo Lucassen

The gap hypothesis very much focuses on the goals and outputs of immigration policy and on the difference between these and the actual results and outcomes, and hypothesizes that the gap may increase hostility against migrants. This is based on three basic ideas: (1) that migration outcomes are the result of a trade-off between different interests—economic forces (employers) often favor immigration, while part of the population (whose voice is represented by politicians) may be opposed for cultural and security reasons; (2) that the (migration) state is somehow a neutral institution that has to juggle these different interests, in order to prevent economic damage, xenophobia, and the erosion of the social contract; and (3) that these are more or less general and autonomous mechanisms, independent of the specific zeitgeist.

Regarding the first idea: Although it is useful to distinguish different interests, reality is much messier and, moreover, depends on the specific historical context and specific migrant group or category we are looking at. Whether citizens of receiving states oppose newcomers depends not only on the (perceived) gap between goals and policy results; at least as important is how politicians, authorities, and media frame the immigration discussion. Politicians are not simply transmitting what citizens think, but play an important role in defining the terms of the debate. We see this clearly in the way radical populist parties have framed migration in the past decades, and more specifically during the "refugee crisis" in 2015.[1] Although the numbers were much less unprecedented than they have often been portrayed as

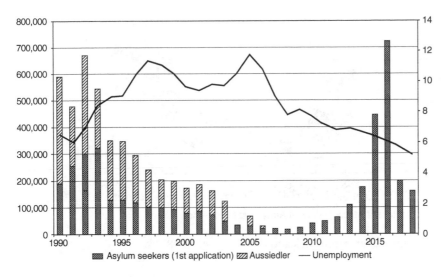

FIGURE 1.3. Asylum seekers and Aussiedler in Germany, 1990–2018
SOURCE: Bamf.de.

(see Figure 1.3), and—like in the 1990s—this migration was caused by clearly defined political crisis in a limited number of countries that were responsible for the bulk of the asylum seekers (Syria, Iraq, Afghanistan, and Eritrea), the impression people got was that asylum migration had spun totally out of control and that Europe faced Armageddon in terms of both cultural and economic impact. The German situation is interesting, as it shows that liberal nation-states can cope with a far greater number of refugees than one might expect given the polarized discussion about refugees. Thus, in the 1990s, when Germany faced the costs of *Wiedervereinigung* (the reuniting of Germans), rising unemployment, and the double inflow of asylum seekers and *Aussiedler* (ethnic Germans) from the Soviet Union, the country was able to accommodate and integrate these newcomers and still remain one of the world's most robust economies.

A second fear that was very much stimulated by politicians, some scholars, and the media since 2015 is that without harsh immigration controls at the outer borders of the EU, Europe will be overrun by poor Africans.[2] This claim is not supported by the data. By far the largest number of such migrants remain within Africa, and even the bulk of West Africans who cross the Sahara to reach North Africa have no intention of going to Europe, but instead look for employment in Libya and Algeria.[3] Furthermore, if we look at the number of asylum seekers from various parts of Africa in the last three decades, this figure remains very low, about 0.02 percent of the population of sub-Saharan Africa (Figure 1.4).

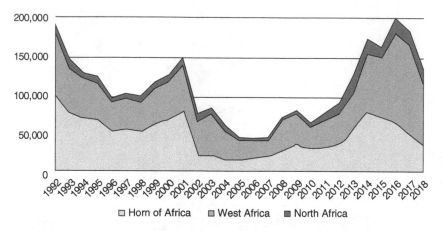

FIGURE 1.4. Asylum seekers from Africa to the EU, 1990–2018
SOURCE: Eurostat.

And despite the apocalyptic visions promoted by politicians and media about the nature and prospects of migration from outside the EU, many European citizens still harbor quite moderate views on immigration. Opinion polls show that, especially in western Europe, where most migrants settle, there still is support for accepting refugees, even after a series of attacks by Islamist terrorists. The role of politicians and government officials in framing the discourse on this subject is illustrated by a recent Pew opinion poll showing that people in countries with dominant populist governments that foster anti-immigrant discourse, such as Hungary and Italy, tend to be much more negative about immigration.[4] The importance of framing by government officials is illustrated by Germany, where Chancellor Angela Merkel in 2015 declared that Germany would be able to integrate hundreds of thousands of refugees—a stance that she repeated subsequently. It seems no coincidence that in a poll preceding the 2019 European elections, Germans (unlike many other Europeans) declared that the environment, not migration, was the most pressing problem.[5]

Apart from the role of framing discourse, it is also important to note that it is not only economic interests that may lead to greater openness; ethical and ideological consideration may also do so. As Saskia Bonjour has argued in a critique of the gap hypothesis, in the 1960s and 1970s many people in the Netherlands expressed rather tolerant views on immigration and stressed that guest workers and other immigrants should be treated equally and not discriminated against once they were allowed to work.[6] At the time, this ethical principle of non-discrimination was shared by many politicians (even those on the right side of the political spectrum) and the media alike.[7]

Regarding the second idea: The example just given makes clear not only that economic interests may generate a more positive stance on immigration but also that government officials and politicians play a crucial role in influencing the public debate—and hence that the "migration state" has its own agency in regard to how to frame immigration. Well-known examples are the way erstwhile colonial powers, such as the Netherlands, the United Kingdom, and France, dealt with postcolonial immigrants after World War II. Whereas the United Kingdom tried to depoliticize the issue by maintaining the Commonwealth and keeping up the pretense of still being an imperial power, other countries, such as the Netherlands, chose to avoid the term "migrant" altogether.[8] Thus the 350,000 newcomers from the former Dutch East Indies (Indonesia) who entered the Netherlands in the period 1946–1964 were consciously defined as "repatriates," although most of them had never been in the Netherlands before and many were of mixed (European and Asian) descent. The reason for labeling them as "repatriates"—engaging in front-stage behavior, to use Goffman's theatrical image—was to create carrying capacity among the population, who had suffered from the war and were generally not enthusiastic about making a place for these newcomers. Backstage, however, the government desperately tried to limit the numbers, because they considered the Netherlands to be already overpopulated, and also tried to stimulate overseas emigration as much as possible. A similar front-stage/backstage strategy was chosen by German governments during the 1990s when they had to cope with massive immigration from the former Soviet Union of people who claimed German citizenship on the basis of some German ancestry (see Figure 1.3), sometimes going back to the eighteenth century when Catherine the Great invited German farmers to settle in the Russian Empire.[9] Here the term *Aussiedler* was deliberately used to soothe anti-immigration atmosphere among parts of the population. The opposite example is Japan, where successive governments after World War II have made it very clear that Japan should remain monoethnic (notwithstanding its multiethnic character) and that even permanent settlement of Koreans, a group that is ethnically quite close, should be avoided at all cost.[10] This state ideology has deeply influenced how the bulk of the population thinks about migration and has even made it difficult to accept descendants of the so-called *nikkeijin*, Japanese emigrants to South America,.[11]

This brings me to the third idea. My point is that history matters. Looking at the postwar period in western Europe, we can distinguish between a period of migration (or integration) optimism (roughly 1950s–1980s, depending on which country we look at) and a period of much more pessimistic mood beginning in the 1980s. The optimism was rooted not only in the booming economy but also in the international humanitarian turn that foregrounded anti-discrimination and anti-racism and was the product of both decolonization and the growing awareness of the enormity of the Holocaust, which led to an "ethical revolution."[12] The pessimism, by contrast, resulted in part from the unexpected settlement of low-skilled guest workers from Islamic countries at a time when the economy was in a protracted recession, and in part from an exacerbation of this economic cause by conscious political strategies to frame immigration (and integration), especially of Muslims, as an existential problem. A good example is the Netherlands, where in the 1970s and 1980s political parties agreed—as an expression of the ethical revolution—not to make migration an electoral issue, because that would lead to xenophobic reactions, something that had to be prevented at all costs. This consensus, however, started to evaporate at the end of the 1980s, and especially following the Rushdie affair—the British author Salman Rushdie was accused of blasphemy by Iranian clerics for his writings, and they issued a fatwa against him encouraging his murder—which was regarded by many (including on the left) as a wake-up call that tolerance for ethnic and cultural differences had reached its limits. The first to change gears was Frits Bolkestein, then leader of the liberal party Volkspartij voor Vrijheid en Democratie (VVD) and later EU commissioner, who started to critically discuss the failing integration of Muslim migrants and in 1994 decided to make refugees an electoral issue. He succeeded, because many more people suddenly declared that limiting the numbers of immigrants was their top priority.[13] Moreover, recent studies have shown that Bolkestein consciously planted the neo-conservative Huntingtonian discourse of a "clash of civilizations" in Dutch politics, and so he should be seen not just as an interpreter of the people's voice from below but rather as having actively engineered the debate from above, on his own terms. With the consequent rise of anti-Islam populists such as Pim Fortuyn (assassinated in 2002) and Geert Wilders (a former political aide of Bolkestein's), integration pessimism came to dominate the public and political debate until this very day.

As a result, the discourse and immigration policies of the Dutch (migration) state became much more restrictive, while integration was increasingly seen not as a joint process involving both newcomers and those already present but only as something to be done by the migrants alone. Naturalization became more difficult, and the rather progressive integration policies of the 1980s were abolished or severely limited.

In this example—and many more can be found in numerous other liberal states—the three points of critique come together, showing that (1) interests other than just economics matter (the VVD was the employers' party); (2) the state is not a neutral agent but is deeply influenced by political actors and the media, which play a role in determining its policies; and (3) history matters.

Notes

1. Lucassen 2018.

2. Collier 2013.

3. Molenaar et al. 2017.

4. Phillip Connor and Jens-Manuel Krogstad, "Many Worldwide Oppose More Migration—Both Into and Out of Their Countries," Pew Research Center, December 10, 2018.

5. Klaus Geiger and Silke Mülherr, "Deutsche halten Umweltschutz für größte Herausforderung der EU," *Die Welt*, May 13, 2019, https://www.welt.de/politik/ausland/article193371401/WELT-Umfrage-Deutsche-halten-Umweltschutz-fuer-groesste-Herausforderung-der-EU.html.

6. Bonjour 2011.

7. Lucassen and Lucassen 2015.

8. Hansen 2000.

9. Panagiotidis 2012.

10. Sharpe and Morris-Suzuki 2001; Lie 2001.

11. Tsuda 2003; Lucassen et al. 2014.

12. Jensen 2016. For the "ethical revolution" concept, see Lucassen and Lucassen 2015.

13. Oudenampsen 2018.

References

Bonjour, S. 2011. "The Power and Morals of Policy Makers: Reassessing the Control Gap Debate." *International Migration Review* 45, no. 1: 89–122.

Collier, P. 2013. *Exodus: Immigration and Multiculturalism in the 21st Century*. London: Allen Lanc.

Goffman, E. 1959. *The Presentation of Self in Everyday Life*. Garden City, NY: Doubleday.

Hansen, R. 2000. *Citizenship and Immigration in Post-war Britain: The Institutional Origins of a Multicultural Nation*. Oxford: Oxford University Press.

Jensen, S. L. B. 2016. *The Making of International Human Rights: The 1960s, Decolonization, and the Reconstruction of Global Values*. Cambridge: Cambridge University Press.

Lie, J. 2001. *Multiethnic Japan*. Cambridge, MA: Harvard University Press.

Lucassen, L. 2018. "Peeling an Onion: The 'Refugee Crisis' from a Historical Perspective." *Ethnic and Racial Studies* 41, no. 3: 383–410.

Lucassen, L., and J. Lucassen. 2015. "The Strange Death of Dutch Tolerance: The Timing and Nature of the Pessimist Turn in the Dutch Migration Debate." *The Journal of Modern History* 87, no. 1: 72–101.

Lucassen, L., et al. 2014. "Cross-Cultural Migrations in Japan in a Comparative Perspective, 1600–2000." In *Globalising Migration History: The Eurasian experience (16th–21st Centuries)*, edited by J. Lucassen and L. Lucassen, 362–411. Leiden: Brill.

Molenaar, F., and F. El-Kamouni-Janssen. 2017. *Turning the Tide: The Politics of Irregular Migration in the Sahel and Libya*. The Hague: Clingendael.

Oudenampsen, M. 2018. "The Conservative Embrace of Progressive Values: On the Intellectual Origins of the Swing to the Right in Dutch Politics." PhD dissertation, University of Tilburg.

Panagiotidis, J. 2012. "Laws of Return? Co-Ethnic Immigration to West Germany and Israel (1948–1992)." PhD dissertation, European University Institute.

Tsuda, T. 2003. *Strangers in the Ethnic Homeland*. New York: Columbia University Press.

COMMENTARY

Multiple Gaps

Christian Joppke

Since the publication of the first edition in 1994, *Controlling Immigration* has been closely associated with the so-called gap hypothesis. This remains one of the key theoretical propositions in a political science literature on immigration policy that has not advanced much conceptually in the past quarter century. It consists of one sentence: "The gap between the 'goals' of national immigration policy . . . and the actual results of policies in this area (policy outcomes) is wide and growing wider in all major industrialized democracies" (Cornelius, Martin, and Hollifield 1994). This is more an observation than a hypothesis because no explanation is provided about what might cause the gap; there isn't even any specification of the content of the "goals" and of the "results" that are said to be in disparity. The gap hypothesis only becomes a hypothesis in conjunction with what James Hollifield (1992) has called the "liberal paradox." This essentially says that liberal states are philosophically open, for trade as much as for people, but that they also have to be closed "in order to protect the social contract" itself (as the introduction to this volume puts it). The liberal state, because of its principled commitments, must take in many more people than its citizens would like, who in turn are pushing this state qua state to recover its original closure function, which it can never fully satisfy as long as it is (or wants to be) liberal.

However, even if taken in combination with the liberal paradox (which should more precisely be called the "liberal *state* paradox," because there is nothing in liberalism itself that calls for closure), it is still not clear what the gap hypothesis is really about. At a minimum, there are two possibilities—call them Gap 1 and Gap 2. In Gap 1, the gap is between rhetoric and practice. In Gap 2, the gap is between action and its consequences. Gap 1 is at the level of a single actor (policymakers or the state). Gap 2 involves several actors, and an actor's intentions can be negated by other actors and/or the circumstances of action. Let me briefly flesh out these possibilities and see how plausible they are.

Gap 1: Rhetoric Versus Practice

In a democracy (or, better, a non-theocracy), politicians act on a public mandate, which is really the majority's mandate. However, as rich-world opinion polls confirm in unison (with the possible exception of Canada's), basing immigration policy on a public mandate would be both unconstitutional and economically harmful, as it would mean zero or at least drastically reduced immigration. This would come close to the "democratic" immigration policy of Switzerland, where public referenda have decreed the *Ausschaffung* (expulsion) of criminal migrants (with "crime" defined as including low-level welfare cheating [*Sozialbetrug*]) and the stopping of the *Masseneinwanderung* (mass migration) of fellow Europeans. Unable or unwilling to deliver, liberal elites don a restrictionist hat to appease the impossible majority preference, and they engage in symbolic politics. But in reality they let in—or have to let in—many more than the public would like, to comply with the rule of law and with what Gary Freeman (1995) called "client interests." The public figures in this scenario are duped, diverted from a liberal reality by restrictionist elite rhetoric. The latter, indeed, had been a reality well *before* the current populist surge, as a famously crisp commentary by Rogers Brubaker (1995) on Freeman's liberal theory pointed out.

The Gap 1 scenario is evidently conspiratorial. But some scholars have seriously proposed it. With a Marxist bent, Stephen Castles (2004) has argued that there is a "hidden agenda": politicians talk the anti-immigrant talk but in reality let immigrants in to meet "important economic or labour market objectives." In short, capitalists have an interest in cheap and docile immigrants (preferably illegal), and compliant, corrupted politicians deliver. Kitty Calavita, a contributor to the first edition of *Controlling Immigration*, delivered a variant of the hidden-agenda hypothesis. In an interesting paper on Spain (1998), she diagnosed an (intentional) Catch-22 between residence permits requiring a work permit and work permits requiring a residence permit, whereby a recurrently illegalized immigrant population is created that is good for capitalists to have. There are two obvious problems with this scenario. First, one must believe in conspiracies to find it plausible. Second, it assumes the unicity of the state, where in reality there is a multiplicity of intrastate actors and interests.

Gap 2: Action Versus Consequences

In fact, most authors in all editions of *Controlling Immigration* support a second version of the gap hypothesis. According to it, rightist politicians, from France's Charles Pasqua in the 1990s to Italy's Matteo Salvini in the new millennium, really want zero immigration (Pasqua) or zero refugees (as one might adapt Pasqua's language to Salvini). But liberal forces in civil society or in the state itself (such as independent courts) prevent this from happening. Note that the mass public figures differently in the Gap 2 scenario: not as duped and sidetracked by conspiratorial elites, but as whipped up by and in turn whipping up certain right-wing politicians and political entrepreneurs, inside and outside the state, who attack the state (or the "elites" that run it) for not delivering what was promised ("security," zero immigration, etc.), in a process that makes right-wing populism grow like mushrooms.

If one looks closer, Gap 2 itself comes in two variants, one that stresses unintended consequences and a second that stresses implementation failures.

Gap 2a: Unintended Consequences. Here the calamity in question, "too many immigrants," is the result of the state's own action. As the Swiss writer Max Frisch famously said, "Workers were called for but human beings arrived." The entire European guest worker experience from the late 1950s on might be understood in these terms.

Gap 2b: Implementation Failures. Here the calamity, failing immigration controls, is the result not of the state's own action but of its failure or incapacity to act. Returning to the European guest worker example, after the stop on recruitment of labor migrants in 1973, migrants continued to arrive as family migrants and asylum seekers. The state was powerless to halt this, because this was as-of-right migration protected by courts, constitutions, and international conventions.

However, if in the end the gap boils down to an implementation problem, one wonders: how does immigration policy differ here from other public policies, which *always* fall short of their original intentions? That "great expectations in Washington get dashed in Oakland," as Pressman and Wildavsky argued in 1973, is a generic experience of all public policy. A proper theorizing of the gap would have to compare immigration policy with other public policies. Apart from Gary Freeman in his classic 1995 paper, hardly anyone has done this. At a minimum, a specific of immigration policy is the difficulty of establishing and factoring in the public preferences that are to guide it. In environmental policy, everyone agrees that the goal is cleaner air, water, and so on, though of course there is disagreement about how to achieve it (for instance, with the market or against it); in social policy, the undisputed goal is justice, though left and right again disagree about its meaning and how to calibrate it against other goals, like efficiency or growth. There is no similar unambiguously shared goal for immigration policy. For one, it can never be a "liberal" goal because the primary function of immigration (as well as citizenship) policy is closure: more have to be rejected than could ever be admitted. If public preferences, as established by opinion surveys, are the benchmark of immigration policy, the result would be, to repeat, unconstitutional and economically harmful, a world of minimal (if any) immigration. So, as Gary Freeman (1995) correctly identified, immigration policy does, and even must, proceed in systematic disregard for public opinion.

But the necessarily unpopular nature of immigration policy in the liberal state leads us back to the Gap 1 scenario, the conspiracy, which isn't really all wrong. This is acknowledged in the editors' introduction to the third edition of *Controlling Immigration* (2019): "Nation-states retain a capacity to control . . . , but that capacity is limited by client politics . . . and by rights-based politics. . . . *Ineffective and symbolic immigration control measures . . . are thus perpetuated because they give the appearance of control*" (49; emphasis added). The challenge would then be to theorize the Gap 1 scenario without succumbing to a conspiratorial and monistic view of the state.

Stemming Versus Soliciting: Immigration Policies Are Plural

Even if there is agreement about what the gap is, it is still misleading to apply it to a singular "immigration policy." This is because immigration policies are always plural. This applies even more in the current neo-liberal era, where states, including previous *keine Einwanderungsländer*, like Germany, are competing for high-skilled immigrants. High-skilled immigration policy follows a logic of "soliciting" that is fundamentally different from the logic of "control" (or "stemming"; see Joppke 2021, chap. 2). Only the logic of stemming corresponds to the conventional view of immigration policy as something singular (a view that this volume also, in both title and content, subscribes to). In a nutshell, a soliciting policy tries to create a flow where none previously existed—typically, high-skilled immigration. By contrast, a stemming policy tries to stop a flow that already exists—typically, illegal immigration, but also much of low-skilled migration, and all as-of-right migration (family and asylum). In soliciting, the demand for immigration exceeds its supply; in stemming, supply exceeds demand. Both policies have radically different relationships to the underlying flows, as either created or contained by the policy. Accordingly, the gaps are very different in both cases.

In "stemming" immigration policy, the gap is structural and it cannot be removed, because the policy postdates the flow by definition. One cannot but decry the policy as deficient, which is why immigration qua stemming (or control) policy has been notoriously politicized, even prior to the current populist moment. Interestingly, the "nativist backlashes" and the "rolling back of immigrant rights," as mentioned in the editors' introduction to the third edition (2019), mostly date back to the 1990s or earlier—that is, *before* the breakthrough of contemporary right-wing populism. The immigration and welfare restriction laws in the United States (notably passed under a Democratic president, Bill Clinton, in 1996), the curtailing of the constitutional asylum right in Germany (1992), the ultra-restrictive Pasqua and Debré Laws in France (1986, 1993, 1997), and the anti-terror laws in the United States and Europe (post-2001) all happened *before* populism was on the map. The talk of "failing" immigration controls at the same time underrates the fearsome police powers of the modern state, with digital fingerprinting, infrared cameras, offshore imprisonment of asylum seekers, and many more instruments of horror. There has been an increasing will for, and effectiveness at, controlling and reducing unwanted family and asylum migration, and if these powers are not activated—as they weren't in the open-border policy of German chancellor Angela Merkel during the 2015 Syrian refugee crisis—this is by choice, not fate.

On the opposite end, in "soliciting" immigration policy, the gap is of an entirely different kind. When German policymakers, under a Left-Green coalition government in the late 1990s, cautiously moved away from the old mantra that Germany is "not an immigration country," they came to see that their ill-conceived (because niggardly restrictive) "green card" for high-skilled immigrants was not sufficient to lure internationally mobile talent to their gray and inhospitable country—the small total quota of 20,000 could never be filled. Considering the reality of "competitive immigration regimes" (Shachar 2006) for high-skilled immigrants, the gap in question is the incapacity of the policy to jump-start a wanted flow.

The different, even contradictory objectives and inefficiencies of stemming and soliciting will become a hallmark of Western states' immigration policies (plural) in the twenty-first century. By the same token, the distinction between "nations of immigrants," "countries of immigration," and "latecomers," which structures this volume, may not do justice to a new migration world that is converging on central policy parameters and imperatives. "Fending off the bottom" and "courting the top"— that is, stemming and soliciting—is the dual signature of contemporary immigration policies from Canada to Denmark to Singapore, everywhere creating similar dilemmas and trade-offs that, of course, are differently resolved (or not) in each case (see Joppke 2021, chap. 2).

The concept of the "liberal paradox" (Hollifield), which works with the binary of closure versus openness, appears too simplistic to capture this constellation. In reality, there are three—not two—competing forces and vectors at play: first, a new populist nationalism, which only reinforces the structural nationalism that is built into the non-liberal nature of immigration and citizenship as closure policies; second, rights-protecting liberalism; and third, neo-liberalism (unacknowledged by the liberal paradox). Neo-liberalism, which needs to be distinguished from liberalism, may push for openness, yes (to the degree that it pays off for capitalists—ever less as they set up shop abroad), but it can also be harshly disciplinary and restrictive, thus allowing for a potential alliance with the new nationalism.

Of these three forces, neo-liberalism seems to be the decisive one: the structure of immigration policies as courting the top and fending off the bottom (with asylum seekers and family migrants being rejected as costly and incapable of "contributing") is fully explicable in neo-liberal terms alone. Importantly, there is little to no transatlantic variation in this structure. The days of the "American" (or, better still, "Canadian") model of a liberal and inclusive, settlement-oriented immigration policy are over. Catherine Dauvergne (2016) wrote with force about the "end of settler societies," as even here a new "economic" logic has replaced an older "nation-building" logic on immigration. The Germans now copy the Canadian model of skill-based migration, while the South Koreans in turn take German policy as the model to emulate. In this convergence there is, for instance, a new proclivity for temporary migration, even with respect to the high-skilled, in the classic nations of immigrants—from the United States to Canada and, in particular, Australia. The nations of immigrants thus embrace the European logic of requiring migrants to gradually "earn" their right to permanent residence through their demonstrated integration efforts, rather than offering settlement from the start on a promissory note (in German legal doctrine, the underlying principle is called *Aufenthaltsverfestigung* [consolidation of residence]). At the same time, especially in Canada, restriction of family migration is on the radar, much as it is in Europe (with the important difference, though, that Canadian restrictiveness aims at the extended family, which in Europe had never been included within the ambit of family reunification). With respect to refugees, finally, the United States, proverbial "land of the free," currently accepts fewer refugees than any other state in the Western world, with a miraculously skimmed-off Muslim component.

The geographical and conceptual distinctions that underlie this volume, fact-filled and illuminating as it is in many respects, distract from the convergent structure of immigration policies in the neo-liberal age.

References

Brubaker, Rogers. 1995. "Commentary on Freeman." *International Migration Review* 20, no. 2: 903–908.

Calavita, Kitty. 1986. "Immigration, Law, and Marginalization in a Global Economy: Notes from Spain." *Law and Society Review* 32, no. 3: 529–566.

Castles, Stephen. 2004. "Why Migration Policies Fail." *Ethnic and Racial Studies* 27, no. 2: 205–227.

Cornelius, Wayne, Philip L. Martin, and James F. Hollifield, eds. 1994. *Controlling Immigration: A Global Perspective*. Stanford, CA: Stanford University Press.

Dauvergne, Catherine. 2016. *The New Politics of Immigration and the End of Settler Societies*. New York: Cambridge University Press.

Freeman, Gary. 1995. "Modes of Immigration Politics in Liberal Democratic States." *International Migration Review* 20, no. 2: 145–170.

Hollifield, James F. 1992. *Immigrants, Markets, and States*. Cambridge, MA: Harvard University Press.

Joppke, Christian. 2021. *Neoliberal Nationalism: Immigration and the Rise of the Populist Right*. Cambridge: Cambridge University Press.

Pressman, Jeffrey, and Aaron Wildavsky. 1973. *Implementation: How Great Expectations in Washington Are Dashed in Oakland*. Berkeley: University of California Press.

Shachar, Ayelet. 2006. "The Race for Talent: Highly Skilled Migrants and Competitive Immigration Regimes." *NYU Law Review* 81: 148–206.

2   NATIONS OF IMMIGRANTS

2 The United States

Whither the Nation of Immigrants?

Philip L. Martin and Pia M. Orrenius

Introduction

The United States is a nation of immigrants.[1] Citing the motto "E pluribus unum" (one from many), US presidents frequently remind Americans that they share the experience of themselves or their forebears leaving another country to begin anew in the United States.[2] Immigration serves the US national interest, meaning that immigrants can better themselves as they enrich the United States. However, there is a persistent gap between the US goal of welcoming immigrants through established front-door channels and the presence of close to 11 million unauthorized immigrants who arrived via side doors as temporary visitors and overstayed or via the back door of unauthorized entry. Closing this gap by dealing with unauthorized immigrants has been the central issue in recent US immigration debates.

The US government began to record the arrival of immigrants in 1820. Since then, over 85 million were admitted; over 10 percent of those were from Mexico and almost 9 percent from Germany, with 90 percent of the Mexicans admitted after 1970 and 90 percent of the Germans before 1970. Despite two centuries of immigration, there are heated debates on the answers to the three major immigration questions: how many immigrants to admit, who has priority to enter, and how immigration laws should be enforced, and the integration of immigrants managed.

Almost 230,000 foreigners enter the United States on a typical day. There are three major entry doors: a front door for permanent immigrants, a side door for temporary visitors, and a back door for the unauthorized, including asylum seekers. Before the border closures associated with the COVID-19 pandemic, almost 3,000 foreigners a day received permanent resident or immigration visas that allow them to live and work in most private sector jobs and to become naturalized US citizens after five years. About 223,000 tourist and business visitors, as well as guest workers and foreign students, collectively known as non-immigrants, arrived each day. Some of these non-immigrants stay only a week or two, while others stay for several years. Finally, about 2,400 unauthorized migrants a day were apprehended just inside US borders in fiscal year (FY) 2019.[3]

The United States admits over a million foreigners a year as permanent immigrants, welcomes over 80 million tourists and other visitors, and, in 2019, apprehended over 800,000 unauthorized immigrants. During the 1990s, there were debates about the relationship of immigrants and their children to the US education, welfare, and political systems—and, more broadly, questions about whether the immigration and integration system served US national interests. Since 2001, the immigration debate has centered on two questions: how to prevent terrorism by foreigners, and what to do about unauthorized migration.

Public opinion polls find widespread dissatisfaction with the "broken" US immigration system, as illustrated by debates over what to do about the nearly 11 million unauthorized immigrants. Congress has debated immigration reforms several times. The House approved an enforcement-only bill in 2005 to deal with unauthorized migration, and the Senate approved comprehensive immigration reform bills in 2006 and 2013 that rested on "three-legged stools" that included more enforcement, a path to legalization for unauthorized migrants, and new and revised programs to allow employers to hire guest (temporary) workers, but neither bill was enacted.

Several economic and political developments have rekindled the immigration reform debate. The 2008–2009 recession, the worst since the Great Depression, exacerbated unemployment and helped to reduce the unauthorized immigrant population from over 12 million in 2007 to under 11 million in 2021 The number of unauthorized workers has declined to under 7 million.

In 2016 presidential candidate Donald Trump made reducing unauthorized immigration a signature promise of his campaign, advocating a wall on the Mexico-US border and more enforcement of immigration laws inside the United States. As president, Trump issued executive orders to build the border wall, to speed up the removal of unauthorized immigrants, and to reduce admissions of refugees and block entries from particular countries, also known as the "Muslim ban." Restricting immigration became a central objective of the Trump presidency, marked by the separation of parents and children in May and June 2018 that resulted in some parents being deported without their children, the requirement that asylum seekers who arrive from Mexico wait in Mexico for hearings before US judges, and the near closure of US borders after March 2020 to prevent the spread of COVID.

After taking office in 2021, President Biden took the opposite approach to immigration, stopping construction of the border wall, ending the wait in Mexico program and the Muslim ban, and increasing refugee admissions. On his first day in office, Biden announced the US Citizenship Act, a bill that would offer an eight-year path to US citizenship for close to 11 million unauthorized immigrants. The transition from Trump to Biden marks major changes in many policy areas, including from closure to openness in immigration policy.

This chapter summarizes US migration patterns, puts the immigration and integration challenges facing the United States in a global context, and reviews the evolution of US immigration and integration policy. Immigration brings newcomers from around the world, making the United States, in the words of former Census director Kenneth Prewitt, "the first country in world history which is literally made up of every part of the world."[4]

Permanent Residents, Temporary Visitors, and the Unauthorized

The United States had 45 million foreign-born residents in 2019, including almost 11 million (about one-quarter of the total) who were illegally present. The United States has the most foreign-born residents of any country, almost four times more than Saudi Arabia, Germany, and Russia, each of which has about 13 million, and more unauthorized residents than any other industrial country.[5] Over 10 percent of the residents of OECD countries were born abroad. The United States, with nearly 14 percent foreign-born residents, has a higher share of immigrants among residents than most European countries, but a lower share than Australia (30 percent of residents were born abroad) and Canada (21 percent).

There are three major types of foreigners in the United States: front-door lawful permanent residents, side-door temporary visitors, and back-door unauthorized immigrants. Lawful permanent residents (LPRs) are immigrants who receive visas that allow them to settle permanently in the United States. LPR visas today resemble credit cards, but they were printed on green paper in the past, explaining why LPRs are sometimes referred to as green card holders.

Permanent Residents

The four major categories of permanent resident visas reflect US immigration priorities. The first and largest category is family reunification: two-thirds of permanent resident visas go to relatives of US citizens and green card holders who are settled in the United States. Settled relatives ask the government to issue visas to family members so that their relatives can live and work in the US.

Table 2.1 shows that over 500,000 or almost half of all permanent resident visas go to the immediate relatives of US citizens, as when a US soldier abroad marries a local resident and brings him or her into the United States, or when a newly naturalized US citizen requests permanent resident visas for his or her parents, spouse, and children. The other family reunification subcategories are for spouses and children of US green card holders and more distant relatives of US citizens, such as their adult brothers and sisters and their families. Over 200,000 immediate relatives of permanent residents and more distant relatives of US citizens are admitted each year.

There are no quotas or waiting times for immediate relatives of US citizens, but families of permanent residents and distant relatives of US citizens sometimes wait a decade or more for visas. Many relatives of permanent residents and US citizens do not wait abroad, which explains why many of the immigrants who are "admitted" in a particular year are already in the United States, in some cases for many years, before they are recognized as lawful permanent residents.

The second-largest category allows almost 140,000 foreigners and their families a year to become permanent residents because they are requested or sponsored by US employers. There are several subcategories of employment-based visas, including one for priority workers or foreigners with "extraordinary ability" in academia or the arts and another for foreigners who invest at least $500,000 in the United States to create or preserve at least ten US jobs.[6] There are more extraordinary-ability visas available than are requested, but this is not the case for the other employment-based visa categories, some of which require a US employer to show that US workers are not available to fill the job for which the employer is requesting a particular foreigner. In many cases, the foreigner is already filling the job while waiting for a permanent resident visa.

The third permanent resident category is for refugees and asylees, who are foreigners admitted on a humanitarian basis to begin anew in the United Sates. Refugees are persons outside their country of citizenship who have a well-founded fear of persecution at home because of race, religion, nationality, membership in a particular social group, or political opinion. Many refugees leave their countries and wait in neighboring countries to be resettled in another country. The United States has been resettling 67,000 refugees a year since 2010, almost all from Asia and Africa.

TABLE 2.1. Immigrants Obtaining Permanent Status, Inflows of Foreign Visitors, and Inflows of Unauthorized Immigrants into the United States, FY 2017–19

Category	2017			2018			2019		
	Number	Percent	Per day	Number	Percent	Per day	Number	Percent	Per day
Persons Obtaining Lawful Permanent Resident Status ("green card")	1,127,167	–	3,088	1,096,611	–	3,004	1,031,765	–	2,827
Immediate relatives of US citizens	516,508	45.8%	1,415	478,961	43.7%	1,312	505,765	49.0%	1,386
Other family-sponsored immigrants	232,238	20.6%	636	216,563	19.7%	593	204,139	19.8%	559
Employment-based	137,855	12.2%	378	138,171	12.6%	379	139,458	13.5%	382
Refugees	120,356	10.7%	330	155,734	14.2%	427	80,908	7.8%	222
Diversity	51,592	4.6%	141	45,350	4.1%	124	43,463	4.2%	119
Asylees	25,647	2.3%	70	30,175	2.8%	83	26,003	2.5%	71
Others (1)	42,971	3.8%	118	31,657	2.9%	87	32,029	3.1%	88
Non-immigrant Admissions	77,643,267	–	212,721	81,279,692	–	222,684	81,563,139	–	223,461
Temporary visitors for pleasure	61,600,219	79.3%	168,768	64,819,854	79.7%	177,589	64,864,687	79.5%	177,711
Temporary visitors for business	8,456,038	10.9%	23,167	8,967,224	11.0%	24,568	9,059,770	11.1%	24,821
Temporary workers and their families	3,969,276	5.1%	10,875	3,919,567	4.8%	10,739	4,106,324	5.0%	11,250
Academic students (F-1)	1,845,739	2.4%	5,057	1,862,828	2.3%	5,104	1,817,724	2.2%	4,980
Others (2)	1,771,995	2.3%	4,855	1,710,219	2.1%	4,686	1,714,634	2.1%	4,698
Unauthorized immigrant apprehensions	310,531	–	851	404,142	–	1,107	859,501	–	2,355
Removals/deportations	387,788	–	1,062	488,656	–	1,339	531,330	–	1,456

(1) Others include 19,200 Iraqis and Afghanis and their families in FY17 who were employed by the US government and 18,100 victims of crimes and their families, among others. (2) Others include exchange visitors, diplomats and transit aliens, among others.

SOURCES: Department of Homeland Security (DHS) Yearbook of Immigrations Statistics; Passel and Cohn (2018); Customs and Border Protection (CBP).

President Trump reduced the refugee ceiling to 45,000 in FY18, but only 22,000 were admitted. The ceiling was only 15,000 for FY21.

Asylum seekers are similar to refugees but more controversial because they first move to the United States and then apply to be recognized as refugees. If the claim is approved, the asylee receives a permanent resident visa to begin anew. In recent years, about 30,000 foreigners a year applied for asylum in the United States, including over half who filed affirmative applications, meaning that they were in the United States as a student or visitor and asked to stay because of persecution at home, such as a Chinese student fearing China's one-child policy. The others filed defensive asylum applications, meaning they were in US custody and requested asylum to avoid deportation or removal, as with Central Americans apprehended just inside the Mexico-US border.

The fourth category includes diversity and other immigrants. Since 1990, some 50,000 permanent resident visas per year are awarded by lottery to nationals of "underrepresented" countries that sent fewer than 50,000 immigrants to the United States during the previous five years. The diversity visa lottery attracts over 10 million entries a year. Other permanent resident visas are available to foreigners who were employed by the US government abroad, as with Afghans and Iraqis who worked for the US government during wars in their countries, and to foreign victims of US crimes, as with victims of sex or labor trafficking.

About half of all green card recipients, and almost 80 percent of employment-based recipients, were already in the United States when their permanent resident visas became available. This adjustment-of-status method of immigration marks a significant change from past immigration patterns, when immigrants set off for the United States from their countries of origin. Many immigrants-in-waiting are in the United States with some type of temporary visitor visa or are unauthorized.

The largest single source of immigrants is Mexico, which has accounted for about 15 percent of permanent residents in recent years. Countries that account for 5 to 10 percent of US green cards include China, India, and the Dominican Republic. California attracts 24 percent of US immigrants, followed by Texas, New York, and Florida, which each attract about 10 percent.

Temporary Visitors

Some 82 million foreigners arrived as temporary visitors in FY19.[7] Most are welcomed. The US travel industry encourages foreign tourists to visit the United States, businesses invite foreign customers and suppliers, and US colleges and universities recruit foreign students. Most temporary visitors are from European and Asian countries and do not need visas; the visa waiver program allows citizens of thirty-eight countries to enter the United States for up to ninety days without a visa, and US citizens may likewise visit these countries without visas.

Other temporary visitors need visas to enter the United States, including foreign students and foreign workers. The United States has more than twenty-five types of visas for temporary visitors, from A-1 for ambassadors to F-1 for foreign students and H visas for foreign workers. There are L-1 visas for intracompany transfers, who are workers employed by a multinational outside the United States who are transferred to the firm's US operations, P visas for foreign athletes and entertainers, and TN visas for Canadian and Mexican professionals admitted under the North American Free Trade Agreement.

Two types of temporary visitors are sometimes controversial: foreign students and guest workers. The United States had 1.1 million foreign students in fall 2019, 35 percent from China. The United States has more foreign students than any other country, but its share of the world's foreign students has been falling as other countries step up efforts to attract students.[8] Trump administration policies and the pandemic also contributed to a sharp drop in student visa applications between 2016 and 2020.

Foreign students faced scrutiny after the September 11, 2001, terrorist attacks because several of those who flew airplanes into the World Trade Center in New York City held student visas, including one who never showed up at the school that admitted him. This led to a new Student and Exchange Visitor Information System (SEVIS), to have the universities and colleges where foreign students are enrolled monitor foreign students.

The major purpose of studying in the United States is to earn a degree. However, foreign students may work part-time while they study, and many foreign graduates of US universities want to stay and work, which raises several issues. First, what should be done about for-profit private universities that admit foreign students whose major reason for enrolling is to work and perhaps not leave the United States when their visas expire?[9]

Second, should the United States worry if half or more of the students in some science and engineering graduate programs are foreign-born? Does the lack of US-born students in rigorous science and engineering doctoral programs reflect deficiencies in US K-12 schools or are foreign students in doctoral programs and postdoctoral apprenticeships low-wage research workers (Teitelbam 2003; Benderly 2010)?

A sixth of the 164 million US workers in 2019 were born abroad, over 28 million. These foreign-born US workers include about 19 million lawful permanent residents and naturalized US citizens, 7 million unauthorized immigrants, and 1 to 2 million temporary foreign workers. There are many types of temporary foreign workers. One of the largest groups is J-1 exchange visitors, foreign youth who come to the United States to work and experience the country. The J-1 visa program is not considered a temporary worker program, so US employers do not have to try to find US workers before hiring J-1 visa holders, who are often employed in seasonal tourism-related jobs.

The United States has three major guest worker programs, H-1B, H-2A, and H-2B. In combination with those holding J-1 visas and other smaller categories of temporary work visas, the number of such workers increased steadily over time until the pandemic (Figure 2.1). Each of these programs is controversial. Employers argue that foreign guest workers are needed to fill vacant jobs, while unions argue that employers prefer guest workers because they are indentured or tied to their employer.

The H-1B program highlights this controversy. The program was created in 1990 to help IT employers to deal with temporary labor market mismatches. The US unemployment rate was above 5 percent during the 1980s, suggesting there were sufficient US workers, but not enough with computer-related skills. The H-1B program was enacted as a bridge to give employers easy access to foreign workers to fill jobs that "require theoretical and practical application of highly specialized knowledge to perform fully" until more US students were trained.

The H-1B program created new types of businesses as it expanded. About 20,000 foreigners a year were admitted under the H-1B's predecessor program, and the number of H-1B visas was capped at 65,000 a year to allow a quick upsurge that was

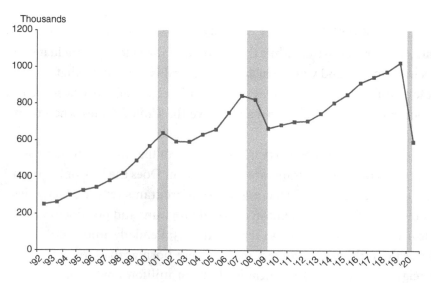

FIGURE 2.1. Temporary Worker Visas Were Rising Before Pandemic
NOTES: Data refers to Temporary Worker Visa issuances (includes H-1A, H-1B, H-1B1, H-1C, H3,1, J-1, L-1, O-1, O-2, P-1, P-2, P-3, Q-1, R-1, TN, H-2A, and H-2B and H-2BR visas). Gray bars indicate US recessions. SOURCES: NBER; US Department of State, *Report of the Visa Office.*

expected to be followed by a decline. Instead, employers requested few visas for H-1B workers until the late 1990s, when employers made a successful effort to raise the quota to 195,000 visas a year for the for-profit sector. After 2004, the cap reverted to 65,000 visas, plus 20,000 visas for foreigners who earned MS and PhD degrees from US universities and an unlimited number for universities and nonprofits.

A new business model emerged under which India-based firms assumed responsibility for developing and maintaining a firm's IT services using some H-1B workers in the United States and sending other IT work to India. These outsourcers had lower costs than firms that hired only US IT workers, and there were several well-publicized cases of major employers laying off US IT workers and replacing them with an outsourcing firm that relied on H-1B workers in the United States and India-based workers. Most US employers may lawfully replace US workers with H-1B workers because when the program was created, it was assumed that there was a shortage of US IT workers.

The debate over the H-1B program illustrates the controversies that surround many aspects of immigration. Many studies suggest that the more H-1B workers in an industry or area, the more patents and the higher the wages of US workers— evidence that supports employers' quest to raise the quota. Other studies emphasize that many H-1B workers have more education than the US workers with whom they work and that employers prefer to hire H-1B workers because, during the six years that an H-1B worker may be employed in the United States, the employer may sponsor the H-1B worker for an immigrant visa, making H-1B workers eager to work long hours and please their employers.

Human capital is the foundation of twenty-first-century service economies, making it difficult to find credible economic arguments against admitting and retaining educated foreigners. The controversy is whether the H-1B program provides a labor subsidy for selected US employers, who might otherwise be forced to train more workers or move IT jobs to India.

The H-2A program admits low-skilled foreign workers to fill seasonal jobs in agriculture, and the H-2B program allows employers to fill seasonal jobs in non-farm industries such as landscaping and roofing. These programs require employers to search for and fail to recruit US workers while offering a wage at least as high as specified by the US Department of Labor (DOL). Employers must explain to DOL why any US workers who responded to their ads were not hired. The number of H-2A workers is not capped, but the number of H-2B visas is limited to 66,000 a year.

The number of jobs certified to be filled by H-2A workers tripled in the past decade to over 275,000 in 2020, so about 10 percent of the average number of jobs on US crop farms were filled by H-2A workers, half of the 20 percent filled by *braceros* at the peak of that program in the mid-1950s. Over 90 percent of H-2A workers are young Mexican men, many of whom replace older unauthorized Mexican men who entered the United States when unauthorized Mexico-US migration peaked in the late 1990s and are now exiting farm work.

The H-2A program is also controversial. Farm employers complain that trying to find US workers to fill seasonal farm jobs is futile because US workers do not want such jobs. They also object to providing housing for H-2A workers and paying them an Adverse Effect Wage Rate (AEWR), a wage set by the Department of Labor that aims to prevent the presence of H-2A workers from depressing wages for US workers. Critics say that farm employers prefer to hire H-2A workers because they are tied to their employers, providing a form of insurance that perishable commodities will be harvested on time. They also complain that the AEWR can become a wage ceiling, since a US worker who would fill the job but wants a higher wage can be deemed unavailable and not hired.

The availability of H-2A workers may have other effects. If H-2A workers are available, will farmers invest in labor-saving machines to replace hand workers? What is the proper response to Florida and Georgia blueberry growers who hire H-2A workers to pick their blueberries and simultaneously seek to block imports of blueberries from Mexico and Peru?

Foreign or guest worker programs are controversial whether they admit skilled workers with university degrees or low-skilled workers who have not completed secondary school. Employers normally assert that they should decide which worker is most qualified to fill a particular job and resent "government interference" when regulations erect hurdles between them and "their" guest workers. Critics allege that guest worker programs give employers "control" over foreign workers, making them loyal and pliable because, if fired, the foreign worker loses the right to be in the United States.

If guest workers could change employers, would they be empowered to escape exploitative employers? The UN's Global Compact for Safe, Orderly and Regular Migration (GCM), which was adopted by 164 of the UN's 193 member states in Marrakesh, Morocco, in December 2018 and then formally adopted by the UN's General Assembly, wants richer countries to open doors wider to guest workers from poorer countries in order to speed development via increased remittances. The GCM is focused on protecting the rights of migrants and urges governments to allow guest workers to be free agents in host country labor markets—that is, to be free to change employers whenever they wish. The United States and a dozen other countries refused to sign the GCM.

Free-agent guest worker programs are a challenge to the current labor migration system, which admits foreign workers in response to labor shortages. Employers begin the admissions process by making attestations or requesting certification to hire guest workers to fill particular jobs, and governments determine whether a labor shortage exists on a job-by-job basis. Admitting guest workers who could change employers easily, perhaps only within a particular industry, occupation, and area, may improve their working conditions but could leave some vacant jobs unfilled or some guest workers unemployed. Free-agent guest workers may improve protections for workers, but they raise a wide range of other issues (Martin 2018).

Unauthorized Immigrants

Unauthorized immigrants enter the United States via the back door. In the past, most were solo Mexican men who slipped across the Mexico-US border, so-called entry without inspection. Today, nearly half of the unauthorized immigrants in the United States entered legally, as a tourist or student or with the border crossing cards available to Mexicans who want to shop in US border areas, and then violated the terms of their legal entry by overstaying or working illegally.[10]

The United States has the largest number and share of unauthorized immigrants among the industrial democracies (Figure 2.2). Half of the almost 11 million

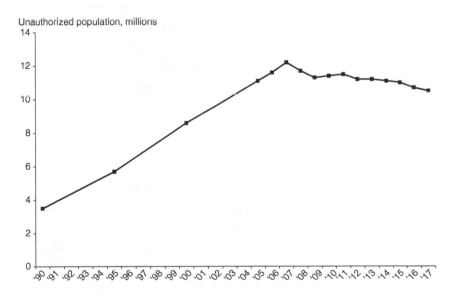

Unauthorized population, millions

FIGURE 2.2. Unauthorized Immigrants in the US, 1990–2017
SOURCE: Jeffrey Passel and D'Vera Cohn. 2019. "Mexicans Decline to Less than Half the U.S. Unauthorized Immigrant Population for the First Time." Pew Research Center. https://www.pewresearch.org/fact-tank72019/06/12/us-unauthorized-immigrant-population-2017/.

unauthorized immigrants in the United States in 2017 were born in Mexico, followed by almost 20 percent from Central America. Unauthorized immigrants were in the United States a median fifteen years in 2017, meaning that half arrived before 2002 (Passel and Cohn 2019). Many unauthorized immigrants have US-born children— some 5 million US-born children live in families with at least one unauthorized parent.

The Mexico-US migration corridor is the world's largest, involving millions of circular migrants who move temporarily from Mexico to the United States as well as the permanent movement of 11 million people, most of whom arrived between 1986 and 2006. Mexico had about 50 million residents in 1970, when there were 750,000 Mexican-born people living in the United States. By 2000, Mexico's population had doubled to 100 million, and the number of Mexico-born US residents increased ten-fold to more than 8 million. In 2021, Mexico has about 130 million people, and 11 million—or almost 10 percent—live in the United States.

Mexico-US migration rose in the two decades between 1987 and 2007 due to economic and policy factors in both Mexico and the United States. Mexico had an inward-oriented economic policy and a series of debt crises and rapid inflation that slowed job growth and led to widespread rural poverty during a demographic boom— a million Mexicans a year entered the labor force in the 1990s, when the economy was creating 300,000 formal-sector or "good" jobs a year. By contrast, the US economy was creating over 3 million jobs a year, many in construction and service industries that already employed Mexicans. These workers informed friends and relatives still in Mexico that if they could cross the border, higher-wage jobs awaited them. The United States legalized 2.3 million unauthorized Mexicans in 1988–1989, making them permanent residents and eventually naturalized citizens, which enabled them to sponsor their families for green cards.

These Mexican push and US pull forces created a Mexico-US migration hump that rose until 2007 and has been on the downslope since the 2008–2009 recession. The reasons for declining Mexico-US migration include fewer young Mexicans entering the labor force each year, more "good" jobs available in Mexico, and a shrinking pool of rural poor residents, as well as tougher US border and interior enforcement against illegal entry and unauthorized workers.

The Mexico-US migration hump demonstrates that the same policies, such as freer trade and investment, that create the jobs needed to reduce unwanted migration in the long run can increase such migration in the short run. Most observers do not expect unauthorized Mexico-US migration to rise again to previous peaks, as when over a million Mexicans a year were apprehended along the border and the number of unauthorized immigrants from Mexico increased by 500,000 a year.

If Mexico-US unauthorized migration is on the downslope of the hump, Central American unauthorized migration may be on the upslope. There were few Central Americans in the United States until civil wars in the 1980s sent people streaming north to find refuge. During the 1990s, many Central Americans who reached the United States were allowed to become permanent residents and naturalized citizens, leading to family reunification. In addition, hurricanes and earthquakes in Central America in 1999 and 2001 prompted the United States to grant Temporary Protected Status, which includes the right to work, to eligible unauthorized Central Americans who were in the United States when these events happened in their home countries.

In recent years, the number of Central Americans from the three Northern Triangle countries of Guatemala, El Salvador, and Honduras apprehended just inside the US border surpassed the number of Mexicans apprehended.[11] Mexicans apprehended at the border are typically young men traveling without their families and seeking US jobs in agriculture, construction, or services. Central Americans, by contrast, often enter the United States as unaccompanied minors or as families and apply for asylum—that is, they ask to stay permanently in the United States as immigrants because of persecution at home.

Over 105,000 foreigners applied for asylum in the United States in FY19, and about half of those applicants were Central Americans. Some Central Americans go to US ports of entry on the Mexico-US border and apply for asylum, but US authorities accept only a few hundred a day, which can lead to long waits in Mexican border cities. Other asylum applicants enter the United States illegally and are apprehended by the Border Patrol. Once in custody, they file defensive asylum applications in order to avoid deportation, often citing domestic and gang violence at home.

The first step to avoid deportation is to pass a credible fear test, meaning that the foreigner must convince a United States Citizenship and Immigration Services (USCIS) officer that they face a "significant possibility" of persecution in their home country. About three-fourths of applicants pass the credible fear test. The next step is to apply for asylum and explain to an immigration judge why the applicant faces a well-founded fear of persecution for reasons of race, religion, nationality, political opinion, or membership in a particular social group at home in order to be recognized as refugees and allowed to settle in the United States. If the judge rules that the applicant does not deserve asylum, the decision can be appealed.

There is a backlog of 1.3 million cases in immigration courts, including 360,000 asylum cases, so the time between illegal entry and a hearing can be several years, and then several more years to consider a denied applicant's appeal.[12] During this time, most asylum applicants can work legally in the United States and their children may attend US schools.

What should be done with apprehended asylum seekers who are awaiting hearings before immigration judges? US law does not allow children under eighteen to be held in jails, so many Central American families have been released while they wait several years for hearings on their asylum applications. The Trump administration criticized this catch-and-release policy, and in May and June 2018 began to prosecute all adults who entered the United States illegally, separating over 5,000 children from their parents. This child-separation policy resulted in public backlash and was quickly ended (Pierce, Bolter, and Selee 2018).

The caravans of Central Americans traveling through Mexico to the United States to apply for asylum have become a major US issue. It is both safer and cheaper for migrants to travel in caravans than to hire smugglers, who in spring 2019 were charging $5,000 to move families through Mexico and into the United States in five days. Smugglers say that half of the migrant-paid fee is used to pay off police and gangs in Mexico.

President Trump believed that a wall on the Mexico-US border would make illegal crossings harder and send a signal that migrants are not wanted. Critics of the wall make two arguments. First, walls are a medieval solution to a twenty-first-century issue, they say, and migrants will find ways to go over or under any wall. Second, a wall does not deter asylum seekers who are seeking out immigration officials to apply for asylum rather than trying to elude them.

Mexico has offered humanitarian work visas to the Central Americans headed for the United States and has agreed that some Central Americans who apply for asylum in the United States can wait for their US hearings in Mexico. Meanwhile, the United States in March 2019 suspended $500 million in aid to El Salvador, Guatemala, and Honduras because these governments did not deter the outmigration of migrants. Trump also threatened to close all, or some, legal ports of entry along the Mexico-US border to prevent Central Americans from arriving and seeking asylum. Two-way Mexico-US trade was $677 billion in 2019, and over 500,000 workers, tourists, and shoppers cross the border daily, prompting businesses to warn of the economic consequences of closing the border.

Central American asylum seekers present the United States with a problem that European nations have been grappling with for years. The longer-term answer to unwanted asylum seekers involves peace and law and order, as well as jobs, in migrant-sending countries. Shorter-term solutions have involved providing aid to transit countries that migrants travel through to persuade them to make it more difficult for asylum seekers to continue their journey, as was done with Turkey, Libya, and Morocco to prevent migrants from passing through to Europe.

Immigration History and Policy

Immigration to the United States occurred in four major waves. Large influxes of foreigners over several decades were usually followed by periods in which there was little immigration due to changes in immigration policy and economic conditions in the United States and abroad. The United States is in the midst of the fourth immigration wave, which began after immigration laws were amended to give priority to relatives of US residents in 1965. While the 2020 coronavirus pandemic put a damper on a lot of migration, pre-pandemic migration trends are likely to resume in 2021–2022, assuming that the virus is brought under control and the pandemic subsides.

Four Waves of Immigrants

The first wave of immigrants arrived in what were then British colonies. In the sixteenth and seventeenth centuries, English colonists established communities at Jamestown and Plymouth, seized control from the Dutch in New York, and overran various French and Spanish settlements. The English were 60 percent of the population in 1790, and English became the most common language and English common law the basis for the US legal system.[13] The word "immigrant" emerged in the 1790s to mean a person who moves voluntarily from one established country into another.

The second wave of immigrants between 1820 and 1860 accelerated the push westward. European peasants displaced from agriculture and artisans made jobless by the industrial revolution were eager to try their luck in the United States, and steamship and railroad companies advertised for passengers. New arrivals sent "American letters" to Europe, encouraging friends and relatives to join them. About 40 percent of the 5 million second-wave immigrants were from Ireland, where an 1840s famine caused by potato blight encouraged emigration. Roman Catholics predominated in the second wave. By 1850, the Roman Catholic Church was the largest denomination in the United States, though Protestants of various kinds outnumbered Catholics.

After the Civil War ended in 1865, there was little immigration during Reconstruction. In 1880 the third wave began, with almost 460,000 arrivals a year. The third wave ended in 1914, with 1.2 million arrivals on the eve of World War I. During the third wave, over 20 million southern and eastern Europeans immigrated to the eastern and midwestern states and several hundred thousand Chinese, Japanese, and other Asians settled in the western states.

The American frontier offering free land to settlers closed by 1890, with almost all viable land claimed. Most newcomers found factory jobs in cities in the Northeast and Midwest. Immigrants were over half of all operatives in the steel and meatpacking industries in 1910, and foreign-born men were over half of the work-force in cities such as New York, Chicago, and Detroit (Briggs 1992, 56–57).[14]

There was an immigration pause between 1915 and 1964, largely because Congress enacted quotas in the 1920s that restricted the arrival of newcomers. The economic depression of the 1930s also discouraged immigration. After World War II, the United States admitted almost 600,000 Europeans who had been displaced by the war, and farmers recruited Mexicans to be *braceros*, or seasonal guest workers, during and after World War II. *Bracero* admissions peaked at 455,000 in the mid-1950s, and additional Mexicans arrived and worked illegally.

Fourth-wave immigrants began arriving in the United States after 1965, when the preference system changed from favoring immigrants from particular European countries under the national origins selection system to favor immigrants with relatives already in the United States and those sponsored by US employers. This change in the selection system, combined with rapid economic growth in Europe, shifted the origins of most immigrants from Europe to Latin America and Asia. During the 1970s, the first decade that the family unification law was in effect, the United States admitted 4.2 million immigrants, including 825,000 Europeans and 621,000 Mexicans. By the 1980s, when immigration rose to 6.2 million, the 1 million Mexican immigrants exceeded the number of European immigrants, 670,000.

There are similarities and differences between immigration at the beginning of the twentieth century and that at the start of the twenty-first century. The number of permanent immigrants is similar, over a million a year. Arrivals from countries that had not previously sent large numbers of immigrants raise questions about integration, including language, religion, and culture. There are also differences. A century ago, there were essentially only permanent and legal immigrants, not temporary visitors and unauthorized immigrants. Immigrants a century ago often found work on assembly lines in factories, while today most newcomers—like most natives—are employed in service occupations. In both eras, there were and are concerns that immigrants may "change us" rather than integrate into the current culture.

Immigration Policy: 1776–1980

During its first two hundred years, US immigration policy went through three major phases: laissez-faire, qualitative restrictions, and quantitative restrictions. For its first hundred years, US immigration policy allowed almost all people who arrived to settle and naturalize. Many businesses promoted immigration to the United States, including shipping companies looking for passengers and developers who had been granted land in exchange for building canals and railroads and needed laborers. The

United States had high tariffs on manufactured goods that kept out lower-cost European goods and created a demand for workers in American factories, which encouraged immigration.

The first major backlash against this open-door immigration policy was the reaction against the Catholics arriving from Ireland and Germany in the 1840s. Protestant opinion leaders formed the Order of the Star Spangled Banner, which urged restrictions on immigration from non-Anglo-Saxon countries. The Order became the "Know-Nothing" movement because members were instructed to say "I know nothing" about the Order, which formed the American Party and won seventy House seats in the congressional election of 1854. Congress did not enact the Order's anti-immigrant agenda, and slavery soon replaced immigration as the major political issue of the day.

The US government introduced qualitative restrictions on immigrants in the 1870s and 1880s, barring certain types of foreigners: convicts and prostitutes in 1875 and Chinese, paupers, and "mental defectives" in 1882. Chinese exclusion was the first ban on immigrants from a particular country.

The third wave of immigration, between 1880 and 1914, featured newcomers observing the Statue of Liberty as they sailed into New York Harbor and being processed at Ellis Island. Arriving ships were boarded by immigration inspectors who checked the first- and second-class passengers before the ships docked in lower Manhattan, and approved passengers went on their way. Passengers in steerage were taken by barge or ferry to Ellis Island, where they were observed by doctors as they climbed a long flight of stairs; they could be returned to their countries of origin if they had contagious diseases.[15] Over 99 percent spent three to five hours at Ellis Island before being admitted, traveling to New Jersey, and from there taking trains to their destinations, often midwestern cities.

There was little migration from Europe to the United States during World War I, but when immigration resumed in the 1920s, restrictionists mounted a campaign to stop immigration from southern and eastern Europe. The congressional Dillingham Commission produced forty-one volumes of reports in 1911 concluding that immigrants from southern and eastern Europe had more "inborn socially inadequate qualities than northwestern Europeans" (quoted in Handlin 1952, 755).[16] Congress used the Dillingham Commission report to impose quantitative limits on immigration in 1921, and revised these quotas in the Immigration Act of 1924 to cap the annual number of immigrants at 150,000 plus accompanying wives and children, giving preference to countries with large numbers of people already in the United States. Between the 1920s and the 1960s over 80 percent of permanent resident visas went to people from northern and western European countries.

After World War II, President Truman tried to abolish the national origins immigration system. However, the McCarran-Walter Immigration and Nationality Act of 1952, which maintained national origins preferences, was approved despite Truman's veto. President Kennedy made another attempt to eliminate the national origins selection system, and in 1965 the Immigration and Nationality Act was amended to substitute the current family unification and employer-sponsor system for national origins in laying out priorities for immigration.

Immigration Policy Since 1980

For most of the past two centuries, US immigration policy changed once a generation, adding restrictions on who and how many immigrants could enter in response to backlashes against the rising number of foreigners who wanted to immigrate to the United States. Beginning in 1980, Congress enacted major immigration laws at least once a decade.

The major immigration laws of the past four decades include:

- *The Refugee Act of 1980.* The United States adopted the UN definition of "refugee"—a person who is outside her country of citizenship and unwilling to return because of a well-founded fear of persecution because of race, religion, nationality, membership in a particular social group, or political opinion.

- *The Immigration Reform and Control Act (IRCA) of 1986.* IRCA was a grand bargain between restrictionists, who won federal penalties on employers who knowingly hire unauthorized immigrant workers (employer sanctions), and admissionists, who won a legalization program (amnesty) for 2.7 million unauthorized immigrants who had been in the United States since 1982 or who were employed in agriculture in 1985–1986; 85 percent of those legalized through IRCA were Mexicans.

- *The Immigration Act (IMMACT) of 1990.* IMMACT raised the worldwide annual ceiling on immigration from 270,000 a year plus immediate relatives of US citizens to 675,000 a year including some relatives but not refugees.[17] IMMACT more than doubled the number of employment-based immigration visas, from 54,000 to 140,000 a year, and created the H-1B and diversity lottery programs.

- *The Anti-Terrorism and Effective Death Penalty Act of 1996.* This law introduced an expedited removal procedure for asylum seekers who cannot convince an immigration officer that they have a credible fear of persecution at home and made it easier to deport foreigners convicted of US felonies.

- *The Personal Responsibility and Work Opportunity Reconciliation Act of 1996.* This legislation turned cash assistance for poor residents from an open-ended entitlement into a federal block grant to states. Most legal immigrants are not eligible for federal means-tested cash assistance until they naturalize or work at least ten years in the United States. US residents who sponsor their relatives for permanent resident visas must prove that they have incomes of at least 125 percent of the national poverty line for themselves and the immigrants they are sponsoring, which means at least $33,125 in 2021 for a couple sponsoring a set of parents (the poverty line in 2021 was $26,500 for a family of four).

- *The Illegal Immigration Reform and Immigrant Responsibility Act of 1996.* This law doubled the number of Border Patrol agents to 10,000 and, via later amendments, to 21,000. It also required several employment verification programs to allow employers to check whether newly hired workers were allowed to work in the United States. E-Verify, as it is now called, is an online verification system that allows employers to submit data provided by newly hired workers to government databases to check their authorization to work in the United States.

- *The Enhanced Border Security and Visa Entry Reform Act of 2001.* Enacted after the September 11, 2001, terrorist attacks, this law created SEVIS to track foreign students inside the United States and required most foreigners seeking visas to appear in person before a US consular officer in their country of citizenship.

Each of these laws reflected the major migration issue of the day, from what to do about Vietnamese boat people in the late 1970s to how to reduce federal spending when there were concerns about welfare dependence and federal deficits in the 1990s and preventing the entry of terrorists after 9/11. Most of these laws were enacted with bipartisan support, as congressional factions with different priorities compromised in an effort to deal with refugees, welfare spending, fraud, border and worksite enforcement, and terrorism.

Since IRCA in 1986, Congress has been unable to agree on another comprehensive law to deal with unauthorized immigration. The two major camps have not changed. Restrictionists want more done to prevent the entry and employment of unauthorized immigrants, while admissionists put priority on legalizing unauthorized immigrants who are already in the United States. The restrictionist approach was embodied in the Border Protection, Antiterrorism, and Illegal Immigration Control Act approved by the Republican-controlled House in December 2005, which would have added more fences and agents on the Mexico-US border and made "illegal presence" in the United States a felony, complicating any future legalization because foreigners convicted of US felonies cannot normally become permanent residents.

There were massive demonstrations against the House bill that culminated in a "day without immigrants" on May 1, 2006, which spurred the Senate to approve the three-pronged Comprehensive Immigration Reform Act (CIRA) later in May 2006.[18] CIRA included many of the enforcement provisions in the House bill but also introduced several earned-legalization programs, so that unauthorized immigrants could have gotten probationary legal status and, if they paid fines, learned English, and continued to work, could become regular permanent residents and eventually US citizens. The third prong was a new H-2C guest worker program that would have allowed employers to attest that they needed to hire foreign workers, and if employers requested all the H-2C visas available, the number could increase.

President George W. Bush supported CIRA in 2006 and encouraged the Senate to enact another version in 2007. Despite support from a bipartisan group of eight senators, CIRA failed to be approved by the Senate in 2007, as Senator John McCain (R-AZ) and other Republicans who were supporters in 2006 changed their views and demanded enforcement before legalization.[19] During the 2008 presidential campaign, Senator Barack Obama (D-IL) promised to support legalization and stressed the need to enforce labor and immigration laws in the workplace to protect all workers, including unauthorized workers.

The 2008–2009 recession, health care reform, and new financial regulation to prevent a future financial meltdown dominated the Obama administration's first term. Legislative action on immigration shifted to the states. Arizona implemented a mandatory E-Verify law in 2007 and enacted SB 1070 in April 2010, a law making unauthorized presence in the state a crime. The E-Verify mandate stuck, but SB 1070 was invalidated by the US Supreme Court in June 2012. Several southeastern states, including Alabama and Georgia, followed Arizona in enacting laws that required all employers to use E-Verify to ensure that newly hired workers were authorized to work in the United States.

President Obama used an executive order in June 2012 to create the Deferred Action for Childhood Arrivals (DACA) program, which provides for unauthorized immigrants brought to the United States as children to receive two-year work permits.[20] The Senate approved another version of comprehensive immigration reform crafted by a bipartisan group of senators in June 2013, but the House did not act.

From Trump to Biden

President Donald Trump issued three executive orders dealing with migration during his first week in office. The first set in motion plans to reduce illegal entries by building a wall on the Mexico-US border and adding more Border Patrol agents, the second aimed to increase deportations from the United States by doubling the number of Immigration and Customs Enforcement (ICE) agents and persuading states and cities to cooperate with ICE, and the third reduced refugee admissions and restricted the entry of foreigners from particular countries, the so-called Muslim ban.

Trump's executive orders were challenged in the courts. Mexico did not pay for the border wall (as Trump had demanded) and Congress did not appropriate the necessary $25 billion, so Trump took funds from the Department of Defense. Efforts to penalize sanctuary states and cities that refuse to cooperate with ICE were blocked by court injunctions. Refugee admissions were reduced sharply, and travelers from particular countries were banned.

Trump took a special interest in the arrival of Central Americans who traveled through Mexico in caravans to the US border to apply for asylum. In May and June 2018, the United States decided to prosecute adults who entered the United States illegally. Since children cannot be detained more than twenty days, parents were separated from their children, and often deported without them. This child separation policy led to a backlash and was soon ended, but not before more than 5,000 children were separated from their parents.

COVID led to new border and immigration restrictions. Trump invoked Title 42 of the Public Health Act in March 2020 to block unauthorized foreigners from entering the United States to prevent the spread of COVID, so foreigners intercepted just inside the Mexico-US border were returned from the United States to Mexico, some several times, since solo men who were apprehended were returned quickly and some tried to reenter the United States.

President Joe Biden changed the direction of US immigration policy, introducing the US Citizenship Act (USCA) to offer an eight-year path to US citizenship for 11 million unauthorized foreigners in the United States and ending or reversing many of Trump's policies. The USCA would allow the 600,000 foreigners who are protected under the DACA program, the 300,000 who have Temporary Protected Status, and up to a million unauthorized farm workers to become lawful "prospective immigrants" who could apply for US citizenship after three years. Other lawful prospective immigrants could apply for US citizenship after eight years.

Congress was unable to enact bipartisan immigration reforms over the past two decades, and President Trump made migration a more partisan issue. Trump's migration actions appealed primarily to the populist wing of the Republican Party, which wants to reduce all types of migration into the United States, while the Republican-leaning US Chamber of Commerce supports the legalization of unauthorized immigrants and more guest workers, a kind of Main Street versus Wall Street divide.[21]

The Democratic Party is more pro-immigration, favoring the legalization of unauthorized immigrants and the removal of quotas that can lead to long waits for immigration visas. Most Democrats oppose aggressive enforcement of immigration laws, including some who want to abolish ICE, the agency that detects and removes unauthorized immigrants from the interior of the United States (Beinart 2017).[22] Unlike bipartisan immigration reform bills approved by the Senate in 2006 and 2013, the USCA does not include funding for more border agents nor require employers to use E-Verify to check the status of new hires.

Second, the nature of unwanted migration has changed. For most of the period since 1970, the typical unauthorized immigrant was a rural Mexican man who entered the United States without inspection by eluding the Border Patrol. As border enforcement increased, more foreigners arrived legally with tourist and other visas and overstayed, yielding a more diverse population of unauthorized immigrants. Over the past decade, more Central American families are arriving at the US border and applying for asylum, citing domestic and gang violence in El Salvador, Guatemala, and Honduras.

The Trump administration responded to caravans of Central Americans by pressuring Central American governments to prevent exits and the Mexican government to prevent caravans from transiting to the US border, threatening tariffs and other penalties for non-compliance.[23] Trump's threats and policies such as the Remain in Mexico program for those who entered the United States reduced the number of Central American asylum seekers, but were widely criticized by migrant advocates. President Biden has promised to invest in Central America to address the root causes of migration but is proceeding carefully in undoing Trump-era policies to reduce the risk of more caravans.

The Trump administration adopted many other policies to reduce immigration. Foreigners who are likely to become "public charges" can be denied immigrant visas, meaning that those who have or are likely to become recipients of federal means-tested benefits (such as those offered via food, medical, and housing programs) can be denied green cards.[24] Under Trump, the public charge rule was expanded, prompting backlashes from advocates who warned of the danger to US public health from immigrants not seeking health care. Biden wants to revert to pre-Trump public charge rules.

The Trump administration's focus on immigration may have pushed migration from normal politics to regime politics. Normal politics involves issues on which there is broad agreement on the ends but disagreement on the means, such as agreement that immigration is mutually beneficial for immigrants and Americans but disagreement on exactly who and how many immigrants should be admitted. Regime politics involves disputes over ends, such as whether the United States should accept immigrants.

Immigration's Impacts

Immigration implies change. The arrival of immigrants increases and changes the composition of the US population, adds workers to the US labor force, and can change political priorities and social norms. Most immigrants are from Latin America and Asia, and some of their children are not fluent in English, raising questions about how best to teach English to children.

Immigration and Population

Immigration changes the size and composition of the US population. As fertility fell from a peak of 3.7 children per woman in the late 1950s to just 1.7 in 2019, the contribution of immigration to US population growth increased. Between 1990 and 2010, the number of foreign-born US residents almost doubled, rising from 20 million to 40 million, while the US population grew from almost 250 million to 310 million. Thus, immigration directly contributed a third to US population growth; taking into account the US-born children and grandchildren of immigrants, immigration contributed half of US population growth.

Immigrants are changing the composition of the US population. The US population rose by over 100 million in the past forty years and is projected to increase by an additional 60 million by 2050.[25] Immigrants and their US-born children contribute over half of US population growth. Since most immigrants are Hispanic and Asian, their share of the population has increased from 5 percent in 1970 to 25 percent today and is projected to increase to 35 percent in 2050 (Table 2.2).

TABLE 2.2. US Population by Race and Ethnic Group, 1970, 2010, 2019, 2050

Race / Ethnicity	Share of population			
	1970	2010	2019	2050
Non-Hispanic white	83.5	63.7	60.0	47.8
Non-Hispanic black	10.9	12.2	12.4	13.3
Hispanic, any race	4.6	16.3	18.4	25.7
Non-Hispanic Asian	0.7	4.7	5.6	8.2
Other	0.4	3.0	3.7	5.0

NOTE: The 2050 population projections are based on the 2010 Census.
SOURCES: 1970 U.S. Census; 2010 U.S. Census; 2019 American Community Survey; Census Bureau Population Projections (2017).

In 1970, about 83 percent of the 203 million US residents were non-Hispanic whites. In 2010, when the United States had 308 million residents, two-thirds were non-Hispanic white and 20 percent were Hispanic or Asian. If current trends continue, the share of non-Hispanic whites in the US population will fall from two-thirds in 2010 to just under half in 2050.

Economic Impacts

Most immigrants come to the United States for economic opportunity. About two-thirds of immigrants are in the US labor force, a figure that is about 4 percentage points higher than the labor force participation rate of US-born persons sixteen and older. A slightly higher share of foreign-born men than US-born men are in the labor force, and a slightly lower share of foreign-born women than US-born women. The overall foreign-born shares of the US population and workforce almost tripled since their lows of 5 percent in 1970 but are not yet at their historical peaks (Table 2.3). In 1910, about 15 percent of US residents were born abroad, and 24 percent of US workers

TABLE 2.3. Foreign-Born Residents and Workers, 1850–2019

Year	Share of population	Share of workers
1850	9.7	
1860	13.2	
1870	14.4	22
1880	13.3	20
1890	14.8	26
1900	13.6	23
1910	14.7	24
1920	13.2	21
1930	11.6	17
1940	8.8	12
1950	6.9	9
1960	5.4	6
1970	4.7	5
1980	6.2	7
1990	7.9	9
2000	11.1	12
2010	12.9	16.3
2019	13.7	17.4

SOURCE: US Census Bureau; Bureau of Labor Statistics.

were foreign-born. Over a century later, 14 percent of US residents and 17 percent of US workers were born abroad.

Immigration increases the number of US workers and the size of the US economy. Most working-age immigrants find jobs, spend most of their wages, pay taxes, and consume public services. Immigration thus expands the economy and employment while slightly depressing wages or the growth in wages, especially for workers similar to the immigrants. For example, over one-half of US adult workers who did not complete high school are immigrants. If these immigrants were not in the US labor force, economic theory predicts that wages for US-born high-school dropouts would be higher.[26] However, without the foreign-born workers, employment, investment, and output growth would be lower and consumer prices would be higher.[27] There is a net economic gain from immigration, but that gain is not distributed equally: employers, investors, land and property owners, and consumers gain, while some workers lose.

During the early 1990s, many of the Mexicans who had been legalized under IRCA in 1987–1988 brought their families into the United States during a recession, prompting several states to sue the federal government, arguing that the federal government's failure to enforce immigration laws saddled them with education and other costs. In 1994, California voters approved Proposition 187, which would have required state-funded institutions, including K-12 schools, to verify the legal status of those seeking services.[28]

Proposition 187 was struck down by the courts, but it unleashed a debate about the economic benefits and costs of immigration that led to a major study concluding that immigrants added a net $8 billion a year to the US economy in 1996, when GDP was about $8 trillion (Smith and Edmonston 1997). The US economy was $200 billion larger because of immigration, according to the study, but $192 billion of this expansion went to immigrants in their wages.[29] According to a stylized model, the presence of immigrants depressed US wages by an estimated 5 percent.[30] Immigrants are a net benefit because the value of what they produce is more than the wages they are paid, so owners of capital and US workers who are made more productive by the presence of immigrants gain from their presence.

As with most immigration-related studies, these results drew opposite reactions. Admissionists stressed the net economic benefits of immigration to the US economy, while restrictionists stressed that the net contribution of immigrants was negligible. The $8 trillion US economy in 1996 was expanding by 3 percent a year, or by $10 billion every two weeks.

Economic theory predicts that US workers who compete with immigrants will have lower wages and employment rates, and the calculation of the economic gain from immigration rests on this assumption. However, most empirical efforts seeking to measure the wage and employment effects of immigration suggest that immigration has either no effect or just a small negative effect on US-born workers.[31] Any negative effects of immigrants are restricted to subgroups of US workers, typically high school dropouts and low-skilled immigrants already in the United States. There is little evidence of negative effects on medium- and high-skilled natives' wages.

The size of the effects on US-born workers depends on how substitutable immigrants are for US-born workers. Natives whose skills are complementary to those of immigrants may see their wages and employment rise due to immigration, while natives with substitutable skills are most likely to lose. Therefore, the brunt of the negative labor market impact falls on earlier immigrants, not natives, because they are most similar to new immigrants and hence compete most closely with them.

Why doesn't immigration have a more negative effect on US workers? There are a number of reasons. First, the number of low-skilled workers in the United States has been declining, so there are fewer native workers competing directly with low-skilled immigrants. Second, the economy—including its workers—is constantly adapting to changing economic forces. When wages fall or rise more slowly, firms hire more workers, so immigration affects the factor mix used by firms to produce output. Immigration can also affect the output mix; firms may begin to produce goods or services that are more labor-intensive.

The decline in the cost of labor also raises the return to capital, so immigration may spur investment and inflows of capital. Immigrants tend to move to booming areas that otherwise might experience labor shortages, relieving growth bottlenecks. US-born workers and other immigrants may also move or change occupations in response to immigration, making adverse wage and employment effects difficult to measure. Any negative effects of immigrants are dampened by the fact that immigrants are consumers and create jobs via their own spending on housing and consumer goods. Last but not least, certain immigrants create jobs via their entrepreneurial activities and innovation, which would further mask any adverse effects.

The other major economic issue is the public finance impact of immigrants. Do immigrants and their children pay more in taxes than they consume in tax-supported services? A 2017 National Academies study concluded that they do: the average immigrant and his or her descendants are expected to pay $58,000 more in taxes (in 2016 dollars) than they would consume in tax-supported services.[32] This conclusion rests on several strong assumptions about the integration of the children of immigrants over their lifetimes as well as the evolution of government spending.

The estimates used in the study for future government spending followed the Congressional Budget Office's long-term budget outlook, admittedly already out of date given recent tax cuts. Projections of the educational attainment of the children of immigrants were based on a regression model that reflects current education transitions between generations.

Labor market and public finance studies emphasize that the major economic impacts of immigration are distributional, meaning that some workers and entities are helped and others are hurt by immigration, leaving a small overall positive economic impact. In the case of taxes and public services, the distributional impact helps the federal government, since most immigrants pay more in federal taxes, primarily social security taxes, than they receive in federally funded services. The reverse occurs at the state and local government levels, especially if the immigrants have low levels of education, lower incomes, and larger families. For example, an average immigrant and his minor children consumed $1,746 more in state and local services in 2013 than they paid in state and local taxes. Interestingly, according to estimates in the 2017 National Academies study, natives were also a net burden on state and local governments in the cross-sectional data, paying about $1,000 less than they consumed in services.[33]

There are other economic effects of immigrants as well. There is a strong correlation between high-skilled immigration and innovation. For example, Hunt and Gauthier-Lauselle (2010) find that immigrants patent new products at double the rate of US natives, a difference explained by immigrants' overrepresentation in STEM occupations. Immigrants also appear to be more entrepreneurial than US natives. They are more likely to own a business: the rate of self-employment is typically one or two percentage points higher for immigrants. Foreign-born business owners make up 18.2 percent of all business owners, which is greater than the immigrant share of the labor force (Fairlie and Lofstrom 2014).

Economic studies agree on one key point. The US government rations front-door visas, reserving two-thirds of permanent resident visas for family reunification and a sixth for employment. If US policy aimed to maximize the economic benefits of immigration to US residents, the US government should admit more high-skilled immigrants and fewer lower-skilled ones. There are several ways to give priority to skilled immigrants, including a Canadian-style points system (as was proposed in the Senate CIRA 2007 bill) or auctioning visas to the highest bidder under the theory that foreigners likely to earn the highest US earnings, or US employers who want to hire them, would be willing to pay the most for permanent resident visas (Orrenius and Zavodny 2010).[34]

Immigration and Politics

Many immigrants become naturalized US citizens and vote; some hold political office, including former California governor Arnold Schwarzenegger. The US government allows legal immigrants who are at least eighteen, have been in the United States at least five years, and pass a test of English and civics to become naturalized US citizens. There are often celebratory naturalization ceremonies on July 4 and other national holidays.

Over half of foreign-born US residents were naturalized US citizens in 2019, about 23 million of 45 million. Naturalization rates vary by country of origin. Immigrants from countries to which they do not expect to return are far more likely to naturalize than immigrants from countries to which they expect to return. Thus, naturalization rates are far higher for Cubans and Vietnamese than for Canadians and Mexicans.

Should the US government make it easier for immigrants to naturalize? Australia, Canada, and New Zealand have shorter residency requirements, simpler naturalization tests, and lower fees, while most European countries have more difficult and expensive naturalization procedures than the United States. During the 1990s, there was a sharp upsurge in naturalizations, with the number topping a million in FY96. There were several reasons for this upsurge, including a green card replacement program that required legal immigrants to obtain new counterfeit-resistant cards, welfare reform that limited the access of legal immigrants to federal means-tested assistance, and migrant-sending countries such as Mexico approving some form of dual nationality so that their citizens could become naturalized US citizens and still retain rights to vote in Mexico.

Foreigners may not feel the need to naturalize if there are few distinctions between legal immigrants and naturalized US citizens. Legal immigrants may live and work (except in some government jobs) where they please and buy houses, land, or businesses without restriction. Both legal and unauthorized immigrants have basic constitutional rights, including the right of free speech and the free exercise of religion. Non-US citizens can vote and hold office in US unions as well as in private organizations such as churches, foundations, and fraternal groups. Welfare reforms in 1996 introduced distinctions between immigrants and US citizens that may have contributed to an upsurge in naturalizations. Increased deportations of green card holders likely also increased incentives to naturalize, since citizens cannot be deported.

Will immigration and naturalization reshape US voting patterns? About 44 percent of US immigrants are from Latin America; they and their US-born children help to explain why there were over 60 million Hispanics and 40 million African Americans in 2019. However, Blacks cast 35 percent more votes than Latinos in the

2016 elections, reflecting the fact that many Hispanics are children and others are not US citizens.

Latinos are often called the "sleeping giant" of US politics, meaning that when they vote in large numbers, their vote may influence the outcome of federal, state, and local elections (DeSipio 1996). Most African Americans and Latinos vote for Democratic candidates, but in 2008 the vote for president was much more evenly split between Democrats and Republicans among Latino voters than among Black voters: 96 percent of Blacks voted for Obama, versus 55 percent of Latinos.[35]

The United States has a *jus soli* principle of citizenship, which means that persons born in the country are US citizens. The large number of unauthorized immigrants in the United States has made *jus soli* contentious. In 2016, about 250,000 babies were born in the United States to at least one unauthorized parent, making up 6 percent of the 4 million births that year.[36] Several bills have been introduced in Congress to end birthright citizenship, which was included in the Fourteenth Amendment to the US Constitution in 1868 to overturn the US Supreme Court's 1857 *Dred Scott* decision that held that blacks could not be US citizens. An October 2010 poll found registered voters were split, with 46 percent favoring an amendment to the constitution to end birthright citizenship and 46 percent favoring no change (Passel, Cohn and Gonzalez-Barrera 2012 13).

Immigrant Integration

Millions of southern and eastern Europeans arrived in the United States during third-wave immigration early in the twentieth century, and the leading metaphor for their integration was a fusion of Europeans and Americans in a "smelting pot" (Ralph Waldo Emerson), "cauldron" (Henry James), or "crucible" in which "immigrants were Americanized, liberated, and fused into a mixed race, English in neither nationality nor characteristics" (Turner 1920, 22–23). The hero of Israel Zangwill's popular 1908 play, *The Melting Pot*, proclaimed: "Germans and Frenchmen, Irishmen and Englishmen, Jews and Russians—into the Crucible with you all! God is making the American!"

Reality was more complex. There is always a tension between the desire of newcomers to retain their language and culture and the need and desire to adapt to their new country. The balance between retention and adaptation changed over time, but three principles have guided US policies. First, the United States was generally open to all immigrants; in the words of George Washington, "The bosom of America is open to receive not only the Opulent and respectable Stranger, but the oppressed and persecuted of all Nations and Religions; whom we shall welcome to a participation of all our rights and privileges." Second, US citizens should act politically as individuals, not as members of officially defined ethnic groups. Third, there was a laissez-faire attitude toward old cultures, so newcomers could maintain their old culture with private support.

Scholars studying the integration of immigrants have proposed two opposing visions: integration and pluralism. Those favoring integration or assimilation emphasize the need for immigrants to become Americans, with an individual identity, while those favoring pluralism or multiculturalism aim to maintain immigrant attachment to their cultures and membership in distinct groups.

Neither extreme characterizes immigrant integration in the United States. The melting pot ignores the importance of the home culture and the fact that ethnic affiliation persists into the second and third generations, long after the language and knowledge of the "old country" have been lost. Pluralism, on the other hand, can favor group loyalties over individual freedom, sometimes overlooking divisions within those from a particular country by allowing some leaders to assert that they speak for all Mexican Americans or Cuban Americans. Such group-based politics ignores the fluidity of people in the United States, where many immigrants work, make friends, and marry outside their ancestral communities.

Integration versus pluralism raises many practical questions. For example, should students in college dorms cluster by race and ethnicity, or should they be assigned to dorms with students from very different backgrounds? Should schoolchildren be taught in their home languages, or should they be brought together in English-language classes from the start? In the workplace, may employees talk to each other in languages other than English?

Historian John Higham proposed that the United States embrace "pluralistic integration," the idea that there is a common US culture shared by all Americans alongside the private efforts of minorities to preserve their culture. Higham emphasized the danger of providing public support to maintain or promote differences between racial and ethnic groups: "No ethnic group under these terms may have the support of the general community in strengthening its boundaries" (Higham 1988, 244).

The use of public funds to support particular racial and ethnic groups is especially contentious in K-12 education. About 80 percent of Americans five and older spoke only English at home in 2019, which means that 68 million Americans spoke Spanish (42 million, 13.5 percent) or other languages.[37] The public policy question is how best to help schoolchildren who do not speak English well, so-called limited English proficiency (LEP) pupils or English-language learners (ELLs).

The federal government in 1970 issued a memo to the 16,000 US school districts that said if the "inability to speak and understand the English language excludes national origin-minority group children from effective participation in the educational program . . . the district must take affirmative steps to rectify the language deficiency in order to open its instructional program to these students."[38] The United States had 50.7 million K-12 pupils in public schools in 2020 plus another 5.7 million in private K-12 schools, and about 10 percent of public school students were English language learners. The federal government did not prescribe the "affirmative steps" school districts should take to help ELLs to learn, but many embraced bilingual education—that is, teaching children math and history in Spanish or other languages as well as English until the child was ready to transition into a regular English-language classroom.

California, which has about a third of ELL pupils, embraced bilingual education, providing extra funds to teach children in their native language. Students were slow to move from native-language to English classrooms, prompting an effort to reform bilingual education.[39] When that failed, Proposition 227, the English for the Children initiative, was approved by California voters to speed the transition to English-only instruction by providing non-English speakers with a year of intensive English instruction, with generally positive results.[40]

Integrating immigrants has never been easy. In the past, US leaders sometimes rebuked their political opponents by slurring their national origins. President Herbert Hoover rebuked Representative Fiorella La Guardia (R-NY), later the mayor of New York City, by asserting in 1930 that "the Italians are predominantly our murderers and bootleggers." Hoover invited La Guardia and Italians who disagreed with him to "go back to where you belong" because "like a lot of other foreign spawn, you do not appreciate this country which supports you and tolerates you" (quoted in Baltzell 1964, 30). By and large, US presidents no longer use such language toward their opponents with immigrant backgrounds.

Studies of immigrant integration paint a mixed picture. Most immigrants are finding the economic opportunity that they sought in the United States, their children are learning English, and some of the children of Asian immigrants are among the top achievers in schools and universities. On the other hand, a significant number of children of Hispanic immigrants lag non-Hispanic whites in US schools, which is likely to limit their economic mobility. Many of those who worry about such integration patterns urge the federal government to fund programs that provide supplemental education, health, and other services to struggling immigrants (Fix 2006). The US Commission on Immigration Reform made similar recommendations: the federal government should do more to "Americanize immigrants" while expecting "immigrants to obey our laws, pay our taxes, respect other cultures and ethnic groups" (USCIR 1997, 28).

Gaps and Convergence?

There is a gap between the goals and the outcomes of US immigration policies. Critics argue that front-door immigration priorities should shift from admitting members of families of US residents (family reunification) to selecting foreigners whose employment in the United States would maximize the economic benefits of immigration. Some want to make it easier for students, guest workers, and other side-door entrants to settle in the United States as immigrants, while others want to reduce side-door entries. The most contentious issue is dealing with unauthorized immigrants in the United States. Does legalization encourage more such migration, or is bringing migrants out of the shadows the morally and economically desirable policy option?

Narrowing the gaps between immigration policy goals and policy outcomes is complicated by disagreement over both means and ends. There is widespread agreement on the need to reduce unauthorized migration, but disagreement on the means to accomplish this goal. A strategy of building more border fences and increasing the number of agents aims to raise the cost of illegal entry and discourage unauthorized migrants, and requiring employers to check the documents provided by newly hired workers in E-Verify could discourage unauthorized entries. Legalization could provide incentives for unauthorized migrants to learn English and obtain skills, allowing them to change jobs, earn more, and contribute more to the United States.

Opinion polls provide mixed signals. A Gallup poll found that until recently, more Americans wanted immigration to be reduced rather than maintained at current levels (Figure 2.3). In 2020, some 36 percent of those polled favored the present level of immigration, and for the first time the share of those who wanted immigration decreased fell below the share of those who wanted immigration increased.

In another Gallup poll, the share of respondents citing immigration as the nation's number one problem rose above 20 percent twice in 2018 (Figure 2.4). Republicans are much more likely than independents and Democrats to consider immigration the most important US problem. In November 2018, some 37 percent of Republicans deemed immigration the most important US problem, compared with 10 percent of Democrats.

Conclusions: Whither US Immigration?

The United States is a nation of immigrants unsure about immigration and integration in the twenty-first century. There is widespread agreement that the US immigration system is "broken," as reflected in the presence of 11 million unauthorized

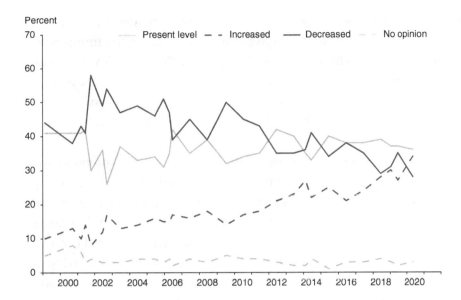

FIGURE 2.3. Gallup: Increase, Maintain, or Decrease Immigration

NOTE: Responses to question "In your view, should immigration be kept at its present level, increased or decreased?"

SOURCE: Gallup, https ://news.gallup.com/poll/1660/immigration.aspx.

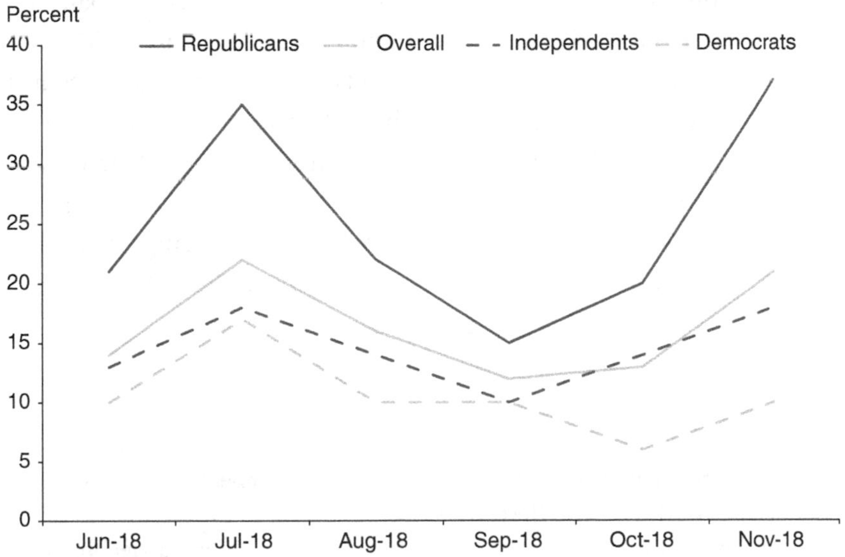

FIGURE 2.4. Gallup: Immigration as Most Important US Problem

NOTE: Share responding that immigration is the most important problem facing the U.S.

SOURCE: Gallup, https://news.gallup.com/poll/237392/satisfaction-important -problem-trends.aspx.

immigrants, long waits for permanent resident visas, and employers complaining of labor shortages. However, there is disagreement on how to fix the immigration system. What should be done to reduce illegal migration? What hurdles should unauthorized immigrants be required to overcome before they can become legal US immigrants and citizens? Should new guest worker programs make it easier for employers to hire migrant workers? What is the proper response to Central American asylum seekers?

Most opinion leaders and interest groups favor the enactment of comprehensive immigration reforms that include the three prongs of more enforcement, an opportunity for unauthorized immigrants to earn legal status, and new guest worker programs. However, they disagree on vital details that range from what burdens to place on employers to prevent unauthorized workers from getting jobs to how many additional guest workers should be admitted. States and cities are complicating the quest for durable migration policies by enacting diverse policies. Some states issue driver's licenses and IDs to unauthorized immigrants, while others require police to check the immigration status of persons they encounter. Some states require employers to use E-Verify to check newly hired workers, while others prohibit employers from cooperating with immigration enforcement agents unless they present a warrant.

The immigration status quo is generally deplored but continues in part because it is the second-best solution for advocates unable to achieve their preferred goal. The status quo allows unauthorized workers to fill jobs and US employers to avoid sanctions for hiring them. Many unauthorized immigrants settle in the United States and develop anchors via US-born (and thus US citizen) children that make them reluctant to leave. Advocates of less immigration believe that time is on their side, as more Americans worry about the demographic, economic, and sociopolitical effects of newcomers, while advocates of more immigration believe that a changing electorate that includes more minorities will insist on generous legalization and integration policies.

Notes

The views expressed here are solely those of the authors and do not reflect those of the Federal Reserve Bank of Dallas or the Federal Reserve System.

1. We use the terms "immigrant," "foreigner," and "foreign-born" interchangeably to refer to individuals in the United States who were born outside the United States to non-US-citizen parents.

2. The exceptions are American Indians who were in what became the United States, slaves brought against their will, and people who became US citizens when the United States acquired the territory in which they were living, such as Mexicans in California after 1848.

3. DHS reported 1 million lawful permanent residents admitted in FY19 and 82 million non-immigrants admitted with I-94 forms (another 105 million Canadian and Mexican border crossers who are exempt from I-94 forms were admitted). Some 860,000 foreigners were apprehended just inside US borders in FY19.

4. Quoted in Lizette Alvarez, "Census Director Marvels at the New Portrait of America," *New York Times*, January 1, 2001.

5. The United Nations Department of Economic and Social Affairs (UNDESA) considers persons born in Puerto Rico who move to the mainland United States to be international migrants and reports 51 million migrants in the United States. The US Census does not and estimated 44.9 million foreign-born US residents in 2019.

6. EB-5 investor visas are available to those who invest at least $1 million and create or preserve at least ten full-time US jobs (or $500,000 in areas with unemployment rates that are 1.5 times the US average). Most foreign investors invest $500,000 via private and public agencies that recruit foreign investors to obtain funds for particular projects—that is, the foreigners generally do not actively manage their US investments. After two years and a check on the investment and jobs, foreign investors can convert probationary resident visas into regular permanent resident visas.

7. DHS reported 186 million temporary visitors on non-immigrant admissions in FY19, including 105 million Canadians and Mexicans who do not need I-94 forms to enter the United States. DHS admissions data count events, not unique individuals, so a tourist who makes three visits in one year is counted three times.

8. The United States has 22 percent of all foreign students, followed by the United Kingdom with 10 percent. China, with 3,000 universities, has become the third-leading destination for international students.

9. A GAO report released in July 2012 found that a third of the 434 US flight schools that admit foreign students were not certified by the states in which they operated to provide flight training, raising questions about their ability to train students. Tri-Valley University of Pleasanton, California, was found to have admitted foreigners so that they could obtain student visas and work part-time. Tri-Valley did not provide classes for the admitted students, most of whom were Indians. "DHS: Border, Interior," *Migration News* 19, no. 4 (October 2012), https://migration.ucdavis.edu/mn/more.php?id=3784.

10. Border crossing cards are available to Mexicans who are established in border areas of Mexico and who want to visit the United States for up to seventy-two hours, remaining within twenty-five miles of the Mexico-US border.

11. In FY19, Mexicans were 166,000 of the 852,000 apprehensions, compared with 90,000 Salvadorans, 264,000 Guatemalans, and 254,000 Hondurans; that is, there were more Central Americans (608,000) apprehended than Mexicans. US Border Patrol, "U.S. Border Patrol Nationwide Apprehensions by Citizenship and Sector in FY2007," https://www.cbp.gov/sites/default/files/assets/documents/2020-Jan/U.S.%20Border%20Patrol%20Nationwide%20

Apprehensions%20by%20Citizenship%20and%20Sector%20%28FY2007%20-%20FY%20 2019%29_1.pdf.

12. There were 1,291,000 cases pending in immigration court in December 2020. About three-fourths involved citizens of Mexico, Guatemala, El Salvador, and Honduras. "Immigration Court Backlog Tool," TRACImmigration, http://trac.syr.edu/phptools/immigration/ court_backlog/.

13. In addition to immigration and colonization, slavery brought Africans to what became the United States. African slaves were 19 percent of the US population in 1790.

14. The 1910 census found that foreign-born residents made up 15 percent of US residents and 24 percent of US workers. Archdeacon (1992, 548) emphasized that third-wave immigrants arrived in a largely rural America: only 35 percent of the 75 million Americans in 1900 were in urban areas. This meant that there could be a great deal of homogeneity in the small communities where most Americans lived even though the country as a whole was becoming more diverse.

15. About 2 percent of the 12 million immigrants who arrived at Ellis Island were rejected for "physical or mental defects." The most common disease that prompted rejection was trachoma, a bacterial infection of the eye.

16. The Dillingham Commission was named for Senator William Dillingham (R-VT).

17. The 675,000 number is a pierceable cap, which can be and is exceeded regularly; see Dittgen 1997.

18. CIRA (S 2611) was approved on a 62–36 vote on May 25, 2006.

19. Campaigning for president in summer 2008, McCain said that after "we have achieved our border-security goal, we must enact and implement the other parts of practical, fair and necessary immigration policy," including a temporary worker program and legalization. Obama repeated his support for CIRA, pledging to bring unauthorized immigrants "out of the shadows" and put them on the path to citizenship after they "pay a fine, learn English, not violate the law, and go to the back of the line for the opportunity to become citizens." Quoted in "Candidates, E-Verify, Visas," *Migration News* 15, no. 4 (October 2008), http:// migration.ucdavis.edu/mn/more.php?id=3431_0_2_0.

20. DACA allows unauthorized immigrants who arrived in the United States before age sixteen, are between the ages of sixteen and thirty and have lived illegally in the United States at least five years, and are enrolled in school, have a high school diploma or equivalent degree, or are honorably discharged veterans to obtain protected status.

21. "Main Street" is considered to refer to the average American consumer, while "Wall Street" includes financial market participants.

22. Beinart (2017) emphasizes that pro-immigration activists and pro-H-1B tech firms combined to convince Democrats that a "growing Latino population gave the party an electoral edge." Leading Democrats downplayed any negative impacts of more immigrants, citing research that concluded that the presence of more immigrants "kicks" similar US workers up the job ladder by increasing competition at the bottom. Oxford's Paul Collier asserted that "social scientists have strained every muscle to show that migration is good for everyone."

23. A record 390,308 people traveling as families, mostly Central Americans, entered the United States illegally in the first nine months of FY19, plus 63,624 unaccompanied children

under eighteen. Since unauthorized children cannot be held for more than twenty days, most families and unaccompanied children are released to join US relatives. The Trump administration in August 2019 announced plans to terminate the Flores settlement, which had established the twenty-day limit on the detention of children, proposing instead to hold families together in detention until decisions are made on their asylum applications. About 85 percent of Central Americans are found not to be in need of asylum.

24. USCIS regulations define public charges as persons likely to become "primarily dependent on the government for subsistence, as demonstrated by either the receipt of public cash assistance for income maintenance, or institutionalization for long-term care at government expense." "Public Charge Fact Sheet," US Citizenship and Immigration Services, last updated March 10, 2021, www.uscis.gov/news/fact-sheets/public-charge-fact-sheet. USCIS estimated that 324,000 people in households with non-citizens would drop out of or not enroll in public benefit programs as a result of the new public charge rule. Advocates think that far more applicants for immigrant visas could be affected. Capps et al. (2018) reviewed immigrants awarded permanent resident visas in recent years and found that almost 70 percent had at least one negative factor under the proposed expansion of the public charge test, while 40 percent had an income of at least 250 percent of the federal poverty line, which is weighed positively for those seeking permanent resident visas.

25. The projections assume that net international migration will be about 1 million per year between 2019 and 2050. Sandra Johnson, "A Changing Nation: Population Projections Under Alternative Immigration Scenarios," report no. P25-1146, US Census Bureau, February 2020.

26. In 2019, there were 10 million US workers twenty-five and older who did not complete high school; 54 percent were foreign-born. The median weekly earnings of the foreign-born high school dropouts were $577 in 2019, versus $617 for US-born dropouts ("Labor Force Characteristics of Foreign-Born Workers," Bureau of Labor Statistics, last modified May 18, 2021, www.bls.gov/news.release/forbrn.toc.htm). Economic theory predicts that wages would rise for the US-born dropouts if there were fewer foreign-born dropouts.

27. See NAS 2017, chap. 4.

28. "Prop. 187 Approved in California," *Migration News* 1, no. 11 (December 1994), http://migration.ucdavis.edu/mn/more.php?id=492_0_2_0.

29. A recent update of the 1997 study concluded that the net impact of immigration on the US economy was $54 billion or 0.31 percent of GDP (NAS 2017).

30. The net gain due to immigration is the size of the triangle in the US labor market due to the supply-of-labor curve shifting to the right; the demand for labor is unchanged. The size of this triangle is half of (1) the share of GDP accruing to labor (65 percent) times (2) the percent of the labor hours that are foreign born (17 percent in 2015) times (3) the decline in wages due to immigration, about 5 percent, or $0.5 \times 0.65 \times 0.17 \times 0.05 = 0.003$, or about $54 billion, which is approximately three-tenths of 1 percent of the $17.5 trillion GDP. The study assumed that the US economy had constant returns to scale (CRTS), which means that doubling the number of workers and the amount of capital doubles output. This assumption means that immigration cannot raise productivity and hence wages.

31. Labor market outcome discussion is based on Orrenius and Gullo 2018; see also NAS 2017, table 5-2.

32. However, immigrants arriving with less than a high school education receive $196,000 more in tax-supported benefits than they pay in taxes, and those with no more than a high school diploma receive a net $47,000 (2016 dollars). Immigrants arriving with some college, a college degree, or more than college have a net positive fiscal present value of $99,000, $280,000, and $547,000, respectively, over the seventy-five-year period. See NAS 2017, table 8-12. All estimates cited here exclude costs of pure public goods, such as national defense and interest on the national debt.

33. See NAS 2017, table 8-2.

34. Canada admitted 341,000 permanent residents in 2019; 58 percent were economic immigrants, 27 percent sponsored family members, 9 percent refugees, and 5 percent asylees. Within the economic category, 56 percent were given permanent residence via the points-based system that awards points for youth, education, and knowledge of English or French. The Canadian points system ensures that immigrant adults have higher levels of education than Canada-born adults. Just over half of Canadian immigrants arriving between 2011 and 2016 had bachelor's degrees or higher, compared with 45 percent of immigrants to the United States.

35. Non-Hispanic whites voted for the Republican McCain (53 percent) over the Democrat Obama (43 percent) in 2008.

36. Pew analysis of 2016 ACS and CPS data. Jeffrey S. Passel, D'Vera Cohn, and John Gramlich, "Number of U.S.-Born Babies with Unauthorized Immigrant Parents Has Fallen Since 2007," Pew Research Center, November 1, 2018, https://www.pewresearch.org/fact-tank/2018/11/01/the-number-of-u-s-born-babies-with-unauthorized-immigrant-parents-has-fallen-since-2007/. Among all 2016 births, 80.7 percent were to US-born women and 19.3 percent were to immigrant women. Gustavo López, Kristin Bialik, and Jynnah Radford, "Key Findings About U.S. Immigrants," Pew Research Center, November 30, 2018, https://web.archive.org/web/20181202012226/https://www.pewresearch.org/fact-tank/2018/11/30/key-findings-about-u-s-immigrants/.

37. Over 60 percent of those who spoke a language other than English at home, 42 million, reported speaking English very well.

38. See J. Stanley Pottinger, "DHEW Memo Regarding Language Minority Children," Department of Health, Education, and Welfare, May 25, 1970, www.ed.gov/about/offices/list/ocr/docs/lau1970.html.

39. Surveys in 1998 found that only a third of the California's ELL pupils were in either bilingual or English-immersion programs—that is, two-thirds got no special help. School districts had little incentive to reclassify ELL pupils as English-proficient, since they received extra funds for these students and suffered no penalties if they did not reclassify children as English-proficient. Ken Ellingwood, "Bilingual Classes a Knotty Issue," *Los Angeles Times*, May 18, 1998.

40. The former head of the California Association of Bilingual Educators changed his mind about English immersion classes. He said: "The kids began to learn—not pick up, but learn—formal English, oral and written, far more quickly than I ever thought they would.

You read the research and they tell you it takes seven years. Here are kids, within nine months in the first year, and they literally learned to read." Jacques Steinberg, "Increase in Test Scores Counters Dire Forecasts for Bilingual Ban," *New York Times*, August 20, 2000.

References

Archdeacon, Thomas. 1992. "Reflections on Immigration to Europe in Light of US Immigration History." *International Migration Review* 26, no. 2: 525–548.

Baltzell, E. Digby. 1964. *The Protestant Establishment: Aristocracy and Caste in America.* New York: Vintage Books.

Beinart, Peter. 2017. "How the Democrats Lost Their Way on Immigration." *Atlantic,* July 2017. www.theatlantic.com/magazine/archive/2017/07/the-democrats-immigration-mistake/528678/.

Benderly, Beryl Lieff. 2010. "The Real Science Gap." *Miller-McCune,* July–August 2010.

Borjas, George. 1990. *Friends or Strangers: The Impact of Immigrants on the US Economy.* New York: Basic Books.

Briggs, Vernon, J. 1992. *Mass Immigration and the National Interest.* Armonk, NY: M. E. Sharpe.

Capps, Randy, Julia Gelatt, and Mark Greenberg. 2020. "The Public-Charge Rule: Broad Impacts, But Few Will Be Denied Green Cards Based on Actual Benefits Use." Migration Policy Institute. https://www.migrationpolicy.org/news/public-charge-denial-green-cards-benefits-use.

DeSipio, Louis. 1996. *Counting on the Latino Vote: Latinos as a New Electorate.* Charlottesville: University of Virginia Press.

Dittgen, Herbert. 1997. "The American Debate About Immigration in the 1990s: A New Nationalism After the End of the Cold War." *Stanford Electronic Humanities Review* 5, no. 2 (online).

Fairlie, Robert, and Magnus Lofstrom. 2014. "Immigration and Entrepreneurship." In *Handbook of the Economics of International Migration,* edited by B. Chiswick and P. Miller, chap. 17. Oxford: Elsevier.

Fix, Michael, ed. 2006. *Securing the Future: US Immigrant Integration Policy, a Reader.* Washington, DC: Migration Policy Institute.

Handlin, Oscar. 1952. "Memorandum Concerning the Origins of the National Origin Quota System." *Hearings Before the President's Commission on Immigration and Naturalization, 82nd Congress, 2nd Sess.* Washington, DC: US Government Printing Office.

Higham, John. 1988. *Strangers in the Land: Patterns of American Nativism, 1860–1925.* New Brunswick, NJ: Rutgers University Press.

Hunt, J., and M. Gauthier-Lauselle. 2010. "How Much Does Immigration Boost Innovation?" *American Economic Journal: Macroeconomics* 2, no. 2: 31–56.

Martin, Philip. 2018. "The GCM and Temporary Labor Migration." *Global Social Policy* 18, no. 3: 339–342. http://journals.sagepub.com/doi/full/10.1177/1468018118799010.

NAS (National Academies of Sciences, Engineering and Medicine). 2017. *The Economic and Fiscal Consequences of Immigration.* Panel on the Economic and Fiscal Consequences of

Immigration. Edited by F. Blau and C. Mackie. Washington, DC: National Academies Press.

Orrenius, Pia M., and Stephanie Gullo. 2018. "The Economic and Fiscal Effects of Immigration: Implications for Policy." In *The Human and Economic Consequences of Twenty-First Century Immigration Policy*, edited by Susan Pozo, 7–31. Kalamazoo, MI: Upjohn Institute.

Orrenius, Pia M., and Madeline Zavodny. 2010. *Beside the Golden Door: US Immigration Reform in a New Era of Globalization*. Washington, DC: American Enterprise Institute.

Passel, Jeffrey, and D'Vera Cohn. 2019. "Mexicans Decline to Less than Half the US Unauthorized Immigrant Population for the First Time." Pew Research Center.

Pierce, Sarah, Jessica Bolter, and Andrew Selee. 2018. "US Immigration Policy Under Trump: Deep Changes and Lasting Impacts." Migration Policy Institute. www.migrationpolicy .org/research/us-immigration-policy-trump-deep-changes-impacts.

Smith, James, and Barry Edmonston, eds. 1997. *The New Americans: Economic, Demographic, and Fiscal Effects of Immigration*. Washington, DC: National Research Council.

Tichenor, Daniel J. 2000. "Voters, Clients, and the Policy Process: Two Faces of Expansive Immigration Politics in America." Unpublished paper.

Turner, Frederick Jackson. 1920. *The Frontier in American History*. New York: Henry Holt.

USCIR (United States Commission on Immigration Reform). 1997. "Becoming an American: Immigration and Immigrant Policy." http://migration.ucdavis.edu/mn/cir/97Report1/ titlepgs/titlepgs.htm.

COMMENTARY

Blinded by the Numbers

Desmond King

Philip Martin and Pia Orrenius present an outstandingly detailed, data-rich account of the way patterns of immigration to the United States (and to a lesser extent US immigration law) have evolved in the twentieth century and in particular the various reforms initiated since the 1986 overhaul. Their encyclopedia style includes numbers about "immigrants" arriving in the United States beginning in the late eighteenth century, with thumbnail sketches of major historical events such as the Know-Nothing mobilization against white Catholic immigrants.

These two outstanding scholars are careful and scrupulous in presenting key data about immigration, offering calibrated descriptions of the categories of immigrants, proposing a potentially useful fourfold periodization of immigration to the United States since 1800, and advancing some remarks about integration in the Trump era. Their descriptive framework finds three types of immigrants in the modern era, depending on which entrance the newcomers use: *front-door* migrants (who arrive properly dressed for dinner and carrying the required gift), *side-door* migrants (often friends of the front-door guests, though always standing dutifully behind, with a smaller gift), and *back-door* entrants (in reality slipping in through cracks around the door hinges and bearing no gifts other than brawn). The level of detail is impressive and the two scholars succeed in putting their numbers-based account into a coherent descriptive narrative of US politics and their evolution.

As an exercise in data mining and data presentation, this is an exemplary chapter and will be a valuable source for students and scholars. As an engagement with the theoretical place, meaning, and significance of immigration in US political struggles, conflicts, and identity, the chapter is less accomplished. The authors are, I fear, blinded by the numbers. Martin and Orrenius retain, promote, and diffuse the conventional Panglossian view of the American story (a narrative long discarded by scholars of America's multiple traditions and identities and its skewed creed—e.g., Smith 1993, 1997). But immigration is a more complex aspect of American political development.

Given how rich the chapter's data is, I will confine my comments to three issues: theoretical developments in understanding the settler colonial origins of the American state, the persistence of racial hierarchies and conflicts embedded in American political development to which immigration is hermetically connected, and the mobilization of Trumpian white protectionism in significant part around historically and racially recognizable caricatures of immigrants.

The chapter opens with the commonplace trope that America is a "nation of immigrants." This conventional stance neglects how comparative political sociologists, historians, and scholars of race now analyze settler colonial societies such as the United States—other obvious examples being Canada, Australia, Israel, and New Zealand (Wolf 2006, Zreik 2016). The arc of the US polity does not begin in 1787. Rather, this date—signaling a break from Britain and a new Constitution—marks the triumph of the settler colonialists, many from England, in consolidating their displacement and dispossession of native peoples on the part of the continent they colonized, and in entrenching racial hierarchy, notably in respect to Africans brought forcibly and involuntarily, as kidnapped people, to be enslaved. The way in which European settler colonialists treated these groups and organized society on their hierarchical inferiority set up the motives informing the structure of the post-1787 American state (Van Cleve 2010). Scholars now emphasize the significance of 1619, when the first enslaved Africans arrived, in the founding of "America" (New York Times 2019); the complex relations with Native American peoples beginning in the late sixteenth century, which shifted from often an agreeable sharing of common land to aggressive dispossession and killings by European colonialists (Greer 2018); and the expansion of patterns of forced labor that extended from enslavement, increasingly justified by an ideology of white supremacy, to indentured and bonded servants.

The central theoretical advance from this new scholarship is the paucity of the moniker "nation of immigrants" as a description of European settlers keen to disrupt and displace existing communities, not commingle with them. A racial contractualism was present from the Europeans' arrival in what they called the "New World"

(Mills 2017). The problem can be illustrated by the following passage by Martin and Orrenius:

> The first wave of immigrants arrived in what were then British colonies. In the sixteenth and seventeenth centuries, English colonists established communities at Jamestown and Plymouth, seized control from the Dutch in New York, and overran various French and Spanish settlements. The English were 60 percent of the population in 1790, and English became the most common language and English common law the basis for the US legal system. The word "immigrant" emerged in the 1790s to mean a person who moves voluntarily from one established country into another.

The footnote in this paragraph reads: "In addition to immigration and colonization, slavery brought Africans to what became the United States. African slaves were 19 percent of the US population in 1790."

This passage is problematic.

First, it overlooks how the settler colonialists came to America to colonize and displace native peoples, not as immigrants seeking to share a society. This is the fundamental difference between colonialism and immigration, and understanding that difference is fundamental to analyzing American political development (Rana 2015; Zreik 2016). The settlers built a particular society with particular hierarchies, which they consolidated in the post-1787 state (Van Cleve 2010; King 2000). As Mahmood Mamdani writes, "Ever since Tocqueville, an important section of America's thinkers have written its autobiography as reflected in a European mirror." This "American autobiography is written as the autobiography of the settler. The native has no place in it" (2015, 596). This settler view is the view that is observable through a white prism, and many of the values celebrated by historians of US immigration—such as a relentless path to equality under America's purportedly inclusive creed—are in practice about only those Americans racialized as white.

The vestiges of these legacies endure. For example, the white-dominant (and, for some, white-supremacist) society assumed after 1787 created institutions to maintain the interests of those dominant before this date (Van Cleve 2010). One of the most important features of American political development is how the United States reinvented and recast itself as an immigrant society, exorcising its colonial history. Probing and acknowledging this history is an indispensable element in placing immigration in American history and political conflicts. Numbers may be blinding, but they are not self-explanatory. The spread of COVID-19 in 2020 and 2021, for example, tragically reproduced elements of this enduring inequality toward Americans racialized as non-white (Hooijer and King 2021).

It is, second, remarkable that the authors' discussion of enslavement and the kidnapping and involuntary passage of Africans to be held in conditions of slavery in the United States sits as a footnote in this passage. Here is a fundamental part of the American population to whom the term "immigrant" is offensive and whose presence has dominated politics since the adoption of the Constitution in 1787. For example, as the United States moved to implement racist quota regimes between the 1920s and the 1960s, African American activists and organizations such as the NAACP underlined how this externally facing racism complemented domestic racist laws embodied in the segregation regime then in place (King 2000). Immigration policy has always been, and remains, intricately connected to America's racial hierarchies. African Americans, for example, were excluded entirely from the debates about assimilation and Americanization in the late nineteenth and twentieth centuries because federal policymakers considered them unassimilable. This stance informed the restrictions placed on types of immigrants. It also helps explain the ease with which a populist like Trump could mobilize anti-immigrant sentiment (Joppke 2021; Smith and King 2020). Immigration is part of how the US polity was and is constituted, and a source of enduring divisions in the political system. Because immigration and the categorization of migrants are constitutive to the American polity, immigration is not merely another policy area.

Starting with the country's formalization as the dominant colonial power in North America, therefore, the United States' political trajectory and its effect on immigration policy have been dominated by the country's racial divisions, and are really only explicable in those terms. Obvious examples include the anti-Catholicism that made Irish immigrants "black," or the way in which being racialized as white gave workers a labor market advantage, what David Roediger (1999)—borrowing from Du Bois—famously calls the "wages of whiteness." The trope with which the chapter opens—"a nation of immigrants"—reifies instead of interrogates the long-standing failure to recognize how kidnapping and involuntary transportation defined the American state's "immigration" policy. The struggles on the streets of America today about racial inequality tell us lots about the enduring consequences of these origins, routinely ignored in conventional "immigration" studies.

Third, this legacy is deep and profound. How else could President Trump have so successfully orchestrated and exploited the image of dangerous migrants in his presidential campaign without widespread negative cultural motifs about foreigners? But this notion of "foreigner" is not just found in attitudes toward the external threat; it is also internal in the United States now, as the title of Arlie Hochschild's runaway bestseller, *Strangers in Their Own Land,* crisply captures, or as Katherine Cramer's politically resentful Wisconsin rural interviewees reveal in her ethnographic study *The Politics of Resentment*. The implicit objects of each scholar's interviewees' ire are African Americans and migrants. American immigration cannot be distinguished analytically from the country's racial-ethnic orders, as many scholars have endeavored to explain. To put it at its simplest, the historical treatment of immigrants is and continues to be far more aggressive and racialized than implied by Martin and Orrenius's chapter—the "nation of immigrants" is paradoxically one in which decisions about exclusion and demarcation have been elemental. Even in 2021 anti–Asian American sentiments were revived in frightening and violent ways, echoing a motif deep in the trajectory of American political development, one seen also in the Chinese Exclusion Act of 1882. Understanding these partial roots is a compelling imperative.

Martin and Orrenius need to theorize the recent changes under Trump in immigration. Following the standard work on how America's racial orders have shaped major policy areas, including immigration (King and Smith 2005), it is clear that the Trump administration's measures were not just isolated responses to immigrants but a crucial part of an agenda to dismantle civil rights and recreate a white-dominant America (Smith and King 2020, 2021). Changes in anti-discrimination enforcement, voting rights and ID checks, urban and housing policy, and welfare measures complemented the reforms to immigration and their implications. These rollbacks fit with what Smith and King call the new white protectionist agenda, which includes the outright rejection of a race-egalitarian agenda—the two racial policy alliances dominating US politics in respect to racial conflicts in the twenty-first century (Schmidt 2021).

Indeed, Trump is best analyzed as the new leader of modern racial conservatives, a group always latent in the electorate but mobilized in 2016 and 2020, as documented by Ashley Jardina, among others (Jardina 2019). A significant group of white voters believe they have become subjects of unfair treatment and even discrimination compared to the treatment of immigrants and African Americans. One survey in 2017 reported that 55 percent of whites believed that whites suffer discrimination in modern America, though less than 20 percent said they had experienced it personally (and most believed racial and ethnic minorities faced discrimination as well) (Gonyea 2017). A substantial part of this white identity group shares also a mostly conservative Christian identity politics, which heightens policy and racial polarization. As Smith and King document from an examination of President Trump's speeches during his campaign for election and in office and his policies once in the White House, Trump's America First crusade promoted a backward-looking reconstruction of white identities and privileges in the twenty-first century, and a reformulation of traditional conservative support of color-blind policies to an explicitly white protectionist agenda (Smith and King 2020).

The Trump administration's immigration policies signaled protectionism. The president made frequent derogatory remarks about migrants from countries that he saw as undesirable (often countries in Africa) compared with attractive sources (often in Europe). His preferences and language fit with the expectations of a racial-orders framework. President Trump's determination—thwarted in part—to build a visible and material wall at the nation's southern border expressed a protectionist agenda. To achieve this end, he had to resort to irregular (and ultimately unsuccessful) use of his constitutional emergency powers. Trump consistently rejected efforts to formalize or improve the position of unauthorized immigrants' children via the Deferred Action for Childhood Arrivals program. Many of his measures faced legal pushback, but the purpose and agenda were pellucid: admitting certain immigrants and ardently discouraging others.

One of Trump's accomplishments was to give traction and further mobilization to a distinct white identity politics in the United States, an aim that his approach to immigration reform and the southern border plainly complemented. As this division over racial policy issues has deepened, more and more whites have come to feel that they, rather than people of color, are the primary victims of unjust racial discrimination in America. Many whites report that they perceive anti-white discrimination to be rising in the United States, and even to be more pervasive than anti-Black bias (Norton and Sommers 2011).

America's racial history and enduring inegalitarian conditions mean that in the United States, pursuing such protectionism effectively means pursuing white protectionism. Evidence from the American National Election Studies, marshaled by Ashley Jardina, revealed that as Americans' anxieties about change mounted during the Obama years, many more self-identified white Americans came to say that their white identities were "extremely" important to them (Jardina 2019, 61). This group of voters were overwhelmingly Trump supporters, and most of those voters believed that he had rewarded them well (Sides, Tesler, and Vavreck, 2017, 16; Jardina 2019, 234, 236–238). A strong sense of racial resentment correlates, according to Ashley Jardina's public opinion research, with being a Trump supporter, because such individuals see in him a protector of white racial in-group values (Jardina 2019). The policy position with which Trump articulated this white protectionism included his stance to limit immigration, criticize many existing migrants, and implicitly promote a preference for white immigrants (Jardina 2019).

Immigration is fundamental to understanding the trajectory of contemporary US politics. In the presidential election of 2020, Biden and Trump garnered, respectively, the first- and second-highest vote totals for presidential candidates ever in US history. This massive and highly polarized mobilization was about the struggle—originating in both seventeenth-century and post-1787 America—over who belongs legitimately in the United States. The powerful Black Lives Matter movement that mobilized in 2020 was one side of this struggle, with roots in anti-enslavement, anti-segregation, and pro-civil-rights movements. The other side was a pro-white protectionism with roots in America's settler colonialists, supporters of segregation, and anti-civil-rights alliances. This is the analytical framework through which the data mobilized by Martin and Orrenius can best be interpreted.

References

Gonyea, Don. 2017. "Majority of White Americans Say They Believe Whites Face Discrimination." NPR, October 24.

Greer, Allan. 2018. *Property and Dispossession: Natives, Empires and Land in Early Modern North America.* New York: Cambridge University Press.

Hooijer, Gerda, and Desmond King. 2021. "The Racialized Pandemic: Wave One of Covid-19 and the Reproduction of Global North Racial-Ethnic Inequalities." *Perspectives on Politics* 19, no. 3: 1–21.

Jardina, Ashley. 2019. *White Identity Politics.* New York: Cambridge University Press.

Joppke, Christian. 2021. *Neoliberal Nationalism.* New York: Cambridge University Press.

King, Desmond. 2000. *Making Americans: Immigration, Race and the Origins of the Diverse Democracy.* Cambridge, MA: Harvard University Press.

King, Desmond, and Rogers M. Smith. 2005. "Racial Orders in American Political Development." *American Political Science Review* 99: 75–92.

Mills, Charles W. 2017. *Black Rights/White Wrongs.* New York: Oxford University Press.

New York Times. 2019. "The 1619 Project." https://www.nytimes.com/interactive/2019/08/14/magazine/1619-america-slavery.html.

Norton, Michael I., and Samuel R. Sommers. 2011. "Whites See Racism as a Zero-Sum Game That They Are Now Losing." *Perspectives on Psychological Science* 6, no. 3: 215–218.

Rana, Aziz. 2015. "Colonialism and Constitutional Memory." *UC Irvine Law Review* 5: 263–288.

Roediger, David. 1999. *The Wages of Whiteness.* New York: Verso.

Schmidt, Ronald, Sr. 2021. *Interpreting Racial Politics in the United States.* New York: Routledge.

Sides, John, Michael Tesler, and Lynn Vavreck. 2017. *Identity Crisis.* Princeton, NJ: Princeton University Press.

Smith, Rogers M. 1993. "Beyond de Tocqueville, Myrdal and Hartz: The Multiple Traditions in America." *American Political Science Review* 87: 549–566.

Smith, Rogers M. 1997. *Civic Ideals: Conflicting Visions of Citizenship in U.S. History.* New Haven, CT: Yale University Press.

Smith, Rogers M., and Desmond King. 2020. "White Protectionism in America." *Perspectives on Politics* 18, no. 2: 1–19.

Smith, Rogers M., and Desmond King. 2021. "Racial Reparations Against White Protectionism: America's New Racial Politics." *Journal of Race, Ethnicity and Politics* 6: 82–96.

Van Cleve, George William. 2010. *A Slaverholders' Union.* Chicago: University of Chicago Press.

Wolfe, Patrick. 2006. "Settler Colonialism and the Elimination of the Native." *Journal of Genocide Research* 8: 387–409.

Zreik, Raef. 2016. "When Does a Settler Become a Native?" *Constellations* 23: 351–364.

COMMENTARY

Activists, Interests, and Parties

Daniel J. Tichenor

Philip Martin and Pia Orrenius provide a valuable overview of US immigration categories, historical trends in migration and federal immigration policy, various impacts, and contemporary policy debates. Covering impressively broad terrain, their chapter offers readers a useful primer on the contours of these subjects. As a political scientist, however, I was struck by the noticeable absence of a careful analysis of the processes and dynamics that shape US immigration policymaking. Consider, for example, these crucial questions about the US case, especially in a volume focused on efforts by governments officials to control international migration: Why has immigration reform been so challenging to achieve not only in the contemporary era but across US history? Why does the United States have, as the authors note, "the largest number and share of unauthorized immigrants among the industrial democracies," and what does this say about federal "controls" over time? Moreover, in a volume that spotlights gaps between policy goals and outcomes, how do we explain the significant contradictions that characterize many US immigration laws and policies? Why has Congress been unable to enact comprehensive immigration reform for more than three decades, and how has this influenced the direction of national policy? Finally, how do we explain the tenacity of nativism and white supremacy in US immigration debate and governance—illustrated by the ascendency of Trumpism—even as newcomers are transforming the demography of American democracy? Martin and Orrenius do not develop an analytical framework or highlight underlying forces that enable us to answer these critical questions. Within the space constraints of a brief commentary, I would like to point to some promising ways to address them.

Research by both historians and political scientists shows that US policymakers long have been buffeted by powerful interest groups, movement activists, and constituencies pursuing rival goals whenever immigration has gained prominence on the public agenda. Throughout the nation's history, a variety of business interests have advocated for policies that facilitate easy access to migrant workers who meet their labor needs. Unions and labor federations traditionally favored immigration restrictions to protect the wages and working conditions of domestic workers, but in the contemporary era they have championed the rights of immigrant union members. Nativist movements and xenophobic groups predictably have pressed for sweeping restrictions and tough enforcement in every period. In turn, ethnic groups and immigrant rights movements have pushed for openness in immigration and citizenship policies. This is only a sample of the diverse organized interests that have mobilized over immigration policy. Because of these clashing interests and beliefs, conflict and stalemate have been recurring challenges for US officials seeking to govern immigrant admissions and rights. As a consequence, policy innovation usually has required strange-bedfellows politics, in which diverse interests and bipartisan coalitions coalesce behind compromise packages that address rival goals and interests.[1]

These defining qualities of American immigration politics have meant that even some of the most restrictive immigration laws in American history have included bargains that create openings for international migration, and that expansive reforms have featured key restrictions. Consider, for example, the infamous Quota Acts of 1924 and 1928. These laws established a racist national origins quota system that dramatically lowered annual admissions while reserving most visas for northern and western Europeans. However, in exchange for their pivotal support of these quota restrictions, southern and western lawmakers kept the door open to Western Hemisphere migrants—thereby winning easy access to cheap, tractable Mexican labor for employers in these regions. In similar fashion, the Immigration and Nationality Act (INA) of 1965 was heralded by immigration champions for dismantling discriminatory quotas and expanding legal admissions, but it also was designed to favor European immigrants and placed new limits on Western Hemisphere migration. The Immigration Reform and Control Act (IRCA) of 1986 extended generous terms of legalization for nearly 3 million undocumented immigrants residing in the country to satisfy immigrant rights activists, created an agricultural worker program to appease grower interests, enhanced border control resources for restrictionists, and launched a weak version of employer sanctions as a bargain between employers and organized labor. In short, major policy innovations typically have hinged upon building uneasy alliances that demand difficult compromises between disparate partisans, lobbyists, and activists. As a result, competing and incongruous elements often are woven into US immigration reform and policy implementation over time.

As noted earlier, the 1920s political bargain to shut down most (south and eastern) European immigration was in exchange for keeping the southern border open to migrant labor from Mexico. Under intense pressure from southern and western agricultural, ranching, and mining interests, members of Congress from those regions supported national origins quotas and other restrictions on overseas immigration so long as access to Mexican migrant labor was not disrupted. This compromise was codified not only in law but also in the implementation process, where few resources were devoted to border control while strict inspection systems were established to deny visas to immigrants beyond Mexico and Canada. From 1942 to 1963, the Bracero Program brought 4.2 million Mexican contract laborers to the United States, many of whom remained as undocumented immigrants or beckoned family and friends to join them without authorization. Pathways for both legal and unauthorized immigration from Latin America were reinforced in the late twentieth century by sustained business demand for their labor, the INA's preference system, and the designed weakness of IRCA's employer sanctions provision. Yet at the same time as undocumented immigrants developed strong social, economic, and cultural ties to their adopted US communities, they also became convenient political scapegoats for drugs, crime, unemployment, the rising costs of public benefits, and other problems. Although a sizable portion of the unauthorized population is not of Latin American descent, political demagogues routinely cast undocumented immigrants as a "Latino threat."[2]

Focusing on the interaction between interest groups, movements, and parties provides crucial insights about the disruption of older patterns of immigration politics and policy formation in recent decades. Whereas lawmakers in the past overcame barriers to policy innovation through crosscutting alliances and bipartisan grand bargains, comprehensive immigration reform has failed repeatedly in modern times, despite significant tries in 2001, 2006, 2007, 2013, and 2014. The reason is that the traditional dynamics of US immigration policymaking have been upended by the enormous influence of movement activists in the base of each party during the contemporary era. In particular, the ability of the nativist and immigrant-rights movements—like labor, civil rights, Christian right, and Tea Party activists—to push the Democratic and Republican parties far from the ideological center has made gridlock on immigration reform a defining feature of the contemporary era. The mobilization of both the conservative and progressive grassroots on immigration, replete with intense media attention, has made grand bargains and bipartisan coalition-building one of the most elusive items on the US public agenda. This deep partisan divide, driven by movement activists, at once stymies major legislative re-form and concentrates extraordinary unilateral power over immigration policy in the hands of modern presidents, who now have strong incentives to unilaterally ad-vance immigration and refugee policies that satisfy activists in their base.[3]

The enormous political traction and influence that conservative anti-immigrant groups have gained in today's Republican Party underscore the staying power of na-tivism in a polarized US polity. Although Martin and Orrenius briefly note back-lashes against early waves of immigration, their chapter tells us precious little about the centrality of race and white nationalism in shaping the politics of US immigra-tion control in both the past *and the present*. Since the nation's founding, signifi-cant shifts in the ethnic, racial, and religious composition of immigration have been viewed by nativists as perilous to the country's well-being. In the 1870s, the California Anti-Chinese Convention proclaimed that "the strong nations of the earth are now, as they always have been, the most thoroughly homogenous nations, that is to say, the most nearly of one race, language, and manners." Decades later, from the other side of the continent, Harvard president A. Lawrence Lowell invoked nearly identical language in response to new southern and eastern European immigration, under-scoring "the need for homogeneity in a democracy." This need, he insisted, stands "as a basis for popular government . . . that justifies democracies in resisting the influx in great numbers of a widely different race." In addition to xenophobic narratives of immigration fueling "race suicide," nativists have also highlighted the economic and national security perils of newcomers. Progressive Era xenophobes, for exam-ple, warned that Italian and Jewish newcomers were prone to "personal violence," "criminality," and "radicalism in politics."[4] Knitting these themes together, Donald Trump's depiction of Mexicans, Muslims, "illegals," and migrant "caravans" as dire threats to public order—like Patrick Buchanan, Peter Brimelow, Tom Tancredo, Samuel Huntington, and Steve King before him—reflects a tenacious vision of ethnic nationalism in which new immigrants imperil the culture, security, and economic well-being of white America.[5] Martin and Orrenius write that Herbert Hoover was the last US president to invoke xenophobic language to rebuke political opponents. Of course, President Trump did just that when he attacked Somalian-born represen-tative Ilhan Omar (D-MN) on the 2020 campaign trail, smiling broadly as his sup-porters chanted "Send her back!"[6] One cannot understand the power of Trumpism as a formidable populist movement in America without taking stock of immigration restriction and nativism as articles of faith for much of his right-wing base.

Undaunted by the political quagmires presented by this issue, the Biden ad-ministration made immigration policy change a top priority during its first 100 days.[7] On his first day in office, the new president unveiled legislative plans for legalizing most of the country's 11 million unauthorized residents, and issued seventeen immigration-related executive orders, including measures to preserve and expand the Deferred Action for Childhood Arrivals (DACA) program, to rescind harsh deportation rules, and to provide a pause on most deportations from the US interior.[8] By mid-February, President Biden's allies in Congress introduced his ambitious reform bill, the US Citizenship Act, whose centerpiece is a pathway to citizenship for nearly all of the country's undocumented population. These blueprints promised the most sweeping overhaul of the nation's immigration policies in generations, calling for "big, bold, inclusive immigration reform" that "leaves no one behind" among immigrants without legal status.[9] Given their narrow control of Congress and the great divide between the major parties, Biden and Democratic lawmakers face daunting headwinds in their quest to achieve major immigration reform, which has eluded policymakers for thirty-five years. Yet, as veterans of more than one previous attempt to overhaul the country's immigration laws, the Biden administration and its legislative allies already have demonstrated a sophisticated understanding of the perils and possibilities of immigration policymaking. Their capacity to translate that knowledge into tangible policy change—great or small—hinges upon structural opportunities and barriers that are difficult to predict. What is certain is that absent significant reform, immigration governance will continue to be driven by the unilateral power of shifting presidential administrations, judicial activism, and variations in state and local regulation.[10] Legislative inertia also will perpetuate a caste system that marginalizes an estimated 11 million undocumented immigrants, reinforcing permanent gradations of membership that make inclusive democracy impossible.[11]

Notes

1. John Higham, *Strangers in the Land* (New Brunswick, NJ: Rutgers University Press, 1955); David Reimers, *Still the Golden Door* (New York: Columbia University Press, 1992); Peter Schuck, "The Politics of Rapid Legal Change: Immigration Policy in the 1980s," in *The New Politics of Public Policy*, edited by Marc Landy and Martin Levin, 47–54 (Baltimore: Johns Hopkins University Press, 1995); Daniel Tichenor, *Dividing Lines: The Politics of Immigration Control* (Princeton, NJ: Princeton University Press, 2002); Aristide Zolberg, *A Nation by Design* (Cambridge, MA: Harvard University Press, 2008); Janice Fine and Daniel Tichenor, "A Movement Wrestling: American Labor's Enduring Struggle with Immigration," *Studies in American Political Development* 23, no. 1 (March 2009): 109–112.

2. Erasmo Gamboa, *Mexican Labor and World War II: Braceros in the Pacific Northwest 1942–1947* (Austin: University of Texas Press 1990); Tichenor, *Dividing Lines;* Douglas Massey, Jorge Durand, and Nolan Malone, *Beyond Smoke and Mirrors* (New York: Russell Sage, 2003); Mario Sifuentes, *Of Forests and Fields: Mexican Labor in the Pacific Northwest* (New

Brunswick, NJ: Rutgers University Press, 2016); Leo Chavez, *The Latino Threat: Constructing Immigrants, Citizens, and the Nation* (Stanford, CA: Stanford University Press, 2008).

3. See, for example, Doug McAdam and Karina Kloos, *Deeply Divided* (New York: Oxford University Press, 2014); Sidney Milkis and Daniel Tichenor, *Rivalry and Reform: Presidents, Social Movements, and the Transformation of American Politics* (Chicago: University of Chicago Press, 2019), chap. 7; Adam Cox and Cristina Rodriguez, *The President and Immigration Law* (New York: Oxford University Press, 2020).

4. Quotes from Tichenor, *Dividing Lines,* 88–94; A. Lawrence Lowell, quoted in Morton Keller, 1998, *Regulating a New Society: Public Policy and Social Change in America, 1900–1933* (Cambridge, MA: Harvard University Press), 230. See also Higham, *Strangers in the Land*; Erika Lee, *America for Americans* (New York: Basic Books, 2019).

5. Daniel Tichenor, "Populists, Clients, and U.S. Immigration Wars," *Polity* 53, no. 3 (2021): 422–448.

6. David Jackson, "Ilhan Omar Responds to President Donald Trump's Attacks," *USA Today,* September 23, 2020.

7. Nick Miroff and Maria Sacchetti, "Biden Says He'll Reverse Trump Immigration Policies," *Washington Post,* December 22, 2020.

8. Michael Shear and Zolan Kanno-Youngs, "Biden Issues Orders to Dismantle Trump's 'America First' Immigration Agenda," *New York Times,* February 2, 2021; "Biden Administration's January/February Executive Actions on Immigration," National Immigration Forum brief, February 12, 2021, https://immigrationforum.org/article/biden-administrations -january-20-executive-actions-on-immigration/.

9. Molly O'Toole and Andrea Castillo, "Democrats Unveil Broad Immigration Reform with Citizenship Path for 11 Million," *Los Angeles Times*, February 18, 2021; Maria Sacchetti, "Democrats Call for 'Big, Bold' Action on Immigration as Biden's Bill Is Introduced," *Washington Post*, February 18, 2021.

10. See, for example, Anna Law, *The Immigration Battle in the Courts* (New York: Cambridge University Press, 2010); Pratheepan Gulasekaram and Karthick Ramakrishnan, *The New Immigration Federalism* (New York: Cambridge University Press, 2015); Tichenor, *Dividing Lines*; Zolberg, *A Nation by Design*; Adam Cox and Cristina Rodriguez, *The President and Immigration Law* (New York: Oxford University Press, 2020); and Allan Colbern and Karthick Ramakrishnan, *Citizenship Reimagined* (New York: Cambridge University Press, 2020).

11. Roberto Gonzalez, *Lives in Limbo* (Berkeley: University of California Press, 2015); Elizabeth Cohen, *Semi-Citizenship in Democratic Politics* (New York: Cambridge University Press, 2009); Joseph Carens, *The Ethics of Immigration* (New York: Oxford University Press, 2013); Linda Bosniak, *The Citizen and the Alien: Dilemmas of Contemporary Membership* (Princeton, NJ: Princeton University Press, 2006).

3 Canada

Continuity and Change in Immigration for Nation-Building

Jeffrey G. Reitz

Despite an intensifying backlash against immigration in many countries, in Canada the basic underlying immigration policy model, emphasizing admission of relatively large numbers of skilled immigrants, supported by language training and other settlement services, with opportunities for family reunification, refugee asylum, and fast-track citizenship, remains in place. Moreover, the concept of multicultural inclusiveness, now rejected in many countries in the wake of terrorist attacks, remains popular in Canada; it is not only a formal policy but also entrenched in law and the country's Charter of Rights and Freedoms. The government introduces modifications to immigration and multicultural policies periodically, in a search for better ways to get new immigrants into the workforce more quickly and to encourage more rapid settlement and social integration. In recent years, these modifications have included revised selection criteria recognizing the importance of language knowledge and other characteristics in job searches, efforts to bring the needs of employers more directly into the selection process, revised administrative procedures for economic immigrants called Express Entry, and expansion of temporary immigration with opportunities for successful workers to transition to permanent status. Whatever impact these innovations may turn out to have, they are part of a pattern of continual adjustment that has characterized the Canadian model since its inception in the 1970s.

The political orientation of successive Liberal and Conservative governments has made some difference to immigration policy, but surprisingly little. After the election of Stephen Harper's Conservative government in 2006, immigration numbers remained high despite greater reservations about immigration among many Conservative supporters. In turn, the Liberals under Justin Trudeau, first elected in 2015 and returned with a parliamentary minority in 2019, have kept most, if not all, of the selection and administrative changes introduced by the Conservatives, including the expansion of temporary immigration despite the controversy it had generated. The most significant difference with the Liberals is greater openness to Muslim and other refugees. Harper had begun severely curtailing such immigration for security reasons, but Trudeau reopened the doors. In addition, the Liberal plan to increase the overall number of immigrants admitted annually has begun to move ahead, though with significant interruption due to the COVID-19 pandemic.

The political success of the broader Canadian immigration program is so well established that many Canadians consider immigration and multiculturalism to be part of national identity, and that supporting them is a civic duty. However, no political sentiment is unconditional. Canadians take control over immigration for granted, but they do so not only because of careful and well-considered policy, what Jonathan Tepperman's op-ed in the *New York Times* called "Canada's ruthlessly smart immigration policy" (2017). Canadians also rely on the good fortune of geography and history. Canada's only land border is with the United States, partially insulating it from large-scale less-skilled immigration. The *Economist* (2016) magazine's issue devoted to "Canada's example to the world" put it well, if somewhat facetiously: "It is easier to be relaxed about immigration when your only land border is protected by a wall the size of the United States." The other important circumstance is that Canada was a former colony, never an imperial power, so it is free from resulting obligations to the populations of former colonies. These lucky circumstances do not mean that Canadian immigration will always remain relatively easy to control, that Canadian policy will always be effective in taking advantage of that potential for control, or that Canada will always look "ruthlessly smart." A review of Canadian immigration should consider how ongoing problems of immigration, and the effectiveness or ineffectiveness of their solutions, may affect perceptions of immigrants as a positive contribution to national well-being.

Canadian Immigration Policy: Long-Standing Goals and New Policy Initiatives

The primary goals of Canadian immigration policy have long been those of nation-building, with a focus on expansion of the economy and the population, meeting the needs of the contemporary labor market, and accommodating the long-term integration of immigrants (Kelley and Trebilcock 2010; Reitz 2012, 2014a; Akbari and MacDonald 2014). The numbers of permanent immigrants (see Figure 3.1) show that a higher priority has been given to immigration in the last two or three decades. Whereas during the period 1971–1990 the annual arrivals of permanent settlers averaged 139,000, from 1991 to 2017 the average increased by nearly 75 percent to 242,000. Over the same period, immigration also increased as a percentage of the population, from 0.5 percent to 0.8 percent. In 2018 and 2019, numbers rose to well over 300,000, phasing in a planned expansion of immigration. The target for 2020 was 340,000, but only just over half this number, 184,000, were admitted, due to international travel restrictions imposed during the COVID-19 pandemic. Immigration has been an increasing source of population growth as well. In the early 1990s, international migration accounted for 44 percent of total population growth; in 2018–2019, it was nearly 82 percent (Statistics Canada 2020, 10). Because of this high level of immigration, the proportion of the population that is foreign-born is greater than that in the United States and most European countries (see Figure 3.2).

The shift in countries of origin of immigrants to Canada from Europe and the United States to elsewhere began in the 1970s (see Table 3.1), and since that time, the specific origins of these new-source immigrants have changed. Initially many were from the Caribbean (predominantly Afro-Caribbean), but after the 1980s, this source declined numerically and as a percentage of the total. Asia quickly became the

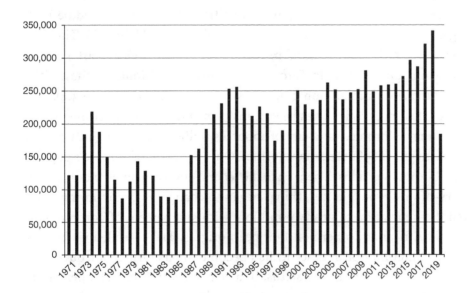

FIGURE 3.1. Annual Numbers of Permanent Immigrants to Canada, 1971–2020
SOURCE: Immigration and Refugees and Citizenship Canada; United Nations, International Migration Report 2015.

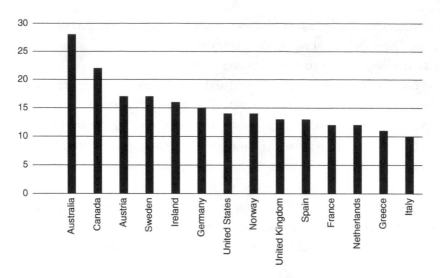

FIGURE 3.2. Immigration Nations: Percent Foreign-Born, 2015
SOURCE: United Nations, International Migration Report 2015.

leading source region, including Hong Kong and South Asia. By the first decade after 2000, over 60 percent of immigrants to Canada were from Asia, including 20 percent from South Asia, 15 percent from China (mostly mainland), and 8 percent from the Philippines. Africa and the Middle East also emerged as important source regions. In the period 2011–2016, South Asia and the Philippines became the leading source regions, and nearly one in four immigrants came from Africa or the Middle East. The shifting of source countries affects the arrival cohorts (see Figure 3.3). The shift from Europe is evident in the origins of immigrants arriving before and after 1990.

Since most immigrants settle in Toronto, Vancouver, and Montreal, these cities rank among the major immigration cities of North America (see Figure 3.4). The composition of their populations has been transformed in racial and ethnic terms. For example, in 1971, Toronto was a city of about 2.5 million, predominantly British in origin but with growing European minorities. Only 4 percent of Toronto's population had non-European origins. Then, once the federal government abandoned previous country-of-origin preferences, things began to change. By 2016, immigration had boosted the population to nearly 6 million, with 51.4 percent of Torontonians claiming Asian, African, or other non-European origins. The so-called visible minorities (those of non-European descent) had become the majority. Vancouver was close to the same majority-minority status; in a city of 2.4 million, 48.9 percent of inhabitants had non-European origins. In Montreal, immigration slowed during the years of the most intense controversy over Quebec sovereignty, but in 2016, the population stood at 4 million, with 22.6 percent of non-European origin.

TABLE 3.1. Immigrants to Canada by Origins, 1961–2016

Origins	1961–1970 Number (,000)	Percent	1971–1980 Number (,000)	Percent	1981–1990 Number (,000)	Percent	1991–2000 Number (,000)	Percent	2001–2010 Number (,000)	Percent	2011–2016 Number (,000)	Percent
Africa and the Middle East	14.0	1.0	64.8	4.5	68.4	5.1	159.5	7.2	291.7	12.3	390.4	24.5
America, Total	246.8	17.5	401.7	27.9	280.4	21.1	294.3	13.3	323.6	13.7	195.9	12.3
Mexico	2.1	0.1	6.1	0.4	6.9	0.5	12.7	0.6	26.6	1.1	23.2	1.5
United States	161.6	11.4	178.6	12.4	75.7	5.7	60.6	2.7	85.5	3.6	48.4	3.0
Other North and Central America	6.2	0.4	2.5	0.2	40.8	3.1	43.6	2.0	14.7	0.6	41.2	2.6
Cuba			0.3	0.0	1.1	0.1	4.7	0.2	10.5	0.4	6.6	0.4
Other Caribbean	52.8	3.7	131.4	9.1	87.3	6.6	97.5	4.4	67.8	2.9	27.3	1.7
South America	24.1	1.7	82.8	5.7	68.6	5.2	75.1	3.4	118.4	5.0	49.2	3.1
Asia and Pacific, Total	140.9	10.0	408.7	28.4	602.9	45.3	1313.6	59.5	1427.0	60.3	810.7	50.9
Hong Kong	36.5	2.6	83.9	5.8	129.3	9.7	240.5	10.9	14.0	0.6	4.5	0.3
Taiwan			9.0	0.6	14.3	1.1	79.6	3.6	27.2	1.1	5.5	0.3
China	1.4	0.1	10.6	0.7	36.2	2.7	181.2	8.2	337.3	14.2	166.6	10.5

(continued)

TABLE 3.1. (*continued*)

Origins	1961–1970 Number (,000)	1961–1970 Percent	1971–1980 Number (,000)	1971–1980 Percent	1981–1990 Number (,000)	1981–1990 Percent	1991–2000 Number (,000)	1991–2000 Percent	2001–2010 Number (,000)	2001–2010 Percent	2011–2016 Number (,000)	2011–2016 Percent
Macao				0.3	2.0	0.2	4.1	0.2	0.3	0.0	0.1	0.0
Vietnam/Laos/ Cambodia			66.2	4.6	100.6	7.6	47.6	2.2	24.9	1.0	14.6	0.9
Philippines			54.1	3.8	65.4	4.9	131.1	5.9	191.1	8.1	233.2	14.6
Japan	0.3	0.0	6.0	0.4	4.2	0.3	9.5	0.4	13.2	0.6	6.6	0.4
South Korea			16.0	1.1	16.5	1.2	43.2	2.0	65.8	2.8	26.9	1.7
South Asia	30.4	2.2	92.1	6.4	108.6	8.2	336.1	15.2	489.7	20.7	330	20.7
Other Asia	72.3	5.1	70.5	4.9	125.8	9.5	240.7	10.9	263.6	11.1	11.5	0.7
Australia	26.4	1.9	14.7	1.0	5.1	0.4	8.6	0.4	10.5	0.4	7.3	0.5
New Zealand	6.8	0.5	5.2	0.4	2.4	0.2	2.3	0.1	4.4	0.2	2.4	0.2
Other Oceania			11.3	0.8	9.9	0.7	11.8	0.5	4.2	0.2	1.5	0.1
Europe and the U.K.	960.8	68.0	531.3	36.9	361.5	27.1	418.3	18.9	296.7	12.5	191.8	12.0
Unidentified Countries	15.8	1.1	2.7	0.2	0.3	0.0	0.0	0.9	9.5	0.4	4.8	0.3
Total	1411.5	100.0	1440.4	100.0	1330.9	100.0	2208.5	100.0	2367.5	100.0	1593.6	100.0

SOURCES: Statistics Canada, *Canada Year Book*, various years; Employment and Immigration Canada 1986, 28–30; 1992, 34 –36; CIC statistics, various years; CIC, "Facts and Figures 2011"; Immigration, Refugees and Citizenship Canada, "Facts and Figures 2016."

NOTE: "Origins" refers to country of last permanent residence.

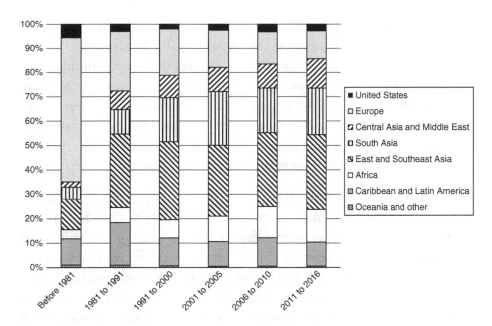

FIGURE 3.3. Birthplace of Immigrants by Period of Arrival, Canada, 2016
SOURCE: Statistics Canada, Census of Canada.

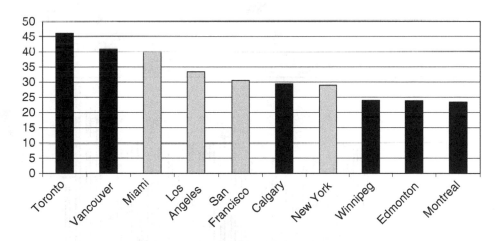

FIGURE 3.4. Percent Immigrant by Urban Area, 2016–2017
SOURCES: Statistics Canada, Census 2016 (https://www150.statcan.gc.ca/n1/daily-quoti-dien/171025/t001b-eng.htm#fn01); U.S. Census Bureau, 2013-17 American Community Survey, as tabulated by the Migration Policy Institute (https://www.migrationpolicy.org/programs/data-hub/charts/us-immigrant-population-metropolitan-area).

Although these three cities continue to dominate the immigration landscape, immigrant settlement has become a bit less concentrated in the largest cities. For example, for a long time Toronto received about 40 percent of Canada's immigrants, roughly 100,000 immigrants per year, but the numbers began to decline in 2006. Since 2011, Toronto has received closer to 30 percent of the immigrants, about 80,000 immigrants per year. However, the recent increase in overall numbers produced a return to higher immigration settlement in Toronto. In 2019, nearly 118,000 new immigrants settled in Toronto, 35 percent of the total for the country.

Economic Class, Family Reunification, Refugees

Over the entire period just described, permanent immigrants to Canada were admitted in three main categories: economic, family, and refugee, with a small group admitted on "humanitarian and compassionate" grounds. As immigration numbers rose in the late 1980s and 1990s, the proportion of economic immigrants remained constant at about half the total (see Figure 3.5). Since the late 1990s, however, there has been a steady increase in economic migrants and a corresponding decrease in the proportions of family-class and refugee immigrants. In the most recent years under the Trudeau government, there has been an uptick in admissions of both family-class and refugee immigrants; nevertheless, the economic class remains more than 50 percent of the total.

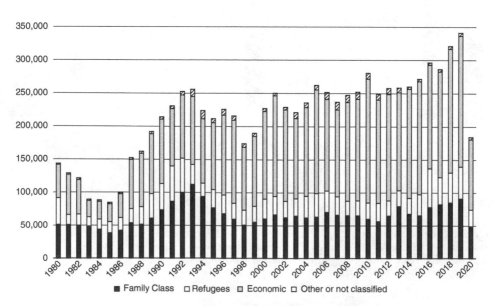

FIGURE 3.5. Immigration to Canada by Class of Entry, 1980–2020
SOURCE: Immigration, Refugees and Citizenship Canada.

Within the economic class, skilled workers are still the largest group, traditionally selected on the basis of a points system emphasizing employability (applied to the principal applicant, though in statistics the skilled worker category also includes spouses and dependents who are admitted at the same time). The points system, in place since 1967, has been altered over time, with the emphasis first shifting from in-demand occupations to more general human-capital criteria, primarily formal education, work experience, and language knowledge. After 2005 the emphasis shifted away from human capital back toward occupations in demand and more direct employer involvement. For prospective skilled worker immigrants indicating an intention to settle in Quebec, applications are processed by the Quebec government, which makes the recommendation for admission.

Evidence clearly shows immigrant skilled workers do well in the Canadian labor market, compared to other immigrant categories. A prime source of such information is longitudinal analyses of immigrant earnings in a data file linking immigration selection criteria to tax records (CIC 1998, 2010a; Ferrer, Picot, and Riddell 2014, 853). A points-based system can bring in large numbers of immigrants, most of whom find employment after arrival. However, there may be a trade-off between numbers and quality because a large intake may necessarily imply lower selection standards on average. Indeed, the essential idea of the points system is to reduce such trade-offs to a simple formula. Thus, the most points are given for high levels of education, but if candidates lack a university degree, sufficient points for admission may be obtained by other indicators of employability, such as an arranged job or relative youth. Canada wants immigrants with a four-year university degree, but in 2002–2005, peak years for the role of education in points-based selection, over 20 percent of points-selected immigrants did not have one.

Credential Recognition and Immigrant Skill Utilization

Even though immigrant selection is based on employability, much attention has focused on the many barriers to employment success for immigrant professionals. Underutilization of immigrant skills is reported to cost the Canadian economy billions of dollars annually (Bloom and Grant 2001; Reitz 2001a, 2001b; Li 2001; Reitz, Curtis, and Elrick. 2014; Grant 2016), and it is one of the most important immigrant complaints about their experiences in Canada, according to the Longitudinal Survey of Immigrants to Canada (see Statistics Canada 2005). Barriers to immigrant skill utilization include employers' lack of familiarity with foreign qualifications, professional licensing procedures set up with Canadian qualifications in mind, immigrants' lack of professional connections and their lack of familiarity with Canadian professional and business lingo, and, of course, their lack of Canadian experience.

These employment problems are reflected in the trend toward lower employment success for immigrants in successive arrival cohorts, despite rising selection standards (Frenette and Morissette 2003). Lack of recognition of immigrant credentials is a problem in many countries (Schuster, Desiderio, and Urso 2013) but looms larger as an issue in Canada because of the significance of immigration and its economic value to the country.

Various government and business programs help immigrants obtain jobs that use their skills, such as Ontario's Fair Access to Regulated Professions and Compulsory Trades Act (2006), intended to ensure that immigrants receive fair access to licensing. Agencies exist in most provincial jurisdictions to provide credential assessment, and there are bridge training programs in specific occupations to top up foreign-acquired skills and provide immigrants with Canadian work experience. Mentorship systems help immigrants to network with professionals in their field, and many websites offer helpful advice for newcomers. Still, circumstances vary greatly across occupations, and efforts to help immigrants are uncoordinated and unevaluated. Among community groups, one of the leaders in promoting immigrant skill utilization is the Toronto Region Immigrant Employment Council (TRIEC). Its annual reports show a range of initiatives and provide some numerical impact assessment. Buoyed by its successes, the TRIEC model has diffused across Canada.

The most highly developed government initiatives are the provincial programs focusing on equivalencies between immigrants' training and training undergone by Canadian-educated professionals. World Education Services, established in Ontario with a government mandate and start-up subsidy, now operates as an independent business, preparing over 10,000 assessment reports annually. Quebec's provincial government provides assessment services, and the federal government has its own program to develop the assessment concept further. The positive impact of credential assessment must be significant given that immigrants (at least in Ontario) are prepared to pay Can$115 for the most basic evaluation and more than double that for a more detailed evaluation.

Still, there has been no systematic effort to evaluate the impact of all these programs. At the same time, immigrant skill levels have risen significantly, magnifying the scale of the problem. If anything, the problem of immigrant employment in Canada has become more difficult over time, and more serious than when it was first identified in the 1990s (Reitz, Curtis, and Elrick 2014).

Linking Immigrant Selection to the Labor Market, and Express Entry
Two additional routes to admission in the economic class have become significant in recent years: Provincial Nominee Programs (PNPs) and the Canadian Experience

Class (CEC) (Ferrer, Picot, and Riddell 2014). Under the various agreements reached since the late 1990s between the federal government and each province individually, provincial authorities make nominations for immigrant admissions based on their assessment of local needs (Quebec has selected immigrants since the 1970s). The Canadian Experience Class is an opportunity for skilled workers, including tradespeople with Canadian work experience as temporary residents and international students, to gain permanent residence status. Both emerging categories are intended to bring the admission decision closer to local conditions in the labor markets where immigrants may settle. Admissions in these categories have grown substantially and together approximately equal the skilled worker category in total numbers. In 2016, skilled workers represented 42 percent of the economic class, provincial nominees accounted for 30 percent, and CEC admissions were 11 percent (see Table 3.2).

A new administrative procedure for processing applications in the economic class, called Express Entry, was launched in January 2015. Under the Express Entry procedure, potential applicants may create an online profile, which is then reviewed for eligibility under economic categories and ranked according to relevant criteria.[1] Those deemed acceptable for admission are invited to apply for permanent residence. Even as it was being launched, Express Entry was reviewed by the Migration Policy Institute as a possible model for managing migration in the European Union (Desiderio and Hooper 2016).

Two features of Express Entry represent important changes from previous practices, one regarding the application backlog, the other regarding new ranking criteria with opportunities for employer involvement. The application backlog was a nagging administrative problem of the previous system, which had specified criteria for admission, but with only limited numbers of openings in any one year. Prospective immigrants would submit applications to be reviewed on a first-come, first-served basis, and those not selected in a given year would be placed on a waiting list. Over several years, a large backlog accumulated, with as many as 600,000 people waiting for their file to be reviewed. Under Express Entry, no backlog is created, since the profiles of those not invited to apply for permanent residence expire after twelve months. In addition, processing times are greatly reduced, since at the point of application a prospective immigrant has already been accepted and the application process is merely a formality. Of course, from the prospective immigrant's point of view, even those who score over the cutoff in the points system may have to submit and resubmit their profile over a period of years and may never be invited to apply. In a sense, they represent an applicant backlog, but an administratively invisible one.

Express Entry also involves new selection criteria.[2] Those seeking admission in the Federal Skilled Worker Program are assessed using a traditional points system,

TABLE 3.2. Canada Permanent Residents by Category, 2011–2016

Category	2011	2012	2013	2014	2015	2016
Economic Class: Total	**156,099**	**160,744**	**148,252**	**165,197**	**170,375**	**156,000**
Skilled workers: principal applicants	36,762	38,571	34,191	28,839	30,430	30,093
Skilled workers: spouses and dependents	52,007	52,846	49,038	38,760	39,706	35,513
Provincial Nominee Program: principal applicants	15,277	17,173	18,782	20,987	20,926	20,487
Provincial Nominee Program: spouses and dependents	23,138	23,707	21,118	26,641	23,609	25,688
Canadian Experience: principal applicants	3,962	5,934	4,356	14,187	11,253	9,726
Canadian Experience: spouses and dependents	2,064	3,422	2,853	9,595	8,807	8,096
Caregiver: principal applicants	5,039	3,688	4,860	11,692	11,179	6,836
Caregiver: spouses and dependents	6,209	5,325	3,939	5,998	16,035	11,632
Investor: principal applicants	2,973	2,607	2,355	2,078	1,547	1,296
Investor: spouses and dependents	7,614	6,754	6,052	5,374	3,913	3,269
Entrepreneur: principal applicants	184	126	114	131	74	38
Entrepreneur: spouses and dependents	521	349	312	368	185	108
Self-employed: principal applicants	113	89	95	159	260	267
Self-employed: spouses and dependents	236	153	170	240	417	418
Skilled trade:* principal applicants	0	0	11	63	971	921
Skilled trade: spouses and dependents	0	0	6	76	1,001	1,507
Start-up business:** principal applicants	0	0	0	4	26	47

Start-up business: spouses and dependents	0	0	0	5	36	58
Family Class: Total	**61,335**	**69,868**	**83,375**	**67,648**	**65,484**	**78,004**
Sponsored spouse or partner	39,059	40,030	45,630	45,067	46,353	56,762
Sponsored children	3,432	3,152	3,108	3,561	3,313	3,826
Sponsored parent or grandparent	14,090	21,810	32,320	18,201	15,489	17,041
Sponsored extended family member	400	508	319	285	329	375
Sponsored family member, H & C §	4,354	4,368	1,998	534	0	0
Refugee CLASS: Total	**27,876**	**23,095**	**24,139**	**24,070**	**32,113**	**58,912**
Government-assisted refugees	7,363	5,425	5,722	7,625	9,488	23,624
Privately sponsored refugees	5,584	4,228	6,332	5,071	9,747	18,645
Blended sponsorship refugee†	0	0	155	177	811	4,434
Protected person in Canada‡	14,929	13,442	11,930	11,197	12,067	12,209
All Other Immigration	**3,391**	**4,054**	**3,266**	**3,377**	**3,844**	**3,430**
Humanitarian and compassionate	3,101	3,445	3,193	3,333	3,799	3,391
Public policy	199	541	29	15	0	0
Other immigrants not included elsewhere	91	68	44	29	45	39
Grand Total	**248,701**	**257,761**	**259,032**	**260,293**	**271,816**	**296,346**

*Established to address shortages in specific skilled trades, such as construction and equipment operation.

** Established as an opportunity for those whose business idea gains the support of a designated organization.

§ Humanitarian and compassionate consideration.

† Persons identified for settlement by the United Nations High Commission on Refugees and matched with private sponsors in Canada.

‡ Persons who applied for refugee status while in Canada.

SOURCE: Immigration, Refugees and Citizenship Canada, "Facts and Figures 2016."

based on age, education, work experience, official language skills (as demonstrated by adequate performance in a language test), the possession of a valid job offer, and "adaptability" (previous education or work in Canada, spouse's language ability, etc.). As in the past, a "passing" score is 67 points out of a possible 100. However, the assessment and weighting of the criteria have changed. Official language ability is now weighted, with a maximum score moved up from 24 to 28 points. Education received outside Canada must be demonstrably equivalent to Canadian education based on an educational credential assessment report by one of the independent agencies that evaluate foreign credentials (the maximum score for education remains 25 points). While credential assessments have been available to all immigrants after arrival in Canada, the Express Entry protocol for those applying under the Federal Skilled Worker Program now mandates assessment as a condition for admission. The maximum score for being young increased from 10 to 12, while the maximum score for work experience declined from 21 to 15.

Once candidates have been accepted into the Express Entry pool, based either on points, as in the Federal Skilled Worker Program, or on criteria, as for the Canadian Experience Class and Federal Skill Trades Program, they are further assessed using the Comprehensive Ranking System, also a points-based system but somewhat more complex. There are two components: "core" points, based on skills and experience of the applicant and spouse, and "additional" points based on a job offer, Canadian connections, a provincial nomination, or a sibling residing in Canada. The system awards up to 600 points for each component, for a possible total of 1,200. There is no minimum or "passing" score to qualify; instead, those selected in any year will be simply those with the highest rank.

The Express Entry pool allows employers to find job candidates for positions not filled by Canadians or permanent residents. Immigration, Refugees and Citizenship Canada (IRCC), the government agency tasked with administering immigration, provides means by which employers may search for non-resident job candidates and find a match to their needs (the Expression of Interest pool). Whereas a job offer has long been part of immigrant selection in the skilled worker program, conferring additional selection points to an applicant, employers' ability to access the applicant pool is new and opens additional opportunities for employers to play a direct role in the recruitment of economic immigrants.

Regular reports on the operation of Express Entry are posted, but many details are sketchy, and specifics are subject to review and change. Selection criteria have been adjusted as administrators gain experience managing the system. It is too early to assess the longer-term value and impact of the new selection procedures. The initial phase-in was slowed as the prior backlog of applications was processed (IRCC

2017b, 16). In recent years, profile submissions have continued to increase, and the system seems likely to generate sufficient submissions to meet annual immigration economic-stream targets. In 2019, 239,115 submissions were deemed eligible for at least one category in that stream (IRCC 2020, 6).

Reduced participation of employers in selection is an example of an administrative adjustment, and an important one, given that such participation had been anticipated as a major benefit of Express Entry. In late 2016, the number of points awarded to candidates with a valid job offer was reduced, particularly in the lower skill categories, to shift selection priorities to more highly skilled candidates even without job offers (IRCC 2016a, 4). In particular, whereas initially all job offers for Express Entry candidates received 600 additional points, this was reduced to 200 points for job offers in the senior management category and 50 points for job offers in managerial, professional, and technical occupations. Subsequently, invitations to apply for permanent residency have been issued to those with arranged employment, who remain a relatively small proportion overall (e.g., 10,905 in 2019; IRCC 2020, 15). Candidates invited to apply have high levels of education: 93 percent have at least a three-year post-secondary credential, and 40 percent have at least a year of Canadian work experience. About one-third have primary occupations in information technology or business and financial services (IRCC 2020, 13–16).

Express Entry's current and very complex selection criteria, a potential political liability if they are perceived to be concealing selection from public scrutiny (Hiebert 2019), could easily be simplified without loss of administrative flexibility. This would also contribute to more effective empirical assessment of the trade-offs inherent in any points-based immigrant selection.

Immigrant Integration Programs

Canadian immigration policy includes several programs that encourage integration in terms of settlement, employment, language training, access to social services, and human rights and equality guarantees. Settlement services involve investments by both federal and provincial governments. In 2015–2016, federal expenditures for the Newcomer Settlement and Integration Program came to $1.1 billion (out of a total IRCC budget of $1.5 billion), representing about $3,000 per new immigrant per year (IRCC 2017c, 33–34).[3] The Language Instruction for Newcomers to Canada (LINC) program, which serves about 100,000 clients each year (IRCC 2017a, 9), represents a significant component of settlement services costs (see also CIC 2010c, 39–40).

Most settlement programs are local initiatives funded by a competitive grant process, and while this process offers the opportunity to link programs to local needs, it also means there is little or no program standardization, so systematic evaluation is difficult. An IRCC evaluation over the period 2011–2016 focused on such issues as continuing need, number of clients, and perceptions of outcomes and costs but did not analyze the impact of specific settlement programs on clients (IRCC 2017a, 12).

Temporary Workers

Canada's admission of temporary workers has expanded greatly. Responding to employer demand for workers to perform jobs requiring lower skill levels, the federal government introduced in July 2002 the Pilot Project for Hiring Foreign Workers in Occupations That Require Lower Levels of Formal Training, a program which had no limits on numbers (Nakache and Kinoshita 2010, 1–2). Since that time, the number of temporary workers in Canada with valid work permits has risen from about 100,000 entrants annually in the 1990s to over 500,000 in years since 2013 (see Figure 3.6). Much recent attention has focused on the Temporary Foreign Worker Program (TFWP). When first introduced in 1973, the TFWP was relatively small and targeted at those with highly specialized skills, including academics, business executives, and engineers. There are also programs for other categories, including seasonal agricultural workers and live-in caregivers, the latter allowing foreign caregivers to apply for permanent residence after two years.

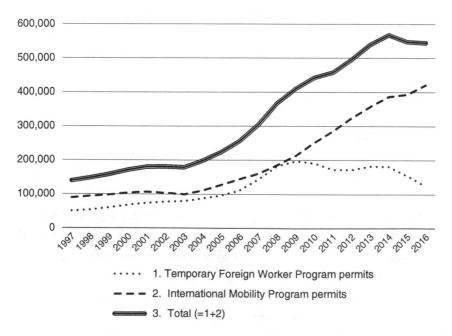

FIGURE 3.6. Temporary Workers with Valid Work Permits in Canada by Program, 1997–2016
SOURCE: IRCC 2016, pp. 14–16.

Long-standing concerns about employment standards prevailing for temporary workers have received some policy attention, though issues remain (McLaughlin and Hennebry 2015).

The recent expansion of the TFWP occurred in part because of rising labor demand in certain industries, notably the booming oil sands industry in Alberta. Employers across Canada took advantage of the opportunity, and controversy peaked in 2014 over highly publicized cases in restaurants and other sectors, where Canadian workers were being displaced despite assurances that a formal labor market impact assessment (LMIA) was required to show no negative impact on Canadian workers, and foreign workers were brought in only when Canadians were not available. The political backlash led to restrictions on program activity and a general review. The review began in June 2014 and was completed after the government transition in 2015. The Liberal government announced plans to tighten the rules governing the TFWP and the enforcement of those rules. Since then, there has been ongoing scrutiny of the TFWP category, and a report concluded that lack of oversight was still a problem (Auditor General 2017; see also Auditor General 2009). Simply stated, the program allows lower-paid foreign workers to take jobs that unemployed Canadians could fill.

One immediate change resulting from the program review is the way in which statistics on the program are published. The IRCC report for 2016 (the basis for Figure 3.6) drew a primary distinction between the TFWP itself and a new category called the International Mobility Program (IMP), admitting workers in categories exempt from the LMIA. As Figure 3.6 shows, the LMIA-exempt category is the one in which expansion has been most rapid, virtually doubling from 213,000 visas in 2016 to 421,000 visas in 2019. It is not clear why this expansion is occurring. About 15 percent of the visas in the IMP category were granted because of international agreements such as NAFTA (North American Free Trade Agreement, now the US-Mexico-Canada Agreement). However, between 80 and 85 percent of them were in a rather nebulous category called "Canadian interests," which included subcategories such as "competitiveness and public policy" (55 percent), "reciprocal employment" (32 percent), "significant benefit" (12 percent), "charitable or religious work" (1.4 percent), and "research, educational, or training programs" (0.2 percent) (IRCC 2016c, 16). The category "competitiveness and public policy" alone grew from 80,000 permit holders in 2010 to 202,000 in 2016.

Some unions are critical of the IMP, saying it is essentially the same program as the TFWP, simply exempting employers from a labor market impact assessment. In the *Tyee*, journalist Jeremy Nuttall said:

Under public pressure in 2014, the government of Stephen Harper made changes to the TFWP, including establishing the IMP as a separate entity. But [Laborers'

International Union of North America's western Canada manager Mark] Olsen said that while use of the TFWP has dropped off, the IMP has grown. The IMP has fewer requirements for employers to prove that efforts were made to find a Canadian resident to fill a job, he said. For example, employers accessing the IMP don't need to apply for a labor market impact assessment, used in part to determine if employers made reasonable efforts to hire a resident. The [Union's policy] paper also says the lack of IMP regulations makes it difficult to know how much employers using the program are paying employees. (Nuttall 2017)

The government response (by Lisa Filipps, a spokesperson for IRCC) pointed out that the IMP increase was mainly "post-graduate students, spouses of students and high-skilled workers, and working holiday visas" (cited in Nuttall 2017). This matches the subcategory of "competitiveness and public policy" on the IRCC website.[4] But what remains unexplained (apart from the labeling of the category) is the reason for such a dramatic increase in the number of visas granted over a short period.

This expansion of temporary work visas also has implications for permanent migration to Canada. The Canadian Experience Class, introduced in 2008, provides new opportunities for temporary foreign workers (with at least two years of experience in a skilled occupation) and for international students (who have graduated in Canada and have one year of experience). Both can apply for permanent residence from within Canada. This extends opportunities, previously available only to live-in caregivers, to all qualifying temporary foreign workers regardless of their admission stream. Experience as a temporary worker may be helpful in the adjustment process for those becoming a permanent resident, but there may also be negative long-term effects of periods of precarious legal status (Goldring and Landolt 2013; Sweetman and Warman 2014).

Under the rules of the Canadian Experience Class, eligible skilled occupations include not only management and professional categories in which a university degree is normally required but also occupations such as carpenter, plumber, bricklayer, and others in the construction trades, where much training may be based on apprenticeship. International students may qualify with university degrees or with degrees from any postsecondary institution. Hence, the educational levels of those qualifying for the Canadian Experience Class may vary considerably. The initial expectation was that the Canadian Experience Class would become a numerically significant category, with 10,000 to 12,000 applicants in the first year (Citizenship and Immigration Canada 2008, 25). As mentioned previously, in 2016 the Canadian Experience Class included 17,822 persons, 11 percent of the total economic class and 6 percent of all immigrants arriving that year.

Role of Employers in Immigrant Selection

A theme in recent policy developments has been a shift away from the "human capital model" of selection and toward one based on labor market demand for specific skills (Akbari and M.acDonald 2014). In the administration of the new demand-driven selection priorities, employers play a larger role in the selection of individual immigrants. Of course, employers have long played a part in the formulation of the criteria for immigrant selection. Now, however, employers have a hand in the selection of specific persons. This is most obvious in the TFWP, where employers apply to bring in specific groups of workers to do specific jobs. This carries over to permanent immigration, since in the Canada Experience Class, temporary workers may qualify for permanent status based on maintaining their jobs over a period of time, and this, in turn, is at the discretion of specific employers. The recommendations of the provinces for admission of immigrants in the Provincial Nominee Programs are often made with input from local employers. And the Express Entry system allows employers to review the Expression of Interest pool to search for potential hires; their interest in hiring a specific applicant person plays an important role in the actual invitations issued. In each of these instances, employers directly affect the admission of permanent immigrants.

In this way, employers have become gatekeepers for initial admission to Canada and for permanent residency. The real and intended advantage is that more immigrants will enter the country with a job in hand. Employer selection is based on immediate need, so at least in the short term, such immigrants will fare better than those who are highly educated but have not yet found jobs. However, integration and accountability also matter, and employer-driven selection schemes raise the question of the longer-term integration of the less skilled. Even if a temporary worker survives in a job for two or more years, his or her potential for longer-term success in employment might be less than for workers with broader skills and higher levels of education (Ferrer, Picot, and Riddell 2014; Reitz 2010).

Meeting the need for less-skilled immigration by allowing employers to make selections also raises the issue of enforcement; the initiative essentially privatizes selection, so the integrity of the selection system is no longer ensured by the public accountability of the government. The potential is there for both abuse and fraud (Reitz 2013, 160–161), and accountability must be built into the private selection system administered by the government to ensure that permanent visas are granted for bona fide employment.

Abuse occurs if those with power over immigration status make unreasonable requests that immigrants feel obliged to fulfill in order to get or maintain status. Such situations may exist in Toronto's construction industry, for example, where temporary foreign workers hoping for permanent status reportedly are sometimes asked to work extra hours without pay. There is also a possibility of fraud because to qualify for permanent status temporary workers must create a formal record of employment. In industries such as construction, where temporary immigrants are numerous, extensive and reliable record keeping is not the norm. Of course, Canadian Experience Class regulations may promote better record keeping, but this cannot be known without effective monitoring. As found repeatedly by the Auditor General (2009, 2017), there are significant problems with monitoring recent immigration initiatives to ensure that the programs are operating as intended.

Another question about temporary foreign workers concerns visa compliance. Formal opportunity to remain in Canada is limited after the expiry of a temporary visa, but experience shows that many such workers overstay their visas and, in effect, become permanently undocumented or "non-status." Until recently, enforcement efforts were ineffective, with little provision even to monitor the extent of visa compliance. This is changing, however, with new legislative authority (in 2018) to collect exit records from airlines and at the US border. There is also concern about the uncertain prospects for the integration of low-skilled non-status immigrants. The rapid increase in temporary immigration reflected in the data in Figure 3.6 suggests this may become a greater concern over time. Based on international experience, Martin (2010) says Canada should be "cautious" in developing temporary worker programs.

Refugees: Generosity and Ambivalence

The number of refugees admitted as permanent residents in Canada, standing at roughly 10 percent of total immigrants for many years, nearly doubled in 2016 primarily due to public concerns about the plight of Syrians. The 58,911 refugees admitted in 2016 were the most since 1992, when there were 51,875. The 34,925 Syrian citizens admitted as immigrants in Canada in 2016, who were mostly refugees, made Syria the third-most-frequent source country for all immigrants admitted in Canada that year, after the Philippines and India, and ahead of China and Pakistan. The refugee doubling occurred in both the "government-assisted" category (identified by the United Nations High Commissioner for Refugees) and for "privately sponsored" refugees (for whom community groups and individuals reach sponsorship agreements with the federal government) (Macklin 2017).

Much attention has been given recently to the refugees who seek asylum from within the country or as they cross the border to enter the country (in Table 3.2, "protected persons in Canada"). The Immigration and Refugee Board of Canada (IRB) reports that during the twenty-five-month period from February 2017 to March 2019, there was a surge in "irregular border crossings" (at the US border), with 41,577 persons making refugee claims.[5] This volume of claims has overwhelmed the system, and the adjudication of claims has been time-consuming. The acceptance rate has been low, fewer than 7,000 as of March 2019. It is difficult to project the significance of the irregular border crossings into the future. Some or many of the claimants were persons who would have sought asylum in the United States but could not do so because of the negative political climate for refugees that existed in the country during the presidency of Donald Trump. Many called for renegotiation of asylum agreements with the United States, such as the Safe Third Country Agreement, but there are no reports of any official movement in this direction.

Public Opinion on Immigration and Politics

Public Opinion

Canadian public opinion is generally supportive of immigration. Canada is clearly an exception to the prevailing pattern across most other industrial countries, where the majority of residents want immigration reduced (Reitz 2012). This "Canadian exceptionalism" (Bloemraad 2012) is evident in the most recent Pew Global Attitudes Survey results, in which the proportion of the population saying immigrants make the country stronger rather than being a burden was higher in Canada than in seventeen other countries, including the United States, Australia, and most countries of Europe (see Figure 3.7; Pew Research Center 2019). A recent Gallup World Poll (2018) showed similar results, using a three-question Migrant Acceptance Index that asked if it was a "good thing" or a "bad thing" if an immigrant lives in the country, becomes a neighbor, or marries a close relative. Canada ranked higher than the United States, Australia, or any other immigration countries surveyed by Pew. These findings follow other international comparisons; for example, the German Marshall Fund (2011) found Canadians were more likely to see immigration as an opportunity than as a problem. In most countries, the reverse is true: there is less immigration, and the majority sees it as a problem and calls for reductions.

Canada's pro-immigration attitudes have been consistent for several decades. From 1975 to 2005, Gallup Canada frequently included the following question in national surveys: "If it were your job to plan an immigration policy for Canada at this time, would you be inclined to increase immigration, decrease immigration, or keep the number of immigrants at about the current level?" In every year but 1982, a recession year, the majority endorsed either staying with existing immigration levels or increasing them (Reitz 2012, 524). In fact, in the Gallup data respondents had become more favorable to immigration since the late 1990s, and this is consistent with

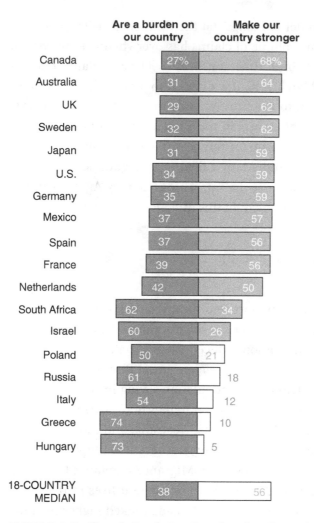

FIGURE 3.7. Canada Leads Pro-Immigration Countries
SOURCE: Pew Global Attitudes Survey.

polling from the Environics Institute (2018; see Figure 3.8). Starting in 1977, their Focus Canada survey has regularly asked whether immigration levels are too high; the proportion *dis*agreeing began rising in the late 1990s and has been the strong majority (about 60 percent) since about 2002, compared to about 35 percent agreeing. Polls by EKOS Research Associates (2010) between 2004 and 2010 asked a similar question. In 2004, the proportion agreeing with current or higher levels was 63 percent, while 31 percent thought there were too many immigrants. In 2010, the proportion agreeing with current or higher levels was 67 percent, compared to 23 percent who thought there were too many immigrants.

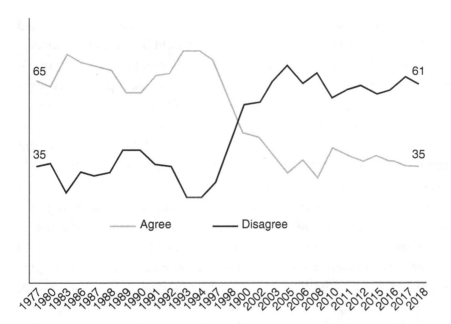

FIGURE 3.8. Opposition to Immigration Weakens over Time in Canada
SOURCE: Environics Institute.

Of course, while majorities of Canadians support present Canadian immigration policy, not all do. In the Gallup surveys, until the late 1990s, the proportion wanting a *decrease* in immigration was often as high as 40 to 45 percent, a sizable minority, much larger than the minority wanting an increase. Ironically, though, when immigration numbers actually increased in the 1990s, the proportion wanting a decrease declined.

In analyses of polling results, emphasis on the salience of particular opinions may vary. Based on recent polls, some even argue that Canadians are currently turning away from support for immigration.[6] However, this interpretation lacks a sufficient empirical basis. Three issues affect the interpretation of polls: the sampling method, the wording of specific questions, and the availability of trend results using constant sampling and question wording. The data cited from Gallup, Environics, and EKOS all use probability samples to which normal statistics apply, and all asked the same question over a number of years. A review of recent polling data purportedly showing a negative turn on immigration in Canada shows that those data do not satisfy the same criteria. For example, a 2018 Ipsos-Reid poll was reported to show half (49 percent) of Canadians saying immigration levels are too high. However, the question asked was about a specific number ("Would you say 310,000 new permanent residents in 2018 is . . . too many, about right, or too few?"), and this was not done in previous surveys. Most surveys on immigration policy have not mentioned particular numbers, and very likely most respondents would be unaware of specific immigration numbers. Another recent Ipsos-Reid poll (2019) reported: "Four in ten (44%) agree . . . that there are too many immigrants in Canada, up 8 points" over the previous eighteen months. No mention was made of how many did not agree, and the 44 percent opposition allows for the possibility that a majority did not agree. More importantly, no source was provided for the previous poll showing an 8 percent change. Sampling is another issue. Poll results from online surveys are frequently cited in the media (the two polls just cited were online panel surveys), often quoting the template survey-accuracy statement, which deflects concern about sampling bias.

The stability of Canadians' attitudes toward immigration has both social and economic roots, as shown in an analysis of an Environics national survey, Focus Canada (Reitz 2011). Canadians are convinced of the positive economic benefits of immigration; they also accept multiculturalism as part of their national identity and accept continued immigration in support of it. These twin pillars of policy support provide a buffer against particular immigration-related issues arising from time to time that might otherwise raise questions about the policy.

On the social and cultural side, support for multiculturalism appears to be a strong force supporting high levels of immigration in Canada. The Focus Canada respondents were asked the question "How important is the following for the Canadian identity?" and were provided with a series of items, one of which was multiculturalism. Fully 85 percent said multiculturalism was either very important or at least somewhat important to national identity and that, compared to other important national symbols, multiculturalism was in the top group behind health care, the flag, and the Charter of Rights and Freedoms but ahead of hockey, bilingualism, and the Royal Canadian Mounted Police. Support for multiculturalism reinforces support for immigration. Those respondents who cited the importance of multiculturalism were significantly more likely to support immigration.

Support for multiculturalism does not mean Canadians do not care whether immigrants conform to mainstream society. Majorities support multiculturalism, but they are concerned that too many immigrants are not adopting Canadian values, and they worry about the implications (Angus Reid Institute 2010). In the Focus Canada survey, an overwhelming 80 percent of respondents agreed that "ethnic groups should try as much as possible to blend into Canadian society and not form a separate community"; 51.3 percent "strongly" agreed. There were also strong concerns that immigrants are not blending in. A majority of Canadians—nearly 70 percent—agreed that "there are too many immigrants coming into this country who are not adopting Canadian values"; over 40 percent "strongly" agreed. These views and others, such as dislike for racial minorities and concerns about "bogus" refugee claims, tended to be associated with less enthusiasm for immigration. Racial difference was also expressed as an issue, leading a small minority to object to immigration.

Concerns about immigrant integration, clearly expressed in the Focus Canada survey, seem heightened specifically regarding Muslims. When asked whether Muslims in Canada "want to adopt Canadian customs and way of life," most respondents felt Muslims "want to be distinct." When asked about the ban on the wearing of head scarves by Muslim women in public places, including schools, respondents diverged, but a slightly greater proportion said it was a good idea. The controversy about Muslims has been particularly prominent in Quebec as reflected in the Focus Canada survey, particularly on the issue of head scarves.

The multiple sources of support for immigration (i.e., both cultural and economic) may be an important reason for the stability of pro-immigration sentiment in Canada over time. Specific issues that might arise and lead to questions about immigration may not do so because of the persistence of other factors supporting immigration. For example, a prolonged recession, visible signs of immigrants experiencing economic difficulty and requiring attention and possibly significant public expenditure, or a dramatic increase in illegal immigration—any of these could threaten pro-immigration sentiment by undermining the positive perceptions of immigration's economic value. On the one hand, in such contexts, cultural and multicultural values (and progressive social values more generally) may help stabilize pro-immigration attitudes because they are as important as the economic views. On the other hand, major developments such as social conflict or a breakdown in immigrant minority communities that increases crime or possible terrorist activities might erode confidence in the belief that multiculturalism fosters Canadian unity. This, in turn, could affect attitudes toward immigration.

Political Parties and Immigration Politics

Immigration in Canada has traditionally been associated with the Liberal Party, and the government of Justin Trudeau continues this tradition while emphasizing refugee protection. At the same time, all major Canadian political parties have pro-immigration policies. The Conservatives under Brian Mulroney (1984–1993) maintained high immigration numbers and introduced legislation in support of multiculturalism and employment equity. Immigration has rarely been an issue in Canadian federal elections.

This cross-party consensus changed only to a degree with the Conservative Party government of Stephen Harper (2006–2015). While Harper maintained immigration numbers and held to a policy of multiculturalism, he focused more intently on increasing the economic benefits of immigration and was less generous to those perceived as posing a security threat to Canadian society or embodying values seen as inconsistent with those of the mainstream. He introduced changes to make citizenship harder to get and keep (Griffith 2018) and amended the immigration act to make it more difficult for potential refugees to come to Canada and make their claim—for example, by requiring visas for all Mexicans and Czechs traveling to Canada. His government banned Muslim women from wearing a facial veil while taking the citizenship oath. And in 2015 it passed the Zero Tolerance for Barbaric Cultural Practices Act (S-7), creating a new criminal status for forced marriage and honor killings, among other provisions, and which, as critics pointed out, had a title that encouraged an association between barbarism and certain cultural groups (the title was changed with the new government).

Conservative Party supporters are less favorable toward immigration than are supporters of the other political parties, mainly for cultural rather than economic reasons (Reitz 2011). In this sense, Harper's immigration policy formula—emphasizing the economic benefit of immigration while enforcing security and conformity to mainstream culture—reflects their concerns. The Conservative Party leader Andrew Scheer seems to pursue a similar direction. He has focused most attention on refugee policy, emphasizing security concerns and underscoring a contrast with the Liberals under Trudeau, who have increased the numbers of refugees.

The Politics of Immigrant Numbers

The issue of immigration numbers may increase in salience in coming years. The Liberal government immigration minister, Marco Mendicino, has posted a target of 420,000 immigrants in 2023 (IRCC 2020, 24), roughly in line with the recommendations of the Advisory Council on Economic Growth (2016), appointed by the finance minister, to set the level at 1.11 percent of the population and to keep that rate into the future. Some prominent groups in the community have advocated similar target levels, including the Conference Board of Canada (2017), the *Globe and Mail* newspaper, and the Century Initiative, a non-profit Toronto advocacy group.

Despite the substantial numbers of Canadians who tell pollsters they want less rather than more immigration, no strong national countermove or backlash has developed in response to the upward revision to immigration targets. The Conservative Party debated the immigration question in its 2017 leadership contest, and one candidate, Kelly Leitch (a surgeon representing a small town in Ontario), attracted attention with a proposal to screen all immigrants for Canadian values. She did not win the leadership, getting only 8 percent of votes, and then lost her parliamentary seat in the 2015 election. Another candidate, former Harper government immigration minister Chris Alexander, advocated increasing immigration to 400,000; he received even fewer votes. Only one candidate made an explicit proposal to reduce immigration numbers—Maxime Bernier, representing a riding south of Quebec City noted as having the highest percentage of whites (2006 census) and the highest proportion identifying "Canadian" as their ethnic origin. Bernier narrowly lost the leadership to Andrew Scheer and subsequently left the Conservative Party to create the People's Party of Canada. Bernier has criticized aspects of multiculturalism, and his supporters have expressed hostility toward certain immigrant groups, causing the media to consider how extreme he might be.[7] However, his proposal for immigration is to drop the number from 300,000 to 250,000, the level maintained during the Harper government years.

Canadian belief in immigration for economic growth has been sustained through many trials. Many predicted that 9/11 and the resulting War on Terror would force Canadians to abandon both immigration and multiculturalism. Despite worries about the loyalties of some groups of immigrants, overall support for immigration remains high. Immigrants now struggle more in the job market. Yet rather than turn against them on that basis, Canadians have rallied, mounting programs to help them find jobs and help employers see the value of foreign-acquired education and experience. The same is true for concerns about temporary foreign workers and refugees. The more negative interpretation of the polling data seems to be that immigration will be a major issue in an upcoming election. A poll released in April 2019 by EKOS Research showed an increase in party polarization on the basis of racial attitudes. Liberal voters were less likely to think racial minorities in Canada were growing too quickly, while Conservative voters were more likely to think so.[8]

It could be shortsighted to think Canadians will always support immigration unconditionally. When foreigners enter Canada without proper documents, as happened with Asian "boat people" some years ago, Canadians react swiftly and often harshly. Canadians are highly suspicious of what are termed "bogus" refugee claims. And despite Canadians' high ideals, minority groups still fight racism and discrimination. Employment audits show job applicants with Asian names have about a 40 percent lower chance of being invited for an interview, even with Canadian education and experience. This is one kind of evidence that a significant minority of Canadians would rather have less immigration and believe immigration damages the economy.

Economic Role and Impact of Immigrants

Immigrant Educational Levels and Labor Market Success

Canada's program of skilled immigration, selecting on employability, has meant that immigrants arriving since 1970 work in relatively highly skilled and well-paid occupations. Yet as mentioned earlier, the extent to which this is true has fluctuated over time. Selection preferences were initially based on occupations in demand in the labor market, but preferences shifted to levels of formal education, and this received a strong boost in the early 1990s. As a result, the proportion of immigrants with bachelor's degrees more than doubled from just over 20 percent in the early 1990s to about 45 percent by 2001 (see Table 3.3). Principal applicants in the economic class led this trend, and among them, the proportion with university degrees doubled from 39 percent in 1994 to nearly 80 percent between 2002 and 2005. Educational levels also rose for spouses and dependents of principal applicants and for immigrants in the family class. For all these immigrants, the proportion with bachelor's degrees more than doubled over the same period.

Then, starting in 2006, when the Conservative government began to shift immigration away from the "human capital" approach and toward selection based on the greater involvement of employers, the educational levels of principal applicants in the economic stream began to decline (Akbari and MacDonald 2014; Ferrer, Picot, and Riddell 2014). Those with university degrees were 79.5 percent of the total in 2005, but only 67.2 percent by 2011. However, the overall proportion of immigrants with a bachelor's degree remained stable (see Table 3.3; the official data reported for 2012 especially may reflect a declining quality of data on immigrant education, as IRCC discontinued their publication after 2012).[9] Moreover, it appears that after about 2012, no further decline in educational levels occurred either for principal applicants or for immigrants in general.[10] Labour Force Survey data indicate that for recent immigrants (in the country for five years or less, and aged fifteen or older), between 45 and 50 percent had university degrees in 2009, 2014, and 2019.

While immigrants with higher education perform well in the labor market over the long term, those with technical and other skills who find early employment also do well, particularly in the first years after arrival. It will be interesting to see how the two criteria affect immigrant success over the longer term (see Reitz 2010).

Declining Earnings and Increasing Poverty Rates

Despite fluctuations in immigrant educational levels relative to those of the native-born, there has been a pervasive downward trend in employment rates and earnings of newly arrived immigrants since the 1970s, for both men and women and in most origins groups. Frenette and Morissette's (2003; see also Reitz 2001b) influential study shows that despite substantial increases in immigrant educational levels and taking account of business cycle fluctuations in labor demand, average entry-level earnings have declined perhaps 20 percent for newly arriving immigrants, for both men and women. Along with this, there has been a decline in employment rates (Reitz 2001b).

TABLE 3.3. Percentage of Permanent Residents 15 Years of Age or Older
with a BA or Higher, by Entry Class and Year, 1994–2012

Year	Economic (principal)	Economic (spouse/dependent)	Family	Refugee	Other	Total
1994	39.0	21.4	12.2	17.5	18.2	20.8
1995	48.3	27.1	12.3	13.6	11.4	25.0
1996	55.0	27.8	13.7	14.0	7.1	28.9
1997	61.6	31.4	14.7	13.0	5.9	33.4
1998	64.5	35.6	17.2	11.9	6.3	35.4
1999	72.4	40.6	20.4	12.0	4.2	40.7
2000	77.3	43.4	21.8	11.1	8.7	43.9
2001	77.5	43.8	23.0	12.6	11.7	45.6
2002	79.2	44.1	21.2	12.2	25.5	46.0
2003	79.9	44.0	28.1	11.9	21.7	44.7
2004	79.6	45.0	29.1	13.7	13.7	45.6
2005	79.5	44.0	28.6	15.8	13.1	45.8
2006	76.7	41.7	28.2	14.4	16.4	42.7
2007	74.3	40.8	30.9	12.1	18.3	43.0
2008	72.4	40.6	32.9	11.3	20.1	44.9
2009	68.7	39.5	33.3	11.7	19.3	43.6
2010	70.8	43.4	33.2	12.0	18.1	46.7
2011	67.2	42.2	26.3	12.0	19.7	42.2
2012*	54.8	37.8	20.1	11.9	17.5	35.5

SOURCES: Years 1994–1995 from CIC 2004; years 1996–2005 from CIC 2006; years 2006–2012
from CIC 2012.
NOTE: Data for 2012 may significantly underestimate education levels. See text.

Some evidence points to at least partial improvement for arrivals in the late 1990s,
but the inter-cohort decline appears to have continued between 2001 and 2006 (Statistics Canada 2008). High and increasing poverty levels are being reported for immigrants in recent studies, based on census data and on the longitudinal immigration
database IMDB (Picot and Hou 2003; Picot, Hou, and Coulombe 2007; see also Kazemipur and Halli 2000; Ornstein 2006). Some of the increase in poverty levels can
be attributed to the business cycle and the difficulty of finding employment during a
recession. The recession of the early 1980s clearly created such difficulties, but there
was an expected rebound for those arriving later in the decade. Weak employment
demand reappeared in the early 1990s and created new employment difficulties, no
doubt exacerbated to a degree by the large numbers of immigrants. The recession of

the early 1990s was the first in which Canada kept immigration levels high, making the numbers of immigrants affected correspondingly higher.

The continuing trend toward declining earnings has extended across several business cycles and appears to have had its roots in more basic changes in the labor market that affected immigrants who had been in Canada for much longer periods of time, and for whom the impact of business cycle factors at time of arrival had faded to insignificance (Reitz 2001b). Analyses of 2001 and 2006 census data confirm that the negative employment trend for immigrants continued during the relatively strong economy.

Various reasons have been put forward for the downward trend in immigrant employment (Reitz 2007). The shift in immigrant origins from Europe to Asia and the increase in racial minorities explain part of the decline, as there was a decline in employment opportunities for all new labor force entrants. In addition, educational levels of the native-born workforce began rising more rapidly than those of immigrants, creating a competitive disadvantage. Many employers wanted evidence of formal education in the new "knowledge economy," making it more difficult for immigrants with foreign-acquired credentials to get hired. Some analysts have noted a decline in returns for foreign experience as well, although no explanation for this trend has been found. Finally, there was an overall increase in labor market inequality; this particularly affected immigrants because their employment is more often near the bottom of the earnings hierarchy.

Evidence on Improving Recognition of Foreign Qualifications

Beginning in 2013, formal credential assessment has been part of the process of skilled immigrant selection, so lack of formal equivalence for this group should no longer be a barrier to employment in Canada. However, this group, while significant, represents only about 13 percent of all immigrants, and those without a job offer or previous Canadian experience may still face barriers to recognition of foreign qualifications. Efforts to address these barriers have received much media attention since the mid-1990s, but any effects are not yet visible in employment statistics.

Overall, the educational level of Canada's immigrants has risen. However, despite having gained substantially in relative skill level since the mid-1990s as a group, the proportion of immigrants in the more highly paid occupations using those skills, such as science, engineering, and nursing, is only marginally higher, and these immigrants' relative earnings have remained unchanged. A close look at trends between 1996 and 2006 also shows that the value of immigrant skills has not significantly improved over time (Reitz, Curtis, and Elrick 2014). In fact, there appears to have been a relative decline in the most recent period, when we might have expected some immigration programs to begin to have an effect. Census data for 2006 show that immigrant skills in terms of both education and work experience have only about half to two-thirds of the value of corresponding skills held by native-born Canadians, and occupational underemployment is a significant reason for this imbalance (see also Fortin, Lemieux, and Torres 2016).

Immigrants with university degrees might be expected to have benefited the most from the new immigration programs, but between 1996 and 2006, the proportion of recently arrived university-educated immigrants working in professional or semi-professional fields actually declined, from 50.4 to 43.5 percent for men, with lower figures for women. At the same time, the proportion of highly skilled immigrants working in low-skilled occupations increased relative to their native-born counterparts. In 1996, the proportion was about 50 percent higher for skilled immigrants, but in 2001 it was 130 percent higher and in 2006 almost 140 percent higher. So despite attention to their plight, highly educated immigrants have been falling further behind.

There are many reasons for the persistence of barriers, including their sheer complexity. Each Canadian professional group—doctors, engineers, accountants—has its own qualifications and evaluation procedures for persons trained abroad. Many occupations outside the regulated professions are seeking analytic and problem-solving skills, and education plays an increasing role as a qualifying criterion. Such occupations include sales supervision, human resource management, and public relations, and in those occupations, addressing barriers to foreign-acquired skills poses even greater challenges. Because of the relative lack of systematic standards in many unregulated fields, it is more difficult for immigrants to demonstrate the value of their specific skills. And while the economic loss for immigrants with professional qualifications is significant, it is even more so for immigrants with a bachelor's degree but without professional certification. Small or medium-sized firms, which represent the majority of employers in Canada, often lack formal human resources departments. They may be less systematic in their approach to job applicants and less able to provide formal opportunities for immigrants to demonstrate their skills (Banerjee, Reitz, and Oreopoulos 2018). Immigrants who fail to get the jobs for which they have specific qualifications may experience even more barriers at lower levels, where they are often dismissed as "overqualified" and find themselves obliged to take jobs for which there are virtually no skill requirements at all.

Impact of Immigration on the Canadian Economy

Large-scale immigration has been justified and motivated by the prospect of economic gains and growth, as seen in public opinion data. Economic research has been guarded in assessing this impact, but most early accounts indicate small but positive effects (e.g., Economic Council of Canada 1991). Some studies have assessed the net impact of immigration on public finance as positive (Akbari 1995); others have cautioned against expectations that immigrants will support an aging population (Beaujot 1999). The geographer Richard Florida (2002) gained public prominence in Canada with his analysis indicating that immigrants are part of a "creative class" and stimulate economic growth. Because he based this analysis on theory and simple inter-urban correlations, it has had limited influence on economic researchers, who use more complex models and data analysis. A simulation study by Dungan, Gunderson, and Fang (2010) using a complete model of the Canadian economy indicated that the economic impacts of immigration depend significantly on how well immigrants are paid. More recent reports recommending increases in immigration numbers, such as by the government's Advisory Council on Economic Growth (2016) and the Conference Board of Canada (2017), also argue immigration contributes importantly to economic growth, partly because of the expansion of the economy overall.

Immigrants may affect the distribution of earnings. In the United States, they are seen to increase overall income inequality, but in Canada, comparative research by Aydemir and Borjas (2007) indicates that immigration may actually reduce income inequality. Immigrants compete for more highly skilled work in Canada, so the labor market impact is at higher levels of employment than in the United States.

Social Issues: Multiculturalism and Race

Canada's Debate over Multiculturalism

Canadian policy defines multiculturalism only in the most general terms, and popular support for multiculturalism is often accompanied by a preference for immigrants to "blend in" with the mainstream society. This means not only acquisition of citizenship but also participation in mainstream institutions, adoption of mainstream values, and, of course, learning at least one of the official languages. This integrationist intention may help explain why multiculturalism remains a positive value in Canada despite its rejection in much of Europe.

There is, nevertheless, a debate about the impact of multiculturalism even in Canada, with strongly contrasting views expressed. In the minds of some critics, multiculturalism is the cause of almost anything that goes wrong in minority communities. They say that multiculturalism, by celebrating diversity, not only encourages minorities to maintain possibly anti-democratic or sexist cultures and extraneous political agendas but also exempts them from criticism based on mainstream values. Incompetence is excused, crimes are condoned, and terrorist threats are ignored because multiculturalism makes people fear that criticism of minority groups, or even individual group members, will draw accusations of racism. In this vein, former British Columbia premier Ujjal Dosanjh at one point blamed multiculturalism for helping promote Sikh extremism because multiculturalism has been distorted to claim that "anything anyone believes—no matter how ridiculous and outrageous it might be, is okay and acceptable in the name of diversity" (MacNair 2010).

For some, multiculturalism is the reason for many of the positive indications of the impact of immigration. For its supporters, multiculturalism helps minority businesses to be successful, helps minority kids to do well in school, and helped Dosanjh to become Canada's first South Asian immigrant premier. Citing such positive experiences, Canadian philosopher Will Kymlicka (1998) once asserted broadly that the multiculturalism program is working.

There is little research to back either the critics or the supporters (for a critical summary, see Reitz 2014b). The most useful research compares countries with and without multicultural policies, and the few existing studies find little effect either way. Kymlicka's (2012) own recent comparative work is fairly guarded. Conclusions derived from analysis of a comprehensive Multiculturalism Policy Index developed with colleagues, including Keith Banting at Queen's University, are, first, that the heralded "retreat from multiculturalism" was more a matter of public rhetoric than an actual change in policy, and, second, that it is still "premature" to make definitive judgments about the success or failure of multiculturalism.[11] One study (Banting et al. 2006) showed that multiculturalism policies in twenty-one countries had little relation to the strength of the welfare state. Such findings undermine critics' claim that multiculturalism is divisive but do not support proponents' claim of enhanced cohesion (see also Banting and Kymlicka 2017). There are many reasons for Canada's relatively positive record on immigrant integration. For example, most analysts attribute successful integration of immigrant minorities to skill-selective immigration policy, not necessarily multiculturalism.

Canadian multiculturalism is often compared to "assimilationist" policies in the United States, although official US policy is actually laissez-faire (according to the overall assessment on the Multicultural Policy Index website, in the 1980s the United States had policies as multicultural as Canada's, though without using the word).[12] The more negative status of specific minorities in the United States, such as African Americans, can be traced to other sources. The legacy of centuries of slavery would not end simply by adopting official multiculturalism any more than multiculturalism solves English-French relations in Canada. Nor could official multiculturalism in the United States transform undocumented immigration from Mexico into a popular cause. Multicultural Canada is also averse to undocumented immigration, as illustrated by the strongly negative reaction to a few Chinese people arriving off the coast of British Columbia in 1999. When we make fair comparisons between Canada and the United States, focusing on similar groups of immigrants—for instance, the highly educated from China, India, or the Caribbean—any differences due to Canadian multiculturalism dwindle. Moreover, rates of economic and social integration for comparable immigrants in the two countries are virtually identical. Some cite the higher rates of intergroup marriage in Canada as showing greater inclusiveness than in the United States, but recent studies reveal this difference to be more a result of demographics and opportunity than of preferences arising from multiculturalism (Hou et al. 2015). The most convincing positive evidence comes from a study (Bloemraad 2006) showing that government funding of ethnic community organizations produces higher citizenship acquisition rates in Canada than in the United States. Still, broader forces may be at work because within Canada, immigrants who participate in ethnic organizations are no more likely to become citizens than those who do not (Laxer, Reitz, and Simon 2020).

Multicultural issues resonate in debates on immigrant religion and the status of women, especially in Quebec, where controversies over "reasonable accommodation" of Muslims and other religious minorities continue to garner attention. The wearing of head scarves and facial veils by Muslim women has been a focus in Quebec and elsewhere. A government-appointed commission (Bouchard and Taylor 2008) recommended that policies define the limits of what is "reasonable" in the accommodation of cultural minorities. The report also recommended that certain government employees—for example, judges, Crown prosecutors, prison guards, and police officers—should refrain from wearing religious attire or symbols. In 2013, the government led by the sovereigntist Parti Québecois introduced a Charter of Quebec Values that would have gone further to limit the wearing of conspicuous religious symbols for all state personnel (including teachers and health care professionals). While this bill did not become law, and the government was defeated in the 2014 election, the subsequent Liberal government of Philippe Couillard passed a bill banning a full face covering for anyone delivering or receiving a public service. However, there has been no proposed legislation banning girls from wearing head scarves in school, as in France.

In Quebec, there has been ambivalence toward multiculturalism from its inception in the 1970s, when multiculturalism was chosen over biculturalism to accommodate immigrant groups, leaving Quebeckers feeling that their interests had been downgraded. Many Quebeckers prefer *interculturalisme*, a difference that, while endorsing cultural pluralism, reserves to the Quebec government the responsibility to support and maintain the French language and culture in Quebec (Bouchard 2015).

Since much of the hypothesized impact of multiculturalism is at the symbolic level, does Quebec's use of a different word make any practical difference to immigrant integration? Results from Statistics Canada's 2002 Ethnic Diversity Survey suggest not. Immigrants in Quebec appear to be as well integrated into society as their counterparts in the rest of Canada (Bourhis et al. 2007). Apparently, then, governments may usefully express support for diversity even without multiculturalism.

One aspect of the debate focuses on the social impact of immigrant enclaves. Findings on such enclaves suggest they help immigrants feel at home but also tend to isolate them (Reitz et al. 2009). Persistent diversity both promotes and slows integration, depending on its aspects. Therefore, multiculturalism policy might consider ways to establish stronger exchanges among Canada's cultural communities.

Racial Disadvantages and Discrimination

The low earnings and high poverty rates for recent immigrants, discussed earlier, apply more specifically to "visible minorities." Ornstein's (2006) analysis of the censuses from 1971 to 2001 focuses on Toronto and shows high rates of poverty for racial minorities. Defining poverty based on Statistics Canada's measure of "low income cut-off" (where a family's basic expenditures for food, clothing, and shelter exceed 55 percent of its income), Ornstein finds racial minorities have poverty rates two or more times higher than whites, with the highest rates among Blacks. Moreover, as racial minorities have grown in Toronto (from 4 percent in 1971 to 40 percent in 2001) income differences among the categories have increased (Ornstein 2006, 80). Within Toronto, racial minorities are more concentrated in low-income neighborhoods, and this pattern has become more striking since 1971 (Hulchanski 2010).

The extent of racial disadvantage in Toronto and Canada generally may be surprising given the high levels of education of racial minority immigrants. The reasons for and significance of racial discrimination are subjects of debate. Compelling evidence of the significance of discrimination come from experimental studies, and the largest such study in Canada found that employers in Toronto and Montreal are 30 percent less likely to call for an interview when applicant résumés have Asian names attached rather than English names, even with Canadian education and work experience (Oreopoulos 2011; Banerjee, Reitz, and Oreopoulos 2018). Some also suggest that immigrants of non-European origin may have qualifications representing lower levels of training or skill, at least partly accounting for their poorer showing in the Canadian labor markets. There is a possibility that disadvantages for immigrant racial minorities net of measured qualifications can be explained in part by the poorer quality of those qualifications and not only by discriminatory treatment (Sweetman

2004). This has been explored in studies focusing on racial minorities educated in Canada. In extensive studies of the largest samples using census data, Pendakur and Pendakur (2002, 2007) find the racial disadvantage for racial minorities born in Canada is significant, although less so than for racial minority immigrants (see also Skuterud 2010; Li 2000).

The Canadian Human Rights Commission has found cases of racial discrimination. In 1997, in a case involving Health Canada, minority qualifications were denigrated. The view that ethnic minorities may possess technical qualifications but lack "soft skills," such as communication and decision-making skills, was found to play a significant role in their low rates of promotion to management. In one tribunal, the commission decided that racial discrimination may be involved when a minority immigrant job candidate is rejected on the basis of being overqualified. Immigrants encounter this complaint almost as often as the proverbial complaint about their lack of "Canadian experience." Such rejections are sometimes defended as standard human resource practice, but the fact that immigrants are so often rejected for jobs for which they are qualified on paper means they must turn to lower-level jobs, where they are vulnerable to the complaint that they are overqualified. Because of this, a human rights tribunal found the practice of rejecting immigrants as overqualified to be discriminatory (Canadian Human Rights Tribunal 2006; Chisholm, Harnden, and Sebold n.d.).

Within minority groups, perceptions of significant racial discrimination in employment are widespread. For example, the 1992 Minority Survey in Toronto found 78 percent of Blacks believed they were being targeted for employment discrimination (Dion and Kawakami 1996). In a 2015 survey in Toronto, 66 percent of men identifying as Black reported experiencing unfair treatment based on race either "frequently" (20 percent) or occasionally (46 percent); for women the figure was virtually the same, 67 percent (Environics Institute 2017, 38). Of all respondents, 28 percent said day-to-day experience with discrimination "bothers me a lot" and another 27 percent said it "bothers me somewhat."

Although immigrant economic experiences do improve over time, and the children of immigrants have attained high levels of education and occupations, perceptions of discrimination are more widespread among immigrants who have been in the country for longer periods, and even more so for the children of immigrants. Evidence from the 2002 Ethnic Diversity Survey documents these trends and indicates that awareness of discrimination is one reason that, despite economic mobility, racial minority immigrants are slower to integrate socially into society than are European immigrants (Reitz and Banerjee 2007; Reitz et al. 2009).

Impacts of Recent Policy Changes

Canada is likely to maintain its high levels of mostly skilled immigration and to continue multiculturalism, or, in Quebec, *interculturalisme*. However, a number of policy innovations to address some of the ongoing problems of immigration, although they offer promise, raise the possibility of new problems. For this reason, a key priority for the future may be timely evaluation to allow for assessment and, if required, adjustment or correction.

The "old problems" of Canadian immigration remain: the difficulties immigrants encounter in securing recognition of their foreign-acquired qualifications, the decline in the economic fortunes of successive cohorts of newly arriving immigrants, the administration of temporary immigration to ensure compliance with regulations, and issues of visa compliance and border control. And despite the popularity of multiculturalism, there are concerns about discrimination against immigrants and racial minorities in various areas of society and questions about immigrants' social and cultural integration.

Each of the new immigration policy initiatives has the potential to lower educational standards for new immigrants, and the evidence supports this trend. What is not yet clear is whether higher rates of early employment among immigrants will prove more important in the long term. Formal requirements for the skilled immigrant category include an explicit shift away from formal education and general work experience toward youth and qualifications in specific occupations in current demand. The provincial nomination program also seems likely to have attracted applicants differing in the same ways. Relatively few permanent visas have been given to temporary foreign workers under the Canada Experience Class, but the categories of eligibility include those who do not have postsecondary education. And, of course, those who become non-status permanent residents are likely to have low skill levels.

A decline in the educational level of immigrants could have an impact on the long-term potential for successful integration. High levels of education have often been cited as a key factor in policy success. An assumption of the new initiatives is that linking immigrants more firmly to the labor market from the outset may be more important in the long run. Which view is correct will have an impact on the future of immigration in Canada. The subtle move to soften multiculturalism is also difficult to assess in terms of impact.

Criteria for attaining citizenship have been tweaked toward a greater emphasis on immigrants acquiring "Canadian values," and officials have openly speculated about the possible limitations of multiculturalism. However, the actual changes appear minor.

Evaluation, then, will be critical. In this regard, it is significant that the Canadian long-form census, which in 2011 was used only in a voluntary National Household Survey, was again in use for the 2016 census. Long-form census data are critical for tracking immigrant progress. Many analysts believe the restoration of the long form to the 2016 census will make assessing the impact of immigration policy changes more accurate and useful.

Notes

1. For additional details, consult the IRCC website description of the Express Entry process: https://www.canada.ca/en/immigration-refugees-citizenship/services/immigrate-canada/express-entry.html.

2. See also Hiebert 2019. This description is based on information on an IRCC website, https://www.canada.ca/en/immigration-refugees-citizenship/services/immigrate-canada/express-entry/eligibility/federal-skilled-workers/six-selection-factors-federal-skilled-workers.html.

3. More recent publications in this series do not report settlement expenditures separately.

4. Government of Canada, "Labour Market Impact Assessment (LMIA) Exemption Codes—International Mobility Program," last modified September 22, 2021, https://www.canada.ca/en/immigration-refugees-citizenship/corporate/publications-manuals/operational-bulletins-manuals/temporary-residents/foreign-workers/exemption-codes.html.

5. Immigration and Refugee Board of Canada, "Irregular Border Crosser Statistics," https://irb-cisr.gc.ca/en/statistics/Pages/Irregular-border-crosser-statistics.aspx#1.

6. A November 23, 2018, article in the *Vancouver Sun* discussed four divergent polling results on immigration: https://vancouversun.com/news/staff-blogs/what-do-canadians-think-about-immigration-levels-three-poll-results.

7. "Bernier Reveals His True Colours," *Hill Times*, February 11, 2019, https://www.hilltimes.com/2019/02/11/bernier-reveals-true-colours/187863; "Maxime Bernier's Alt-Right Problem," *Toronto Star*, February 8, 2019, https://www.thestar.com/politics/federal/2019/02/08/maxime-berniers-alt-right-problem.html.

8. "Increased Polarization on Attitudes to Immigration Reshaping the Political Landscape in Canada," Ekos Politics, April 15, 2019, http://www.ekospolitics.com/wp-content/uploads/full_report_april_15_2019.pdf. See also Tasha Kheiriddin, "Commentary: Will the 2019 Vote Be the Election of Hate?," Global News, May 6, 2019, https://globalnews.ca/news/5235846/canada-immigration-election/.

9. Adjusted data (thanks to Feng Hou of Statistics Canada) based on imputation of education where accurate data were not available indicate that in 2012, 69.5 percent of principal applicants had university degrees, and 47.3 percent overall for immigrants. Release of education data was not included in subsequent "Facts and Figures" publications (for example, IRCC 2016b).

10. Adjusted data for 2013–2015 show that the proportion of principal applicants in the economic category with university degrees remained stable at around 68–70 percent, and the overall proportion of immigrants with university degrees remained between 45 and 50 percent. Data from the 2016 census on educational levels of immigrants by category and year of arrival support this conclusion (data again thanks to Feng Hou).

11. A summary of the Multiculturalism Policy Index project is available at https://www.queensu.ca/mcp/about.

12. One can scroll through the decades for the assessment across twenty-one Western democracies in the Multiculturalism Policy Index: https://www.queensu.ca/mcp/.

References

Advisory Council on Economic Growth. 2016. *Attracting the Talent Canada Needs Through Immigration.* Ottawa: Minister of Finance.

Akbari, A. H. 1995. "The Impact of Immigrants on Canada's Treasury, Circa 1990." In *Diminishing Returns: The Economics of Canada's Recent Immigration Policy*, edited by D. DeVoretz, 113–127. Toronto: C. D. Howe Institute.

Akbari, A. H., and M. MacDonald. 2014. "Immigration Policy in Australia, Canada, New Zealand, and the United States: An Overview of Recent Trends." *International Migration Review* 48, no. 3: 801–822.

Angus Reid Institute. 2010. "Canadians Endorse Multiculturalism, but Pick Melting Pot over Mosaic." November 8, 2010. http://angusreid.org/canadians-endorse-multiculturalism-but-pick-melting-pot-over-mosaic/.

Auditor General of Canada. 2009. "Fall Report of the Auditor General of Canada," chap. 2. Office of the Auditor General of Canada, Ottawa. http://www.oag-bvg.gc.ca/internet/English/parl_oag_200911_02_e_33203.html.

Auditor General of Canada. 2017. Spring Reports of the Auditor General of Canada to the Parliament of Canada. "Report 5—Temporary Foreign Worker Program—Employment and Social Development Canada." Government of Canada, Ottawa. http://www.oag-bvg.gc.ca/internet/English/parl_oag_201705_05_e_42227.html#.

Aydemir, A., and G. J. Borjas. 2007. "Cross-Country Variation in the Impact of International Migration: Canada, Mexico, and the United States." *Journal of the European Economic Association* 5, no. 4: 663–708.

Banerjee, R., J. G. Reitz, and P. Oreopoulos. 2018. "Do Large Employers Treat Racial Minorities More Fairly? An Analysis of Canadian Field Experiment Data." *Canadian Public Policy/Analyse de Politiques* 44, no. 1: 1–12.

Banting, K., R. Johnston, W. Kymlicka, and S. Soroka. 2006. "Do Multiculturalism Policies Erode the Welfare State? An Empirical Analysis." In *Multiculturalism and the Welfare State: Recognition and Redistribution in Contemporary Democracies*, edited by K. Banting and W. Kymlicka, 49–91. New York: Oxford University Press.

Banting, K., and W. Kymlicka, eds. 2017. *The Strains of Commitment: The Political Sources of Solidarity in Diverse Societies.* New York: Oxford University Press.

Beaujot, R. P. 1999. "Immigration and Demographic Structures." In *Immigrant Canada: Demographic, Economic and Social Challenges*, edited by S. S. Halli and L. Driedger, 93–115. Toronto: University of Toronto Press.

Bloemraad, I. 2006. *Becoming a Citizen: Incorporating Immigrants and Refugees in the United States and Canada*. Berkeley: University of California Press.

Bloemraad, Irene. 2012. *Understanding "Canadian Exceptionalism" in Immigration and Pluralism Policy*. Washington, DC: Migration Policy Institute.

Bloom, M., and M. Grant. 2001. *Brain Gain: The Economic Benefits of Recognizing Learning and Learning Credentials in Canada*. Ottawa: Conference Board of Canada.

Bouchard, G., and C. Taylor. 2008. "Building the Future: A Time for Reconciliation." Report of the Consultation Commission on Accommodation Practices Related to Cultural Differences. Quebec: Government of Quebec. https://www.mce.gouv.qc.ca/publications/CCPARDC/rapport-final-integral-en.pdf.

Bouchard, G. 2015. *Interculturalism: A View from Quebec*. Toronto: University of Toronto Press.

Bourhis, R. Y., A. Montreuil, D. Helly, and L. Jantzen. 2007. "Discrimination et linguicisme au Québec: Enquête sur la diversité au Canada." *Études Ethniques au Canada/Canadian Ethnic Studies* 39, nos. 1–2: 31–49.

Canadian Human Rights Tribunal. 2006. "Gian S. Sangha and the Canadian Human Rights Commission v. Mackenzie Valley Land and Water Board." Reasons for Decision, Feb. 24.

Chisholm, R., E. Harnden, and M. Sebold. n.d. "Hiring: Over-qualification and the Law." Hire Immigrants, Ottawa. http://www.hireimmigrantsottawa.ca/hiring-overqualification-and-the-law/.

CIC. 1998. "The Economic Performance of Immigrants: Immigration Category Perspective." IMDB Profile Series, Citizenship and Immigration Canada, December.

CIC. 2004. "Facts and Figures 2003: Immigration Overview—Permanent and Temporary Residents." Citizenship and Immigration Canada, Research and Evaluation Branch.

CIC. 2006. "Facts and Figures 2005: Immigration Overview—Permanent and Temporary Residents." Citizenship and Immigration Canada, Research and Evaluation Branch.

CIC. 2010a. "Facts and Figures 2009: Immigration Overview—Permanent and Temporary Residents." Citizenship and Immigration Canada, Research and Evaluation Branch.

CIC. 2010b. "Evaluation of the Federal Skilled Worker Program." Citizenship and Immigration Canada, Research and Evaluation Branch.

CIC. 2010c. "Evaluation of the Language Instruction for Newcomers to Canada (LINC) Program." Citizenship and Immigration Canada, Research and Evaluation Branch.

CIC. 2012. "Facts and Figures 2012: Immigration Overview—Permanent and Temporary Residents." Citizenship and Immigration Canada, Research and Evaluation Branch.

Conference Board of Canada. 2017. "450,000 Immigrants Annually? Integration Is Imperative to Growth." Conference Board of Canada, Ottawa.

Desiderio, M. V., and K. Hooper. 2016. "The Canadian Expression of Interest System: A Model to Manage Skilled Migration to the European Union?" Migration Policy Institute Europe, Brussels.

Dion, K. L., and K. Kawakami. 1996. "Ethnicity and Perceived Discrimination in Toronto: Another Look at the Personal /Group Discrimination Discrepancy." *Canadian Journal of Behavioural Science* 28, no. 3: 203–213.

Dungan, P., M. Gunderson, and T. Fang. 2010. "Macroeconomic Impacts of Canadian Immigration: An Empirical Analysis Using the FOCUS Model." Presentation at the CERIS seminar, October 10, 2010.

Economic Council of Canada. 1991. *Economic and Social Impacts of Immigration*. Ottawa: Supply and Services Canada.

Economist. 2016. "Liberty Moves North: Canada's Example to the World." October 29. https://www.economist.com/leaders/2016/10/29/liberty-moves-north.

EKOS Research Associates. 2010. "Annual Tracking Survey—Winter 2010." Submitted to Citizenship and Immigration Canada, April.

Environics Institute for Survey Research. 2017. "The Black Experience Project in the GTA: Overview Report." Environics Institute, Toronto.

Environics Institute for Survey Research. 2018. "Canadian Public Opinion About Immigration and Minority Groups." Environics Institute, Toronto. https://www.environicsinstitute.org/docs/default-source/project-documents/focus-canada-winter-2018---immigration-and-minority-groups/focus-canada-winter-2018-survey-on-immigration-and-minority-groups---final-report.pdf?sfvrsn=ede94c5f_2.

Ferrer, A. M., G. Picot, and W. C. Riddell. 2014. "New Directions in Immigration Policy: Canada's Evolving Approach to the Selection of Economic Immigrants." *International Migration Review* 48, no. 3: 846–867.

Fortin, N., T. Lemieux, and J. Torres. 2016. "Foreign Human Capital and the Earnings Gap Between Immigrants and Canadian-born Workers." *Labour Economics* 41: 104–119.

Florida, R. 2002. *The Rise of the Creative Class: And How It's Transforming Work, Leisure, Community and Everyday Life*. New York: Basic Books.

Frenette, M., and R. Morissette. 2003. "Will They Ever Converge? Earnings of Immigrant and Canadian-Born Workers over the Last Two Decades." Analytical Studies Branch Research Paper Series, catalogue no. 11F0019MIE—no. 215, Statistics Canada, Ottawa.

Gallup World Poll. 2018. "Revisiting the Most- and Least-Accepting Countries for Migrants." Gallup Inc., Washington, DC. https://news.gallup.com/opinion/gallup/245528/revisiting-least-accepting-countries-migrants.aspx.

German Marshall Fund of the United States. 2011 *Transatlantic Trends: Immigration—Key Findings 2010*. Washington, DC: German Marshall Fund of the United States.

Goldring, L., and P. Landolt, eds. 2013. *Producing and Negotiating Non-Citizenship: Precarious Legal Status in Canada*. Toronto: University of Toronto Press.

Grant, M. 2016. *Brain Gain 2015: The State of Canada's Learning Recognition System*. Ottawa: Conference Board of Canada.

Griffith, A. 2018. "What the Census Tells Us About Citizenship." *Policy Options*, March 20.

Hiebert, Daniel. 2019. "The Canadian Express Entry System for Selecting Economic Immigrants: Progress and Persistent Challenges." Migration Policy Institute, Washington, DC.

Hou, F., Z. Wu, C. Schimmele, and J. Myles. 2015. "Cross-Country Variation in Interracial Marriage: A USA-Canada Comparison of Metropolitan Areas." *Ethnic and Racial Studies* 38, no. 9: 1591–1609.

Hulchanski, J. D. 2010. *The Three Cities Within Toronto: Income Polarization Among Toronto's Neighbourhoods, 1970–2005.* Toronto: Cities Centre Press.

Ipsos-Reid. 2018. "Immigration in Canada: Does Recent Change in Forty Year Opinion Trend Signal a Blip or a Breaking Point?" Angus Reid Institute. https://angusreid.org/canadian-immigration-trend-data/.

Ipsos-Reid. 2019. "Canadians Becoming More Nervous About Immigration." Ipsos Global Public Surveys, Toronto. https://www.ipsos.com/sites/default/files/ct/news/documents/2019-01/factum.pdf.

IRCC. 2016a. "Express Entry Year-End Report 2016." Immigration, Refugees and Citizenship Canada, Ottawa. https://www.canada.ca/content/dam/ircc/migration/ircc/english/pdf/pub/ee-2016-eng.pdf.

IRCC. 2016b. "Facts and Figures 2016: Immigration Overview—Permanent Residents." Immigration, Refugees and Citizenship Canada, Ottawa. http://www.cic.gc.ca/opendata-donneesouvertes/data/Facts_and_Figures_2016_PR_EN.pdf.

IRCC. 2016c. "Facts and Figures 2016: Immigration Overview—Temporary Residents." Immigration, Refugees and Citizenship Canada, Ottawa. http://www.cic.gc.ca/opendata-donneesouvertes/data/Facts_and_Figures_2016_TR_EN.pdf.

IRCC. 2017a. "Evaluation of the Settlement Program." Reference no. E2-2016. Immigration, Refugees and Citizenship Canada, Ottawa.

IRCC. 2017b. "Express Entry Year-End Report 2017." Immigration, Refugees and Citizenship Canada, Ottawa. https://www.canada.ca/content/dam/ircc/documents/pdf/english/pub/express-entry-year-end-report-2017.pdf.

IRCC. 2017c. "Departmental Plan 2017–2018." Immigration, Refugees and Citizenship Canada, Ottawa.

IRCC. 2020. "Express Entry Year-End Report 2019." Immigration, Refugees and Citizenship Canada, Ottawa.

Kazemipur, A., and S. S. Halli. 2000. *The New Poverty in Canada: Ethnic Groups and Ghetto Neighbourhoods.* Toronto: Thompson.

Kelley, N., and M. Trebilcock. 2010. *The Making of the Mosaic: A History of Canadian Immigration Policy.* Toronto: University of Toronto Press.

Kymlicka, W. 1998. *Finding Our Way: Rethinking Ethnocultural Relations in Canada.* Oxford: Oxford University Press.

Kymlicka, W. 2012. "Multiculturalism: Success, Failure and the Future." In *Rethinking National Identity in the Age of Migration*, edited by Migration Policy Institute, 33–78. Berlin: Verlag Bertelsmann Stiftung.

Laxer, E., J. G. Reitz, and P. Simon. 2020. "Muslims' Political and Civic Incorporation in France and Canada: Testing Models of Participation." *Journal of Ethnic and Migration Studies*, forthcoming.

Li, P. S. 2000. "Earnings Disparities Between Immigrants and Native-Born Canadians." *Canadian Review of Sociology and Anthropology* 37, no. 3: 289–311.

Li, P. S. 2001 "The Market Worth of Immigrants' Educational Credentials." *Canadian Public Policy* 27, no. 1: 23–38.

Macklin, A. 2017. "Resettler Society: Making and Remaking Citizenship Through Private Refugee Sponsorship." Toronto: Pierre Elliott Trudeau Foundation, Fellowship Program. http://www.trudeaufoundation.ca/sites/default/files/macklin-project-web-en.pdf.

MacNair, A. 2010. "Ujjal Dosanjh Speaks the Truth About Honour Killings." *National Post*, June 17, 2010. https://nationalpost.com/full-comment/adrian-macnair-ujjal-dosanjh -speaks-the-truth-about-honour-killings.

Martin, P. 2010. "Temporary Worker Programs: U.S. and Global Experiences." *Canadian Issues/Thèmes Canadiens*, Spring, 122–128.

McLaughlin, J., and J. Hennebry. 2015. "Managed into the Margins: Examining Citizenship and Human Rights of Migrant Workers in Canada." In *The Human Right to Citizenship: A Slippery Concept*, edited by R. Howard Hassmann and M. Walton-Roberts, 176–190. Philadelphia: University of Pennsylvania Press.

Nakache, D., and P. J. Kinoshita. 2010. "The Canadian Temporary Foreign Worker Program: Do Short-Term Economic Needs Prevail over Human Rights Concerns?" IRPP Study 5. Institute for Research on Public Policy, Montreal.

Nuttall, J. J. 2017. "Increase in Foreign Workers Through Federal Program Still a Problem, Says Union," *Tyee*, July 27, 2017. https://thetyee.ca/News/2017/07/27/ Increase-in-Foreign-Workers-Still-a-Problem/.

Oreopoulos, P. 2011. "Why Do Skilled Immigrants Struggle in the Labor Market? A Field Experiment with Thirteen Thousand Resumes." *American Economic Journal: Economic Policy* 3, no. 4: 148–171.

Ornstein, M. 2006. "Ethno-Racial Groups in Toronto, 1971–2001: A Demographic and Socio-Economic Profile." Institute for Social Research, York University, Toronto.

Pendakur, K., and R. Pendakur. 2002. "Colour My World: Have Earnings Gaps for Canadian-Born Ethnic Minorities Changed over Time?" *Canadian Public Policy/Analyse de Politiques* 28, no. 4: 489–512.

Pendakur, K., and R. Pendakur. 2007. "Minority Earnings Disparity Across the Distribution." *Canadian Public Policy/Analyse de Politiques* 33, no. 1: 41–62.

Pew Research Center. 2019. "Around the World, More Say Immigrants Are a Strength Than a Burden." Pew Research Center, Washington, DC.

Picot, G., and F. Hou. 2003. "The Rise in Low-Income Rates Among Immigrants in Canada." Catalogue no. 11F0019MIE—no. 198. Analytical Studies Branch Research Paper Series, Business and Labour Market Analysis Division, Statistics Canada, Ottawa.

Picot, G., F. Hou, and S. Coulombe. 2007. "Chronic Low Income and Low-Income Dynamics among Recent Immigrants." Catalogue no. 11F0019MIE—no. 294. Business and Labour Market Analysis, Statistics Canada, Ottawa.

Reitz, J. G. 2001a. "Immigrant Skill Utilization in the Canadian Labour Market: Implications of Human Capital Research." *Journal of International Migration and Integration* 2, no. 3: 347–378.

Reitz, J. G. 2001b. "Immigrant Success in the Knowledge Economy: Institutional Change and the Immigrant Experience in Canada, 1970–1995." *Journal of Social Issues* 57, no. 3: 579–613.

Reitz, J. G. 2007. "Immigrant Employment Success in Canada, Part II: Understanding the Decline." *Journal of International Migration and Integration* 8, no. 1: 37–62.

Reitz, J. G. 2010. "Selecting Immigrants for the Short Term: Is It Smart in the Long Run?" *Policy Options* 31, no. 7: 12–16.

Reitz, J. G. 2011. "Pro-Immigration Canada: Social and Economic Roots of Popular Views." IRPP Study 20. Institute for Research on Public Policy, Montreal.

Reitz, J. G. 2012. "The Distinctiveness of Canadian Immigration Experience." *Patterns of Prejudice* 46, no. 5: 518–535.

Reitz, J. G. 2013. "Closing the Gaps Between Skilled Immigration and Canadian Labour Markets." In *Wanted and Welcome? Policies for Highly Skilled Immigrants in Comparative Perspective*, edited by P. Triadafilopoulos, 147–163. New York: Springer.

Reitz, J. G. 2014a. "Canada: New Initiatives and Approaches to Immigration and Nation Building." In *Controlling Immigration: A Global Perspective*, 3rd ed., edited by J. F. Hollifield, P. L. Martin, and P. M. Orrenius, 88–116. Stanford, CA: Stanford University Press.

Reitz, J. G. 2014b. "Multiculturalism Policies and Popular Multiculturalism in the Development of Canadian Immigration." In *The Multiculturalism Question: Debating Identity in 21st Century Canada*, edited by J. Jedwab, 107–126. Kingston: McGill-Queen's University Press.

Reitz, J. G., and R. Banerjee. 2007. "Racial Inequality, Social Cohesion, and Policy Issues in Canada." In *Belonging? Diversity, Recognition and Shared Citizenship in Canada*, edited by K. Banting, T. J. Courchene, and F. L. Seidle, 489–545. Montreal: Institute for Research on Public Policy.

Reitz, J. G., J. Curtis, and J. Elrick. 2014. "Immigrant Skill Utilization: Trends and Policy Issues." *Journal of International Migration and Integration* 15, no. 1: 1–26.

Reitz, J. G., R. Breton, K. K. Dion, and K. L. Dion. 2009. *Multiculturalism and Social Cohesion: Potentials and Challenges of Diversity*. New York: Springer.

Schuster, A., M. V. Desiderio, and G. Urso, eds. 2013. *Recognition of Qualifications and Competences of Migrants*. Brussels: International Organization for Migration.

Skuterud, M. 2010. "The Visible Minority Earnings Gap Across Generations of Canadians." *Canadian Journal of Economics/Revue Canadienne d'Économique* 43, no. 3: 860–881.

Statistics Canada. 2005. "Longitudinal Survey of Immigrants to Canada: A Portrait of Early Settlement Experiences." Special Surveys Division, Statistics Canada, Ottawa.

Statistics Canada. 2008. "Earnings and Incomes of Canadians over the Past Quarter Century, 2006 Census: Findings." Catalogue no. 97-563-X. Minister Responsible for Statistics Canada, Ottawa.

Statistics Canada. 2020. "Annual Demographic Estimates: Canada, Provinces and Territories (Total Population Only)." Catalogue no. 91-215-X. Statistics Canada, Ottawa.

Stoffman, D. 2002. *Who Gets In: What's Wrong with Canada's Immigration Program—And How to Fix It*. Toronto: Macfarlane, Walter & Ross.

Sweetman, A. 2004. "Immigrant Source Country Educational Quality and Canadian Labor Market Outcomes." Catalogue no. 11F0019MIE—no. 234. Statistics Canada, Analytic Studies Branch, Business and Labour Market Analysis Division, Ottawa.

Sweetman, A., and C. Warman. 2014. "Former Temporary Foreign Workers and International Students as Sources of Permanent Immigration." *Canadian Public Policy* 40, no. 4: 391–407.

Tepperman, J. 2017. "Canada's Ruthlessly Smart Immigration System." *New York Times*, June 28, 2017. https://www.nytimes.com/2017/06/28/opinion/canada-immigration-policy-trump.html.

COMMENTARY

Canadian Exceptionalism

Antje Ellermann

In this age of populism, Canada (with the partial exception of Québec) stands out by the lack of public contestation surrounding its immigration and multiculturalism policies. As Jeffrey Reitz points out in this chapter, at a time when most democratically elected governments are struggling to contain populist opposition to immigration, Canadian political elites and the Canadian public have remained largely supportive of immigration. In fact, one of the basic assumptions underlying the four editions of *Controlling Immigration*—that there is a growing gap between the goals and the outcomes of immigration policy, fueling popular demands for immigration restriction—is not borne out by Canadian immigration politics. Various explanations have been put forward to account for this "exceptionalism" (Bloemraad 2012). Reitz emphasizes economic and cultural explanations. Thus, Canadians believe that immigration is economically beneficial—a belief that in large part is driven by the high-skill bias of Canadian immigration policy. And the fact that multiculturalism itself is part of Canadian identity has ensured cultural support for continued immigration. Reitz also reminds us that Canada has had the good fortune of geography. Being located far from any immigrant-sending region has made it much more feasible to manage immigration and to closely align policy goals and migration outcomes. Clearly economic selection, a pluralistic conception of national identity, and geography matter. However, I do not think that they are sufficient to explain Canadian exceptionalism.

As Reitz notes, public support for immigration quickly dissipates when Canadians are confronted with "non-selected" immigrants—most importantly, asylum seekers. Similarly, Canadian support for multiculturalism goes hand in hand with the expectation that immigrants blend into Canadian society. Canadian attitudes, when confronted with trigger events, easily align with those commonly seen in Europe or the United States. I argue that, in addition to having the good fortune of geography, Canadian exceptionalism rests on political institutions that have facilitated the creation of a high-skilled immigration and multiculturalism policy in the first place. Two sets of institutions in particular nurture Canadian exceptionalism by discouraging the politicization of immigration. First, the making of Canadian immigration policy takes place in a much more politically insulated environment than is the case for most other democracies. Policymaking insulation has prevented the politicization of immigration and thus the mobilization of anti-immigration attitudes. Second, Canada's electoral geography rewards party issue positions that appeal to immigrants and ethnic minority voters, thereby cementing an elite pro-immigration consensus. After discussing these factors, I will shift our attention to some recent changes in Canada's economic immigration policy. While these reforms represent continuity in having been passed without much public notice, they also mark a departure from Canada's long-standing practice of admitting immigrants as permanent residents.

Explaining Canadian Exceptionalism

Canadian immigration policy is made in settings that are well insulated from public scrutiny and debate. Many of the most important immigration reforms since World War II—including the introduction of the points system and the shift from family-dominated to economically driven immigrant admissions—were passed by the executive branch through orders-in-council before being eventually affirmed by parliament. Canada's immigration acts take the form of framework legislation: they delegate key aspects of policymaking to the regulatory process.[1] Whereas in the United States, something as relatively minor as increasing the number of skilled worker visas is subject to congressional approval, whereas in Canada far-reaching decisions like the setting of overall immigration levels, the balance between family, economic, and humanitarian admissions, and the points system's selection criteria and their relative weight are routinely made by the executive branch.

All of this matters because policy that takes the form of orders-in-council or regulation attracts little parliamentary scrutiny and even less public attention. It allows executive officials to pursue their preferences in the absence of parliamentary and public debate. While executive-dominated policymaking does not preclude public consultation—the Canadian government routinely consults with major societal interests as well as the provincial governments before adjusting policy—consultation is typically limited to (mostly pro-immigration) organized interests and provincial governments and rarely finds its way into broader public debate. Immigration officials tend to exercise tight control over this process and primarily use these consultations to gauge the state of elite opinion. In a similar vein, Canada's immigration ministry conducts annual public opinion polls in order to preempt any need for damage control.

Even when immigration reform is passed in the form of new legislation or legislative amendments, the executive branch continues to dominate policymaking. Except in times of minority government, Canadian governments have little to fear from opposition parties. Canada's Westminster parliamentary system, with its congruence of government and parliamentary majority and strong norms of partisan discipline, ensures that parliamentary decision-making will not deviate much from the government's preferences. Moreover, since the 2000s, governments (including minority governments) have increasingly resorted to the use of omnibus bills to push through immigration amendments without parliamentary debate. Budget and other omnibus bills lump together multiple unrelated issues that are then voted on in their entirety. Because of the length of these bills, specific proposals attract little attention, which allows governments to pass immigration reforms without much parliamentary and public debate. Because policy reforms pass without attracting much attention, most Canadian opinion polls therefore measure attitudes that are *not mobilized*. When public opinion is mobilized, as happens when there is an influx of asylum seekers or, in Québec, when immigration becomes linked to questions of religious accommodation, we see polling results that no longer are "exceptional" but resemble those in other immigrant-receiving democracies.

Political institutions thus play a critical role in facilitating or impeding the mobilization of anti-immigration attitudes. So far I have emphasized the importance of executive-dominated decision-making as a constraint on popular mobilization. A second factor driving Canadian exceptionalism is the country's electoral geography. Canada's single-member district electoral rules reward geographically concentrated interests. Because of the interaction of high levels of immigration, exceptionally high naturalization rates, and immigrant settlement in large urban areas, parties can only win a majority government with the support of immigrant and ethnic minority voters (Besco and Tolley 2019). As a result of ethnic minority electoral strength, today all of Canada's major federal parties share a pro-immigration consensus, including the Conservative Party (Marwah, Triadafilopoulos, and White 2013). While this does not preclude taking restrictionist positions on specific issues of immigration (in particular asylum policy), it removes key questions of immigration and multiculturalism policy from the political agenda. Equally importantly, Canada's electoral geography has prevented the rise of a successful radical far-right party at the federal level. Canada is one of the few remaining countries in the Global North without a viable far-right party. Its mainstream parties thus do not have to fear voter defection when adopting pro-immigration and pro-immigrant positions.

Recent Changes to Canada's Economic Immigration Policy

As the title of this chapter suggests, Canadian immigration policy has long been driven by the imperative of nation-building. Like in other settler colonial states, immigration was central to the colonial project of territorial domination and erasure of indigenous presence. Ethnically selective immigration allowed for the building of a European settler society that eventually claimed jurisdiction over the lands it had settled on. As colonial settlers became transformed into immigrants and the white settler nation became reinvented as a multicultural nation of immigrants, past and present settler colonialism became written out of the national narrative (Volpp 2015). Thus, Canada became a "nation of immigrants" where, today, ideas of nation-building live on in the form of economic and demographic arguments in favor of immigration. These arguments have historically been premised on the admission of immigrants as settlers—that is, as permanent residents. Yet while these arguments live on, over the past two decades Canada's economic immigration policy has undergone far-reaching changes that have prompted some to declare "the end of settler society" (Dauvergne 2016). As outlined by Reitz, these changes not only have increased the role of employers in the selection of economic immigrants but also have expanded the admission of temporary foreign workers and created new pathways to permanent residence. It is these latter developments—the rise of temporary foreign worker recruitment and the establishment of "two-step immigration"—that mark a fundamental departure from the ways in which economic immigration was used for the purposes of "nation-building" in the past.

Until recently, the vast majority of economic immigrants (and their dependents) arrived in Canada as permanent residents through the Federal Skilled Worker (FSW) program (which, until the creation of Express Entry in 2015, was equivalent to the points system; CIC 2010b). With the proliferation of new entry programs, however, the FSW program has declined in significance. Comparing the pathways of economic immigrants who gained permanent residence in 2015 to those who had done so in 2000, the FSW program's share dropped from nearly 90 percent to about 40 percent (Figure 3.9). Annual FSW admissions also declined in absolute terms during this

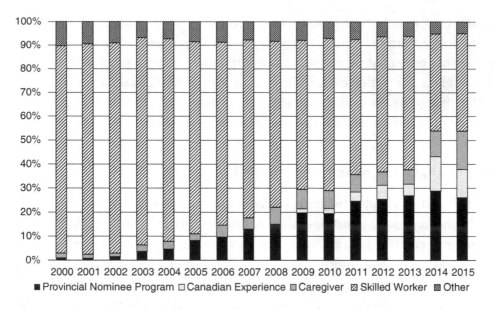

FIGURE 3.9. Skill Composition of Temporary Workers Transitioning to Permanent Residence (2005–2014)

SOURCE: IRCC, Facts and Figures 2005, 2006, 2014, 2015; Quarterly Reports, 2016, 2017.

period, falling from 120,000 to 70,000. The drastic decline of FSW admissions is largely the result of the expansion of the Canada Experience Class and the Provincial Nominee Program. By 2015, these two pathways together accounted for close to 40 percent of permanent residents in the economic stream. Unlike the one-step admissions under the FSW program, the CEC and PNP are examples of two-step immigration programs.[2] Instead of admitting newcomers right away as permanent residents, "two-step" programs first admit applicants on a temporary basis, before offering some the option of applying for permanent residence. With the creation of these programs, Canada followed New Zealand and Australia in creating legal pathways for employer-sponsored migrants on temporary visas to become permanent residents. Since the beginning of the COVID-19 pandemic (which at the time of writing is in its second year), the Canadian government's decision to maintain high immigration levels has further accelerated this trend. With border restrictions hindering the recruitment of economic immigrants from overseas, Canada has further opened up its immigration pathways to foreign workers on temporary visas already in the country, particularly through the Canadian Experience Class and through the issuance of postgraduate work permits, which facilitate subsequent immigration through the CEC.

This shift from one-step to two-step immigration has important implications. As Reitz points out, two-step immigration introduces a degree of legal precarity not

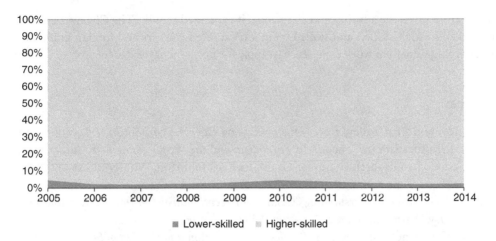

Lower-skilled ■   **Higher-skilled** ■

FIGURE 3.10. Economic Permanent Resident Admissions, by Program, 2000–2015
SOURCE: IRCC, 2016 Annual Report to Parliament on Immigration; CIC, Facts and Figures.

traditionally associated with "countries of immigration" such as Canada. Only if they succeed in establishing themselves in the labor market and secure the support of their employer can temporary foreign workers and international students qualify for permanent residence. Two-step immigration matters not only because it introduces precarity into Canadian immigration policy but also because it largely reserves access to permanent residence to high-skilled workers. Because Express Entry rewards human capital in addition to employment, well over 90 percent of those who manage to transition from temporary to permanent residence are high-skilled (Figure 3.10). Thus, while certain aspects of Canadian immigration policy and politics do not fit this book's hypothesis of cross-national convergence, the shift from one-step to two-step immigration has moved Canada closer toward the economic migration policies of more recent countries of immigration. In expanding temporary economic admissions and attaching new conditionalities on the transition to permanent residence, Canada has moved closer to the economic immigration policies of many European states. In other words, while the depoliticized mode of Canadian immigration politics continues to show continuity with the past, immigration policy itself has undergone significant change—far more than the limited nature of public debate would suggest.

Notes

1. There have been only two major immigration acts since the abolition of national-origins-based immigration, passed in 1976 and 2001, respectively.

2. The PNP was established in 1995 to allow provinces with low levels of immigration to nominate immigrants on the condition that they fill a specified job. By 2007, the program was in place in all provinces (except for Québec) and two northern territories, and after the

government removed the admissions cap in 2008, it expanded rapidly. The CEC was created in 2008 to allow high-skilled and skilled temporary foreign workers and foreign graduates with qualifying Canadian work experience to apply for permanent residence.

References

Besco, Randy, and Erin Tolley. 2019. "Does Everyone Cheer? The Politics of Immigration and Multiculturalism in Canada." In *Federalism and the Welfare State in a Multicultural World*, edited by Elizabeth Goodyear-Grant, Richard Johnston, Will Kymlicka and John Myles, 291–318. Kingston: Queen's School of Policy Studies.

Bloemraad, Irene. 2012. *Understanding "Canadian Exceptionalism" in Immigration and Pluralism Policy*. Washington, DC: Migration Policy Institute.

Dauvergne, Catherine. 2016. *The New Politics of Immigration and the End of Settler Societies*. Cambridge: Cambridge University Press.

Marwah, Inder, Triadafilos Triadafilopoulos, and Stephen White. 2013. "Immigration, Citizenship and Canada's New Conservative Party." In *Canadian Conservatism in Comparative Context*, edited by James Farney and David Rayside, 95–119. Toronto: University of Toronto Press.

Volpp, Leti. 2015. "The Indigenous as Alien." *UC Irvine Law Review* 5, no. 2: 289–325.

4 Australia and New Zealand

Classical Migration States?

Alan Gamlen and Henry Sherrell

Introduction

In this chapter, we review the histories of Australian and New Zealand migration, focusing on the evolution of immigration controls and channels over the course of around two centuries. Australia and New Zealand are both classical countries of immigration, formed by indigenous arrival, transformed by British settler colonialism, and systemically dependent on immigration for economic and demographic growth (Castles, Vasta, and Ozkul 2014). These South Pacific neighbors share one of the most open bilateral borders in the world—a fragment of the former British Imperial migration system—and both have geopolitically reoriented toward the Asia-Pacific region since the 1970s, overturning racist colonial migration policies in favor of economic entry criteria, and attracting growing numbers of temporary migrants in addition to a more diverse range of permanent settlers.

But Australia and New Zealand are quite different in important ways. Although both are islands, Australia is a continent of some 7.7 million square kilometers, which dwarfs the 268,000-square-kilometer archipelago of New Zealand to its southeast. Australia is also more populous, weighing in at some 25 million inhabitants compared to New Zealand's 5 million. Australia was colonized earlier and even more brutally than New Zealand, and has done less to address the legacy of colonization—a difference that has shaped national identity, citizenship, and immigration policy in both countries (see Bedford 2019; Veracini 2010). As a result of their many similarities, connections, and contrasts, Australia and New Zealand are ideal candidates for a comparative study of controlling immigration.

Australia and New Zealand are classical immigration countries, but are they also migration states? James Hollifield has highlighted the growing need for governments to manage a "liberal paradox," in which they are pressured to allow more migration for economic reasons, even though this raises major political and security risks (Hollifield 1992). The response, Hollifield argues, has been the emergence of "migration states," whose central purpose is to balance these competing pressures by controlling immigration (Hollifield 2004). In migration states, Hollifield argues, migration has risen to the sphere of "high politics," where issues impinge upon national security and geopolitics and governments must therefore please both pro- and anti-immigrant factions. To do so, they often talk tough on border control, but implement controls that are designed to fail—leading to a "policy gap" over migration (Hollifield 1986; also see Freeman 1994; Joppke 1998; Castles 2004; Boswell 2007; Zolberg 2009; Czaika and De Haas 2013; Lutz 2019).

To what extent do Australia and New Zealand conform to this conception of "the emerging migration state"? This chapter argues that both Australia and New Zealand must be thought of as migration states—but that in order to define them as such, the concept of the migration state itself needs to be subtly but significantly revised. The chapter makes this argument through a historical narrative divided into five main periods: (1) the first great settler boom and bust, 1841–1900; (2) Britain's "white dominions" in the Pacific, 1901–1945; (3) the end of empire and the push to populate, 1946–1973; (4) globalization, diversification, and multiculturalism, 1974–1995; and (5) the second great migration boom, 1996–2020. Finally, the chapter raises key questions about the future of Australian and New Zealand migration in the wake of the 2020 pandemic before returning to draw conclusions about the nature of "migration states" in this part of the world.

The First Great Settler Boom and Bust: 1841–1900

Australia and New Zealand's patterns of indigenous arrival and settlement are very different. Aboriginal Australians arrived via Melanesia and settled swiftly by land around the continent's perimeter some 50,000–65,000 years ago, developing into more than 250 distinct ethno-linguistic groups (O'Connell et al. 2018). Māori settled Aotearoa (the Māori name for New Zealand) via Polynesia some 700 years ago and developed a single language grouping with a variety of dialects (Walter et al. 2017). No known contact occurred between Aboriginal and Māori peoples prior to British-led colonization in the modern era. But both countries fell into the British colony of

New South Wales from 1788, when the First Fleet, bearing convicts, established Australia's first penal colony in what is now Sydney. This merger lasted until 1841, a year after New Zealand's Treaty of Waitangi was signed (Orange 2015).

The treaty marks a formative difference in the histories of Australia and New Zealand. In the early nineteenth century, growing numbers of rusticated British mariners, missionaries, whalers, sealers, traders, trappers, fugitives, and flâneurs were reaching the South Pacific, often transiting through Australia's growing penal colonies (Salmond 1997). Though few in number, they wreaked havoc, running flax, timber, and guns across the Tasman Sea, which upended a delicate intertribal balance of power in Aotearoa and fueled its catastrophic Musket Wars of 1806–1837 (Belich 2001a; Crosby 2017). By 1839, many Māori chiefs wanted Britain to bring its diaspora in line, and so they signed the treaty to make the Crown responsible for operational *kawanatanga* (governance), without ceding their *tino rangatiratanga* (absolute chieftainship) (Kawharu 1989). But the distinction was lost in translation: the British claimed "sovereignty"—then an alien concept—over New Zealand and commenced large-scale, commercially organized settlement. The non-Māori population skyrocketed from around 2,000 in 1841 to 59,000 in 1856 and to 299,000 in 1871. The Māori population shrank from 80,000 to 47,000 in the same period (Pool and Jackson n.d.).

Judging themselves usurped, many Māori fought back in the New Zealand Wars of 1845–1872, and a Māori King movement emerged to uphold the treaty's guarantee of *rangatiratanga* (Belich 1986). This provided justification for the British to systematically confiscate large tracts of Māori land (Williams 1999). Māori nationalism was further galvanized by opposition to conscription in World War I, and then by the distinguished contribution of the Māori battalion during World War II. A Māori middle class began to emerge with large-scale urbanization of Māori after World War II (Grace, Ramsden, and Dennis 2001), and by the 1960s and 1970s the treaty was once again the focus of Māori protests, which eventually led to the 1975 Treaty of Waitangi Act. The act elevated the treaty to the status of a semi-constitutional document and led to the establishment of the Waitangi Tribunal, which has since settled Māori land and fisheries claims worth over $2.2 billion at the time of payout (Hayward and Wheen 2016). Though far from perfect, the process has helped sustain a growing Māori elite that is sophisticated, articulate, internationally mobile, and ambivalent about immigration and foreign land ownership (Kukutai and Rata 2017).

By contrast in Australia, late eighteenth- and nineteenth-century colonists— most either forced or free immigrants from Britain and Ireland—signed no treaty with the indigenous inhabitants, whom they brutally displaced and dismissed as nomads, classifying the continent as *terra nullius*: unoccupied land, free for settlement

(Banner 2005). A successful court challenge to this legal sleight of hand was not mounted until 1992, over 200 years later, when the Mabo Decision recognized native title to Australian land for the first time (Secher 2007). This facilitated significant land compensation and has had a number of positive social effects but is still perceived by many Australians to have fallen short of addressing issues of social justice, sovereignty, and constitutional change (Smith and Morphy 2007). In sharp contrast with New Zealand, Aboriginal Australians lacked basic citizenship until 1967. They moved to cities in fewer numbers than Māori and into segregated circumstances, and today the indigenous middle class is smaller, less resource-rich, and more marginalized, with fewer global connections, than New Zealand Māori (Markham and Biddle 2018). Thus, despite its flaws, New Zealand's Treaty of Waitangi has left Māori better off by most measures than Aboriginal Australians—a fact with implications for national identity, citizenship, sovereignty, race relations, and immigration control to this day (Kamp et al. 2018; Moran 2017).

Australia and New Zealand were both shaped by population movement within the British Empire, where all inhabitants held the status of "British subject," with rights to free movement throughout Britain's global realm (Hansen 2000). In the nineteenth century, rapid European urbanization spilled into the antipodes, which became Britain's new agricultural hinterlands (Belich 2009). Unlike in North America, these far-flung colonies required "assisted migration," sponsored by government and businesses, to overcome the huge distances and costs involved and ensure the right balance of capital and labor needed for growth. In the 1830s and 1840s, over half of all migrants to South Australia and New South Wales received government assistance (Department of Labour and Immigration 1975, 2). Across the Tasman, the New Zealand Company brought 14,000 of the 18,000 new settlers in 1840–1852 (Spoonley and Bedford 2012, 30).

Spontaneous migration also occurred in the nineteenth century, creating immigration booms and busts and rapid population changes. During the gold rush, Victoria's population grew by 220 percent in three years (from 97,489 in 1851 to 312,307 in 1854), with many arrivals drawn from the 1848–1855 California gold rush (Serle 2014, 382). From 1850 to 1860 Australia's population grew by 183 percent (from 405,000 to 1,145,000); three-quarters of the increase came from net migration (Department of Labour and Immigration 1975, 3). Soon after, gold rushes in New Zealand's South Island drew massive inflows, including many California and Australia veterans. Streets and buildings in California, Australia, and New Zealand began to look similar (Hamer 1990). From 1853 to 1870 New Zealand's non-Māori population mushroomed from 30,000 to 250,000 (Spoonley and Bedford 2012, 30–31). During the 1860s net migration increased New Zealand's population by almost 6.5 percent per year, some

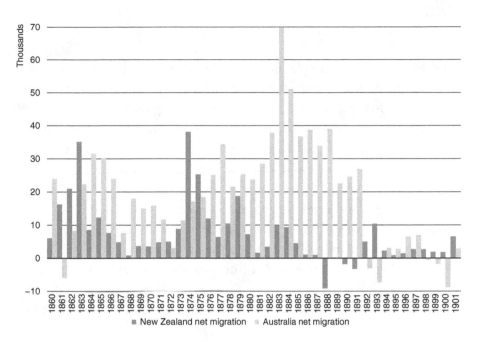

FIGURE 4.1. Net Migration, New Zealand and Australia, 1860–1901
SOURCE: Multiple official sources, Gamlen's analysis.

five times higher than the rate in Australia (Figure 4.1). (For a sense of scale: in 2016, Britain voted to exit the European Union in protest at roughly half this immigration rate.) Not everyone stayed: around 100,000 people left New Zealand to go to Australia, other British colonies, or "home" to Britain itself.

After a lull in the late 1860s–1870s, the so-called Great Migration began. Net migration rates neared all-time peaks, and relative to population size they shot far higher than ever before or since. New Zealand offered free passage to European migrants in 1873; in 1874 net migration spiked to over 38,000—a raw intake that was unequaled for thirteen decades, and was at the time equivalent to 11 percent of New Zealand's total population. However, weak commodity prices soon hit New Zealand's export-dependent economy, driving average net migration below 10,000 per year for a decade. Meanwhile, numbers kept climbing in Australia, where Melbourne—then one of the world's largest, most populous, and richest cities—was the epicenter of a massive real-estate bubble. As money and migrants jostled to get a piece of the colony, net migration to Australia grew from 17,121 in 1873 to 34,384 in 1877 and to 69,865 in 1883, then hovered around 30,000 per year until the bubble burst in 1891. When that happened banks and businesses failed en masse, and immigration dwindled to a trickle for the next decade.

Britain's "White Dominions" in the Pacific: 1901–1945

Australia and New Zealand were planned as white British colonies. By 1900 their foreign-born population shares were 23 percent and 33 percent respectively, mostly from Britain. In 1901, 79 percent of Australia's 857,000 immigrants and 80 percent of New Zealand's 256,613 immigrants were from the United Kingdom, which at the time included Ireland. Migrants also moved across the Tasman Sea. In 1901 Australia had 25,700 New Zealand–born people, and New Zealand had about 27,000 Australian-born. The colonies only tolerated non-British immigration if it was white: in 1901 Australia had 38,352 German-born residents and New Zealand had 4,217. The largest non-European groups were the Chinese: in 1880s Victoria, one adult male in four was Chinese (McQueen 2004). By 1901 Australia had 29,907 Chinese-born people (about 3 percent of the foreign-born population), while New Zealand had 2,902 Chinese-born (about 1 percent of all foreign-born). The first active efforts at immigration control in both places aimed to curb Chinese immigration and keep the colonies white.

Indeed, race-based immigration controls represent some of the earliest independent government actions of any kind in both these fledgling nation-states. At the end of the Victorian imperial period, Australia became a unified state and New Zealand formed its own semi-independent dominion of Britain (McIntyre 2007). Able to make their own territory-wide migration policies for the first time, both states moved to restrict Chinese immigration. In 1881, following the Canadian and Australian examples, New Zealand imposed a £10 poll tax on each Chinese immigrant, and limited arriving ships to one Chinese passenger per ten tons of cargo. In 1896, the restriction was tightened further, and the poll tax reached around $20,000 in today's money (Ministry for Culture and Heritage 2020; Spoonley and Bedford 2012, 36–37). Restrictions on Chinese immigration were eased in 1907, but new legislation gave the government great discretion to exclude Chinese: the 1919 Undesirable Immigrants Exclusion Act and the 1920 Immigration Restriction Amendment Act. Meanwhile, the unfederated Australian states actively deselected Chinese immigrants throughout the 1890s (Yarwood 1964). This approach culminated in the *Immigration Restriction Act 1901*—commonly known as the White Australia Policy—one of the first major pieces of national legislation for the new federation (Willard 1967). Rather than explicitly excluding race groups, the policy operated through language skills: immigrants had to take a "dictation test" in any European tongue, and it became standard practice to make non-white migrants take the test in an obscure language that they were almost certain not to know (Palfreeman 1958; Atkinson 2015). Conservatives, liberals, the trade union movement, and the world's first national labor government all supported this "white Australia" policy (Jupp 1995, 207–208). Rates

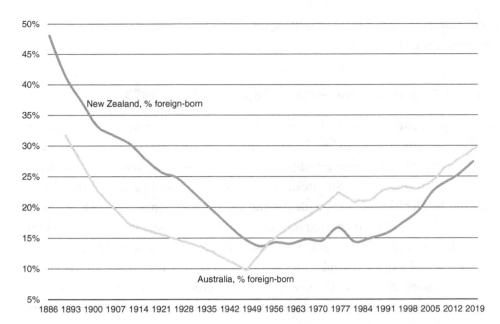

FIGURE 4.2. Foreign-Born as a Percentage of the Population, Australia and New Zealand, 1886–2019

SOURCES. Australian Bureau of Statistics and Statistics New Zealand, multiple sources; Gamlen's analysis.

NOTE: As population figures for New Zealand are from censuses at 5-to 10-year intervals, other years are interpolated.

of net migration slowed and Australia and New Zealand became known as Britain's "white dominions" in the Pacific (Bridge and Fedorowich 2003).

However, the immigration bust in this era was not only about immigration control. Despite their zealous racism, the colonial governments—with their weak infrastructures and limited autonomy—had much less control over immigration than governments today. It was normal, for instance, for immigrants to arrive without documents. As much or more than immigration control, the slowdown reflected falling supply and demand. Would-be emigrants faced a riskier international environment, with World War I, the Great Depression, racist totalitarian regimes, World War II, the Holocaust, and the atom bomb. Those who took the risk met growing hostility in settler societies marked by rising nativism, racial discrimination, and political opposition to non-white immigration—based on a complex of fears, including wartime paranoia about foreign "enemies within," as well as the perception that "cheap" Asian labor migrants would steal the jobs of Australian and New Zealand workers. Against this background, immigration to Australia and New Zealand remained low until after World War II—but immigration control was more a function of contemporary society, culture, politics, and economy rather than of formal state immigration control.

The End of Empire and the Push to Populate: 1946–1973

Britain's empire, battered by both world wars, continued to crumble. The colonies themselves were also itching to break free. Canada was first, establishing its own citizenship in 1946. India broke free and partitioned the following year. Both Australia and New Zealand enacted the Statute of Westminster (in 1942 and 1948, respectively), establishing full legislative independence and separate national citizenships. As its empire slipped away, Britain enacted legislation intended to hold its peoples together, automatically granting citizens of Commonwealth countries a new status, "citizenship of the United Kingdom and colonies," created by the 1948 British Nationality Act (Hansen 2000). A vestige of imperial free movement persisted in the de facto open border between Australia and New Zealand, which was later formalized in the 1973 Trans-Tasman Travel Arrangement. But the newly independent settler societies now urgently needed population growth to survive, and in this period "controlling immigration" meant that if immigrants wouldn't come of their own accord, they had to be assisted.

Alarmed at declining immigration after World War I, when population growth was considered the foundation of national economic and military strength, Australia resumed active recruitment. The Empire Settlement Scheme contributed to the arrival of some 300,000 new settlers during the 1920s (Phillips and Simon-Davies 2016). The Chifley government (1945–1949) began a program of mass migration under the slogan "populate or perish." Arthur Calwell, Australia's first immigration minister, endorsed Britain as the main source. But when Britain couldn't supply enough immigrants, Australia quickly recruited postwar European refugees and assisted passage from the Netherlands, Germany, Malta, Italy, Greece, Spain, and elsewhere. Unassisted migration was also embraced. The Menzies government (1949–1967) welcomed skilled and family migrants from Asia, abolishing the dictation test in 1957. By 1967 various visas allowed increasing Asian immigration, and the residency requirement for Australian citizenship was slashed from fifteen to five years. Together these changes fueled Australia's largest-ever migration boom (Figure 4.3).

New Zealand's foreign-born population also dropped after World War II, and it remained less diverse than Australia's. A postwar Population Committee formed an assisted migration program, first from Britain and Ireland in 1947, then later from the Netherlands, which delivered 2,600 Dutch immigrants in its first year (1952) and over 10,000 at its peak in 1954 (Belamy 2008). Pacific immigration also spiked during

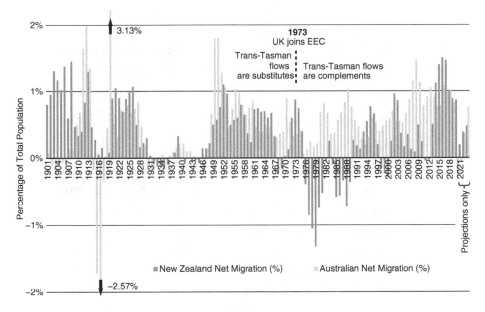

FIGURE 4.3. Net Migration as a Percentage of Total Population, New Zealand and Australia, 1901–2023
SOURCE: Multiple official sources, Gamlen's analysis.
NOTE: 2020–2023 data are official projections.

the 1970s, adding to an already substantial diaspora in New Zealand. Nonetheless, New Zealand's foreign-born population only began to fully revive and diversify after David Lange's Fourth Labour Government abolished the country's racist "traditional source country preferences" in 1987, as part of wholesale restructuring and liberalization of the economy. Contrary to its own mythmaking, New Zealand was not a race-relations paradise: it retained a white immigration policy for even longer than Australia.

The imperial migration system finally collapsed in 1973. Britain's preferential Commonwealth trading ties, once a source of its imperial strength, had become an unbearable cost. Britain severed these ties and joined the European Economic Community instead. The main source of antipodean export earnings evaporated, hitting particularly hard in New Zealand, which remained dependent on Britain both economically and culturally (Belich 2001b). Beginning in 1973, the small South Pacific archipelago began forging a more independent path, involving occasional defiance of Anglo-American doctrine (for example, over nuclear weapons) and a gradual reorientation toward the Asia-Pacific region. After withdrawing New Zealand troops from Vietnam and establishing diplomatic ties with China, Prime Minister Norman Kirk (1972–1974) declared in 1974 that "New Zealand has, in many ways, reached full nationhood. It stands on its own feet, it makes its own judgements, it charts its own course of action . . . [a]s a country of the Asian and Pacific region" (Kirk 1974). New Zealand's immigration system began changing to reflect this geopolitical shift.

Globalization, Diversification, and Multiculturalism: 1974–1995

The political and economic upheavals of the 1970s catalyzed sweeping changes to immigration policy in Australia and New Zealand. The oil shocks and global recession led to an era of economic transformation and rising globalization. Agriculture and manufacturing employed a shrinking share of Australian workers, while professional, scientific, technical services, health care, social assistance, education, and training industries were growing dramatically (Australian Bureau of Statistics 2020). Manufacturing's share of New Zealand's GDP halved from 26 percent to 13 percent between 1972 and 2009, while the share of finance, insurance, and business services almost doubled, from 15 percent to 29 percent (Statistics New Zealand 2012). The 1970s was also a decade of profound shifts in national identity, associated with Britain's withdrawal from Commonwealth trade, divisions over the ongoing Vietnam War, and fallout from the May 1968 social movements. In this climate, both Australia and New Zealand began to overhaul the race-based colonial-era "populate or perish" paradigm, replacing it with economic admission criteria and "multicultural" policies toward immigrant settlement.

As demand fell following the oil shocks, Australia dismantled its postwar system of assisted immigration through bilateral agreements with European countries. Unskilled immigration was slashed, and intake nosedived from 185,000 in 1969–1970 to 80,000 in 1974–1975. Though formally abolished in 1973 by the Whitlam government (1972–1975), the "white Australia" policy continued to operate in practice till well after the Vietnam War. Preference was given to "spouses, dependent children and aged or otherwise dependent parents . . . sponsored by residents of Australia"—the vast majority of them European (Richards 2008). Vietnamese refugee migration was restricted, and Laotian and Cambodian refugees, including many anti-Communists, were refused (Viviani and Lawe-Davies 1980). As Saigon fell in mid-April 1975, Whitlam told his immigration minister, Clyde Cameron, "I'm not having hundreds of fucking Vietnamese Balts coming into this country with their political and religious hatreds against us" (Cameron 1980, 233). And this attitude was not restricted to Whitlam: it was bipartisan and continued after his dismissal. The "white Australia" policy was finally put to rest only when, in deference to Australia's alliance with the United States, over 52,000 Vietnamese refugees were resettled in Australia between 1977 and 1982 (Stevens 2012, 526–541).

The overhaul of immigration priorities and the end of the "white Australia" policy allowed the evolution of a distinctive Australian model of multiculturalism. Seeded from Canada, where it emerged in the late 1960s and 1970s (Kymlicka 2003), the idea of multiculturalism gained influence in the Fraser government (1975–1983). In 1978, the government's Galbally Report on Migrant Services and Programs outlined a new multicultural approach to settlement, involving assistance to new migrants and refugees and a new multicultural Special Broadcasting Service (SBS). In 1987, the Hawke government (1983–1991) created the Office of Multicultural Affairs (OMA) within the Prime Minister's Office, signaling both the growing importance of multiculturalism and the government's desire to carefully manage it. As non-white immigration increased, and with it considerable anti-immigration sentiment, the Fraser and Hawke governments both prioritized issues of settlement and multiculturalism over immigrant recruitment and admission.

In the background, the policy focus was shifting to economics. In 1979, emulating Canada's immigration points system, Australia introduced the Numerical Multifactor Assessment System (NUMAS), which assessed applicants against demographic, education, employment, and family criteria (Hawkins 1991, 144–145; Meyers 2002, 129). A sharp break with past immigration policy, it allowed the Australian government to prioritize economically relevant traits rather than socio-cultural ones: officials could filter for younger migrants with existing work experience or qualifications, without needing to search and recruit them through an international network of staffed offices. Though issues of family reunification and multiculturalism took center stage under both Fraser and Hawke, behind the scenes a new system of controlling immigration was beginning to cohere around three main policy levers: the refugee quota, the immigration quota, and—importantly—the points-based economic criteria set out in NUMAS (Richards 2008, 275).

The new economic migration policy framework moved decisively to center stage when the Keating government (1991–1996) took power during a deep recession. For Keating, "tolerance and respect for diversity" and "access and equity regardless of ethnic origin" should continue, but multiculturalism was to be reframed as a "potentially huge national economic asset" (Keating 1992). "Productive diversity" became a catchword. In 1995, the Keating government subtly deprioritized the OMA by moving it to the Department of Immigration and Ethnic Affairs, and established a Committee of Inquiry into the Temporary Entry of Business People and Highly Skilled Specialists, chaired by the prominent Indian-born Australian businessman Neville Roach. Alongside NUMAS, the changes introduced as a result of the Roach Review (Roach 1995) made a major contribution to the migration boom after 1996, and particularly the rise of temporary migration (see next section).

Meanwhile, immigration to New Zealand was also globalizing and diversifying (Bedford 2005). Beginning in the 1950s there was growing Pacific immigration through various work, family, humanitarian, and colonial-era channels (Statistics New Zealand n.d.). Soon after World War II, large-scale Pacific labor migration to New Zealand began for the first time, through a wide range of channels (Bedford 2007). So long as demand for labor remained high, Pacific immigration was welcomed and there was a relaxed attitude toward people overstaying their visas. New Zealand's Pacific population grew from 3,600 in 1951 to over 50,000 in 1972 and to well over 65,000 at the 1976 census—over 2 percent of the total population (Ongley and Pearson 1995). But when demand fell, Pacific peoples quickly became scapegoats for rising unemployment, and the government infamously launched a barrage of "dawn raids" on Pacific communities harboring visa overstayers—an epoch seared into Pacific identity (Anae 1997). Nonetheless, New Zealand's Pacific population continued to grow, based on a high fertility rate and a diverse range of channels into New Zealand, including at various times assisted migration, work permits, family reunification, and—in the case of Cook Island Māori, Niueans, and Tokelauans—automatic right to New Zealand citizenship under the provisions of the 1948 New Zealand Citizenship Act. Large Pacific diaspora communities evolved in New Zealand from these roots: several Pacific nationalities are now more numerous in New Zealand than in their island homelands, and in the 2018 census, 8.1 percent of New Zealand's population identified with a Pacific ethnicity. Two-thirds of those who did were born in New Zealand (Statistics New Zealand 2019).

That said, multiculturalism took hold later and more lightly in New Zealand than in Australia. In the 1970s and 1980s New Zealand progressives, unlike their Australian counterparts, were focused not on multiculturalism but on biculturalism, to address Māori grievances regarding colonial breaches to the Treaty of Waitangi (Ritchie 1992). Following large-scale Māori protests, in 1975 the Treaty of Waitangi Act passed into law, establishing the Waitangi Tribunal to address Māori land claims and paving the way for the semi-constitutional recognition of Māori identity and rights in the 1980s. When the 1986 Immigration Review introduced multiculturalism into New Zealand policy discourse, many Māori sympathized with other ethnic minorities. But many also feared that hard-won recognition of their status as *tangata whenua* (the people of the land)—equal to the British Crown in the country's founding treaty—would be watered down if they became just one among many minorities clamoring for state recognition (Spoonley, Bedford, and Macpherson 2003; Pearson and Ongley 1996; Simon-Kumar 2019). This response tempered the growth of formal multiculturalism in New Zealand. Today the country is often described as multi-cultural in the sense of being home to many cultural groups. But to the extent that New Zealand government services target cultural groups, they still tend to follow a bicultural rather than a multicultural model.

Then came the 1986 Review of Immigration Policy and 1987 Immigration Act— a watershed. Until then, New Zealand had abandoned its colonial-era immigration policies more slowly than Australia, admitting fewer southern and eastern Europeans and opening up later to Asia. From 1970 to 1990, the foreign-born share of Australia's population hovered around 20 percent, while New Zealand's remained around 15 percent (Figure 4.2). New Zealand still maintained colonial-era race controls for more than a decade after the end of the "white Australia" policy (Trlin 1992). The 1987 act removed these "traditional source-country preferences," enabling New Zealand's overseas-born population to double between 1986 and 2006, from 500,000 to over 1 million people. The Asian-born population rose from 32,712 to 251,121, a sixfold increase (Spoonley and Bedford 2012, 85; Bedford 2002). And New Zealand's immigration policy drew closer to Australia's. A points system modeled on those of Australia and Canada was introduced in 1990–1991. Starting in 1992 New Zealand participated in the new Council of Australian Governments as a de facto seventh state in the Australian federal system, which allowed further synchronization of the countries' immigration policies (Bedford 2003).

Thus, 1974–1995 was a period of "rapid and radical" shifting from a race-based colonial-era immigration regime to an economic immigration system more oriented toward Asia and the Pacific (Spoonley and Bedford 2012, 94). The rapid changes met with significant resistance in both countries, particularly among the older age groups in the population. In 1988 John Howard, then leader of the Australian opposition, advocated curbing Asian immigration in line with "the capacity of the community to absorb" (Van Olsen and Errington 2008, 157). The Hawke government responded by strongly defending Australia's non-discriminatory admission policy and rejecting the main elements of the 1988 FitzGerald Review of Immigration Policy, which had advocated a shift from family reunification toward economic migration (Fitzgerald 1988). Meanwhile, in New Zealand, the "grey" (elderly) vote was galvanized by the populist politician Winston Peters, who won electoral support during the mid-1990s by complaining of an "Asian invasion"—and who continued this approach into the early 2000s, claiming immigration was "out of control" and that the country was being swamped by "alien cultures" (Bedford 2002, 9). As in the "emerging migration states" Hollifield writes of, immigration began shifting from the margins to the center of political debate in both countries.

The Second Great Migration Boom: 1996–2020

Beginning in the mid-1990s, both Australia and New Zealand entered a sustained period of growing migration unequaled since the nineteenth century. By 2017 net migration accounted for 64 percent of population growth in Australia, where almost half all residents either were born abroad or had at least one parent born abroad (Simon-Davies 2018). In New Zealand in 2014–2018, net migration added the equivalent of the entire population of the city of Wellington, accounting for 71 percent of population growth (Statistics New Zealand 2018). This was the height of the second great migration boom.

Cities received the most immigrants, despite decades of trying to divert immigration toward rural and regional centers through extra points and visa channels for applicants specifying a regional destination. In 1947, 62 percent of Australia's overseas-born lived in major urban areas (Hugo 1999). By 2016, 83 percent lived in capital cities alone (compared to 61 percent of the Australian-born) (Australian Government 2019). From 1981 to 2016 the foreign-born share of Melbourne's population grew from 29 percent to 40 percent, while Sydney's population grew from 28 percent to 43percent (Hugo 1999). In many suburbs of both cities the overseas-born share topped 50–60 percent. Almost 64 percent of Melbournians and 67 percent of Sydney-siders had at least one overseas-born parent. Urban diversity was also growing in New Zealand. From 1996 to 2018 the foreign-born share of Auckland's population grew from 37 percent to 42 percent (Statistics New Zealand 2014, 2020a). Some 51 percent of the overseas-born population lived there, but only 33 percent of the total population (Statistics New Zealand 2020b). This clustering of immigrants in larger cities also drove concerns about unsustainable population growth, lagging infrastructure, and urban congestion—which rose to the top of political agendas, driving infrastructure plans budgeted at over $100 billion (Australian Government 2019). However, these plans were called into question somewhat when the 2020 pandemic struck, accelerating a long-term trend toward remote work and sharply reducing commuter traffic.

During the second great migration boom, policy shifted even more definitively toward economic outcomes and "skills" (Bedford 2004), and all categories of immigration expanded: humanitarian, permanent, and especially temporary inflows. These trends are discussed in turn.

Humanitarian Migration

Both New Zealand and Australia accept humanitarian migration flows, having ratified the United Nations Convention on Refugees and 1967 Protocol. Australia has accepted more than 880,000 refugees since World War II and has participated in the

United Nations High Commissioner for Refugees (UNHCR) resettlement scheme since 1977—Australia's program is the world's third-largest, after the United States and Canada.[1] From 1990 to 2010 an average of 8,990 refugees and "special humanitarian" migrants were resettled in Australia every year, with larger numbers during crises such as the Vietnam War. Similarly, from 2015 to 2017 Australia granted 12,000 additional visas to Syrian and Iraqi refugees. Thus, the country prides itself on a refugee resettlement program that is generous by international standards, humane, fair, orderly, and compliant with international law.

However, Australia takes a very different approach to asylum seekers who arrive by boat without visas. Past surges have arrived from Vietnam (1976–1981), Indochina (1989–1998), and the Middle East (1999–2003). The Keating government (1991–1996) introduced mandatory detention for all boat arrivals after 224 mostly Cambodian asylum seekers arrived without visas in 1989–1990 (Phillips 2015). In August 2001, the Australian military boarded a Norwegian cargo ship, the *Tampa*, which was carrying 433 asylum seekers rescued in waters between Indonesia and Australia. The Howard government (1996–2007) turned the boat away. Howard's tough stance was domestically popular and buoyed him to reelection, after which he established extraterritorial detention and asylum-processing centers on Christmas Island and Nauru and on Manus Island in Papua New Guinea, to prevent asylum seekers from ever setting foot in Australia. The first Rudd government (2007–2010) abandoned this approach, known as the Pacific Solution, resulting in a large surge of boat arrivals in 2009–2013 (Figure 4.4).

Based partly on campaign promises to "stop the boats," Tony Abbott was elected prime minister in 2013 and launched Operation Sovereign Borders, a zero-tolerance campaign of naval interceptions, mandatory detention, offshore processing, and information blackouts surrounding the matter. The rationale is that treating asylum seekers harshly deters others. The UNHCR criticizes Australia's "punitive measures," which it says "can significantly impair . . . mental health and general well-being." The award-winning Kurdish Iranian novelist Behrouz Boochani, detained on Manus Island from 2013 to 2017, called it "the island of the damned" (Baker 2019). Boat arrivals are referred to as "illegal maritime arrivals" and cast as line jumpers who risk lives and embolden human traffickers (Richards 2008, 263). Refugee advocacy groups contend that maritime arrivals are not illegal because everyone has a right to apply for asylum under international law.

New Zealand's approach to humanitarian migration has in some ways been the mirror image of Australia's. For example, it has periodically offered to accept the asylum seekers Australia will not take. It took 131 of the asylum seekers from the *Tampa* in 2001, and offered to resettle 150 refugees from Manus and Nauru in 2017, but was

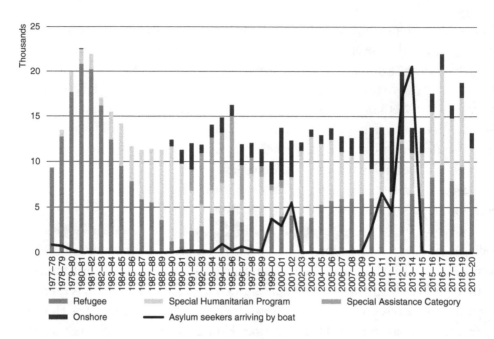

FIGURE 4.4. Australian Humanitarian Program Visa Grants, 1977–1978 to 2019–2020

SOURCE: Australian Government, Gamlen's analysis. Note that "Asylum seekers arriving by boat" are sometimes captured in the "Onshore" category, but other times not. This series is therefore treated separately from other categories, rather than cumulatively.

rejected by the Turnbull-Morrison government (2015–present). Boochani himself was granted refugee status in New Zealand in July 2020. Such offers have contributed to a widespread international perception that New Zealand is more generous toward humanitarian migration than Australia. This is perhaps too simplistic: unlike Australia, New Zealand receives zero boat arrivals because of its remote location. It is separated from its nearest major landmass (Australia) by over 2,500 kilometers of open sea, and can afford to appear generous occasionally without fear of being overwhelmed. Meanwhile, New Zealand's refugee intake has always been less generous than Australia's on a per capita basis. Only 4,582 World War II refugees came from 1949 to 1952. It joined the UNHCR resettlement program a decade later than Australia, in 1987, with a far smaller per capita quota than Australia (Figure 4.5). New Zealand did institute two unique refugee categories, for solo parents and for children with disabilities, and its humanitarian intake includes a quota of 1,100 Samoans and a "Pacific Access Category" quota (established in 2002), comprising 75 iKiribati, 75 Tuvaluans, 250 Tongans, and 250 Fijians, all selected by ballot. But it was still only accepting 750 refugees per year in 2015.

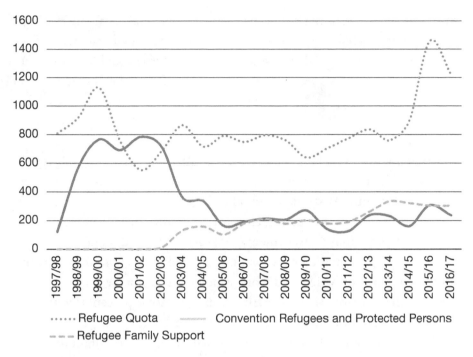

FIGURE 4.5. New Zealand, Number of Residence Grants Under International and Humanitarian Policies, by Source Country and Category, 1997/98–2016/17
SOURCE: Authors' analysis of Migration Trends 2016–17 (residents), Ministry of Business, Innovation, and Employment.

Things shifted briefly in 2013: the Key government (2008–2017) aped Australia, introducing "mass arrivals" legislation that allowed detention of undocumented asylum seekers arriving in groups of thirty or more, to send "a clear message to potential people smuggling ventures that New Zealand is not a soft touch" (Woodhouse 2013). This helped fuel a backlash movement demanding a doubling of the refugee quota, which came to a head during the 2015 Mediterranean refugee crisis. Under public pressure to support multilateral humanitarian efforts, Key's government announced a token increase. The Ardern government (2017–present) then raised the quota to 1,000, committed to reaching 1,500 during its first term, and abolished rules limiting resettlement from Africa and the Middle East. However, just as New Zealand has escaped criticism for a whites-only immigration policy that lasted much longer than Australia's, New Zealand has not quite fairly earned an international reputation for greater generosity toward refugees. Australia helps a great many people through humanitarian migration while angering many and hurting a few through its severe, utilitarian approach to the risks of irregular migration. New Zealand faces far less risk and helps far fewer people but has made symbolic gestures of compassion that gain international praise. On both sides of the Tasman, policymakers are increasingly aware of both growing forced migration pressures, including climate change and the economic fallout of the 2020 pandemic, and shrinking international humanitarian coordination over migration issues, despite the signing of two global compacts on migration in 2018.

Permanent Migration

Permanent immigration flows, long the mainstay of Australia's and New Zealand's migration systems, changed markedly in both size and composition during the second great migration boom. Australia's annual quota of permanent residency visas grew from 70,000 to 160,000 under the Howard government (1996–2007) and to 190,000 under the Rudd-Gillard government (2007–2013). Howard mandated that 60 percent of permanent visas should be economic and only 30 percent family; the family stream's share of visas duly dropped from 55 percent to 29 percent from 1994 to 2006, while the skilled stream's share rose from 29 percent to 68 percent (Figure 4.6).

Similar shifts occurred in New Zealand. A decade after the 1987 act, large and consistent net migration losses had been replaced with historic net migration gains

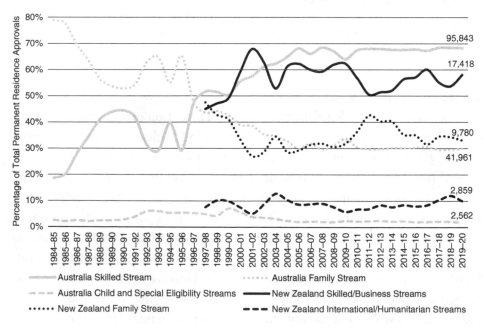

FIGURE 4.6. Permanent Immigration to Australia and New Zealand, by Stream, 1984–85 to 2019–20

SOURCE: Australian Department of Home Affairs; New Zealand Ministry of Business, Innovation and Employment, Gamlen's analysis. Australian data on permanent residence represent visa grants, while New Zealand data reflect arrivals.

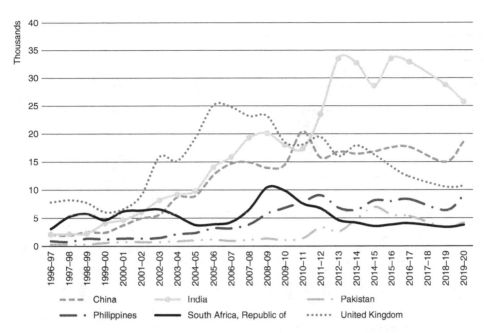

FIGURE 4.7. Australian Skilled Migration Stream Outcomes, by Selected Citizenships, 1996–1997 to 2019–2020
SOURCE: Australian Government, Gamlen's analysis.
NOTE: 2017–2018 figures are interpolated.

(Figure 4.3). New Zealand also adopted the new 60/30 economic-to-family rule, introducing new visas for entrepreneurs, investors, businesspeople, and "talented" people and tweaking English-language requirements. The family stream rallied briefly around 2012, as family applicants with sufficient personal or family wealth were fast-tracked. But the skilled/business stream soon recovered, accounting for 60 percent of all permanent immigrants by 2017–2018. Many of these new permanent economic immigrants came from new source countries, notably India and China (Figures 4.7 and 4.8). From 2007 to 2017, the United Kingdom fell from the top source of new permanent residents to a distant third place in both countries.

In both countries, the shift from selection by origin to selection by economic potential has been effected through tweaks to the points systems. In 2003 New Zealand introduced an Expression of Interest (EOI) procedure; this dramatically reduced processing time and application backlogs, which had previously let other countries poach the best applicants while they waited. Applicants now register via a simplified EOI form, and those with the highest number of points are issued an invitation to apply in full. Those with fewer points may be invited to apply for a two-year "work-to-residence" visa, providing the opportunity to "demonstrate their ability to settle and gain relevant employment" (immigration minister Lianne Dalziel, quoted in

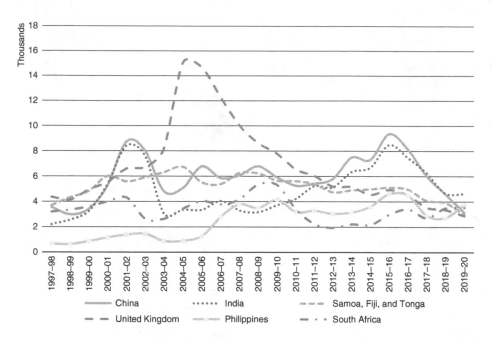

FIGURE 4.8. New Zealand Permanent Immigration, by Source Country, 1997–1998 to 2019–2020
SOURCE: New Zealand Ministry of Business, Innovation and Employment, Gamlen's analysis.

Bedford and Spoonley 2014, 895). Australia and Canada, the traditional benchmarks for New Zealand's immigration policies, have since adopted similar systems (Martin 2014). Over time there has been decreasing emphasis on generic skills and increasing emphasis on employer sponsorship, based on increasing evidence that immigrants performed better on a range of settlement outcomes if they secured a job before arriving, rather than after.

Temporary Migration

The two-track EOI system relates to a second trend: the rise of temporary migration. Both countries had occasionally used temporary permits to control immigration from "racially undesirable" countries during acute labor shortages. Australia had used them to regulate Chinese admission during the 1920s and 1930s (Markus 1995, 356), and New Zealand had used them in the 1950s and 1960s for Pacific labor migration. But permanent migration remained the dominant paradigm until the 1990s.

In 1995, the Roach Report argued for a more flexible immigration system: Australia must import the changing skills and innovation needed by knowledge economies, but should not resort to a European "guest-worker program" (Sherrell 2019, 38). Consequently, in 1997 the Howard government introduced a temporary skilled migrant visa—the 457 Visa—allowing employers to sponsor migrants in eligible occupations and skills categories, provided they had adequate English skills. From 2010 to 2020, temporary visas came to outstrip permanent visas by a factor of three or four to one (see Figure 4.9). The 457 Visas in particular came under fire for over-empowering employers, weakening unions, and enabling worker exploitation—concerns encapsulated in the title of Peter Mare's 2016 book *Not Quite Australian: How Temporary Migration Is Changing the Nation* (Mares 2016). Meanwhile, New Zealand's employer-sponsored Essential Skills Visa mimicked the 457 Visa, with its high- and low-skill distinction, skills-shortage list, and requirement to show that no existing resident could fill the role. From April 2017, temporary migrants in "low-skilled" occupations could receive a one-year visa, twice renewable, and then had to leave New Zealand for at least a year before applying again (Bedford and Didham 2018).

Since the late 2000s, temporary migration policies in both countries have been influenced by United Nations–level consensus surrounding "migration and

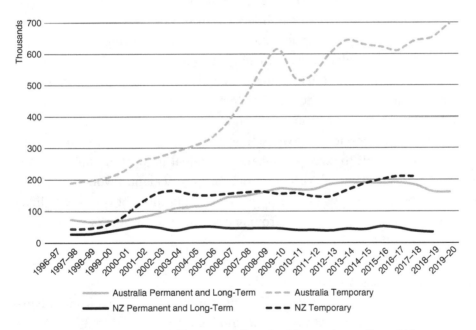

FIGURE 4.9. Permanent vs. Temporary Immigration to Australia and New Zealand, 1997–1998 to 2019–2020

SOURCE: New Zealand Ministry of Business, Innovation and Employment, authors' analysis; Department of Home Affairs, Parliamentary Library, authors' analysis. Australian temporary immigration is the sum of international students, working holidaymakers, and temporary business visa holders. New Zealand temporary immigration is the sum of international students, working holidaymakers, and essential skills visa holders. Australian permanent immigration is the sum of skilled, family, child, and special eligibility streams. New Zealand permanent immigration is the sum of skilled/business, family, and international/humanitarian streams.

development" (Annan 2006). This has focused on shared benefits of temporarily "circulating" migrants from countries with high unemployment to countries with seasonal labor shortages. New Zealand's Recognised Seasonal Employer (RSE) program received global attention for bringing in Pacific island citizens to work in the agricultural and horticultural industries so that they could send remittances and savings back home (Gibson and McKenzie 2014). Australia's small Seasonal Worker Program later emulated the RSE program. By 2020 the two programs granted a combined total of over 26,000 visa grants per year, generating substantial remittance flows to developing Pacific island states (Lawton 2019; Curtain et al. 2018). These programs have become a model for a new generation of guest-worker programs around the world.

However, the biggest temporary migration channels are for those on "working holidays" and international students. People on working holidays began coming to Australia in the 1970s under agreements aimed at fostering cultural exchange with the United Kingdom, Ireland, and Canada (1975), followed soon by Japan (1980), South Korea (1995), and Malta (1996). These agreements allowed young people (aged eighteen to thirty-five), regardless of skill level, to travel in the country for twelve months and work, with restrictions, for some of their time. Working-holiday agreements have since proliferated: forty-two are now in place, and an additional thirteen are under negotiation. They have also changed focus, from cultural exchange to labor market management. In the mid-2000s, the Howard government allowed working-holiday participants in Australia to extend their stay for a year if they choose agricultural employers. A further one-year extension was allowed beginning in 2018, bringing the total time available to three years—and consolidating working-holiday labor as a vital force within Australia's rural economies. New Zealand's working-holiday program also expanded rapidly. From 2006 to 2020 the number of working-holiday agreements rose from 23 to over 40, and from 1997 to 2017, the number of participants increased from 6,761 to over 70,000.

International students had also been coming to Australia at least since the 1950s, when Asian students began arriving under the Colombo Plan. By 1983, there were 13,700 overseas students attending Australian institutions of higher education. During the 1980s, governments of both Australia and New Zealand reduced funding to universities but allowed them to recoup losses by setting their own fees. The sector began aggressively recruiting international students, turning them into a major export industry. New Zealand's share of the "international student market" rose from almost nothing in 2000 to some 3 percent in 2004 (Chiou 2014). International students contributed significantly to the historic net migration figures from 2016–2017 onward, compensating for a dip in temporary business visas around 2012–2013 in the wake of Australia's mining boom. In addition to propping up universities, numbers

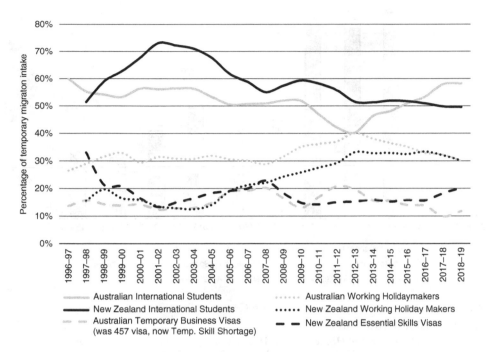

FIGURE 4.10. Temporary Visa Grants to Australia and New Zealand, 1997–1998 to 2018–2019

source: New Zealand Ministry of Business, Innovation and Employment, authors' analysis; Department of Home Affairs, Parliamentary Library, authors' analysis.

of these students grew to form a major portion of the labor force, particularly in the retail and hospitality sectors of both countries, where they often worked over their allowed hours and fell vulnerable to employer exploitation. The sustainability of this model has been questioned further in the wake of the 2020 pandemic, as temporary migrants are concentrated in many of the industries hardest hit by lockdowns and social distancing regulations.

International study and other temporary visas are now often treated as a first step toward permanent immigration—the two-step immigration path mentioned previously (Hawthorne 2010). From 2000 to 2014 about 15 percent of international students in Australia transitioned to permanent residence (Figure 4.11). Since 2013–2014 the prospect of post-study work visas has driven international student migration to new heights. In the three years beginning in November 2013, the number of people remaining in Australia from a previous temporary visa tripled to 46,000. After a sharp increase from 2010–2011 to 2012–2013, Australia quickly imitated the New Zealand EOI approach, thus restricting numbers of two-step migrants. From 2006–2007 to 2011–2012, almost 130,000 prior temporary-visa holders were granted a residency

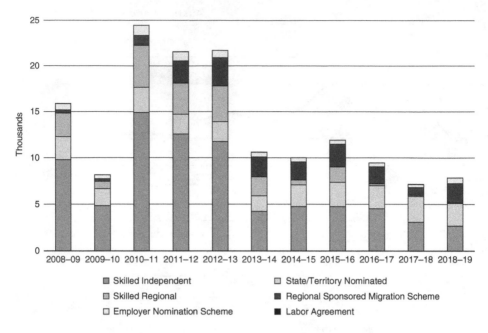

FIGURE 4.11. Australian Permanent Migration Grants to Former International Students, 2008–2009 to 2018–2019

SOURCE: Australian Department of Home Affairs, Gamlen's analysis. These figures exclude multi-step temporary visas (e.g., if someone moved from a student visa to a temporary work visa to a permanent visa).

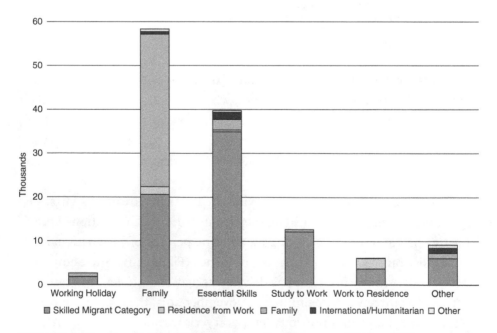

FIGURE 4.12. New Zealand Visa Pathways for Temporary Workers Who Transitioned to Residence by Work Visa Type and Resident Visa Type (2006–07 to 2011–2012 Cohorts Combined)

SOURCE: Authors' analysis of Table 5.6, Migration Trends 2016-17, New Zealand Ministry of Business, Innovation and Employment.

visa, accounting for 49 percent of all residency visas granted in the period (Bedford et al. 2010). The two-step migration trend is a major driver of the expansion in temporary inflows to New Zealand and Australia, with the "skilled migrant" residency category now the dominant form of transitioning to residency for all temporary migrants except family members.

Trans-Tasman Migration

Alongside any discussion of temporary migration in the South Pacific, we need to discuss the rise of a population of permanent migrants who hold restricted residence rights—namely, New Zealanders in Australia. From the 1970s, an increasing share of Australia's net migration came from New Zealand, which experienced net emigration in all but one of the fourteen years from 1976 to 1989 (inclusive), with losses totaling 236,959 across the period. The country was losing, on average, half a percent worth of its total population every year, mostly to Australia; in 1977–1980 alone the country lost 126,000 net migrants. Whereas migration flows to Australia and New Zealand had previously been complementary, they now became substitutes—when one gained, the other lost—and the balance tipped decisively toward Australia. Between the censuses of 1971 and 2016–2018, the number of Australians in New Zealand rose modestly from 44,080 to 75,700—an increase of 72 percent in just under half a century. But in the same period, the number of New Zealanders living in Australia rose from 74,000 to 518,460—an increase of over 600 percent. Fears of a New Zealand "brain drain" grew in the 1980s (Reserve Bank of New Zealand 1986) but were dismissed by Prime Minister Robert Muldoon, who famously quipped that the New Zealanders moving to Australia raised the average IQ of both countries.

Australia took an opposite and equally exaggerated stance, complaining of Kiwi (and especially Māori and Pasifika) "dole bludgers" (welfare recipients) at Bondi Beach, and eventually curtailing the reciprocal health and social security entitlements of New Zealanders. Race was a factor; as Bedford writes, "Australia was prepared to accept, with reluctance, entry of Māori migrants on the same basis as New Zealanders of European heritage, but extending uninhibited rights of entry to Pacific Island (and Asian) New Zealanders long remained a bridge too far for Australia" (Bedford 2019, 216; cf. Hamer 2007; Hamer 2014, 93). They were still useful to Australia as a reserve pool of laborers, and could still live and work freely in Australia on a "Special Category Visa." But they now lacked any social safety net, and could be deported for bad behavior. There has since emerged a cohort of Australians born in Australia to New Zealand parents but who, unbeknownst to them, may lack Australian citizenship (Gamlen 2007; Hamer 2007). When they commit crimes, Australia now deports them to New Zealand, where they have never lived and have no connections (Weber and Powell 2018). In February 2020, New Zealand prime minister Jacinda Ardern remarked bluntly that "Australia is well within its rights to deport individuals who break your laws; New Zealand does the same. But we have a simple request: send back Kiwis, genuine Kiwis. Do not deport your people and your problems."

The Politics of Immigration Boom

In both Australia and New Zealand, the latest immigration boom has led to a "policy gap" characteristic of migration states, in which politicians claim to oppose immigration while enacting policies to increase it, or vice versa (McNevin 2007, 2010; McKenzie and Hasmath 2013; Walsh 2015). On one hand, Australia has a strong anti-immigrant constituency. Anti-immigration arguments find polite expression in a continuing post–World War II debate about "population growth," in which the case to "populate or perish" has gradually given way to concerns about "congestion" and "environmental carrying capacity." Each new wave of immigrants is still targeted by openly racist newspaper headlines and political scaremongering about "ethnic gangs"—the latest being humanitarian migrants from Africa (Windle 2008). The most vocal anti-immigrant politician is populist Pauline Hanson, leader of Australia's One Nation political party, who infamously opined, "I and most Australians want our immigration policy radically reviewed and that of multiculturalism abolished. I believe we are in danger of being swamped by Asians" (Hanson 1996). It would be an exaggeration, however, to describe Hanson as an outlier in Australian politics.

On the other hand, despite its serious problems with racism, Australia remains one of the most diverse and successful multicultural countries in the world. Concerns about congestion and environmental carrying capacity have not driven major immigration restrictions, but rather have resulted in plans to divert immigration toward rural areas and regional towns, where outmigrating Australian youths have left labor shortages—trends that appear to have accelerated during the 2020 pandemic, as urban populations have sought larger blocks of land for lockdowns and remote working. Meanwhile, for all Hanson's tirades against it, multiculturalism remains deeply institutionalized at every level in Australia, from local to state and federal governments. In sum, Australia has developed a version of Hollifield's "liberal paradox," in which politicians talk tough to appease anti-immigration groups while keeping the country open to immigration for business reasons.

New Zealand, too, has sometimes displayed the liberal paradox. In 2013 the Key government enacted a tough-looking Australian-style policy against mass boat arrivals of asylum seekers. Such arrivals were unrealistic, but the policy had symbolic importance: it was flattering to Australian allies and it burnished Key's credentials with right-leaning anti-immigrant groups. Meanwhile, however, Key's government oversaw the highest net inflows in the country's history, designed to turbocharge the economy and rebuild the earthquake-stricken city of Christchurch. Peaking with a net inflow of 70,588 in 2016, equivalent to 1.5 percent of the population, immigration drove rapid inflation in real estate prices, particularly in Auckland, leading to concerns not only about the country's potential exposure to a property bubble but also to debates about foreign ownership of land, housing affordability, social inequality, congestion and failing infrastructure—particularly in Auckland.

However, in New Zealand the policy gap has sometimes worked the opposite way. In 2015 the opposition Labour Party saw an opportunity to exploit concerns about Key's immigration boom by courting the anti-immigrant vote. They promised to "cut immigration by tens of thousands" per year, and published research showing that almost 40 percent of Auckland homebuyers had "Chinese-sounding names." But the approach divided rather than united the Labour Party's pro- and anti-immigration factions, and party leader Andrew Little was replaced by his thirty-seven-year-old deputy, Jacinda Ardern, just seven weeks out from the 2017 election.

Ardern took the exact opposite approach: instead of talking tough on immigration while remaining open, she looked very open while acting fairly closed. On one hand, she was everything Labour's pro-immigration liberal elites asked for: a young woman with a pro-diversity outlook who could satisfy their fixation with *not* being seen as a party of faintly bigoted-sounding middle-aged white men. On the other hand, Arden retained Little's restrictionist immigration policy, and allied with the anti-immigrant New Zealand First Party, offering their leader, Winston Peters, the position of deputy prime minister and minister of foreign affairs. With Ardern at the helm, the party's share of the popular vote rose from below 24 percent under Little to almost 37 percent in the election, giving them control of forty-five seats in the legislature. The National Party won fifty-eight seats, but Ardern's coalition of Labour, the Greens (seven seats), and New Zealand First (nine seats) controlled a majority and thus formed the next government. Instead of a liberal paradox, the Ardern coalition's immigration policy gap created what we might call an *illiberal* paradox: rather than feigning toughness, they feigned openness to immigration, and in this way they united what Aristide Zolberg called "strange bedfellows" into an unlikely majority (Zolberg 2009).

The Next Migration Bust?

The global financial crisis of 2008 signaled a turning point in global economic fortunes, but it took several years for this to translate into immigration to Australia and

New Zealand—partly because the banking systems of both countries were relatively insulated from the crisis. However, the rising anti-immigrant sentiment and growing resistance to global trade and finance that have characterized the post-crisis period have seeped into the South Pacific during the mid-2010s. As shown in Figure 4.1 permanent and long-term immigration flows to both countries peaked just after the middle of the decade and have declined sharply since. The final years of the 2010s mark the beginning of the end, but it is the COVID-19 pandemic of 2020, with its complete lockdowns on all forms of mobility and the prospect of long-term migration restrictions, that marks the decisive end of the second great migration boom in Australian and New Zealand history.

What does the future hold for migration in the South Pacific after the 2020 Pandemic? Will Australia and New Zealand curtail labor migration in order to reduce native unemployment, which has skyrocketed during lockdown? Will would-be migrants to and from this region wait for a less risky moment to fulfill their plans, or be forced to move by the dire economic impacts of the pandemic? Will anti-immigrant sentiment continue to grow, with migrants and minorities being used as scapegoats for the spread of the disease? Will politics in the region follow the authoritarian-populist trends currently seen in the United States and United Kingdom, and lead to similar efforts to suppress diversity? Will migration restrictions continue to proliferate globally, reducing the overall volume of migration to and from this part of the world? Will Australia and New Zealand manage to form a trans-Tasman "travel bubble," and how will the "air bridges" and "travel corridors" emerging between new clusters of countries affect global production and supply chains? Will international student migration ever recover, or will Australian and New Zealand universities have to fundamentally revise their current business models? At the urban scale, will commuter travel decline as more and more people work from home, taking advantage of unprecedented information and communications technologies? Will such new patterns of immobility reshape cities, reducing demand for inner-city commercial real estate and increasing demand for residential properties in rural and regional areas suitable for telecommuting? Will the age-specific mortality impacts of the pandemic shunt demographic and mobility transitions in new directions, altering dependency ratios and/or changing the pace or direction of urbanization? At the time of writing in early 2021, the answers remain to be seen.

Conclusions

Whatever the future holds, Australia and New Zealand are undoubtedly migration states. Both were formed by immigrants who became indigenous peoples between

700 and 65,000 years ago. Both were transformed by British colonization in the modern period. Both grew ever more dependent on white settlers to fuel population growth even as they became more independent of Britain in the twentieth century. And both have diversified their selection of immigrants since the 1970s in order to sustain economic growth. As a result of this history, Australia and New Zealand have evolved expansive and sophisticated institutional systems for controlling immigration, designed to maintain socio-economic stability while managing immigration flows that often exceed 1 percent of the population each year—an extraordinarily high rate by international standards. Indeed, in these countries, government migration control has been more about proactively recruiting immigrants than about turning people away. A migration system dominated by permanent colonial settlement has transformed into one dominated by temporary and step-wise migration, and the colonial goals of nation-building and race-based immigrant recruitment have given way to the goals of economic management via skills-based recruitment—but the key point is that recruitment remains the focus of immigration control. Governments increasingly find themselves in a liberal paradox, playing off pro- and anti-migration factions against each other by promising one thing and doing another when it comes to migration policy. But controlled immigration has always been central to the identity of the nation and the purpose of the state.

However, studying immigration control in Australia and New Zealand suggests a need to modify the concept of the "migration state." In theory, migration states are discrete, sealed units, but in practice, Australia and New Zealand are fragments of an imperial conglomeration that formally existed until the mid- to late twentieth century, and they remain joined by an open border today. In theory, migration states are competitive strategic actors, and sometimes Australia and New Zealand have competed on migration issues, such as when Australia cut entitlements for New Zealanders in Australia or began deporting Australian criminals with New Zealand passports. But much more often the two countries collude rather than compete. New Zealand immigration ministers and officials routinely participate alongside Australian state governments in Australian councils, forums, and meetings concerning immigration policies. Immigration control in these two countries has evolved symbiotically—and other countries, especially Canada, have been part of this symbiosis. In theory, migration states treat migration as an issue of "high politics," along with matters of security and diplomacy where reasons of state outweigh moral and legal considerations. In practice, the opposite is true in Australia and New Zealand: as the periodization of this chapter suggests, there have only been half a dozen or so major politically driven changes to migration policy in the last two centuries. Most legislation has tinkered around the edges of existing political settlement: business as usual, carried out by professional migration experts in a large, sophisticated migration bureaucracy that is well integrated not only across branches of government but includes key sections of the academy, the mainstream press, and civil society. They are migration states not because migration is part of high politics but because it is pre-political: immigration is fundamental to national identity, and migration management is fundamental to the machinery of state.

This matters not least because it means Australia and New Zealand have almost entirely avoided the political convulsions over migration currently occurring elsewhere in the world. In 2016 about 14 percent of the United Kingdom's population was born abroad: fears of "out-of-control" migration drove the country to leave the European Union. In the United States, which has a similar share of foreign-born residents, Donald Trump was elected to the presidency in 2016 over similar anti-immigrant hysteria. The foreign-born share of total population in these countries has averaged more than 20 percent for over a hundred years, has often risen well above 25 percent, and has never fallen below 10 percent. Yet most people in both Australia and New Zealand view immigration positively (Spoonley and Gendall 2010), and neither country has ever experienced a political conflagration over migration like those currently occurring across the Western world. A great deal of credit for this is due to the sophisticated migration management systems these countries have evolved over the past two centuries. In Australia and New Zealand, immigration control is now the preserve of mandarins, not emperors.

Note

1. Most refugees living in developing countries. "Resettled" refugees are the small fraction of refugees who have been transferred "from an asylum country to another State that has agreed to admit them and ultimately grant them permanent settlement" (UNHCR n.d.).

References

Anae, M. 1997. "Towards a NZ-Born Samoan Identity: Some Reflections on 'Labels.'" *Pacific Health Dialog* 4, no. 2: 128–137.

Annan, K. 2006. "Address of Mr. Kofi Annan, Secretary-General, to the High-Level Dialogue of the United Nations General Assembly on International Migration and Development." New York, September 14, 2006.

Atkinson, David C. 2015. "The White Australia Policy, the British Empire, and the World." *Britain and the World* 8, no. 2: 204–224.

Australian Bureau of Statistics. 2020. "Labour Force Australia, Detailed." Series no. 6291.0.

Australian Government. 2019. *Planning for Australia's Future Population*. Canberra: Australian Government.

Baker, N. 2019. "'A Victory for Humanity': Manus Island Refugee Behrouz Boochani Wins Major Literary Prize." SBS News, February 1, 2019. https://www.sbs.com.au/news/a-victory-for-humanity-manus-island-refugee-behrouz-boochani-wins-major-literary-prize.

Banner, S. 2005. "Why Terra Nullius? Anthropology and Property Law in Early Australia." *Law and History Review* 23, no. 1: 95–131.

Bedford, R. 2002. "Contested Ground: The Politicisation of Immigration and Belonging." *New Zealand Journal of Geography* 114, no. 1: 8–16.

Bedford, R. 2003. "New Zealand: The Politicization of Immigration." *Migration Information Source*, January 1, 2003.

Bedford, R. 2004. "The Quiet Revolution: Transformations in Migration Policies, Flows and Outcomes, 1999–2004." *New Zealand Geographer* 60, no. 2: 58–62.

Bedford, R. 2005. "International Migration and Globalization: The Transformation of New Zealand's Migration System Since the Mid-1980s." In *Sovereignty Under Siege: Globalization and New Zealand*, edited by R. Patman and C. Rudd, 129–156. Aldershot: Ashgate.

Bedford, R. 2007. "Pasifika Mobility: Pathways, Circuits and Challenges in the 21st Century." Report for the Pasifika Project, Institute of Policy Studies, Wellington. https://www.academia.edu/48372224/Pasifika_Mobility_Pathways_Circuits_and_Challenges_in_the_21_ST_Century.

Bedford, R. 2019. "Australasia and the Pacific Islands." In *The SAGE Handbook of International Migration*, edited by C. Inglis, W. Li, and B. Khadria, chap. 21. London: SAGE.

Bedford, R., and R. Didham. 2018. "Immigration: An Election Issue That Has Yet to Be Addressed?" *Kōtuitui: New Zealand Journal of Social Sciences Online* 13, no. 2: 177–194.

Bedford, R., E. Ho, and C. Bedford. 2010. "Pathways to Residence in New Zealand, 2003–2010." *New Zealand and International Migration: A Digest and Bibliography* 5: 1–49.

Bedford, R., and P. Spoonley. 2014. "Competing for Talent: Diffusion of an Innovation in New Zealand's Immigration Policy." *International Migration Review* 48, no. 3: 891–911.

Belich, J. 1986. *The Victorian Interpretation of Racial Conflict: The Maori, the British, and the New Zealand Wars*. Montreal: McGill-Queen's University Press.

Belich, J. 2001a. *Making Peoples: A History of the New Zealanders, from Polynesian Settlement to the End of the Nineteenth Century*. Honolulu: University of Hawaii Press.

Belich, J. 2001b. *Paradise Reforged: A History of the New Zealanders from the 1880s to the Year 2000*. Honolulu: University of Hawaii Press.

Belich, J. 2009. *Replenishing the Earth: The Settler Revolution and the Rise of the Angloworld*. New York: Oxford University Press.

Bellamy, P. 2008. "Immigration Chronology: Selected Events 1840–2008." Parliamentary Library Research Paper 2008/01.

Boswell, C. 2007. "Theorizing Migration Policy: Is There a Third Way?" *International Migration Review* 41, no. 1: 75–100.

Bridge, C., and K. Fedorowich. 2003. "Mapping the British World." *Journal of Imperial and Commonwealth History* 31, no. 2: 1–15.

Cameron, C. 1980. *China, Communism and Coca Cola*. Melbourne: Hill of Content.

Castles, S. 2004. "Why Migration Policies Fail." *Ethnic and Racial Studies* 27, no. 2: 205–227.

Castles, S., E. Vasta, and D. Ozkul. 2014. "A Classical Immigration Country in Transition." In *Controlling Immigration: A Global Perspective*, 3rd ed., edited by J. F. Hollifield, P. L. Martin, and P. Orrenius, 128–150. Stanford: Stanford University Press.

Chiou, B. 2014. "International Education, Student Migration and Government Policy: A Comparative Study of Australia and New Zealand." PhD dissertation, Auckland University of Technology.

Crosby, R. D. 2017. *The Musket Wars: A History of Inter-Iwi Conflict, 1806–1845*. Auckland: Oratia Books.

Curtain, R., M. Dornan, S. Howes, and H. Sherrell. 2018. "Pacific Seasonal Workers: Learning from the Contrasting Temporary Migration Outcomes in Australian and New Zealand Horticulture." *Asia and the Pacific Policy Studies* 5, no. 3: 462–480.

Czaika, M., and H. De Haas. 2013. "The Effectiveness of Immigration Policies." *Population and Development Review* 39, no. 3: 487–508.

Department of Labour and Immigration. 1975. *1788–1975: Australia and Immigration*. Canberra: Australian Government Publishing Service.

Fitzgerald, S. 1988. "Immigration: A Commitment to Australia." Report of the Committee to Advise on Australia's Immigration Policies.

Freeman, G. P. 1994. "Can Liberal States Control Unwanted Migration?" *Annals of the American Academy of Political and Social Science* 534, no. 1: 17–30.

Gamlen, A. 2007. "Making Hay While the Sun Shines: Envisioning New Zealand's State-Diaspora Relations." *Policy Quarterly* 3, no. 4: 12–21.

Gibson, J., and D. McKenzie. 2014. "The Development Impact of a Best Practice Seasonal Worker Policy." *Review of Economics and Statistics* 96, no. 2: 229–243.

Grace, P., I. Ramsden, and J. Dennis, eds. 2001. *The Silent Migration: Ngāti Pōneke Young Māori Club, 1937–1948: Stories of Urban Migration*. Wellington: Huia Publishers.

Hamer, D. 1990. *New Towns in the New World: Images and Perceptions of the Nineteenth-Century Urban Frontier*. New York: Columbia University Press.

Hamer, P. 2007. *Māori in Australia: Ngā Māori i Te Ao Moemoeā*. Wellington: Te Puni Kokiri.

Hamer, P. 2014. "'Unsophisticated and Unsuited': Australian Barriers to Pacific Islander Immigration from New Zealand." *Political Science* 66, no. 2: 98–118.

Hansen, R. 2000. *Citizenship and Immigration in Postwar Britain*. New York: Oxford University Press.

Hanson, P. 1996. "Maiden Speech." *Commonwealth of Australia, Parliamentary Debates (1st Session–2nd Period)*, 3860–3863.

Hawkins, F. 1991. *Critical Years in Immigration: Canada and Australia Compared*, vol. 2. Montreal: McGill-Queen's University Press.

Hawthorne, L. 2010. "How Valuable Is 'Two-Step Migration'? Labor Market Outcomes for International Student Migrants to Australia." *Asian and Pacific Migration Journal* 19, no. 1: 5–36.

Hayward, J., and N. Wheen, eds. 2016. *The Waitangi Tribunal: Te Roopu Whakamana i te Tiriti o Waitangi*. Wellington: Bridget Williams Books.

Hollifield, J. F. 1986. "Immigration Policy in France and Germany: Outputs Versus Outcomes." *Annals of the American Academy of Political and Social Science* 485, no. 1: 113–128.

Hollifield, J. F. 1992. *Immigrants, Markets, and States: The Political Economy of Postwar Europe*. Cambridge, MA: Harvard University Press.

Hollifield, J. F. 2004. "The Emerging Migration State." *International Migration Review* 38, no. 3: 885–912.

Hugo, G. J. 1999. "Regional Development Through Immigration? The Reality Behind the Rhetoric." Department of the Parliamentary Library Information and Research Services Research Paper No. 9.

Joppke, C. 1998. "Why Liberal States Accept Unwanted Immigration." *World Politics* 50, no. 2: 266–293.

Jupp, J. 1995. "From 'White Australia' to 'Part of Asia': Recent Shifts in Australian Immigration Policy Towards the Region." *International Migration Review* 29, no. 1: 207–228.

Kamp, A., K. Dunn, Y. Paradies, and K. Blair. 2018. "Aboriginal and Torres Strait Islander People's Attitudes Towards Australian Multiculturalism, Cultural Diversity, 'Race' and Racism, 2015–16." *Australian Aboriginal Studies* 2: 50–87.

Kawharu, I. H. 1989. *Waitangi: Māori and Pākehā Perspectives of the Treaty of Waitangi*. New York: Oxford University Press.

Keating, P. 1992. "Speech at the Productive Diversity in Business Conference." Melbourne, October 28, 1992.

Kirk, N. 1974. "New Directions in New Zealand's Foreign Policy." *Millennium* 3, no. 2: 91–99.

Kukutai, Tahu, and Arama Rata. 2017. "From Mainstream to Manaaki: Indigenising our Approach to Immigration." In *Fair Borders? Migration Policy in the Twenty-First Century*, edited by David Hall, 30–39. Wellington: Bridget Williams Books.

Kymlicka, W. 2003. "Canadian Multiculturalism in Historical and Comparative Perspective: Is Canada Unique." *Constitutional Forum/Forum Constitutionelle* 13, no. 1: 1–8.

Lawton, H. 2019. "Australia's Seasonal Worker Program Now Bigger than New Zealand's." Development Policy Centre, Australian National University, July 25, 2019.

Lutz, P. 2019. "Reassessing the Gap-Hypothesis: Tough Talk and Weak Action in Migration Policy?" *Party Politics* 27, no. 1: 1–13.

Mares, P. 2016. *Not Quite Australian: How Temporary Migration Is Changing the Nation*. Melbourne: Text Publishing.

Markham, F., and N. Biddle. 2018. *Indigenous Residential Segregation in Towns and Cities, 1976–2016*. Canberra: Centre for Aboriginal Economic Policy Research, ANU.

Markus, A. B. 1995. "Chinese Immigration Under the 'White Australia' Policy." In *Histories of the Chinese in Australasia and the South Pacific*, edited by P. Macgregor, 354–360. Melbourne: Museum of Chinese Australian History.

Martin, J. E. 2014. "Immigration." Parliamentary Library Research Paper. https://www.parliament.nz/en/pb/research-papers/document/00PLEcoC51111/immigration.

McIntyre, W. D. 2007. *Dominion of New Zealand: Statesmen and Status, 1907–1945*. Wellington: New Zealand Institute of International Affairs.

McKenzie, J., and R. Hasmath. 2013. "Deterring the 'Boat People': Explaining the Australian Government's People Swap Response to Asylum Seekers." *Australian Journal of Political Science* 48, no. 4: 417–430.

McNevin, A. 2007. "The Liberal Paradox and the Politics of Asylum in Australia." *Australian Journal of Political Science* 42, no. 4: 611–630.

McNevin, A. 2010. "Border Policing and Sovereign Terrain: The Spatial Framing of Unwanted Migration in Melbourne and Australia." *Globalizations* 7, no. 3: 407–419.

McQueen, H. 2004. *A New Britannia*. Brisbane: University of Queensland Press.

Meyers, E. 2002. "The Causes of Convergence in Western Immigration Control." *Review of International Studies* 28, no. 1: 123–141.

Ministry for Culture and Heritage. 2020. "Poll Tax on Chinese Immigrants Abolished." https://nzhistory.govt.nz/poll-tax-on-chinese-immigrants-abolished. Last updated March 13, 2020.

Moran, A. 2017. "Aboriginal and Multicultural Imaginaries: Tensions, Accommodations, Reconciliation." In *The Public Life of Australian Multiculturalism*, 207–240. Cham: Palgrave Macmillan.

O'Connell, J. F., J. Allen, M. A. Williams, A. N. Williams, C. S. Turney, N. A. Spooner, J. Kamminga, G. Brown, and A. Cooper. 2018. "When Did *Homo sapiens* First Reach Southeast Asia and Sahul?" *Proceedings of the National Academy of Sciences* 115, no. 34: 8482–8490.

Ongley, P., and D. Pearson. 1995. "Post-1945 International Migration: New Zealand, Australia and Canada Compared." *International Migration Review* 29, no. 3: 765–793.

Orange, C. 2015. *The Treaty of Waitangi*. Wellington: Bridget Williams Books.

Palfreeman, A. C. 1958. "The End of the Dictation Test." *Australian Quarterly* 30, no. 1: 43–50.

Pearson, D., and P. Ongley. 1996. "Multiculturalism and Biculturalism: The Recent New Zealand Experience in Comparative Perspective." *Journal of Intercultural Studies* 17, nos. 1–2: 5–28.

Phillips, J. 2015. *Boat Arrivals and Boat "Turnbacks" in Australia Since 1976: A Quick Guide to the Statistics*. Canberra: Parliamentary Library.

Phillips, J., and J. Simon-Davies. 2016. *Migration to Australia: A Quick Guide to the Statistics*. Canberra: Parliamentary Library.

Pool, I., and N. Jackson. n.d. "Population Change—Key Population Trends." *Te Ara: The Encyclopedia of New Zealand*. http://www.TeAra.govt.nz/en/graph/28720/new-zealand-population-by-ethnicity-1840-2013. Accessed March 29, 2020.

Reserve Bank of New Zealand. 1986. "Migration and the New Zealand Labour Market." *Reserve Bank of New Zealand Bulletin* 49: 332–335.

Richards, E. 2008. *Destination Australia: Migration to Australia Since 1901*. Sydney: UNSW Press.

Ritchie, J. E. 1992. *Becoming Bicultural*. Wellington: Huia Publishers.

Roach, N. J. 1995. *Business Temporary Entry: Future Directions*. Canberra: Australian Government Publishing Service.

Salmond, A. 1997. *Between Worlds: Early Exchanges Between Maori and Europeans, 1773–1815*. Honolulu: University of Hawaii Press.

Secher, U. 2007. "The High Court and Recognition of Native Title: Distinguishing Between the Doctrines of Terra Nullius and Desert and Uncultivated." *University of Western Sydney Law Review* 11, no. 1: 1–39.

Serle, G. 2014. *The Golden Age: A History of the Colony of Victoria 1851–1861.* Melbourne: Melbourne University Press.

Sherrell, H. 2019. "Evolving Role of Temporary Migration." In *Effects of Temporary Migration*, 38. Melbourne: Committee for Economic Development of Australia.

Simon-Davies, J. 2018. "Population and Migration Statistics in Australia." Department of the Parliamentary Library Information and Research Services Research Papers, December 7, 2018. https://www.aph.gov.au/About_Parliament/Parliamentary_Departments/Parliamentary_Library/pubs/rp/rp1819/Quick_Guides/PopulationStatistics.

Simon-Kumar, R. 2019. "The Multicultural Dilemma: Amid Rising Diversity and Unsettled Equity Issues, New Zealand Seeks to Address Its Past and Present." *Migration Information Source*, September 2019.

Smith, B. R., and F. Morphy. 2007. *The Social Effects of Native Title: Recognition, Translation, Coexistence.* Canberra: ANU Press.

Spoonley, P., and R. Bedford. 2012. *Welcome to Our World? Immigration and the Reshaping of New Zealand.* Auckland: Dunmore Publishing.

Spoonley, P., R. Bedford, and C. Macpherson. 2003. "Divided Loyalties and Fractured Sovereignty: Transnationalism and the Nation-State in Aotearoa/New Zealand." *Journal of Ethnic and Migration Studies* 29, no. 1: 27–46.

Spoonley, P., and P. Gendall. 2010. "Welcome to Our World: Attitudes to Immigrants and Immigration." *New Zealand and International Migration: A Digest and Bibliography* 5: 136–158.

Statistics New Zealand. 2012. "What New Zealand Actually Does for a Living: From Manufacturing to a Services-Orientated Economy." http://archive.stats.govt.nz/browse_for_stats/economic_indicators/NationalAccounts/Contribution-to-gdp.aspx#gsc.tab=0.

Statistics New Zealand. 2014. "International Migration to and from Auckland Region: 1996–2013." http://archive.stats.govt.nz/browse_for_stats/population/Migration/international-travel-and-migration-articles/international-migration-to-from-auckland.aspx.

Statistics New Zealand. 2018. "Migration Drives High Population Growth." https://www.stats.govt.nz/news/migration-drives-high-population-growth.

Statistics New Zealand. 2019. "New Zealand's Population Reflects Growing Diversity." Press release, September 23, 2019. https://www.scoop.co.nz/stories/PO1909/S00296/new-zealands-population-reflects-growing-diversity.htm.

Statistics New Zealand. 2020a. "2018 Census Place Summaries: Auckland." https://www.stats.govt.nz/tools/2018-census-place-summaries/auckland-region.

Statistics New Zealand. 2020b. "2018 Census Data Allows Users to Dive Deep into New Zealand's Diversity." April 21, 2020. https://www.stats.govt.nz/news/2018-census-data-allows-users-to-dive-deep-into-new-zealands-diversity.

Statistics New Zealand. n.d. "Demographics of New Zealand's Pacific Population." http://archive.stats.govt.nz/browse_for_stats/people_and_communities/pacific_peoples/pacific-progress-demography/population-growth.aspx#.

Stevens, R. 2012. "Political Debates on Asylum Seekers During the Fraser Government, 1977–1982." *Australian Journal of Politics and History* 58, no. 4: 526–541.

Trlin, A. D. 1992. "Change and Continuity: New Zealand's Immigration Policy in the Late 1980s." In *New Zealand and International Migration: A Digest and Bibliography* no. 2, edited by A. D. Trlin and P. Spoonley. Palmerston North: Massey University.

UNHCR. n.d. "Resettlement." https://www.unhcr.org/en-au/resettlement.html.

Van Onselen, P., and W. Errington. 2008. *John Winston Howard: The Definitive Biography.* Melbourne: Melbourne University Press.

Veracini, L. 2010. *Settler Colonialism: A Theoretical Overview.* Houndmills, UK: Palgrave Macmillan.

Viviani, N., and J. Lawe-Davies. 1980. *Australian Government Policy on the Entry of Vietnamese Refugees, 1976 to 1978.* Queensland: Griffith University, School of Modern Asian Studies, Centre for the Study of Australian-Asian Relations.

Walsh, J. P. 2015. "Border Theatre and Security Spectacles: Surveillance, Mobility and Reality-Based Television." *Crime, Media, Culture* 11, no. 2: 201–221.

Walter, R., H. Buckley, C. Jacomb, and E. Matisoo-Smith. 2017. "Mass Migration and the Polynesian Settlement of New Zealand." *Journal of World Prehistory* 30, no. 4: 351–376.

Weber, L., and R. Powell. 2018. "Ripples Across the Pacific: Cycles of Risk and Exclusion Following Criminal Deportation to Samoa." In *After Deportation*, edited by S. Khosravi, 205–229. Cham: Palgrave Macmillan.

Willard, M. 1967. *History of the White Australia Policy to 1920.* London: Frank Cass & Co.

Williams, D. V. 1999. *"Te Kooti Tango Whenua": The Native Land Court 1864–1909.* Wellington: Huia Publishers.

Windle, J. 2008. "The Racialisation of African Youth in Australia." *Social Identities* 14, no. 5: 553–566.

Woodhouse, M. 2013. "Mass Arrivals Bill Passes into Law." Press release, June 14, 2013.

Yarwood, A. T. 1964. *Asian Migration to Australia: The Background to Exclusion, 1896–1923.* Melbourne: Melbourne University Press.

Zolberg, A. R. 2009. *A Nation by Design: Immigration Policy in the Fashioning of America.* Cambridge, MA: Harvard University Press.

COMMENTARY

Australia: Legitimizing Immigration Through Contrast

Matthew J. Gibney

In their impressive chapter on Australia and New Zealand as migration states, Gamlen and Sherrell offer a *tour d'horizon* across two centuries of immigration in these countries. They describe the transformation in these countries' respective migration regimes from immigration informed by race-based, nation-building goals through most of the twentieth century to step-wise, skill-based recruitment today. This is careful and convincing scholarship that helps us to understand what these countries share and how they differ as migration states. While I could hardly improve on their account of New Zealand, I want to say something here about the political logic that drives Australian immigration policy, if only to acknowledge the distinctively belligerent and illiberal flavor of some of the country's recent migration control practices.

Gamlen and Sherrell are too perceptive to ignore the dark side of Australian migration control that exists alongside the country's continued openness toward skill-based economic immigration. They note the anti-Asian One Nation Party and recognize that its xenophobic leader, Pauline Hanson, is *not* an outlier in Australian politics. They mention Australia's recent restrictive policies toward refugees and practices of deportation. And they highlight recent complaints about congestion in the major cities linked to immigration. However, the force of these anti-immigration currents is somewhat diminished by Gamlen and Sherrell's reassurance that multiculturalism is deeply institutionalized across governance in Australia and that the country has not (yet) had a political conflagration on immigration similar to those seen in some other democratic countries. Australian political elites, we are told, have thus far navigated the liberal paradox of conflicting demotic calls for closure and economic liberalism by "talk[ing] tough" about immigration "while keeping the country open to immigration for business reasons."

This description makes it sound like Australian governments have responded to restrictive pressures simply through rhetoric and that the driving forces of exclusion come from *outside* government. But this is somewhat misleading. In my view, it is more accurate to see the contemporary battle by political elites to preserve openness to (economic) migration as one fought by proxy against other immigrant groups, who have recently been subject to highly illiberal treatment by the Australian state. We see this clearly if we look more closely at practices toward asylum seekers deemed as entering unlawfully and non-citizens on temporary and permanent visas who commit crimes.

Over the last two decades Australia has established a worldwide reputation for hostility toward the asylum seekers arriving by boat without visas. This reputation has its origins largely in the early 1990s, when the Labour government, hoping to stem the arrival of Cambodian refugees, introduced a new policy of mandatory detention (typically in isolated parts of Australia) for unauthorized boat arrivals during the consideration of their asylum claims. Less than a decade later, the Liberal government, faced with an upsurge in arrivals from countries such as Afghanistan, Iran, and Iraq, toughened policy further. John Howard's government drew international attention when it initiated a stand-off in August 2001 when it refused to allow a Norwegian freighter that had picked up imperiled asylum seekers at sea to land on the Australian territory of Christmas Island. Australian special forces boarded the ship and the government arranged to process the asylum seekers' claims in New Zealand and on the destitute island nation of Nauru (Gibney 2004). Through legislation passed in September 2001, the government excised the Australian territories of Christmas Island and Ashmore Reef from its formal migration zone, thus excluding refugees arriving there from many of the protections of Australian domestic law (including access to appeals). The law also formalized regional processing centers in Manus Island in Papua New Guinea and Nauru. Thus began what was to become known as the "Pacific Solution."

The Pacific Solution aimed to deter asylum claims by enmeshing those arriving by boat in long processing delays in insalubrious locations. It was publicly justified on a number of grounds. The Howard government steadfastly proclaimed its sovereign right to decide who enters Australian territory; questioned the character of the asylum seekers (they were accused alternately of being line jumpers and possible terrorists); and emphasized its duty to prevent perilous sea crossings in unsafe vessels

(Gibney 2004). Little attempt was made to deny the obvious: that the vast majority of those arriving were refugees under the 1951 UN Convention.

The policy on asylum seekers softened when the Labor government came to power in 2007 and closed the centers on Nauru. But offshoring returned again in the early 2010s, when the number of arrivals began to rise precipitously, reaching a high of 7,604 in 2013–2014 (Australian Refugee Council 2021). And when the Liberals under Tony Abbott returned to power in 2013, a new, far tougher policy, Operation Sovereign Borders, was implemented (McAdam 2013). Abbott committed his government to the position that no asylum seekers arriving by boat would *ever* be settled on Australian territory. In effective violation of international law pertaining to refugees, the government announced that people on boats intercepted at sea would be returned from whence they came (Kaldor Centre 2019).

With the government's goal of securing resettlement places moving at a glacial pace after 2014, Nauru and Manus Island became international bywords for the inhumane treatment of refugees. Those on the islands found themselves spending many years of limbo in centers where suicide, mental health breakdown, and sexual abuse were common (see, for example, Human Rights Watch 2016). Yet the Liberal government did not yield. Indeed, a battle of wills ensued as domestic and international human rights groups decried the baleful effects of Operation Sovereign Borders and the government resisted any attempts that would facilitate refugee arrival in Australia, including onshore medical treatment and resettlement of the detainees by New Zealand (whose overtures to take the refugees were long rejected by the Australian government, as it might enable backdoor entry to Australia under the Trans-Tasman Agreement). While numbers on Nauru and Manus have fallen over time as a result of agreements with other countries and small compromises, the world has been left in no doubt as to how far Australia will go to deter and control unwanted migration.

During the last decade a similar type of muscular border control policy has also played out against immigrants (non-citizens on temporary or permanent visas) who breach the conditions of their Australian residency. Section 501 of the Australian Migration Act has long granted the Australian state wide-ranging powers to deport non-citizens unable to prove they are of good character. However, a change to the law in 2014 made deportation mandatory for certain crimes and anyone sentenced to jail for twelve months or more. During the second reading of the bill creating these powers, the immigration minister stated that "those who choose to break the law, fail to uphold the standards of behaviour expected by the Australian community or try to intentionally mislead or defraud the Australian government should expect to have . . . [the privilege of residence] removed" (Parliament of Australia 2014). The effect of this law upon resident non-citizens has been dramatic. Between 2013–2014 and

2019–2020, the number of visa cancellations (which make individuals concerned eligible for detention and deportation) increased by 1,240 percent, from a yearly average of 107 between 2012 and 2014 to 980 between 2018 and 2020 (Australian Department of Home Affairs 2020).

As the numbers have risen so has controversy. It soon became apparent that many of those deported were New Zealanders, primarily of Pacific Island and Maori descent, who were long-term residents of Australia and had few connections to New Zealand. This was hardly the only source of tension. In a manner redolent of its treatment of asylum seekers, the Australian government has detained a large number of those awaiting deportation in detention facilities on Christmas Island. Some deportees have been held in these detention facilities for more than a year, geographically isolated from family and friends in centers originally designed to deter refugees. Children have also been caught up in the new deportation sweep. In 2018 the Australian government was criticized by the acting New Zealand prime minister for holding in immigration detention a seventeen-year-old New Zealand citizen. In 2021, New Zealand officials again complained publicly when a fifteen-year-old child was deported from Australia and sent unaccompanied to New Zealand. In both of these cases, state officials have argued that Australia's actions violate the UN Convention on the Rights of the Child (Fernando 2021).

What is notable in this case is not the deportation of non-citizens who commit crimes per se (there has been a move toward more vigorous enforcement of such expulsions across many Western states in recent years) or even perhaps the lack of discernment in Australia's enforcement of its visa cancellation laws. It is how breezily Australian officials have dismissed criticism from human rights groups, UN bodies, and officials from other countries. Gamlen and Sherrell rightly note that in 2020 the New Zealand prime minister, Jacinda Ardern (in a press conference with the Australian prime minister), characterized Australia's policy as "corrosive" and asked Australia not to "deport your people and your problems." But it is worth remembering that the request of the leader of Australia's closest ally was simply brushed aside. Indeed, early in 2001, the Australian home affairs minister, Peter Dutton, remarked that he made "no apology" for having "ramped up" deportation and "done it in a dramatic way." Such a policy, he said, makes "Australia a safer place" by "taking the trash out" (Fernando 2021). His comments were not well received in New Zealand.

What should we make of these muscular displays of toughness against asylum seekers and visa-holding residents who commit crimes? One way of seeing them is simply through the dynamic of electoral politics: the Liberals (who are the equivalent of Conservatives in other countries) implement very tough policies in order to outfox their moderate and more rights-respecting opponents on issues like irregular immigration and crime. This logic is evident in many liberal democratic countries, not least the United Kingdom, where the Conservatives court the Labour Party's working-class constituency through tough border policies. But this harshness has hardly been confined to the right in the Australian political context (it was, as we saw, Labour that introduced mandatory detention in the early 1990s and reintroduced offshoring in the 2010s), even if it has been most clearly exemplified there.

Another way we might see such practices is as a way that governments committed to liberal policies toward economic/skills-based immigration legitimize this type of migration through contrast. By offering up certain groups—asylum seekers, criminal non-citizens—as sacrificial lambs for public anxiety about migration, governments draw hostility away from the economic immigration they favor while simultaneously appealing to anti-immigration sentiment. If this is right—and I think it certainly helps to describe part of what is going on in the Australian case—we can see how illiberal policies toward some groups may be used to enable more liberal and open policies toward others, like skilled migrants.

If there is nothing particularly novel about this logic, what makes the trade-off notable in the Australian case is that it is a country with such weak institutional buffers on the illiberal treatment of non-citizens. The president of the Australian Human Rights Commission, Gillian Triggs, lamented in 2017 that she had presided over a period when Australia's human rights "are regressing on almost every front." She attributed this to a Liberal government "ideologically opposed to human rights" and the fact that, "unlike almost every other comparable country, Australia has no bill of rights against which government policies can be benchmarked" (Slezak 2017). Without a bill of rights, Australian courts have been unable to correct recent policies against asylum seekers and visa-holding residents. Courts in the country lack even the power "to consider whether an individual's detention is arbitrary, unreasonable or unnecessary and they cannot order the government to release a person from immigration detention" (Australian Human Rights Commission 2009). Moreover, such constraints as the judiciary do provide can often be evaded by governments through new legislation.

That said, it is not easy to determine just how effective such harshness has been in influencing public support for immigration generally. Suggestively, public support for decreasing the overall level of immigration during the 2000s tracked fairly well the presence of Liberal governments in power. That is, under the governance of the more restrictionist party (the Liberals), the number of people supportive of reducing immigration tended to be at its lowest levels (McAllister and Cameron 2016, 100). A similar trend is less clear in the 2010s, however. Research by the Lowy Institute in Sydney in 2020 suggested that public perception that the total number of migrants coming to Australia each year is "too high" has grown significantly (but unevenly) since 2014 (a period of Liberal Party governments), currently standing at about 47 percent (Lowy Institute 2020). Of course, many factors other than government policies (let alone policies toward asylum and deportation) shape public attitudes to migration.

Nonetheless, to the extent that Australian governments have tried to navigate the so-called liberal paradox in recent years, I think it safe to say that they have not relied solely on their oratorical skills or taken public opinion simply as an immutable constraint. They have instead used some groups of entrants and non-citizen residents as lightning rods to concentrate anti-immigration attitudes while continuing to keep an open door to favored groups.

References

Australian Department of Home Affairs. 2020. "Visa Statistics: Key Visa Cancellation Statistics." https://www.homeaffairs.gov.au/research-and-statistics/statistics/visa-statistics/visa-cancellation.

Australian Human Rights Commission 2009. "Human Rights and Asylum Seekers and Refugees." https://www.youtube.com/watch?v=Jeil9S2exIU&list=RDTfVyneuCsS4&index=9.

Australian Refugee Council. 2021. "Statistics on Boat Arrivals and Boat Turnbacks." https://www.refugeecouncil.org.au/asylum-boats-statistics/.

Fernando, Gavin. 2021. "Australia Accused of Flouting International Obligations." SBS News, March 17, 2021. https://www.sbs.com.au/news/australia-accused-of-flouting-international-obligations-over-child-s-disturbing-deportation-to-new-zealand.

Gibney, Matthew J. 2004. *Ethics and Politics of Asylum*. Cambridge: Cambridge University Press.

Human Rights Watch. 2016. "Appalling Abuse, Neglect of Refugees on Nauru." August 2, 2016. https://www.hrw.org/news/2016/08/02/australia-appalling-abuse-neglect-refugees-nauru.

Kaldor Centre. 2019. "Fact Sheet: Turning Back Boats." Sydney. https://www.kaldorcentre.unsw.edu.au/sites/kaldorcentre.unsw.edu.au/files/Factsheet_Turning%20back%20boats_Apr2019.pdf.

Lowy Institute. 2020. "Poll 2020." Sydney. https://poll.lowyinstitute.org/charts/immigration-rate/.

McAdam, Jane. 2013. "Australia and Asylum Seekers." *International Journal of Refugee Law* 25, no. 3: 435–448.

McAllister, Ian, and Sarah M. Cameron. 2016. "Trends in Australian Political Opinion: Results from the Australian Election Study, 1987–2016." Australian National University.

Parliament of Australia. 2014. *House of Representatives Debates*. 10325. September 24, 2014.

Slezak, Michael. 2017. "Australian Government Ideologically Opposed to Human Rights." *Guardian*, July 26, 2017. https://www.theguardian.com/australia-news/2017/jul/26/gillian-triggs-australian-government-ideologically-opposed-to-human-rights.

3 COUNTRIES OF IMMIGRATION

5 Immigration and the Republican Tradition in France

James F. Hollifield and François Héran

Unlike other European countries, France has a long history of immigration dating back to the middle of the nineteenth century, when industrialization began in earnest. France was not the only European country compelled to import labor to feed the fires of industrialization. British industry relied upon Irish workers throughout the nineteenth century, while Germany brought in Poles and others from east-central Europe to work in mining and heavy industry in the Ruhr, especially during the period of intensive economic development in the 1880s and 1890s (Herbert 1986). What distinguishes France from other European countries is the early willingness to accept immigrants as settlers and citizens, whether as a benediction or as a necessary vice. The acceptance of foreigners as potential citizens is nowadays commonly justified by the principles of a republican tradition that stems from the French Revolution and holds that immigrants must adhere to the social contract as individuals, never as members of a minority. The symbolic force of the republican tradition is undeniable, but, as we shall see, demography and economics played a big role in French immigration history as well.

Republicanism is strongly egalitarian, anti-clerical (*laïque*), and opposed to monarchy. It stresses popular sovereignty, citizenship, and the rights of man. It can be nationalist and imperialist while at the same time promoting universal political values, such as equal protection of all individuals before the law. Republicanism, as an ideology and a form of government, was bitterly contested in France throughout the nineteenth century and well into the twentieth (Hoffmann 1963; Hollifield and Ross 1991).

Early in the twentieth century, the French state began to lay the legal foundations for nationality, which would be based not only on blood (*jus sanguinis*), as in Germany (Weil 2002; Noiriel 1988), but also on the birthright principle of soil (*jus soli*). Hence, the republican tradition found its expression in a more open and expansive notion of citizenship, similar (but not identical) to the birthright principle enunciated in the Fourteenth Amendment of the US Constitution ("All persons born or naturalized in the United States, and subject to the jurisdiction thereof, are citizens of the United States") and in stark contrast to the narrow, ethno-cultural vision of citizenship evolving in Germany during the Second Reich (Brubaker 1992; Hollifield 2021). While Germany was struggling with the issues of national and territorial unification and would continue to do so—one could argue—until 1989–1990, France was becoming more comfortable with its revolutionary and republican heritage, as reflected in an expansive policy of immigration and naturalization. The relationship between immigration and nation-building is critical in enabling democratic states to manage immigration and finesse the gap between policy outputs and outcomes (Hollifield 1986, 1997, 2021). Thus, a key argument in this chapter is that the more closely associated immigration is with the political myths that legitimate and give life to the regime, the easier it is for governments to justify immigration and immigrant policies and to manage the ethnic and distributional conflicts that inevitably arise.

Immigration accelerated in France during the second half of the nineteenth century. It was associated not only with the triumph of republicanism but also with industrialization, which was slow and late by comparison with Britain and even Germany. To sustain a surge in economic growth during the Belle Époque, French industry needed access to additional supplies of labor, which could not be found at home. There were two reasons for the labor shortages during this period of industrialization and rapid economic growth. Because of the revolutionary land settlement, which gave French peasant farmers legal control of their land, there was no large rural exodus in France in the nineteenth century comparable to what happened in Germany and Britain (Weber 1976; Le Bras 1986b). The labor shortage was compounded by anemic population growth, because a demographic transition occurred earlier in France than in any other society (Spengler 1938). Taken together, these two factors—a stagnant population and a weak rural exodus—set the stage for a rise in immigration in the latter half of the nineteenth century.

The Demographic and Republican Nexus

Throughout the nineteenth century, France was the only European country with a positive net migration (based on comparison of censuses at ten-year intervals). From

1861 to 1910, France was gaining 190,000 inhabitants per decade on average just from immigration, while Italy was losing 890,000, Germany 670,000, England and Scotland 470,000, Ireland 620,000, Sweden 200,000, and Austria and Hungary 530,000. The de facto acceptance of immigration compensated somewhat for the Malthusian behavior of the French population—their fear of shortages made the French risk-averse and contributed to the falling birth rate. French families were having fewer children since the second part of the eighteenth century in large part to avoid further fragmentation of their smallholdings (Le Bras 1986a; Van de Walle 1986). From 1800 to 1950, total fertility was lower than the English rate by around 1.5 children per woman (Vallin and Caselli 1999). The surplus of births over deaths ("natural growth" in demographic terms) remained very low in France, in sharp contrast with the rest of Europe. The net reproduction rate (the ratio between female births in two successive generations, taking mortality into account) remained close to 1 from the time of the Revolution. As a result, France had no excess population to send out to the New World. Public and private companies constantly complained of labor shortages (*le manque de bras*).

While French peasants contributed their labor in the first phase of the Industrial Revolution through seasonal migration or contract work, this was no longer the case under the Second Empire (1852–1870), when industrialization accelerated in textiles, coal mining, steel, and railroads (Noiriel 1988). Before World War I, France recruited permanent immigrant workers from neighboring countries—mainly Belgium and Italy, and secondarily from Germany and Switzerland (Figure 5.3). Later, for purposes of post–World War I reconstruction, the recruitment pool expanded to Spain and distant regions like Poland and even the Maghreb. This surge in immigration posed a challenge for the republican tradition from the middle of the nineteenth century through the interwar period, but not in ways that one might have expected.

During World War I, the state attempted to assert control over immigration through the establishment of national identity cards. By forcing all residents to have a national identity card, the state created a national/legal identity for the population, native as well as foreign (Noiriel 1988). After World War I, French industry was again faced with dramatic labor shortages, this time because of the crippling effects of the war itself. In the early 1920s two major interest groups emerged that would influence French immigration policy for decades to come. First were employers, who created the Société Générale d'Immigration (SGI), a private organization that, with the blessings of the divided and stalemated governments of the 1920s, took as its mission to organize the recruitment and placement of immigrant (primarily Italian and Polish) labor. Second were the pro-natalists of the Alliance Nationale pour l'Accroissement de la Population Française, long active in Third Republic politics.

Employers were interested in securing an unlimited supply of cheap foreign labor, and the pro-natalists were inspired by a nationalist impulse to increase birth rates and grow the population.

A decade later the pro-natalists were closely identified with the fascist Vichy regime, only to be rehabilitated and transformed into the populationists of the Fourth and Fifth Republics (Teitelbaum and Winter 1985). Beginning with the provisional Tripartite Government, the populationists took immigration as one of their primary concerns. Immigration provided a new rallying cry during the period (1945–1950) when population policies were still viewed with suspicion because of their association with eugenics, *pétainisme*, and fascism. The thrust of the populationists' immigration policies was outlined in the French demographic journal *Population* in two articles by Alfred Sauvy (1946, 1950; see also Héran 2016). He made the case for large-scale recruitment of immigrant workers and their families from Italy and Spain, arguing that such a strategy would give the French population (and by extension the economy) a fighting chance to catch up with more powerful European competitors, primarily Germany and Britain, and restore a demographic balance between generations.

In Charles de Gaulle the populationists had a powerful ally who helped them shape postwar French immigration policy. The thinking of the early Gaullist reformers, especially Jean Monnet, who was to head the newly created national planning agency—the Commissariat Général du Plan—was that all necessary resources should be mobilized to modernize the economy (Debré and Sauvy 1946). For technocrats like Monnet, modernization should be done quickly to take advantage of the political honeymoon between business and government after Liberation. The political stalemate of the Third Republic was broken, and a new consensus in favor of immigration was emerging. Recruitment policies were supported by major segments of the republican right (especially the Gaullists) oriented toward big business and rapid economic growth, and by segments of the old republican left (the radicals, the socialists, and eventually the Communists as well).

The *ordonnances* of 1945, signed by de Gaulle before the restoration of Parliament, laid down the basic outline of immigration and naturalization policy in postwar France, or what Patrick Weil (1991, 61) has called *la règle du jeu*. Thanks to the firm intervention of René Cassin, who headed the Conseil d'État (Council of State), the *ordonnances* rejected the idea of selecting immigrants on the basis of ethnicity or national origins. French immigration policy since 1945 must be understood in terms of the demographic and republican nexus, which helped to forge a consensus for the recruitment of foreign workers. Nevertheless, many of the crises and controversies involving the issue of immigration control from the 1960s to the present stem from the turbulence of decolonization and the dismantling of the French Empire, which was itself a creation of nationalist and republican forces. The liberal side of the history of immigration in postwar France cannot be told without reference to decolonization and the Algerian War, which created ethnic and racial fault lines in French society that persist today.

A look at the size and evolution of the foreign and immigrant populations will help to round out the historical picture. From Figures 5.1 and 5.2 we can see the changes in the foreign and immigrant populations in France from 1850 to 2020. Certainly by 1931, France was statistically a country of immigration—6.6 percent of the population was foreign (without French nationality), comparable to other immigrant-receiving countries. The foreign population dropped slightly during the war years and the early period of reconstruction (falling to 4.1 percent in 1954), but it rose again with successive waves of immigration in the 1950s and 1960s, reaching a high of 6.8 percent in 1982; it settled around 5.5 percent at the turn of the twenty-first century, then rose again rapidly to a historical high of 7.4 percent in 2020. Note, however, that the immigrant (total foreign-born) population (Figure 5.2), which includes naturalized citizens, has been rising consistently throughout the postwar period: it was 5 percent of total population in 1946, remained around 7.3 percent in the last two

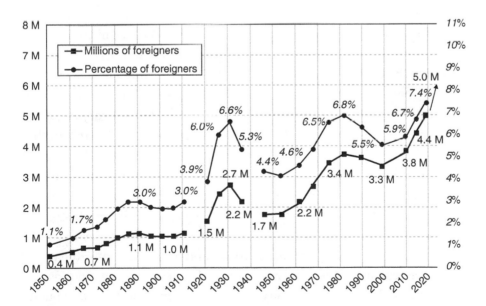

FIGURE 5.1. Foreign Population of France

Number and percentage of foreigners in mainland France since 1851 (census series interrupted during the two world wars).

SOURCE: SGF (Statistique générale de France) and INSEE (French National Statistical Office), authors' graph.

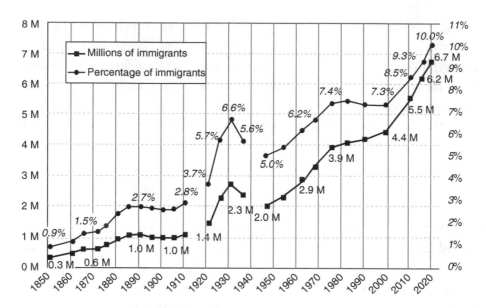

FIGURE 5.2. Immigrant Population of France

NOTE: Number and percentage of immigrants in mainland France since 1851 (census series interrupted during the two world wars).

SOURCE: SGF (Statistique générale de France) and INSEE (French National Statistical Office), authors' graph.

decades of the twentieth century, and then rose another 2.5 points to a historical high of 10 percent in 2020. The first waves of immigration in the postwar period were settler (as opposed to temporary) in nature, with a heavy labor component. The more permanent nature of immigration during the Trente Glorieuses (thirty glorious years of economic growth from 1945 to 1975) and the weight of the colonial legacy make the French and German experiences quite different (see Martin and Thränhardt in this volume).

Looking only at the numbers, especially the size of the foreign population, the argument can be made that France has been a country of immigration since early in the twentieth century (Héran 2012). Yet despite the long and continuous history of immigration in modern France, immigration never achieved the legitimacy that it has enjoyed in the United States, Canada, Australia, and New Zealand—all nations of immigrants (see various chapters in this volume). Immigration did not play the role of a "founding myth" in any of the various political regimes in France (republican or otherwise) in the nineteenth or twentieth centuries. Policies pursued by postwar French governments, especially after 1974, were designed to discourage settler immigration and encourage some nationalities, particularly those from countries in North Africa and sub-Saharan Africa, to return to their countries of origin. From the beginning of the postwar period there was a sort of rotation logic embedded in French immigration policy (similar to the German *Gastarbeiter* policy), which helps to explain why governments in 1974 and 1993 could seriously contemplate a halt to all types of immigration (the so-called zero immigration option). In order to understand the abrupt shifts from recruitment after the war to suspension in the 1970s, "zero immigration" in the 1990s, and selective immigration (*l'immigration choisie et non subie*, "immigration as a choice, not an imposition") in the 2000s, we must look at the origins of postwar immigration policy in the 1950s and 1960s. It was during this period that immigration control was defined in the highly statist terms of economic and demographic planning.

Economic Planning and Population Policy

The postwar French system of immigration control was created in a very short period of time after Liberation. The two principal agencies for managing immigration and refugee flows, the Office National d'Immigration (ONI) and the Office Français pour la Protection des Refugiés et Apatrides (OFPRA), were established in 1946, and population/family policies in general were given a boost by the creation of the Institut National d'Études Démographiques (INED). The ONI was touted (by Gaullists on the right and by Communists on the left) as a model agency for the recruitment and placement of foreign workers in various sectors of the French economy. Trade unions (represented by the Confédération Générale du Travail, CGT, and the Confédération Française des Travailleurs Chrétiens, CFTC) were especially pleased to have a "neutral" state agency to oversee foreign worker and immigration policy. They lobbied hard to avoid a return to the interwar system of the SGI, where immigration was organized and controlled by and for business. Business associations, such as the Conseil National du Patronat Français (CNPF), were not sufficiently well organized in the immediate postwar period to have any formal influence on the creation of this system for regulating immigration. Big business offered little resistance to the new directions in immigrant worker policy, except, ironically, to question the wisdom of importing large numbers of immigrant workers at a time of high unemployment, when many French forced laborers were returning from Germany (Hollifield 1992b; Schor 1985; Martin and Thränhardt in this volume).

Throughout the period of the Trente Glorieuses, each of the economic plans published by the CGP contained specific targets for the importation of foreign labor, ranging from 430,000 in the First (Monnet) Plan of 1946–1947 to 325,000 for the Fifth Plan, 1966–1970. These figures, while not irrelevant, had little bearing on actual levels of immigration, because the system of immigration control during this period of high growth and rapid decolonization quickly slipped into private hands. The ONI became little more than a clearinghouse for employers, who went directly to the sending countries to find the labor they needed, bring the workers to France, get them integrated into the workforce, and then seek an adjustment of status (*régularisation*). This practice of bypassing the institutions created to manage immigration flows came to be known as "immigration from within" (*l'immigration interne*), and the legalization rate (*le taux de régularisation*) was the most important statistic for measuring the ability or inability of the state to control immigration. By the late 1960s, according to this measure, almost 90 percent of new immigrants were coming to France, finding a job, and then requesting an adjustment of status (Hollifield 1992b, 45–73). Meanwhile, Italy had given way to Spain and Portugal, as well as former colonies in North and West Africa, especially Algeria and Morocco, as the principal recruiting grounds for foreign workers (see Figure 5.3).

It was also during this period that the confused and ambiguous status of immigrants from North and West Africa began to pose a problem. Following the Evian Agreements, which granted independence to Algeria in 1962, the status of these former "citizens" was unchanged. They had the right to move freely between France and their home countries. The continued arrival of hundreds of thousands of Algerians, which accelerated in the late 1960s and 1970s, led the French government to renegotiate the freedom-of-movement clause of the Evian Agreements. France was reluctant to unilaterally impose restrictions on the movement of Algerian nationals, but in 1968 the government of Georges Pompidou succeeded in convincing the Algerian authorities to give France greater control, provided there was no restriction on tourist visas for Algerians.

Morocco and Tunisia became major sending countries in the period 1968–1973, and they retained a privileged status as ex-colonies. The same was true for the states of francophone West Africa, even though immigration from these countries (Senegal, Ivory Coast, Cameroon, and others) remained very low (until the late 1980s and 1990s; again, see Figure 5.3) by comparison with North Africans. In effect, the process of decolonization created a special category of protected immigrants who were quasi citizens of France. High rates of economic growth (demand/pull) combined with a relatively open (rights-based) immigration regime made control difficult. The ambiguous status of North and West Africans played havoc with attempts by the French government to control immigration in the 1960s and 1970s, since those individuals in former African colonies who were born during the time of French rule had the legal right to ask for "reintegration into French nationality." Thus, a cohort of former French nationals (most of them in their forties) constituted a latent reservoir of African immigration to France.

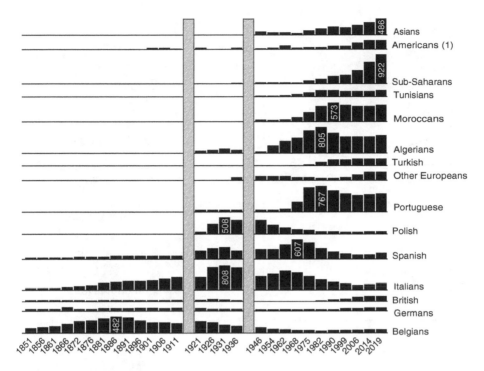

FIGURE 5.3. Foreigners and Naturalized Migrants by Origin, 1851–2019
NOTE: Evolution of the number of immigrants (in thousands) enumerated in France from 1982 to 2019, according to the main countries of origin.
(1) Mostly Haitians and Brazilians.
SOURCE: French Census, SGF and INSEE, authors' calculations.

Stopping Immigration

The consensus for an open immigration regime held until 1973–1974, when the Trente Glorieuses abruptly ended as a result of the Yom Kippur War and Arab oil embargo. However, stopping immigration (*l'arrêt de l'immigration*) would prove difficult, because the mechanisms and instruments of control had not yet been developed by the French state, and cutting ties with former African colonies would not be easy. Reestablishing control over the flows of worker immigration (*travailleurs permanents*) would take many years (Hollifield 1992b). Simply decreeing an immigration stop proved insufficient to master all the different flows (see Figure 5.4).

Apart from worker immigration, French authorities, like their German counterparts, struggled to deter family immigration, which remained at high levels (over 50,000 per year from 1974 to 1980), even after the immigration stop imposed in 1974 (see Figure 5.4). The mercantilist justification for stopping worker immigration was clear in both countries: with the decline in economic growth and the rise of

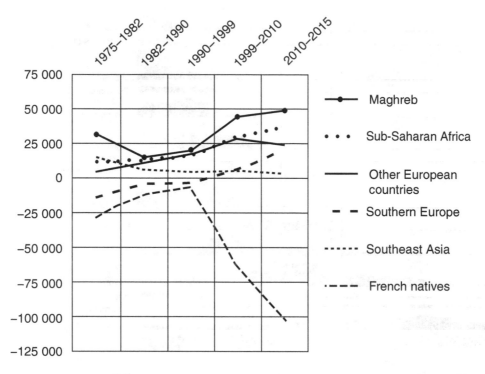

FIGURE 5.4. Net Migration Flows in France by Origin Since 1975
SOURCE: INSEE, authors' graph.

unemployment—especially in France—employers should no longer be allowed to recruit foreign labor, and the denial of visas (external control) and work permits (internal control) was seen as a necessary policy response to worsening economic conditions. The new control policies were also seen as a way to head off a rising tide of xenophobia, which was increasingly evident not just in France but also in neighboring countries like Switzerland and Belgium (de Wenden 1988; Thränhardt 1997). The shift in policy reflected a widespread Malthusian and mercantilist impulse in Europe and France in particular: if the receiving states could stop immigration, they could solve the problem of unemployment, the reasoning being that there are a limited number of jobs in each national economy and that stopping immigration will create jobs and weaken xenophobic political movements.

One of the principal sending countries, Algeria, took steps in 1973 to prevent the free emigration of its nationals to the former metropole because of the growing hostility toward Algerians in France. Yet immigration from Algeria and elsewhere continued throughout the 1970s, in large part due to increases in family reunification, which was much more difficult to control. The economic rationale for stopping worker immigration did not apply to family immigration, which was humanitarian in nature and constitutionally protected. Nevertheless, French and German authorities tried to impose internal (labor market) controls to slow the influx of family members, denying them work permits. In both instances, however, the courts ruled these policies to be unconstitutional (Weil 1991; Hollifield 1992b, 1999, 2000; Ellermann 2021). The French also had to cope with the continued inflow of seasonal workers, employed primarily in agriculture. From 1974 to 1987, the number of seasonal workers entering each year hovered around 60,000. Many of these workers came from Spain and Portugal; however, the enlargement of the European Community and the extension of the freedom-of-movement clause of the Rome Treaty to cover Spanish and Portuguese nationals partially resolved the issue of seasonal migration (Tapinos 1975, 1982). In the late 1970s and early 1980s, Moroccans made up the bulk of seasonal flows, whereas in the 1990s, North Africans were replaced by eastern Europeans, especially Poles.

During the presidency of Valéry Giscard d'Estaing (1974–1981), there was a radical shift away from the open immigration regime of the earlier Gaullist years and toward a more closed regime. The methods used to stop immigration were heavy-handed and statist—consistent with the centralized Jacobin state—and they produced many unintended consequences (Hollifield 1992a). The most important consequence, which was certainly not unique to France, was to freeze the foreign population in place. By simply decreeing an immigration stop, France, like the United States (Martin and Orrenius in this volume; see also Massey 2020) and other western European states, inadvertently accelerated the processes of settlement and family reunification. Moreover, having raised expectations among the French public that the state could simply decree a halt to immigration, the government found that its hands were tied both by the law and by the uncontrollable effects of chain migration (Hollifield 1999). The governments of Jacques Chirac (1974–1976) and Raymond Barre (1976–1981) tried to stop family reunification by denying visas and deporting family members. The Barre government also tried to encourage return migration by paying foreigners to leave (Hollifield 1992b; Weil 1991, 107ff.).

The socialists came to power in 1981 with the election of François Mitterrand. They opted to maintain tight (external) control of borders and stepped up (internal) control of the labor market to inhibit the development of a black market for undocumented workers (*travail au noir*). Regulation of the labor market was carried out by *inspecteurs du travail*, who conducted surprise inspections of firms and imposed sanctions on employers caught using undocumented workers (Marie 1992). At the same time, the new socialist government, led by Prime Minister Pierre Mauroy, offered a conditional amnesty to undocumented immigrants and longer (ten-year) residency and work permits for all immigrants. Anyone who had entered France prior to January 1, 1981, was eligible for a temporary residency permit, valid for three months, which gave individuals time to complete an application for an adjustment of status (*régularisation exceptionnelle*). By the end of the amnesty period in 1983, over 145,000 applications had been received (Weil 1991).

In a liberal and republican polity like France, strict control of entries together with an amnesty for the undocumented came to be seen as a good way to integrate permanent resident aliens, or as Tomas Hammar (1990) called them, "denizens." In addition to the amnesty, to make foreigners residing in France more secure, the Mauroy government (1981–1984) relaxed prohibitions against associational and political activities by foreigners. No changes were made to the nationality law or naturalization policy, leaving this key element of the republican model intact. Foreigners were welcome within strict guidelines of labor market rules and regulations. They would be integrated on the (republican) basis of respect for the separation between church and state (*laïcité*), and they were expected to assimilate quickly.

Having thus reaffirmed the previous governments' commitment to strict immigration control, while at the same time taking steps to speed the integration of foreigners, the socialists, it seemed, were forging a new consensus on the contentious immigration issue. Nonetheless, the issue exploded onto the political scene in 1984 with the municipal elections in the city of Dreux, an industrial town just west of Paris. The Front National—a grouping of extreme right-wing movements under the charismatic and flamboyant leader Jean-Marie Le Pen—won control of the city on a platform calling for a complete halt to immigration and for the deportation of African immigrants. The electoral breakthrough of a neo-fascist, xenophobic, and racist movement profoundly changed the politics of immigration in France and throughout western Europe (Thränhardt 1997; Givens 2005). For the first time since the end of World War II, an extremist party of the right was making itself heard and finding a new legitimacy, garnering support from large segments of the French electorate. Within a matter of years, it would become, in the words of the political scientist Pascal Perrineau, "the largest working-class party in France" (Perrineau 1995). From its beginning, the Front National was a single-issue party, taking a stand against immigration, and its leader, Le Pen, called for a physical separation of the races. His discourse mixed xenophobia, nationalism ("la France aux Français"—France for the French), and anti-Semitism with appeals to the economic and physical insecurities of the French working class.

Crises of National Identity

The rise of the Front National contributed heavily to a sense of crisis in French politics, with immigrants at the center of the maelstrom, from the immigrant suburbs—dubbed by some "les banlieues de l'Islam ou de la République" (the Islamic suburbs of the Republic) (Kepel 2012), to a common depiction of a veiled Marianne. Suddenly immigrants were seen as the cause of the economic and cultural decline of the French nation, provoking a loss of confidence in the republican model, especially on the right, but also on the left. Immigrants were accused of taking jobs away from French citizens, thereby contributing to high levels of unemployment, and Muslims were deemed to be hostile to republican values and impossible to assimilate. The socialist left under the leadership of President Mitterrand as well as the neo-Gaullist right—led by Jacques Chirac—had different responses to the Front National's populist appeals to economic insecurity, xenophobia, and racism.

One of the first steps of the new government of cohabitation—a combination of neo-Gaullists (Rassemblement pour la République, RPR) and liberals (Union pour la Démocratie Française, UDF) under Prime Minister Jacques Chirac—was to reform immigration *and* naturalization policy. Chirac handed the dossier to the tough Corsican minister of the interior, Charles Pasqua, whose name would become synonymous with immigration restriction. Pasqua's approach was quite different from those taken by his predecessors. He viewed immigration control primarily as a police matter, and he moved quickly to reinforce border controls by giving sweeping new powers to the Police de l'Air et des Frontières (PAF) to detain and immediately deport anyone who did not have proper papers. He also reinforced the power of the (internal) police forces to conduct "random" identity checks of any foreign- or suspicious-looking individual. It was during this time (1986) that there was a wave of terrorist bombings in Paris that were connected to the Middle East, specifically Iran. The violence helped to further legitimize the new get-tough policy with respect to foreigners, shifting the immigration debate away from markets and rights and toward security and culture (see the introduction to this volume). The immediate effect of these measures was to restrict the civil liberties of foreigners, specifically from the Maghreb, thereby launching a psychological campaign against immigrants and immigration. The policies were explicitly designed to win back supporters of the Front National and to prevent any further loss of votes to the extreme right on the issue of immigration (Perrineau 1997), moves that would be repeated by the center-right governments of Sarkozy and Macron (discussed later). These get-tough policies also heightened the sense of crisis and contributed to the growing debate over insecurity and a loss of national identity.

Yet if we look at the inflows, what we find is considerable continuity. The number of immigrants fluctuated between 100,000 and 200,000 annually throughout the 1980s. The only noticeable increase, as in other European states, was in the number of asylum seekers, which peaked at 61,400 in 1989. With the end of the Cold War and the gradual implementation of the Schengen Agreement in the 1990s, the rate of rejection of asylum applicants rose from 57 percent in 1985 to 84 percent in 1995, and the number of applicants fell precipitously to below 20,000 a year by the mid-1990s (see Figure 5.5). So if flows were not raging out of control, what was the purpose of the first Pasqua Law of 1986? The most controversial aspect of the reform was the attempt to weaken the birthright principle of *jus soli* by putting an end to the practice of automatically conferring citizenship at age eighteen on children born in France of foreign parents. The reform was symbolic, intended to placate right-wing nationalists and win back Front National voters, but its effects were real (Perrineau 1995, 1997; Viard 1996). Any immigrant who had been sentenced to more than six months in prison was deemed excludable and would not be allowed to naturalize. West Africans were no longer allowed to naturalize under the streamlined procedure known as "reintegration into French nationality." And foreign spouses of French nationals would have to wait two years (rather than one) before they could apply for naturalization (Figure 5.6).

The thrust of the proposed law was to require young foreigners to affirm their commitment to the Republic by formally requesting French nationality and taking a loyalty oath. What effect such a change might have on immigration flows was unclear, but the intended message was clear: the acquisition of French citizenship was a privilege, not a right, and it should be withheld from those who have not made a clear commitment to the French nation. The first Pasqua Law provoked a firestorm

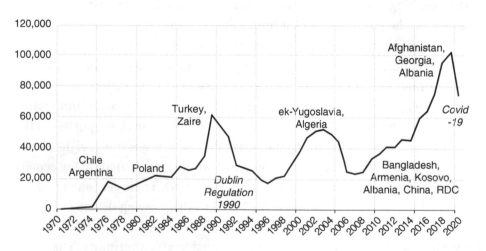

FIGURE 5.5. Asylum Seekers, 1972–2020

Annual number of new asylum seekers registered in France by OFPRA, showing the main countries of origin.

SOURCE: Ministries of Justice and Interior.

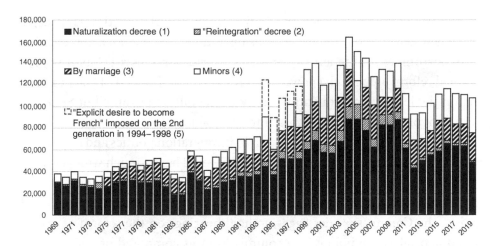

FIGURE 5.6. Acquisition of French Citizenship Since the Pompidou Presidency
In absolute numbers.

SOURCE: French Ministry of Justice and Ministry of Social Affairs.

NOTES:

1. Positive decision on requests for naturalization processed by the prefects on assimilation criteria (mainly linguistic and professional). Includes the accompanying minor children.
2. Women married to foreigners, who can recover their French citizenship after divorce or widowhood.
3. French citizenship granted to the foreign spouse by simple registration.
4. Children born in France to immigrants who become French on anticipated demand before age 18.
5. "Desire to acquire French nationality," which children born in France to immigrant parents had to declare between age 16 and 21 (law of July 1993 abolished by the Socialists in March 1998).

N.B.: The 2nd generation children, if born in France and living in France for at least five years, become automatically French at age 18. There are no official statistics on them if they do not apply before age 18. In total, the state has a margin of action in matters of naturalization policy only through procedures 1, 2, and 5.

of protest, as various civil and immigrant rights organizations, such as La Ligue des Droits de l'Homme, GISTI, SOS-Racisme, MRAP, and others, mobilized against the reform, leading the government eventually to withdraw the bill from consideration. The law did not affect second-generation Franco-Algerians, those who were born in France of parents who were born in Algeria prior to 1962, the year of Algerian independence. In such cases both the parents and the children were French by birth (double *jus soli*) and therefore eligible to naturalize (Weil 1991, 2002; Feldblum 1999; Schnapper 2000).

The withdrawal of the bill was a major setback for the Chirac government, which had provided the increasingly active French civil rights movement with a new rallying cry: "Touche pas à mon pote!" (Don't touch my buddy!). Tens of thousands marched in Paris under this banner. In addition to altering the political landscape, launching a new debate about French citizenship and national identity, and creating political opportunities for the left (Ireland 1994; Kastoryano 1997; Feldblum 1999), the attempted reform brought the power and prestige of the Council of State to bear. In ruling on the legality and constitutionality of the bill, the Council of State put the government on notice that the rights of individual foreigners and the republican tradition must be respected. This was a lesson in immigration politics and law, which Minister Pasqua would not soon forget. In 1993, he would have a much stronger hand to deal with the judiciary (discussed later), but in this first round of reforms, the government was forced to compromise and the decision was made to appoint a special commission, the Commission des Sages, to hold hearings on the reform of immigration and naturalization policy. The commission was composed of political and intellectual elites, and it was chaired by Marceau Long, who, as vice president of the Council of State, had the moral and legal authority to tackle this difficult policy issue.

After hearing the testimony of many experts on immigration, the commission simply reaffirmed the importance of the republican tradition by defending the birthright principle of *jus soli*, while at the same time stressing the importance of integrating foreigners into public and civic life (Long 1988). The whole episode of reform during the first government of cohabitation had little discernible impact on immigration flows, which remained well over 100,000 during the late 1980s and into the 1990s. The number of naturalizations averaged around 50,000 annually during the same period (see Figure 5.6). However, if we look at changes in the ratio of naturalizations by declaration or acquisition (*par déclaration*) to those by decree or attribution (*par décret*) for the period 1984–2010, what we find is an upsurge in naturalizations in 1985–1986 and again in the late 1990s and 2000s. This indicates that many individuals were filing for naturalization during the key years of the Pasqua reforms, while the number of those qualifying for "automatic" naturalization (by declaration, as opposed to by decree) remained relatively constant. The exception is 1994, when, with the implementation of the second Pasqua Law (discussed further shortly), the number of those declaring themselves to be French shot up to 43,000, twice the average of 19,900 for the period 1973–1992 (see Figure 5.6). The big question, which was difficult to answer in France before the introduction in 2003 of questions on the migration origins of parents in the main surveys conducted by the Institut National de la Statistique et des Études Économiques (INSEE), is what happens with the integration of the second generation. According to the annual Labor Force Survey in 2003, 11 percent of adults have at least one immigrant parent. It is estimated that by 2008, 20 percent of the total French population was either an immigrant (first generation) or the child of one or two immigrants (second generation) (see Héran 2012, 32–33). The proportion reached 26.6 percent among those between twenty-five and fifty-four years of age (Bouvier 2012, 19).

The coalition of liberals and the republican right (UDF-RPR) lost its battle to defeat the Front National, and it also lost the elections of 1988. The new left-wing government, led by two old socialist rivals, François Mitterrand and Michel Rocard, essentially returned to the grand-bargain policies of the early 1980s, increasing regulation of the labor market, campaigning against illegal immigration, and taking steps to integrate immigrants. Prime Minister Rocard created the Haut Conseil à l'Intégration to study ways of speeding the integration of the foreign population, which still constituted over 6 percent of the total population (Haut Conseil 1991). For the period 1988–1993, socialist governments fell back on a strategy of strictly controlling inflows in order to integrate those foreigners already in the country. The hope was to depoliticize the issue and defuse the national identity crisis. However, no sooner had the left returned to power than it found itself confronted with a highly symbolic controversy, which struck at the heart of the republican tradition itself and risked splitting the Socialist Party into competing factions.

The controversy arose when three girls of Moroccan descent came to a public school wearing Islamic head scarves (*foulards*). The event immediately became a cause célèbre for both the anti-immigrant right and the republican left, with more liberal (pluralist or multicultural) elements of the political and intellectual elite, including Prime Minister Rocard, caught in the middle. (A similar controversy, discussed later, erupted in 2020–2021, this time with President Emmanuel Macron in the eye of the storm.) Allowing the girls to wear the head scarves was bound to offend both the left and the right, but forcing them to remove the scarves could open a Pandora's box concerning the dividing line between the public and private spheres. Banning the scarves would raise questions about the wearing of other religious symbols in the classroom, such as a crucifix or a Star of David. The event also heightened the sense of a cultural crisis with respect to immigration control, because of the widespread fear that the new immigrants from North Africa, especially the second generation, were prone to Islamic fundamentalism and therefore impossible to assimilate into a secular, republican society, where the individual should keep his or her private life and religious beliefs completely separate from the public sphere (Roy 1991; Schnapper 1990). One of the leaders of the Socialist Party who was most adamant in his opposition to such overt violations of the republican principle of *laïcité* was Jean-Pierre Chevènement, erstwhile leader of the Centre d'Études, de Recherche et d'Éducation Socialistes (CERES), the strongest republican wing of the Socialist Party. Chevènement held ministerial posts in various socialist governments in the 1980s and 1990s.

Prime Minister Rocard and his minister of education and future prime minister, Lionel Jospin, made the decision to allow the girls to wear the scarves so long as they agreed not to proselytize or in any way disrupt classes. As happened frequently with the issue of immigration and integration, when the rights of the individual vis-à-vis the state come into question, the Council of State is invoked. In this case, the Council of State simply ratified the compromise put forward by the Rocard government. But the compromise did little to allay growing fears of Islamic fundamentalism among the French public, and the "*foulards* affair," as it came to be known, raised a new specter of American-style multiculturalism, seen as yet another threat to French unity and national identity (exemplified by the "one and indivisible Republic"). *Le droit à la différence* (the right to be different) became the new rallying cry of those defending multiculturalism and the rights of immigrants (Roy 1991; Kastoryano 1997), and the terrorist attacks of the 2000s would add a security dimension and new sense of urgency to these debates about integration (see the model of the policy process, Figure 1.1, in the introduction to this volume).

Yet despite the almost continuous atmosphere of crisis in French politics over immigration, integration, and national identity, dating back at least to the early 1980s, very little changed in terms of either policy outputs (policies for controlling immigration) or policy outcomes (levels of immigration) (Hollifield 1986, 1992a, 1997; Simon 2012; introduction to this volume). The first experience of cohabitation (1986–1988) did little to alter the republican model and the rules of the game, as spelled out in the *ordonnances* of 1945 (Weil 1991). Flows, which are the best measure of policy outcomes, continued at the level of 100,000 or more immigrants a year, and the liberal nationality code allowed for the relatively quick naturalization of the foreign population (see Figure 5.6).

Zero Immigration

When asked about immigration policy in 1991, President Mitterrand suggested that every society, including France, has a "threshold of tolerance" (*seuil de tolérance*), beyond which instances of xenophobia and racism are likely to increase. However, he did not say what that threshold might be in the case of France. Charles Pasqua, soon to be (for the second time in his career) minister of the interior, stated bluntly that "France has been an immigration country, but she wants to be no longer." Like any good nationalist and populist, Pasqua claimed to be speaking in the name of the French people. As a powerful member of the second cohabitation government, elected by a landslide (the coalition of Gaullists and liberals won over 80 percent of the seats in the Assembly) in the spring of 1993, Pasqua made clear what the immigration policy of the new government would be: "The goal we set, given the seriousness of the economic situation, is to tend toward *zero immigration*" (Le Monde 1993).

Faced with a badly weakened, divided, and demoralized socialist opposition, and having won an overwhelming majority in Parliament, the new right-wing government, headed by Prime Minister Édouard Balladur, had a virtually free hand to pursue draconian policies for (1) stopping all immigration, (2) reducing the number of asylum seekers to an absolute minimum, and (3) reforming the nationality code to block naturalization of as many resident foreigners as possible. What distinguishes this 1993 round of reforms from earlier attempts to limit immigration (in 1974 or 1986, for example) is the clear focus on rolling back the rights of foreigners. The second Pasqua Law presented a direct challenge to the republican model, as defined by the *ordonnances* of 1945. Equal protection and due process (civil rights) were denied to foreigners by cutting off possibilities of appeal for asylum seekers and by giving the police much greater powers than ever before to detain and deport foreigners.

To constrain worker and family immigration in France, the second Pasqua Law, enacted in 1994, required workers and foreign students to wait two years (rather than one) before bringing any family members to join them. To inhibit permanent settlement of foreigners and to control illegal immigration, the law prohibited adjustment of status (*régularisation*) for any undocumented individual who married a French citizen. Mayors were given the authority to annul any suspected marriage of convenience (*mariage blanc*). With these provisions the state inserted itself directly into the private lives of French citizens, as well as foreigners. Finally, under the second Pasqua Law, any foreigner expelled from France would be denied reentry into French territory for one year. These reforms indicate the lengths to which liberal states are willing to go in rolling back the rights of foreigners in order to restrict immigration, much like the Trump administration in the United States (see Martin and Orrenius in this volume).

The efforts of the Balladur government to move France to "zero immigration" did little to calm the national identity crisis. If anything, the second Pasqua Law heightened the sense of crisis and fanned the flames of xenophobia, leading to a full-blown constitutional debate. One objective of the reforms, however, seems to have been met: the average annual rate of immigration for the period 1993–1999 fell below 100,000 for the first time since the late 1940s and early 1950s. But, as we shall see in the crisis over the Debré Law in 1997, many of the formerly legal flows were simply pushed underground, increasing the size of the undocumented population and raising the level of insecurity among the foreign population as a whole. The number of individuals caught trying to enter the country illegally (*refoulements à la frontière*) rose steadily from 1993 on, jumping from 8,700 in 1993 to 10,100 in 1995 and over 12,000 in 1996, providing (indirect) evidence of greater unauthorized immigration (cf. Massey 2020 on the United States).

The Limits of Immigration Control

The election of Jacques Chirac as president of the Republic in 1995 by a narrower-than-expected margin over the leftist candidate, Lionel Jospin, did little to change French immigration policy, even though the Front National received 15 percent of the vote in the first round of the presidential elections. In the summer of 1996, the tough control policies (described in the preceding section) were challenged by a group of Africans, mostly from Mali, who were caught in the Catch-22 of the second Pasqua Law (unable to obtain a residency permit, even though they had resided in France for many years and could not be legally deported) and whose applications for political asylum had been rejected. The undocumented or *sans-papiers*, as they were called, occupied the Saint-Bernard church in Paris, demanding that they be given an adjustment of status, and several of them launched a hunger strike. Apart from occasional acts of civil disobedience by the African *sans-papiers*, which continued throughout the period 1995–1997, whether in the form of occupying churches or, in one case, the offices of UNESCO, the civil war in Algeria also had an impact on French immigration control policy. The abrupt cancellation of the Algerian elections in 1992—which Islamic fundamentalists were poised to win—had sparked a civil war in the former French colony. The conflict pitted the Islamic radicals against the long-ruling revolutionary party, the Front de Libération Nationale (FLN), which controlled the military. The elections were canceled with the blessing of the French government, which made no attempt to hide its support for the Algerian military. French involvement in Algerian politics led to a number of terrorist attacks by Islamic militants against targets in France. These attacks forced the government of Alain Juppé to increase security throughout the country. The security sweeps by the police and the military, known as Operation Vigipirate, focused public attention on the Muslim (and African) communities in France, brought the full power of the French state to bear in an effort to catch the perpetrators, and shifted the debate about immigration further in the direction of security and culture.

As in the 1950s, French relations with former colonies, especially Algeria, were a driving factor in immigration and refugee policy. Various governments felt compelled to grant asylum (or at least temporary residence) to many members of the

Algerian political and intellectual elite (from 1992 to 1997, over 400,000 affluent Algerians fled the civil war, with most going to France or Canada), while at the same time stepping up pressure to keep other Algerians out and maintain a close watch on the established Algerian community in France. This atmosphere of crisis and public insecurity together with continuing pressure from the Front National led the Juppé government late in 1996 to propose a new law, supported by the minister of the interior, Jean-Louis Debré, designed to resolve the ambiguous status of some of the *sans-papiers*, particularly the French-born children of illegal immigrants and the foreign spouses of French citizens. Under the proposed law, foreign children under sixteen years of age would have to prove continuous residence in France for ten years, and foreign spouses would have to have been married for two years in order to be eligible (like the children) for a one-year residence permit.

The Debré Law had some liberal intent. It got a lot of publicity and became the focal point of controversy and protest because of a provision added to the bill by the conservative National Assembly. The provision required all private citizens to notify local authorities whenever they received in their homes any non-EU foreigner. Moreover, mayors would be given the authority to verify that a foreign visitor had left the private citizen's home once the visitor's visa had expired. What is most interesting about the Debré Law is not so much the effect (or lack thereof) that it had on immigration control but the response it received both from certain groups in civil society and from institutions of the liberal-republican state. Minister Debré, paraphrasing his predecessor Pasqua, stated, "I am for zero *illegal* immigration. . . . The State must be given the means to deter foreigners who want to enter France without resources, papers or jobs" (Le Monde 1993). The focus in this statement is on those clearly outside the law—that is, illegal immigrants—but public attention was focused on the effect that the law would have on French citizens, who would (by law) be compelled to inform on foreign visitors. Such an intrusion by the state into the private lives of individuals and families was deemed by many to have crossed the invisible line beyond which liberal states are not supposed to go (Hollifield 1999). The Debré Law was denounced as an infringement of personal freedom and a threat to the basic civil liberties of all citizens. The European Parliament even went so far as to pass a resolution condemning the law and equating it with Vichy-era laws that required French citizens to inform on their Jewish compatriots so that they could be deported by the Gestapo to death camps.

The Debré Law also seemed to violate the liberal principle that an individual is innocent until proven guilty. In order to renew their ten-year residence permits, foreigners would be required to prove that they were not a threat to public order and that they had maintained a regular residence in France, thus shifting the burden of proof from the state to the individual. This provision of the law, along with another that would have given police access to the fingerprints of all asylum seekers, was subsequently struck down by the Constitutional Council, which, unlike the Council of State, has powers of judicial review. The final version of the Debré Law was passed by the French Parliament in March 1996. Provisions concerning notification of the whereabouts of foreigners were watered down. The law required African visitors to prove that they have adequate accommodations for their visit, the funds necessary to live in France during their stay, and the funds to return home afterward. Throughout this period of policy reform, a major concern of the French government was to devise a system for controlling entry by Africans (and other foreign visitors coming from developing countries), but without imposing American-style quotas or overtly targeting specific ethnic or national groups. The resistance to quotas is born of the republican desire to maintain an egalitarian approach to the issuing of visas—where all or most applicants coming from developing countries would be treated equally— as well as a desire to construct a system that would not overtly discriminate against individuals coming from former French colonies in West and North Africa. But regardless of intent, the effect of both the second Pasqua Law (1993) and the Debré Law (1997) was to restrict legal immigration of Africans to France and feed the fires of xenophobia.

A New "Republican Pact"

To the surprise of many, President Chirac dissolved the National Assembly and called early elections in May and June 1997. The French socialists and their allies (a mixture of Communists, radicals, and Greens) won control of the National Assembly, launching the third period of cohabitation in a little over a decade, only this time the right would control the presidency and the left would control the Parliament. The new left-wing government, headed by Lionel Jospin, took steps to return French immigration policy to its republican roots and to resolve the ambiguous status of the *sans-papiers*. In his opening speech to the new Parliament on June 19, 1997, Jospin announced that he would establish a "new republican pact." He laid out a detailed republican vision of immigration policy, reminiscent of earlier periods in French immigration history (beginning at the turn of the century and extending through the 1920s, the 1945 *ordonnances*, and the early Mitterrand years in the 1980s) (Weil 1991). To quote Jospin: "France, with its old republican traditions, was built in layers that flowed together into a melting pot, thus creating an alloy that is strong because of the diversity of its component parts. For this reason, birthright citizenship [*le droit du sol*] is inseparable from the French nation [*consubstantiel à la nation française*].

We will reestablish this right. Nothing is more alien to France than xenophobia and racism. . . . Immigration is an economic, social, and human reality, which must be organized and controlled. France must define a firm, dignified immigration policy without renouncing its values or compromising its social balance" (Jospin 1997).

To accomplish this goal, Jospin called for (1) a new republican integration policy that welcomes immigrants and respects their human rights but combats illegal immigration and labor black markets, thus returning to the "grand bargain" strategies of earlier socialist governments; (2) a new policy of cooperation with the sending states to address the root causes of migration; and (3) a comprehensive review of immigration and nationality law, which was carried out by an inter-ministerial task force chaired by the immigration scholar Patrick Weil (1997). During the campaign, Jospin promised to repeal the Pasqua and Debré Laws—a promise that would come back to haunt him (discussed later). Finally, (4) steps were taken to review, on a case-by-case basis, the situation of all undocumented foreigners caught in the maze of regulations and contradictions surrounding the Pasqua and Debré Laws. The government issued orders to the prefects (the direct arm of the administrative state in the provinces) to immediately begin reviewing as many as 40,000 cases. Foreigners who had waited months or years for their dossiers to be reviewed suddenly found the administrative authorities newly willing to help them by issuing temporary residence permits.

The Weil report, published in August 1997, contained 120 propositions for modifying immigration and nationality law. For the most part, the report (like the bills that would be presented to Parliament later that year) tried to steer a middle course: reestablishing the centrality of the principle of *jus soli* in French nationality law, going back to the naturalization procedure that existed before the 1993 Pasqua Law, with a few modifications, but not creating a blanket birthright citizenship, as exists in the United States; reinforcing the rights of asylum seekers and the rights of family reunification; but cracking down on illegal immigration—a policy similar to the old socialist grand bargain and to the policies of Democratic administrations in the United States from Clinton to Obama. Finally, the report appealed to the republican tradition, linking immigration with an open, welcoming, but secular tradition in French politics and law.

By giving such a high priority to reform of immigration and nationality law, the Jospin government signaled its desire to confront the issue. And by appealing to French republican values as a way of resolving the immigration crisis, the government clearly hoped to return to the earlier "republican consensus," defuse the immigration issue, and seize the political and moral high ground. Attempts by right-wing governments to steal the thunder of Le Pen and the Front National by cracking down on immigrants and thereby appealing to the electorate's insecurities and xenophobia—what might be called the Pasqua-Debré approach to immigration policy—did little to reduce levels of support for the Front National (Perrineau 1997). Whether the socialists and their left-wing allies could reconstruct the republican consensus would depend heavily on their ability to reach out to elements of the liberal and republican right. This was the strategy adopted in the Weil report (1997) and subsequently by the government itself.

Two bills were drafted and presented to the National Assembly late in 1997. The Guigou Law dealt with reform of the nationality code, whereas the Chevènement Law dealt with reform of immigration policy. Both laws openly appealed to the republican tradition in an attempt to gain support from a broad spectrum of politicians on the left and the right. The Guigou Law was adopted in early December 1997 by a narrow margin (267 deputies voting for it and 246 against, with many Communists and Greens abstaining because they thought the law too harsh). The pro-immigrant left wanted to send a message to the government expressing its displeasure with the strategy of amending rather than repealing the Pasqua and Debré Laws. This pink-Green coalition, dubbed the "moral left," took a strong stand in favor of birthright citizenship, meaning an end to all restrictions on the naturalization of individuals born on French territory. The right-wing opposition denounced the reform as unnecessary and detrimental to the national interest. One UDF (liberal) deputy, François Bayrou, following the lead of former president Valéry Giscard d'Estaing, called for a referendum on the issue. Meanwhile, the sole representative of the Front National in the Assembly, Jean Marie Le Chevalier, called for the elimination of *jus soli* in favor of *jus sanguinis* as the organizing principle for French nationality law.

The Guigou Law in effect reinforced the principle of *jus soli*, so that anyone born in France of foreign parents can acquire French nationality at the age of majority (eighteen) as long as that individual can show continuous or discontinuous residence in France for at least five years after the age of eleven. Any minor born in France of foreign parents can request naturalization as early as age thirteen if his/her parents give their consent and if s/he has resided in France for at least five years since age eight. To ensure that naturalization is voluntary, the law stated that any young foreigner can refuse French citizenship in the six months before s/he turns eighteen or in the twelve months after his/her eighteenth birthday. To avoid having individuals fall through the cracks of the law, as happened with the *sans-papiers* under the second Pasqua Law, the Guigou Law created a "republican identity card" (note the symbolism of the name) to be given to every minor born in France of foreign parents. Finally, the law rolled back the waiting period for foreign spouses to request naturalization from two years to one year after the date of the marriage.

The Chevènement Law changed the 1945 *ordonnances* governing the status of foreigners in France. The Chevènement Law eliminated the "legal entry requirement" imposed by the second Pasqua Law on any foreigner seeking to adjust his/her status. However, the law kept "threat to public order" as grounds for exclusion. Under the law, one-year residence permits were issued to (1) all minors entering under the auspices of family reunification, (2) all foreigners who entered France before the age of ten and who reside in France, (3) any foreigner who can prove that s/he has resided in France for fifteen years, and (4) foreign spouses of French nationals as well as the foreign parents of French children. These changes were intended to emphasize the importance and sanctity of the family under French law. The one-year permits also will be issued to foreigners who are infirm. Special consideration in the issuance of residence and work permits also must be given to (1) foreign scholars and professors invited to work in France and (2) any foreigner who has a special personal or family situation. Foreigners who pose a threat to public order or who engage in polygamy are prohibited from receiving residence permits. A special residence permit for retired people, valid for ten years and renewable, also was created.

The Chevènement Law established two new forms of asylum for individuals persecuted because of their activities "on behalf of freedom." This is called "constitutional asylum." The law created a French equivalent of the American Temporary Protected Status, giving the French minister of justice the power to grant "territorial asylum" (independent of the Geneva Convention) to individuals who would be in imminent personal danger if they were returned to their country of origin. In another nod to the right, the length of administrative detention for irregular migrants was increased from ten to twelve days, but foreigners have additional time to appeal a deportation order.

The shift in policy toward greater external (border) controls seems to have had a discernible effect on flows, which rose from 95,757 in 1996 to 139,533 in 1998 but went back down to 119,250 in 2000 (Lebon 2001). These numbers were more in line with the annual averages of the 1980s and early 1990s (around 100,000), and they reflected a partial amnesty of individuals with an irregular status. Over a three-year period (1997–2000), 76,300 individuals benefited from a review of their cases that allowed them to obtain residence permits.

Choosing Immigrants

Following the victory of Jacques Chirac and the parties of the traditional republican right (rebaptized as the Union pour la Majorité Présidentielle, UMP) in the presidential and legislative elections of May and June 2002, there was little immediate change in immigration policy, despite the fact that Jean-Marie Le Pen and the Front National garnered 17 percent of the vote in the first round of the presidential elections, eliminating Lionel Jospin (16 percent) and the fractured left from the second round of voting. The new government under Prime Minister Jean-Pierre Raffarin promised to crack down on crime and increase spending on public security, and the new "law and order" minister of the interior, Nicolas Sarkozy, wasted little time in reframing the debate about immigration, vowing that France, as a sovereign nation, had the right to choose immigrants, rather than having immigrants choose France. "Oui à l'immigration choisie, non à l'immigration subie" (yes to immigration as a choice, no to the imposition of immigration) became the slogan and the cornerstone of French policy in the 2000s, a decade that saw the passage of no fewer than four new immigration laws. Although the thrust of these reforms was toward greater restriction—especially with respect to family immigration—the terms of the debate shifted from stopping immigration (the so-called zero immigration option, discussed earlier) to managing immigration in the "national interest." In practice this meant limiting unskilled (worker) immigration in favor of the highly skilled, cracking down further on illegal immigration, and requiring immigrants to demonstrate their willingness and ability to integrate not only into the labor market (by finding employment) but also into society (by showing mastery of the French language and acceptance of "republican" values).

The debate about immigrant integration took on greater urgency as the so-called War on Terror heated up with further terrorist attacks in Madrid (2004) and in London (2005), followed in the fall of 2005 by riots and civil unrest across France, but especially in the working-class and heavily immigrant suburbs of Paris (Kepel 2012). The republican model appeared to be in crisis, as mostly second-generation (African) immigrants took to the streets to protest high levels of unemployment, poor living conditions (in the public housing projects or *habitations à loyer modéré*), bleak prospects for future mobility within French society, and harassment by the police. Rioting continued off and on for almost one month, prompting President Jacques Chirac to declare a state of emergency in November 2005 and leading Interior Minister Sarkozy famously to declaim that the rioters were *racailles* (scum) and that he would use a sort of steam cleaner (*Kärcher*) to cleanse the suburbs of these hoodlums (*voyous*). By dialing up the rhetoric and vowing to rid the suburbs of undesirable elements, Minister Sarkozy placed himself at the center of debates about immigration and integration, and he would be the author of two new restrictive laws on immigration. Sarkozy I, passed in November 2003, strengthened the hand of administrative authorities to detain and deport undesirable or undocumented migrants, tightened restrictions on granting residency permits, especially for family members and spouses of French citizens, and linked residency to a willingness on the part of

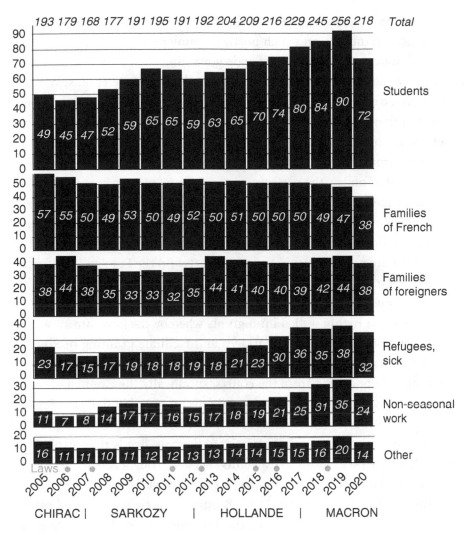

FIGURE 5.7. Annual Number of Residence Permits Granted by France to Non-Europeans

Numbers are in thousands. Minors and asylum seekers awaiting decision are not included. The decline observed in 2020 is due to the Covid pandemic.

SOURCE: French Ministry of Interior, authors' calculations.

immigrants to demonstrate "republican integration." Three years later, near the end of the second Chirac administration, Sarkozy II—passed in 2006—again tried to tighten restrictions on family immigration, making it more difficult for immigrants to bring their relatives to join them, and creating new administrative barriers for obtaining residency permits. But family immigration continued to increase in the 2000s, along with growing numbers of foreign students (Figure 5.7).

At roughly the same time (2005) the venerable *ordonnances* of 1945, which had laid down the republican principles on which postwar immigration and naturalization policy was based, were replaced by a new code governing the admission and residence of foreigners and asylum seekers in France (Code de l'entrée et du séjour des étrangers et du droit d'asile, CESEDA). In keeping with the idea that the French state should choose immigrants rather than having immigrants choose France, the making and implementation of immigration policy were centralized in the Ministry of Interior. Somewhat ironically, at the same time that the government was tightening its grip on immigration policy, the prefects were given new powers in making critical decisions about the conditions that immigrants would have to fulfill to obtain residency permits, to marry, and to reunify their families. The net result was to create greater bureaucratic obstacles for immigrants and to strengthen the hand of the police and administrative authority vis-à-vis the courts and the Foreign Ministry in "managing" migration.

The crackdown on family and worker migration was accompanied by a new kind of quota system for highly skilled immigrants whereby the government would identify certain professions with skill shortages and facilitate granting of visas to immigrants meeting critical labor market needs. But, just as in the 1970s, the government encountered opposition from the courts, specifically the Council of State, which ruled that the right of families to live together is protected both by the French Constitution and by European (and international) law. Thus, at the beginning of the Sarkozy administration (in 2007), with the parties of the right firmly in control of the government—Nicolas Sarkozy easily defeated his socialist rival, Ségolène Royal, and his party (the UMP) had a large working majority in the National Assembly—the government was frustrated in its efforts to limit immigrant rights, civil and otherwise, and to establish a more selective immigration policy. Nevertheless, two more immigration laws would be passed by President Sarkozy and his new government. The first (in 2007), named for the minister of the interior, Brice Hortefeux, provoked a firestorm of controversy and intense opposition from civil liberties groups, like GISTI and SOS-Racisme. The law required immigrants seeking family reunification to use expensive DNA tests to prove that those who were applying were blood relatives. Opponents argued that DNA testing was unethical and unconstitutional and that if immigrants refused to undergo or pay for the tests, their applications could then more easily be rejected by administrative authorities on the grounds that they were fraudulent. Even though the law was upheld (with some reservations) by the Constitutional Council, its DNA testing provision was never implemented. The controversy would return in 2009, however, when Hortefeux's successor, Eric Besson, announced that he would open the way for the use of DNA tests. A second law, named for Besson, was passed in 2011 and targeted illegal immigrants by increasing administrative detention and strengthening the hand of the police, particularly the border police (PAF). In France, as in other major receiving countries (Ellermann 2009), the majority of illegal immigrants are actually visa overstayers, and the legal and administrative difficulties associated with deportation are numerous. In the 2000s, deportation orders ranged from 50,000 to 80,000 per year, with actual expulsions from 10,000 to 20,000. In 2010, for example, 73,500 individuals were ordered to leave the country, but only 16,100 were actually deported (Régnard 2010; Breem 2011).

With all the twists and turns of immigration policy in the first two decades of the twenty-first century, the presence of immigrants (those of foreign origin) in France continued to grow, rising from 7.3 percent of the total population in 2000 to 10 percent in 2020 (see Figure 5.2). As a result, attention shifted from control of entry (admission) to integration. Three of the four laws passed during the decade linked the granting of visas and residency permits to a willingness to integrate and, in the case of Sarkozy II, potential immigrants were obliged to sign a "reception and integration contract" (*contrat d'accueil et d'intégration*). The real issue—the proverbial elephant in the room—was the integration of a large and growing Muslim population, and especially the fate of the second generation and those who arrived in France as young children (known as the "1.5 generation") (Tribalat 1996, 2011–2012; Héran 2012; Simon 2012). Understanding immigrant integration requires information about the ethnicity of individuals, including their religious practices and affiliations. The first survey that broached the issue of immigrant origins and ethnicity, conducted in the early 1990s, was highly controversial (Tribalat 1995, 1996). The survey provoked a bitter public debate within the scientific community over the appropriateness of collecting and analyzing information about ethnic origins (Le Bras 1998). This evolved into a general political and constitutional argument about so-called ethnic statistics (Simon 2003, 2005, 2017), a question that eventually came before the Constitutional Council at the same time (2007) as the DNA testing controversy. The council ruled against the use of survey questions about ethnicity or religion, on the grounds that such intrusive questions are a violation of Article 1 of the French Constitution, which states that "la France est une République indivisible, laïque, démocratique et sociale. Elle assure l'égalité devant la loi de tous les citoyens sans distinction d'origine, de race ou de religion" (France is an indivisible republic, religion-neutral, democratic, and social. Equality before the law is guaranteed for all citizens irrespective of national origin, race, or religion).

The number of practicing Muslims in France is estimated to be 4 million, or 6 percent of the total population, compared with a similar number in Germany (5 percent of the population) and 2.4 million in the United Kingdom (4 percent of the population) (Simon and Tiberj 2013). The preoccupation with assimilation of Muslim immigrants is not unique to France. Similar concerns about the effects of Islam on civic life have arisen across Europe, particularly in the Netherlands, Britain, Germany, and Switzerland (see chapters by Maas, Hansen, and D'Amato in this volume), as well as in the United States. In France, highly symbolic measures—such as the deportation of several hundred Roma in 2010, the 2011 ban against women wearing the burqa in public, and the debate over halal meat stirred up by the Front National candidate Marine Le Pen, daughter of Jean-Marie, in the presidential elections of 2012—are symptomatic of the surge in identity politics, which has gained in intensity, especially during the Macron presidency (discussed later).

In January and July 2016, Nicolas Sarkozy published two campaign booklets for the presidential primary of the center right (the republicans). He would lose in the first round in November to François Fillon, his former prime minister, who took a harder line on immigration, and to Alain Juppé, a former prime minister under Jacques Chirac, with a moderate line. In these professions of faith, Sarkozy returned to the policies he had pursued from 2005 to 2012. He explained that his only mistake was to have been right before everyone else. He felt that he should have stuck with the program that linked immigration and security (defined in a speech given in Grenoble on July 30, 2010). He pointed to three "historical errors" that had led to the "current disaster": (1) the recruitment of large numbers of immigrant workers in the postwar years, (2) the authorization of family reunifications in 1974, and (3) the power of a pro-migration "single-issue lobby" (*pensée unique*). All his predecessors were guilty of these errors—those on the left, of course (Mitterrand and Hollande), but even more so those on the right (de Gaulle, Giscard d'Estaing, Chirac).

Such rewriting of history was not normal for the mainstream right. Sarkozy took a page from the playbook of the extreme right, which persisted in blaming the decline of France on high levels of immigration, using immigrants as scapegoats for France's social and economic problems. Candidate Sarkozy thus avoided any mention of his own policy failures as president. According to him, his efforts to reform immigration policy had fallen victim to the entrenched legacy of the right and the left. He felt trapped by the weight of history. His biggest regret was his inability to break the "path dependency" of earlier policies.

In retrospect, it is easy to identify the objectives of the Sarkozy immigration policy. In January 2007, in the middle of the presidential campaign, a low-circulation journal published a manifesto by Sarkozy entitled "Demography and Politics" (Sarkozy 2007). The stated goal was to ensure the replacement of the "French" population by supporting the birth rate instead of relying on immigration to sustain population growth. Strict control of immigration was presented as a way to avoid closing borders. The manifesto was in the classic right-wing tradition of pro-natalist policies (discussed earlier). The novelty was in the tone: it was necessary to break with "taboos," to end the "politically correct" policies of the past, to defend harsh restrictionist policies without apologies, and to reform immigration laws without flinching. Such rhetoric is more familiar today, especially with the surge in reactionary populism in Europe and the United States, but it sounded extreme at the time (Sarkozy 2007).

Nicolas Sarkozy had the upper hand in French immigration policy for nine years: four years as minister of the interior (May 2002–March 2004, June 2005–March 2007) and five as president of the Republic (May 2007–May 2012). As minister of the interior, he adhered to the migration policy framework of the 1990s, but in 2005 he began to implement a more radical program, which included four laws passed in July 2006, November 2007, August 2008, and June 2011 (see previous discussion). His goal was a complete overhaul of French immigration policy. Never before had reformist zeal reached such intensity in the French immigration debate. Every week for nine years, Sarkozy the politician and policymaker dominated the media cycle on the immigration issue. There was nothing equivalent under the subsequent presidencies of François Hollande and Emmanuel Macron, who were content to stick with Sarkozy's harsh reforms.

The immigration policy of the Sarkozy era remains to this day an exceptional experience in French politics, even though his legacy is uncertain. Did Sarkozy really change the French immigration policy game, or did he simply crack down on entry conditions for migrants and tighten controls? Looking again at the numbers (Figure 5.7), we can offer an assessment of the Sarkozy policies, focusing on the composition of migration flows, legal constraints on policy, and the reaction of the European Union (Héran 2007, 2017; Carvalho and Geddes 2012; for more details, see Geddes and Hadj-Abdou in this volume). Here our analysis draws on two sources: the personal recollections of Sarkozy's advisor for immigration and homeland security, which show the decision-making process (Tandonnet 2014), and the quantitative gap between the proclaimed objectives of the policy and the outcomes, especially the actual distribution of residence permits, hence producing the policy gap (see Figure 5.7).

As early as the 1980s, scholars familiar with demographic data drew our attention to the relative autonomy of the logic of rights as a major source of immigration in France, as in the United States (Hollifield 1986, 1992a, 1992b). Because of the lack of data, until the late 1990s French policymakers did not understand immigration dynamics very well. Under pressure from INED demographers and various European directives, the Ministry of the Interior in the 2000s worked to build a unified database of new residency permits issued every year by the prefectures in France (see Figure 5.7 for a summary). This administrative file keeps track of the flow of permanent-residence permits broken down by countries of origin and categories of migrants (workers, family members, students, refugees). It is now an indispensable source of information for the government and policymakers. These figures are regularly cited during television debates by political candidates. Two numbers stand out: the total number of permits and the number of permits for family reunification.

During the Sarkozy era (beginning in 2005, and including his two ministries plus his presidency) and under the Hollande administration, the number of new residence permits remained remarkably stable, around 190,000 per year. It surpassed the 200,000 threshold during the Hollande presidency, and reached a high of 273,000 in 2019, two years into the Macron presidency (see Figure 5.7). This is due mainly to two factors: first, a steady increase in the number of international students (from the Maghreb, China, and various OECD countries), which is a global trend; and, second, the impact of the "refugee crisis" that unfolded in 2015–2016.

Paradoxically, the much-debated issue of family reunification does not show up in these statistics: the trends in those migrant flows show little impact of policy changes over the past twenty years. The consistency of the numbers can be traced to the two subcategories of family migration: French citizens marrying foreigners (including foreign-born residents) and spouses and minor children of foreigners already settled in France. How can we explain these trends? Since 1994, with a new immigration law passed every two years on average, the inflows of family migration have remained stable. Steps have been taken to combat fraudulent marriages; to check the level of household resources, the adequacy of housing, and the language skills of the spouse; and to assess the written commitment of the newcomers to respect "republican values." Each new law set the bar for entry and integration higher. In this sense, family migration has been "controlled."

On the other hand, the share of family members in the total number of residency permits remains one of the highest in Europe. The attempt to deter family-related migration and attract high-skilled workers failed. The slogan proclaimed by Nicolas Sarkozy in 2006, "Oui à l'immigration choisie, non à l'immigration subie," has remained a dead letter. The number of permits granted to highly skilled workers increased slightly after 2006 but is still well behind the number of permits issued for family reunification and very far from the levels reached in Canada through that country's points system, considered as a model for French policy (see Reitz in this volume). The government suspended the recruitment of workers in 1974, letting other categories of migrants enter the labor market only after they had entered the country and in an indirect way with adjustment of status. Sarkozy's major policy innovation was to reopen the door for labor immigration in 2006, but there were so many bureaucratic obstacles that the policy fell flat. The stated goal of favoring worker over family immigration while lowering the numbers for both forms of migration was never achieved (Héran 2007). This is a good example of a policy gap. The policy outputs during the Sarkozy era (speeches, laws, decrees) never resulted in the desired policy outcomes (as measured by the number and mix of residence permits). One explanation for the failure to reach the policy goals is "specification error" conveyed by the slogan "l'immigration choisie . . . non subie." It is problematic to say that immigration is imposed when it is legal by definition. Nicolas Sarkozy suggested implicitly that the constitutional principles that govern the right to family reunification and asylum were an exogenous force, a pressure from the outside, not a part of France's legal and constitutional heritage. But here again we see the power of rights-based politics.

The consistent trend in the number of residence permits issued in France since 2005 is in sharp contrast with the huge fluctuations observed in Germany (see Martin and Thränhardt in this volume). The main reason for this disparity is the low proportion of asylum seekers who are granted official protection in France. Germany regularly grants protection to large numbers of asylum seekers under the Geneva Convention and under its generous refugee laws. Germany has experienced several waves of asylum seekers, the result of conflicts across the crescent of instability from North and West Africa to the Middle East and South Asia, as well as the Balkan wars after the breakup of Yugoslavia, the repatriation of ethnic Germans (*Aussiedler*) from Russia and the post-Soviet republics, the Kosovo conflict, and wars in Syria, Iraq, and Afghanistan. In each instance, the number of asylum petitions approved in France has been one-eighth that in Germany (see Figure 5.8).

French refugee policy is not very generous, yet France respects the principle of family reunification more than any other EU country. According to OECD data, France has the highest share of residence permits for family reunification of any country in Europe: 40 percent, far above Germany's 12 percent or the United Kingdom's 8 percent (of course, the highest level of family immigration is in the United States, where that category accounts for 65 percent of admissions). These OECD figures do not include students (unless they change their status) but do include an estimate of the new residents coming from other EU states under the freedom-of-movement clause. Compared with the German-speaking countries, France attracts fewer EU migrants (one-third of new arrivals, as opposed to two-thirds), but France gets more migrants from the global South (the Maghreb and sub-Saharan Africa)

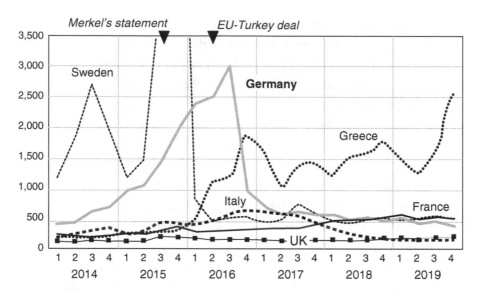

FIGURE 5.8. Quarterly Number of First-Time Asylum Applicants per Million Inhabitants

SOURCE: Eurostat, Asylum and managed migration database. Authors' calculations.

through family reunification. This sharp contrast is related to geopolitical and historical (colonial) legacies: the post-unification German sphere of influence includes Poland, the Baltic countries, Hungary, the Czech Republic, the southern Slavic countries, and even Turkey, whereas the French sphere is in the southern Mediterranean, especially North and West Africa. Migration from Italy, Spain, and Portugal to France has declined since the 1980s, while France continues to receive many migrants from its former colonies in Africa (see Figures 5.3 and 5.4).

Opening the parliamentary debate in 2006, Nicolas Sarkozy—at that time minister of the interior—explained that controlling immigration flows and their composition would shape the demographic destiny of France for generations to come. In 2009 President Sarkozy asserted that "immigration is nothing but France in thirty years" (Bonal and Équy 2009). This was his way of saying that France should not have "too many" immigrants and that it should screen migrants, especially from the global South, according to economic and cultural criteria. For good measure, he made the altruistic and paternalistic argument that the countries of origin had to avoid the negative effects of the brain drain and that it was for their sake that emigration from the South had to be restrained. But this fooled nobody. The explanation of the 2006 law pretended to draw a third way between two excesses, the "zero immigration" advocated by right-wing governments in the 1990s and the unconditional welcome proposed by the humanitarian left. In reality, though, the promise to reestablish control of borders was a political gambit—a not-so-subtle move to seduce the right and the far right, even as voters from the center and the left might consider it reasonable to call upon a migrant labor force "strictly adjusted to the needs of the economy."

For Nicolas Sarkozy, labor migration should be offset by a drastic reduction in family immigration. He stated, "I will not accept the fact that labor immigration accounts for only 7% of migration flows to France. We must change the paradoxical system, under which immigration has been governed for the past thirty years. On the pretext of protecting national employment, a system of ex ante controls by the labor ministry has been introduced to admit foreign workers into France. And at the same time, against all logic, we have admitted an increasing number of family migrants creating imbalances in the labor market, bringing into our country foreign residents, who are poorly qualified and difficult to integrate!" (Ministry of the Interior 2007).

Many countries have policies for the selective recruitment of highly skilled migrants (see chapters by Reitz, on Canada, and by Gamlen and Sherrell, on Australia, in this volume), which the OECD used to classify as "discretionary immigration." Romano Prodi, president of the European Commission between 1999 and 2004, proclaimed the need to "choose our migrants" (Prodi 2004). What was problematic was to consider all of the rest of the migration flows as "imposed"—that is, unwanted, even though legal. The provisions of the 2006 law and the following laws promulgated in 2007 and 2011 sought to tighten the conditions of family reunification and marriage of French nationals with foreigners, but without formally challenging the rights of family unification, for fear of a negative ruling by the Council of State or the Constitutional Council, not to mention the European courts. A few "skills and talents" residence permits were reserved for researchers, senior executives, and investors. Foreign students who received a master's or doctoral degree were given six months to apply for a position with a French company, an opportunity welcomed by leading business schools (leading to approximately 6,000 adjustments of status in 2010). When the minister of the interior and immigration, Claude Guéant, decided to restrict this provision in 2011, it caused an uproar.

This new policy for high-skilled immigration was confusing at first. Should the government organize a sort of human capital competition, like the Canadian points system? Such a policy would imply a preference for French-speaking candidates with graduate degrees and several years of work experience, not too young or too old. This idea proved to be popular for some MPs from the majority. In the end, however, the government opted for the recruitment of foreigners in sectors with skill shortages where there were no comparable French workers—a system borrowed from the Italians, who themselves borrowed it from the Swiss, a classic example of policy learning and transfer. The two policies correspond to different philosophies. The Canadian formula does not match labor supply and demand in the macroeconomy. It operates on an individual, case-by-case basis rather than focusing on labor shortages (see Reitz in this volume). In Switzerland since the 1970s, stakeholders (employers, trade unions, local elected officials, delegates of the Ministry of Labor) have to identify—each year, branch by branch, canton by canton—the sectors suffering from skill shortages (see D'Amato in this volume). The administrative agencies must then prepare a decree that enumerates for the next calendar year the local and sectoral list of occupations to meet these needs. Each approach has a bureaucratic cost: that of a national competition for the first, of a sectoral competition and local planning for the second. In the French case, there was no attempt to compare the costs and benefits of the two approaches, nor to examine their long-term implications. Having finally opted for the second approach without any public hearings, the Ministry of Immigration and the Ministry of Labor set about the difficult task of identifying shortages in specific occupations, region by region and sector by sector, in order to write the regulations necessary to implement the 2006 law (compare this with the labor certification process in the United States, as described by Martin and Orrenius in this volume). However, this new policy was complicated by existing bilateral agreements with the sending countries, agreements that were legally binding on the French state and which thereby seriously disrupted the work of the regional labor directorates.

The outcome of this "migratory diplomacy" was unusual. A December 20, 2007, circular drew up two lists of sectors suffering from labor shortages that would be open to foreigners. For example, 150 professions were opened to Romanians and Bulgarians, while non-Europeans could apply only in 30 highly skilled professions. Algerians and Tunisians were excluded from some positions, while nationals of Senegal, Gabon, and Congo were eligible to apply only for a limited number of jobs. The lists were revised subsequently through a series of hearings and negotiations. Candidates for work visas from the Maghreb and sub-Saharan Africa could access a limited number of highly skilled jobs for which demand was tight. It was out of the question for them to apply for low-skilled service jobs, where they would run the risk of competing with French and other EU nationals. The idea of carefully selecting immigrants turned out to be a non-starter. Migrants from the Southern Hemisphere were constrained from the outset in their bid to enter the French labor market.

The system was subject to two very different criticisms. The first came from the Haute Autorité de Lutte contre les Discriminations et pour l'Égalité (HALDE; Anti-Discrimination and Equal Opportunity Commission), then chaired by Louis Schweitzer, the former CEO of Renault. In October 2008 HALDE issued a statement denouncing the "ethnic selection criteria" that discriminated against African workers. HALDE recommended a uniform list of professions by countries, with no ethnic distinctions, but it got no response from the government. The second criticism came from the economist Gilles Saint-Paul, author of a detailed outside evaluation of the program. He noted that there was no significant correlation between the number of professions open to immigration and unemployment rates in the sectors concerned (Saint-Paul 2009).

Sarkozy's immigration policy was a failure. Non-seasonal professional migration peaked around 20,000 people at the end of the Sarkozy-Fillon government, while immigration in all other legal categories combined never fell below 150,000. The selective immigration policy launched in 2007 was abruptly suspended in March 2011 by Claude Guéant, newly appointed minister of the interior and immigration, who replaced Eric Besson. Ironically, the report to Parliament on French immigration policy, published by the same ministry, still reiterated that the official objective was "to redirect migratory flows toward France to favor high-skilled immigration." The same report welcomed the rise in professional immigration as "the realization of government policy to attract workers whose skills match the needs of our economy" (République Française 2011).

The minutes of the meeting with Sarkozy's immigration counselor show precisely the moment (April 1, 2011) when the president put an end to this recruitment policy, which had played such an important role in the 2007 presidential campaign. Nicolas Sarkozy was chairing a meeting on immigration, which addressed several issues, when Claude Guéant, newly appointed, made this quiet announcement: "I have issued orders to limit labor immigration. We have enough unemployment in France!" He was backed by the president, who stated, "The French labor force is growing by 100,000 every year. Germany may need labor immigration. But this is not the case in France!" The president then moved on to other topics. No mention was made of the possible needs of some companies for skilled migrants. The president's immigration advisor who reported this exchange could not help confiding to the reader his amazement at this "profound change of doctrine," a "true ideological shift" (Tandonnet 2014, 332, 335).

Was the global financial crisis of 2008 a sufficient motive to discourage the recruitment of highly skilled immigrants in sectors with a skill shortage? In the end, the numbers involved were too small. High-skilled immigration, half-opened by the 2006 law, had not taken off. The number of such immigrants never exceeded 20,000 a year, out of a total of 200,000 permits issued to third-country nationals—less than 10 percent of the total, a proportion well below the European average (20 percent in northern and western Europe) and far behind the 60 percent achieved in Canada (if one adds up the winners of the points system and their families). The sudden turnaround by President Sarkozy in March and April 2011 simply closed a door that had been slightly ajar.

The abandonment of Sarkozy's signature reform by his government had no rational economic basis. The 20,000 high-skilled immigrants represented only 0.8 percent of the 2.7 million unemployed registered at the time. Why was the reform abandoned? Not because of high rates of unemployment, but because of political pressure from the Front National, which seized upon the economic crisis to demand cuts in immigration. The timing of the cuts makes this quite clear. Three weeks earlier, *Le Monde* published an article entitled "A New Survey Shows Increasing Support for Marine Le Pen." For the first time, she was outpolling Sarkozy, 23 percent to 21 percent, with only twelve months remaining before the first round of the presidential election (Le Monde 2011). The president of the Front National was focusing on immigration as a major issue in the campaign: "The sharp increase in labor immigration is particularly reprehensible in the midst of the economic crisis, as unemployment explodes in our country and purchasing power collapses. In 2007, high-skilled immigration reached 19,985 foreigners in France. It was 32,132 in 2010, a 61% increase in just a few years!" (République Française 2012).

The government did not deny the increase in immigration. No official bothered to point out that these numbers were only a small percentage of the residence permits issued each year in France and that a 60 percent increase was not unusual given the institution of a new category of immigration with the passage of the July 2006 law. Claude Guéant highlighted the need to stop labor immigration in the face of rising unemployment, and he never undertook to refute Marine Le Pen's assertions. Taking advantage of that void, the Front National could easily discredit the policy: "Labor immigration has risen dramatically in the midst of a deep recession, in a context of mass unemployment. Marine Le Pen denounces labor immigration—which penalizes all French people, from workers to engineers—as criminal. She calls for the abolition of Sarkozy's policies, including the issuing of permits for skilled professions and seasonal workers. The government must stop catering to big business, greedy for immigration that will lower wages" (Le Pen 2011).

In addition to the heated rhetoric, the symbolic effect of Le Pen's critique appealed to the average voter. Le Pen resorted to a tried-and-true method for exaggerating the numbers (25,432 permits) without saying that these numbers were a small percentage of overall immigration (in fact, not even 1 percent) of the labor force; she used percentages only to describe the progression of a phenomenon that had just begun (referring to an increase of "112%"). The government could easily have refuted these allegations and demonstrated how Le Pen was playing fast and loose with the numbers, but Guéant simply announced the end of the recruitment policy, thus capitulating to pressure from the Front National and playing the game of the far right.

Was this a deliberate strategy on the part of the president and his minister, ignoring the true levels of immigration in order to undermine their own policy in which they had lost confidence, or did it simply reflect a desire to hide an obvious policy gap? Either of these explanations is plausible. Historians eventually will delve into the archives of the Élysée Palace and the Ministry of the Interior to tell us what actually happened. One thing is clear, however: one day in March 2011, Nicolas Sarkozy and Claude Guéant decided to abandon their policy because it was criticized by Marine Le Pen, who was rising in the polls. The decision was based purely on an electoral logic, not an economic one.

At least 90 percent of the 200,000 migrants admitted on an annual basis to France during the Sarkozy era (and later on as well) were not admitted for economic reasons, even though most of them eventually would enter the labor market. They did not fill gaps in the age pyramid or shortages in the labor market. Rather, they entered France because they had the right to. This right applies because the judiciary protects it (yet more evidence of the power of rights-based politics) under the watchful eye of vigilant NGOs. It is the logic of rights that feeds immigration in France in the twenty-first century, not the logic of the market. The shift in French immigration policy dates from the mid-1970s, when France, like Germany, decided to stop the recruitment of foreign workers. Since then, flows have been fueled by marriage migration, family reunification, international student mobility, and asylum seeking, all largely disconnected from the business cycle (see Hollifield and Wilson 2011 on the US case). Policy proposals to make immigration more responsive to economic needs ignore the rights-based reality of immigration flows.

The presidential elections of 2012 once again saw immigration taking center stage in French politics. The candidate of the Front National, Marine Le Pen, received almost 18 percent of the vote in the first round, a result comparable to that achieved by her father, Jean-Marie Le Pen, in 2002; however, it was not enough to get her to the second round. Her biggest impact on the election was to shift the debate about immigration to the right, and the incumbent president, Nicolas Sarkozy, chose to compete directly with Le Pen for the nativist vote, taking a hard line on immigration control and integration. During the campaign, Sarkozy criticized the European Union for not being sufficiently Christian and promised that if reelected he would renegotiate the Schengen Agreement and reimpose national border controls. As a result, in the second round Sarkozy lost many moderate voters in the center, and François Hollande, the socialist candidate, was elected with almost 52 percent of the vote. The socialists consolidated their power by winning a comfortable parliamentary majority in the legislative elections that followed. The Hollande government took a cautious approach to immigration reform in the hopes of depoliticizing the issue. Given the power of republican ideology, especially the principle of *laïcité*, Hollande adhered to the policies of previous socialist governments. He followed the "grand bargain" strategies of the Mitterrand era—cracking down on illegal immigration to better legitimize legal immigration—and returned to the "republican pact" of the Jospin government, under which immigration was deemed to be consubstantial with the Republic.

Immigration, "Macronisme," and Resurgent Republicanism

In May 2017, France experienced a political earthquake with the election of a young, liberal technocrat, Emmanuel Macron, as president of the Republic. He was swept to power on a wave of *dégagisme* against the traditional elites (from the rude injunction "dégage!" [bugger off!]) more than by any enthusiasm for political reform. His political movement, first called En Marche! and then La République en Marche (LREM), gained a comfortable majority in the National Assembly. Immigration was not at the top of Macron's agenda. Nevertheless, a new immigration bill was introduced in April 2018 and the bill became law on September 10 of that year. Put forward by Gérard Collomb, the minister of the interior, a defector from the right wing of the Socialist Party, the bill had an impressive title: For Strict Immigration Control, Effective Asylum Policy, and Successful Integration. It linked the right of asylum to migration policy. The Council of State, in its first review of the draft Collomb Law, pointed out that since 1993, France has adopted a new immigration law every sixteen months, with little regard for the actual effects—policy gaps abound. The minister of the interior defended yet another immigration reform as a response to the migration crisis that had begun in 2015, citing public concern about asylum seeking in particular and immigration in general. He alluded to the pressures placed on French society and the administration by the rapid rise in asylum seeking.

In a speech to the prefects, President Macron called for a complete review of migration policy, but no sooner had he said this than his government had to scale back its ambitions. The bill relied mainly on psychological deterrence to slow immigration, a tactic that has become all too common in other countries of immigration (see Martin and Orrenius, on the United States, in this volume). The first objective of the policy was to cut in half the time it takes to review asylum applications, from twelve months to six. Upon arrival in France, an asylum seeker will have 90 days (instead of 120) to file his/her application and only 15 days to file, if necessary, an appeal to the National Court of Asylum Rights—little time for such a complex process. The government ignored warnings by the major humanitarian organizations, which drew attention to the fact that these shortened deadlines would adversely affect the most vulnerable asylum seekers. In response, the Republicans (the mainstream right-wing party, some of whose members had agreed to enter the Macron government) and the Front National (now rebaptized as the Rassemblement National) competed with each other to demand even tighter deadlines, in the name of the sovereign right of France to choose which immigrants and refugees to accept. It was easy for the government to advocate a middle line between the extreme positions of closure and openness.

Another classic objective of the Collomb Law was to accelerate the deportation of rejected asylum seekers to "safe" third countries. To combat illegal immigration more efficiently, the law doubled the possible duration of "administrative detention" of undocumented migrants from forty-five to ninety days. Only a small number of deputies objected to the discriminatory nature of the law and the creation of new bureaucratic hurdles for migrants and asylum seekers. Still, proponents of the law incurred the wrath of the Rassemblement National, with its leader, Marine Le Pen, criticizing the law for encouraging more irregular migration (Le Parisien 2018). The law, however, extended the rights of several categories of asylum seekers: refugees threatened with torture in their country of origin, persecuted homosexuals, young women exposed to the risk of genital mutilation, and victims of domestic violence. Moreover, minors already placed under the protection of OFPRA would benefit from family reunification with siblings, a measure adamantly opposed by the right for its presumed magnet effect, despite the very low number of cases. On the more liberal side, the law facilitated the entry into the labor market of international students and allowed asylum seekers to work after six months in the country instead of nine. The government allowed an amendment to the bill to grant special residence permits for migrants working in humanitarian organizations (NGOs).

A highly controversial provision of the Collomb Law concerned the "solidarity offense" (*délit de solidarité*) committed by those working in the non-profit sector aiding undocumented migrants. In April 2018, the government urged the National Assembly to reject all the amendments to the bill, including those introduced by MPs from the majority REM party. A good Samaritan who helped an illegal migrant would be exposed to legal jeopardy. On July 10, 2018, to everyone's surprise, the Constitutional Council issued a remarkably bold ruling (Décision 2018-717/718) on the legality and constitutionality of the articles concerning the *délit de solidarité* when it considered the charges against Cédric Herrou, a French farmer who had been helping hundreds of refugees at the French-Italian border for some months. The council partially overturned the "anti-solidarity" provisions of the bill by affirming the constitutionality of the "fraternity principle." The word *fraternité* has been part of the motto of the French Republic since 1880, together with *liberté* and *égalité*, but to that point it had been considered merely a moral obligation and a matter of social conscience, not an overarching principle of law.

The Constitutional Council, however, did not simply eliminate the anti-solidarity clause. On one hand, the ruling says: "It follows from the principle of fraternity that individuals are free to help others for humanitarian reasons, whether they are legally resident in France or not." However, the council went on to say that it was up to the government authorities to reconcile this principle with the necessities of "public order." Humanitarian assistance for illegal migrants should not encourage illegal crossings of the national border; the fraternity principle applies only *within* French territory, not *across* the border. The question remains open: is humanitarian assistance for illegal migrants legal? On March 31, 2021, the Court of Cassation, the supreme legal body in France, took an important step in this direction. It rejected the appeal filed by the general prosecutor's office against the release of Cédric Herrou. The young humanitarian farmer thus won a final legal victory, which follows directly from the constitutional affirmation of the "principle of fraternity," interpreted in a broad sense.

It will take time to assess the full impact of the various measures that came into effect with the Collomb Law. The government contends that accelerating the processing of asylum applications will reduce the uncertainty and anxiety suffered by asylum seekers and those seeking a residence permit. So far, the result of the reform has been to make life more difficult for NGOs that provide legal assistance to migrants by adding a new layer of bureaucracy with each regulation. Without the help of NGOs, migrants are lost in the bureaucratic labyrinth. During the debate in the National Assembly the Rassemblement National accused the NGOs of profiting from the "misery of the world" because they receive public subsidies for their work.

In the European elections of May 26, 2019, the candidate list supported by Marine Le Pen and the Rassemblement National did slightly better than that of Emmanuel Macron: 23.3 percent versus 22.4 percent. While the Rassemblement National celebrated its victory, the press pointed to the continued success of the majority in power (LREM). The real surprise, however, was the utter collapse of the Republicans, heirs of Jacques Chirac and Nicolas Sarkozy (down to 8.5 percent), while the Green Party increased its vote tally significantly (to 13.5 percent). Support for the left (the Socialist Party and others) also collapsed, because of deep divisions among the various left-wing parties.

Immigration played a relatively minor role in the electoral debates of 2019. While the Rassemblement National continued to exploit the issue, the party of President Macron, LREM, had a consistent message, similar to that of former president François Hollande: to talk about immigration as little as possible, to refrain from direct engagement with the extreme right, and to seize the "middle ground" by opposing the extremes of open or closed borders, thereby preserving French leadership on the issues of immigration and asylum in Europe. The "yellow vests" movement, which held demonstrations every Saturday between October 2018 and June 2019, spoke very little about immigration. Instead, the yellow vests focused on the "forgotten sectors" of rural society, which have seen a constant decline in their purchasing power. The yellow vests targeted fiscal and regulatory measures that affect those with long commutes to work by car (higher taxes on gasoline in particular), and they sought to eliminate tax benefits for high-income groups, to raise the purchasing power of retirees and the rural population, and more generally to seek redress from a technocratic and out-of-touch president who seemed caught up in his elite milieu and who appeared to look down on the "little people." That said, when France formally adopted the UN Global Compact for Safe, Orderly and Regular Migration (2018), some self-proclaimed leaders of the yellow vests embraced the position taken by Marine Le Pen and the Rassemblement National—that the Global Compact was little more than an international conspiracy to swamp France in a sea of migrants. This shift in focus by the yellow vests did not last long, however. The protest movement remained committed to the struggle against economic and social inequalities (Noiriel 2019). Taken aback by such large-scale and disorganized social protest, Emmanuel Macron decided to launch a "national debate" to quell the yellow vests' unrest, conducting a three-month marathon of town hall meetings around France. He toyed with the idea of including migration as one of the themes of the debate, but in the end he decided against it. Migration did not reappear as a major issue in the debates that followed, but it would explode back onto the political agenda with the murder in Conflans-Sainte-Honorine, a small town south of Paris, of a high school history teacher, Samuel Paty, beheaded on October 16, 2020, by a young jihadist of Chechen origin raised in France, because he had shown his young students caricatures of the Prophet Muhammad borrowed from the satirical weekly *Charlie Hebdo*. This event aroused considerable emotion in the country, as it rekindled the memory of the killings perpetrated on January 7, 2015, at the headquarters of *Charlie Hebdo* and two days later at the Hyper Cacher store, both in Paris. President Macron delivered a vibrant tribute to Samuel Paty at the Sorbonne, extolling the French tradition of satire and caricatures. This led to a new debate about the limits of free speech and religious liberty (Héran 2021).

Sticking to his strategy of trying to appeal to all sides in the emotional debate— reflected in his constant use of the expression "at the same time" (*en même temps*)— President Macron denounced discrimination against "young people" (meaning young people with an immigration background) and the colonial abuses by the French in Algeria, while "at the same time" taking the initiative of proposing a big new law against "separatism" (which in fact targets the visibility of Muslim communities). To avoid the accusation of religious discrimination, the government preferred to rename the project as "a law reinforcing respect for the principles of the Republic." Adopted on August 25, 2021, the law makes it a crime to impose religious rules in home schooling and it requires a "republican" commitment and greater transparency for private associations.

In late 2020 and early 2021, as the country faced the COVID-19 pandemic and struggled to carry out testing and vaccinations, several of Macron's ministers— Education Minister Jean-Michel Blanquer, Minister for Higher Education Frédérique Vidal, and Interior Minister Gérald Darmanin—embarked on repeated diatribes against "Islamo-leftist" teachers, scholars, and university leaders, whom they accused of practicing "racist anti-racism" and of being the "intellectual role models" for jihadist terrorists (see Fassin 2021). They claimed that ideas "imported from American campuses," such as postcolonial studies, decolonial studies, and intersectional and gender theories, were infiltrating French academia, undermining the principle of equality and destroying French republican values. Salvation, in their eyes, is to be expected when a *laïcité de combat* (fighting secularism) is deployed against the Islamist threat—a metaphorical call to arms that reflects the tough ideological stance of an influential republican club, appropriately named the Republican Spring (Le Printemps Républicain).

Their political statements played down the prevalence of Islamophobic attitudes, to the point that the word "Islamophobia," in their view, should be banned from the French vocabulary. Yet many surveys and field experiments using state-of-the-art statistical methods over the past twenty years have provided strong evidence on the extent of ethno-racial and religious discrimination in France (Adida et al. 2010; Petit et al. 2013; Valfort 2015; Beauchemin et al. 2016). The same political and intellectual circles reject the idea of "systemic racism," which they see as an affront to the French Republic. They ignore the fact that since 2001 French law has incorporated the ideas of unintentional or "indirect discrimination," as defined in EU directives promulgated in 2000.

This virulent campaign against the Americanization of anti-racist discourse in France appears to be aimed at stealing the thunder of Marine Le Pen and the Rassemblement National to prevent her and her party from "hijacking" republican discourse on *laïcité* and Islam. Some scholars and intellectuals, who are far removed from ethnographic field work and lack knowledge of techniques of statistical analysis, have trouble understanding social science research on these issues (see Corcuff 2020). This bitter debate among the elites has resulted in a deep division of the French left, which is torn between the supporters of a "universalist" and completely color-blind approach to social policy (such as Manuel Valls, Jean-Pierre Chevènement, Élisabeth

Badinter, Jean-Michel Blanquer, and Pierre-André Taguieff) and the defenders of an open, more tolerant version of *laïcité*. The latter consider it essential to be able to measure the gap that separates objective social reality from the egalitarian, republican ideal, especially on issues of race and religion (Baubérot 2017; Cadène 2020; Défenseur des Droits 2020; Héran 2021).

Opinion polls conducted in March and April 2021 by Ipsos provide some interesting insights into the current debates. For those age twenty-five to thirty-four, Marine Le Pen was slightly ahead among those intending to vote in the 2022 presidential election (at 21 percent), but Emmanuel Macron had a decisive lead among those eighteen to twenty-four years old (at 29 percent), while the number of those who said they planned not to vote or were undecided remained quite high. Another survey from March 2021, this one by IFOP, revealed that high school students age fifteen or older are much more tolerant than adults when it comes to religious diversity: 52 percent are in favor of allowing individuals to wear conspicuous religious symbols at school, even though such symbols have been banned by law since 2004. This compares to only 25 percent of adults. And 57 percent of the young (compared to only 26 percent of adults) believe that parents of students accompanying children on a school trip should be permitted to wear religious symbols. Commentators are split on how to interpret these results: some see inroads and the growing influence of Islam in the schools, while others see it simply as the fact that students of the younger generation are more at ease with diversity and more tolerant than their parents.

Now more than ever, French society is sharply divided over how to deal with ethno-racial and religious issues. Whatever people think about changes in laws governing migration and ethnicity, French attitudes reflect many of the same divisions that are evident in American society. Strong attachments to republicanism are not enough to shield French society from ethno-racial and religious discrimination. France is an increasingly multicultural society de facto, if not de jure, and the French must recognize that relations between the native and foreign-born populations and attitudes toward immigration will remain fraught for decades to come.

Conclusion

Historically immigration has had greater legitimacy in France than in the other major receiving countries of western Europe. Even though France became a country of immigration because of fundamental economic and demographic pressures, what is most important from the standpoint of the politics and policies of control is to understand how the early waves of immigration were legitimized. In this respect, France looks less like its European neighbors and more like the United States

(Horowitz and Noiriel 1992). In both France and the United States, immigration was legitimized through an appeal to republican ideas and ideologies. From the very earliest days of the French Republic, politicians have appealed to republican ideals of universalism, egalitarianism, nationalism, and *laïcité* as a way of legitimizing immigration and integrating foreigners. Hence, it is was surprising to hear former prime minister Lionel Jospin call in 1997 for a new "republican pact" as a way of resolving the social and economic crises associated with immigration, or to hear President Emmanuel Macron and his ministers demanding that migrants adhere to a strictly secular (*laïque*) vision of the Republic.

Yet immigration, like republicanism, remains highly contested in France. Immigration is not a founding myth of the French Republic; therefore, we cannot say that France is, like the United States, Canada, or Australia, a nation of immigrants. Still, attacking immigrants and their rights is viewed by many as tantamount to attacking the Republic. Conversely, one of the best ways for a government to defend immigrants is to cloak itself in the values and symbols of the Republic. When Jacques Chirac sought to rally left- and right-wing voters to his side in the runoff with Jean-Marie Le Pen in the second round of the 2002 presidential elections, he appealed to all French voters to defend "the values of the Republic" and reject extremism. But republicanism is a double-edged sword, as we can see in debates about immigration, race, religion, and *laïcité* during the Macron presidency.

Clearly, immigrants and immigration have come under attack in large part because of the shift in the composition and ethnic mix of the flows from predominantly Christian and European to Muslim and African. This shift was the result of two developments. First, decolonization in the 1960s contributed to an exodus of North and West Africans to France. Second, European integration gradually eliminated immigration from neighboring states, such as Italy, Spain, and eventually Portugal. In the early 1970s, the justification for stopping immigration was primarily economic. France had high levels of unemployment, so, consistent with a strong strand of Malthusian and mercantilist thinking, the reasoning went: if the state can stop immigration, this will solve the problems of unemployment. But this rationale for stopping immigration—although still present today—quickly gave way in the 1980s and 2000s to the arguments advanced by Jean-Marie Le Pen and his daughter Marine: that the French nation was being destroyed by an influx of inassimilable African immigrants. In this view, Muslims could never be good citizens of the Republic because of their refusal to accept the secular principle of *laïcité* and to keep their private, religious views separate from their public life.

As politicians began to play on these fears as a way of getting votes, the republican argument (a double-edged sword) seemed to cut the other way. Throughout the 1980s and 1990s, the tactic of appealing to xenophobic fears and instincts led to further polarization of the electorate on the issue of immigration and contributed to the rise of the Front National and its successor, the Rassemblement National (Perrineau 1997; Viard 1996; Thränhardt 1997). In the 2002 elections in the wake of terrorist attacks in New York, Madrid, and London, and again after the horrific attacks at the offices of *Charlie Hebdo* and the Bataclan Theater in 2015, immigration was linked to issues of terrorism and security. The same was true in the 2007 elections in the aftermath of the civil unrest (violence in the suburbs) that rocked France in 2005, and again in the 2012 and 2017 elections when the specter of an inassimilable, radicalized Muslim population seemed to haunt segments of the French electorate. Whether these fears are rational or irrational is open to debate, but there is no doubt that politicians have exploited them for political gain (or, in the case of Nicolas Sarkozy in the 2012 presidential election, loss). In the aftermath of the murder of Samuel Paty, President Macron has fallen back on a harsh republicanism to shore up his support on the right (and the left).

By the mid-1990s, the strategies for immigration control in France began to change dramatically. Instead of relying exclusively on the external mechanism of border controls—which were nonetheless being reinforced and further externalized and Europeanized through the Schengen and Dublin systems—or on the more classic mechanisms of internal regulation of labor markets (employer sanctions and the like), the first right-wing government of the 1990s began to roll back and limit the rights of immigrants, by undercutting civil rights and liberties (due process and equal protection) and by going after certain social rights, specifically health care. Finally, political rights, naturalization, and citizenship were challenged, through a reform of the nationality code and the erosion of the principle of birthright citizenship. This trend intensified during the presidency of Nicolas Sarkozy and has continued under President Macron.

We can see quite clearly the progression of control strategies: the imposition of external controls (in the form of new visa regimes) in the early 1970s; the restriction on hiring foreign workers (in 1974) coupled with return policies and employer sanctions; attempts to roll back the right to family reunification in the late 1970s; increased labor market regulation during the socialist years of the 1980s (internal controls); a return to external strategies of control with ratification of the Schengen and Dublin Agreements; limits on social and civil rights (the first and second Pasqua Laws, as well as the Debré Law); attempts to limit citizenship by changing the nationality law (the first and second Pasqua Laws); and a somewhat confused flurry of laws in the first decades of the twenty-first century, when strategies for immigration control shifted again in favor of migration management (and the highly skilled) and selecting immigrants on the basis of their potential contributions to the French economy. But the policy of "choosing immigrants" for economic purposes, focusing on discretionary flows of worker migration, was quickly overwhelmed by a crackdown on humanitarian (non-discretionary) flows of family immigration, asylum seekers, and the like, putting the Sarkozy government at odds with the EU and domestic (constitutional) law. Whenever the state crossed the invisible line between controlling immigration and threatening civil society, thereby putting the state at odds with the founding, republican principles, institutional/constitutional, ideational, and societal checks came into play (Hollifield 1997, 1999). As in other liberal republics, immigration control in France is not purely a function of markets, economic interests, or national security. It is heavily dependent on the interplay of ideas, institutions, and civil society, and we can see the enduring power of republicanism in debates about immigration, religion, race, and ethnicity.

References

Adida, Claire L., David D. Laitin, and Marie-Anne Valfort. 2010. "Identifying Barriers to Muslim Integration in France." *Papers of the National Academy of Sciences*, May 21, 2010.

Baubérot, Jean. 2017. *Histoire de la laïcité en France.* Paris: Que Sais-Je?

Beauchemin, Cris, Christelle Hamel, and Patrick Simon, eds. 2016. *Trajectoires et origines: Enquête sur la diversité des populations en France.* Paris: Institut National d'Études Démographiques.

Bonal, Cordélia, and Équy, Laurie. 2009. "L'identité nationale selon Sarkozy." *Libération*, November 2, 2009.

Bouvier, Gérard. 2012. "Les descendants d'immigrés plus nombreux que les immigrés: Une position française originale en Europe." *INSEE Références*, INSEE, Paris.

Breem, Yves. 2011. *Rapport du SOPEMI pour la France.* Paris: Ministère de l'Intérieur.

Brubaker, Rogers. 1992. *Citizenship and Nationhood in France and Germany.* Cambridge, MA: Harvard University Press.

Cadène, Nicolas. 2020. *En finir avec les idées fausses sur la laïcité.* Paris: Éditions de l'Atelier.

Carvalho, João, and Andrew Geddes. 2012. "La politique d'immigration sous Sarkozy. Le retour à l'identité nationale." In *Les politiques publiques sous Sarkozy*, edited by Jacques De Maillaerd and Yves Surel, 279–298. Paris: Presses de Sciences Po.

Corcuff, Philippe. 2020. *La grande confusion. Comment l'extrême droite gagne la bataille des idées.* Paris: Textuel.

Debré, Robert, and Alfred Sauvy. 1946. *Des français pour la France, le problème de la population.* Paris: Gallimard.

Défenseur des Droits. 2020. "Rapport annuel d'activité 2020." République Française, Paris.

Ellermann, Antje. 2009. *States Against Migrants: Deportation in Germany and the United States.* Cambridge: Cambridge University Press.

Ellermann, Antje. 2021. *The Comparative Politics of Immigration: Policy Choices in Germany, Canada, Switzerland, and the United States.* New York: Cambridge University Press.

Fassin, Didier. 2021. "Are 'Woke' Academics a Threat to the French Republic? Ask Macron's Ministers." *Guardian*, March 12, 2021.

Feldblum, Miriam. 1999. *Reconstructing Citizenship: The Politics of Immigration in Contemporary France.* Albany, NY: SUNY Press.

Hammar, Tomas. 1990. *Democracy and the Nation-State: Aliens, Denizens, and Citizens in a World of International Migration.* Aldershot: Avebury.

Haut Conseil à l'Intégration. 1991. *La connaissance de l'immigration et de l'intégration.* Paris: La Documentation Française.

Héran, François. 2007. *Le temps des immigrés. Essai sur le destin de la population française.* Paris: La République des Idées/Seuil.

Héran, François. 2012. *Parlons immigration en 30 questions.* Paris: La Documentation Française.

Héran, François. 2016. "Alfred Sauvy and Immigration: Commentary on the Short Paper Published in 1946 in the First Issue of *Population*." *Population* [English version] 71, no. 1: 11–14.

Héran, François. 2017. *Avec l'immigration. Mesurer, débattre, agir.* Paris: La Découverte.

Héran, François. 2021. *Lettre aux professeurs sur la liberté d'expression.* Paris: La Découverte.

Herbert, Ulrich. 1986. *Geschicte der Ausländer—beschäftigung in Deutschland 1880 bis 1980.* Bonn: Dietz.

Hoffmann, Stanley, ed. 1963. *In Search of France.* Cambridge, MA: Harvard University Press.

Hollifield, James F. 1986. "Immigration Policy in France and Germany: Outputs vs. Outcomes." *Annals* 485: 113–128.

Hollifield, James F. 1992a. "L'état français et l'immigration." *Revue Française de Science Politique* 42, no. 6: 943–963.

Hollifield, James F. 1992b. *Immigrants, Markets, and States.* Cambridge, MA: Harvard University Press.

Hollifield, James F. 1997. *l'immigration et l'état nation: À la recherche d'un modèle national.* Paris: L'Harmattan.

Hollifield, James F. 1999. "Ideas, Institutions and Civil Society: On the Limits of Immigration Control in Liberal Democracies." *IMIS-Beiträge* 10 (January): 57–90.

Hollifield, James F. 2000. "Immigration and the Politics of Rights." In *Migration and the Welfare State in Contemporary Europe*, edited by Michael Bommes and Andrew Geddes, 109–133. London: Routledge.

Hollifield, James F. 2021. "General Perspectives on Membership: Citizenship, Migration, and the End of Liberalism?" In *Handbook of Citizenship and Migration*, edited by Marco Giugni and Maria Grasso, 101–117. London: Edward Elgar.

Hollifield, James F., and George Ross, eds. 1991. *Searching for the New France.* New York: Routledge.

Hollifield, James F., and Carole J. Wilson. 2011. "Rights-Based Politics, Immigration, and the Business Cycle: 1890–2008." In *High-Skilled Immigration in a Global Labor Market*, edited by Barry R. Chiswick, 50–80. Washington, DC: AEI Press.

Horowitz, Donald L., and Gérard Noiriel, eds. 1992. *Immigrants in Two Democracies: French and American Experience.* New York: New York University Press.

Ireland, Patrick. 1994. *The Policy Challenge of Ethnic Diversity.* Cambridge, MA: Harvard University Press.

Jospin, Lionel. 1997. "Le discours de Jospin." *Libération*, June 20, 1997.

Kastoryano, Riva. 1997. *La France, l'Allemagne et leurs immigrés: Négocier l'identité.* Paris: Armand Colin.

Kepel, Gilles. 2012. *Banlieues de la République.* Paris: Gallimard.

Lebon, André. 2001. *Immigration et présence étrangère en France.* Paris: La Documentation Française.

Le Bras, Hervé. 1986a. "Coït interrompu, contrainte morale et héritage préférentiel." *Communications* 44: 47–70.

Le Bras, Hervé. 1986b. *Les trois France.* Paris: Seuil.

Le Bras, Hervé. 1998. *Le démon des origines.* Paris: Éditions de l'Aube.

Le Monde. 1993. "France, pays d'immigration: Fixé de manière ambiguë par Charles Pasqua l'objectif 'zéro immigré' est un mythe." *Le Monde*, June 8, 1993.

Le Monde. 2011. "Un nouveau sondage illustre la dynamique Marine Le Pen." *Le Monde*, March 5, 2011.

Le Parisien. 2018. «Chiffres de l'Ofpra : Marine Le Pen blâme la loi Immigration . . . pas encore promulguée,» August 23, 2018. https://www.leparisien.fr/politique/chiffres-de-l-ofpra-marine-le-pen-blame-la-loi-immigration-pas-encore-promulguee-23-08-2018-7862388.php

Le Pen, Marine. 2011. "Guéant: Des mots contre l'immigration de travail mais des actes pour la favoriser comme jamais!" Front National website, May 24, 2011.

Long, Marceau. 1988. *Être français aujourd'hui et demain.* Paris: La Documentation Française.

Marie, Claude Valentin. 1992. "Le travail clandestin." *Infostat Justice* 29 (September): 1–6.

Massey, Douglas. 2020. "Immigration Policy Mismatches and Counterproductive Outcomes: Unauthorized Migration to the U.S. in Two Eras." *Comparative Migration Studies* 8, no. 21: 1–27.

Ministry of the Interior. 2007. "Prefectural Meeting on Immigration." Marseille, March 5, 2007.

Noiriel, Gérard. 1988. *Le creuset français.* Paris: Seuil.

Noiriel, Gérard. 2019. *Les gilets jaunes à la lumière de l'histoire.* Paris: Le Monde/L'Aube.

Perrineau, Pascal. 1995. *Le vote de crise.* Paris: Presses de la FNSP.

Perrineau, Pascal. 1997. *Le symptôme Le Pen: Radiographie des électeurs du Front national.* Paris: Fayard.

Petit, Pascale, Emmanuel Duguet, Yannick l'Horty, and Loïc du Parquet. 2013. "Discrimination à l'embauche: Les effets du genre et de l'origine se cumulent-ils systématiquement?" *Economie et Statistique* 464, no. 1: 141–153.

Prodi, Romano. 2004. "Romano Prodi: Les nouvelle priorités de l'Union européenne élargie." Canal Académies, December 31, 2004. https://www.canalacademies.com/emissions/2004-leurope/les-nouvelles-priorites-de-lunion-europeenne-elargie.

Régnard, Corrine. 2010. *Rapport du SOPEMI pour la France.* Paris: Ministère de l'Intérieur.

République Française. 2011. "Déclaration de M. Claude Guéant, ministre de l'intérieur, de l'outre-mer, des collectivités territoriales et de l'immigration, en réponse à une question sur l'immigration, à l'Assemblée nationale le 1er mars 2011." Vie Publique. https://www.vie-publique.fr/discours/181545-declaration-de-m-claude-gueant-ministre-de-linterieur-de-loutre-mer.

République Française. 2012. "Programme de Mme Marine Le Pen, candidate du Front national à l'élection présidentielle de 2012, intitulé: 'Mon projet, pour la France et les Français,' le 14 janvier 2012." Vie Publique. https://www.vie-publique.fr/discours/184668-programme-de-mme-marine-le-pen-candidate-du-front-national-lelection.

Roy, Olivier. 1991. "Ethnicité, bandes et communautarisme." Esprit, February, 37–48.

Saint-Paul, Gilles. 2009. Immigration, qualifications et marché du travail. Rapport du Conseil d'Analyse Economique. Paris: La Documentation Française.

Sarkozy, Nicolas. 2007. "Démographie et politique." Agir: Revue de la Société de Stratégie 29: 11–16.

Sauvy, Alfred. 1946. "Evaluation des besoins de l'immigration française." Population 1, no. 1: 91–98.

Sauvy, Alfred. 1950. "Besoins et possibilités de l'immigration en France." Population 5, no. 3: 417–434.

Schnapper, Dominique. 1990. La France de l'intégration. Sociologie de la nation. Paris: Gallimard.

Schnapper, Dominique. 2000. Qu'est-ce que la citoyenneté? Paris: Gallimard.

Schor, Ralph. 1985. L'opinion française et les étrangers, 1919–1939. Paris: Publications de la Sorbonne.

Simon, P. 2003. "Les sciences sociales françaises face aux catégories ethniques et raciales." Annales de Démographie Historique, "Politique des Recensements" 1: 111–130.

Simon, P. 2005. "The Measurement of Racial Discrimination: The Policy Use of Statistics." International Journal of Social Science 183: 9–25.

Simon, P. 2012. "Les revirements de la politique d'immigration." Cahiers Français 369: 86–91.

Simon, P. 2017. "The Failure of the Importation of Ethno-Racial Statistics in Europe: Debates and Controversies." Ethnic and Racial Studies 40, no. 13: 2326–2332.

Simon, Patrick, and Vincent Tiberj. 2013. "Sécularisation ou regain religieux: la religiosité des immigrés et de leurs descendants." Document de travail no. 196. INED.

Spengler, J. J. 1938. France Faces Depopulation. Durham, NC: Duke University Press.

Tandonnet, Maxime. 2014. Au cœur du volcan: Carnets de l'Elysée, 2007–2012. Paris: Flammarion.

Tapinos, Georges. 1975. l'immigration étrangère en France. Paris: Presses Universitaires de France.

Tapinos, Georges. 1982. "European Migration Patterns; Economic Linkages and Policy Experiences." Studi Emigrazione 19, no. 67: 339–357.

Teitelbaum, Michael S., and Jay M. Winter. 1985. Fear of Population Decline. Orlando, FL: Academic Press.

Thränhardt, Dietrich. 1997. "The Political Uses of Xenophobia in England, France, and Germany." In Immigration into Western Societies: Problems and Policies, edited by Emek Uçarer and Donald Puchala, 175–194. London: Pinter.

Tribalat, Michèle. 1995. *Faire France: Une enquête sur les immigrés et leurs enfants*. Paris: La Découverte.

Tribalat, Michèle. 1996. *De l'immigration à l'assimilation: Enquête sur les populations d'origine étrangère en France*. Paris: La Découverte/INED.

Tribalat, Michèle. 2011–2012. "Dynamique démographique des musulmans de France." *Commentaire* 136: 971–980.

Valfort, Marie-Anne. 2015. "Discriminations religieuses à l'embauche: Une réalité." Institut Montaigne, October 2015. https://www.institutmontaigne.org/publications/discriminations-religieuses-lembauche-une-realite.

Vallin, Jacques, and Graziella Caselli. 1999. "Quand l'Angleterre rattrapait la France." *Population et Sociétés* 346: 1–4.

Van de Walle, Etienne. 1986. "La fécondité française au XIXe siècle." *Communications* 44: 35–45.

Viard, Jean, ed. 1996. *Aux sources du populisme nationaliste*. Paris: Editions de l'Aube.

Weber, Eugen. 1976. *Peasants into Frenchmen: The Modernization of Rural France, 1870–1914*. Stanford, CA: Stanford University Press.

Weil, Patrick. 1991. *La France et ses étrangers*. Paris: Calmann-Lévy.

Weil, Patrick. 1997. *Mission d'étude des législations de la nationalité et de l'immigration*. Paris: La Documentation Française.

Weil, Patrick. 2002. *Qu'est-ce qu'un français?* Paris: Grasset.

Wihtol de Wenden, Catherine. 1988. *Les immigrés et la politique*. Paris: Presses de la FNSP.

COMMENTARY

Republicanism in Question

Catherine Wihtol de Wenden

France is the oldest immigration country in Europe, but the French have difficulty accepting this reality. During the late nineteenth century, bringing in workers via immigration was necessary both because of labor shortages in the new industrial sectors in a period of demographic decrease and in light of the French-German conflict during World War I. The debate over *dépopulation* and *dénatalité* was intense in the interwar period, marked by strong assimilationism. In the 1930s, the percentage of immigrants in the total population was the same as in the United States despite a rise in anti-immigrant feelings and especially anti-Semitism. After World War II, public policy actors decided both to undertake a populationist program (a move supported by Charles de Gaulle and Alfred Sauvy) and to recruit foreign workers to rebuild France in the Trente Glorieuses period (1945–1974). The debate about depopulation was at first depoliticized, only to become highly politicized after the emergence of the extreme rightist National Front in the 1980s, which narrowed the terms of the debate. However, the presence of foreigners in France has been rather stable over the past decades.

Given the crises that have shaped European immigration and refugee policies in recent years, the French case bucks the trend seen in many other European countries. France was less affected by the economic crisis of 2008 than Spain, the United Kingdom, Ireland, and Italy, for example. It was, however, caught up in the refugee crisis sparked by the 2011 Arab revolutions and then by the so-called refugee crisis of 2015 (when Germany was the most affected). France still received a lot of asylum seekers during this period (100,000 in 2017, 122,000 in 2018, and 130,000 in 2019), while most other EU countries (in particular Germany, Italy, and Greece) are seeing a large decrease in asylum applications. In 2020, the COVID-19 pandemic revealed the extent to which the French economy is dependent on foreign labor in some key sectors (agriculture, care jobs, services), but in this respect France was not different from its European neighbors. In spite of a general trend toward an emphasis on security issues in the debate over immigration, the immigration debate is seeing input from new actors, including NGOs.

Europe as a Key Player in France's Immigration and Asylum Policy

This chapter focuses almost exclusively on France and does not take the European dimension of immigration policy into account. However, when it comes to managing migrant flows (through entrance policies for immigration and asylum and through external border control), Europe has become the main player in terms of policymaking, even though EU member states, like France, still have discretionary power for granting asylum, legalizing undocumented migrants, and welcoming unaccompanied minors. In the past thirty years, European immigration and asylum policy emanating from Brussels defined most entrance policies and legal principles (regarding family reunification, students, highly skilled workers, and refugees under the Dublin Agreement) as well as border controls (with the 1985 Schengen Agreement, the externalization of borders in 1990, and repatriation agreements). Since 1993, European directives and regulations have been fully integrated into French immigration and asylum policy, beginning with the Pasqua Laws in 1993. The immigration debate shifted from a conflict between the priorities of a liberal economy and security concerns (a key aspect of the liberal paradox) to an exclusive focus on security. This trend (a shift of emphasis from economics to security) accelerated with the 1997 Treaty of Amsterdam; no longer are immigration and asylum a question of labor markets and social affairs, as was the case after adoption of the 1957 Treaty of Rome. According to the subsidiarity rule put forward in the Amsterdam Treaty, migration flows are to be governed in the first instance by Brussels, whereas integration remains the prerogative of national and local governments. The new European pact on immigration and asylum presented by the EU Commission in September 2020 follows this trend toward an emphasis on security. Most of the pact's provisions do not change EU refugee policy (there is no reform of the Dublin system, even though it was hotly criticized, and no compulsory mechanisms of solidarity are imposed on reluctant eastern European countries). Moreover, immigration policy reforms receive even less attention than the refugee question, because no EU country wants to be vulnerable to criticism by radical right parties if Brussels proposes a safer way of recruiting much-needed foreign workers. The COVID-19 crisis once again demonstrated how dependent EU countries are on non-EU countries for workers in agriculture, care jobs, and tourism, and if anything the pandemic further highlighted the security dimension of migration policy.

In 2004 France was the second-most-important destination in western Europe for migrants from eastern Europe. But this was still during a period of economic growth, and this migration flow did not have a strong impact on the political debate over immigration during the years 1990–2004 compared to the issue of integration of Islamic populations.[1] In the United Kingdom, the supposed competition from Polish migrants on the labor market was mentioned as a major reason to vote for Brexit in 2016 (and on this issue employers and the state were on opposite sides), but in France it would be strange to see the Polish presence mentioned as the main immigration challenge.

Which Republicanism?

Republicanism is usually defined as a democratic regime in which the law is the same for all citizens. However, there can be republicanism without democracy (as in Venice until the nineteenth century), and democracy without republicanism (as in the United Kingdom). France's *laïcité* is not even a symbol of republicanism, because a similar principle exists in regimes with few democratic principles (such as Tunisia, Turkey, and the former Soviet republics). As for the nationality code, since 1889 France has been ruled by an equilibrium between *jus soli* and *jus sanguinis* that has nothing to do with republicanism. *Jus sanguinis* was introduced by Napoleon I in the Civil Code, inspired by the ideas of the French Revolution, and *jus soli* (which was the principle of citizenship under the ancien regime) is predominant in the British Isles, where peasants and landlords were linked by the soil. The principle of *jus soli* has been increasingly important in most EU nationality codes only since the 2000s, particularly in Germany, where the aim is to be more inclusive toward newcomers.

If republicanism defines the background of France's laws (and sometimes constitutional decisions) about immigration generally (the chapter mentions "ethnic statistics," head scarves at school, solidarity in civil society, diversity in public housing, and the *contrat d'accueil et d'intégration*), French immigration policy has rarely been analyzed through the lens of republicanism, as that concept does not play a role in other European immigration and refugee policies that follow the EU trend. The control of external European borders, which plays a huge role in immigration and refugee policy, is less and less in Europe a national decision, even if in many countries the debates around immigration center on national-level decisions in an effort to soothe voters and to respond to public opinion. The shifts of position during the Sarkozy period (2002–2012)—such as the launch of the *immigration choisie* approach to policy in 2006 after years of closed-border policy, the attempts to respond to extreme rightist trends in the country, the 2011 crisis with Italy after the Arab revolutions in Tunisia and Libya, the failed policy of *identité nationale,* the Grenoble discourse on security issues—are all illustrations of this political reaction.

From the early 2000s until now, it has been very difficult to perceive any liberal trend in immigration policy. Employers' voices (e.g., the Mouvement des Entreprises de France, the largest French employer federation, and the Fédération Nationale des Syndicats d'Exploitants Agricoles, for agriculture) are calling for more flexibility in the labor market in a context of labor shortages in agriculture, restaurants and other services, industry, construction, information technology, and medicine—shortages made worse by the COVID-19 pandemic. But employers have little voice in public debates relating to migration. Furthermore, it is very difficult to define their position on immigration, in part because they hold contradictory positions—for example, in favor of more open borders so as to increase the labor force, but sharing anti-immigrant feelings with the right wing (and the extreme right in some regions, such as in the South of France).

So in recent debates the trade-off has been more between security and human rights than between economy and security. At the same time, we must take into account the role of less visible actors who are strong advocates for the human rights of migrants, more often at the local level. These include left-wing groups, like MRAP and SOS-Racisme, as well as charitable organizations on the right (such as Caritas and Secours Catholique), the Social Democrats, and NGOs such as CIMADE, Jesuit Refugee Service, Amnesty International, and the Ligue des Droits de l'Homme. All of these organizations are in favor of more rights for foreigners (mainly for irregular migrants and asylum seekers), and they condemn the persecution of the so-called *justes,* individuals who assist migrants in clandestine crossings of the border (like Cédric Herrou). As noted in the chapter, in summer 2018 the Constitutional Council ruled that Herou's actions were legal, citing the principle of *fraternité,* a cornerstone of the republican ideal.

I should mention the local-level networks built to welcome irregular migrants or unaccompanied minors (such as the network of welcoming cities called ANVITA, Association Nationale des Villes et Territoires Accueillants). At the local level, ethics has more impact than any other republican value besides *laïcité.,* which many towns and cities are reluctant to embrace. In some big cities, there is a reluctance to embrace policies built around the idea of equality (such as in public housing, schooling, and policing). The principle of equality has emerged as a motive for a variety of social movements (think of the 1983 March for Equality and Against Racism—the "Marche des Beurs"—in 1983 during Mitterrand's presidency and the 2005 riots in Clichy-sous-Bois), but such movements for equality have largely been embraced by younger people.

There is considerable variation in the acceptance of specific republican values at different levels of government. For example, France's ratification of the Marrakech Global Compact in December 2018 commits French immigration policymakers to be respectful of multilateral governance of migration and refugees (the compact calls for "safe, organized, and regular" migration), which means opening the borders to legal immigration for workers in particular, providing irregular immigrants with avenues to legalize their status, and avoiding the confusion between economic migration and refugee flows. At the European level, the EU has been implementing restrictive security approaches. At the national level, countries have introduced a variety of discretionary practices. And we have seen generous, liberal interventions by non-state actors at the local level.

Conclusion: Challenging the Liberal Paradox in the French Case

Employers and trade unions were very strong between 1945 and 1975, but they lost influence between 1980 and 2000, with deindustrialization and soaring unemployment. Consequently, French policymakers have been less influenced by employers' interests than by their need to lure back voters from the extreme right. As the overwhelming majority of legal immigrants in France are not workers but family members entering through family reunification policies, along with asylum seekers and students, the weight of the liberal paradox (Hollifield 1992) (which highlights the role of business and employers) is lessened.

In the decision-making process, the most important actor is public opinion. For quite a long period (1945–1975), immigration was a depoliticized issue.[2] This was largely because the booming economy needed immigrant workers. The rise of the extreme right in the 1980s and the way it placed immigration at the core of its political program transformed immigration from an issue of "low politics" (which, as described in the introduction to this volume, is concerned with problems of domestic governance, especially labor and demographics) to one of "high politics" (problems affecting relations between states), where security issues predominate and symbolic policies are used to reassure the right-wing electorate. The role of civil society has been important; NGOs (such as human rights and solidarity associations), churches, migration experts, and journalists are all powerful groups in France. But when immigration becomes an issue of high politics, opportunities for discussion, negotiation, and bargaining between civil society organizations and decision-makers are limited. Short-term thinking prevails, along with pressure coming from public opinion and campaign platforms. The conflicting objectives of immigration policy in France are thus less a matter of closing the borders versus an open economy and more a question of solidarity of civil society versus national security.

Notes

1. Sibylle Regout, "Ouverture à l'est de l'Union européenne en 2004: L'approche différenciée franco-germano-britannique," *Migrations Société* 175 (January–March 2019): 47–62. See also Emmanuel Comte, *The History of the European Migration Regime: Germany's Strategic Hegemony* (London: Routledge, 2017).

2. Catherine Wihtol de Wenden, *Les immigrés et la politique. Cent-cinquante ans d'évolution* (Paris: Presses de la FNSP, 1988).

COMMENTARY

France's Children of Immigrants

Jean Beaman

In *The Suffering of the Immigrant*, Algerian sociologist Abdelmalek Sayad (1999) wrote of the "double absence" of migrants. They are absent both from their country of origin and within their destination country or host society. This duality is also present for children of immigrants, who often navigate between the culture of their immigrant parents and the culture of the society where they were born and raised. As sociologist Richard Alba has noted, "In all immigration societies, the social distinction between immigrant and second generations, on the one hand, and natives, on the other . . . is, in a sense, a fault line along which other differences and distinctions pile up" (2005, 41). It is for this reason that an examination of the immigrant second generation is crucial.

That France has never had immigration as part of its national myth despite its long history of immigration means that children of immigrants, or the second generation, have posed a challenge to questions of French national identity and values. In what follows, I complement Hollifield and Héran's chapter by providing an overview of France's children of immigrants, particularly those who have origins in former French colonies, thereby representing the "visibility" of French colonialism and subsequent migration to the metropole in the postcolonial era. In doing so, I will focus on their integration, assimilation, inclusion, and belonging. This is a population who were born and raised in France and attended French schools. Many may have relatives in other countries, which they visited during summer holidays (this is particularly true for the Maghrébin second generation). They were therefore raised in the republican ethos of *liberté*, *égalité*, and *fraternité*. Yet, as I will later discuss, for many, their everyday experiences belied this promise of equal treatment.

Demographic Overview

In definitions used by the Institut National de la Statistique et des Études Économiques (INSEE), "children of immigrants" refers to the second generation, or individuals born in France to at least one immigrant parent. According to INSEE, as of 2015, about 11 percent of the French population has at least one immigrant parent (and half of this second-generation population has only one immigrant parent). This is a heterogeneous population, with origins in southern Europe as well as former French colonies in the Maghreb and sub-Saharan Africa. As Hollifield and Héran noted, gathering demographic information on immigrants and their descendants can become complicated. Partly due to France's republican model, collecting data on race and ethnicity (what is known as "ethnic statistics") is prohibited, and seen as a challenge to French uniformity and societal cohesiveness.

Many large-scale surveys are able to capture this second generation by combining the respondent's place of birth with that of their parents. Using data from the Étude de l'Histoire Familiale (Study of Family History), Meurs, Pailhé, and Simon (2006) compare the labor force participation of first-generation and second-generation immigrants. Based on measures such as access to employment, occupational status, and access to jobs in the civil sector, they find that though second-generation immigrants experience less occupational segregation overall than first-generation immigrants, they persist in experiencing high unemployment rates and low job security relative to "white" French individuals. Particularly for those of North African or sub-Saharan African origin, there is an "inherited disadvantage" from the first generation to the second generation. For example, among first-generation Moroccan and Tunisian immigrants, men had a 24.6 percent unemployment rate and women had a 26.1 percent unemployment rate. Among second-generation Moroccan and Tunisian immigrants (ages eighteen to forty), men had an unemployment rate of 19.4 percent and women had an unemployment rate of 21.7 percent. First-generation Algerian immigrant men had an unemployment rate of 29.6 percent and women had a 30.5 percent unemployment rate. Among second-generation Algerian immigrants (ages eighteen to forty), 23.2 percent of men were unemployed and 22.3 percent of women were unemployed. Those of Italian, Spanish, and Portuguese origin had lower unemployment rates compared to the Maghrébin second generation. Similarly, the researchers find that educational trajectories of the second generation vary according to the parents' country of origin, yet there is more gender convergence regarding educational outcomes for the second generation vis-à-vis their immigrant parents.[1] In sum, Meurs, Pailhé, and Simon (2006) demonstrate the persistence of an "ethnic penalty" for the second generation, particularly those with origins in sub-Saharan Africa, North Africa, and Turkey, who are more vulnerable than children of immigrants from southern Europe. There is therefore a mismatch between cultural assimilation and educational attainment, on the one hand, and labor market participation, on the other, for the second generation.

More recently, the 2008 Trajectoires et Origines (Trajectories and Origins) survey, the largest survey thus far conducted of French minority populations and their experiences, surveyed approximately 21,000 immigrants, descendants of immigrants, French migrants from overseas departments (in French, *départements d'outre-mer*, DOMs), descendants of DOM migrants who were born in mainland France, and people born in mainland France without an immigrant background (Beauchemin et al. 2010). Of the first- and second-generation migrants surveyed, a majority had origins in Spain, Italy, Morocco, Algeria, or Tunisia. On average, the second generation had slightly higher self-reported experiences of discrimination than the first generation across ethnic categories.[2] This study also reports a mismatch between those of the second generation who identify as French and those who are perceived by others as French, especially for the second generation from Turkey, sub-Saharan Africa, and North Africa compared to those from other ethnic backgrounds (Simon 2012). There is increased residential integration in the second generation, in that they are less concentrated in the most disadvantaged neighborhoods than the first generation (Shon 2011). The second generation also has more education than their immigrant parents. Yet their trajectories are still shaped by the social characteristics of their immigrant parents (including their educational attainment and countries of origin), which is evidence of an ongoing ethnic penalty. They also experience more difficulties than native students (students born to non-immigrant parents) (Ichou 2014).

Assimilation and Societal Belonging for the Second Generation

The French republican model suggests that the lack of statistical visibility actually affords the second generation social mobility, including the benefits of integration. The republican ideology frames the second generation as French, particularly when they subscribe to republican values. Yet, as this commentary has mentioned, available data indicates that this is not how the second generation experiences being perceived (Meurs, Pailhé, and Simon 2006); rather, the second generation is still socially visible. While I follow scholarly conventions in using the terms "second-generation immigrants" and "children of immigrants," I recognize issues associated with this terminology. Constant (2009) notes that applying the term "immigrant" to the second generation implies that they inherited an immigrant status. Additional terms applied to this population include *les issus de l'immigration* (literally "issued from immigration"), *les descendants des immigrées* (descendants of immigrants), *les jeunes qui sont nés en France* (youth who were born in France), *les jeunes ethniques* (ethnic youth), and *les descendants des peuples colonisés* (descendants of colonized people).[3]

These issues become increasingly clear when considering the realities of ethnic minority second-generation populations. As revealed in the Trajectories and Origins study, despite being born and raised in France, these individuals are often made to feel different by and from their compatriots (Bidoux 2012). They may be referred to as "immigrants" or "foreigners" even though they are not (Kastoryano 2006; Tin 2008). As Hollifield and Héran note in the chapter, the visibility of the second generation was brought into sharp relief with the 2005 uprisings, which were sparked by the deaths of two ethnic second-generation youth, Zyed Benna and Bouna Traoré, while they were being chased by police. Both their deaths and the ensuing uprisings challenged the success of France's assimilationist republican model and revealed the diversity and differentiation of France's population. Another example of the visibility of the second generation was the 2004 ban on religious symbols in public places, and the related controversy of Muslim girls wearing head scarves to school (Bowen 2006). France's preoccupation with Islam also extends to children of immigrants amid the general concern that Islam and Muslims threaten existing French culture and values.

In the 2004 French film *Le grand voyage* (The great journey) by director Ismaël Ferroukhi, who was born in Morocco before moving to France as a young child, Réda, the teenage son of Moroccan immigrants, accompanies his father on a pilgrimage to Mecca from southern France. His father insists on communicating in Arabic, while the son speaks French. Their tense interactions across eight different countries capture how children of immigrants—particularly from former French colonies—live in dual worlds: in their parents' traditional culture and in the Westernized French culture in which they have grown up. Here, it is also important to note the importance of national myths (in this case French republicanism) for the second generation as well.

In analyzing the assimilation of the "new" second generation (stemming from waves of immigration in the 1950s and 1960s), Simon (2003) identified three different trajectories: maintenance of the social position of the first generation, upward mobility through education, and mobility hindered by discrimination. There is also evidence of French-language transmission across generations, as French is often the primary language of the second generation (Borrel and Lhommeau 2010).

Upward mobility has led to increased representation of the second generation throughout French society. For example, Rachida Dati, the daughter of an Algerian immigrant mother and Moroccan immigrant father, served as minister of justice and member of the European Parliament. And Nicolas Sarkozy, the son of a Hungarian immigrant father, served as French president.

Remaining Challenges

But the question remains as to who can be seen as authentically French or included in French society, particularly when children of immigrants are treated as foreigners or feel that France has rejected them (Esman 2009). Moreover, how can the second generation demonstrate integration or assimilation into French society when France is the only society they have ever known? As evident in the ongoing discussions about Muslim integration or President Macron's concern about the influence of US ideas in French academia, France remains uncomfortable with the multicultural nature of its population. Invoking race or racism challenges French ideas of oneness.

Moreover, France needs to address the ongoing discrimination and mistreatment that second-generation immigrants experience, as discussed earlier. This was highlighted by France's 2018 World Cup victory. Despite claims by some that this was an "immigrant victory" due to the fact that the French team, known as Les Bleus, had many players who were children of immigrants, France was quick to clarify that Kylian Mbappé, Paul Pogba, and the other Les Bleus players were French. A similar narrative occurred when France won the World Cup in 1998 and the motto "Blanc-Black-Beur" (White-Black-Arab) became popular.

The 2019 French film *Les Misérables* aptly demonstrates the issues at stake for France's inclusion of its second generation. The film, which takes place in a housing project in the *banlieue* (suburb) of Montfermeil following the 2018 World Cup victory, illustrates the tensions between the state, here represented by the local police, and second-generation (as well as later-generation) populations living on the margins of mainstream society. Watching this film, I wondered if the Les Bleus players would be treated as French if they were not winning World Cup championships. And how much do narratives like those insisting on the Frenchness of the national-team players belie the difficulties children of immigrants face? Yes, they are part of French society, but their presence challenges France's republican ethos. French society insists upon the singularity of Frenchness—but only when it suits them.

Notes

1. They also demonstrate how the Maghrébin second generation "compensate[s] for a lack of cultural and social resources through over-investing in education" relative to non-immigrant origin families (Meurs, Pailhé, and Simon 2006, 251).

2. There were more self-reported experiences of discrimination for children of two immigrant parents than children of just one immigrant parent.

3. In addition, children of Maghrébin immigrants are often referred to as, or included in the category of, Muslims; however, this privileges a religious identification over other identities and presumes that everyone of North African origin claims a Muslim identity. See Alba and Silberman 2002.

References

Alba, Richard. 2005. "Bright vs. Blurred Boundaries: Second-Generation Assimilation and Exclusion in France, Germany, and the United States." *Ethnic and Racial Studies* 28: 20–49.

Alba, Richard, and Roxane Silberman. 2002. "Decolonization Immigrations and the Social Origins of the Second Generation: The Case of North Africans in France." *International Migration Review* 36: 1169–1193.

Beauchemin, Cris, Christelle Hamel, Maud Lesne, and Patrick Simon. 2010. "Les discriminations: Une question de minorités visibles." *Population et Societés* no. 466: 1–4.

Bidoux, Pierre-Emile. 2012. "Les descendants d'immigrés se sentent au moins autant discriminés que les immigrés." INSEE Île-de-France à la Page no. 395.

Borrel, Catherine, and Bertrand Lhommeau. 2010. "Être né en France d'un parent immigré." INSEE Première no. 1287.

Bowen, John R. 2006. *Why the French Don't Like Headscarves: Islam, the State, and Public Space.* Princeton, NJ: Princeton University Press.

Constant, Fred. 2009. "Talking Race in Color-Blind France: Equality Denied, 'Blackness' Reclaimed." In *Black Europe and the African Diaspora*, edited by D. C. Hine, T. D. Keaton, and S. Small, 145–160. Urbana: University of Illinois Press.

Esman, Milton. 2009. *Diasporas in the Contemporary World.* Malden, MA: Polity Press.

Ichou, Mathieu. 2014. "Who They Were There: Immigrants' Educational Selectivity and Their Children's Educational Attainment." *European Sociological Review* 30, no. 6: 750–765.

Kastoryano, Riva. 2006. "Territories of Identities in France." *Items* (Social Science Research Council), June 11, 2006. http://riotsfrance.ssrc.org/Kastoryano.

Meurs, Dominique, Ariane Pailhé, and Patrick Simon. 2006. "The Persistence of Intergenerational Inequalities Linked to Immigration: Labor Market Outcomes for Immigrants and their Descendants in France." *Population* 61, nos. 5–6: 645–682.

Sayad, Abdelmalek. 1999 *The Suffering of the Immigrant.* Cambridge: Polity.

Shon, Jean-Louis Pan Ké. 2011. "Residential Segregation of Immigrants in France: An Overview." *Population et Societés* no. 477.

Simon, Patrick. 2003. "France and the Unknown Second Generation." *International Migration Review* 37: 1091–1119.

Simon, Patrick. 2012. *French National Identity and Integration: Who Belongs to the National Community?* Washington, DC: Migration Policy Institute.

Tin, Louis-Georges. 2008. "Who Is Afraid of Blacks in France? The Black Question: The Name Taboo, the Number Taboo." *French Politics, Culture, and Society* 26, no. 1: 32–44.

6 UK Immigration and Nationality Policy

Radical and Radically Uninformed Change

Randall Hansen

It was a provocative image: a large placard showing a seemingly endless column of people moving forward, their dark faces accentuated by the bright red color of the poster itself. The words "Breaking Point" were emblazoned in a large red font, supplemented below with "The EU has failed us all." The UK Independence Party (UKIP) leader, Nigel Farage, unveiled the poster on June 16, 2016. The message was simple enough: if Britain stays in the EU, these swarthy, threatening young men will come to Britain. The claim was both racist and inaccurate: they were not future migrants but past ones, and their destination was not the United Kingdom but Germany. Nonetheless, the picture was worth more than the proverbial thousand (or, in this case, nineteen) words: it fed into an old trope about an overcrowded island threatened by immigrants.

Simple lies have more power than complex truths, and the United Kingdom voted to leave the European Union a week later. The reasons for doing so were complex, but immigration was undoubtedly one of them. For many, perhaps most, Brexit voters, "Take Back Control" (Vote Leave's slogan) was about taking back control over immigration.

The vote to leave the European Union ruptured British politics, split the two main political parties, brought back the Irish question, and reinvigorated Scottish nationalism. Brexit and its aftermath are thus an appropriate endpoint for this chapter, which reviews UK immigration policy since 1997. It examines the Labour Party's public embrace of high-skilled immigration, the Conservatives' "hostile environment" strategy, its tragic consequences for Black Britons, and UK immigration policy after Brexit.

The chapter will begin with a brief historical overview of postwar migration to Britain, followed by an examination of the 1997–2010 Labour governments' (liberal) migration policies, and the (restrictive) migration policies pursued by Conservative and coalition governments from 2010 to the present. It will ask four questions. First, why is the British case characterized by such radical swings in policy relative to France or Germany, where policy evolution is much more gradual? Second, what role did migration play in the 2016 referendum on remaining within the European Union? Third, what were the deeper reasons behind the *Empire Windrush* scandal of 2018? Fourth, does the UK's post-Brexit immigration policy match its economic needs?

British Immigration Policy: A Brief History

A historical flyover of UK immigration history is relevant for two reasons. First, it highlights the radical policy shifts—expansive, restrictive, expansive, and once again restrictive—that are fundamental to UK immigration policy history. Second, the largest post-Brexit immigration crisis, the Windrush scandal, was directly linked to policy decisions made just after World War II.

Immigration and nationality policy are conceptually and legally distinct, but they have been intertwined in the United Kingdom since the 1940s. From 1905 until 1948, British policy distinguished two types of migrants: British subjects (who could enter the United Kingdom largely freely from anywhere in the empire) and aliens (who could not). In 1948, the British government passed its first citizenship law in response to Canada's 1946 decision to create its own nationality (under which Canadians were Canadian citizens first and British subjects second). The United Kingdom introduced an umbrella nationality—citizenship of the United Kingdom and colonies (CUKC)—for Britain and British colonial subjects (Hansen 1998). Subjecthood is a feudal concept based on a vertical status attaching each subject to the monarch; citizenship is a modern concept based on a horizontal relationship of equality among citizens.

The British intention was to generalize the Canadian logic: if British subjects in Canada were citizens first and subjects second, so would they be across the empire: CUKCs first and British subjects second. To keep the independent dominions in the scheme, the United Kingdom introduced a second umbrella citizenship: citizenship of an independent Commonwealth country (CICC). In 1948, CICCs were Canadians, Australians, New Zealanders, and South Africans (whose movement British politicians supported as a reflection of close ethnic links between them and the

United Kingdom) as well as Indians, Pakistanis, and Ceylonese (whose movement they opposed). As more colonies became independent, their nationals moved from the CUKC to the CICC column. For those countenancing the end of empire, the very British idea was that UK citizenship would organically emerge as the last colony dropped off (Hansen 2000, 169).

Odd though it seems today, when the British government adopted the British Nationality Act of 1948, it expected few Commonwealth migrants to come. Few had in the past, and Britain was in a dire financial position after the war, so the UK government assumed, as most of us do, that tomorrow would be like today. As the British economy recovered in the 1950s, however, labor demand surged. The British government did not encourage the immigration of Black or Asian citizens; on the contrary, it actively discouraged non-white Commonwealth immigration. The 1948 legislation meant, however, that there was little that governments could do to stop it. It was thus the pull of the market, not of politics, that brought Commonwealth immigrants to Britain. There were, it is true, a few recruitment schemes, for nurses and London Transport, for instance, but most Asian and West Indian migrants used citizenship to enter the United Kingdom and searched for jobs once they had arrived. Over the 1950s, some 500,000 came. Conservative governments tolerated them for a time because, as much as they disliked Black and Asian immigrants, they disliked the alternative even more: blocking the entry of white immigrants from Canada, Australia, New Zealand, and South Africa (Hansen 2000; Joppke 1998; Wright 2011). In 1962, however, as numbers surged and domestic public opposition became intense, a Conservative government rather reluctantly placed controls on British subjects' migration (both CUKCs and CICCs) to the United Kingdom.

From 1962 until 1971, British subjects from colonies and former colonies enjoyed privileged access under a work-permit scheme. From 1973, however, they were on the same legal footing as aliens, with a few exceptions. The Immigration Act of 1971, which took effect two years later, is the anchor of UK immigration policy to this day. Under it, individuals wishing to migrate to the United Kingdom could come only as family members or with a work permit. For the latter option, they had to have an employment offer. The work permit allowed them to work in one job for up to four years. They could then apply for permanent residency. In 1973, in the same bill that ended British subjects' privileged access to the United Kingdom, European Economic Community workers were given the right to work in the country. In 1981, the relic of imperial citizenship, CUKC, was replaced with citizenship of the United Kingdom of Great Britain and Northern Ireland. From 1983 (when the British Nationality Act of 1981 took effect), almost everyone in what had been the British Empire was a citizen of the United Kingdom, an independent Commonwealth country, or an overseas territory (the last without entry rights). British subjecthood was a residual status possessed by the few people who did not fit into any other citizenship scheme.

From the 1970s to the 1990s, there was very little primary immigration (immigrants with no familial connection) to the United Kingdom. Prime Minister Margaret Thatcher, "instinctively, without effort or much apparent thought, on the hard right of the party" on the issue, maintained a tight immigration policy for the next decade (Young 1991, 233). The Home Office only begrudgingly offered work permits. From 1973 to 1989, between 10,000 and 20,000 work permits were issued each year (Wright 2011, 149). Family migration continued, although the Conservatives limited that too through harsh application of the "primary purpose" rule (spouses wishing to migrate had to prove that the "primary purpose" of their marriage was not immigration to the United Kingdom) and eventually by ending the unqualified right to bring foreign spouses. Asylum seekers were almost non-existent. Throughout these years, governments were able to maintain the control regime partly because Ireland, then a net-emigration country, constituted an ideal temporary labor supply: English-speaking workers who could easily travel to the United Kingdom and were more likely to return home if the economy soured. It also helped that the economy was, at least for workers, generally sour: there was high unemployment and little demand for immigrants throughout much of the 1980s and the early 1990s.

Enter (New) Labour

The Labour Party came to power in 1997 armed with a massive majority. There was no mention of immigration during the election, but over the next decade, the government adopted a series of measures that led to a sharp increase (Consterdine 2018, 70–71; Wright 2011, 155–161):

- The government issued more work permits under the 1971 legislation and further liberalized the system in 2000. Permits rose from 24,000 in 1995 to 96,740 in 2006.
- Students graduating from undergraduate, MA, or PhD programs were given a temporary work permit.
- The quota for the Seasonal Agricultural Workers Scheme was raised from 10,000 in 1997 to 25,000 in 2002.
- In 2003, the government created the Sectors Based Scheme for the food and hospitality sectors. The quota ranged from 7,500 to 15,000.
- The Working Holidaymaker Scheme was transformed from a cultural exchange to a labor market program.

Two further changes followed. First, the government introduced—tentatively in 2002 and fully in 2008—a skills-based points system allowing people with the right

FIGURE 6.1. Net Migration of Non-British Nationals, 2000–2010

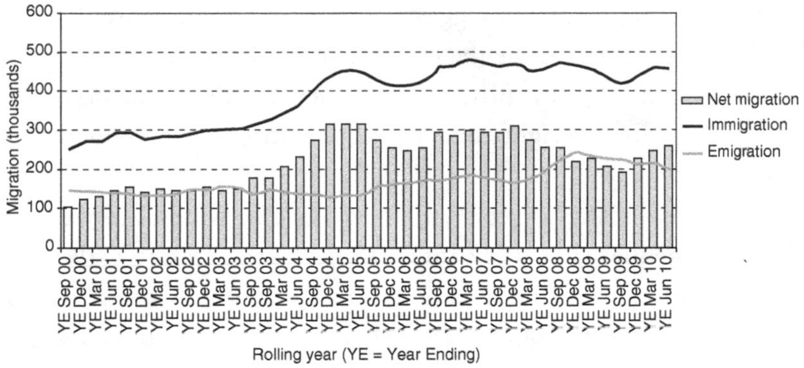

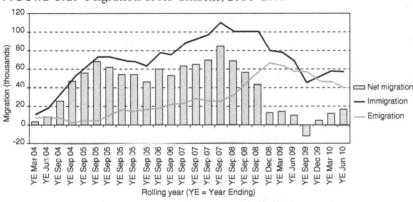

source: Migration Statistics Quarterly Report, no. 8, February 2011, Office for National Statistics, London.

FIGURE 6.2. Migration of A8 Citizens, 2004–2010

source: Migration Statistics Quarterly Report, no. 8, February 2011, Office for National Statistics, London.

educational, linguistic, and professional qualifications to migrate (more on this below). Second, the United Kingdom allowed immediate free movement for nationals from member states joining the EU in 2004.

The policy effects were significant. Within a few years, migration doubled, and net migration from newly acceded EU states reached over 60,000 annually.

Why Did the Door Swing Open?

In a commentary on Zig Layton-Henry's chapter for the 2004 edition of this volume, I suggested that British immigration policy needed to be theorized in terms of markets rather than rights (Favell and Hansen 2002). That is, the key factor determining immigration policy was neither activist courts nor pro-migrant civil society actors (both of whom rely on the language and law of rights) but, rather, the double demand for migrants found at both the top and the bottom of the pay scales. Morgan

Stanley and McDonald's, not judges and juries, drove immigration policy. The experience of the last Labour governments suggests a more complex picture. Markets are undoubtedly relevant as they generate the labor demand that is at the basis of almost all migration movements, but the British state played a decisive role in making economic immigration possible (Wright 2011). Expansive immigration policy was a choice rooted in economic theory.

Gordon Brown was the leading player (Wright 2011, 162). An unusually powerful Chancellor of the Exchequer (Rawnsley 2010, 62–63), Brown was an early advocate of increased immigration. He made two arguments (Wright 2011, 162–163). First, skilled immigration would raise the country's human capital and improve its lagging productivity levels. Second, unskilled immigrants would fill the labor shortages that would otherwise further inhibit productivity growth.

Labour launched its new immigration policy soon after taking office. For the first three years, the Department for Education and Employment (DEE) increased the issuing of work permits (Spencer 2007, 349). When it paid no political price, the government went one step further. Minister of State for Asylum and Immigration Barbara Roche gave a speech, approved by the Treasury and the Prime Minister, at the Institute for Public Policy Research on September 11, 2000. The delivery was uninspiring, but the content revolutionary: The UK is "in competition for the brightest and best talents—the entrepreneurs, the scientists, the high technology specialists who make the economy tick . . . [and] we need to explore carefully [the] implications for immigration policy" (quoted in Somerville 2007, 30). As she spoke, Roche was surrounded by a handpicked panel of academics ready to sing immigration's praises; thus, the speech was an official endorsement of skilled immigration.

Happily experiencing no political blowback, the government waited until after the June 2001 election. Following another decisive victory, Blair moved David Blunkett from the DEE to the Home Office, and he took with him responsibility for labor migration (Spencer 2007, 350). In 2002, Blunkett created the Highly Skilled Migrant Entry Programme (HSMP). Based on the points system invented by Canada in the 1960s (although the British gave Australia credit out of a fear that Canadians seemed too soft on immigration), skilled workers could for the first time migrate to the United Kingdom without a job. The scheme lasted from 2002 to 2008, but relatively few migrants took advantage of it. Most came on Home Office-issued work permits.

By the early 2000s, the British government had successfully shifted both rhetoric and policy on immigration, and it had in place the policy levers for both demand-driven migration (the work permit scheme) and human-capital migration (the HSMP). It was a sharp policy reversal from the 1979–1997 period, and, somewhat incredibly for a country not known for its warm welcome of migrants, the government paid no political price. These halcyon days would not last long.

Caught Unaware: Asylum Policy

In the 1980s, Britain was a no-go zone for refugees. Whereas Germany frequently had over 100,000 asylum applications per year, the UK peaked at 17,000 in 1989 (Gibney and Hansen 2003). Beginning in the mid-1990s, however, the British numbers shot up, reaching over 84,000 in 2002. The Conservative opposition, desperate for an issue that would put a dent in Labour's dizzyingly high popularity, seized on immigration. Shadow Home Secretary Ann Widdecombe, from the hard right of the Conservative Party, made the issue her own and bitterly denounced the government's supposed laxity on asylum (BBC News 2001).[1] "By the end of 2002," a senior advisor remarked, "we were just getting slaughtered on asylum. It wasn't unusual for there to be an asylum story on the front page of a tabloid every day of the week" (quoted in Spencer 2007, 345).

Labour responded by turning the screw. The government passed a series of acts designed to make obtaining asylum much more difficult. Legislation in 2002 withdrew social support for those who did not apply for asylum on arrival (later overturned by the courts; Spencer 2007, 344). Asylum seekers lost the right to work (Goodfellow 2020, 100). In 2004, legislation further limited appeal rights while excluding failed asylum seekers from specialist health care (Spencer 2007, 344).

At the same time, the government attempted to balance restrictions in the asylum sphere with continued liberalization of labor migration. The strategy worked: whether because of the policy or a change in conditions abroad, asylum applications fell steadily from a peak of over 80,000 to 30,000 in time for the 2005 election (Migration Observatory 2019).

EU Enlargement

In 2004, the European Union experienced the greatest enlargement in its history. Ten central European countries, most of them poor, joined the EU at once. In early May 2004, the press began to run stories about eastern European Roma opting for welfare rather than work (Spencer 2007, 352). Blunkett stood his ground, maintaining that there was demand for low-skilled workers that would otherwise be filled by undocumented migrants (Spencer 2007, 352). Whitehall supported the decision. Most departments had worked closely with their opposite numbers in central Europe, and there was a general feeling that Britain's strong support for enlargement placed the country under a moral obligation to open its doors (Wright 2011, 173; personal communication with Charles Clarke, London, November 10, 2014).

The cost-benefit calculation also supported the decision. The Home Office estimated that only some 5,000 to 13,000 central Europeans would arrive per year.

Several other studies came to similar conclusions (IPPR 2004, 12–13). The fact that almost every other EU country (except Sweden and Ireland) invoked the seven-year waiting period for granting mobility rights permitted under the accession treaty had little effect on British deliberations. If anything, it bred a degree of self-satisfaction. The decision was a repeat of 1948: the UK government adopted a policy that opened great new migration channels to poorer countries while blithely assuming that few people would use them.

It did not turn out that way. Over 700,000 EU 8 nationals applied for registration after the 2004 enlargement (Galgóczi et al. 2011). Arrivals fell after the 2007–2008 financial crisis but picked up again with the economic recovery. As of 2019, there were 1,858,000 EU 8 and EU 2 migrants in the country (Migration Observatory 2022; Pollard 2008).

Labour's last significant reform to immigration was the introduction of a five-tiered immigration system replacing all other immigration visas. The new Home Secretary, Charles Clarke, had promised to rationalize the immigration system, root out abuse, and maintain support for continued immigration (Home Office 2005, 5–6). The effort reflected the post-2002 balancing act: see off Conservative opposition and assuage public opinion by reducing asylum applications (with frequent references to "abuse" of the asylum system) and by strictly controlling borders while maintaining open channels for economically beneficial migration (Home Office 2005). The evidence of that effort's success is mixed.

The tiered system rationalized the multiple entry paths into the United Kingdom (HSMP, general work permits, the Seasonal Agricultural Workers Scheme, the Sectors Based Scheme, forty non-permit routes such as "UK ancestry" and the Working Holidaymakers Scheme, and specialist routes, such as au pairs and academic visitors) by grouping them all under five categories (Home Office 2005, 16). Government documents and public communications called the new regime an Australian "points system," but that description only applied to the first tier, for high skilled migrants. The tiers broke down as follows:[2]

- Tier 1, replacing the HSMP, the only group that did not need a sponsor to migrate to the United Kingdom.
- Tier 2, replacing the work permit scheme, for workers with A-levels or above and a job offer in a shortage area (such as nurses, teachers, and administrators).
- Tier 3, replacing the Sectors Based Scheme, for employer-sponsored low-skilled worker. The availability of EU workers meant that no places were ever offered under it.
- Tier 4 for students, seconded workers, and working holidaymakers.

- Tier 5, replacing all temporary schemes for youth mobility and temporary workers (such as Working Holidaymakers and visiting faculty).

Dependents were allowed and could work under Tiers 1 and 2 and were allowed but unable to work under Tiers 4 and 5 (Home Affairs Committee 2009, 18).

Every Tier except 1 depended on a sponsor. Depending on the category, points were allocated for age, qualifications, earnings, job offer, place on a course, nationality, and language. Rather than a guarantee of entry, the points guided a decision-making process that had been left under the previous work permit scheme to the discretion of adjudicating officials (Home Office 2006, 15–18).

The Conservatives and Immigration

As Ann Widdecombe's unsubtle interventions made clear, the Conservatives recognized early on that they might exploit immigration for electoral gain. During the 2005 election, the Party made it a central campaign issue. The Conservatives, rather defensively declaring that "it's not racist to impose limits on immigration," promised enhanced border security, the offshore processing of refugees, an upper limit on annual refugee intake, and (what else?) an "Australian" points system.

 The results were mixed. Anti-immigration sentiment reduced Labour and Liberal Democratic voting, and this may have helped the Tories maintain seats (particularly in the Home Counties), but the strongest anti-immigration preferences were found among non-voters (Ford 2006). As Robert Ford presciently concluded, "analysis of party evaluations and future vote intentions . . . suggest the party best placed to win over voters worried about immigration is not the Conservatives, but the United Kingdom Independence Party" (Ford 2006, 23). Labour continued to defend immigration's economic benefits, and the issue played a small role in the campaign.

 By 2010, the politics of immigration had shifted in important ways. Over the course of the Parliament, Ipsos Mori conducted monthly opinion polls and found that immigration was regularly listed as one of the five "most important issues facing Britain today," and usually one of the top two (Carey and Geddes 2010, 852–853). The Labour Party was dangerously exposed on the issue. Just how exposed was made clear by a disagreeable voter who caught up with the prime minister on her way back from the shops.

 On April 28, 2010, Gordon Brown was visiting Rochdale in Greater Manchester. A sixty-five-year-old widow, Gillian Duffy, heckled him as he spoke. He ignored her, but aides then arranged a one-on-one meeting in a hopeless effort to show his common touch. Duffy ranted about immigrants from "eastern Europe," and then asked where they were "flocking from" (the clue, Brown might have remarked, was in the question). Brown politely defended immigration and then thanked her. He had done rather well, but it soon went wrong. Back in his car, with the microphone on, he spoke his mind: "She was just a sort of bigoted woman." He wasn't wrong: Duffy certainly walked and talked like a bigot. She would, predictably, vote Leave in 2016. The press nonetheless had a field day. Journalists played Brown's words back to Duffy, who feigned appropriate horror that anyone could think such a sweet lady a bigot. The nightly news replayed them to the nation, and an ashen-faced Brown was forced into a series of humiliating apologies.

The encounter became a seminal moment (even acquiring the suffix "gate"—Bigotgate) because Duffy was working-class and a Labour Party member. The exchange strengthened the view, taking shape even before the election, that the party's immigration policy alienated working-class voters. In 2009, Communities Secretary Hazel Blears, a straight-talking MP for the northern constituency of Salford (her hometown), argued that politicians were ignoring low-income white workers' "acute fear" of immigration (Goodfellow 2020, 172; Summers 2009). In the same period, a divided Cabinet, with Brown tipping the matter, agreed that (a) immigration was a major concern to voters and (b) that the party's policies had to change (Cavanagh 2010, 31).

After that, leading figures in the Labour Party went further still. In the run-up to the 2010 Labour leadership contest, Ed Balls told the papers that Labour had been "wrong to allow so many eastern Europeans into Britain" as they undercut the wages of poorer Britons (Balls 2010). Ten months later, the victor in the contest, Ed Miliband, who hails from the unionist left of the party, told the *Daily Telegraph* that the Labour government "got it wrong" and failed to see the impact that immigration would have on low-skilled British workers (Porter 2011).

As this was going on, the Conservatives played their cards carefully. In the years preceding the election, they had tried to shake the impression that they were what Theresa May, then casting herself as a moderate, called "the nasty party": harshly right-wing, uncaring, and beholden to extremists. That they had elected three of the most right-wing party leaders since Margaret Thatcher—William Haig (Thatcher's choice), Iain Duncan Smith (a virulent Euroskeptic), and Michael Howard (a "hang 'em and flog 'em" Home Secretary)—certainly had not helped. The election of a young, urbane David Cameron in 2005 (in a not very subtle effort to imitate Tony Blair) was designed to shake this image. Conscious that they enjoyed an advantage over Labour on the issue, they did not make immigration the center of the campaign (Carey and Geddes 2010). But they made a promise that would come to haunt them: reducing net annual immigration from hundreds of thousands to tens of thousands. The Tories went on to win a plurality of seats, and they entered a coalition government with the Liberal Democrats.

Two months into the coalition, in July 2010, the government announced a temporary cap on Tier 1 and Tier 2 visas at 24,100 as well as an increase in the points required under Tier 1 from 95 to 100. Intensive lobbying by corporations, backed by Vince Cable of the Liberal Democrats, followed, with some companies threatening to move overseas. In late October, the prime minister announced a significant concession: the cap would not apply to intra-company transfers, subject to a minimum salary of 40,000 pounds sterling. In 2009, such transfers made up 40 percent of all Tier 1 and Tier 2 entrants (22,030 out of 55,165; Migration Advisory Committee 2010, Table 3.2) When then Home Secretary Theresa May announced the cap in February 2011, the global figure for Tiers 1 and 2 was reduced to 21,700, and the sorting changed. Tier 1 became a "route for high-value entrepreneurs, investors, and persons of exceptional talent." Investors and entrepreneurs faced no limit; the exceptionally talented (who needed an endorsement from a Designated Competent Body) were limited to 1,000. In 2009, 13,930 migrants had come under Tier 1 (Migration Advisory Committee 2010, Table 3.2). Tier 2 (General, subject to the labor market test) was capped at 20,700; 8,555 had come under it in 2009 (Migration Advisory Committee 2010, Table 3.2). The policy was thus a marked shift back toward a work-permit-based immigration system. Tier 3, for the low-skilled, was never activated (UK Parliament 2011). In addition, high earners—those making over 150,000 pounds per year—were exempt from the cap, as were several other special categories (e.g., ministers of religion and elite sports personalities) (Travis 2011a; Travis 2011b). Finally, students entering under Tier 4 had to prove proficiency in English (de Lotbinière 2011). The cap took effect in April 2011.

The Chimera of 100,000 Minus One

The effort failed to reduce migration to tens of thousands annually, and it was destined to fail. There were two categories of migrants that the British government could limit only at the margins: family migrants (who enjoyed entry rights under UK legislation and the European Convention on Human Rights, which Labour incorporated into English law) and European Union citizens. The only categories the British could fully control were non-EU nationals with no family members in the United Kingdom, including students. Moreover, net migration is a poor measure. In good economic times, fewer Britons leave the United Kingdom for opportunities elsewhere, meaning that net migration could increase without a single new immigrant landing in Britain. The "tens of thousands" promise was a politically foolish one: it was easy to remember but impossible to keep.

A quick look at the data should have made that clear. In 2009, just over 55,000 Tier 1 and Tier 2 entries were granted (Migration Advisory Committee 2010, table 3.2).

Once the exempt categories of investors (13,930), intra-company transfers (22,030), elite athletes (265), and ministers of religion (370) are subtracted, the figure becomes 18,570, *a figure lower than the cap for Tier 1 & 2.* The government left high-skilled immigration untouched. The Migration Advisory Committee, a non-partisan experts committee created by Labour and maintained by the coalition, calculated that the government would have had to reduce the net migration of non-EU nationals (184,000 in 2009) by 146,000 (Migration Advisory Committee 2010, 129). Doing so would have meant brutally cracking down on the remaining tiers, above all students. The government did try to limit student visas and root out fraudulent degrees and applications (with disastrous results—addressed later in the chapter) (Ali 2016). However, with an underfunded university sector wholly dependent on international students' high fees, a radical reduction of Tier 4 visas was never in the cards. Indeed, the inclusion of students, whose stay is usually temporary, in the net migration figures was another ham-fisted decision. It made the <100,000 target impossible to achieve, and there was no need for it: students are rarely a political issue since the public thinks of them as visitors rather than immigrants.

The predictable result was that, as the British economy recovered from the crash, labor demand increased, fewer Britons emigrated, and net migration remained well above 100,000 per year throughout the 2010s.

As the table indicates, the closest the UK government came to achieving its target was in 2012, when the economy was still recovering from the late 2000s recession. At over 150,000 net migrants, it was not even particularly close. Even a sharp fall in migration after the EU referendum left net migration well above 100,000. From

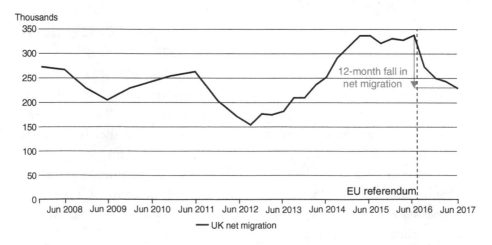

FIGURE 6.3. UK Net Migration, Years Ending December 2007 to June 2017

2012–2019, non-EU migration likely averaged 175,000 per year (Sumption and Vargas-Silva 2020).

The Hostile Environment

Irony has never been Theresa May's strength. Two years into the coalition government, when it was obvious that the migration target would not be reached, the Home Secretary who had denounced her own party as "nasty" showed no compunction about embracing an unremittingly nasty policy—and naming it as such. Pressed on her failure to hit the immigration target, she told the *Daily Telegraph*, "[Our] aim is to create here in Britain a really hostile environment for illegal migration" (Kirkup and Winnett 2012). The idea, popular among hardline anti-immigration politicians in the United States, is that if you make life awful for undocumented migrants, they will go home voluntarily (or, to use their infelicitous compound verb, "self-deport"). For the Home Office, the policy had two advantages: it would reach a larger number of people than any raid could, and "self-deportation" was much cheaper than forced removals (Gentleman 2019, 118). In the summer of 2013, the campaign's early public face was a government-sponsored van driving through six London boroughs with an injunction painted on it: "In the UK illegally? GO HOME OR FACE ARREST. Text HOME TO 78070." May had her officials deny her complicity in the campaign, but this is not credible; an immigration minister later confirmed her involvement (Elgot 2018).

In the run-up to the 2015 election, the Conservatives again burnished their restrictionist credentials by adopting the 2014 Immigration Act. The legislation:

- creates penalties for landlords who did not confirm a "right to rent" by making "reasonable enquiries" into renters' immigration status (Part 3, chapter 1, section 22);
- prohibits banks and building societies from opening accounts for people without "leave to remain" in the United Kingdom (Part 3/1/40(2));
- obligates the bank/building society to carry out immigration status checks (Part 3/1/4(1)); and
- denies driver's licenses to anyone not normally a resident in the United Kingdom or on a course there (Part 3/1/46(1)).

"The stated intention," concluded the Independent Chief Inspector of Borders and Immigration, "was to deny illegal migrants access to public and other services . . . in the expectation that this would persuade large numbers to depart the UK voluntarily and would reduce the 'pull factor' for anyone thinking to come to the UK to settle illegally" (Independent Chief Inspector of Borders and Immigration 2016, 2). Both Cameron and May backed the policy as the best way to keep Tory voters from switching to UKIP (Gentleman 2019, 130).

The 2015 Conservative Party manifesto adopted a much harsher tone in touch with the public mood. Pollsters found that immigration was one of the three most important issues—along with health care and the economy—facing the country (YouGov 2015). The Labour Party, meanwhile, reverted to 1980s form and elected on ideological grounds an unelectable leader, Ed Miliband, who was ill-inclined to defend immigration (Goodfellow 2020: 121–124). Labour instead decided to enter a restrictionist contest that, given the Conservatives' record on immigration, it would inevitably lose. In the run-up to the election, the party sold bright-red mugs emblazoned with the slogan, "Controls on Immigration. I'm voting Labour" (Gentleman 2019: 137).

To exploit its natural advantage over Labour, the Tory manifesto had to confront the fact that the Conservatives had failed in their promise to reduce immigration to the tens of thousands annually. The manifesto attempted to turn a policy failure into a success: non-EU migration was down, but EU migration was up because of the strength of the British economy. This was true, but rather than leaving it at that and offering anti-immigration generalities, the Conservatives, scarred by the defection of two MPs to UKIP (Gentleman 2019, 137), doubled down on the <100,000 promise: "We will keep our ambition of delivering *annual net migration in the tens of thousands, not hundreds of thousands*" (CPM 2015, 29; emphasis in original). The next lines specified the mechanisms for achieving his unachievable goal: clamping down on illegal migration, enhancing border security, and controlling migration from the EU through welfare policy. The manifesto then set in motion events that would cost David Cameron his job:

> We will negotiate new rules with the EU, so that people will have to be here for a number of years before they claim benefits, including the tax credits that top up low wages. Instead of something-for-nothing, we will build a system on the principle of something-for-something. We will then put these changes to the British people in a straight in-out referendum on our membership of the European Union by the end of 2017 (CPM 2015, 30).

The referendum promise dated to 2013, when the Conservatives panicked about the United Kingdom Independence Party's rise in public opinion polls. Placing the promise in the manifesto *may* have helped the Conservatives at the 2015 general election, but it generated three serious problems. First, it fed the myth that EU migrants committed benefit fraud and were a drain on the economy when the best analysis made it clear that they provided a net fiscal benefit to the country (for details, see Dustmann and Frattini 2013, 19). Second, the party once again established the same simplistic, easily remembered yardstick—the 100,000 goal—against which its policies would almost assuredly be judged a failure. And, finally, the government anchored its future, to say nothing of the country's, to the vagaries of a referendum that would be about migrants over which the government would at best have limited control: EU nationals. That the free movement of workers was one of the four pillars of the single market, one taken particularly seriously by Britain's allies in the newly acceded central European states, should have been a secret to no one, above all a prime minister who studied politics at Oxford. Following negotiations trumped up by the British press—in its inimitable fashion—as a great battle between London and Brussels, Prime Minister David Cameron came back with predictably modest changes, notably an agreement that allowed any member state to declare an "emergency break" to limit access to in-work benefits (the income-based Jobseeker's Allowance). It required European Parliament approval, did not allow restrictions on EU migration for work, and was unlikely to warm the heart of Euroskeptics seeking to restore British "sovereignty" over immigration policy (but, then again, nothing but full withdrawal would).

Cameron went on to lose the referendum that he had so cavalierly called. Immigration played a substantial role in the campaign and an oversized role in the result: polling done in the immediate aftermath of the 2016 vote showed that 33 percent of "Leave" voters cited immigration control as the main reason for their vote; overall, it was the second-most important reason after the "principle that decisions about the UK should be taken in the UK" (Ashcroft 2016). The referendum, designed to keep the Conservative Party together, split it. In another irony, both EU immigration and public concern over it fell after the referendum.

The *Empire Windrush* Scandal

In 2014, Renford McIntyre, a sixty-year-old Briton of Jamaican descent living in the United Kingdom since 1968, was subject to an employment eligibility check (Gentleman 2018). He had worked for some thirty-five years as a tool setter, deliveryman, and National Health Service driver. But he had neither a British passport nor a certificate of naturalization, and so, following a routine employment check, he was sacked. Unable to find another job without papers, he slipped into depression, lost his flat, and was soon homeless.

He was not alone. Up and down the country, people who had lived in the United Kingdom for decades and never dreamed of living anywhere else lost their bank accounts, driver's licenses, flats, and jobs (Committee of Public Accounts 2019). They were denied hospital treatment and employment benefits. Many provided documents showing decades of National Insurance contributions—meaning they had worked and paid taxes—but to no avail. The Home Office told Joycelyn John, who moved from Grenada on a CUKC passport in 1963, that 75 pages of documentation—National Insurance and tax slips, bank statements, records from dentists and doctors, school letters—were insufficient (Gentleman 2019, 171). In total, 57,000 people without British nationality, who had entered the United Kingdom perfectly legally before 1973, and whom the 1971 Immigrant Act defined as citizens in everything but name, now faced exclusion from public services and the country itself (Home Affairs Select Committee 2018). The Home Office arrested people, held them in detention, and placed them on planes to the West Indies (Gentleman 2019). A simple holiday abroad could result in denied reentry. Reports on the number deported vary. Official statistics put it at 63 as of April 2018, but subsequent estimates arrived at a figure at 83 (164 were detained or deported) (Agerholm 2018). At least 19 people died before the Home Office could contact them to make amends, and another 27 could not be traced (Gentleman 2019, 279; Rawlinson 2018).

Technically, any British subject who entered the United Kingdom before 1973 could have been affected, but the cases had a pronounced race and class bias: almost all were Black, from the West Indies, and low- to medium-income earners. They were people who spent all their time in the United Kingdom and lacked the means and/or inclination for holidays, sabbaticals, or postings abroad—privileges that would have led them to apply for British passports as a matter of course. In a sad irony, they were classic "somewheres" rather than "anywheres," to use Goodhart's terms, for whom Theresa May claimed to speak in her 2016 Conservative Party conference speech: they lived in, worked in, and knew only the United Kingdom (Goodhart 2020).

How Did It Happen?

In August 1995, I interviewed Enoch Powell, author of the racist 1968 "rivers of blood" oration, for my doctoral dissertation. As we started, he gave me an intense stare and asked, "may I give a speech?" I replied affirmatively. Speaking in his usual prophetic way, he said, "You must apply your mind to the study of citizenship." He was wrong about most immigration issues, but he was right about that: the *Empire Windrush* scandal was the product of the seven-decade, messy intersection of British nationality law and immigration to Britain. As noted earlier, until 1962, all CUKCs and CICCs (Jamaican, Indian, or Canadian nationals) could enter the country freely, and until 1973, they had privileged access (Hansen 2000). During those years, hundreds of thousands of CUKCs/CICCs and their children migrated to the United Kingdom and were granted admission. Section 2 1(c) of the 1971 Immigration Act guaranteed the "right of abode" to all CUKCs who had been ordinarily resident in the United Kingdom for five years. Section 7 1 extended, in effect, permanent leave to remain to all Irish and Commonwealth citizens who had been ordinarily resident in the United Kingdom for five years.

From 1983, when 1981 the British Nationality Act took effect and created British citizenship, all CUKCs renewing or applying for a passport would have received one for "the United Kingdom of Great Britain and Northern Ireland." The government amended Section 2 of the 1971 Immigration Act to make it clear that all Commonwealth immigrants with the right of abode (for instance, a Jamaican national arriving in 1965) would be "construed" and "treated" as British citizens. Under the 1981 Act, they could also obtain British citizenship by proving five years' residence, speaking English (or Welsh or Scottish Gaelic), and being free of a criminal record.

Under the 1971 Immigration Act, the burden of proof rested with the individuals claiming a right of abode (Gentleman 2019, 182). If they lost the CUKC or independent Commonwealth country passport with which they entered the country, or if they never had one because they came on their parents' passport, they had no proof. Nonetheless, tens of thousands of people in this situation lived undisturbed, working and paying their taxes, for decades. What changed was the environment, which became "hostile" as a result of the Immigration Acts of 2014 and 2016. The laws placed an obligation on a wide range of actors—employers, landlords, banks, and all manner of public agencies—to act as border guards and informants at every level of British society. The move was curious, if not hypocritical, for a party whose leader had mocked national identity cards as an anti-British bit of continental illiberalism.[3] Implemented in a country whose officials and private citizens had little experience with identity checks, the policy accorded far too much discretion to ill-trained (indeed mostly untrained) actors (Bulman 2018).

The human consequences were devastating (details from Gentleman 2019). Paulette Wilson was a sixty-two-year-old cook who came to Britain in 1968 as a CICC from Jamaica and worked at the House of Commons canteen. She was arrested, sent to an immigration detention center, and narrowly escaped deportation. Joycelyn John did not: the Home Office, unconvinced by the 75 pages of documentation she provided, hounded her into accepting "voluntary" removal to Grenada.

Others who left for visits abroad were not allowed back. Under the 1988 Immigration Act anyone with indefinite leave to remain who went abroad for more than two years would lose that right (Gentleman 2019, 260). Vernon Vanriel came to the

United Kingdom from Jamaica in 1962 as a CUKC on his mother's passport. He had a right to post-1983 British nationality but lacked the money to apply for it. After visiting Jamaica for two years on his Jamaican passport (the United Kingdom accepts dual citizenship), border officials refused to allow him back into the country. Vanriel speaks in an unmistakable (north) London accent and was a feted boxer who entered the fight at Royal Albert Hall to a crowd chant of "Vernon Vanriel, Vernon Vanriel. We'll support you ever more. We'll support you ever more" (Gentleman 2019, 259–260).

In 2010, the Home Office made the task of challenging sackings, loss of benefits, evictions, denials of bank accounts, and deportation even more difficult by destroying documentation on Commonwealth immigrants who arrived before 1973. What is not clear is precisely which documentation and how difficult. The papers referred to destroyed "landing cards," but they were only filled out after 1973. Journalist Ian Cobain, then at the *Guardian*, sent a Freedom of Information request to the Home Office. The reply was cryptic, condescending, and Kafkaesque:

> As you may be aware, the destruction of registry slips was made public knowledge in 2010 and was part of a destruction programme dating back to 2009. This was then misinterpreted [by journalists] as landing cards, and, possibly, landing cards of members from the Windrush generation.
>
> Registry slips and landing cards are not one and the same. Registry slips were index cards/finding aids for Home Office files which were no longer required following the digitization of Home Office records and therefore could be destroyed; landing cards are the records passengers complete on their arrival in the UK and are (and always have been) subject to a data retention policy and *routinely* destroyed. (emphasis in original) (FOI 2018)

The reply settled nothing. If finding aids were destroyed, the obvious question is "finding aids to what?" and the "what" might have been documentation confirming date of arrival. The Home Office declined to provide further details. Another possibility is that the Home Office destroyed "sea arrival cards," required by the 1906 Merchant Shipping Act for arrivals by ship. In that case, CUKCs and CICCs who arrived by ship could have secured proof of when they moved to the United Kingdom had the destruction not occurred.

In either case, the destroyed documentation might have helped some CUKCs/CICCs prove their arrival date. However, many people arrived on their parents' passports and, furthermore, there were two distinct requirements for proving a right of abode: date of arrival and continuous residence. The latter meant three to four pieces of official documentation demonstrating place of residence for each year a person lived in the United Kingdom (Gentleman 2019, 181). It was the hostile environment policy itself, not the destruction of the documents, that ensnared thousands of Black Britons.[4]

As *Guardian* journalist Amelia Gentleman's stories about the treatment suffered by the "Windrush Generation" gathered attention, and as outrage grew among readers and the wider public, the Home Office reacted in a manner that was both incompetent and callous. It was incompetent in that it had no idea of how to respond; in implementing the 2014 and 2016 acts it had revealed its profound ignorance of past legislation drafted and implemented by the Home Office in 1962 and 1973. Ignorance of citizenship law is broad and deep in the United Kingdom—senior politicians speak of "British subjects" when the status all but vanished in 1983, and even the most sympathetic journalists often reveal only a faint understanding of why people in the country for so long should have such difficulties establishing their right to be there—but the Home Office has no excuse for sharing such ignorance.

It was callous because the requirement imposed on people wishing to prove their right of abode would defeat anyone who was not a professional archivist (Younge 2018). The scandal eventually cost Home Secretary Amber Rudd her job, but the hostile environment's legacy lives on. In April 2019, the Home Office informed a thirty-four-year-old woman born in the United Kingdom that she was not British (Ellis 2019). In September of the same year, a report by the public accounts committee, which drew a parallel with the Windrush scandal, concluded that the Home Office falsely accused 30,000 international students of cheating on English language tests and deported 2,500 of them (7,200 left voluntarily on the threat of deportation) (Syal 2019). As in the Windrush scandal, the ideological obsession with achieving the unachievable reduction to fewer than 100,000 net migrants resulted in overzealousness, callousness, and absurd decisions (Skapinker 2019). The department responsible for the disaster is now, post-Brexit, managing 3.5 million EU nationals who need confirmation of their right to remain in the United Kingdom (Gentleman 2019, 287).

UK Immigration Policy after Brexit

Following the UK's formal departure from the European Union on January 31, 2020, the Conservatives made good on their promise to reform immigration. In February 2020, the government replaced the Tier 1 visa (the quota for which had been raised to 2,000 in 2017) with the Global Talent Visa. The visa is for "leaders or potential leaders" in the academic or research, arts and culture, or digital technology fields endorsed by government-recognized organizations. Like Tier 1, there is no requirement of a job offer, and like Tier 1 few will benefit: 1,669 came to the United Kingdom with the visa in 2020 (although Covid-19 resulted in fewer visas in all categories) (Home Office 2021).

A few months later, the new Home Secretary, Priti Patel, a hardened Euroskeptic and far-right Home Secretary in the mold of Michael Howard, launched a broader reform. In May, she introduced the Second Reading of the Immigration and Social Security Coordination (EU Withdrawal) Bill, and the law received Royal Assent in November. The bill abolished the 1973 immigration rules and made EU nationals, except Irish citizens, subject to the 1971 Immigration Act. The 1971 legislation gave the Home Secretary the power to draw up immigration rules, and Patel used these to develop the UK's new immigration system. On October 22, 2020, the Home Office published its new immigration rules (Home Office 2020a). They reinvent the wheel. The government yet again made much of "introducing" an Australian points system (Johnson made repeated reference to it) (Hetherington 2020). Under the new rules, applicants nominally, as in Canada, receive points for various attributes—a job offer (20 points), English-language skills (10 points), a PhD in a relevant subject (20 points), and so on—and with 70 points they can apply for work in the United Kingdom. In fact, the system is a mirage: it is mathematically impossible to reach 70 points without a job offer, and a job offer by an approved sponsor at the appropriate skill level and English language skills are mandatory (UK Government 2021). The rules mention a new, unsponsored route for skilled migrant workers, but the details are limited to a promise of a future announcement.

The current rules are thus much like the old points-based system, in place since 2008, which was itself an update on the 1971 work permit scheme. In a real points system like Canada's, an applicant can achieve the minimum points needed based on skills and characteristics alone, particularly age, education, and language.

Under the October 2020 UK rules, a new Skilled Worker route replaces the Tier 2 visas. The rules drop the minimum skill level from the Required Qualifications Framework (RQF) level 6 (roughly a bachelor's degree) to level 3 (roughly A-levels); reduce the minimum salary threshold from 30,000 pounds to 25,600 pounds (20,400 for shortage occupations); suspend the annual cap; and allow the visas to be renewed indefinitely (after six years, visa holders can apply for indefinite leave to remain). The government abolished the never-deployed Tier 3, making it a four-tier system with an awkward jump from "2" to "4." The only clear improvement on previous policy is the abandonment, at last, of the <100,000 promise; the government's policy statement of early 2020 only offers a vague commitment to "reduce overall immigration levels" (Home Office 2020b). Such an easily escapable promise in 2015 would have spared the United Kingdom much agony.

At the time of writing, Home Secretary Patel is also proposing new asylum rules. Given the number of applications—35,737 in 2019, around the same average as 2004–2009 and well below the late 1990s spike—the changes are arguably a solution in search of a problem (Sturge 2022, 13 for the statistics). But anti-refugee posturing plays well with the Tory base and in the northern Brexit heartlands.[5]

Brexit required one part of the reform: replacing the Dublin Convention. Under it, asylum applications are to be processed in the first signatory state reached; the United Kingdom now must negotiate bilateral agreements with all EU countries. But it also involves a series of harsh measures. The plan criminalizes (the word "illegal" is peppered throughout the document) any asylum seeker who arrives without a visa by boat, lorry, or plane or who passes through a safe third country (UK Government 2021). If they cannot be deported (expanded deportation is a key part of the plan), they will be given not refugee status but temporary protection, with regular reassessment for deportation, limited family reunion rights, and no public funds except in cases of destitution. If, as is likely, other countries refuse to accept asylum seekers for processing (the return provisions of the Dublin Convention were largely a failure, and the United Kingdom has burned many bridges in its behavior toward the EU), they would remain in limbo and forever liable for deportation. The plan also promises to shift asylum policy toward resettlement (processing refugees abroad, generally in first-country-of-asylum refugee camps) outside the refugee convention. The rules also empower the Home Secretary to create, along Australian lines, overseas processing and detention. UNHCR has condemned the plan (Grierson and Marsh 2021), and the extent to which it will be implemented is uncertain. The offshore processing proposal already faces substantial political resistance, faster deportation has been tried many times before (Gibney and Hansen 2003), and expanding resettlement policy is extremely costly. But one thing is clear: the Home Secretary has used the power of her office to score cheap political points by demonizing refugees.

Returning to labor migration, the UK's current immigration system will allow skilled immigrants (including of course EU nationals who enjoyed free entry until early 2021) such as bankers, professors, and senior managers, and the reduced RQF will now allow technicians, electricians, plumbers, office managers, sales executives, estate agents, shopkeepers, ticket inspectors, gardeners, chefs, fitness instructors, teaching assistants, and child minders (assuming they are paid enough) to migrate to the UK (Kingsley Napley 2021). The rules however, make no allowance for low-skilled workers: waiters, hairdressers, administrative assistants, cashiers, retail assistants, waiters, fast-food employees, and most hotel and tourism workers (Kingsley Napley 2021). With the exception of the disinterred Seasonal Workers Scheme (packaged as an innovation) for a small number of agricultural laborers, the UK government provides no migration routes for low-skilled migrants in a country that is highly dependent on cheap labor. Fully 18.1 percent of UK workers are low-paid (understood as less than 2/3 of median earnings), the highest in Western Europe and the 7th highest in the OECD (OECD data). Sixteen percent of the UK labor force is made up of immigrants (up from 7 percent in the early 1990s and 13 percent in 2009, although down from 18 percent pre-Covid), and EU nationals make up 6 percent of the labor force (down from 7 percent pre-Brexit) (Anderson and Ruhs 2012, 24; Fernández-Reino and Rienzo 2021). EU nationals born in the ten post-2004 EU states, which made up the majority of EU migrants, have the highest employment rate among any group, immigrant and non-immigrant (93 percent for EU-2 men and 89 percent for EU-8 men, vs. 79 percent for UK-born men) (Fernández-Reino and Rienzo 2021). They concentrate heavily in low-skilled sectors: 58 percent of EEA migrants[6] work in RQF levels 1 and 2 (GCSEs) (Walsh 2021, 11). Brexit has blocked their entry: 74 percent of those who entered after 2004 would not have met the minimum salary thresholds (Walsh 2021, 11–12). Multiple sectors are entirely dependent on low-skilled (RQF 1–2) and low-paid workers: 63 percent of accommodation and hospitality jobs [23 percent of low-skilled jobs in the sector are migrant workers]; 29 percent of agricultural employment [7 percent migrant workers]; 57 percent of food and beverage manufacturing [31 percent migrant workers]; 44 percent in residential and social care [19 percent migrant workers]; 73 percent in transport [21 percent migrant workers]; 64 percent in warehousing [30 percent migrant workers]; and 57 percent in wholesale and retail trade [13 percent migrant workers] (Migration Advisory Committee 2021).

The new immigration rules thus shut out immigrants with the highest labor-participation rates and on which multiple sectors depend. Should the government succeed in its ambitions to provide better training for British workers and "level-up" poorer parts of the country, that demand will not disappear. Instead, native-born UK workers will be even less inclined to take low-skilled jobs, thus increasing demand for low-skilled migrants. The putative logic behind the decision to end free movement was, as a UK government policy document put it, that the country needed "to shift the focus of our economy away from reliance on cheap labor from Europe and instead concentrate on investment in technology and automation" (MacLellan 2020). Automation may well eliminate jobs in some sectors in the future, but that does nothing for the low-skilled labor shortages that sectors will face as the economy recovers from the Covid-19 pandemic. What's more, faith in science and technology is hard to credit when expressed by a government that has presided over the largest real cut to education funding since 1950 (Bolton 2020). Rather like Brexit itself, confidence in current UK immigration policy requires suppressing judgment and adopting a religious faith ("believing in Brexit," as the Tory papers put it) in some glorious but distant future.

Conclusion: The Longue Durée

The United Kingdom stands out among the countries examined in this volume in its radical policy shifts. British immigration policy shifted from periods of great liberality (the 1950s and 1960s), to great restrictiveness (the 1970s-mid-1990s), to (relative) liberality again (the mid-1990s to 2010), and back to great restrictiveness (2010 to present). British institutions make these jarring shifts possible (Freeman 1995, Joppke 1998, Hansen 2000). The absence of checks on the executive in the United Kingdom, such as those that exist in the United States or Germany, mean that the United Kingdom can maintain policies that fly in the face of public opinion—such as open immigration—for relatively long periods. When governments do make restrictive moves, however, those same institutions allow sudden policy reversals. Thus, in the 1960s, Roy Jenkins articulated a vision of an inclusive society (partly out of principle, partly because it did him a lot of good with the intellectual wing of the Labour Party). In the 1980s, Prime Minister Thatcher was utterly hostile to immigration. In the 1990s, Chancellor Gordon Brown saw in immigration a partial solution to the UK's deficits in human capital and productivity. And after 2010, the Conservatives once again pursued the chimera of low immigration levels, with Theresa May's control-obsessed Home Office playing a leading role. Somewhat paradoxically, British institutions made UK immigration policy both excessively liberal and excessively illiberal.

Westminster institutions' ability to effect radical policy shifts has not been matched in the case of immigration policy by an understanding of the implication of those shifts. Repeatedly, UK governments have launched major policy changes while remaining, at best, blithely ignorant and, at worst, deluded about their long-term effects. In 1948, politicians from all sides of the political spectrum lined up to extend full citizenship rights to hundreds of millions of people without anyone even raising the possibility that hundreds of thousands might just exercise them. In 2004, the Labour government extended free movement rights to tens of millions of people with immediate effect without taking seriously the possibility that hundreds of thousands might just exercise them. In 2010, the coalition articulated, and later stuck to, a target that any respectable analyst would have dismissed as unattainable. In 2014 and 2016, the government shifted immigration control from the border to sub-state and private actors, once again launching a significant policy change with little regard to long-term and unintended consequences. And, finally, in 2021, the government all but ended low-skilled immigration with little regard to either an economy wholly dependent on it or the human trafficking that the Home Office claims it wishes to stop (on this, see Goodfellow 220, 245). For decades, UK immigration policy has been both radically transformed and radically uninformed. Given the concentration of power in the UK executive, the far too extensive remit of the Home Office, and the ignorance that pervades both Whitehall and the political class regarding the basic intersection between immigration law and nationality law, there is little evidence that either will change.

Notes

I am grateful to Alisa Gorokhova, Joseph Hawker, and Frederick Hayward for research assistance; to Ian Cobain and Amelia Gentleman for advice and comments on the Windrush section; and to Matthew Gibney, François Héran, James F. Hollifield, Desmond King, Philip L. Martin, Riva Kastoryano, Pia M. Orrenius and the other participants at the June 2019 Paris conference that led to this volume. For editorial advice, my thanks to Erin at Newgen. The University of Toronto's Munk School and my Canada Research Chair in Global Migration provided research funding, which I gratefully acknowledge.

1. She later joined Nigel Farage's Brexit Party.

2. A probably unconscious imitation of the work permit scheme in place for Commonwealth immigrants from 1962 to 1973. Hansen (2000), 110.

3. See Cameron's "Where are your papers" comment in a bad German accent: https://www.youtube.com/watch?v=Sp4nwcBgx0A

4. An email exchange with Amelia Gentleman clarified these points.

5. A conversation with Matthew Gibney clarified this section.

6. EU plus Iceland, Lichtenstein, and Norway.

References

Agerholm, Harriet. 2018. "Windrush: Government Admits 83 British Citizens May Have Been Wrongfully Deported Due to Scandal but Will Only Apologize to 18." *Independent*, August 22.

Ali, Aftab. 2016. "More than 30 Fake UK Universities Shut Down by Government in Past Year." *Independent*, August 15, 2016.

Anderson, Bridget and Martin Ruhs. 2012. "Reliance On Migrant Labor: Inevitability or Policy Choice?" *Journal of Poverty and Social Justice* 20/1: 23–30.

Ashcroft, Michael. 2016. "How the United Kingdom Voted on Thursday . . . and Why." Lord Ashcroft Polls. June 24. Available at: https://lordashcroftpolls.com/2016/06/how-the-united-kingdom-voted-and-why/.

Balls, Ed. 2010. "We Were Wrong to Allow So Many Eastern Europeans into Britain." *The Guardian*, June 6.

BBC News. 2001. "Tories Renew Asylum Attacks." *BBC News*. April 25.

Bolton, Paul. 2020. *Education Spending in the UK*. London: UK Parliament. October 28.

Bulman, May. 2018. "Windrush: The Biggest Political Scandal of the Last 12 Months had Nothing to Do with Brexit." *Independent*, December 21.

Carey, Sean and Andrew Geddes. 2010. "Less is More: Immigration and European Integration at the 2010 General Election." *Parliamentary Affairs* 63, no. 4: 849–865.

Cavanagh, Matt. 2010. "Numbers Matter." In *Immigration under Labour*, edited by Tim Finch and David Goodhart. London: IPPR and Prospect.

Committee of Public Accounts. 2019. *Windrush Generation and the Home Office*, March 6.

CPM. 2015. Conservative Party Manifesto. *Strong Leadership. A Clear Economic Plan. A Brighter, More Secure Feature*. Available at: http://ucrel.lancs.ac.uk/wmatrix/ukmanifestos2015/localpdf/Conservatives.pdf.

Consterdine, Erica. 2018. *Labour's Immigration Policy: The Making of the Migration State*. Cham, Switzerland: Palgrave Macmillan.

Dustmann, Christian and Tommaso Frattini. 2013. *The Fiscal Effects of Immigration to the UK. CREAM Discussion Paper* 22/13. London: UCL Centre for Research and Analysis of Migration.

Elgot, Jessica. 2018. "May Was Not Opposed to 'Go Home' Vans, Official Accounts Suggest." *The Guardian*. April 19.

Favell, Adrian and Randall Hansen. 2002. "Markets against Politics: Migration, EU Enlargement and the Idea of Europe." *Journal of Ethnic and Migration Studies*. 28, no. 4: 581–601.

Fernández-Reino, Mariña and Cinzia Rienzo. 2021. *Briefing: Migrants in the UK Labour Market: An Overview*. Oxford: The Migration Observatory.

Ford, Robert. 2006. "An Iceberg Issue? Immigration at the 2005 British General Election." Paper presented at the Political Studies Association's Annual Conference.

FOI. 2018. Freedom of Information Request 48193. Internal Review. November 16. I am grateful to Ian Cobain for providing me a copy of this FOI request.

Freeman, Gary P. 1995. "Modes of Immigration Politics in Liberal Democratic States." *International Migration Review*. 29, no. 4: 881–902.

Galgóczi, Béla, Janine Leschke and Andrew Watt. 2011. "Intra-EU Labour Migration: Flows, Effects and Policy Responses." *European Trade Union Institute Working Paper* 2009/3. Available at: https://www.etui.org/sites/default/files/11%20WP%202009%2003%20Update%20WEB.pdf (consulted February 27, 2011).

Gentleman, Amelia. 2018. "'I've Been Here for 50 years': The Scandal of the Former Commonwealth Citizens Threatened with Deportation." *The Guardian*, February 21.

Gentleman, Amelia. 2019. *The Windrush Betrayal: Exposing the Hostile Environment*. London: Guardian Faber.

Goodhart, David. 2020. *The Road to Somewhere: The Populist Revolt and the Future of Politics*. Oxford: Oxford University Press.

Grierson, James and Sarah Marsh. 2021. "UN Refugee Agency Hits Out at Priti Patel's Plans for UK Asylum Overhaul." *The Guardian*. March 24.

Ellis, Brian. 2019. "'I Should Not Have to Prove I Am British.'" *Lancashire Post*, May 18.

Ford, Rob. 2006. "Immigration at the 2005 British General Election." Reading: Paper presented at the Political Studies Association Conference.

Gibney, Matthew J. and Randall Hansen. 2003. "Deportation and the Liberal State: The Forcible Return of Asylum Seekers and Unlawful Migrants in Canada, Germany and the United Kingdom." *New Issues in Refugee Research*, Working Paper No. 77. Geneva: UNHCR.

Goodfellow, Maya. 2020. *Hostile Environment: How Immigrants Became Scapegoats*. London: Verso.

Goodhart, David. 2020. *The Road to Somewhere. The Populist Revolt and the Future of Politics*. Oxford: Oxford University Press.

Hansen, Randall. 1998. "The Politics of Citizenship in 1940s Britain: The British Nationality Act." *20th Century British History* 10, no. 1: 67–95.

Hansen, Randall. 2000. *Citizenship and Immigration in Postwar Britain*. Oxford: Oxford University Press.

Hetherington, Philippa. 2020. "This Is Why the Myth of the 'Australian Points-Based System' Is So Damaging." *Prospect*, February 20.

Home Affairs Committee—Thirteenth Report. 2009. *Managing Migration: The Points Based System*. London: House of Commons. Available at:
https://publications.parliament.uk/pa/cm200809/cmselect/cmhaff/217/21714.htm#a39.

Home Affairs Select Committee Report. 2018. *The Windrush Generation*.

Home Office. 2005. *Controlling Our Borders: Making Migration Work for Britain*. London: HM Government.

Home Office. 2006. *A Points-Based System: Making Migration Work for Britain*. London: HM Government.

Home Office. 2020a. *Statement of Changes in Immigration Rules*. Presented to Parliament pursuant to section 3(2) of the Immigration Act 1971. London: House of Commons, October 22, 2020.

Home Office. 2020b. *Policy Paper. The UK's Points-Based System: Policy Statement*. February 19. Available at: https://www.gov.uk/government/publications/the-uks-points-based-immigration-system-policy-statement/the-uks-points-based-immigration-system-policy-statement (consulted March 27, 2021).

Home Office. 2021. *National Statistics: February 25 2021*. Available at: https://www.gov.uk/government/statistics/immigration-statistics-year-ending-december-2020/summary-of-latest-statistics (consulted March 25, 2021).

Independent Chief Inspector of Borders and Immigration. 2016. *An Inspection of the "Hostile Environment" Measures Relating to Driving Licenses and Bank Accounts. January to July 2016*. London: HMSO.

IPPR (Institute for Public Policy Research). 2004. *EU Enlargement and Labor Migration: an IPPR Factfile*. London.

Joppke, Christian. 1998. *Immigration and the Nation State: The United States, Germany, and Britain*. Oxford: Clarendon.

Kingsley Napley. 2021. *The UK Has a New Immigration System from January 1 2021*. January 5.

Kirkup, James and Robert Winnett. 2012. "Theresa May Interview: 'We're Going to Give Illegal Migrants a Really Hostile Reception.'" *The Daily Telegraph*. May 25.

De Lotbinière, Max. 2011. "UK Tells Foreign Students: 'Speak English or Stay Out.'" *The Guardian*. April 12.

MacLellan, Kylie. 2020. "UK Heralds End of 'Cheap Labor from Europe' with Post-Brexit Immigration System." *Reuters*. February 18.

Migration Advisory Committee. 2010. *Limits on Immigration*. Croydon: the Home Office.

Migration Observatory. 2019. *Migration to the UK: Asylum and Refugees*. January 4. Available at: https://migrationobservatory.ox.ac.uk/resources/briefings/migration-to-the-uk-asylum/.

Migration Observatory. 2022. *EU Migration to and from the UK*. Available at: https://migrationobservatory.ox.ac.uk/resources/briefings/eu-migration-to-and-from-the-uk/.

Migration Advisory Committee. 2021. *Annual Report*. Available at: https://www.gov.uk/government/publications/migration-advisory-committee-annual-report-2021/migration-advisory-committee-mac-annual-report-2021-accessible-version.

Pollard, Naomi. 2008. "Feeling the Pull of Home?" IPPR. London: Institute for Public Policy Research.

Porter, Andrew. 2011. "Ed Miliband: Immigration Lost Labour Votes." *Daily Telegraph*. April 20.

Rawlinson, Kevin. 2018. "Windrush: 11 People Wrongly Deported from UK Have Died—Javid." *The Guardian*. November 12.

Rawnsley, Andrew. 2010. *The End of the Party: The Rise and Fall of New Labour*. London: Penguin Books.

Syal, Rajeev. 2019. "Home Office 'Rushed to Penalise' Students Accused of Cheating." *The Guardian*. September 18.

Skapinker, Michael. 2019. "Theresa May's Poisonous Immigration Legacy." *Financial Times*. May 7.

Somerville, Will. 2007. *Immigration under New Labour*. Bristol: Policy Press.

Spencer, Sarah. 2007. "Immigration." In Anthony Seldon, ed. *Blair's Britain 1997–2007*. Cambridge: Cambridge University Press.

Sturge, Georgina. 2022. *Asylum Statistics*. London: House of Commons Library.

Summers, Deborah. 2009. "White Working Class Feels Ignored over Immigration, Says Hazel Blears." *The Guardian*, January 2, 2009.

Sumption, Madeleine and Carlos Vargas-Silva. 2020. *Briefing: Net Migration to the UK*. Oxford: The Migration Observatory.

Travis, Alan. 2011a. "High Earners Exempted from Immigration Cap." *The Guardian*. February 15.

Travis, Alan. 2011b. "Immigration Cap Exclusions Turn Policy Into Gesture, Say Critics." *The Guardian*. June 28.

UK Parliament. 2011. "Government Response: Immigration Cap—Home Affairs Committee." Available at: https://publications.parliament.uk/pa/cm201011/cmselect/cmhaff/717/71704.htm (consulted March 24, 2021).

UK Government. 2021. *UK Visas and Immigration. An Introduction for Employers*. January 4. Available at: https://www.gov.uk/government/publications/uk-points-based

-immigration-system-employer-information/the-uks-points-based-immigration
-system-an-introduction-for-employers#:~:text=Under%20the%20points%2Dbased
%20immigration,which%20they%20will%20score%20points.&text=The%20system
%20provides%20flexible%20arrangements,number%20of%20different%20immigration
%20routes (consulted March 23, 2021).

Walsh, Peter William. 2021. *Policy Primer: the UK's 2021 Points-Based Immigration System*. Oxford: The Migration Observatory.

Wright, Chris. 2011. *Policy Legacies and the Politics of Labour Immigration Selection and Control*. Cambridge: Cambridge University PhD dissertation.

YouGov. 2015. "General Election 2015: How Britain Really Voted." Available at: https://yougov .co.uk/topics/politics/articles-reports/2015/06/08/general-election-2015-how-britain -really-voted.

Young, Hugo. 1991. *One of Us: A Biography of Margaret Thatcher*. London: Pan.

Younge, Gary. 2018. "The Veneration of the Windrush Generation." *The Nation*. April 25.

COMMENTARY

Anti-Immigrant Sentiments and the "Brexit Moment"

Desmond King

Professor Randall Hansen is the leading academic authority on British immigration and nationality policy since 1945. Hansen contributes here an original and important essay on this vital area of UK policy.

The British (largely English) response to and engagement with immigration has been problematic for well over seventy years, and in that historical context the contemptuous dismissal of European citizens of non-UK origin after the Brexit referendum is unremarkable. Disdain for the foreigner is deep and wide, and the frequent object of "bracing" critiques by commentators and intellectuals. It coincides with a revitalized defense of whiteness and whites' distinct interests. Remarkably, not only did Brexit orchestrate more hostility toward migrants, but the Conservative government managed concurrently to concoct another pernicious colonial-legacy scandal in its callous treatment of the *Windrush* generation. Both topics are addressed brilliantly in Hansen's chapter.

The English antipathy to foreigners helped shape the Brexit moment. Not imbibed by every Leaver, this antipathy was nonetheless unignorable and pretty widespread during and after the referendum in June 2016: immigration was a key concern for Leavers, according to public opinion polls. The ethnographic evidence for bigotry was distressing but unsurprising. Thrilled to have at last told "those Europeans" to take a hike, the ardent Brexiteer could cheerfully instruct longtime permanent residents (for example, Germans or French or Italians married to British citizens) that they would presumably be packing their bags that afternoon and journeying to

Stansted Airport, as their legal right to remain had been terminated. Uninformed about the precise details of Brexit, other Leavers assumed that they would also be evicting Asian and Caribbean Britons, whether these were first-generation immigrants or citizens whose parents had moved to the United Kingdom. Immigration was one of the strongest indicators that Brexit was not an economic question but a political, ideological, and cultural one (and there was strong support for Brexit in the leafy suburbs, not just in lower-income areas).

This tsunami of built-up resentment—first framed by Powell's "rivers of blood" speech in 1968 and fanned regularly by politicians worried about "swamping" or "marauding" or cosmopolitan undesirables—seemed at last to be delivering redemption to Little England. This sea of people felt redeemed and celebrated at once. Judging by the stream of books by Black or Asian Britons about the challenge of being able to feel they belong, and the demands for integration from white Britons who were part of the dominant white culture, the picture of an often excluding polity is hard to disregard.[1] In one of these books, Afua Hirsch devotes a chapter to "The Question"—that is, "Where are you from?" (Similar tales are recounted in the United States, of course.)

These reactions to Brexit and the massive political mobilization generated by the ambition of getting the United Kingdom to leave the EU are comprehensible only by reference to Britain's colonial-imperial legacies. Whether promoted by absent-minded imperialists, casual purveyors of white superiority, complacent defenders of class hierarchy, or authentic racists, the vision of Britain as a white nation dominates. By 2020 and 2021, this white hegemony faced multiple and far-ranging challenges. Echoing the US protest movement that erupted after the murder of George Floyd in Minneapolis, UK Black Lives Matter activists launched wide protests in support of Floyd's case, broadening them into a deeper engagement with racism in Britain and the roots of that racism in the country's colonial-imperial values: statues and memorials to slave owners and slave traders were torn down or renamed, while a stream of official reports documented lamentable memorializations and racism in national institutions.[2]

Hansen's chapter has many strengths. First, it offers a detailed and lucid analysis of how UK immigration and nationality policies have developed in the twentieth century and especially after World War II, identifying contradictions and tensions within these two policy trajectories and their costs. He unearths a four-stage uneven trajectory of policies regarding migrants ("extremely expansive, equally restrictive, expansive again, and once again highly restrictive") and sets out a persuasive analytic narrative to understand this trajectory.

Second, in an analysis rich in nuance about how policy affects many people's lives in distressing ways, Hansen provides a timely and detailed account of how the *Windrush* scandal unfolded, its consistency with inherited UK policy, and what it reveals about Tory politicians evading blame after embracing martinet-like aims. The Wendy Williams report, issued by the House of Commons in March 2020, confirmed many of the worst aspects of this scandal, and its multiple recommendations included directing that Home Office civil servants be educated in the United Kingdom's colonial-imperial history and its negative effects.

Reflections on the Text

Randall's chapter uses the excellent research he has conducted over two decades to rehearse the essence of UK immigration and nationality policy, highlighting key moments and texts such as the 1948 British Nationality Act and laws enacted from the late 1970s onward. Here are some comments.

First, Hansen cites the number of non-UK EU citizens who moved to the United Kingdom after 2005. And later he notes that by 2015 "non-EU migration was down, but EU migration up because of the strength of the British economy." I think it is necessary to reflect on language and description here: is "EU migration" a helpful term, since until January 2021 the United Kingdom was part of a twenty-eight-member EU in which the right of citizenship and freedom of movement is neither legally nor geographically constrained? Does this language run the danger of reifying the UK Brexit framework rather than probing it as a malicious perversion of legal status? The issue arises again when Randall rightly points out that although the referendum about Europe centered on immigration (with immigration the dominant issue for most Leavers), UK state power over migrants was limited. However, this limitation has to do with the status of EU citizens across the twenty-eight member states, rather than with state policy. Second, the account of the "hostile environment" under Theresa May's reign as home secretary (a reign that was sustained when she made the improbable transition to 10 Downing Street as prime minister) is brilliantly recounted. Both Brexit and this punitive policy regime have ended the movement of non-UK EU citizens to the United Kingdom, and many who have lived in the United Kingdom are departing. There is no understanding among many "Leave" voters of how successful and prosperous German and French cities are and how urban areas such as Warsaw, Prague, and Budapest will boom in the coming decade. The severe effects of this regime on the so-called *Windrush* generation are meticulously laid out. The new regime's targets were racially non-random, with low-income and Black migrants disproportionately affected. Third, I would like to see more about how migrants and immigration have been constructed by British intellectuals/thinkers and the state. As he notes, "the most recent immigration debate was as much about white (and Christian) immigrants from eastern Europe as it was about non-white ones and/or Muslim ones from the Middle East or Africa." Enoch Powell set the dominant motif in his 1968 speech, to which Hansen alludes; it dominated subsequent accounts up to and including the recent statements on behalf of white English people. Randall might want to cite also James Hampshire's important book on how the Home Office and London police decided to construct Black immigrants as problematic in 1950s and 1960s England.[3] These engagements led directly to the modern Powellite celebration of whiteness. Commenting on this recent upsurge, Hampshire writes that this new project aims "to legitimise and argue for the political recognition of 'white ethno-traditionalism.'"[4] Hansen may also want to look at the resurgence among English normative political theorists of cultural liberal nationalism.

Throughout the text there is need for a fuller discussion of Ireland and Irish citizens' position. Reference to the 1948 agreement's inclusion of the free travel area and what that meant is important. The account here also glosses over anti-Irish discrimination and hatred, which was profound in the 1950s—the famous window poster declaimed "No blacks, no dogs, no Irish," as Hansen of course knows from his previous work.[5] The experience of Irish workers—the "navvies"—is perhaps also worth discussing: many were on the so-called lump system, with unscrupulous employers failing to pay National Insurance, which left generations of male Irish workers destitute when old age arrived. This is a part of the migration narrative that is distinct to the UK experience and needs more attention.

Notes

1. Recent examples are Akala, *Natives: Race and Class in the Ruins of Empire* (London: Two Roads, 2018); Jeffrey Boakye, *Black, Listed: Black British Culture Explored* (London: Dialogue Books, 2019); and Afua Hirsch, *Brit(ish): On Race, Identity and Belonging* (London: Vintage, 2018). For an older perspective, see Sam Selvon, *The Lonely Londoners* (Penguin, 1956). And for a non-metropolitan-centered perspective set in colonial Cairo, see Waguih Ghali, *Beer in the Snooker Club* (London: Andre Deutsch, 1964).

2. These included a study of how the United Kingdom treated its colonial soldier war dead in World War I and the neglect of enslavement as a source of wealth in great national houses and institutions.

3. See James Hampshire, "The Legitimation of Racial Resentment," Discover Society, December 4, 2018, https://discoversociety.org/2018/12/04/the-legitimation-of-racial-resentment/.

Also, James Hampshire, *The Politics of Immigration: Contradictions of the Liberal State* (Cambridge: Polity Press, 2013).

4. Hampshire, "The Legitimation of Racial Resentment."

5. For contemporary issues, see Maureen McBride, "Is Anti-Irish Racism Still a Problem? You Can Bank on It," Discover Society, March 6, 2019, https://discoversociety.org/2019/03/06/is-anti-irish-racism-still-a -problem-you-can-bank-on-it/.

7 Germany

Managing Migration in the Twenty-First Century

Philip L. Martin and Dietrich Thränhardt

Immigrants in Germany

Germany has Europe's largest economy and is the major EU magnet for migrants. Foreigners were 12.4 percent of the 83 million German residents in 2019, when 26 percent of all residents had a migrant background (defined as not being a German citizen at birth or being born as a German to at least one non-German parent).

The 10.1 million foreign residents present in Germany at the end of 2019 included 1.5 million Turks, 863,000 Poles, 748,000 Romanians, and 646,000 Italians. The foreign population increased by 313,000 in 2019, led by increases in the stock of Romanians, Syrians, and Bulgarians.

Table 7.1 shows that more foreigners have moved to Germany than left in most years since 1991. Several dates stand out in terms of adding to or subtracting from the population of foreigners in Germany. In 1991–1992, the foreign population rose by over 1.3 million as a result of wars in the former Yugoslavia. Since 2011, Poles and citizens of other new EU member states have been free to work in Germany, and they arrived in high numbers. Romanians and Bulgarians have been able to work freely in Germany since 2014. In 2015 the foreign population increased by 1.1 million with the arrival of Syrian and other asylum seekers. The foreign population rises and falls with entries and exits, and also due to deaths and naturalizations. In 2019, almost 129,000 foreigners became naturalized Germans, including 12 percent who had been Turks and almost 12 percent who had been British.

TABLE 7.1. Entries and Exits of Foreigners, 1991–2020

	Entries	Exits	Net
1991	1,198,978	596,455	602,523
1992	1,502,198	720,127	782,071
1993	1,277,408	815,312	462,096
1994	1,082,553	767,555	314,998
1995	1,096,048	698,113	397,935
1996	959,691	677,494	282,197
1997	840,633	746,969	93,664
1998	802,456	755,358	47,098
1999	874,023	672,048	201,975
2000	841,158	674,038	167,120
2001	879,217	606,494	272,723
2002	842,543	623,255	219,288
2003	768,975	626,330	142,645
2004	780,175	697,632	82,543
2005	707,352	628,399	78,953
2006	661,855	639,064	22,791
2007	680,766	636,854	43,912
2008	682,146	737,889	−55,743
2009	721,014	733,796	−12,782
2010	798,282	670,605	127,677
2011	958,299	678,969	279,330
2012	1,080,936	711,991	368,945
2013	1,226,493	797,886	428,607
2014	1,464,724	914,241	550,483
2015	2,136,954	997,552	1,139,402
2016	1,865,122	1,365,178	499,944
2017	1,550,721	1,134,641	416,080
2018	1,585,112	1,185,432	399,680
2019	1,558,612	1,231,552	327,060
2020	1,120,000	897,000	223,000

SOURCE: Statistisches Bundesamt, "Population: Overview of External and Internal Migration," https://www.destatis.de/EN/Themes/Society-Environment/Population/_Graphic/_Interactive/overview-migration.html.

NOTE: 2020 data cover January through November.

Foreigners arrived in Germany at different times and for different purposes. Italians were some of the earliest arrivals, migrating to Germany in the 1950s to work in agriculture before spreading to factories and construction sites. Most Italian migrant workers returned to Italy after several years in Germany, but some settled and elected not to become German citizens, so over 6 percent of foreigners in Germany are Italians. The performance of the children of Italian migrants in German schools is uneven (Thränhardt and Winterhagen 2013).

The largest group of foreigners in Germany, Turks, began to arrive in the 1960s and early 1970s as guest workers. Some settled and formed or unified families in Germany, and there were several waves of Turks who sought asylum in Germany during the 1980s and 1990s. Family unification and migration for work, study, and asylum continues, and Turks today are a sixth of the foreigners in Germany.

Italians migrated within what is now the European Union, while Turks are third-country nationals, that is, from a country that is not an EU member state. In May 2004, ten eastern European countries joined the EU, followed by Bulgaria and Romania in 2007, and today Poles and Romanians are the largest groups of migrants from other EU member states in Germany, together accounting for more than a sixth of foreigners in Germany. Labor migration from Poland to Germany has a long history, and Poles work in many German industries, from construction and meatpacking to services such as providing care to children and the elderly. Romania is a populous and poor EU member state, sending abroad workers with skills as well as low-skilled workers seeking higher wages.

Since 2014, many of the foreigners arriving in Germany have been asylum seekers from Middle Eastern countries; some 745,500 asylum applications were filed in 2016, with 207,200 in 2017. The Syrian civil war began with the Arab Spring uprising of 2011, displacing millions of people within Syria and encouraging millions more to move into neighboring countries such as Turkey. Some Syrians, Afghans, and others in Turkey went to the country's west coast and boarded small boats and rubber dinghies to travel to nearby Greek islands in 2015. After arriving on the Greek mainland, they traveled northward through the Balkans and Hungary to Austria and Germany to apply for asylum.

Under the EU's Dublin regulations, Syrian and other asylum seekers should have applied for asylum in Greece, the first EU country they reached. However, Greece allowed the migrants to travel north through the Balkan countries to Hungary, which blocked their entry and transit. In response, German chancellor Angela Merkel in August 2015 suspended the Dublin regulations to allow Syrians, Afghans, Iraqis, and others who traveled through other EU countries to reach Germany to apply for asylum.

The number of asylum seekers from Middle Eastern countries reaching Germany and other EU countries was already falling when the EU made an agreement with Turkey in March 2016 to stop the flows and provide aid to improve conditions for Syrians in Turkey.[1] Some 76,000 foreigners made first requests for asylum in Germany in 2020, led by citizens of 3the same countries that dominated arrivals in 2015, Syrians, Afghans, and Iraqis.

Emigration and War

Germany was a major country of emigration in the nineteenth century. Some 7.3 million Germans left for the United States between 1820 and 1920, making Germany a leading source of immigrants to the United States (Bade 1984). As a result of World War II, pre-war Germany lost a quarter of its territory and post-war West Germany absorbed 12 million ethnic German refugees from the east Meanwhile, prisoners of war and 7.5 million foreign workers brought to Germany during the war were repatriated to their home countries.

The Federal Republic of Germany, founded in 1949, had a war-wrecked economy and massive unemployment. Currency reform, Marshall Plan aid, and the development of the "social market economy" put West Germany on a path to sustained economic growth and helped the new country absorb the millions of ethnic and East Germans who arrived (Abelshauser 2005).[2]

Complaints about labor shortages surfaced in the 1950s, prompting the German government to sign a labor recruitment agreement with Italy in 1955 that permitted German farmers to hire Italian workers to harvest their crops. Italy wanted jobs for its unemployed workers but insisted that they be recruited and employed under the terms of a bilateral labor agreement. As the German economy began to boom in the 1950s, the need for additional foreign workers shifted from farms to German factories producing cars, machine tools, and consumer durables for growing export and domestic markets.[3]

Guest Worker Recruitment: 1960–1973

In 1960, the number of job vacancies exceeded the number of registered unemployed workers, and German employers requested permission to recruit additional foreign workers. The German government made labor recruitment agreements with Greece and Spain in 1960, with Turkey in 1961, with Morocco in 1963, with Portugal in 1964, with Tunisia in 1965, and with Yugoslavia in 1968 (Molnar 2019)3. German employers also recruited a few miners and nurses in South Korea.

Many European countries followed similar labor recruitment strategies, recruiting foreign workers in southern Europe and North Africa. European countries signed over sixty recruitment agreements during the so-called guest worker era between 1945 and 1973 (Rass 2012, 53).

Germany recruited foreign workers who were expected to be guests, saving some of their higher German wages before returning to their countries of origin. The so-called rotation principle envisioned experienced guest workers working in Germany a year or two, departing, and being replaced by newcomers eager to earn high German wages. Some guest workers were expected to settle, but employers cooperated with government ministries to minimize opposition to temporary workers becoming settled residents in the name of promoting economic growth (Oswald, Schönwälder, and Sonnenberger 2003, 24, 22).

Guest worker recruitment expanded faster and lasted longer than anticipated. There were four major reasons for guest worker settlement. First, the German labor force was shrinking in the early 1960s due to a delayed baby boom that limited female labor force participation, more educational opportunities that kept youth in school longer, and shorter working hours and improved pensions that prompted earlier retirements. Second, political leaders who had experienced postwar destruction and unemployment were reluctant to risk what was perceived to be a fragile economic recovery on alternatives to foreign workers such as mechanization or foreign investment (Kindleberger 1967). Unions did not oppose recruiting foreign workers because there was full employment and foreign workers received the same wages and work benefits as German workers.

Third, a keystone of the European Economic Community (EEC; now the European Union), founded in 1957, was freedom of movement, meaning that workers from any EEC country could move to another and seek jobs on an equal basis with local workers. Italy was the poorest of the first six EEC member states and had the most jobless workers, so Italians had to wait a decade for freedom of movement. By allowing German employers to recruit Italian guest workers before 1967, the German government was regulating the free movement that would soon occur without any regulation.[4] The fourth reason to prefer guest workers over labor-saving alternatives involved currency misalignments. European currencies were undervalued in the 1960s, which made Germany and other European nations magnets for foreign investment that created jobs.[5] American multinationals invested so much in Europe in the 1960s that French writer Jean-Jacques Servan-Schreiber warned in 1968 of the "American challenge" to Europe's independence and identity.

In 1960, there were 329,000 foreign workers in Germany. After the Berlin Wall was constructed in 1961, slowing migration from East to West Germany, the number of guest workers rose rapidly, topping 1 million in 1964. Guest worker employment fell during the 1966–1967 recession, seemingly verifying the rotation principle that unemployed guest workers would return to their countries of origin if they lost their jobs. The economic boom between 1968 and 1973 allowed the employment of foreign workers in Germany to increase to 2.6 million, making foreign workers an eighth of all wage and salary workers. In the early 1970s, many guest workers had been in Germany over five years, making them permanent residents with the right to stay even if they lost their jobs.

German employers could hire guest workers only after failing to recruit German workers. However, the extraordinary low German unemployment rate prompted the German Employment Service to establish offices in Turkey and other countries so that potential guest workers could register, making it easy for German employers to recruit them. Over time, guest workers in Germany recommended family members and friends to their German employers so that they could be recruited by name. Employers often arranged housing for newly arrived guest workers, but most workers moved out of barracks and into regular housing after several years.

During the 1960s, almost all foreigners in Germany were employed. However, the gap between the foreign population and the foreign workforce began to widen as guest workers formed or united families in Germany. Surveys reported that most guest workers planned to return when they retired, a finding that came to be known as the myth of return, as migrants who had children and grandchildren eventually retired in Germany.

From Workers to Minorities: 1973–1980

Guest worker programs aim to add workers temporarily to the labor force but not settlers to the population. Most foreign workers employed in Germany returned to their countries of origin as expected, but the number of workers arriving in Germany was so large that a significant immigrant community developed. According to one estimate, over 70 percent of the 30 million foreigners who lived in Germany sometime during the forty years between 1960 and 2000 returned as expected, but the nearly 30 percent who stayed generated a foreign population of 9 million.

Guest workers earned the higher wages they sought, but they also learned that German living costs were higher than at home, so some stayed abroad longer to achieve their savings goals. Migrants could reunify their families in Germany after a year of satisfactory work, so settlement was a logical next step that some employers encouraged in order to retain experienced migrants and to employ migrant spouses. Rotation and return made sense to policymakers who wanted to avoid turning

Germany into a country of immigration, but rotation was not always in the interests of migrants and employers (Miller and Martin 1982; Castles 1989).

The settlement of foreign workers and their families in a non-immigrant Germany led to confusion about integration. For example, how should the children of settled foreign workers be educated? Some German states taught them in German to help them integrate into Germany, while others taught Turkish and Italian children in their own language so that they could integrate into their country of citizenship after their expected return. German politicians reinforced the notion that the guest workers and their children would eventually leave by declaring, as Chancellor Helmut Kohl did, that "Germany is not a country of immigration" (Sontheimer 2017).

The German government in 1973 halted the recruitment of more guest workers in the wake of the October 1973 Arab-Israeli War (which led to a sharp increase in the price of oil and an economic shock), but it also promised that it would not force foreigners who had earned the right to settle in Germany to leave, even if they lost their jobs. Employers did not want to lose experienced workers, and young guest worker families with children in German schools did not want to return to countries of origin that were also experiencing high unemployment.

The settlement of guest workers represented a gap between the policy goal of rotating foreign workers in and out of the country and the reality that Germany had become a country of immigration. In November 1973, there were 2.6 million employed foreign workers among 4 million foreign residents, so two-thirds of foreigners in Germany were employed (Figure 7.1). The number of employed foreigners fell to 2 million by 1980, while the foreign population rose to 4.5 million, reducing the share of foreigners in Germany who were employed to less than half (Bade 1984).

The German government appointed its first commissioner for foreigners in 1979. Heinz Kühn called for new policies to accelerate the integration of settled migrants, and urged birthright citizenship, so that babies born in Germany would be German citizens. However, the recession that followed the Iranian Revolution in 1979 shifted the government's focus from integration to reducing the number of foreigners. Chancellor Helmut Schmidt, a member of the Social Democratic Party (SPD) who was reelected in October 1980, acknowledged the economic contributions made by guest workers during the 1960s and said that Germany had to integrate those who settled, but went on to say that "four million is enough" (Vinocur 1982) at a time when West Germany had 56 million residents.[6]

Helmut Kohl, of the Christian Democratic Union (CDU), who replaced Schmidt as chancellor in 1982, offered departure bonuses of $5,000 to migrants who gave up their work and residence permits, copying a similar French departure bonus

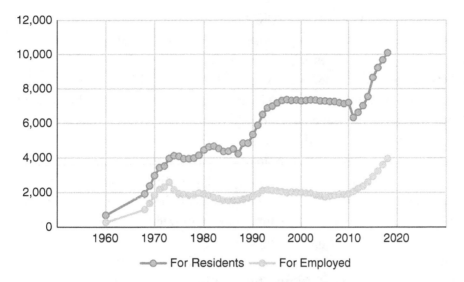

FIGURE 7.1 Foreign Residents and Employed Foreigners in
Germany, 1960–2018

program. Departure bonuses had only a short-lived effect on the foreign population, which fell from 4.7 million in 1982 to 4.4 million in 1984–1985, then rose to 4.5 million in 1986 and to 5.8 million in 1991.[7] Departure bonuses encouraged those who were going to return to leave with the payments, but not the majority of foreigners, who elected to stay.

Even as the foreign population rose, the Kohl government insisted that "Germany is not, nor shall it become, a country of immigration" (Sontheimer 2017). Integration policies in the 1980s and 1990s remained contradictory. The first policy goal was to integrate legally resident foreigners and their families who elected to stay. However, the second goal was to encourage voluntary returns and reintegration at home, while the third was to reduce the arrival of more non-EU job seekers such as Turks.

Turks were never more than a third of the foreigners in Germany, but because they arrived in large numbers in the early 1970s and were Muslims, Turks were often considered "problem foreigners." Many of the Turks in Germany had had little education, and some brought Turkish cultural norms such as the different treatment of men and women to Germany. The Turkish government made demands on its citizens abroad, requiring Turkish boys born abroad to perform eighteen months of military service in Turkey or pay a fee equivalent to an average two years' income in Turkey to reduce their military obligation to two months.[8]

Turkey played a special role in the German migration story because of Turkey's desire to join the EU, which would mean that Turks could move freely to Germany and other EU countries and seek jobs. The Ankara Association Agreement of 1963 and the Additional Protocol of 1973 promised Turkey a reciprocal lowering of tariff and migration barriers and anticipated Turks having "free access" to European labor markets by December 1986.[9] Turkey applied to join the EU in 1987, when the Turkish economy was expanding rapidly. Negotiations for full membership started in 2005. They were slow and stalled in 2016, due to the authoritarian turn in Turkey after a failed coup and tensions with Greece.

Higher oil prices and the switch from manufacturing to services prompted a restructuring of the German economy in the 1970s and 1980s that displaced many guest workers from their jobs. During the 1960s, foreigners had a lower unemployment rate than Germans, but during the 1980s the unemployment rate of foreigners was twice the rate of Germans, and has remained higher since.

The economic boom in the late 1980s associated with the lowering of economic barriers between EU member states and the creation of an EU single market increased the demand for labor in Germany and attracted foreign workers from Poland and other eastern European countries. Germany allowed eastern Europeans to arrive as tourists or asylum seekers and then work illegally in agriculture, restaurants, and other industries employing seasonal workers in the hopes of speeding the end of the Cold War that divided East and West Germany.

East Germans, Ethnic Germans, Asylum

After World War II, Germany was divided into four zones and occupied by troops from France, the United Kingdom, the United States, and the Soviet Union. Some 730,000 Germans moved from the Soviet zone of Germany to the other three zones during the late 1940s, and 3.8 million moved from East to West Germany between 1949 and the building of the Berlin Wall in August 1961, which blocked migration from east to west. Another 600,000 East Germans moved west between 1961 and 1988, including many pensioners who were permitted to leave East Germany.

The fall of the Berlin Wall in November 1989 opened a new chapter in internal German migration. Migration hastened the demise of the Communist regime in East Germany, setting off a wave of migration from east to west. Chancellor Helmut Kohl, fearful of unification in West Germany, undertook a costly economic stabilization program that sought to rapidly improve economic conditions in the former East Germany. Nonetheless, almost 800,000 former East Germans moved to West Germany in 1989–1990, including many young people seeking jobs, and net migration from east to west continued until 2018.

Ethnic Germans and Jews

Germany's Expelled and Refugee Law of 1953 gave ethnic Germans in eastern Europe and the Soviet Union the right to move to Germany and be received as German citizens because they suffered persecution after World War II due to their German heritage. Some 4.5 million ethnic Germans moved to Germany between 1950 and 2000 in two major waves. The first wave, between 1950 and 1990, brought 1.4 million ethnic Germans (mostly from Poland, 62 percent, or Romania, 15 percent). Many knew some German and had maintained at least some of their German culture.

The second wave of ethnic German migration, between 1989 and 2005, brought 2.6 million migrants from the former Soviet republics who knew less German and in many cases had not maintained much German culture. These newcomers put a strain on the local governments charged with assisting their integration, especially because some of the younger ethnic Germans considered themselves to be Russian rather than German, making them reluctant to participate in German-language classes aimed at helping them find jobs. About three-fourths of the "ethnic Germans" who arrived from the former Soviet Union were the (non-German) family members of ethnic Germans, prompting the German government to introduce a language test in 1996 and take other steps to slow entries, so only 6,000 arrived in 2015.[10] Persons born after 1993 are no longer eligible for automatic German citizenship on arrival in Germany, and most ethnic Germans today are well integrated. By 2020, this immigration was being considered a success; post-Soviet migrants were no longer discussed in public, having become "invisible" in the population.

There was a related influx of Jews from the former Soviet Union. Only 15,000 of the 525,000 Jewish German citizens in 1933 remained in 1945. The number of Jews rose gradually to 29,000 by 1990, when Germany opened the door to Jews in the former Soviet Union, attracting 218,000 between 1990 and 2017 (BMI 2020, 117). Local governments provide Jewish immigrants with housing and integration services similar to those provided to immigrating ethnic Germans. As with ethnic Germans, regulatory changes made entry more difficult after 2005. For example, Jews from the former Soviet area who want to move to Germany must now be recognized as Jewish by the Central Welfare Office of Jews in Germany, and only 789 were accepted in 2019 (BMI 2020, 117).[11]

Asylum Seekers

The challenge of integrating the high numbers of East Germans, ethnic Germans, and Russian Jews was complicated by a fourth inflow in the early 1990s: asylum seekers from the former Yugoslavia and other countries. Under the Nazi government of 1933–1945, some Germans and others perished because other countries refused to provide them with asylum (the right to settle in another country because of governmental persecution at home). This history explains why Article 16 of Germany's 1949 Basic Law includes an open-ended commitment to provide asylum: "Persons persecuted for political reasons shall enjoy the right of asylum."

The 1951 Geneva Convention signed by Germany and many other countries defines a refugee as a person who, "owing to a well-founded fear of being persecuted for reasons of race, religion, nationality, membership in a particular social group, or political opinion, is outside the country of his nationality, and is unable to, or owing to such fear, is unwilling to avail himself of the protection of that country."[12] An asylum seeker is a person who arrives and asks to be recognized as a refugee by submitting evidence of persecution at home. Germany and most European countries register asylum seekers and provide them with housing and food for the several months or years that are typically required to make a first decision about status. If a foreigner's application is rejected, there can be an appeal.

Germany received relatively few asylum applications until 1980, when a military coup in Turkey prompted some Turks to travel to Germany and apply for asylum.[13] First decisions and appeals took several years, which enabled applicants to work and achieve the higher earnings they could no longer obtain by arriving as guest workers. Turks were over half of Germany's 110,000 asylum applicants in 1980, but the government found a quick fix by requiring Turks to obtain visas to travel to Germany and prohibiting asylum applicants from working during their first five years in Germany. The number of asylum applications dropped to less than 20,000 in 1983.[14]

This quick fix left Germany unprepared for the flood of asylum applications in the early 1990s that followed the breakup of Yugoslavia. Asylum applications rose from 103,000 in 1988 to 438,000 in 1992—over 1,000 a day—and local governments complained that they could not afford to provide asylum applicants with housing and food while their applications and appeals were considered.[15] The presence of young men who received tax-supported benefits rather than working prompted attacks on foreigners, including 600 arson attacks on asylum housing in 1992. Attackers did not distinguish between asylum seekers and other foreigners, prompting Japanese and other foreign investors to warn the German government that they would reconsider investing in Germany.

The major political parties struggled to find an agreement on how to deal with the upsurge in asylum seekers and the backlash of attacks on foreigners. Chancellor Kohl's Christian Democratic Union–Christian Social Union (CDU-CSU) government wanted to amend the Basic Law to eliminate Article 16's open-ended right to asylum, while the opposition SPD and Greens wanted to preserve Article 16's right to asylum and develop an immigration system that allowed Germany to select immigrants. A compromise preserved Article 16 but required foreigners in search of asylum to apply in the first "safe country" they reach after escaping persecution, such as Hungary if fleeing Serbia.[16] Germany also urged the EU to standardize the processing of asylum seekers to discourage them from seeking out countries such as Germany that offered better housing and benefits (Zaun 2018). The Yugoslav asylum crisis was defused by changes in Germany and the EU and the 1995 Dayton Peace Agreement.

New Guest Workers and Green Cards

Poles and other eastern Europeans began to work in Germany during their summer vacations in the late 1980s, often filling seasonal farm jobs. Wages in Germany were significantly higher than at home, so Poles could earn the equivalent of a year's wages at home by picking apples or wine grapes for several months in Germany. The German government was reluctant to "re-create the Berlin Wall" on its eastern borders, but it was also unwilling to tolerate the widespread employment of unauthorized foreigners. The resulting compromise was new guest worker programs that allowed up to 350,000 eastern Europeans a year to work temporarily in Germany. These programs ended when Poland and other countries joined the EU in 2004 (Hönekopp 1997).[17]

These new guest worker programs reflected the lessons learned from the 1960s. First, many of the eastern Europeans were not considered German workers, so they did not necessarily earn German wages and the right to settle in Germany. Under the project-tied worker program, German construction firms could subcontract with a Polish firm that provided both materials and workers, so Polish employees who were assigned or posted to a German worksite were covered by Polish rather than German wage and benefit laws. By contrast, many Turkish workers in the 1960s were employees of the German firms Opel and Volkswagen who received the same wages and benefits as German workers.

Second, the 1990s guest worker programs limited seasonal workers to less than ninety days in Germany to avoid the development of ties between employers and workers that could lead to settlement. Border-commuter status allowed Czechs and Poles living within fifty kilometers of Germany's eastern borders to work and stay overnight in Germany up to two days a week, another effort to avoid settlement.

These new guest worker programs added flexibility to the German labor market and reduced the employment of unauthorized migrants in agriculture and seasonal services (Werner 1985). Most of the new guest workers complemented German workers; the negative effects of their presence, if any, fell mostly on settled foreign workers. Whereas the recruitment of the 1960s and 1970s had been tightly regulated by the government, the 1990s programs allowed some subcontractors to abuse workers, especially in construction and meat processing, leading to more government regulation (Hunger 2000).[18]

After Poland and other eastern European countries joined the EU in 2004, their citizens could move freely to Germany and other EU countries. After a seven-year wait that ended in 2011, Poles and others had the right to work in other EU member states. Bulgaria and Romania joined the EU in 2007 and, after their citizens got freedom-of-movement rights in 2014, many Bulgarians and Romanians moved to Germany in search of higher-wage jobs. Germany continues to attract migrants from EU countries with lower wages and fewer opportunities.

Naturalization

In 2000, Germany's naturalization policy was transformed from one of the most restrictive to one of the most liberal. The 1913 Reichs- und Staatsangehörigkeitsgesetz (RuStAG), which gave local officials a great deal of discretion to reject applicants seeking to become naturalized Germans, was reformed to allow persons born in Germany to at least one foreign parent who was legally resident in Germany for at least eight years to be considered German citizens at birth, and allowed children to also retain their parents' citizenship. Since 2014, these dual-citizen children may keep both their German and their parents' citizenship indefinitely if they stay in Germany as adults.[19]

Some 2.2 million foreigners became naturalized German citizens between 2002 and 2017. After peaking at 187,000 in 2000, naturalizations have declined to about 100,000 a year (Thränhardt 2018). In 2019, there were 128,900 naturalizations, among them 16,200 Turks and 14,600 Britons. Citizens of EU nations have low naturalization rates because their EU citizenship provides them with rights equal to Germans', while foreigners from outside the EU often naturalize in order to have a secure status in Germany. This explains the upsurge in naturalization applications from British citizens.

Computers and Green Cards

During the late 1990s, employment in computer-related industries expanded rapidly amid fears of a Y2K problem that would shut down computers that recorded only two-digit years. Employers in many countries complained of too few IT workers, including the German computer association BITKOM, which asserted that there were 75,000 unfilled computer-related jobs in 2000.

The government response was a "green card" program that offered five-year work and residence permits to non-EU workers who were offered jobs in Germany that paid at least $45,000 a year. A quarter of the 14,000 green cards issued in 2000 went to Indians, prompting a failed political movement with the slogan "Kinder statt Inder" (children instead of Indians—that is, to substitute German-born babies for foreign workers).

Compared to the United States, which was issuing hundreds of thousands of H-1B visas to Indian IT workers early in the twenty-first century, Germany issued relatively few green cards. The United States proved more attractive to IT migrants because English was the language of the workplace and the larger society (many German multinationals adopted English as their workplace language in the twenty-first century). IT jobs in the United States generally offered higher wages, lower taxes, and stock options, and employers were allowed to sponsor their H-1B workers for immigrant visas. Germany's more restrictive green card program required more of employers and did not lay out an easy transition to immigrant status.

Migration Act of 2005

The green card program helped to unravel the myth that Germany was not a country of immigration. SPD interior minister Otto Schily nonetheless opposed an immigration law in 1999, saying: "There is no need for an immigration law because, if we had one, the quotas would be zero" (Aust, Knaup, and Mascolo 2001). A 2000 poll found that 66 percent of Germans thought immigration was "too high and has exceeded the limits of what is bearable," while 75 percent believed that Germany's asylum policies should limit the maximum stay of a refugee in Germany to nine months (Fetzer 2011).

The SPD-Green government nonetheless appointed the Süssmuth Commission to propose a future-oriented immigration policy, and the commission's report of July 4, 2001, declared that "Germany is and should be a country of immigration" (Economist 2001) The commission noted that family unification brought 75,000 newcomers a year to Germany, and recommended the admission of an additional 50,000 professionals a year selected under a Canadian-style points system that would give preference to foreigners who are young, have high levels of schooling, and know German.

The SPD-Green government embraced many of these recommendations in the Migration Act of 2005, which aimed to attract more skilled foreigners and to promote the integration of low-skilled foreigners and their children.[20] Skilled foreigners—defined as those who were offered a German job that paid at least €66,000 ($93,600) a year, investors who invest at least €250,000 and create at least five jobs in Germany, or foreign students who graduate from German universities and get a job offer from a German employer—were given the easiest path to enter or stay in Germany.

The Migration Act also dealt with immigrant integration. Foreigners were less than 10 percent of German residents in 2000 but 20 percent of those receiving government cash assistance for poor people. The Migration Act required non-EU foreigners who had been in Germany less than six years and received government assistance to enroll in 600 hours of German language and culture classes or face potential problems renewing their residence permits.[21] After 2007, foreigners seeking to join family members in Germany must pass a German-language test before arrival, and the maximum age at which children abroad can automatically join parents in Germany was reduced to twelve, with children between twelve and sixteen required to demonstrate some knowledge of German before being allowed to join their parents in Germany.

Germany lies at the center of Europe and has millions of foreigners entering and exiting each year. EU freedom of movement and the Schengen Agreement mean that there are no border controls with neighboring countries, so efforts to deter the entry and employment of unauthorized foreigners center on checks inside Germany, as when residence and work permits must be presented to employers and to receive government services. Separate systems register authorized residents and workers, and these lists are compared to detect anomalies. Local aliens authorities report resident foreigners to the state government and the federal Ministry of the Interior, while the local work permit registries and labor inspectors are the responsibility of the state government and the federal Ministry of Labor.[22]

Germany's labor market was made more flexible by the so-called Hartz reforms in 2003.[23] The duration of unemployment benefits was reduced for all workers to encourage them to seek jobs. New "mini-jobs" exempted workers earning up to €400 a month from payroll taxes, and €1 public service jobs were created for those unable to find employers to hire them.[24] The government stepped up the fight against illegal work with more inspectors, aiming to detect unauthorized foreigners and Germans and resident foreigners who worked for cash wages while collecting government benefits.

Labor markets were also affected by the rising number of foreign workers who were posted to Germany from other EU member countries. In response to the exploitation of posted workers in construction, meatpacking, and other sectors, Germany introduced its first national minimum wage of €8.50 an hour in 2015, so that Polish and other workers posted to Germany by their Polish employers would receive at least €8.50 an hour (€9.50 in 2021).[25] There are still cost savings involved in hiring posted workers due to lower payroll taxes and the willingness of posted workers to work long hours.

Turks and Integration

When Angela Merkel became chancellor in 2005, foreigners were 8 percent of German residents and opinion polls found that a majority of Germans agreed that "there are too many foreigners living in Germany." Merkel's coalition government took steps to accelerate the integration of foreigners, especially Turks, who some feared would become a "parallel society."

The integration of Turks and other foreigners today can be seen as a glass half full or a glass half empty. A quarter of German residents are immigrants or have at least one parent who is an immigrant, meaning that one in four people in Germany has a migrant background.

Integration commissioner Maria Böhmer in 2010 noted that eleven of the twenty-three players on the German national soccer team had migrant backgrounds, reflecting successful integration in sports. On the other hand, the unemployment rate among foreigners in summer 2010 was almost twice that of Germans, 12.4 percent compared to 6.5 percent. About 82 percent of Germans between the ages of twenty-five and sixty-five were in the labor force in 2008, compared to 75 percent of the foreign-born, largely because foreign-born women were less likely to work or look for jobs.

Economist Thilo Sarrazin in 2010 wrote a polemical bestselling book, *Deutschland schafft sich ab* (Germany does away with itself), that concluded that Muslim immigrants were dependent "on the social welfare state" and "connected to criminality." Researchers and migrant advocates disagreed with Sarrazin's conclusions, emphasizing that the integration of foreigners had been delayed during the decades when Germany denied that it was an immigration country, but was proceeding successfully in the twenty-first century.

Immigration means change, and integration raises the question of change to what. Should foreigners "become German," or should they retain their own language and culture? Should governments subsidize centers and groups that help migrants to retain their language and culture, so that Germany becomes a multicultural country? Should governments provide services in the migrants' own language or expect migrants to learn German?

Merkel, a critic of multiculturalism, encouraged migrants and persons with migration backgrounds to improve their German-language skills to get better jobs and to participate in German society. Some leaders of migrant countries of origin disagreed. Turkish prime minister Recep Tayyip Erdogan in 2011 urged Turks living in Germany to teach their children Turkish first and German second, asserting that "our children must learn German, but first they must learn Turkish." Integration minister Böhmer countered that "the German language takes precedence. Only those with good German have opportunities to advance in our country" (Gezer and Reimann 2011).

The prospect of more Turkish migrants in Germany has shadowed Turkey's half-century quest to join the EU. EU leaders put Turkey on a list of countries eligible for future EU entry in 1999, and Turkish-EU accession negotiations began in 2005. However, progress has stalled due to changes in Turkey, including an increasingly authoritarian Erdogan government that repressed protests in 2014, curbed civil liberties after a failed July 2016 coup attempt, fired many public employees, and jailed journalists. There was a net migration of Turks from Germany to Turkey between 2008 and 2014 as optimism about economic growth and EU membership rose, but the flows reversed beginning in 2015, as educated and professional Turks joined others in seeking a safe haven in Germany.

Labor Reforms and Asylum Again

Germany's economy benefited from labor market reforms during the recovery from the 2008–2009 recession, as employment rose to record levels while unemployment fell. However, a strong push to develop a "welcoming culture" to attract skilled foreigners was interrupted by an upsurge of asylum seekers in 2015–2016.

The Hartz labor market reforms helped to turn Germany into the economic powerhouse of Europe, with a low unemployment rate and many unfilled jobs. German employers want more skilled foreign workers, and Germany issues most of the visas granted under the EU blue card program, offering four-year work and residence permits to foreigners with university degrees and their families if they receive job offers from German employers.

Many southern Europeans (from Portugal, Italy, Greece, and Spain) moved to Germany in the aftermath of the 2008–2009 recession. The introduction of the euro in 2002 lowered interest rates, increased borrowing, and ended with severe recessions and high unemployment rates in southern European nations. Germany's strong economy attracted skilled workers from poorer EU member states, and Germans were urged to develop a "welcoming culture" to attract more foreigners.

The number of asylum applications rose above 100,000 in 2012 and continued to increase despite a government effort to reduce welfare benefits that were thought to attract asylum seekers.[26] The rising number of asylum applications prompted a group called Patriotic Europeans Against the Islamization of the West (known by the German acronym Pegida) to hold Monday night protests against immigration in Dresden beginning in October 2014, in memory of the Monday night protests that had toppled the East German regime.

The year 2015 changed Germany forever. During the summer of 2015, a million Syrians, Afghans, and Iraqis used inflatable rafts to travel ten to twenty miles from Turkey's western coast to nearby Greek islands such as Lesbos. Under the EU's Dublin Convention, the Greek government should have screened the new arrivals and determined the fate of those who applied for asylum. However, the bankrupt Greek government allowed migrants to pass through and travel north toward Germany and other countries.

Many migrants made their way north through Albania, Montenegro, and Serbia into Hungary, the next EU member state. The Hungarian government responded with fences on its border with Serbia and refused to allow asylum seekers in Budapest to board trains for Austria and Germany, saying that it would handle asylum for the migrants from Greece. Chancellor Merkel, fearful of a new wave of fences in eastern Europe, declared, "Wir schaffen das," meaning that Germany would accept and integrate Syrian refugees who were allowed to travel from Hungary to Germany.[27] Merkel urged Germans to welcome the newcomers (Thränhardt 2019).

Merkel's welcome prompted a million migrants to move to Germany, Sweden, and other EU countries in 2015, including 12,000 migrants who arrived in Munich on September 12, 2015. Most Germans welcomed the newcomers, volunteering at shelters that housed them and sometimes opening their homes to them. However, there were also arson attacks on housing meant for asylum seekers; most Germans did not want solo male Muslim migrants housed in group quarters near their homes (Liebe et al. 2018).

EU leaders took steps to stop the influx of migrants, resulting in the EU-Turkey agreement that had the Turkish government discourage illegal exits to Greek islands and accept the return of migrants who reached Greek islands without proper documents in return for €6 billion to improve conditions for migrants in Turkey. Inside Germany, the government speeded up the asylum application and appeals process and created various levels of protection, from full refugee status to temporary protected status. About half of the 2015–2016 asylum seekers were recognized as refugees, and most of the others received temporary protections that allowed them to live and work in Germany; 11 percent of the asylum applications were rejected (Brücker, Kosyakova, and Schuss 2020).

Many of the 2015–2016 asylum seekers were young men who had not completed secondary school and did not speak German. Three-fourths of the asylum seekers in 2018 were from eight countries: Afghanistan, Eritrea, Iraq, Iran, Nigeria, Pakistan,

Somalia, and Syria. There were significant differences by country of origin. For example, the Syrians were typically better educated than the Afghans and Iraqis (Brücker, Kosyakova, and Schuss 2020).

Of those who arrived after 2014, 8 percent were employed at the end of 2015, and 28 percent were employed in mid-2018. Brücker, Kosyakova, and Schuss (2020) report that half of the foreigners arriving as asylum seekers between 1990 and 2013 were employed fifty months after arrival, but half of the 2015–2016 asylum seekers were employed within forty-six months of their arrival, perhaps reflecting the favorable German labor market and the availability of German language and culture courses for 2015–2016 arrivals. Two-thirds of those who were employed had full- or part-time jobs; many of the others were in paid training or internships.

Refugees in Germany were asked about the skills required to do their jobs at home and after they found employment in Germany. At home, refugees and Germans had a similar distribution of skill requirements, with 16 percent of refugees and 13 percent of Germans in jobs that did not require skills and 65 and 60 percent, respectively, in jobs that required skills. Once in Germany, refugees got lower-skilled jobs—44 percent had jobs without skill requirements and 52 percent had jobs that required skills. Most refugees reported that they had more skills than required for their German jobs, but 10 percent moved up in the labor market, meaning that their German jobs required more skills than their jobs at home. In 2018, all refugees who were employed had average pretax earnings of less than €1,300 a month, and those employed full-time earned less than €2,000 a month. Germans with full-time jobs had average pretax earnings of €3,390 a month (see Table 7.2 and Brücker, Kosyakova, and Schuss 2020).

Most analysts believe that the recent wave of asylum seekers is being integrated successfully, reflecting the greater investments made by the government in language and culture courses to prepare newcomers for jobs in Germany. Low unemployment rates encouraged many employers to hire migrants, making it easier for them to gain a foothold in the German labor market.

A twenty-five-member expert commission released a report in January 2021 that highlighted both the importance of employment for migrant integration and the struggles of low-skilled immigrants, who are less likely to be employed and who typically earn less than native-born workers.[28] The reasons low-skilled migrants have difficulty finding jobs range from lack of German-language skills and low levels of education and training to discrimination against non-Germans. The expert commission emphasized that migration can generate win-win outcomes if migrants are integrated successfully into employment.

TABLE 7.2. Skills Required for Jobs Held by Refugees Before and After Their Arrival in Germany, 2018 (%)

| Skill Level | All | Before Arrival | | All | After Arrival | | Germans | | |
		Men	Women		Men	Women	Total	Men	Women
Unskilled tasks	16	17	9	44	44	45	13	12	14
Skilled tasks	65	66	60	52	53	45	60	57	63
Specialist tasks	6	6	6	2	2	2	14	16	11
Expert tasks	14	11	26	3	2	8	14	16	11
Number	2,423	1,914	509	1,113	953	160	#######	15,366,308	13,947,334

SOURCE: Brücker, Kosyakova, and Schuss 2020.

The commission urged the government to replace the term "persons with migrant backgrounds" with "immigrants and their descendants." There are 21 million residents of Germany with a migrant background, and most of them were born in Germany.

After Merkel and COVID-19

Merkel's decision to accept asylum seekers was widely praised and led to her being named *Time* magazine's Person of the Year in 2015.[29] Not all Germans welcomed the latest wave of migrants, however. Dissatisfaction with migration policies helped the anti-migrant Alternative for Germany (AfD) to win 13 percent of the vote in September 2017 elections and emerge as the second-largest party in many states of the former East Germany, the part of Germany with the fewest migrants. Merkel's CDU-CSU-SPD coalition government that took office in 2017 promised to cap the number of asylum seekers at 200,000 a year and to develop policies to "permanently reduce the number of people fleeing to Germany and Europe in order to prevent a repeat of the situation such as in 2015," while CSU interior minister Horst Seehofer asserted that migration was the "mother of all problems" and the major reason voters turned to parties such as the AfD (Dostal 2017).

In the five years between 2015 and 2020, there was not another mass movement from Turkey to Greece and on to Germany, and many of the 2015 arrivals are integrating successfully. The locus of asylum-seeking migration to Europe has shifted to the central Mediterranean route from Libya to Italy, prompting reactions that include providing boats to the Libyan Coast Guard to prevent migrants from leaving. The EU continues to struggle with managing migration across its external borders and with sharing the burden of processing and caring for asylum seekers between EU member states.

The German government in June 2019 enacted a new law to attract skilled non-EU workers. The Fachkräftezuwanderungsgesetz ended labor market certification, the requirement that employers prove there are no EU workers available before receiving visas for non-EU workers. Skilled non-EU workers may enter Germany for up to six months to search for a job, and foreigners with a temporary protected status who cannot be deported may stay in Germany up to thirty months if they have jobs or are in training. In June 2018, 174,000 of the 230,000 rejected asylum seekers were being allowed to stay in Germany de facto, despite their irregular status de jure.

The COVID-19 pandemic closed many of the world's borders to non-essential travelers, including immigrants and migrant workers. Governments made limited exceptions for some essential workers, including those employed in health care and agriculture. However, migrant flows to most countries fell by half or more in 2020 compared to 2019, and the unemployment rate of migrants in rich countries such as Germany rose more than for native-born workers, in part because of the concentration of migrants in sectors such as hotels and restaurants that were forced to close. The generally rapid integration of asylum seekers who arrived after 2013 may be slowed by the pandemic and the subsequent recession.

Conclusions

For most of the post–World War II period, Germany was the major European country that admitted foreigners, but it did not have a formal immigration policy to explain why the arrival of foreigners was in the national interest or lay out a clear path for foreigners to integrate into the labor market and society. The CDU-CSU, which dominated governments between 1982 and 1998, argued that Germany was not and should not become an immigration country despite the arrival and settlement of an increasing number of foreigners.

One reason that Germany was able to avoid declaring itself a country of immigration is that during the 1970s and 1980s, governments pursued flawed policies that nonetheless worked the first time they were tried. For example, the guest worker programs of the 1960s were based on the rotation principle: that guest workers would rotate in and out of Germany rather than settling. When this premise was tested during the recession of 1966–1967, it worked because many of the foreign workers who lost jobs were newcomers without the right to remain unemployed in Germany.[30] However, rotation failed in the 1970s because many guest workers had been in Germany for more than five years and had permanent residence rights, so they could remain and form or reunify families even if they had lost their jobs.

Similarly, when Germany experienced an upsurge of Turkish asylum seekers in 1980, the immediate crisis was solved by requiring Turks to obtain visas to travel to Germany. However, requiring visas did not work when even more Yugoslavs fled civil war in the early 1990s. The short-lived apparent success of earlier policies delayed the development of durable immigration policies until the twenty-first century.

Germany is now an acknowledged country of immigration with the most foreigners in Europe and is second only to the United States among the world's countries in hosting international migrants. Workers from other EU countries continue to move to Germany for higher wages and more opportunities, but there are projections that intra-EU migration from Romania, Poland, and other EU countries will decline as wages rise in these countries (Fuchs, Kubis, and Schneider 2019). This means that most analysts expect more non-Europeans (from Middle Eastern countries, China, and India) entering Germany in the future.

Germany is not a traditional country of immigration and does not have an immigration narrative like the United States, a nation of immigrants whose history and culture were shaped by newcomers from Germany and elsewhere. Instead, Germany was shaped by emigration, with stories of those who left for better opportunities passed down through the generations (Bade 1984). Germany successfully integrated Poles and other foreigners early in the twentieth century, but post–World War II political leaders denied that Germany was or would become a country of immigration. Today there is no debate that Germany is a country of immigration.

Migration is a process to be managed rather than a problem to be solved. When governments react to migration issues, sometimes they solve one problem while creating another. Germany and other industrial democracies are struggling to answer the fundamental immigration questions of how many, from where, and in what status newcomers should arrive and how they should be integrated. German political and economic leaders agree that more immigration is needed for demographic and economic reasons, and that the German economy and society can integrate diverse newcomers successfully.

Notes

1. The EU also promised to give Turks visa-free entry to Schengen countries if Turkey satisfied a certain list of requirements, but these were not fulfilled. Turkey encouraged migrants to cross the Greek land border in 2020, but Greece closed the border and rebuffed the migrants. Migrants on the Greek islands suffer under bad conditions, and some hundred of the most vulnerable were allowed to move to Germany.

2. Over 4 million East Germans moved to West Germany between 1949 and 1990.

3. Thirty countries expressed an interest in sending migrants to Germany, but Germany followed a European-only strategy, with a few exceptions.

4. Freedom of movement within the EEC meant that a worker from any member state could enter another and remain for up to three months in search of a job; if the migrant found employment, the host country had to grant any necessary work and residence permits. Under subsequent EU freedom-of-movement rights, EU nationals do not need residence permits to move to another EU member state, although they can be required to register after stays of three months and show that they are enrolled in school, are employed or self-employed, or have sufficient resources and health insurance to support themselves during their stay abroad (or be a member of a family that includes someone who satisfies these study, work, or sufficient-resources criteria).

5. If the exchange rate was $1 = DM 4.2 when it "should" have been $1 = DM 3, a $100 investment in Germany was worth DM 420 to the investor rather than its "true" DM 300 value.

6. In 1980 foreigners were 6 percent of German residents. Schmidt continued to be pessimistic about integrating foreigners. In a 2002 book, *Hand on Heart*, Schmidt wrote that Germany "brought in far too many foreigners as a result of idealistic thinking that resulted from the experience of the Third Reich. We have seven million foreigners today who are not integrated, many of whom do not want to be integrated and who are also not helped to integrate. We Germans are unable to assimilate all seven million. The Germans also do not want to do this. They are to a large extent xenophobic."

7. Studies showed that most of the foreigners who took departure bonuses would have left in any event, so the scheme bunched normal emigration during the two years that bonuses were available (Hönekopp 1990).

8. The fee in the late 1980s was DM 10,000. Turkish men who failed to perform military service or pay the fee could not get their Turkish passports renewed. In 2020, the fee stood at €5,261 ($6,000).

9. The European Communities were three international organizations governed by the same set of institutions: the European Coal and Steel Community (ECSC), the European Economic Community (EEC), and the European Atomic Energy Community (EAEC or Euratom). The European Union replaced the EEC, which regulated economic affairs and migration, in 1993, and the ECSC expired in 2002. Euratom is integrated into the EU..

10. For example, after July 1, 1990, ethnic Germans had to fill out a lengthy questionnaire and be approved as ethnic Germans before departing for Germany. Winning recognition as an ethnic German required passing a German language test, which a third of test-takers failed (retakes were not permitted). After 1993, there was a quota of 220,000 ethnic Germans a year accepted; this quota was later reduced. People born after 1993 are not eligible.

11. Jewish law holds that religion is transmitted via the mother, so many of those considered Jewish in the former Soviet Union were not considered Jewish by Jewish religious authorities in Germany.

12. Refugees leave their countries and may either wait in another country (often a neighboring one) for an opportunity to return to their native land or seek to resettle elsewhere; a

contemporary example is Syrians in Turkey. Asylum seekers move to the country in which they want to resettle and ask for asylum—that is, they ask to be recognized as refugees.

13. There were 1,737 asylum applications in 1967, and 10,000 in 1970.

14. Germany was able to deal other asylum surges in similar ad hoc ways. For example, Germany did not require foreign children under sixteen to have visas to come to Germany, so some Sri Lankan Tamils and Iranians sent their children to Germany by air to request asylum. After 2,500 unaccompanied minors applied for asylum in 1988, Germany imposed fines on airlines carrying minors without documents and began to require visas of unaccompanied foreign minors, and the problem was solved.

15. The Königstein key assigns asylum seekers to states using a formula based on the state's economy (two-thirds) and its population (one-third).

16. Other provisions of the compromise included rejecting applications from nationals of safe countries of origin, accelerating non-admission or return procedures at airports, and shifting from cash to in-kind assistance for asylum seekers waiting for decisions on their applications.

17. Most of these "new guest workers" are employed for less than a full year, so they add the equivalent of about 150,000 full-time-equivalent workers to the German workforce,

18. The effects of subcontracting are apparent in the membership of construction union IG BAU, which had only 247,000 members in 2018, down from 720,000 in 1996. IG Metall, the largest union that represents workers in manufacturing, has maintained its membership of 2.2 million, of whom a quarter are immigrants (Karakayali et al. 2017).

19. Thränhardt (2017) estimated that almost two-thirds of foreigners naturalizing in 2017 kept their original citizenship. There may be 10 million dual citizens in Germany, but only 3 million actively use two passports.

20. The official title was "Gesetz zur Steuerung und Begrenzung der Zuwanderung und zur Regelung des Aufenthalts und der Integration von Unionsbürgern und Ausländern." The opposition CDU-CSU preferred steering and limiting in-migration to immigration in the title of the law. Reflecting the contentious nature of immigration, the new law was approved in 2002, found invalid by the constitutional court, and reenacted in 2004.

21. The Federal Office for Migration and Refugees (BAMF) contracts with a variety of entities to offer these integration courses.

22. Germany has 396 *Ausländerbehoerden* (foreigners authorities) in cities and counties, and these offices issue *Aufenthaltserlaubnisse* (residence permits). Police in the late 1990s located 130,000 to 140,000 foreigners a year who were suspected of being unlawfully in Germany (such as by overstaying their visas) and charged 10,000 a year with falsifying documents (European Commission 2001, 72–73).

23. A fifteen-member commission chaired by Peter Hartz, then Volkswagen's personnel director, recommended these reforms, which took effect in 2003, 2004, and 2005. The first set of reforms, Hartz I, allowed for private employment agencies (Personal-Service-Agenturen or PSAs) and modified unemployment insurance; the second set, Hartz II, allowed the creation of "mini-jobs" that offered lower wages for employees and lower benefit costs to employers as well as simplifying self-employment (Ich-AG). Hartz I and II went into effect January 1, 2003.

Hartz III, in 2004, restructured the German Employment Service, while Hartz IV, in 2005, combined long-term unemployment insurance (*Arbeitslosenhilfe*) and welfare assistance (*Sozialhilfe*) and reduced unemployment benefits to welfare assistance levels.

24. Employer payroll taxes are 23 percent of wages paid in mini-jobs, much less than the 40 percent or more paid to higher-wage workers. Beginning January 1, 2005, Germans unemployed more than a year receive €345 ($450) a month plus money to cover their rent, and they were required to take "one-euro" public service jobs (which paid €1.50 an hour) for up to twenty hours a week.

25. Drivers who deliver cargo in Germany or transit Germany. They can be employed and paid by eastern European firms at their prevailing wages rather than German wages.

26. Germany's constitutional court in 2012 held that Article 1 of the constitution, protecting human rights, does not allow lower welfare payments to asylum seekers than to German citizens.

27. Merkel may have been referring to Germany's postwar *Wirtschaftswunder* (economic miracle), saying "Wir haben schon so viel geschafft, wir schaffen das" (we have accomplished so much, we can do this too).

28. Fachkommission Integrationsfähigkeit, "About Us," https://www.fachkommission -integrationsfaehigkeit.de/fk-int-en/.

29. In naming Angela Merkel its 2015 Person of the Year, *Time* called her the "Chancellor of the Free World": http://time.com/time-person-of-the-year-2015-angela-merkel/.

30. Between 1966 and 1967, for example, the employment of guest workers fell by 25 percent, while German employment fell only 3 percent, suggesting that guest workers could be rotated in and out of the labor market as needed.

References

Abelshauser, Werner. 2005. *Deutsche Wirtschaftsgeschichte von 1945 bis in die Gegenwart*. Munich: Beck.

Aust, Stefan, Horand Knaup, and Georg Mascolo. 2001. "Otto Schily zur Einwanderungspolitik: 'Es gibt noch Stolpersteine': Bundesinnenminister Otto Schily (SPD) über seine Pläne für ein Zuwanderungsgesetz." *Der Spiegel*, June 1, 2001.

Bade, Klaus J., ed. 1984. *Das Manifest der 60: Deutschland und die Einwanderung*. Munich: Beck.

Brücker, Herbert, Yuliya Kosyakova, and Eric Schuss. 2020. "Low-Skilled Mobility and Jobs." In *Integrating Low-Skilled Migrants in the Digital Age: European and US Experience*, edited by Gudrun Biffl and Philip Martin, 51–80. Krems: Donau University Press. https://door .donau-uni.ac.at/view/o:982.

Castles, Stephen. 1989. "Migrant Workers and the Transformation of Western Societies." Western Societies Program, paper no. 22, Cornell University, Ithaca, NY.

Dostal, Jörg Michael. 2017. "The German Federal Election of 2017: How the Wedge Issue of Refugees and Migration Took the Shine off Chancellor Merkel and Transformed the Party System." *Political Quarterly* 88, no. 4: 589–602.

Economist. 2001. "German Immigration Help Wanted." *Economist*, August 11, 2001.

European Commision. 2001. "Die Folgen der Attentate in den Vereinigten Staaten für die Luftverkehrsbranche." European Commission, Brussels. https://eur-lex.europa.eu/Lex UriServ/LexUriServ.do?uri=COM:2001:0574:FIN:DE:PDF.

Fetzer, Joel S. "The Evolution of Public Attitudes Toward Immigration in Europe and the United States, 2000–2010." Unpublished paper, Pepperdine University.

Gezer, Özlem, and Anna Reimann. 2011. "Erdogan Urges Turks Not to Assimilate: 'You Are Part of Germany, but Also Part of Our Great Turkey.'" *Der Spiegel*, February 28, 2011.

Hönekopp, Elmar. 1990. *Zur beruflichen und sozialen Reintegration türkischer Arbeitsmigranten in Zeitverlauf.* Nuremberg: Bundesanstalt für Arbeit, Institut für Arbeitsmarkt und Berufsforschung.

Hönekopp, Elmar. 1997. "The New Labor Migration as an Instrument of German Foreign Policy." In *Migrants, Refugees, and Foreign Policy: U.S. and German Policies Toward Countries of Origin*, edited by Rainer Münz and Myron Weiner, 165–182. Providence, RI: Berghahn Books.

Hunger, Uwe. 2000. "Der rheinische Kapitalismus in der Defensive. Eine komparative Policy-Analyse zum Paradigmenwechsel in den Arbeitsmarktbeziehungen am Beispiel der Bauwirtschaft. Baden-Baden." Unpublished PhD dissertation, Universität Münster.

Kindleberger, Charles. 1967. *Europe's Postwar Growth: The Role of Labor Supply.* Cambridge, MA: Harvard University Press.

Liebe, Ulf, Jürgen Meyerhoff, Maarten Kroesen, Caspar Chorus, and Klaus Glenk. 2018. "From Welcome Culture to Welcome Limits?" *PLOS One*, August 1, 2018. https://journals .plos.org/plosone/article?id=10.1371/journal.pone.0199923.

Miller, Mark J., and Philip L. Martin. 1982. *Administering Foreign-Worker Programs: Lessons from Europe.* Lexington, MA: Lexington Books.

Molnar, Christopher A. 2019. *Memory, Politics and Yugoslav Migration to Postwar Germany.* Bloomington: Indiana University Press.

Oswald, Anne von, Karen Schönwälder, and Barbara Sonnenberger. 2003. "Einwanderungsland Deutschland: A New Look at Its Post-War History." In *European Encounters: Migrants, Migration and European Societies Since 1945*, edited by Rainer Ohliger, Karen Schönwälder, and Triadafilos Triadafilopoulos, 19–37. Aldershot: Ashgate.

Rass, Christoph A. 2012. "Die Anwerbeabkommen der Bundesrepublik Deutschland mit Griechenland und Spanien im Kontext eines europäischen Migrationssystems." In *Das "Gastarbeiter"-System*, edited by Jochen Oltmer, Axel Kreienbrink, and Carlos Sanz Díaz, 53–69. Munich: Oldenbourg.

Servan-Schreiber, Jean Jacques. 1968. *The American Challenge.* New York: Atheneum.

Schmidt, Helmut, with Sandra Maischberger. 2002. *Hand aufs herz* [Hand on Heart]. Munich: Econ.Sontheimer, Michael. 2017. "Warum Kohl kein großer Kanzler war." *Der Spiegel*, June 22, 2017.

SVR. 2019. *Bewegte Zeiten: Rückblick auf die Integrations- und Migrationspolitik der letzten Jahre.* Berlin: Sachverständigenrat deutscher Stiftungen für Migration und Integration.

Thränhardt, Dietrich. 2019. "Welcoming Citizens, Divided Government, Simplifying Media: Germany's Refugee Crisis 2015–2017." In *Refugee News, Refugee Politics: Journalism, Public*

Opinion, and Policy Making in Europe, edited by Giovanna dell'Orto and Irmgard Wetzstein, 15–25. London: Routledge.

Thränhardt, Dietrich, and Jenni Winterhagen. 2013. "Three Catholic Transnationalisms—Italian, Croat and Spanish Immigrants Compared." In *Migration and Organized Civil Society*, edited by Dirk Halm and Zeynep Sezgin, 175–194. Milton Park: Routledge.

Vinocur, John. 1982. "Germany's Season of Discontent." *New York Times*, August 8, 1982.

Werner, Heinz. 1985. "The Employment of Foreigners in Western European Industrial Countries." *Intereconomics*, January/February, 10–15.

Zaun, Natascha. 2018. "States as Gatekeepers in EU Asylum Politics: Explaining the Non-adoption of a Refugee Quota System." *Journal of Common Market Studies* 56, no. 1: 44–62.

COMMENTARY

General and Special Integration Policies in Germany

Friedrich Heckmann

Introduction

Martin and Thränhardt note that the development of migration policies has been accompanied by integration policies. This commentary reviews these integration policies in a systematic way.

The openness to migrants of the central societal institutions, such as the labor market and the education, training, and health care systems, is a crucial element of general integration policies. However, special integration policies are necessary to enable migrants to fully participate in social institutions, including language courses, anti-discrimination and empowerment measures, and intercultural contact programs.

These special integration policies originate from different levels of government and civil society, but are mainly implemented at the local level. They include policies at the EU level, the national level, the state (*Länder*) level, the local level, and the neighborhood level.

The EU Level

Since the Tampere conference of 1999 and follow-up conferences in The Hague (2004) and Stockholm (2009), the EU has taken a stronger role in integration policies that affect its member states. The strongest policy implements are EU directives that member states are to transpose into national law. Directives 2000/43 and 2000/78 obliged the member states to enact laws against discrimination, particularly racial discrimination, while Directive 2003/109 established a right to safe residence status for third-country nationals after five years of legal residence. A 2003 directive for family reunion also supports integration.

In 2004 the EU council of ministers of justice and the interior proclaimed eleven basic principles to facilitate the integration of immigrants into the European Union. The EU created the EU Integration Fund for the fiscal period 2007–2013 to measure integration and conduct projects and research in EU countries. Support continues under the new and more comprehensive Asylum, Migration, and Integration Fund (AMIF). Despite these EU policies, individual nation-states still have the largest influence on general and special integration policies, including the right to allocate the AMIF funds.

The National Level

In 2001 the federal government of Germany established an independent commission (the Süssmuth Commission) to review the status of migration and integration. This commission was made up of representatives of the most important groups in German society and laid the foundations for a more systematic integration policy.

The milestones of Germany's integration policies include (Heckmann 2015, 247–250):

- The citizenship law of 2000
- The immigration law of 2005
- The institutionalization of an anti-discrimination policy in 2006
- The German Islam Conference, initiated in 2006
- The national integration plan of 2007
- Initiatives for monitoring and evaluation of political measures since 2005
- Launching a comprehensive anti-racism policy at the highest level of government in 2020

The citizenship law of 2000 established the principle of *jus soli*, allowing for individual and collective identity by permitting those born in Germany to be German without being the descendant of German parents.

The immigration law of 2005 founded a systematic integration policy, including integration courses, but officially announced that Germany is an immigration country and thus established a new societal definition and a new framing of the immigration process.[1]

The institutionalization of an anti-discrimination policy was initiated by the European Union and led to passage of an anti-discrimination law and the creation of a federal office for anti-discrimination.

The ongoing German Islam Conference tries to define and improve relations between state and Islamic organizations and officially recognizes Islam as a major religion in Germany.

Recognizing migrant organizations as partners and relevant players in integration policies is an important component of the national integration plan, an ongoing coordinated effort by major state and civil society institutions to improve and evaluate integration policies. These policies are evaluated periodically during integration summits in the chancellery in Berlin.

There are many monitoring and evaluation measures. Since 2005 the micro census has been able to identify persons with a migration background and to measure variables connected with the integration process, as indicated by the Fachkommission Integrationsfähigkeit (2021).

After several deadly racist and anti-Semitic incidents, the federal government in 2020 initiated a comprehensive and well-funded program against racism and right-wing extremism.

The Role of the *Länder*

Germany's *Länder*, or states, have significant control over taxes, education, and the police, reflecting their sovereign status until 1871. Since education is the key to migrant integration and social mobility for the children of migrants, the *Länder* have a major responsibility in the integration process. State policies to help immigrant children in schools include transition classes for newly arriving schoolchildren, preschool language training, mentoring, and increasing the number of all-day schools. However, the *Länder* do not yet have a systematic and solidly financed educational support concept for youth with a migration background. The *Länder* are developing various programs for religious instruction of Muslims within the school system.

Police are another major responsibility of the *Länder*, and relations between migrants and police are an important aspect of integration. Four types of policies affecting the interaction of police with migrants are (Lüken-Klaßen and Heckmann 2010, 80–86):

- Intercultural education of police officers
- Recruitment of police with a migration background
- Information on the police for migrants

- Institutionalized dialogue between police and migrant organizations

The Länder also support local integration projects financially, and some have created integration ministries and integrations laws.[2]

The Role of the Local Level

"Integration happens at the local level" is a frequently heard aphorism, especially in cities where a third or more of residents have a migration background. Counties have fewer migrants but similar programs. Policies directly addressing intercultural and interethnic relations include:[3]

- The development of local integration concepts
- Avoiding segregation and developing desegregation strategies
- Establishing political structures to link cities and their minority residents
- Adapting local administration to the needs of migrants and minorities
- Policies for improving inter-group relations

Local Integration Concepts
Many local governments have made integration policies a top priority, with the mayor often taking a leading role in advancing integration policies. Most cities in Germany have developed a local integration concept (*Leitbild*) that outlines needs, goals, and policies to improve integration. In most cases, integration policies are developed in a participatory manner, meaning that interested citizens (migrants and non-migrants), civil society organizations including migrant organizations, and representatives of the city government participate in developing policies, sometimes with the help of consultants.

Avoiding Segregation and Developing Desegregation Policies
Germany has less segregation than most countries of immigration because of ongoing efforts to avoid the concentration of "problem groups" including migrants. Second, the welfare state promotes communal housing whose managers avoid concentrations of migrants.

The Council, the Mayor, and Their Migrant Partners
The city council can initiate basic concepts and rules concerning local integration policies. As the body with budgetary responsibility, the council also has to decide whether a department in the administration should be created that has the primary responsibility for designing and executing integration policies, whether these policies should be organized as a cross-departmental task, or both. Funding decisions also

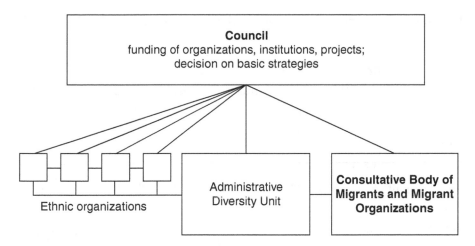

FIGURE 7.2. The Council and Intercultural Policies

have to be made by the council regarding larger projects of immigrant integration and support for migrant and minority organizations.

Most cities and counties have both created a special administrative integration policy unit and at the same time promote integration as a cross-departmental task.

Relations between the city councils and migrant groups may involve migrant representatives on the council or having the council consult with groups of migrants (Figure 7.2). The proportion of persons with a migration background in elected political positions is small but increasing, making representatives of migrant organizations important to articulate migrant concerns.

In most cities relations between the integration department and single-ethnic-group organizations are largely informal, with the intensity of contacts depending on issues and personalities. Most cities in Germany have done a mapping of migrant and minority organizations, and support them directly with funding or by providing them with resources such as rooms.

Mayors and heads of county administrations are key players in integration policies, with the authority to make integration policies a top priority in city work via the city council and local media.

Adapting to Migrants

Bureaucracies may not be welcoming to migrants, so many aim to promote an intercultural opening and thus to create a welcoming culture by providing translation services, recruiting staff with a migration background, and adapting regulations in public institutions concerning housing and construction, food, dress codes, sports, slaughtering, burials, and other issues. The improvement of intercultural competence among city employees through special training measures is also part of these policies.

Policies for Improving Inter-Group Relations

These are policies that are often practiced in close cooperation with and are established through initiatives of civil society organizations, including:

- Institutionalized inter-religious dialogue
- Inter-cultural contact programs
- Encouraging migrants to participate in majority organizations and voluntary associations
- Intercultural events
- Anti-prejudice and anti-discrimination measures and campaigns
- Inter-ethnic mediation

The Neighborhood Level

Migrant integration measures often deal with particular neighborhoods and public spaces where different ethnic and religious groups meet and interact, such as markets, public parks, public institutions, and street corners. Because these spaces are enjoyed by many different groups, interactions in such spaces can be a source of conflict.

A useful means of managing intercultural conflict is by establishing mediation services to deal with neighborhood conflicts. Conflicts over the use of public spaces often revolve around noise, the amount of rubbish left behind, or barbequing in park areas without suitable facilities, prompting local governments and neighborhood organizations to create partnerships to better manage public spaces.

Conclusion

A strong motivation for upward mobility among migrants and the openness of social institutions to migrants are the most important factors for successful integration. Special policies can ensure that migrants participate in societal institutions generally. However, the fact that policies are undertaken by different levels of government creates many problems of coordination, as does the temporary nature of many integration policies. Overall, Germany's institutions and society are united in striving for successful migrant integration.

Notes

1. The generously funded integration course is mainly a language course, but it has a civics component.
2. For a detailed discussion, see Sachverständigenrat Deutscher Stiftungen 2012.
3. Kommunaler Qualitätszirkel zur Integrationspolitik 2014.

References

Fachkommission Integrationsfähigkeit. 2020. "Gemeinsam die Einwanderungsgesellschaft gestalten." Berlin. https://www.bmi.bund.de/DE/themen/heimat-integration/integration/fachkommission.

Heckmann, Friedrich. 2015. *Integration von Migranten—Einwanderung und neue Nationenbildung.* Wiesbaden: Springer.

Kommunaler Qualitätszirkel zur Integrationspolitik. 2014. "2009–2014 Einblicke, Rückblicke, Ausblicke." Stuttgart.

Lüken-Klaßen, Doris, and Friedrich Heckmann. 2010. "Intercultural Policies in European Cities." European Foundation for the Improvement of Living and Working Conditions. http://www.eurofound.europa.eu/pubdocs/2010/32/en/1/EF1032EN.pdf.

Sachverständigenrat deutscher Stiftungen für Integration und Migration. 2012. "Integration im föderalen System: Bund, Länder und die Rolle der Kommunen. Jahresgutachten 2012 mit Integrationsbarometer." Berlin.

Unabhängige Kommission Zuwanderung. 2001. "Zuwanderung gestalten, Integration fördern." Berlin.

COMMENTARY

Can Germany Master the Integration Challenge?

Ingrid Tucci

Immigration, asylum, and integration have always been contentious issues in Germany, and they have been even more so in recent years with the return of right-wing extremism to the political scene. Germany's late recognition of itself as an immigration country is responsible for the lack of an immigration narrative in German politics and society, even though the country relies heavily on immigration as a solution for future problems in the domains of demography, the labor market, and pensions. The year 2016 was a historic one: 722,370 persons in need of protection requested asylum (37 percent of them Syrians and 18 percent Afghans). This new migration reinforces the already existing social, cultural, and religious diversity of Germany's population, but it is at the same time a challenge. The negative image of the Muslim population among parts of German society (Foroutan 2013) and concerns over migration (which are stronger in the former East Germany [SVR 2019]) compete with the solidarity toward asylum seekers that first emerged in the summer of 2015 and led to a large movement of civic engagement (hosting newcomers, supplying them with urgent necessities, teaching German, helping with administrative paperwork, and so on).

Integration as a Societal Challenge

Counting foreigners is recognized as an important part of acknowledging the reality of migration and integration. Even when they become German citizens, migrants and their children face specific problems as a result of discrimination, social exclusion, and other factors. While foreigners represented 12 percent of the population in Germany in 2017, 24 percent of the population—that is, 19.258 million people—had a migration background (a statistical administrative category introduced in 2005; see Elrick and Schwartzman 2015 and Figure 7.3). Among the population with a migration background, 68 percent were migrants and 32 percent were descendants of migrants.

Integration is an individual challenge for migrants and their children, but it is also a societal challenge that needs to be taken seriously by governments. Germany recognized the importance of social policy in this domain beginning in the mid-2000s. Integration was acknowledged as a two-sided process that involves not only migrants but also German society as a whole. A strong signal of Germany's recognition of itself as an immigration country were the changes in naturalization policy that occurred at the beginning of 1999 and to a lesser extent in 2014. The concept of German citizenship as based mainly on ancestry was enlarged in 2000 to encompass *jus soli*, meaning that children born in Germany to foreign parents could become German citizens. In addition, the number of years of residence needed before migrants can naturalize was reduced from fifteen to eight, leading to a significant increase in 2000 (when 187,000 naturalizations took place). But becoming German is not necessarily the end of the integration process. Doubt is regularly cast on the migrant population's willingness to integrate, in particular those labeled as "Muslim."

In the mid-2000s, the government began a vast integration effort, organizing summits to set the agenda and develop so-called integration plans. One factor that was identified was providing support for migrants to learn the German language. In the past, the vast majority of guest workers did not benefit from language courses upon their arrival; rather, integration was meant to occur primarily through work. And indeed, questions about the German-language proficiency of migrants (and their descendants) are frequently raised when discussing a possible lack of integration, although three-quarters of the population with a migration background declare that they speak German "well" or "very well" (Schacht 2018). The focus on language acquisition allowed Germany to set up a huge program of language and social integration courses directed at a variety of targets (youth, women, parents, and so on). In a way, this helped Germany be relatively well prepared to host the newcomers fleeing war and terrorism in recent years. But the demand for such courses exceeds the supply: asylum seekers wait eight months on average before being able to find space in such a course. Attending language and integration courses also became a condition for asylum seekers to get permanent resident status and later to apply for German citizenship.

The question of the incorporation of recently arrived asylum seekers and refugees is crucial both for individuals and for society. Several programs have been set up to help avoid some of the mistakes that were made with the influx of guest workers. Asylum seekers do not have the same rights as refugees. But a new German law now allows asylum seekers who have a good chance of being recognized as refugees to work. Young men constitute a significant share of the group of persons in need of protection who arrived most recently in Germany (Juran and Broer 2017), and within that segment there is a major split in terms of qualifications, with many having little education and others having the equivalent of a high school degree. Only a minority have a job; the vast majority are unemployed or enrolled in integration courses. Those who can search for jobs typically look in domains where German proficiency plays a secondary role, such as cleaning, logistics, and kitchen help. Among refugees who arrived in 2013, 17 percent say they speak good or very good German. The language courses put in place to serve recently arrived refugees show positive results, in particular when there are no children in the household (Brücker et al. 2019). However, the presence of children in the household has been shown to negatively affect women's German proficiency and their labor market integration. This is a real challenge for the near future, as many of these women arrived with relatively low education levels and less work experience compared to men (Fendel 2019).

Integration takes time, and so the duration of residence is a crucial factor explaining achievement in several domains. It is also an intergenerational process, as migrants bring or build families. Children with a migration background grow up in Germany, go to German schools, and very often build their lives far from their or their parents' country of origin. Three-quarters of these children are German citizens, born in Germany. Calculations based on data from the micro census show that among the migrant population, 40 percent have German citizenship. Those figures testify that migration is now at the foundation of Germany today: a country in which a large number of German citizens have a link to migration, whether near or far. Two central issues involve the capacity of the population to live "together in diversity" and to attenuate the boundaries between "we" and "them" that have an effect on public opinion.

A Facilitating Structural Context?

With a strong decrease in the unemployment rate since 2009 (reaching 5.8 percent in 2018) and even a lack of workers foreseen in some sectors (such as health care, education, and the social sector [Fuchs, Kubis, and Schneider 2019]), the German context can be considered to be economically favorable to the incorporation of migrants. But there is still room to improve the situation of many migrant families in Germany.

The poverty rate of people with a migration background (29 percent) is almost three times higher than for natives (12 percent) (Statistisches Bundesamt 2019). This has implications for children in terms of social, cultural, and political participation. One main reason for this economic vulnerability is the occupational structure: those with a migration background are less likely to work full-time, are more likely to be unemployed, and are less likely to have jobs as higher-level professionals or civil servants (this is true in particular for those of Turkish origin). No doubt the 2012 law facilitating the recognition of foreign credentials was helpful for third-country nationals. But there is still overrepresentation of migrants in the lower levels of the occupational hierarchy, and underrepresentation in the higher ones.

At the end of March 2016, 59,000 unaccompanied minors in need of international protection were counted by the German authorities. This group presents challenges for the German education system. The German dual training system is an advantage, as it provides a way to train young newcomers for specific occupations, making the path to regular employment somewhat easier.

The education level of the second generation of immigrants has long been lower than that of the children of natives. Their lower social background is an important factor explaining this difference. Children of migrants have less chance to get a place in kindergarten, and are still underrepresented in the preschool system (which affects the likelihood for further education) until the age of three years. The German dual training system is unique and facilitates labor market entrance. But children of migrants tend to have more difficulties finding training opportunities (see Beicht 2017 and Figure 7.4). They are still overrepresented in transitional training programs—a sort of "waiting room" system, offering qualifications that do not lead to a recognized training degree.

Despite a favorable structural context for integration, the recurrent discourse about migrants' "unwillingness" to integrate brings complexity to the context of reception. A heated discourse about the existence of "parallel societies" in Germany first emerged in the mid-1990s. At the time, it expressed the fear of a possible "ethnic withdrawal"—that is, the likelihood that migrants in many poor urban areas (which some politicians consider to be "ghettos") interact mostly or exclusively with other members of their community. But that is primarily a social matter, and thus it brings in other issues related to migrants' integration into German society—for example, having access to education, which leads to better jobs, which leads to increased income, making it possible to obtain housing outside of such areas. In this debate about parallel societies, research confirmed that they exist (Halm and Sauer 2006). More recently, the debate over Sarrazin's book and the Pegida movement also contributed to a division of opinion, with some questioning the compatibility of Islam with the values of Germany and fearing the "elimination" of Germany as a Christian country. Germany's search for a new way to "make society" is a challenge in a context characterized by the presence of right-wing extremists in the Bundestag and in the government of some federal states.

Acceptance and Discrimination

What does it mean to be German today? As in any other state of the European Union, the question of what it means to be a citizen is influenced by history and the political forces in play, and it is further complicated for those with migration experience. Boundaries between Germans with and without a migration background still persist, even if possessing German citizenship is a significant predictor of the feeling of belonging to Germany. On the other side, having experienced discrimination is negatively correlated with this feeling of belonging and more generally with life satisfaction (Tucci and Eisnecker 2014). Discrimination on the grounds of race, ethnicity, or religion was not an issue in Germany for many decades, and as a consequence Germany was slow to implement the EU directive against discrimination of all kind. Germany's anti-discrimination board was established only in 2006, and the last European Commission Against Racism and Intolerance (ECRI) report stressed the lack of the resources needed to render this board operational across the entire country. While discrimination is not easy to prove, much less measure, it is hard to argue that it is not a problem. A large study on all kinds of discrimination in Germany indicates that 23 percent of people with a migration background experienced ethnic or racial discrimination in the prior two years (Beigang et al. 2017, 101). Most of the time individuals experienced discrimination because of their religion, mainly Islam. Discrimination was experienced most frequently in the workplace, in public areas, and during off hours. Another recent study shows the strengthening of extreme rightist opinion among the German population (Krause, Zick, and Küpper 2019): the proportion of study respondents who expressed negative attitudes toward asylum seekers rose from 49.5 percent in 2016 to 54 percent in 2018, despite the decrease in asylum migration during this period. The feeling of not being accepted might be something that increases the longer a migrant has been resident in Germany: the share of recently arrived refugees who worry a lot about xenophobia (8 percent) is significantly lower than for those who have resided in the country longer (37 percent) (Schacht 2018). This indicates that the fight against xenophobia might need to be put at the forefront of the German policy agenda, as this more positive outlook among newcomers is a factor that might help further their smooth incorporation into German society. And social cohesion depends on one's opinion toward immigration:

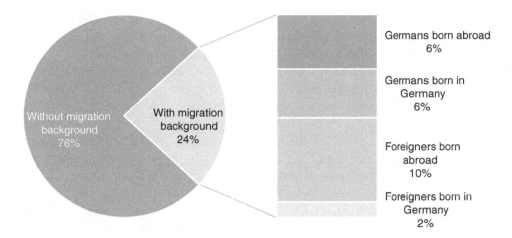

FIGURE 7.3. Population with and Without Migration Background in Germany 2017, Microcensus
SOURCE: German Federal Statistical Office.

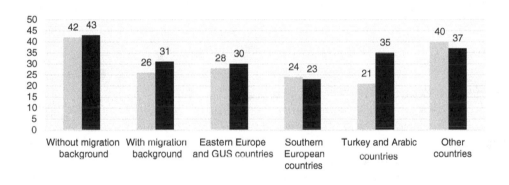

FIGURE 7.4. Share of Entries in Vocational Training
SOURCE: Beicht 2017.

non-migrants who feel threatened by migrants and immigration in Germany tend to avoid having relationships with migrants (Eisnecker 2019). This shows how important the political and media discourse on migration can be for the future of a multicultural German society.

References

Beicht, U. 2017. "Ausbildungschancen von Ausbildungsstellenbewerbern und-bewerberinnen mit Migrationshintergrund. Aktuelle Situation 2016 und Entwicklung seit 2004." Bundesinstitut für Berufsbildung.

Beigang, Steffen, Karolina Fetz, Dorina Kalkum, and Magdalena Otto. 2017. *Diskriminierungserfahrungen in Deutschland. Ergebnisse einer Repräsentativ- und einer Betroffenenbefragung. Hg. v. Antidiskriminierungsstelle des Bundes.* Baden-Baden: Nomos.

Brücker, Herbert, Johannes Croisier, Yuliya Kosyakova, Hannes Kröger, Giuseppe Pietrantuono, Nina Rother, and Jürgen Schupp. 2019. "Second Wave of the IAB-BAMF-SOEP Survey: Language Skills and Employment Rate of Refugees Improving with Time." IAB-Kurzbericht, Nürnberg.

Eisnecker, Philipp Simon. 2019. "Non-Migrants' Interethnic Relationships with Migrants: The Role of the Residential Area, the Workplace, and Attitudes Toward Migrants from a Longitudinal Perspective." *Journal of Ethnic and Migration Studies* 45, no. 5: 804–824.

Elrick, J., and L. Farah Schwartzman. 2015. "From Statistical Category to Social Category: Organized Politics and Official Categorizations of 'Persons with a Migration Background' in Germany." *Ethnic and Racial Studies* 38, no. 9: 1539–1556.

Fendel, Tanja. 2019. "Die Arbeitsmarktintegration geflüchteter Frauen." WISO-Direkt.

Foroutan, Naika. 2013. *Identity and (Muslim) Integration in Germany.* Washington, DC: Migration Policy Institute.

Fuchs, Johann, Alexander Kubis, and Lutz Schneider. 2019. *Zuwanderung und Digitalisierung: Wie viel Migration aus Drittstaaten benötigt der deutsche Arbeitsmarkt künftig?* Gütersloh: Bertelsmann Stiftung.

Halm, D., and M. Sauer. 2006. "Parallelgesellschaft und ethnische Schichtung." *Aus Politik und Zeitgeschichte* 1, no. 2: 18–24.

Juran, S., and P. N. Broer. 2017. "A Profile of Germany's Refugee Populations." *Population and Development Review* 43, no. 1: 149–157.

Krause, D., A. Zick, and B. Küpper, eds. 2019. *Verlorene Mitte—Feindselige Zustände: Rechtsextreme Einstellungen in Deutschland 2018/2019.* Bonn: Friedrich-Ebert-Stiftung.

Schacht, Diana. 2018. "Die Lebenssituation von Migranten und Migrantinnen und deren Nachkommen." Datenreport 2018, 272–279. BPB.

Statistisches Bundesamt. 2019. "Migration und Integration. Integrationsindikatoren 2005–2017."

Tucci, Ingrid, Philipp Eisnecker, and Herbert Brücker. 2014. "Diskriminierungserfahrungen und soziale Integration: Wie zufrieden sind Migranten mit ihrem Leben?" In "Die IAB-SOEP-Migrationsstichprobe: Leben, lernen, arbeiten—wie es Migranten in Deutschland geht," 29–35. IAB-Kurzbericht, Nuremberg.

8   The Netherlands

From Consensus to Contention in a Migration State

Willem Maas

Introduction: The Netherlands as a Migration State

The Netherlands has always been a migration state.[1] Immigrants played crucial roles in the formation of the Dutch state and its subsequent Golden Age in the seventeenth century, when many were drawn to the country for its relative religious tolerance. At least 150,000 people, primarily Calvinists and other Protestants—merchants, artists, and others—fled Flanders and Brabant during the war of independence from Spain (1568–1609) and settled in the northern Netherlands, where they constituted one tenth of the new country's population (Maas 2013a). As the new Dutch Republic overtook northern Italy as Europe's most urbanized region, immigrants quickly outnumbered locals in many cities.[2] Immigrants from present-day Belgium and northern France were joined by Sephardic Jews from Portugal and Spain, Germans, Scandinavians, Scots, Ashkenazi Jews from central and eastern Europe, Huguenots from France, and others, who helped transform the Netherlands from a mostly rural and agricultural backwater into an urbanized society, a world center of economic, industrial, intellectual, financial, artistic, and scientific activity (*Algemene Geschiedenis Der Nederlanden* 1977). Immigration continued more slowly in the eighteenth century (see Table 8.1) and then gradually decreased in the nineteenth century, increasing again in the twentieth century (Lucassen and Penninx 1997). Only in the twenty-first century has the proportion of immigrants in Dutch society surpassed the previous peak reached during the Golden Age: by 2018, people born outside the

Netherlands accounted for around 12 percent of the total resident population of the Netherlands (see Table 8.2), while they and individuals with at least one parent born outside the Netherlands accounted for almost one quarter of the population (see Table 8.3). As Leo Lucassen (whose commentary follows this chapter) noted at the launch of a website about migration to the Netherlands, the image of a stable Dutch population which was transformed by immigration only in the past half century demonstrates a lack of historical insight and is in dire need of correction.[3]

Almost as important as immigration has been large-scale emigration. Over half a million persons born in the Netherlands—over 5 percent of the country's population—emigrated between 1946 and 1969, not counting the many who emigrated and subsequently returned (Elich 1983, 1987), encouraged by government emigration subsidies. Emigration of the Dutch-born population slowed slightly in the 1970s and 1980s but then once again increased, driven by free movement within the EU which allows individuals to more easily relocate to other EU countries; Belgium and Germany are particularly popular with the Dutch because of lower taxes and house prices, and there is also significant retirement migration to southern Europe (Maas 2009). Between 1995 and 2017, there was net emigration of some 437,445 individuals born in the Netherlands (see Table 8.4), roughly the same number (averaging around 20,000 annually) as during the postwar emigration boom.[4] Of course the postwar emigration of people born in the Netherlands was proportionately more significant, as the resident population has increased from approximately 10 million in 1950 to over 17 million by 2019. Because of a significant increase in the emigration of foreign-born Dutch residents (whether returning to their countries of origin or moving elsewhere), however, there is now more emigration than ever before: 0.89 percent of the total population emigrates every year. Immigration is even more significant than emigration, however, with annual inflows equivalent to 1.36 percent of the population. Taken together, the population of the Netherlands is increasingly mobile.

Dutch public opinion is not more hostile to immigrants than public opinion in other European states and the political salience of immigration in the Netherlands is generally below the EU average. For example, the Fall 2019 Eurobarometer survey asking Europeans to choose the two most important issues facing their country showed that only 13 percent of Dutch respondents chose immigration, below the EU27 average of 17 percent and far lower than neighboring Belgium (where immigration was the most mentioned issue, chosen by 26 percent of respondents) and Germany (where likewise 26 percent of respondents chose it and immigration was the second-most mentioned issue). In that survey, Dutch respondents ranked immigration behind the environment, energy, and climate change (chosen by 66 percent of Dutch respondents as one of the two most important issues facing the Netherlands; by far the highest in the EU), health and social security (31 percent), the education system (25 percent), housing (15 percent), crime (15 percent), and pensions (14 percent).[5]

In another survey conducted in October 2017, asking Europeans whether they would feel comfortable or uncomfortable having an immigrant as a family member or partner, Dutch respondents were the most open of all EU28 member states, with 78 percent saying they would be totally comfortable and only 5 percent saying they would be uncomfortable, far more open than the EU28 average of 40 percent comfortable and 23 percent uncomfortable.[6] On questions of whether immigration from outside the EU is more of a problem or more of an opportunity, on whether integration of immigrants is successful, and on the impact of immigrants on society Dutch respondents similarly were more positive than the EU28 average.[7] Nevertheless, immigration by individuals from non-Western societies aroused a mixture of responses, and by the end of the twentieth century the Netherlands could be described—along with many other western European states—as a reluctant immigration country (Entzinger 2004). In the same survey as above, Dutch respondents were the most likely of all EU28 member states to say that successful integration of immigrants requires being able to speak Dutch (87 percent versus the EU28 average of 68 percent for being able to speak the country's language) and being committed to the way of life in the Netherlands by accepting the norms and values of society (79 percent of Dutch respondents, compared to the EU28 average of 56 percent). As detailed below, the political situation in the Netherlands in the first decades of the twenty-first century challenges immigration advocates, though policies and their implementation were not as restrictionist as in some other European states.

The Dutch tradition of consensus-building, where all views are carefully considered and the result is generally middle-of-the-road policies and bureaucratic inertia, coupled with the purely proportional electoral system, allowed anti-immigrant parties not only to enter parliament but also to affect government policy. In the twenty-first century, the depoliticization of migration and citizenship policy that had been the norm in the Netherlands was shattered by populist parties, most famously those led by Pim Fortuyn (LPF), Geert Wilders (PVV), and Thierry Baudet (FvD)—for descriptions of all recent Dutch political parties see below, and especially Table 8.8. The shift from consensus-building to factiousness or discord characterizes recent Dutch politics and undermines a key assumption of the gap hypothesis. As discussed elsewhere in this book, the gap hypothesis holds that the gap between the goals of national immigration policy and actual policy outcomes is increasing. But this assumes that the goals of national immigration policy can be defined and are relatively fixed. The Netherlands provides a context in which this does not hold, because there is lack of consensus about almost every aspect of migration politics and policies, and this lack of consensus is translated into shifting national immigration policies.

The Migration Tradition

Whether caused by geography, political culture, economic links, or other factors, migration has been a central issue in the Netherlands since its foundation as a state. In the seventeenth century Golden Age, the Netherlands was an economic and cultural magnet, with Dutch cities drawing the best and brightest from far and wide. This role waned during the eighteenth century, and during the nineteenth century the Netherlands was a country of emigration. Like other colonial states, the Netherlands exported people abroad during the colonial period, but it also imported highly skilled immigrants.

In the first quarter of the twentieth century (1900–1924), the Netherlands became a net immigration country, drawing roughly the same proportion of immigrants as in the third quarter (1950–1974). Only from the late 1920s until the early 1960s was the Netherlands a net emigration country—until the country briefly became an emigration country again during a period of five years from 2003 to 2007, a situation unique in western Europe until the economic crisis, as Ireland also once again became an emigration country. Immigration outpaced emigration strikingly in the final quarter of the twentieth century, as net immigration averaged 0.20 percent of the population

TABLE 8.1. Average Annual Migration, 1796–2017

	Immigration	Emigration		Immigration	Emigration	
	(thousands)		Net	(per 1,000 population)		Net
2000–2017	148.9	123.6	25.2	9.0	7.5	1.5
1975–1999	98.4	69.4	28.9	6.7	4.7	2.0
1950–1974	63.9	59.8	4.1	5.4	5.1	0.3
1925–1949	41.3	45.7	−4.5	4.8	5.3	−0.5
1900–1924	35.6	34.1	1.5	5.7	5.5	0.2
1865–1899	12.5	15.8	−3.3	2.9	3.7	−0.8
1796–1864	1.6	3.0	−1.4	0.6	1.1	−0.5

SOURCES: Data adapted from Nicolaas and Sprangers 2007, except for 2000–2017, which is calculated from Statistics Netherlands figures.

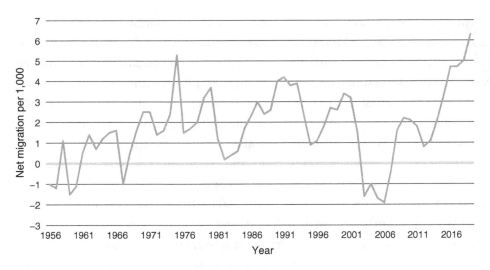

FIGURE 8.1. Net Migration to the Netherlands, per 1,000
Population, 1956–2019

annually. Since 2000, both immigration (averaging 0.90 percent of the population annually) and emigration (averaging 0.75 percent of the population annually) are the highest ever, as the Netherlands joins the trend across western Europe of increasing mobility.

Figure 8.1 shows net migration to the Netherlands between 1956 and 2019. Despite substantial postcolonial and labor immigration, the Netherlands was essentially an emigration country from the late 1920s until the 1960s. Peak net immigration years included the 1970s (labor migration and the independence of Suriname), the late 1980s and early 1990s (asylum and family reunification), 1998–2001, and the period since 2014.

Postwar Emigration

In the immediate aftermath of World War II, the Dutch government started exploring the possibility of encouraging emigration. In order to build a welfare state, the government wanted to promote industrialization and export industries and reduce the reliance on farming. As a result, agricultural workers—who also had a very high birth rate—were considered surplus. In his New Year's address on January 1, 1950, Prime Minister Willem Drees famously announced that "part of our people should venture, as in previous centuries, to seek their future in larger realms than our own country."[8]

To encourage emigration, the government offered information and courses, facilitated transportation, signed international agreements such as the Netherlands Australian Migration Agreement (1951), and offered financial subsidies to those willing to leave. Farmers' associations, women's groups, and Protestant and Catholic emigrant organizations assisted emigrants in their journey, and the government established a Netherlands Emigration Service.[9] From 1950 to 1959, roughly 350,000 Dutch emigrants settled in Canada (127,900), Australia (106,100), the United States (59,900), South Africa (29,100), New Zealand (19,900), and elsewhere. The peak year was 1952, when 52,000 Dutch emigrants left (Nicolaas and Sprangers 2007).

The war had devastated the country's infrastructure, there were worries about the Cold War and insufficient work and food, and a prevailing pessimism. A novelist captured the bleak mood: "The Netherlands is overpopulated. Every child that is born sets back civilization and makes us poorer. In ten years we will be bankrupt." (Hermans 1951, my translation). Severe storms on February 1, 1953, destroyed dykes and flooded large parts of the provinces of Zeeland, South Holland, and North Brabant, killing roughly 1800 and causing the evacuation of approximately 72,000 people. The tragedy galvanized government spending on infrastructure and laid the groundwork for the Delta Plan, intended to prevent future disasters. The rise of social programs introduced by the social democratic government headed by Willem Drees stabilized the situation. The standard of living started to rise, industrialization increased, and the 1959 discovery of natural gas in Groningen added to the economic resurgence. Emigration slowed and by the 1960s there were efforts to recruit workers, first from southern Europe (especially Italy, Spain, and Portugal) and then elsewhere (see section on Labor Migration, below).

Postcolonial Immigration

The Netherlands had postcolonial immigration from Indonesia, Suriname, and the Netherlands Antilles. I will examine the effects of this immigration in the following sections of the chapter.

Indonesia

The largest immigration to the Netherlands was the movement of over 400,000 people from the former Dutch East Indies following the independence of Indonesia and its subsequent annexation of Netherlands New Guinea from 1945 to 1968. Many of these immigrants were among the roughly 300,000 people who had moved there from the Netherlands between 1900 and 1940 (and thus were simply returning emigrants), but others were born in what became Indonesia (Beets, van Imhoff,

TABLE 8.2. Foreign-Born Residents of the Netherlands, by Country of Birth (thousands)

	Germany	Indonesia	Suriname	Turkey	Morocco	Other countries	Total	% of total population
2018	105.4	100.9	176.4	191.5	169.0	1336.1	2079.3	12.1
2015	104.8	107.5	179.2	192.3	168.5	1108.6	1861.0	11.0
2010	120.5	140.6	186.8	196.7	167.4	1020.5	1832.5	11.1
2005	117.7	155.9	190.1	195.9	168.5	907.9	1736.1	10.6
2000	124.2	168.0	185.0	178.0	152.7	748.4	1556.3	9.8
1996	130.1	177.7	181.0	167.5	140.7	610.1	1407.1	9.1
1971	128.9	204.4	29.0	28.2	20.9	194.9	606.3	4.6
1960	129.2	203.2	12.9			103.3	448.6	3.9
1947	135.5	79.9				76.6	292.0	3.0
1930		32.6				245.1	277.7	3.5

SOURCE: Calculated from Statistics Netherlands figures and Nicolaas and Sprangers 2007 for the pre-1996 numbers. "Indonesia" figures for 1930 and 1947 include Suriname and the Netherlands Antilles. Poland has now joined the historically five most important sources, as shown in Table 8.3.

and Huisman 2003). The Indonesian-born group quickly became the largest group of foreign-born residents in the Netherlands.

Of particular note within the Indonesian-born population are the Moluccans, who are mostly Christian, Dutch-speaking, and were part of the Dutch colonial elite.[10] In 1950, Moluccan soldiers who had served with the Royal Netherlands Indies Army (KNIL) declared an independent Republic of the South Moluccas (Republik Maluku Selatan, RMS). Within six months, most of the RMS forces were defeated by the troops of the new Republic of Indonesia. The RMS leadership retreated to the Netherlands, where they established a government-in-exile, accompanied by some 12,500 soldiers and their families. Initially housed in camps, many Moluccans never adopted Dutch citizenship, expecting that they would be able to return to an independent South Moluccan state. Frustrated with the inaction of successive Dutch governments, some Moluccan exiles engaged in violent action in the 1970s, including occupations, hostage-takings, and the hijacking of two trains ("Moluccan exiles will settle for autonomy" 2009).[11] By 2017 the Moluccan community numbered approximately 45,000, of whom approximately 40 percent live in special residential districts reserved for Moluccans, although many of these districts were disappearing ("Nog 45 gemeenten hebben aparte Molukse wijk" 2017).

The total Indonesia-born population also remained significant although aging fast: by 2018, approximately 100,900 people born in Indonesia resided in the Netherlands, down by about half from the 1960s and 1970s. Subsequent generations are much larger: by one estimate from 2001 there were over 280,000 second-generation Indonesians (a person with at least one parent born in Indonesia) resident in the Netherlands (Beets, van Imhoff, and Huisman 2003, 65). More recent estimates put the number of second-generation Indonesians at around 260,700 in 2018, for a total first- and second-generation population of 361,500 Indonesians (Table 8.3), although almost three-quarters of the second generation have only one parent born in Indonesia. Statistics Netherlands does not count individuals with foreign heritage beyond the second generation, but many second-generation Indonesians now have children,

TABLE 8.3. Residents with a Migration Background, 2018

	Total (thousands)	First Generation (thousands)	Second Generation Total (thousands)	One Parent (thousands)	Two Parents (thousands)	Percentage of Those with Migration Background	Percentage of Total Population
Turkey	**404.5**	191.5	212.9	51.9	161.0	10.2	2.35
Morocco	**396.5**	169.0	227.5	46.2	181.3	10.0	2.31
Indonesia	**361.5**	100.9	260.7	191.9	68.8	9.1	2.10
Germany	**354.1**	105.3	248.8	229.9	18.9	8.9	2.06
Suriname	**351.7**	176.4	175.3	68.3	106.9	8.9	2.05
Poland	**173.0**	135.0	38.0	19.8	18.2	4.4	1.01
Antilles and Aruba	**156.2**	84.5	72.6	40.9	31.6	3.9	0.91
Belgium	**118.7**	45.5	73.2	67.5	5.7	3.0	0.69
Syria	**90.8**	81.8	9.0	1.0	7.9	2.3	0.53
United Kingdom	**88.4**	49.4	39.0	34.7	4.3	2.2	0.52
Former Yugoslavia	**83.0**	49.7	33.2	14.2	19.0	2.1	0.48
China	**74.2**	51.5	22.7	4.9	17.8	1.9	0.43
Former USSR	**64.6**	44.0	20.6	10.8	9.7	1.6	0.38
Iraq	**61.3**	43.9	17.4	2.6	14.8	1.5	0.36
Italy	**53.7**	31.4	22.3	18.9	3.4	1.4	0.31
Afghanistan	**47.8**	35.0	12.8	0.96	11.8	1.2	0.28
France	**45.6**	25.1	20.5	17.4	3.1	1.1	0.26
Others	**1046.2**	659.3	387.0	239.7	146.5	26.7	6.63
Total	**3971.8**	2079.3	1892.5	1061.6	830.7	100.0	22.92

SOURCE: Calculated from Statistics Netherlands.

grandchildren, and great-grandchildren, while only the original immigrants and their children appear in the statistics.

Suriname

The other significant spurt of postcolonial migration occurred around the 1975 independence of Suriname. One of the Dutch government's motivations for granting independence (neighboring French Guiana was never granted independence and remains an overseas department of France) had been to reduce the immigration of Surinamese to the Netherlands (van Amersfoort 1999, 143). This plan backfired spectacularly, as many Surinamese moved to the Netherlands in anticipation of independence, fearing that independence would have negative consequences and wanting to make use of their Dutch citizenship rather than lose it. Soon after independence, over one third of Suriname's population had moved to the Netherlands, where they rivalled the Indonesians as the largest group of foreign-born residents.

Suriname's population is ethnically diverse. The four largest groups are the Hindustani or East Indians (descendants of nineteenth century contract workers from northern India), the Creoles (of mixed African and European, mostly Dutch, heritage), the Javanese (descendants of contract workers from the former Dutch East Indies), and the Maroons (descendants of West African slaves who escaped to the interior). One estimate placed the proportions at 37 percent Hindustani, 31 percent Creole, 15 percent Javanese, 10 percent Maroon, 2 percent Amerindian, 2 percent Chinese, 1 percent white, and 2 percent other.[12] In particular, the Chinese community in Suriname has grown since the 1990s (Tjon Sie Fat 2009). The size of the Surinamese community resident in the Netherlands has also continued to grow, though more slowly after 1980, when visa restrictions were introduced. By 2018, approximately 176,400 individuals born in Suriname resided in the Netherlands (Table 8.2) along with a similar number of second-generation Surinamese (Table 8.3), for a total of around 351,700 Surinamese resident in the Netherlands, compared with a total population in Suriname of around 600,000.

Netherlands Antilles

Dutch settlers colonized various islands in the Caribbean in the seventeenth century, running slave plantations and engaging in trading. After the 1814 Anglo-Dutch Treaty, the Dutch retained control of two sets of islands: Aruba, Bonaire, and Curaçao (off the coast of Venezuela) and Sint Eustatius, Saba, and Sint Maarten (in the Leeward islands). Following the postwar decolonization, the Netherlands Antilles became one of three constituent units of the Kingdom of the Netherlands (along with Suriname and the Netherlands). Aruba separated from the rest of the Netherlands Antilles in 1986 and Curaçao and Sint Maarten followed in 2010, when Bonaire,

Sint Eustatius, and Saba became Dutch municipalities. The islands had a combined population of around 335,000 (approximately 150,000 on Curaçao; 117,000 on Aruba; 42,000 on Sint Maarten; 20,000 on Bonaire; 2900 on Sint Eustatius; and 1800 on Saba). Antillians hold Dutch citizenship and migration to the Netherlands is unrestricted, although several islands limit migration from the Netherlands by requiring residence permits and establishing quotas. Migration from the Antilles to the Netherlands was for a long time chiefly temporary, as local youth sought opportunities to work or study in the Netherlands before returning. In the late 1990s, however, the economic situation in the Caribbean deteriorated and many Antillians moved to the Netherlands: there was net migration of over 28,000 between 1997 and 2002, before the migration flow reversed. By 2018, there were an estimated 84,500 first-generation Antillians residing in the Netherlands, alongside another 72,600 second generation.

The increase in the number of Antillians and the fact that some Antillian youth in the Netherlands became involved in criminal activities prompted the Dutch government in 2006, under immigration minister Rita Verdonk, to propose regulations allowing for the repatriation of Antillian youth between the ages of sixteen and twenty-four who were unemployed and had no good employment prospects. Later proposals specified that only individuals who were convicted of a crime or who threatened national security could be repatriated. There were other public discussions advocating restricting the migration rights of *all* Antillians to the Netherlands (Emmer 2007). But these ran into the fundamental problem that Dutch citizenship is unitary, with equal status and no distinctions between any of the constituent units of the Kingdom of the Netherlands.[13] In 2010, the disjuncture between the Antilles being able to limit migration from the Netherlands without the reverse resulted in a draft law on free movement within the Kingdom (Rijkswet Personenverkeer 2010), but this was abandoned. The relationship between the European and Caribbean Netherlands remains politically sensitive (Sharpe 2014). As detailed in Sharpe's commentary following this chapter, there are significant migration issues in the Caribbean Netherlands, particularly relating to Venezuela. The integration of three of the Caribbean islands as special municipalities of the Netherlands also led to more immigration from the European part of the Netherlands, and the mostly white immigrants are relatively well off compared with their local fellow citizens.[14]

Labor Migration

In common with other western European states such as Germany, the Netherlands in the 1960s signed several labor recruitment agreements with foreign countries, intended to bring workers to the Netherlands who would work for some period of time and then return to their home countries. Such agreements were signed with Italy

(1960), Spain (1961), Portugal (1963), Turkey (1964), Greece (1966), Morocco (1969), Tunisia (1970), and Yugoslavia (1970). Free movement within the European Community (Maas 2007) soon made obsolete the agreement with Italy and later the ones with Greece (which joined the EC in 1981) and Spain and Portugal (which joined in 1986). The labor migration that resulted from these agreements was first mostly circular: the mostly young, male workers would work and then indeed return. The 1973 oil crisis altered this pattern significantly. Following the Egyptian and Syrian attack on Israel in October 1973 (the Yom Kippur War), the Organization of Petroleum Exporting Countries (OPEC) first raised the price of oil and then set a total embargo on oil exports to the United States and the Netherlands, later extending the embargo to other west European states and Japan. The resulting oil crisis, coupled with a stock market crash and high inflation, resulted in recession across Europe and rising unemployment. Rather than returning home, however, many of the labor migrants who had moved to the Netherlands decided to stay.

The Netherlands during this time had relatively liberal family reunification and formation policies, allowing labor migrants to bring their families to the Netherlands. For example, a comparison of the growth of the Turkish populations in the Netherlands and Germany since the informal end of the guestworker system in 1974 shows that the Turkish population grew much faster in the Netherlands, mostly because of Germany's more restrictive family reunification and formation policies and Germany's relative success during the 1980s at enticing unemployed Turkish workers to leave (Muus 2004, 269).

The legacy of pillarization—known as *verzuiling* in Dutch, meaning the vertical segregation of society into distinct, usually denominational, social pillars each with its own social, cultural, and political institutions, and even sports leagues—resulted in publicly-funded Muslim and Hindu denominational schools and broadcasting facilities. The welfare state provided high benefits and low unemployment while promoting cultural diversity, meaning that the Netherlands was widely perceived as one of the few clear examples of multiculturalism, alongside Canada and Australia (Maas 2010, 227–8). But as discussed in the Sharpe commentary following this chapter, the commitment to multiculturalism has arguably been replaced by an "ethnorepublican" nationalism that undermines respect for diversity and inclusion.

By 2018—as shown in Tables 8.2 and 8.3—the largest group of residents of the Netherlands born outside the country were born in Turkey, followed by Suriname, Morocco, and then Poland, ahead of Germany. Indonesia, which had been the largest source country until the 1990s, dropped to sixth place as the first generation died: most immigrants from Indonesia had arrived by the mid-1950s, while most postcolonial and labor immigrants arrived twenty or more years later.

One way of examining the relative size of immigrant groups is to look at the statistics on the background of immigrants and their children. Until 2016, these statistics employed the term *allochtoon*, in use since the 1970s and taken from the Greek roots *allos* (other) and *chthon* (land or earth), the opposite of the word *autochtoon* (autochthonous, in English). Statistics Netherlands defined an *allochtoon* as someone born abroad with at least one parent who was born abroad (first generation *allochtoon*) or someone born in the Netherlands who had at least one parent born abroad (second generation *allochtoon*). For adopted children, the birthplaces of the adoptive rather than genetic parents counted. In the debate about terminology, it was sometimes remarked that because Geert Wilders' mother was born in the Netherlands Indies (now Indonesia), he is a second-generation *allochtoon* with a western background, because Statistics Netherlands defines Western background as Europe (excluding Turkey), North America, Oceania, Indonesia, and Japan. The Dutch royal family, too, are *allochtonen*: King Willem-Alexander's father and grandfather were born in Germany, and because Queen Maxima was born in Argentina, the crown princess and her sisters are second-generation *allochtonen* with a non-western background. Such examples highlight the difficulties with statistics, and is one reason (following advice from a government thinktank in 2012) the Dutch government introduced new terminology in 2016, ending the use of the term *allochtoon* and the western and non-western distinction and suggesting many alternatives, including persons with a migration background (Bovens et al 2016).

Table 8.3 shows the top sources of persons with a migration background resident in the Netherlands. By 2020, almost one-quarter of residents of the Netherlands (24.1 percent) had a migration background either directly or through one or both parents, roughly half first generation and half second generation, a total of 4.2 million people. Just under half of this population originated in five countries of origin: Turkey, Morocco, Indonesia, Germany, and Suriname. Noteworthy are the intermarriage rates in the second generation: 80 percent of Morocco-background, 76 percent of Turkey-background, and 61 percent of Suriname-background residents of the Netherlands born in the Netherlands are the children of two parents both born in that country of origin, compared with less than 8 percent of those with a background in Germany or Belgium.

Recent Migration Patterns

Examining annual immigration and emigration statistics by the citizenship (Dutch or non-Dutch) of the migrant shows stable immigration of Dutch citizens (return migration and immigration of those who acquired citizenship abroad, such as by marriage or birth to a Dutch citizen) from the 1970s to the 1990s and growing immigration of Dutch citizens since then. Emigration of Dutch citizens has grown, particularly after 2000. For non-Dutch citizens, the immigration trend is considerably more varied (with many ups and downs), while the emigration trend is stable and growing, particularly after 2002; in 2009 more than 57,000 non-Dutch citizens emigrated, the highest number ever.

Figure 8.2 shows net immigration not by citizenship status but by country of birth for the period of 1972 to 2017. Suriname and the Antilles, which were the most important source of immigrants throughout the 1970s (postcolonial immigration), were joined by Turkey and then Morocco (labor immigration). The ever-growing importance of immigration from European Union member states is noteworthy, particularly since the 2004 enlargement—most notably from Poland (Pool 2011). The most dramatic rise in recent years is immigration from Syria: while in 2010 there were only 6916 individuals born in Syria living in the Netherlands, by 2018 that number had jumped to 81,811.

Figure 8.3 shows net immigration (immigration minus emigration) by country of birth for the top ten sources, ranked by total net immigration over the 1995–2019 period (shown beside the country name). Most striking is Poland, by far the largest source of recent immigrants settling in the Netherlands, followed by Syria (spiking due to the civil war; it is unclear whether these people will stay or return to Syria), and then the former Soviet Union and China, ahead of Turkey and Morocco. Germany, the second EU country after Poland, appears ninth, while other EU member states are even further down the list—but this is only because of high emigration compensating for high immigration. The numbers for net immigration mask the

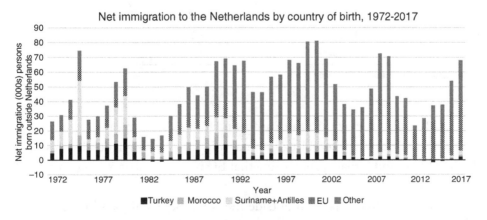

FIGURE 8.2. Net Immigration (in 000s) by Country of Birth, 1972–2017
SOURCE: Calculated from Statistics Netherlands.

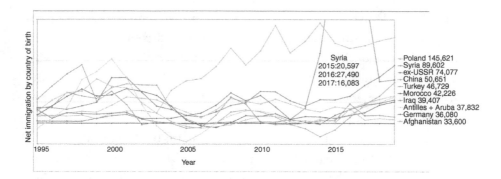

FIGURE 8.3. Net Immigration by Country of Birth, Top Countries, 1995–2019

TABLE 8.4. Emigration of Persons Born in the Netherlands, by Destination, 1995–2009 (thousands)

	Emigration	Return	Net Emigration	
Belgium	102.5	50.3	52.2	23.6%
Germany	80.8	44.8	36.0	16.3%
Other Europe	82.8	48.3	34.6	15.6%
United Kingdom	45.5	22.0	23.5	10.6%
France	30.8	15.0	15.7	7.1%
Spain	30.8	18.2	12.6	5.7%
United States	37.4	25.9	11.6	5.2%
Canada	13.1	5.2	7.9	3.6%
Antilles and Aruba	35.4	27.7	7.7	3.5%
Australia	17.0	9.3	7.7	3.5%
Other	94.1	82.5	11.6	5.3%
Subtotal	570.4	349.2	221.2	100.0%
Unknown	92.2	0	92.2	
Total	662.6	349.2	313.4	

SOURCE: Calculated from Statistics Netherlands figures.

growing circular migration within the European Union, as Europeans move within the EU in a "churn" pattern resembling internal migration within federal states such as the United States and Canada, something that EU institutions have long promoted (Maas 2007; 2017).

Immigration by individuals born outside the Netherlands dipped in the middle of the first decade of the twenty-first century (especially 2002–2006) at the same time that emigration of those born in the Netherlands increased. Table 8.4 shows the most important destination countries of these Dutch-born emigrants. The significant "churn" in migration within the European Union is evident, as thousands of Dutch-born individuals both emigrate to and return from other EU member states. The top five destinations of net emigration (emigration minus immigration) are all European, in contrast to postwar emigration overseas. Indeed, net emigration to European destinations now accounts for almost four-fifths of all emigration by persons born in the Netherlands.

Free movement within the EU has always been key to European integration (Maas 2020, 2021a, 2021b), but recent Dutch People's Party for Freedom and Democracy or VVD-led governments have been among the most vocal proponents of restricting intra-EU free movement rights, and have pursued restrictive interpretations of what constitutes "sufficient resources" for economically inactive EU citizens while adding higher income and working hours conditions to qualify for residence rights as a "worker" under EU law (Mantu 2021; Schrauwen 2021).

Citizenship

Within the wide range of citizenship and naturalization policies in Europe, the Netherlands was long situated at the liberal end of the spectrum. For example, a 1998 study of foreigners' rights in France, Germany, and the Netherlands found that the Netherlands had provided foreigners the most rights, because foreigners could vote in local elections and their cultural rights were guaranteed under the minorities policy (Guiraudon 1998, 274). In addition, the Netherlands has had one of the highest naturalization rates among European states.

Table 8.5 shows the percentage of residents who were born abroad and the percentage who have foreign nationality for nine European states in1998, 2003, and 2007. The ratio is inexact because birth abroad does not necessarily mean foreign citizenship—for example a child born abroad of citizen parents usually acquires citizenship automatically through *jus sanguinis*, acquisition by descent. However, the relative ratios are illustrative of the difference in naturalization rates; the Netherlands emerges as having the lowest proportion of foreign-born residents who do not naturalize (conversely, the highest proportion of foreign-born who do naturalize).

In the Netherlands, the 1990s witnessed a debate about whether granting citizenship should be seen as a means of encouraging integration or rather as the statement of its successful conclusion. Political parties on the left tended to promote the former view; those on the right the latter, arguing that naturalization should be seen as the "crowning moment" at which a completely integrated person finally achieved

TABLE 8.5. Percentage of Residents Who Are Foreign Born and Have Foreign Nationality

	1998			2003			2007		
	Foreign Born	*Foreign Nationality*	*Ratio*	*Foreign Born*	*Foreign Nationality*	*Ratio*	*Foreign Born*	*Foreign Nationality*	*Ratio*
Netherlands	**9.6**	**4.2**	**44%**	**10.7**	**4.3**	**40%**	**10.7**	**4.2**	**39%**
Sweden	11.0	5.6	51%	12.0	5.3	44%	13.4	5.7	43%
United Kingdom	7.4	3.8	51%	8.9	4.7	53%	10.2	6.5	64%
Germany	12.2	8.9	73%	12.9	8.9	69%			
France	7.3	5.6	77%	8.1	5.6	69%			
Belgium	10.0	8.7	87%	11.4	8.3	73%	13.0	9.1	70%
Denmark	5.4	4.8	89%	6.3	5.0	79%	6.9	5.5	80%
Switzerland	21.4	19.0	89%	23.1	20	87%	24.9	20.8	84%
Spain	3.2	1.9	59%	8.8	7.2	82%	13.4	11.6	87%

SOURCE: Calculated from OECD figures. Figures for France are for 1999 and 2005; for Germany, 1998 and 2005.

complete legal equality. The right-wing leaders argued that that granting citizenship too easily would cast doubt on the recipient's loyalty, while others argued that naturalization inherently provided a source of loyalty (Groenendijk 2005, 194).

Between 1992 and 1997, the view of the parties of the left held sway: "Nationality is an expression of connection, not of indivisible loyalty. Because that connection can be of many kinds, it is possible for an individual to have connections to more than one country. Nationality should therefore no longer be seen as an exclusive link with a single country; dual nationality not a phenomenon that should automatically be opposed" (Driouichi 2007, 123, my translation). The toleration of dual nationality that resulted from this kind of argument resulted in large-scale naturalizations, peaking at over 80,000 acquisitions of Dutch nationality in 1996 (Figure 8.4).

Subsequently, however, the openness towards dual nationality waned, and policies once again became more restrictionist (Penninx 2005). By 2007, the far-right politician Geert Wilders was proposing that dual citizens should not be cabinet ministers, a jab at two new cabinet members, one Turkish-Dutch and the other Moroccan-Dutch. His proposal was defeated, but the government did propose making it harder for those who naturalize as adults to retain their other nationality, and new laws made it easier to strip individuals of their Dutch citizenship.

Despite the perceived "restrictive turn in Dutch citizenship policy" (Van Oers 2008, 40) the demographic data paints a more nuanced picture. The proportion of the Dutch population with a nationality other than Dutch has been growing while the proportion of the population with only Dutch nationality has declined. The number of individuals resident in the Netherlands holding both Dutch and one or

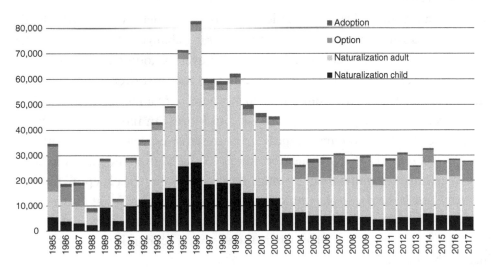

FIGURE 8.4. Acquisition of Dutch Nationality Other than by Birth, 1985–2017

TABLE 8.6. Nationality of Foreigners Resident in the Netherlands (twelve largest nationalities, in thousands)

1998		2008		2020	
Moroccan	135.7	Turkish	93.7	Polish	155.9
Turkish	114.7	Moroccan	74.9	German	79.5
German	53.9	German	62.4	Syrian	79.5
British	39.2	British	40.2	Turkish	77.0
Belgian	24.4	Belgian	26.2	British	47.9
Italian	17.4	Polish	26.2	Italian	43.3
Spanish	16.6	Italian	19.0	Chinese	39.4
Bosnian	14.6	Spanish	16.5	Indian	37.4
Somali	13.6	Chinese	16.2	Bulgarian	36.8
Iraqi	13.0	French	15.1	Belgian	35.9
American	13.0	American	14.5	Moroccan	35.8
Surinamese	11.8	Portuguese	12.9	Spanish	35.6

SOURCE: Calculated from Statistics Netherlands data.

more other nationalities increased from just over 400,000 (2.6 percent of the total Dutch population) in 1995 to just over 1.3 million (7.7 percent of the total population) in 2014, tripling in less than two decades. At the same time, both the number and proportion of residents of the Netherlands who do not hold Dutch nationality declined from 749,061 individuals (4.9 percent of total population) in 1995 to 677,795 individuals (4.1 percent of total population) in 2007, growing again subsequently but not to previous levels; the story here is one of stability.

Table 8.6 shows the twelve largest nationalities of the residents of the Netherlands who do not hold Dutch nationality. The most striking change is the decline in the number of citizens of Morocco and Turkey, from over 250,000 (approximately 37 percent of all foreign residents) in 1998 to around 117,700 (just over 13 percent of all foreign residents) by 2016 and around 112,800 (9.5 percent of all foreign residents) by 2020. This reflects the acquisition by Turkish and Moroccan individuals of Dutch nationality, so that they no longer appear in these statistics. The contrast with the numbers of citizens of other EU member states in the Netherlands is stark: with some fluctuations, the numbers of citizens of other EU countries keep increasing. Noteworthy here is the rise in the number of citizens of Poland resident in the Netherlands, but more generally this reflects an outward migration from eastern and southern EU member states to states where there is more economic opportunity, including the Netherlands.

TABLE 8.7. Dutch Citizens Resident in the Netherlands with Dual Nationality, 2014 (by country of second nationality, top fifteen nationalities, in thousands)

1	Morocco	320.8	24.6%
2	Turkey	312.1	23.9%
3	Germany	61.0	4.7%
4	United Kingdom	45.1	3.5%
5	Belgium	34.0	2.6%
6	Italy	25.0	1.9%
7	Poland	20.4	1.6%
8	France	19.8	1.5%
9	Iran	19.1	1.5%
10	Surinam	17.7	1.4%
11	Bosnia	16.7	1.3%
12	Spain	15.8	1.2%
13	Egypt	15.3	1.2%
14	United States	15.0	1.1%
15	Vietnam	13.3	1.0%
	Other EU	47.7	3.7%
	Other	212.1	16.2%
	Unknown	95.4	7.3%
	Total	1306.3	

That the declining number of Dutch residents who are citizens of Turkey or Morocco but not citizens of the Netherlands is due to naturalization is evident from the data in table 8.7, which disaggregates Dutch citizens resident in the Netherlands who hold dual nationality by the country of their second nationality. Roughly half of all citizens of the Netherlands resident in the Netherlands who held dual nationality in 2014—over 630,000 people—had Turkish or Moroccan nationality. Those who, besides Dutch nationality, also hold an EU nationality account for roughly another quarter of all dual citizens residing in the Netherlands.

The reason the data is from 2014 is that a change to the civil registry in January 2014 stopped new registrations of other nationalities for Dutch citizens. This followed years of debate, including an attempt in 2009 to stop registering dual or additional nationalities for Dutch citizens, which ultimately resulted in the 2013 law that enacted the stop.[15] There had been political commotion following the news that the tax authorities had targeted individuals on the basis of dual citizenship.[16] Later some parties raised doubts about whether it was in fact a good idea to stop registering second nationalities, as subsequent policies intended to deprive citizens of their Dutch citizenship for engaging in terrorism depended on ensuring they have another nationality, to avoid statelessness.[17] In the benefits scandal that caused the fall of the Rutte government in 2021, dual citizens in particular were targeted for extra attention from the tax authorities. As of this writing, an estimated 26,000 parents responsible for 80,000 children were incorrectly accused of fraud and had their child benefit payments revoked, with the forced repayment leading to stress and lost jobs and homes.

Dutch laws regarding dual citizenship remain restrictive, though several parties and interest groups support broadening dual citizenship, and the coalition agreement for the government that served from 2017 to 2021 had promised to "modernize nationality law" by broadening the possibilities for dual citizenship. Despite the agreement, no such law was passed. A different law passed in June 2020 would temporarily allow dual citizenship for Dutch citizens residing in the UK if parliament later determined that their rights were being infringed. As of this writing, that has not yet occurred.

Meanwhile, in February 2021 MPs approved motions to pressure Morocco to interpret its Code de la nationalité to make it easier for Dutch citizens of Moroccan background to renounce Moroccan citizenship, and more broadly for all Dutch citizens to be able to renounce undesired second or other citizenship (only the PVV voted against),[18] to set up a register for Dutch citizens wishing to renounce Moroccan nationality (only VVD and PVV voted against),[19] and to coordinate in implementation of the policy with the governments of Belgium, France, and Germany and report back by summer 2021 (only PVV voted against).[20] This followed a 2020 parliamentary initiative[21] inspired by a 2019 manifesto from Dutch citizens of Moroccan background: "we Dutch citizens with a second nationality, Moroccan, which we have not chosen of our own free will, turn to Dutch society and the Dutch government to help relieve us of the fear and lack of freedom inseparably connected with that second nationality."[22] Salima Belhaj, a Dutch-born D66 Rotterdam city councilor with Moroccan background led a similar initiative in 2008: "we are citizens of the Netherlands and disapprove of any interference by the Moroccan government in our lives."[23] Belhaj became an MP in 2016, and led the 2021 parliamentary motions above.

Immigrant Integration and Dutch Norms and Values

Immigrant integration in the Netherlands is coupled with the question of ethnic minorities. Dutch minorities policy became formalized with a parliamentary report drafted in 1981 and finalized in 1983, when it had become clear that both postcolonial migrants and labor migrants were going to remain in the Netherlands rather than returning to their countries of origin. The report recognized that the Netherlands had become a "de facto immigration country" (Netherlands 1981, 1983). Since then, a multitude of policies have aimed to integrate immigrants and ethnic minorities.

Immigration is an area of policy where the desires of the national government and those of the municipalities and other decentralized authorities tasked with executing national policy do not always coincide. Consider the case of asylum. In the decade between 1992 and 2001, the Netherlands was the third largest recipient of asylum applications in Europe, behind Germany and the United Kingdom. Per capita, this made the Netherlands (along with Switzerland and Sweden) one of the most popular destinations in the world, at 2.27 applications per thousand inhabitants. (By comparison the rate for the United States was 0.45 and Canada's was 0.94.) By the end of the decade, however, asylum policy had become decidedly less welcoming (Van Selm 2000).

At least some of this change can be attributed to a former sociology professor who styled himself as the leading Dutch advocate of the "clash of civilizations" thesis, Pim Fortuyn. In his book *Against the Islamicization of our Culture*, first published in 1997, Fortuyn warned that Muslims living in the Netherlands threatened traditional Dutch values: "Because of their advanced individualization, Dutch people are not aware of their own cultural identity and the rights they have gained: the separation of church and state, the position of women and of homosexuals. Their indifference makes the Dutch an easy and vulnerable prey" (Fortuyn 2002, my translation).

At first dismissed, then vilified, Fortuyn could no longer be ignored after his party won the March 2002 Rotterdam municipal elections. Nine days before the May 2002 national elections, he was assassinated by an ethnically Dutch environmental activist. The 2002 elections were among the most volatile in European history, leading commentators to argue: "after many years of stability and predictability, it is more important than ever to understand the nature of the increasing volatility of the Dutch electorate and the sudden changes in the Dutch political landscape" (van Holsteyn and Irwin 2003). Fortuyn's party won a landslide, going from zero to twenty-six seats in the 150-seat lower house of parliament, becoming the second-largest party. The List Pim Fortuyn (LPF) formed a governing coalition with the Christian democratic CDA and the conservative VVD. Without Fortuyn, however, the party imploded. An LPF deputy minister resigned within hours of being sworn in after it emerged that she had lied about her involvement in the Surinamese militia.[24] After further tensions within the LPF, the entire cabinet resigned within three months and new elections were called. The LPF dropped to 8 seats in the January 2003 elections before disappearing.

Fortuyn's harsh line towards immigration was taken up by others, including Geert Wilders, a former protégé of conservative politician (later European Commissioner) Frits Bolkestein.[25] As VVD leader, Bolkestein had published a book in 1997 on Muslims in the Netherlands that advocated cultural assimilation.[26] Wilders was a municipal councilor for the VVD in 1997 and then a VVD member of parliament from 1998 to 2004, when he left the VVD to campaign against the EU constitution (which was defeated in a June 2005 referendum by a vote of 61.5 percent against, with 63.3 percent turnout) and then formed his own party, Partij voor Vrijheid (PVV), which won 9 seats in the 2006 elections and then grew spectacularly to 24 in the 2010 elections, becoming the third-largest party. The government formed after the 2010 elections was a coalition of the VVD (31 seats) and CDA (21 seats) who, because they lacked a majority of over 75 seats, required the parliamentary support of Wilders' party. This arrangement, whereby the government depended on Wilders' support but did not include ministers from his party was criticized for giving Wilders influence but no responsibility.[27]

The success of anti-immigration politicians had effects on policy. One observer noted that "the supposedly difference-friendly, multicultural Netherlands is currently urging migrants to accept 'Dutch norms and values' in the context of a policy of civic integration that is only an inch (but still an inch!) away from the cultural assimilation that had once been attributed to the French" (Joppke 2007, 2). One example of more stringent immigration policy was a new citizenship exam coupled with the requirement that applicants for a residence permit pass an integration test before admission. The test was required of all applicants with the exception of citizens of Australia, Canada, Japan, Monaco, New Zealand, South Korea, Switzerland, the United States of America, and Vatican City. The United Nations Committee on the Elimination of Racial Discrimination warned the Netherlands that this was discriminatory.

Yet it would be a mistake to portray the harder line that emerged starting in the late 1990s as a seismic shift. There were earlier examples of restrictionist policies and contrasting examples of more open ones. For example, in mid-2007 the government granted amnesty to approximately 28,000 individuals who had been living in the Netherlands without authorization, and many mayors and municipal councils asked organizations working with illegal migrants to forward only those applicants who fulfilled the requirements, thereby tolerating the continued presence of "illegal" residents. Other large-scale efforts include a petition to allow children who had lived at least eight years in the Netherlands to stay, together with their families.[28]

Despite such open tendencies, the Netherlands emerged as one of the most restrictive states in Europe regarding benefits for migrants, with immigrants barred from many benefits for lengthy periods after arrival (Koning 2020). Furthermore, a series of laws on benefits levels coupled with restrictive enforcement practices made it more difficult for non-citizens and mixed status families (where one partner is a non-citizen) to meet residence requirements; and because residence permits are withdrawn retroactive to the moment when the right of residence was lost, prior benefits received may need to be paid back (De Jong and De Hart 2021).

Political Fragmentation and Fractiousness about Migration and Citizenship

The 2021 elections (discussed further below) resulted in a postwar record of seventeen parties entering parliament. Such fragmentation was possible because the Netherlands electoral system applies pure proportional representation with no threshold: only 0.67 percent of the vote suffices for a party to win one of the 150 seats in the lower house. Unlike in other countries, where constituencies or thresholds make it harder for new parties to emerge, this means that new parties can quickly find representation in parliament, including those based on the issue of immigration. The Dutch People's Union (Nederlandse Volks-Unie) won 2.2 percent of the vote in the 1974 municipal elections in The Hague (Their slogans were: "The Hague must stay white and safe" and "Free our city from the plague of Surinamese and Antillians") and 0.4 percent in the 1977 national elections, but this was not enough for a seat (Van Gorp 2012). Hans Janmaat of the anti-immigrant Centrumpartij (Center party slogans included: "Neither left nor right," "Full = full," and "Resist mass immigration to our overpopulated country") was first elected to parliament in 1982 with 0.8 percent of the vote. Despite the party winning 2.6 percent of the vote in the 1984 European Parliament elections (almost enough for a seat) and strong showings in some municipal elections, the party was divided and expelled Janmaat, who formed the slightly more moderate Centrum Democraten (Center Democrats, CD). The two anti-immigrant parties split the vote in 1986, but Janmaat returned to parliament in 1989 with 0.9 percent of the vote. Opinion polls in 1993 placed the CD at 5.5 percent nationally, and the party's result in the 1994 municipal elections was strong, but divisions and scandals within the party kept its score in the 1994 parliamentary elections to 2.4 percent of the vote and three seats. This was the party's zenith, as further scandals, divisions, and convictions for incitement to racial hatred kept the CD to 0.6 percent in the 1998 parliamentary elections, just below the 0.67 percent needed for a seat. As discussed above, the next parliamentary elections, in 2002, resulted in a landslide twenty six seats for the List Pim Fortuyn, but this included a large sympathy vote for Fortuyn's murder nine days previously.

Geert Wilders' twenty four seats (15.5 percent) in the 2010 elections rivaled Fortuyn's result, but the 2010–2012 governing coalition under new VVD prime minister Mark Rutte, which became the government only with PVV support, was unstable. Several elements of the coalition agreement would contravene European Union treaties and legislation if enacted. They would require agreement from some or all other EU member states and, in some cases, the European Parliament, and so were infeasible. Wilders withdrew his support from the coalition in April 2012. During the subsequent election campaign, he attempted to blend Euroskepticism and anti-immigration sentiments, but this strategy did not succeed: in the September 2012 elections, his party lost over one third of its votes, dropping to 10.1 percent of the vote (15 seats) and making its support no longer necessary for the new governing coalition of VVD and PvdA.

This two-party coalition served for its entire term, only the second time in the postwar period that this occurred.[29] But in common with the decline of social democratic and labor parties elsewhere in Europe, the 2017 elections were a disaster for the PvdA: it dropped from 24.8 percent of the votes to only 5.7 percent (from 38 seats to only 9). Meanwhile, Wilders regrew a little bit to 13.1 percent of the votes, and 20 seats, becoming second-largest party as thirteen parties won seats in parliament. Two new parties are noteworthy: Forum for Democracy (FvD), which won two seats, and Denk, which won three seats. Denk (which means "think" in Dutch, and "equal" or "equivalent" in Turkish) was formed in 2015 by Tunahan Kuzu and Selçuk Öztürk, who had been elected as PvdA MPs but left the party over dissatisfaction with the PvdA's integration policy. Denk has been described as the "long arm of Erdogan" for its sympathies with the Turkish president.[30]

FvD was cofounded in 2016 by the then-33-year-old Thierry Baudet, who four years earlier had offered a copy of his PhD dissertation (entitled "The significance of borders: why representative government and the rule of law require Nation States") to French far-right politician Jean-Marie Le Pen and had since become known for his strident views. He called the EU a "cultural Marxist" project out to destroy European culture, supported Hungarian leader Viktor Orbán's moves to close borders and stop immigration, and strongly opposed multiculturalism. Although the FvD won only 1.78 percent of the votes (2 seats) in the 2017 parliamentary elections, Baudet's strident pronouncements against the established parties, the EU, immigration, and feminism, and denying the existence of climate change quickly won the party many converts. FvD vaulted to first place in the March 2019 provincial elections, winning 14.5 percent of the votes, while the SP, Wilders' PVV, D66, CDA, PvdA, and VVD all lost votes. FvD won a total of 86 of the 570 seats in the provincial assemblies, becoming the largest party in the provinces North Holland, South Holland, and Flevoland.

In his victory speech, Baudet underlined the need to protect the "boreal world," understood as a euphemism for whiteness.[31]

Looked at from a comparative perspective, the "more 'acceptable' Dutch far-right parties" since the year 2000 "changed the relationship between the mainstream right and the far right" as, in the six elections contested by either the LPF or PVV between 2002 and 2017, those parties were included twice (2002 in cabinet and 2010 with support) while being excluded because of concerns about coalition stability in 2003 and because the mainstream right and far right did not have enough seats for a majority in 2006, 2012, and 2017 (Twist 2019, 101).

In the May 2019 European Parliament elections, FvD became the fourth largest party with 11 percent of the votes (3 seats), while Wilders' PVV sank from 13.3 percent of the votes (4 seats) to only 3.5 percent and no seats. The Eurosceptic Socialist party (SP) also dropped to zero seats, from two—possibly because the PvD had taken over the anti-immigration, Eurosceptic, and anti-establishment ground. The mainstream and Europhile parties did quite well: PvdA doubled its votes share to over 19 percent (6 seats), with the VVD and CDA each at 4 seats, all ahead of the FvD, with GreenLeft (GL) at three seats and D66 at two.[32]

The 2017–2021 government was a four-party coalition led by Mark Rutte's VVD with CDA, D66, and CU. Issues relating to immigration and citizenship continue to play a significant role in the political debates. For example, in August 2019 the Netherlands introduced a policy that people wearing face coverings would be denied public services or be fined. The policy was understood to target women wearing the full-face burka, following such bans in Denmark, Belgium, France, and elsewhere, although the transport companies immediately said they would not enforce the policy, rendering it toothless. Yet it would be a mistake to assume that such developments are due entirely to anti-immigration sentiment on the political right: Lucassen and Lucassen (2015, 25) have argued that feelings of discomfort towards immigration and Islam also have deep roots in the Dutch political left and that various leaders across the political spectrum share a "cultural nonconformist stance and a communitarian conception of the people"—a description that could also be compared to the victories in 2019 of social democratic parties in Denmark and Sweden combining rigorous integration policies with promises to protect the native welfare state.

Table 8.8 shows the parties that have won seats in parliament since 1982. The Christian democratic CDA and social democratic PvdA (Labor) together used to dominate Dutch politics, but the PvdA shared the decline of many other European social democratic parties and the CDA suffered from the fragmentation of the political landscape. The March 2021 national elections resulted in further fragmentation of the political landscape, as seventeen parties entered parliament. VVD gained a

TABLE 8.8. Parties Winning Seats in Parliament

	1982	1986	1989	1994	1998	2002	2003	2006	2010	2012	2017	2021
VVD	36	27	22	31	38	24	28	22	31	41	33	34
D66	6	9	12	24	14	7	6	3	10	12	19	24
PVV								9	24	15	20	17
CDA	45	54	54	34	29	43	44	41	21	13	19	15
SP				2	5	9	9	25	15	15	14	9
PvdA	47	52	49	37	45	23	42	33	30	38	9	9
GL	9	3	6	5	11	10	8	7	10	4	14	8
FvD											2	8
PvdD								2	2	2	5	6
CU	3	2	3	5	5	4	3	6	5	5	5	5
Volt												3
JA21												3
SGP	3	3	3	2	3	2	2	2	2	3	3	3
Denk											3	3
50plus										2	4	1
BBB												1
Bij1												1
Lijst Pim Fortuyn						26	8					
LN						2						
AOV/Unie55+				7								
CD			1	3								
CP	1											

VVD: conservative center-right   D66: centrist liberal
PVV: right-wing populist   CDA: Christian democratic
SP: socialist   PvdA: social democratic labor
GL: Green left   FvD: right-wing nationalist
PvdD: leftist animal rights   CU: centrist Christian
Volt: progressive European   JA21: right-wing conservative
SGP: Christian right   Denk: center-left identity
50plus: pensioners   BBB: farmers
Bij1: left egalitarian
Historical:
LPF: right-wing populist   LN: populist direct democracy
AOV/Unie55+: pensioners   CD: right-wing nationalist
CP: right-wing nationalist

seat while D66 matched its 1994 result and the CDA continued its slide. Wilders' PVV dropped from twenty seats to seventeen, but the FvD rose to eight seats despite internal turmoil and scandals about antisemitic, fascist, and homophobic statements, possibly helped by strident anti-vaccine and anti-lockdown rhetoric. A third far-right party, JA21 (founded by MPs who had left FvD over the turmoil), also entered parliament, with three seats. JA21 also included breakaway FvD Senators, members of the European Parliament, and members of provincial parliaments. On the left, the Socialists and GreenLeft lost seats, the PvdA stalled rather than regrowing, the leftist animal rights party PvdD continued to grow, and Denk maintained its three seats.

Besides JA21, three other new parties entered parliament: the progressive pan-European Volt, the farmer-oriented BBB, and Biji (*bijeen* means "together"), headed by the Suriname-born Black activist and former television presenter Sylvana Simons, who had earlier joined and then left Denk in 2016, won 0.3 percent of the vote in the 2017 elections, and in 2018 had won a seat on Amsterdam city council. A record number of 28 MPs had a migration background,[33] though this number could change as MPs might join cabinet and be replaced. The VVD looked set to stay in government together with D66 and two or more additional parties necessary to reach a majority in the lower house, although the new parliament voted to censure outgoing prime minister Rutte (VVD) for lack of honesty during the coalition negotiations. As of this writing, it is unclear whether Rutte will survive the lack of trust that other parties have in his leadership.

From Consensus to Fractiousness in Dutch Migration and Citizenship Policies

By way of conclusion, the case of the Netherlands offers a corrective to the gap hypothesis. The hypothesis holds that the gap between the goals of national immigration policies and the actual policy outcomes is increasing, thereby provoking greater public hostility toward immigrants in general and putting pressure on political parties and government officials to adopt more restrictive policies. Yet in order for the gap hypothesis to be testable the goals of national immigration policy must first be clear. Such clarity is lacking in the Netherlands, where both public opinion and the government's approach are fractious and volatile. At the same time, the declining relative net immigration from traditional source countries and their replacement with new source countries such as Poland, coupled with the increasing emigration of Dutch-born citizens mostly within the European Union, changes the picture of both the immigrant and the emigrant. When a growing share of both "immigration" and "emigration" is simply mobility within the EU, which is both difficult to regulate (because of EU citizenship) and largely accepted politically (despite periodic grumblings about eastern Europeans taking jobs), it becomes unclear what the goals of Dutch immigration policy should be. Looking comparatively at other European cases suggests that polarization about the goals of migration and citizenship policy are no longer restricted to the Netherlands, which suggests a process of "Dutchification" of other European countries. "As long as immigration continues to be a concern for the public, far-right parties will likely remain a fixture of Western European politics," concludes an analysis comparing the Netherlands with other cases and suggesting that the mainstream right will want to form a government with the far right when the latter is useful to them, as they would with any other party (Twist 2019 149, 144). Across the continent, politics lurch from *wir schaffen das* to draconian border controls, from welcoming certain migrants to demonizing others. And of course, the COVID-19 pandemic introduces a new element of uncertainty.

Notes

1. The concept of the migration state is drawn from James Hollifield (2004), who uses it to mean a situation where regulation of international migration is as important as providing for the security of the state and the economic wellbeing of the citizenry. Grateful thanks to James Hollifield, Leo Lucassen, and Michael Sharpe, participants at the book workshop held at the Collège de France in 2019, and also to Amanda Sears for assistance with the tables and figures.

2. Amsterdam's population ballooned from 13,500 in 1514 to 104,900 in 1622 and 200,000 in 1675; Leiden's from 14,300 in 1514 to 44,800 in 1622 and 65,000 in 1675. In 1622, immigrants constituted 33 percent of the population of Amsterdam and Dordrecht, 38 percent of Gouda's, 40 percent of Rotterdam's, 51 percent of Haarlem's, 63 percent of Middelburg's, and 67 percent of Leiden's.

3. From the press release at https://www.knaw.nl/nl/actueel/nieuws/grootste-migratiewebsite-van-nederland-gelanceerd for the website https://vijfeeuwenmigratie.nl/.

4. There is significant variation in the annual numbers in the 1995–2017 period, from a low of 9,794 net emigrants in 1998 to a high of 35,821 net emigrants in 2006.

5. Standard Eurobarometer 92 (fall 2019). In the subsequent survey (Eurobarometer 93), done in summer 2020 during the pandemic, the economic situation, health, and unemployment vaulted to the top of Europeans' responses. Dutch respondents listed health (47 percent), the environment and climate change (35 percent), the economic situation (34 percent), housing (17 percent), and unemployment (15 percent) ahead of immigration (11 percent). Only in 2016, during the height of the Syrian refugee crisis, did Dutch respondents mention immigration as the top issue facing the Netherlands, a view that was widely shared across Europe.

6. Special Eurobarometer 469 (2018), question A6.5. Dutch respondents were among the most welcoming on most measures.

7. Special Eurobarometer 469 (2018), questions A2, A8T, A9T.

8. "Een deel van ons volk moet het aandurven zoals in vroeger eeuwen zijn toekomst te zoeken in grotere gebieden dan eigen land."

9. "Nederlandse emigranten in Australië," https://www.nationaalarchief.nl/onderzoeken/zoekhulpen/nederlandse-emigranten-in-australie.

10. Portugal controlled some of the islands of Indonesia in the fifteenth century, when Islam had only recently been introduced. Portuguese missionaries quickly set about to Christianize the population. When Spain took control, Portuguese missionaries were replaced by Spanish missionaries, including Francis Xavier, who later co-founded the Jesuits.

11. In the 1975 train hijacking, in the northern province of Drenthe, the Moluccan hijackers killed three hostages, shooting one in full view of the police and the press. There was a simultaneous hostage-taking at the Indonesian consulate in Amsterdam, which ended when the train hijackers surrendered after two weeks. The 1977 train hijacking on the Drenthe-Groningen border was simultaneous with the hostage-taking of 105 students and their five teachers at a primary school in Drenthe. Lasting twenty days, the train hijacking resulted in the deaths of two hostages and six hijackers. The hostage-takers at the school (who had earlier released the children, keeping only the teachers) surrendered after hearing about the military action at the train. In 1978 there was another hostage-taking at the Drenthe provincial hall; the hostage-takers executed one hostage in front of a window, then threw his body out. Dutch marines raided the building the next day, freeing the hostages.

12. CIA World Factbook, available at https://www.cia.gov/library/publications/the-world-factbook/geos/ns.html (accessed June 10, 2019).

13. In this way, Dutch citizenship can be compared to citizenship in federal states, where "citizenship" in a subnational jurisdiction does not preclude free movement rights to and from other subnational jurisdictions, such as California to New York, Quebec to Ontario, or England to Scotland. See Maas 2013b, 2013c.

14. "De makamba moet inburgeren: 'Het mag hier dan warm zijn, maar dan ga je niet driekwart naakt over straat,'" *De Volkskrant*, August 12, 2019, referring to the idea that white Dutch immigrants must integrate into local Dutch Caribbean culture.

15. https://www.trouw.nl/nieuws/stop-automatische-registratie-tweede-nationaliteit~bff55ebc/.

16. https://www.volkskrant.nl/columns-opinie/discrimineren-mag-niet-maar-registratie-van-de-dubbele-nationaliteit-afschaffen~b66a7c11/.

17. https://www.ewmagazine.nl/nederland/achtergrond/2017/09/registratie-dubbele-nationaliteiten-alles-is-weg-538471/.

18. https://www.tweedekamer.nl/kamerstukken/detail?id=2021Z02312&did=2021D05076.

19. https://www.tweedekamer.nl/kamerstukken/detail?id=2021Z02313&did=2021D05077.

20. https://www.tweedekamer.nl/kamerstukken/detail?id=2021Z02315&did=2021D05079.

21. https://www.parlementairemonitor.nl/9353000/1/j9vvij5epmj1ey0/vl91na1cfjwi.

22. My translation from https://debalie.nl/artikel/manifest-voor-keuzevrijheid-in-nationaliteit/.

23. My translation from https://www.volkskrant.nl/nieuws-achtergrond/nederlandse-burgers-geen-onderdanen-marokko~b74af6bf/.

24. Philomena Bijlhout was elected LPF member of parliament in the May 2002 elections, then resigned to become deputy minister of emancipation and family affairs in the cabinet

sworn in on June 22, 2002. She resigned the same day when a TV station aired photos of her in the militia uniform of Surinamese military leader Dési Bouterse. The photos were taken in 1983, after the December 1982 murders (in which fifteen prominent opponents of Bouterse's military regime, mostly journalists and lawyers, were shot dead); Bijlhout had earlier claimed she left the militia in 1981. She was replaced by LPF member Khee Liang Phoa.

25. Interestingly both Bolkestein's and Wilders's mothers were of Indo (mixed European and indigenous Indonesian) ancestry, as is the mother of Eddie and Alex van Halen (of the band Van Halen), who emigrated from the Netherlands to California with their parents in 1962, part of the postwar emigration discussed earlier.

26. The VVD grew from thirty-one seats in 1994 elections to thirty-eight seats in the May 1998 elections, but Bolkestein stepped down as party leader; he was European commissioner for internal market from 1999 to 2004. Bolkestein lamented in 2010 that Wilders had become "completely radicalized."

27. Bolkestein, interviewed in *De Volkskrant*, "Rutte is goud, Wilders is strovuur," March 5, 2011.

28. The petition, submitted to parliament in September 2012, was signed by 130,000 people and supported by 135 of the country's 415 municipal councils. It reflected a draft law proposed by PvdA, CU, SP, GL, D66, and PvDD.

29. The other was the PvdA-VVD-D66 coalition under PvdA prime minister Wim Kok, which served from 1994 to 1998; that same coalition continued in office after the 1998 elections, serving until twenty-nine days before the scheduled 2002 elections. The cabinet resigned to take responsibility for the July 1995 murder of over 8,000 Bosnian men and boys by troops led by Bosnian-Serbian general Ratko Mladi in the town of Srebrenica, which was under the protection of a "Dutchbat" of the United Nations Protection Force (UNPROFOR).

30. The phrase is by VVD parliamentary leader (later foreign minister) Halbe Zijlstra after Kuzu spoke at a September 2016 rally in Rotterdam of the Turkish AKP. Denk's proposal to renew diplomatic links with Turkey (which had been cut after the 2016 crackdown by Erdogan) was rejected in April 2017, several weeks after Öztürk had accused Dutch Socialist MP Sadet Karabulut of being a PKK sympathizer. In November 2017 Denk was the only party to vote against a motion to pressure Turkey to release Taner Kılıç, a human rights activist and chair of Amnesty International Turkey; in February 2018 Denk was the only party to vote against recognizing the Armenian genocide; and in June 2018 Denk was the only party to vote against a motion asking Turkey to release Turkish MPs opposed to Erdogan.

31. "Like all the other countries in our boreal world we are being destroyed by the very people who are supposed to protect us. We are being undermined by our universities, our journalists. By people who get art subsidies and who design our buildings." https://www.theguardian.com/commentisfree/2019/apr/03/thierry-baudet-dutch-rightwing-populism.

32. The Christian Union / SGP stayed at two seats, the animal rights party stayed at one, and the retirees' party 50PLUS gained a seat. Turnout increased to just under 42 percent, from 37.3 percent at the previous elections.

33. https://www.stemdivers.nl/selectie/gekozen/?filter_afkomst=meer-dan-nederlands&query_type_afkomst=or.

References

Algemene Geschiedenis Der Nederlanden. 1977. Haarlem: Fibula-Van Dishoeck.

Beets, Gijs, Evert van Imhoff, and Corina Huisman. 2003. "Demografie van de Indische Nederlanders, 1930–2001." In *Bevolkingstrends, 1e kwartaal 2003*, Centraal Bureau voor de Statistiek.

Bovens, M., M. Bokhorst, J. Jennissen and G. Engbersen. 2016. *Migratie en Classificatie: Naar een Meervoudig Migratie-idioom.* The Hague: Wetenschappelijke Raad voor het Regeringsbeleid.

De Jong, Judith, and Betty de Hart. 2021. "Divided Families and Devalued Citizens: Money Matters in Mixed-status Families in the Netherlands." In *Money Matters in Migration*, edited by De Lange, Tesseltje, Willem Maas, and Annette Schrauwen, 297–316. Cambridge: Cambridge University Press.

Driouichi, Fouzia. 2007. *De casus Inburgering en Nationaliteitswetgeving: Iconen van Nationale Identiteit: Een Juridische Analyse.* Amsterdam: Wetenschappelijke Raad voor het Regeringsbeleid.

Elich, J. H. 1987. *Aan De Ene Kant, Aan De Andere Kant: De Emigratie Van Nederlanders Naar Australië 1946–1986.* Delft: Eburon.Elich, J. H. 1983. *Emigreren.* 1st ed. Utrecht: Spectrum.

Emmer, Piet. 2007. "Postkoloniale Migratie: Stop de Antillianen." *NRC Handelsblad.* http://www.nrc.nl/nieuwsthema/antillen/article1890483.ece/Postkoloniale_migratie_Stop_de_Antillianen.

Entzinger, Han. 2004. "Commentary." In *Controlling Immigration: A Global Perspective*, 289–292. Stanford, CA: Stanford University Press.

Eurobarometer. 2019. https://data.europa.eu/data/datasets/s2255_92_3_std92_eng?locale=en.

Eurobarometer. 2020. https://europa.eu/eurobarometer/surveys/detail/2262.

Fortuyn, Pim. 2002. *De Islamisering van Onze Cultuur: Nederlandse Identiteit als Fundament.* Uithoorn: Karakter.

Groenendijk, Cees A. 2005. "Het Desintegratiebeleid van de Kabinetten Balkenende." *Migrantenrecht.*

Guiraudon, Virginie. 1998. "Citizenship Rights for Non-Citizens: France, Germany, and The Netherlands." In *Challenge to the Nation-State: Immigration in Western Europe and the United States*, edited by Christian Joppke, 272–319. Oxford: Oxford University Press.

Hermans, Willem Frederik. 1951. *Ik heb Altijd Gelijk.* Amsterdam: Van Oorschot.

Hollifield, James F. 2004. "The Emerging Migration State." *International Migration Review* 38, 3: 885–912.

Joppke, Christian. 2007. "Beyond National Models: Civic Integration Policies for Immigrants in Western Europe." *West European Politics* 30, no. 1: 1–22.

Koning, Edward A. 2020. *Immigration and the Politics of Welfare Exclusion.* Toronto: University of Toronto Press.

Lucassen, Jan, and Rinus Penninx. 1997. *Newcomers: Immigrants and Their Descendants in the Netherlands 1550–1995.* Amsterdam: Het Spinhuis.

Lucassen, Leo, and Jan Lucassen. 2015. "The Strange Death of Dutch Tolerance: The Timing and Nature of the Pessimist Turn in the Dutch Migration Debate." *The Journal of Modern History* 87: 1–30.

Maas, Willem. 2007. *Creating European Citizens*. Lanham: Rowman & Littlefield.

Maas, Willem. 2009. "Unrespected, Unequal, Hollow?: Contingent Citizenship and Reversible Rights in the European Union." *Columbia Journal of European Law* 15, 2: 265–280.

Maas, Willem. 2010. "Citizenship and Immigrant Integration in the Netherlands." In *Migrants and Minorities: The European Response*, edited by Adam Luedtke, 226–244. Newcastle upon Tyne: Cambridge Scholars.

Maas, Willem. 2013a. "Immigrant Integration, Gender, and Citizenship in the Dutch Republic." *Politics, Groups, and Identities* 1, 3: 390–401.

Maas, Willem. 2013b. "Varieties of Multilevel Citizenship," In *Multilevel Citizenship*, edited by W. Maas, 1–21. Philadelphia: University of Pennsylvania Press.

Maas, Willem. 2013c. "Equality and the Free Movement of People: Citizenship and Internal Migration," In *Democratic Citizenship and the Free Movement of People*, edited by Willem Maas, 9–30. Leiden/Boston: Martinus Nijhoff.

Maas, Willem. 2017. "Boundaries of Political Community in Europe, the US, and Canada." *Journal of European Integration*, 39, 5: 575–590.

Maas, Willem. 2020. "Citizenship of the European Union." *Oxford Research Encyclopedia of Politics*. https://doi.org/10.1093/acrefore/9780190228637.013.1096

Maas, Willem. 2021a. "Citizenship, refugees and migration in the European Union." In *Handbook of Citizenship and Migration*, edited by Marco Giugni and Maria Grasso, 211–223. Cheltenham: Edward Elgar.

Maas, Willem. 2021b. "European Citizenship during the Brexit Process," *International Studies* 58, no. 2: 168–183.

Mantu, Sandra. 2021. "Women as EU citizens: Caught between Work, (Sufficient) Resources, and the Market." In *Money Matters in Migration*, edited by De Lange, Tessletje, Willem Maas, and Annette Schrauwen, 188–204. Cambridge: Cambridge University Press.

Muus, Philip. 2004. "The Netherlands: A Pragmatic Approach." In *Controlling Immigration: A Global Perspective*, 263–288. Stanford, CA: Stanford University Press.

Netherlands. 1981. "Ontwerp-minderhedennota." Nederland. Ministerie van Binnenlandse Zaken.

Netherlands. 1983. "Minderhedennota." Organisatie: Historisch Centrum Overijssel (HCO).

The Netherlands-Australia Migration Agreement. 1951."Nederlandse emigranten in Australië." https://www.nationaalarchief.nl/onderzoeken/zoekhulpen/nederlandse-emigranten-in-australie

Nicolaas, J. M. M., and A. H. Sprangers. 2007. "Buitenlandse Migratie in Nederland, 1795–2006. De Invloed op de Bevolkingssamenstelling." In *KNAW*, 19–50. The Hague.

Penninx, Rinus. 2005. "Dutch Integration Policies after the Van Gogh Murder." In *Expert Panel on Social Integration of Immigrants*. Ottawa: House of Commons.

Pool, Cathelijne. 2011. *Migratie van Polen naar Nederland in een tijd van Versoepeling van Migratieregels*. The Hague: Boom Juridische uitgevers.

Schrauwen, Annette. 2021. "Pushing Out the Poor: Unstable Income and Termination of Residence." In *Money Matters in Migration*, edited by De Lange, Tessltje, Willem Maas, and Annette Schrauwen, 112–129. Cambridge: Cambridge University Press.

Sharpe, Michael O. 2014. *Postcolonial Citizens and Ethnic Migration: The Netherlands and Japan in the Age of Globalization*. New York: Palgrave.

Tjon Sie Fat, Paul B. 2009. *Chinese New Migrants in Suriname: The Inevitability of Ethnic Performing*. Amsterdam: Amsterdam University Press.

Twist, Kimberly A. 2019. *Partnering With Extremists: Coalitions between Mainstream and Far-Right Parties in Western Europe*. Ann Arbor: Michigan University Press.

Van Amersfoort, Hans. 1999. "Immigration Control and Minority Policy: The Case of the Netherlands." In Brochmann, Grete and Tomas Hammar, *Mechanisms of Immigration Control. A Comparative Analysis of European Regulation Practices*, 135–168. Oxford: Berg.

Van Gorp, Johannes. 2012. "Party System Change in the Netherlands: Intra-Party Cohesion, Discourse, and the Socio-Cultural Cleavage." PhD dissertation, Boston University.

Van Holsteyn, Joop J.M., and Galen A. Irwin. 2003. "Never a Dull Moment: Pim Fortuyn and the Dutch Parliamentary Election of 2002." *West European Politics* 26, 2: 41–67.

Van Oers, Ricky. 2008. "From Liberal to Restrictive Citizenship Policies: The Case of the Netherlands." *International Journal on Multicultural Societies* 10, 1: 40–59.

Van Selm, Joanne. 2000. "Asylum in the Netherlands: A Hazy Shade of Purple." *Journal of Refugee Studies* 13, 1: 74–90.

COMMENTARY

Mind the Gap

Leo Lucassen

The Rise of Integration Pessimism in Postwar Netherlands

In his insightful overview of migration and policies, Willem Maas argues that the gap hypothesis for the Netherlands does not work because it wrongly assumes that there is a clear agreement on who to admit and what integration entails. In my contribution I would like to point at another "gap" that has developed in the last three decades, which has received much less attention in scholarship on migration and integration. This concerns the opposition between alarmist, and at times apocalyptic, politicians throughout the political spectrum and large parts of the media, on the one hand, and, on the other hand, what is happening on the ground. And the facts are—as Maas shows—that the integration of children whose parents settled in the Netherlands as low-educated migrants in the 1970s and 1980s (especially from Turkey and Morocco) is advancing quite well. Especially when considering the unfortunate timing of their immigration, during the recession of the 1980s and the rise of Islamophobia and labor market discrimination since the 1990s. In this contribution I will first explain the causes and effects of integration pessimism, and then proceed to answer the question of whether, in the end, there really is such a discrepancy between policy aims and outcomes. Or in other words whether "multiculturalism" has failed, as a number of pessimistic journalists in various European countries claim.[1]

The End of History and the Clash of Civilizations

In his chapter, Willem Maas shows that the large-scale settlement of former guest workers and their family members, which peaked around 1980, overlapped with the start of a long recession. Due to the unintended combination of social and legal "embedded rights" and restrictive immigration policies, labor migrants whose freedom of movement was severely restricted, Turks and Moroccans (but not Italians), decided to remain and use their right to family reunification. Because they realized that once they would return to their homeland, they would find the door closed. Initially most of them were still employed, but soon the closure and displacement of industries (like shipbuilding and the textile industry) to Asia, resulted in mass unemployment. In hindsight we can conclude that the starting point of their integration process was therefore very badly timed. Moreover, most of them could only find affordable housing in the worst neighborhoods of the major cities, like Amsterdam, Rotterdam, The Hague, and Utrecht. Finally, we should realize that these (former) guest workers were selected on the grounds of low human capital and initially still harbored hopes to return to their country of birth, which made it extra difficult for them and their families to find their place in the new society.

Remarkably, the public opinion concerning immigration in the 1970s and 1980s was moderately optimistic. Most politicians and the media were wary of xenophobia and stressed the importance of tolerance, multiculturality, and anti-discrimination. Although the social problems in the urban centers were evident, especially for the migrants themselves, the dominant idea was that the greatest danger was stigmatization and racism. New anti-immigration parties therefore were not very successful and were completely marginalized, both in parliament and in the media. This can be explained by what we have termed the "ethical revolution", which developed in the 1960s as part of the broader cultural revolution, which arose from the realization of the atrocities of the Nazi regime and the Holocaust in particular. As in other countries this was a belated response which was triggered by television series on the Second World War and the persecution of Jews in particular, which bloomed in the 1960s. This awareness of the ultimate consequences of stigmatization overlapped with a growing conviction that equality (in all domains) should be the guiding principle of politics and policies in general, including between citizens and aliens.[2]

In the course of the 1980s, however, this ethical revolution began to lose steam and would almost entirely evaporate from the 1990s onwards. The main reason for this was another key element of the cultural revolution in the Netherlands, which was the dramatic and radical deconfessionalization which led to a widespread secularization and put the ax to the roots of the pillarized nature of Dutch society.[3] This resentment to organized religion in general was especially strong among the left and deeply influenced the generation of baby boomers, many of whom turned their back on religion and became outspoken atheists. It should therefore not come as a surprise that the rise of institutionalized forms of Islam among former guest workers from Morocco and Turkey was considered as worrisome, especially among left wing politicians and journalists. This became evident in 1989 when Dutch Muslims, inspired by their coreligionists in Iran and Pakistan, took to the streets to demand that Rushdie's book *The Satanic Verses* be banned, while the Dutch publisher of the translation received death threats.

For many, not in the least on the left, this "coming out" of Dutch Muslims was regarded as a frontal attack on everything the cultural revolution of the 1960s represented: separation of church and state, freedom of speech, and—somewhat remotely—gender equality. It should therefore not come as a surprise that the first very negative reactions came from high profiled left-wing journalists and writers, who pictured "Islam" and "the Muslims" as highly problematic and as a backward religion, unfitting in the modern secularized, democratic, and open-minded Dutch society. This "left-wing moment" however was soon eclipsed by the right, when the leader of the liberal party (VVD), Frits Bolkestein, introduced the Huntingtonian *Clash of Civilizations* framework, in direct opposition to Fukuyama's *End of History* (1992) perspective.[4] This successful importation of an American ideological framework in the dying days of global communism was a major game changer in Dutch society and opened a window to criticize immigration and integration, focused on Muslims, with cultural and political arguments which appealed to both the right and the left.

A second crucial step was the unilateral decision by Bolkestein in the run-up to the elections in the Spring of 1994 to make migration an electoral theme, although leaders of the major political parties had agreed not to do this, bearing in mind the danger of stigmatization. The result was that immigration as a major issue was ranked significantly higher within a few weeks. And thus, the "ethical revolution" lost steam and was gradually replaced by a much more pessimistic mood in which "Islam" became the major stumbling stone. This shifted into higher gear when Pim Fortuyn, a former member of the social democratic party and openly gay, started his own right-wing political movement, with the dangers of migration, multiculturalism, and Islam as major themes. Although heavily criticized and accused of extreme right sympathies by left-wing politicians, his mix of progressive and conservative positions gave him much more credibility and made him acceptable also for parts of the left. After his success in the municipal elections of Rotterdam, where his party became the largest in March 2002, he was assassinated by an animal rights activist in May just before the national elections, where his party gained 17 percent of the votes.

This electoral potential was valued by a former member of the Liberal Party, and one-time Bolkestein protégé, Geert Wilders, who started his own political party in 2004 and ever since has followed a populist racist and extremely Islamophobic agenda, calling for the closure of mosques, the seizure of Korans, even those in private homes, and the closing of borders to "non western" immigrants, especially refugees.

How much the public debate on migration and multiculturalism had changed since the 1990s was shown by the enormous impact of a newspaper article entitled "The Multicultural Drama," by Paul Scheffer, member of the Labour party.[5] In this essay he portrayed the integration of migrants from Islamic countries as a major problem and Islam as a serious threat to the core values of an open society. Moreover, he accused the political elites of refusing to set clear integration goals and neglecting the importance of the Dutch national identity. This mix of Huntingtonian and welfare state chauvinism, with the Dutch workers portrayed as being under threat,[6] became very dominant throughout the political spectrum and was further deepened by the murder of Theo van Gogh in November 2004 by a radicalized Dutch born Islamist, of Moroccan background. Van Gogh had directed the movie "Submission: Part 1," on the misogynic treatment of women in Islamic countries (written by Hirsi Ali).[7]

Another important cause of the turn to integration pessimism were the media, where journalists, especially those from left-wing newspapers and journals, blamed themselves for having supported, for much too long the in their eyes, suffocating "political correctness" which made it impossible to discuss the real problems with migration and integration.

This "Pim Fortuyn Trauma" had two effects. First of all, it led to a highly critical attitude and the reproduction of the anti-Islam frame by virtually all news media. The dominating idea was that politicians and journalists had ignored integration problems for far too long and naively pushed for a multiculturalist model that clashed with the core values of Dutch society. In reality, however, most civil servants and politicians who were responsible for the "integration while retaining its own identity", were well aware of the big problems that the badly timed settlement of uneducated labor migrants posed, and which moreover had coincided with the large-scale immigration from the former Dutch colony of Suriname in the mid-1970s. The bulk of the state budget that went into integration policies was therefore spent on the "hard" domains such as education, housing, and the labor market, and much less on typical multicultural/identity issues, such as subsidies to migrant associations and multicultural policies.[8] Furthermore, politicians, not in the least those from the Labour party, had been quite critical of immigration and integration from the end of the 1980s. A good example is the minister of Internal Affairs, Ien Dales (Labour), who in 1991 called for immigration restrictions to avoid the existing stock of migrants continually being replenished by newcomers, which would make integration like mopping with the tap open.[9] Since the 1990s several high profiled members of the Labour party would join the integration-pessimist choir, often with essentialist notions of immigrants cultural and religious characteristics. What lowered the bar and had a bridging effect for progressives, and here the Netherlands diverges in important respects from the United States,[10] constituted the idea that migrants from Islamic countries threatened the emancipation and equality of the LGBTQ community and women.

The second effect of the "Fortuyn trauma" was that most Dutch media, who blamed themselves for not having recognized the electoral potential for right-wing populist parties, shifted to the other extreme and gave any new right-wing populist contender a wide platform to express their ideas. The result being that they failed to critically scrutinize—and recognize—their often-inflammatory rhetoric and outright racist and discriminatory proposals. This in contrast to French speaking Belgium and Luxemburg, where media (and mainstream political parties) provided little space for such politicians and where they imposed an effective cordon sanitaire.

In the Netherlands—at least until the national elections in March 2021—most media are still imprisoned by this idea, afraid to miss a next new kid on the block. Although the public opinion about migration seems rather immune to such populist fear mongering,[11] the problematization and stigmatization of immigrants and their offspring—especially those from Islamic countries—has real consequences and has led to institutional discrimination in various domains like the housing and labor market.[12] Furthermore the positions on migration and integration have become more polarized. Together with the reproduction of the populist integration-pessimist frame by mainstream political parties this has created a public sphere that facilitates the national visibility of such parties and partly legitimizes their ideas.[13]

This development is well illustrated with the appearance of Thiery Baudet and his "Forum for Democracy" party in 2017 that explicitly strives for a "dominant white Europe". Building on fear of Islamist terrorism, the flow of refugees and buttressed by white supremacist persuasions integration-pessimism has radicalized. Especially by the spreading of various conspiracy theories about the deliberate "replacement" of the Dutch and European population by Baudet and his inner circle. This racist enemy image, rooted in a "clash of civilization" discourse, has more recently been propagated by extreme right ideologues and politicians like Jean Marie le Pen,

Renaud Camus, and Jared Taylor. These conspiracy theories have clear antisemitic elements, with George Soros as the evil genius behind the scenes who would deliberately scheme to send massive streams of asylum seekers to Europe, with the aim to destabilize societies and "replace" their native populations. These ideas can be found in Wilders' Party for Freedom.

As we saw above, the interesting paradox is that these apocalyptic racist frames have not resulted in a more negative opinion on immigration in the last decades, showing that integration-pessimism has its limits. Surveys even show, as Maas rightly argues, that despite the pessimist mood in the public debate, an increasing share of the population has a (slightly) more positive opinion. What has changed since the beginning of the century, is that populist parties have become more successful in mobilizing the anti-immigrant vote.

This is in tune with the actual trends and developments of integration and migration, which are a reason for optimism. Despite the unfortunate timing of the immigration of former guest workers at the end of the 1970s and stubborn patterns of institutional racism in the labor market and beyond,[14] differences between native Dutch and the descendants of unskilled labor migrants pertaining to educational levels, criminality, and labor market participation show a constant decrease over time. As the yearly "integration monitors" by Statistics Netherlands (CBS) and The Netherlands Institute for Social Research (SCP) show, this is even more the case for children of the hundreds of thousands of refugees who arrived in the 1990s, the bulk coming from the Middle East and the Horn of Africa. Part of this group, especially those from Iran, even outperform their native Dutch peers. There remain worries about part of the second generation that is attracted to Salafist orthodox beliefs, but so far this has led to barely any of the violent radicalization or terrorism, witnessed (from a very small minority) in France and Belgium.

Migration Policies and Their Effect

Having shown the gap between the pessimist public debate, public opinion, and the integration facts on the ground, I now turn to the real gap hypothesis and answer the question, also central in Willem Maas' chapter, whether we can speak of a gap between policy aims and outcomes in the Netherlands in the last half a century. Although Maas is right to point at the fact that there have been many, and sometimes contradictory, migration policies, I would argue that at a macro level the gap is much smaller than often assumed.

This has especially been the case since the 1980s. Hollifield's "embedded rights" concept does a good job in explaining the unintended and unforeseen settlement of former guest workers and their families as discussed above. This is also true for post-colonial migrations from Indonesia and Suriname, who successfully claimed citizenship on the basis of a joined imperial legacy.[15] Since the 1990s, however, immigration is more and more in line with policy aims and the legal frameworks that regulate and enable immigration. In the remainder of this commentary, I will illustrate this by looking briefly at the four most important categories of migrants:

1: *Non-EU labor (and self-employed) migrants.* Since the Second World War the main policy is to be very selective and only admit immigrants from other continents when they are considered an asset to the economy, as high, medium, or low skilled labor.[16] The permit system is meant to close the gap between demand and supply of workers in certain sectors and—in the case of labor migrants— employers have to convince bureaucrats that they have tried in vain to find employees in the Dutch labor market. This has resulted in a steady stream of highly skilled immigrants (termed "expats") from mostly Asian countries like India, Malaysia, Indonesia, and China.

2: *EU migrants*: Since the 1950s, freedom of movement and pick up work increasingly became the rule within the European Economic Community (EEC), of which The Netherlands was one of the driving nation states.[17] With the formation of the European Union in 1993 (and its gradual enlargement) the freedom of mobility of capital, services, and labor became a top priority. Gradually this has also included inhabitants of Eastern European countries like Poland (2007), Romania, and Bulgaria (2014). The result is that, given the pull of the Dutch labor market, in the last decade the total number, as well as the share, of EU citizens in the yearly immigration has risen and now constitutes the majority. Most of them come for work, and a part stay on temporarily, but many also come to study or for family reasons, joining kin or as partners of Dutch citizens. Although the welfare state has become more and more "immigration proof" and many labor migrants contribute more to the system than they take out in terms of benefits,[18] there is discussion about the desirability of their presence. This concerns especially Eastern Europeans, with low pay and flexible contracts in sectors like distribution, agriculture, and slaughterhouses. Thus far, however, no government has introduced limitations, which would go against EU agreements. In other words, as with non-EU labor migrants, their arrival and stay are the consequence of explicit policy decisions, but this is often not perceived as such in the public debate and often ignored by politicians.

3: Then there is the category of *non-EU asylum seekers*. Although only some six percent of the total yearly inflow, they generate by far the most—often heated—controversy. Especially since 2015 many politicians suggest that the EU borders should be better protected, and that they should be received in "the region", meaning outside the EU, while public opinion remains more positive. Politicians regularly doubt whether most asylum seekers have legitimate motives and express fears that the welfare state will implode as a consequence of constant immigration of asylum seekers. This argument is not very convincing, though, because if the strain on welfare was really that great, this problem should have arisen much earlier, especially during the 1990s, when considerably more asylum seekers arrived than in the 2010s (350,000 versus 250,000).[19] Notwithstanding heated debates on the desirability to accept refugees, the basic right of people to ask for asylum in the Netherlands, as laid down in the 1951 Refugee Convention (and signed by the Netherlands in 1955), remains intact and as such constitutes the foundation of the policy.

4: Finally, there is the category of *non-EU family migration*, of both family members and spouses. As Saskia Bonjour has shown there is no clear gap, because especially from the 1990s onwards policy makers are well aware of the possibilities to regulate and block the coming of migrants with these motives. This started with legislation limiting the marriage partners of the children of Moroccan and Turkish migrants and spread to marriage migration and family reunification in general. Here the results were very much what politicians and policy makers intended.[20]

Conclusion

The chapter by Willem Maas does a good job in giving a systematic overview of the postwar migration trends, both into and from the Netherlands. Furthermore, he shows that when rethinking the gap hypothesis, we should realize that that policies are not that clear cut, they change and may be contradictory. In this commentary I have raised two other points that both complicate and elucidate the original gap hypothesis. The first pertains to integration and is a suggestion to also consider gaps between public (and political) opinion and developments in the key domains of integration, such as the labor market, education, and housing. As I have shown for the Netherlands, periods of integration optimism and pessimism alternated, whereas the prevailing mood often lingers on beyond what one would expect on the basis of what is really happening, both with respect to integration and the general economy. This explains the extension of the optimist trend during the *Trente Glorieuses* into the gloomy 1980s when integration problems were obvious, but political correctness and anti-racism prevailed. And vice versa, the prolonged apocalyptical pessimism into the 2010s (and 20s), when the economy boomed again after the Financial Crisis of 2008 and integration trends all pointed in the right direction.[21]

Finally, as to the original gap hypothesis, which focusses more on migration than integration, a case can be made that at a higher and more systemic level the outcomes of the policies are overall much more in tune with the outcomes than is often assumed and than politicians realize.

Notes

1. Caldwell 2009; Scheffer 2011; Goodhart 2013.
2. Bonjour 2011; Lucassen and Lucassen 2015.
3. Dekker and Ester 1996.
4. For the reconstruction of this ideological shift, see Oudenampsen 2021.
5. Scheffer 2000.
6. This position was not unique for the Netherlands, as the role of David Goodhart in the UK shows (Goodhart 2004), as well as the more recent policy change by the Danish social democrats (Kuisma 2020).
7. Buruma 2007.
8. Scholten 2007.
9. Lucassen and Lucassen 2018, 203.
10. Foner and Lucassen 2012.
11. Rooduijn 2020.
12. Thijssen 2020.
13. De Jonge 2019.
14. Thijssen 2020.
15. Bosma et al. 2012.
16. De Lange 2007 and 2018.
17. Heinikoski 2021.
18. Kremer 2016.
19. Lucassen 2018.
20. Bonjour 2011.
21. Lucassen 2005; Lucassen and Lucassen 2018.

References

Bonjour, S. 2011. "The Power and Morals of Policy Makers: Reassessing the Control Gap Debate." *International Migration Review* 45, 1: 89–122.

Bosma, U., et al., Editors. 2012. *Postcolonial Migrants and Identity Politics: Europe, Russia, Japan and the United States in Comparison.* New York: Berghahn.

Buruma, I. 2007. *Murder in Amsterdam: the Death of Theo van Gogh and the Limits of Tolerance.* London: Atlantic Books.

Caldwell, C. 2009. *Reflections on the Revolution in Europe: Immigration, Islam and the West.* London: Allen Lane.

De Jonge, L. 2019. "The Populist Radical Right and the Media in the Benelux: Friend or Foe?" *The International Journal of Press/Politics* 24, 2: 189–209.

De Lange, T. 2007. *Staat, Markt en Migrant. De Regulering van Arbeidsmigratie naar Nederland 1945–2006.* Nijmegen: Boom.

De Lange, T. 2018. "Welcoming Talent? A Comparative Study of Immigrant Entrepreneurs' Entry Policies in France, Germany and the Netherlands." *Comparative Migration Studies* 6, 27.

Dekker, P. and P. Ester. 1996. "Depillarization, Deconfessionalization, and De-Ideologization: Empirical Trends in Dutch Society 1958–1992." *Review of Religious Research* 37, 4: 325–341.

Goodhart, D. 2004. "Too Diverse?" *Prospect,* February 20, 2004.

Foner, N. and L. Lucassen. 2012. Legacies of the Past. In *The Changing Face of World Cities: Young Adult Children of Immigrants in Europe and the United States,* edited by M. Crul and J. Mollenkopf, 26–43. New York: Russell Sage.

Goodhart, D. 2013. *The British Dream: Success and Failures of Post-War Immigration.* London: Atlantic.

Heinikoski, S. 2021. *The History and Politics of Free Movement within the European Union.* London: Bloomsbury.

Hollifield, J. F. 1992. *Immigrants, Markets, and States: the Political Economy of Postwar Europe.* Cambridge Mass: Harvard University Press.

Huntington, S. P. 1993. "The Clash of Civilizations?" *Foreign Affairs* 73, 3: 22–49.

Kremer, M. 2016. Sociale Zekerheid "Migratie-proof." In *Sociale (on)zekerheid. De Voorziene Toekomst,* edited by P. V. Lieshout, 133–161. Amsterdam: Amsterdam University Press.

Kuisma, M. 2020. "Nordic Social Democrats: Still Europe's Progressive Vanguards?" *Constellations. An International Journal of Critical and Democratic Theory* 27: 594–607.

Lucassen, L. 2005. *The Immigrant Threat: The Integration of Old and New Migrants in Western Europe since 1850.* Urbana and Chicago: The University of Illinois Press.

Lucassen, L. 2018. "Peeling an Onion: The 'Refugee Crisis' from a Historical Perspective." *Ethnic and Racial Studies* 41, 3: 383–410.

Lucassen, L. and J. Lucassen. 2015. "The Strange Death of Dutch Tolerance: the Timing and Nature of the Pessimist Turn in the Dutch Migration Debate." *The Journal of Modern History* 87, 1: 72–101.

Lucassen, L. and J. Lucassen. 2018. *Vijf Eeuwen Migratie: een Verhaal van Winnaars en Verliezers.* Amsterdam: Atlas Contact.

Oudenampsen, M. 2021. *The Rise of the Dutch New Right: An Intellectual History of the Rightward Shift in Dutch Politics.* Milton Park: Routledge.

Rooduijn, M. 2020. "Immigration Attitudes Have Barely Changed—So Why Is Far Right on the Rise?" *The Guardian,* March 2, 2020.

Scheffer, P. 2000. "Het Multiculturele drama." *NRC-Handelsblad*, January 29, 2000.

Scheffer, P. 2011. *Immigrant Nations*. Cambridge: Polity Press.

Scholten, P. 2007. *Constructing Immigrant Policies. Research-policy relations and immigrant integration in the Netherlands (1970–2004)*. Enschede: University of Twente.

Thijssen, L. 2020. *Racial and ethnic discrimination in Western labor markets: empirical evidence from field experiments*. Utrecht: University of Utrecht.

COMMENTARY

Who Is Truly Dutch? The Politics of Law, Policy, and Practice

Michael Orlando Sharpe

In the run-up to the 2017 Dutch parliamentary elections, Prime Minister Mark Rutte of the VVD attempted to capture supporters of the far-right Geert Wilders PVV by publishing full-page advertisements in several Dutch dailies[1] and an open letter on the party website[2] indirectly admonishing immigrants who come to the Netherlands for freedom or reject Dutch values to "Doe normaal of ga weg" (act normal or leave). By January 2021, Prime Minister Rutte and his cabinet had resigned, and elections were called over a racial profiling scandal targeting people of ethnic minority background or dual nationality and their alleged scamming of child benefits. In the subsequent March 2021 national election, Rutte's VVD claimed "overwhelming" victory; second place went to the progressive pro-European D66, and third place to Wilder's anti-Islam PVV. Despite the PVV's loss of three seats, the anti-immigrant/Covid denying/anti-lockdown Thierry Baudet's FVV gained six seats, and together far-right populists had the best combined results in recent history. Contrary to contemporary anti-immigrant and anti-Muslim discourse, the Netherlands has always been a migration state, welcoming and tolerant of immigrants and political and religious refugees, as immigration is critical to its own development. In the twentieth and twenty-first centuries, the Netherlands continues to be a country of emigration and immigration. One can see evidence of both in foods that have become commonplace and "normal" in the Netherlands, particularly in the major cities, including Indonesian *rijsttafel* (rice table), *tokos* (small shops selling Chinese, Indonesian, Surinamese and Antillean foods), Turks *brood* (Turkish bread), potato fries with Indonesian/

Javanese-inspired curry or peanut sauce, the ubiquitous Vietnamese *loempia*, and Javanese/Surinamese *bami*. Maas argues that the political salience of immigration in the Netherlands is below the EU average and that the Dutch public is not more hostile to immigration than other states. Despite the fact of the distinction between the temporary intent and the end result of the permanent residence of guest worker programs, Maas is correct about the gap hypothesis and lack of clear goals or consensus in the Dutch case. However, I argue that the Netherlands is decidedly more assimilationist and exclusionary, with a rather recent construction of Dutch nationalism and membership (Sharpe 2014). This extends Bloemraad's (2014) argument that these developments in Dutch society may undermine the current goals of immigrant integration and the attraction of high-skilled immigration in the face of "low fertility," an "ageing workforce," and an "expensive social safety net" (276). Moreover, as the Netherlands is, in many respects, a model liberal state, a permanent excluded underclass of migrants and their descendants corrodes the social contract, civil society (Hollifield and Sharpe 2017), and overall democratic legitimacy, with a potentially damaging message for the liberal world order. This unwelcoming and restrictive turn in Dutch attitudes and society is reflected in this new iteration of Dutch nationalism, the treatment of minorities (including fellow citizens from the Dutch Caribbean), and a right-wing populist-infused electoral politics that has influenced Dutch law, policy, and practice.

Dutch Nationhood and New Dutch Nationalism

The contemporary concerns about Dutch nationhood and identity are novel as there has never been a culturally homogenous established understanding of them (Oostindie 2011, 16). It is important to remember that from the late nineteenth century to the late 1960s the Netherlands was a deeply divided society organized in a system of blocs or *zuilen* (pillars, that is Protestants, Catholics, Liberals, and Socialists) that accommodated religious and ideological differences. This system of "consensual" and "consociational" democracy was noted for compromise, power sharing, relative group autonomy and a high level of democracy (Lijphart 1968, 1999, 1969). De Jonge (2010) writes that "an identity of *being* Dutch had to reconcile with robust bloc identities . . . contact among the blocks was limited to the elite level, to run the nation's public affairs" (45–46). For Oostindie (2011), "the *verzuilde*, 'pillarized', Netherlands had no strong tradition of directed nation-building" (40). By the late 1960s, the pillarization system broke down as the Netherlands was embracing secularization and individualization, as well as a profound liberalism (Lechner 2008,

133), and this coincided with the coming of guest workers who were preceded and followed by waves of postcolonial and other migrants. During the 1980s, Dutch society initially accepted a "multiculturalism" by way of a minorities policy that was very much influenced by the old *verzuiling* or "pillarization" system, in which it was thought that migrants could better integrate by retaining their own language and culture, and many of the guest workers were presumed to return home. This soon fell out of favor as it was criticized for not facilitating the integration of immigrants and replaced with an assimilatory integration policy and law during the 1990s. It is at this point that a new Dutch nationalism seems to have emerged in opposition to immigrant groups, asylum seekers, multiculturalism, and the larger Europe (Maas 2007; Sharpe 2014). This has initiated an attachment to an imagined pre-immigrant past, "the archetype of a pure bred *autochton* [native Dutch, my emphasis] with deep roots in the Dutch polder—a liberal-secular white Dutch majority that at long last defines a collective Dutch identity" (De Jonge 2010, 21, 64, 75, 74; Sharpe 2014, 57). One commentator identifies this an "ethno-republican" conception of citizenship, or the uniting of liberal-democratic principles with an ethnic conception of nationhood and an assumption of cultural assimilation (De Haart 2004, 150). Hence, an exclusionary idea of nationhood and nationalism has developed in which ethno-cultural identity and nationality are joined, which is ironically similar to ideas of nationhood in Japan and South Korea (later in this volume) and other parts of the world. The question here to consider is, How do immigrants and their descendants fit into this more recent iteration?

Differentiated Citizenship—Minorities, Allochtonen, or New Dutch?

Some changes in policy indicate a move towards a differentiated or tiered citizenship. Since the 1985 minorities policy, Turks, Moroccans, Surinamese, Antilleans, and Arubans became officially recognized minorities with consultative bodies and government funded organizations (Vermeulen and Penninx 2000, 23; Van Hulst 2000, 4). This was very much influenced by the previously described the *verzuiling* or pillarization system that dominated Dutch society until the Christian democrats, once its main proponent, did not form part of a Dutch cabinet for the first time in 1994 (Entzinger 2003, 77). After the PVDA, VVD, and D66 secular parties took control of the cabinet in 1994 and the integration policy was in place, the establishment of ethnic and cultural organizations became the migrant's responsibility with the option of applying for state subsidies (Entzinger 2003, 78). Many migrant organizations fell by the wayside or dissolved due to lack of funding and/or leadership. The formal national minorities consultative structure (LOM) was discontinued in 2011 and formally ended in 2015 with some calling for its reestablishment as there is no longer a formal link for ethnic minority communities and the government to voice concerns and mitigate social tension.[3]

Maas points out some of the distinctions around the term *allochtoon*. Another indicator of the change of policy in the 1990s was the use of the terms *allochtoon, autotochton, westerse allochtoo*n, and *niet westerse allochtoon*. These classifications are used by government authorities to statistically count residents (including legal Dutch citizens) in the Netherlands While *Allochtoon* roughly translates as 'non-native', referring to those of foreign background (Van Hulst 2000, 20), *Autotochtoon* defines the "native Dutch" or those people whose parents were both born in the Netherlands regardless of where they themselves were born.[4] *Westerse allochtoon* or western *allochtoon* includes most western European countries, North America and curiously Oceania, Japan, and Indonesia. Finally, *Niet westerse allochtoon*, or non-Western *allochtoon,* is just about everyone else and includes those of first- and second-generation ethnic background from Turkey, Morocco, the former Dutch Antilles, Aruba, Suriname, Africa, Latin America, and Asia.[5] It is notable that Antilleans or Arubans are classified as *Niet westerse allochtoon* non-Western *allochtoon* when in fact they are internal migrants, born and raised Dutch citizens as their islands are constituent parts of the Kingdom of the Netherlands. Although Dutch King Willem-Alexander's father and grandfather were born in Germany and his Argentinian-born wife, Queen Maxima, can be called *allochtoon*, the colloquial use of the word *allochtoon* usually implies "non-Western *allochtoon*," or people of color, and is commonly understood as such in the media and popular discourse. De Haart (2004) makes the point that even those who have been naturalized remain *allochtoon* and not belonging "to the Dutch 'Us'" (161). Some in parliament have advocated doing away with these classifications or using something more objective like "*Nieuwe Nederlander,*" or New Dutch, to deemphasize origins and play up belonging in the Netherlands, but the consensus in parliament was that these terms had become too enmeshed in Dutch society and were necessary to identify problems impacting vulnerable minorities.[6] At the end of 2016, the Scientific Council for Government Policy (WRR) and the Central Agency for Statistics (CBS) formally changed the term *allochtoon* to "person with a migration background." Children who have one Dutch-born parent and one parent born abroad are also considered "person with a migration background."[7] Since then, the government has adopted the new terms in their policies. However, the old terms are very much still relevant because nothing has changed in the division between *autochtonen* and *allochtonen.* These are tangible policies and practices that reflect a change in attitudes around who is entitled to full membership and belonging.

Minorities, or *Allochtoon,* as the Miner's Canary

One can tell a lot about a society from the way it treats its minorities. In this way, minorities can act as a miner's canary for the quality of democratic inclusion. Minorities in the Netherlands tend to live in the major urban centers, with just over half of the residents of Amsterdam, The Hague, and Rotterdam being of foreign background.[8] As *allochtoon* comprise some 23 percent of the population in 2018, this is a very important issue. In 2017, the unemployment rate for *westerse allochtoon* (western *allochtoon*) was 6 percent and for *Niet westerse allochtoon* (non-Western *allochtoon*) was 11 percent, compared to the *Autochtoon* (native Dutch) average of 4 percent. The unemployment rate for those of non-Western background is starkly different from that of native Dutch. There are also distinctions when it comes to generation as it seems the second generation does better. Labor participation in 2017 for first-generation Turks was 56.7 percent; Moroccans, 50.6 percent; Surinamese, 59.3 percent; and Antilleans, 51.1 percent, compared to second-generation Turks at 59.7 percent; Moroccans, 60.1 percent; Surinamese 65.6 percent; Antilleans 63.0 percent; and 68.3 percent for the native Dutch.[9] People from Turkish, Moroccan, Surinamese, and Antillean backgrounds get their incomes less often from work than do migrants from the new EU countries, particularly those from Poland, who rely on employment or profits from their own businesses, similar to the native Dutch. Poles have some of the highest rates of labor participation; refugees from Eritrea and Syria have some of the lowest.[10] Minorities pursue higher education in higher numbers than ten years ago, but still lag behind the native Dutch with some variation.[11] The crime rate has dropped in recent years, but of the four largest minority groups, the highest number of registered suspects are of Antillean background, at some 4.4 percent in 2017. This means that Antilleans are six times more likely to be registered suspects than the native Dutch at 0.7 percent, a rate that is also higher than that of migrants from the new EU countries and refugees. Non-Western *allochtonen* are also more likely than the native Dutch to be the victims of crime.[12] Since the 1994 change of the party system, ethnic minority representation has become progressively better, and by 2003 was in proportion to the population, with 10 percent of the Lower House of foreign origin. Despite this, Antilleans and Aruban co-citizens have some of the lowest political participation rates of any ethnic minority group (Fennema and Tillie 2001; Sharpe 2005, 2014). By several measures, there is progress, but still much to be done in terms of full inclusion that will likely benefit the society.

Rounding the Circle: Multiculturalism, Integration, and Foreign Talent

Paradoxically, the "ethno-republican" move occurs as the Netherlands makes varied policy attempts to successfully integrate migrants, in an environment that some may not find necessarily inviting, while simultaneously trying to attract foreign talent. With the end of multiculturalism, there was a tendency toward more assimilatory integration policies. For example, the loss of original nationality upon naturalization was reintroduced in 1997 (Van Oers et al 2006, 392), along with the law of integration requiring foreigners from non-EU counties to pass an integration test including Dutch language, knowledge of Dutch society and the Dutch labor market; more restrictive "civic integration" courses and naturalization tests (Van Oers et al 2006, 404, 408); and the transformed perception of naturalization from a tool of integration to an "end point" of successful integration (Van Oers et al 2006, 403). The effect of the more restrictive turn in access to citizenship is evidenced in the dramatic reduction in naturalizations after the 2000 nationality law took effect in 2003. The Central Bureau of Statistics records in 2003 a substantial reduction in the number of naturalized Turks and Moroccans. Whereas in 2003 some 3000 Turks and 6000 Moroccans were granted Dutch nationality, six years prior "ten times as many Turks were naturalized . . . and in the preceding three years almost twice as many [Moroccans] were granted the Dutch nationality."[13] In addition to the in-country integration courses and tests, there is now a similar requirement for persons who want a temporary long-term-stay resident permit to complete prior to their travel to the Netherlands. Maas points out that a number of advanced countries, including the United States, Canada, Australia, and Japan, are exempt from this requirement and this was warned as discriminatory by the United Nations Committee on the Elimination of Racial Discrimination. At the same time, laws such as the Modern Migration Act,[14] which came into force in 2013, were enacted to encourage non-EU "knowledge migrants"—foreign investors, entrepreneurs, research scientists, start-ups, and highly educated professionals—to reside in the Netherlands through relaxed residence requirements and to strengthen the Dutch economy so that it could more effectively participate in the global economy.

Right-Wing Populism and Its Impact

As suggested above, concerns about immigration, integration, and Islam had already been voiced by the VVD and others in the 90s with related policy changes. From the year 2000, right-wing populism captured these concerns, built on them, and helped to frame the agenda and pressure mainstream parties to move to the right (Akkerman 2018, 11). Both LPF and PVV played an important role in shaping the immigration and integration policy agenda (Akkerman 2018, 4). LPF was able to capitalize on the sentiments of the 90s raised by Pim Fortuyn around multiculturalism and the alleged incompatibility of Islam and Western culture when they briefly became the second-largest party with the 2002 parliamentary election and entered coalition with VVD and CDA and were able to frame the consensus that integration has not been successful. When the LPF lost support in the 2003 election and dissolved in 2008, the VVD moved further to the right on immigration and integration, and leaders like Geert Wilders were ready to take advantage (Akkerman 2018, 8–9).

Some evidence of the influence of right-wing populism in rhetoric and language includes the idea that immigration threatens social cohesion, cultural values, and national identity and the emphasis on individual responsibility in civic integration for learning Dutch language and civic values. In the 2017 elections, the CDA proposed a ban on foreign governments financing mosques and Islamic organizations, and the VVD suggested banning the wearing of burqas in public. It is now a criminal offense to reside unauthorized in the Netherlands (Akkerman 2018, 2).

In 2017, Prime Mister Rutte barred a Turkish minister from landing to prevent her from addressing a rally in Rotterdam in support of a referendum expanding the powers of the Turkish president. He cited security but this was also an attempt to enforce loyalty over dual nationality or dual allegiance and show that Dutch Turks could not be politicized by the Turkish government.[15] In 2016, the government began to enforce strict evidentiary rules for family reunification that can be particularly difficult for asylum seekers who lack documents.[16] Baudet's FVD presents itself as the refined voice of the alt-right, simultaneously railing against multiculturalism while advocating the superior place of European culture; it had electoral success in three provinces in the 2019 elections as well as the 2021 national elections at the expense of Wilders PVV.

Conclusion

Many of the recent laws, policies, and practices add up to creating an experience of alienation and permanent outsider status for immigrants and their descendants but particularly those from non-Western backgrounds. Despite their shared citizenship, Antilleans and the native Dutch view each other as foreigners. With Antillean immigrants numbering only 153,469, or less than 1 percent (0.9 percent) of the population of the Netherlands, Dutch historian Piet Emmer suggested that unlimited Antillean immigration has caused a "national trauma" and extensive damage to Dutch society.

(Emmer 2007) Laws have been proposed to restrict the movement of young Antilleans to the Netherlands. The Netherlands expanded its border to the Caribbean in 2010 with the dissolution of the Netherlands Antilles; three islands were integrated as "special municipalities" (*Openbare Lichamen*) of the Netherlands and the remaining islands became semi-autonomous countries of the Dutch Kingdom. A host of problems and controversies remain, including the ongoing migration crisis in nearby Venezuela, disagreements about the responsibilities of the Netherlands to the islands, as well as internal conditions on the islands and the status of Dutch Caribbean co-citizens (Sharpe 2020).

In recent years, scholars have examined the history and vestiges of Dutch racism (Nimalko and Willemsen (2011) and the brutal involvement of the Dutch in the transatlantic slave trade and its legacies as central in the contemporary Netherlands; Essed (1990) analyzed the country's persistent characterization of racism as something unimaginable in Dutch society and how that denial belies and reinforces the practice of everyday racism. The Black Lives Matter protests of 2020 raised the issues of systemic racism and police brutality in the Netherlands. The BLM movement coincided with an ongoing spirited national debate about the pros and cons of the Dutch Christmas tradition of *Sinterklaas* in which St. Nicholas is accompanied by his helper *Zwarte Piet* (Black Pete) who appears in blackface in minstrel-like fashion. Despite a rigorous defense by populists and liberals alike that it is a critical nondiscriminatory part of Dutch national identity, in 2015 the United Nations Committee for the Elimination of Racial Discrimination (CERD) called on the Netherlands to eliminate or alter the practice to protect the dignity of people of African descent, who compose a large segment of the Surinamese and Antillean minorities.[17]

The government's recent focus on fiscal austerity and criticism of public expenditure on social, cultural, and educational programs have impacted many organizations, such as the National Institute for the Study of Dutch Slavery and Its Legacy (NINsee), which was defunded in 2011 and terminated in 2013 but then reestablished in 2019 with some government funding allocated to commemorate the end of slavery.[18] Some suggest that there is a desire for this history of slavery to be extricated from the Dutch master national narrative of tolerance, freedom, and democracy (Cain 2015, 231, 239). In June 2020 the governing coalition parties called for a nationwide discussion and state apology for the Netherlands' role in slavery but this was rejected by Prime Minister Rutte.[19]

Rotterdam and Arnhem have very well-liked mayors of Moroccan descent, and there are widely appreciated hosts and artists of ethnic minority backgrounds on Dutch national TV. The 2021 election signaled a general ambivalence about these issues, with results favoring the status quo, disappointing outcomes for the left, losses and gains for right-wing populists, an emergent antiracist party Bijl winning one seat, and the anti-populist pro Europe Volt party winning three seats.

There is a need to go beyond a rhetoric of tolerance to create a genuine consensus around the need to address systemic racism as well as acceptance and respect for diversity and inclusion in the broadening of Dutch national identity, belonging, and membership.

Notes

1. https://nos.nl/artikel/2154459-rutte-ga-weg-als-je-nederlandse-waarden-afwijst.html (accessed June 21, 2019); https://www.nrc.nl/nieuws/2017/01/24/het-normaal-doen-van-rutte-sluit-migranten-uit-6368512-a1542701 (accessed June 21, 2019).

2. https://www.vvd.nl/nieuws/lees-hier-de-brief-van-mark/ (accessed June 21, 2019).

3. https://nltimes.nl/2017/02/27/dutch-govt-reinstate-regular-meetings-ethnic-minorities-report (accessed June 22, 2019).

4. Central Bureau of Statistics of the Netherlands, Voorburg/Heerlen, 2006, http://www.cbs.nl/CmsSiteEngine/Presentation/Functional/Template/Special Page Template, December 6, 2006.

5. Ibid.

6. http://n.expatica.com/nl/news/Parliament-says-term-allochtoon-is-indispensable_3216.html (accessed March 30, 2013); http://www.expatica.com/nl/news/community_focus/Dutch-minister-wants-immigrants-to-integrate-better_58184.html (accessed March 30, 2013).

7. https://www.cbs.nl/nl-nl/faq/specifiek/wat-verstaat-het-cbs-onder-een-allochtoon-#:~:text=De%20term%20'allochtoon'%20is%20eind,in%20het%20buitenland%20is%20geboren (accessed April 4, 2021).

8. https://www.cbs.nl/en-gb/background/2018/47/population (accessed June 23, 2019).

9. https://www.cbs.nl/nl-nl/achtergrond/2019/08/arbeidspositie-naar-migratieachtergrond-2003-2017 (accessed June 23, 2019).

10. https://www.cbs.nl/nl-nl/achtergrond/2018/47/sociaaleconomische-positie (accessed June 23, 2019).

11. https://www.cbs.nl/nl-nl/achtergrond/2018/47/onderwijs (accessed June 23, 2019).

12. https://www.cbs.nl/en-gb/background/2018/47/crime (accessed June 23, 2019).

13. http://www.cbs.nl/en-GB/menu/themas/bevolking/publicaties/artikelen/archief/2004/2004-1528-wm.htm (accessed September 11, 2012).

14. https://www.government.nl/latest/news/2013/03/06/modern-migration-policy-act-coming-into-force-on-1-june-2013 (accessed June 22, 2019); https://www.government.nl/latest/news/2013/03/06/modern-migration-policy-act-coming-into-force-on-1-june-2013 (accessed June 22, 2019).

15. https://www.migrationpolicy.org/article/migration-netherlands-rhetoric-and-perceived-reality-challenge-dutch-tolerance (accessed June 24, 2019).

16. https://www.migrationpolicy.org/article/migration-netherlands-rhetoric-and-perceived-reality-challenge-dutch-tolerance (accessed June 24, 2019).

17. http://stopblackface.com/kozp/664-2/ (accessed January 28, 2018); https://www.inde pendent.co.uk/news/world/europe/zwarte-piet-black-pete-racist-christmas-character-pro test-sinterklaas-a8640611.html (accessed January 28, 2018).

18. https://nltimes.nl/2019/06/11/dutch-govt-commits-eu1-million-annually-commemo rating-slavery-past (accessed April 1, 2021).

19. https://www.dutchnews.nl/news/2020/07/as-keti-koti-is-celebrated-the-netherlands -is-slowly-facing-up-to-its-slavery-past/ (accessed April 1, 2021); https://www.politico.eu/ article/dutch-coalition-parties-call-for-formal-apology-for-slave-trade-history/ (accessed April 1, 2021).

References

Akkerman, Tjitske. 2018. *The Impact of Populist Radical-Right Parties on Immigration Policy Agendas: A Look at the Netherlands.* Washington, DC: Migration Policy Institute.

Bloemraad, Irene. 2014. "A Restrictionist Shift That Matters." In Controlling Immigration: A Global Perspective. 3rd ed., edited by James F. Hollifield, Philip L. Martin, and Pia Orrenius. Stanford, CA: Stanford University Press.

Cain, Artwell. 2015. "Slavery and Memory in the Netherlands: Who Needs Commemoration." *Journal of African Diaspora, Archaeology, and Heritage* 4, no. 3: 227–242.

Central Bureau of Statistics of the Netherlands. 2006. Voorburg/Heerlen.

Emmer, Piet. 2007. "'Van de Antillen blijf je af.' Hoezo?" *NRC Handelsblad,* November 10, 2007.

Entzinger, Han. 2003. "The Rise and Fall of Multiculturalism in the Netherlands." In *Toward Assimilation and Citizenship: Immigrants in Liberal Nation-States*, edited by Christian Joppke and Ewa Morawska. New York: Palgrave Macmillan.

Essed, Philomena. 1990. Everyday Racism: Reports from Women of Two Cultures. Cape Town: Hunter House.

Fennema, Meindert and Jean Tillie. 2001. "Civic Community, Political Participation and Political Trust of Ethnic Groups." *Connections* 24, no. 1: 26–41.

De Haart, Betty. 2004. "Political Debates on Dual Nationality in the Netherlands 1990–2003." *IMIS–Beitrage* 24: 149–62.

De Jonge, Lammert. 2010. *Being Dutch, More or Less.* Amsterdam: Rozenberg Publishers.

Hollifield, James F., and Michael Orlando Sharpe. 2017. "Japan as an 'Emerging Migration State.'" *International Relations of the Asia Pacific* 17, no. 3: 371–400.

Lechner, Frank J. 2008. *The Netherlands: Globalization and National Identity.* New York: Routledge, Taylor & Francis Group.

Lijphart, Arend. 1968. *The Politics of Accommodation: Pluralism and Democracy in the Netherlands.* Berkeley: University of California Press.

Lijphart, Arend. 1969. "Consociational Democracy." *World Politics* 21: 207–25.

Lijphart, Arend. 1999. *Patterns of Democracy: Government Forms and Performance in Thirty Six Countries.* New Haven, CT: Yale University Press.

Maas, Willem. 2007. *Creating European Citizens.* Lanham, MD: Rowman and Littlefield.

Nimalko, Kwame and Glenn Willemsen. 2011. *The Dutch Atlantic: Slavery, Abolition, and Emancipation*. London: Pluto Press.

Oers, R. van, B. de Hart, and K. Groenendijk. 2006. "The Netherlands." In *Acquisition and Loss of Nationality: Volume 2, Country Analyses*, edited by R. Bauböck, E. Ersbøll, K. Groenendijk, and Harald Waldrauch, 391–434. Amsterdam: University of Amsterdam Press.

Oostindie, Gert. 2011. *Postcolonial Netherlands: Sixty Years of Forgetting, Commemorating, Silencing*. Amsterdam: Amsterdam University Press.

Sharpe, Michael O. 2005. "Globalization and Migration: Post-Colonial Dutch Antillean and Aruban Immigrant Political Incorporation in the Netherlands," *Dialectical Anthropology* 29, no 3–4: 291–314.

Sharpe, Michael O. 2014. *Postcolonial Citizens and Ethnic Migration: The Netherlands and Japan in the Age of Globalization*. Houndmills, Basingstoke: Palgrave Macmillan.

Sharpe, Michael O. 2020. "Extending Postcolonial Sovereignty Games: The Multilevel Negotiation of Autonomy and Integration in the 2010 Dissolution of the Netherlands Antilles and Dutch Kingdom Relations." *Ethnopolitics*, April 2, 2020: 1–26.

Van Hulst, Hans. 2000. "A Continuing Construction of Crisis: Antilleans, Especially Curacaoans, in the Netherlands." In *Immigrant Integration: The Dutch Case*, edited by Hans Vermeulen and Rinus Penninx. Amsterdam: Het Spinhuis.

Vermeulen, Hans and Rinus Penninx (eds). 2000. *Immigrant Integration: The Dutch Case*. Amsterdam: Het Spinhuis.

9 Governing Immigration in the Scandinavian Welfare States

Control and Integration

Grete Brochmann

The welfare model has been called the sacred cow of Scandinavia. As compared to the United States, Scandinavia is famous for its mixed economy, combining efficiency and economic growth with a comprehensive social state. All three Scandinavian countries (Sweden, Denmark, and Norway) have the welfare state as a central part of their self-understanding, to the extent that this political framework has become part of the Scandinavian national concept. Scandinavia is the area where trust in political institutions and the state is the greatest in the world. Political actors in the three countries now compete for the honor of having created and developed the welfare state.

The Nordic welfare model, as it is often labeled internationally, largely came about in the post–World War II era, the basic features being in place by the late 1960s.[1] Both idealistic and pragmatic, the model was initially formed as a grand social insurance system, aimed at taking care of citizens from cradle to grave. It can initially—in broad strokes—be seen as a societal integration project with three central ingredients: democracy, modernization, and citizenship.

International migration was clearly not in the minds of the Scandinavian welfare architects in the postwar period. The new universalistic and redistributive system was designed with the national population in mind. It was a "bounded universalism," in the words of Seyla Benhabib (2002). At the time, the inflow of immigrants was meager and immigration was not a politicized topic; none of the governments could have known the degree to which immigration would increase in the years to come.

In this chapter I will describe and analyze the contradictory impact of immigration—institutionally and politically—on these three advanced welfare states in Europe's northern periphery. Similarities and differences between the countries will be discussed through a historical exploration of the period after the 1970s. Public documents and historical analyses form the empirical basis of the chapter, which will be delineated by three policy areas: immigration, integration, and naturalization. Theoretically, the chapter draws on conceptual tools from political economy, citizenship discourse, and institutional theory.

The Historical Account

Denmark, Norway, and Sweden have received immigrants for centuries, but predominantly from neighboring Scandinavian countries; immigration from outside the OECD is mainly a post-1960s phenomenon.[2] The first of these "new immigrants" were labor migrants from Turkey, Yugoslavia, Morocco, and Pakistan. This inflow lasted only till the early/mid-1970s, when strict new regulations were introduced— the "immigration stops."[3] Labor migration became an issue again around the turn of the century, particularly after 2004, when the EU enlarged to include central European countries. The stops of the 1970s were a milestone in immigration policies in Scandinavia, introducing policy mechanisms with wide-reaching consequences. The new policies were intended to curtail unwanted, unskilled immigration while allowing the admission of skilled workers in demand, especially in Norway, where there was an oil boom in the early 1970s.[4] Yet the legacy of the stops is to a large extent their unforeseen consequences.

As was the case in most receiving European countries, immigration changed character in the mid-1970s. When the legal channel was closed for low-skilled labor, foreigners arrived via other entry channels, as refugees/asylum seekers or family members of already settled migrants. The number of immigrants from non-OECD countries has increased because of international conventions and the general humanitarian platform of the Scandinavian social democracies.

The Nordic welfare state or "the Nordic model" is *comprehensive* regarding the kinds of social needs it tries to satisfy.[5] It is *institutionalized* via social rights that give all citizens—in practice, all legal residents—a right to a decent standard of living. It is solidaristic and *universal* in the sense that the welfare policy serves the entire population, not just particularly exposed groups.[6] The Nordic model turns many of life's risks over to the state, lightening the load of care obligations for families.[7] It is service-intensive, with local governments playing key roles in providing welfare services. By contrast with other welfare states in Europe, women's rate of employment is high.

The Nordic welfare model is structurally linked to the highly centralized organization of working life. The regulation of the labor market via collective agreements, tripartite cooperation (business, labor, and the state—the neo-corporatist arrangement), an active labor market policy, and welfare security throughout life have contributed to productive economies with good flexibility and high human capital. Working life and welfare have represented mutual buffer functions, with a high rate of employment needed both to finance welfare and to reduce public spending. Income security has been a fundamental pillar in this context, both in the form of social assistance and as social insurance. The system has been encompassing and generous, and has contributed to the three Scandinavian states having the world's most equal income distribution.[8] State control and planning have constituted major ingredients in the system, which is basically tax-based.[9] Equal treatment has been a key element in the system, and the only criterion for accessing basic income security is legal residency.[10]

There are important structural, humanitarian, and ideological reasons for the setup of the model. The Nordic states are basically social investment states, aiming at economic growth and social equality. Humanitarian ideals, first spelled out in terms of international solidarity in the wake of wartime devastation and later on in the form of political radicalization in the 1960s and 1970s, supported this policy ideologically. The Scandinavian approach has been labeled "something for nothing" in comparison to the "something for something" market logic that couples benefits to contributions in other welfare state systems.[11]

In all three countries the wide-ranging development of the welfare state was interconnected with nation-building—the creation of nationhood and social cohesion based on historical myths and realities, facilitated by the oneness and homogeneity of the population. The welfare state project implied much more "than a mere upgrading of existing social policies," in the words of Gösta Esping-Andersen.[12] Apart from economic redistribution, the welfare state was a moral construct, an entity for institutionalized solidarity and part of the nation-building process that took place after World War II. This essentially political project was necessary since a fully developed citizenship was seen as a precondition for the stabilization of vulnerable postwar democracy.

A homogenization had taken place in the Scandinavian populations in the first half of the twentieth century, including a rather forceful streamlining of the few existing minorities in Sweden and Norway.[13] The new welfare state was seen as something that should be built by individuals, liberated from old collectives and bonds, ready to enter a new and perhaps paradoxical fusion of modern individualism and a new sense of societal responsibility. This general homogenization—or assimilation— is usually seen as a precondition for the development of the specifically Nordic form of welfare state, and also for its continued support and legitimacy.[14] The fact that all three countries were small in terms of population most likely facilitated this process.

The "moral construct" of this nation-building project relied on rights and duties that forged a basic reciprocity between the individual and society through principles of solidarity.[15] Historically rights and duties have been closely intertwined, epitomized by the labor union slogan "Do your duty, claim your rights!" (*gjør din plikt, krev din rett*). The collective imposes duties (to work and to pay tax) on the individual, who in turn is reaffirmed by the collective while strengthening his or her bonds to the group, with the possibility of acquiring goods—or rights—from it. This reciprocity dynamic applies both to civil society and to the state. In the Scandinavian context, the dialectic between rights and duties can be seen as the core philosophy of the welfare state.

The concept of *folkhemmet*, "the people's home," emerged as a central concept of Swedish social democrats before World War II. It imagined a grand class alliance replacing the former class struggle and helping to steer society toward a social democratic goal. "The integrative idea of the '*folkhemmet*,' in which society was organized as a grand family, with the home as a metaphor, subordinated the class struggle to the national welfare."[16] This concept, appropriated from the conservatives, was used as an instrument for modernization after the war. National social citizenship was secured through an egalitarian order, heavily state-sponsored, yet at the same time preserving individual autonomy.[17]

In Denmark and Norway similar tendencies were prevalent, and the *folk* turned out to be a politically attractive concept in these countries as well— *folkefællesskabet* (the people's community) in Denmark and *hele folket i arbeid* (all the people to work) in Norway. Particularly in Norway and Sweden, the concept of the *folk* was closely entangled with the nation. Legitimacy for this broad plea for popular mobilization was, according to Bo Stråth, a combination of the national question and a specific Protestant ethic prevailing among popular movements. This ethic was marked by pietistic value orientation, emphasizing individual freedom and radical claims of equality.[18] Pietism and duty often go hand in hand. Accordingly, the twin metaphors of home and people indicated, through their collective connotations, the sacrifices expected of the individual in return for social security.

Among the sacrifices, work holds a strategic position. Active labor market policies have been a basic characteristic of the Scandinavian welfare model from an early stage, and they bring with them a sort of duality—as Lundberg and Åmarks characterized it, one side is "work for everyone; the other is that everyone has to work."[19] In other words, a high employment rate is a precondition for the necessarily high taxation in the model. And besides, having people work keeps them off the public budgets. "Labor market policy has been developed as a form of preventive social policy" in Scandinavia, according to Joakim Palme.[20]

All these features—the (relative) homogeneity, the subtle balance between rights and duties, and the structural composition of the welfare model—potentially predict a troubled relationship between the Scandinavian welfare state and immigration.

Institutional Prerequisites for Immigration Policy in Scandinavia

The Scandinavian welfare state's tradition of regulation, its large public sector, its economic transfers to weak groups, and its principle of equal treatment have in practice had two central implications for the "new immigration." First, controlling inflow into the country has been seen as a prerequisite for maintaining the specific character of the system. The generous welfare model, which includes everyone but which can be undermined by excessive burdens, necessitates selection and delimitation in relation to potential new members from outside. This logic has been reemphasized along with the expansion of rights in the region.[21] Social rights are a cornerstone of modern welfare states and are an important prerequisite if the ideals of such systems are to be realized for all their members. Yet the more rights, the more caution. And caution has been manifested both in the form of border control and, increasingly, via differentiation through categories of immigrants.[22] Different kinds of immigrants (distinguished partly by the motives for immigration) are given different residence statuses, which activate different sets of rights and thereby also affect the scope of expenditure. An intricate and tightly defined status hierarchy, reflected in what are known as the "foreign laws," has been developed over the years in this respect. The juxtaposition of access control and extension of rights sets up the basic tension between generous welfare structures and immigration.

Second, the emphasis on equality and welfare rights has a logical corollary in integration policy. If the policy framework of the welfare state is to be maintained, new, legally accepted inhabitants must be made part of it. Good welfare states do not tolerate substantial elements of persons or groups who live on the edge, disturb the regulated world of work, and burden social budgets—a Marshallian recognition that a society cannot function smoothly if a large section of the population is marginalized and socially excluded.[23] What would eventually come to be called the "work line" (between those employed and those who are not) was the central element here, for in order to maintain the expensive welfare state, people had to be integrated into productive work to the greatest extent possible. Sweden, which was the first of the Scandinavian countries to become an immigration country, was also the first to formulate the baseline of the immigration regime in these terms, clearly underlining the expectation of self-sufficiency among immigrants (Borevi 2014). They saw that the sustainability of the Nordic welfare model depends on what today we might call economic absorption capacity (Collier 2013; Brochmann and Grødem 2019). The states had to balance the volume and composition of the inflow, on the one hand, with the institutional and economic integration capacities of the receiving nation-state, on the other. Later, the issue of a state's *cultural* absorption capacity also became a subject of concern to varying degrees in the region. The Scandinavian welfare model based itself on a specific kind of communitarianism, which sees the need to "balance individual rights and liberties with the interest of the community as a whole" (Brandal et al. 2013 , 183). This fine-tuned approach, similar to what the Swedish historian Lars Trägårdh (1997) depicts as "statist individualism," can be thrown off by immigration.

The combination of an intentionally restrictive access policy and an inclusive and equality-oriented labor-market/welfare approach emerged in the 1970s and would mark the three countries in the following decades. Yet it was developed within a context of labor immigration and was based on national interests. Both these premises proved to be inadequate when the immigration pattern changed. This approach has been challenged first by the international human rights regime and, after the turn of the century, by free movement of labor within the EU. The immigration that occurred after the stops (asylum seekers and family migrants) could not be regulated with previously developed tools. International obligations and a genuine desire for a humanitarian immigration practice meant that new arrivals could not easily be dismissed merely with reference to the capacity of the national welfare state or demand in the labor market. After the extension of the European Union in 2004 and 2007, immigration control was intentionally abolished in relation to EU citizens seeking employment. Thus, in terms of institutional prerequisites, these two externalities drastically changed preconditions for governance in the area of immigration. The tensions and contradictions between the considerations needed to secure the sustainability of the welfare state (that is, the boundedness of the welfare contract) and the ascending human rights regime provided the core quandary for the three Scandinavian states from the 1970s till today.[24]

Theoretical Approaches to the Welfare State–Immigration Nexus

Is immigration a threat to welfare states? Gary Freeman highlighted the fundamental contradiction between inclusive welfare policies and comprehensive international migration, emphasizing that welfare states need to be closed to protect "the collective good component" from overexploitation by outsiders. Freeman said that immigration has a tendency to erode the normative consensus on which generous welfare systems depend: "When the welfare state is seen as something for 'them' paid by 'us,' its days as a consensual solution to societal problems are numbered" (Freeman 1986, 62).

Today, there are four major arguments about immigration and welfare states. The first focuses on economic sustainability, in line with Freeman: generous welfare distribution depends on a restrictive selection of its new members to avoid being overburdened. Michael Walzer in his *Spheres of Justice* (cited in Freeman's article) provided some basic philosophical premises for this position: "The idea of distributive justice presupposes a bounded world within which distributions take place: a group of people committed to dividing, exchanging and sharing social goods, first of all among themselves" (Walzer 1983, 31). Christian Joppke states it more bluntly: "Because rights are costly, they cannot be for everybody" (Joppke 1999, 6). Seyla Benhabib's (2002) concept of "bounded universalism" pinpoints this logic, in which internal redistribution is combined with economically motivated access restrictions.

The second argument deals with the interconnection between boundaries and bonds. This is Freeman's "normative consensus": the popular support necessary to sustain the basic structure of a redistributive welfare state in democratic societies. This "social cohesion" asserts that increasing ethnic diversity weakens the normative consensus, gradually undermining the foundation of the welfare state (Alesina and Glaeser 2004; Goodhart 2004). In the Scandinavian context, the emphasis on reciprocity norms for the sustainability of the Nordic welfare model belongs in this group.

A third argument seeks to disprove the "social cohesion" approach. Banting and Kymlicka (2006) find no empirical proof for the cohesion hypothesis, and argue that good welfare states can cushion the potential negative effects of immigration and diversity. Markus Crepaz (2008) takes this institutional argument further to argue that institutions shape the success of integration. In comparing the United States and the Europe, he says that the United States was racially divided when it developed a welfare system, while in Europe institutionally strong welfare states were already in place when immigrants arrived. According to Crepaz, this fact has made the European welfare states more robust in withstanding pressure against generalized trust, as the ability to include newcomers as eligible for welfare and care was already established. The social investment approach of the Scandinavian welfare states represents this basic thinking: educating and socializing newcomers through equal treatment and extension of social rights are supposed to counteract the problems related to low-skilled and culturally different immigrants.

Fourth, Ruud Koopmans (2010) argues that particular combinations of welfare and multiculturalism policies are unsustainable. Where scholars such as Banting, Kymlicka, and Crepaz find evidence that generous and inclusive welfare states handle immigration better, Koopmans finds that immigrants fare worst in welfare states that combine generosity with multiculturalism policies "which do not provide strong incentives for host-country language acquisition and for interethnic contacts" (2010, 3). In this perspective, this type of welfare state is bad for the immigrants themselves, as it may lead to dependence "on welfare-state arrangements and thereby to social and economic marginalization" (2010, 2). Koopmans claims that giving immigrants easy access to equal rights, in combination with a generous welfare state, leads to weak labor market participation, high levels of spatial segregation, and overrepresentation in crime statistics. Poor socio-economic integration of immigrants is thus blamed on the welfare state and multiculturalism policies. This argument makes welfare generosity toward newcomers not only bad for immigrants but also bad for the larger society.

All four perspectives are present in current Scandinavian policymaking and public discourse on welfare and immigration. The Walzer-Freeman perspective is one of the constituting features of the Scandinavian migration policy as such, and is premised on the restrictive immigration regulation instituted in the early 1970s in the region: because rights are costly but should be for all (to twist Joppke's words), only a select few can be let in. Since the 1990s, the authorities as well as the public have been increasingly concerned about the pressure on welfare costs imposed by low-skilled immigration. A large proportion of these newcomers have proven difficult to integrate into the Scandinavian labor market, which is characterized by high demands in terms of skills and a compressed wage structure that makes low-skilled labor comparatively expensive. The universalistic welfare approach, implying a generous inclusion of legal newcomers from day one, in combination with the highly regulated and knowledge-intensive labor market, has made the three states particularly exposed to disincentive challenges as concerns the absorption of immigrants in gainful work.

The Koopmans perspective has gained attention, particularly in Denmark. The OECD's annual International Migration Outlook for 2018 (OECD 2018) reveals that the Scandinavian countries are at the bottom of a scale that measures the gap between the employment rate of immigrants and that of the native-born. Sweden performs worst of all. Concurrently, the Migrant Integration Policy Index (Mipex) for 2020 places Sweden at the very top among twenty-eight European states when it concerns integration *policies* (i.e., the formal extension of rights to immigrants), with 86 out of 100 possible points.[25] Seen together, these figures leave the impression that the extension of rights to immigrants may not imply a state's ability to include these newcomers in productive work. There are definite weaknesses in both these comparative exercises, yet the juxtaposition highlights the current political superstructure for the retrenchments on the rights side—again particularly in Denmark. If it is the rights in question that hinder the entry of immigrants into productive work, the causal link is not evident. There are incentive problems in Scandinavia for low-skilled individuals, given the relatively high compensation level of social benefits, but it can also be argued that social rights may serve a social investment logic: people are given these rights in order to facilitate their (long-term) labor market participation.

The social cohesion issue has increasingly been a focus, particularly in Denmark, but also in Norway over the last decade. Cultural conflicts have been connected to welfare state sustainability and used as fuel for discussion on the limits of solidarity. Public discourse has nonetheless been somewhat simplistic and polarized between restrictionists, who want to keep immigrants out so as to sustain welfare and cohesion for the established citizens, and admissionists, who want maximum inclusion and a generous access policy and disregard the cohesion problem as such. General support for the welfare state system is overwhelming in all three countries, yet policymaking regarding access and inclusion of immigrants increasingly differs between countries within the Scandinavian region. Broad political support of restrictions both on access to family reunification and citizenship and on welfare support for newcomers in Denmark is an indication of Freeman's theorem: a majority not wanting a welfare system as something for "them" paid for by "us." Sweden, on the other hand, has exemplified a Crepazian system, trying to use its institutional basis to withstand any erosion of welfare state legitimacy for all.

The "Welfare Contract" Under Challenge

An attentiveness to the failure of immigrant inclusion, both in the labor market and more generally in society, has developed in Scandinavia since the 1990s. Multicultural immigration has "matured" as a policy field, with ever more conflicts and contradictions amid more general structural and economic problems.

Economic crises hit all three countries in the 1980s and early 1990s (with different momentum and slightly different timing), making the Nordic model "sclerotic," with rigid obstacles to economic change and competitiveness. Generous income security was believed to create perverse incentives and to fail to respond to new needs, thereby adding to inactivity. Sweden, Norway, and Denmark embarked on significant reforms, succeeding economically to the extent that before the financial crisis hit in 2008, all three were rated as leading the world in terms of growth rates, economic efficiency, and equality (Dølvik 2008).

Despite the soundness of the economies, a relatively high share of the Scandinavian labor force has been out of work over the past decades because of sick leave, rehabilitation, and long-term disability. The immigrant population has been overrepresented in certain welfare arrangements, particularly those receiving social assistance—the basic form of income security.[26] And in all three countries, the unemployment rate for immigrants was roughly three times the rate for the majority population, and their rate of employment is significantly lower.

According to the traditional argument, these newcomers have been given residency on legitimate grounds and are thus eligible for the support that the system offers. The moral aspect of the resurrected duty ethics has nevertheless affected immigrants more than others, at least in Denmark and Norway. Even though universality and solidarity have been pillars of the Scandinavian welfare state, legitimacy is a subtle underlying dimension in all welfare policy: who deserves support, and who should be able to care for themselves?

Welfare benefits to newcomers who have not contributed through work and taxpaying highlight this inherent tension in the welfare system. Traditionally there was considerable shame attached to receiving welfare benefits in Scandinavia, and one of the merits of the welfare state was to diminish this sense of inferior status among recipients. At the same time, the system has depended on a certain feeling of unease among potential beneficiaries, in order to avoid overburdening or direct abuse of the system. There have been worries that immigrants not socialized into the subtleties of the welfare contract could more readily come to depend on transfers over time. Labor market participation and welfare dependency among immigrants are of course complex issues, with structural factors and discriminatory elements, but the focus among the public has been increasingly on the implicit constituents of duty attached to the principle of a generous welfare system. The most basic duty in the system is "obligatory solidarity"—that is, the duty to support the institutionalized redistributive system. This is done in practical terms: through work, according to an individual's capacity, and through paying tax.

All three states have realized the very basic challenge posed by the influx of low-qualified persons in a labor market that demands high levels of education and

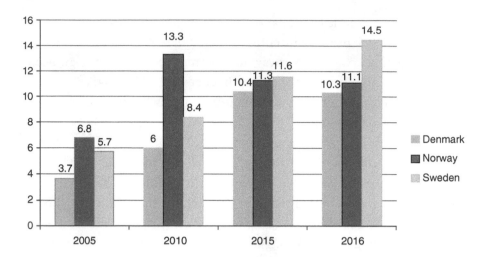

FIGURE 9.1. Migration Inflo per 1,000 Inhabitants
SOURCE: OECD, International Migration Outlook 2018.

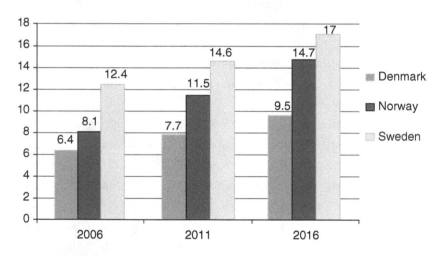

FIGURE 9.2. Stock of Immigration (Foreign Born), Percentage of Population
SOURCE: OECD, International Migration Outlook 2018.

productivity. Like any other state, the Nordics want newcomers who can support themselves and contribute to diversity and innovation. Generous welfare rights and a compressed wage structure may serve to hamper this objective.

Three Approaches to the Immigration Challenge

The types of immigrants that have entered the three Scandinavian countries since the 1970s have been similar: first, an influx of labor migrants, followed by relatively high proportions of humanitarian migrants after the introduction of immigration stops in the mid-1970s, followed by a new surge of labor migrants after the EU enlargement of 2004. The political mechanisms and measures implemented were also initially similar in the three countries, but since 2000 significant variation has developed in immigration and integration policies. Multiculturalism has been under attack, particularly in Denmark. Sweden is referred to as the most multicultural country of the three, whereas Denmark is moving in the opposite direction with its more majority-dominated policy, which many call assimilationist.[27] Norway is somewhat in the middle, trying to muddle through by recognizing diversity and cultural traditions and emphasizing the need for "some common values in society" as well as the majority's heritage.[28] On the access side, all three states have wanted to restrain immigration that is considered a burden on welfare budgets while at the same time upholding their humanitarian responsibilities—that is, following the UN Refugee Convention and more generally international principles of human rights. It is thus interesting that three states that are basically very similar in terms of economic governance, welfare systems, and political traditions in practice interpret the limits of these responsibilities differently.

In the following sections, the national approaches to immigration taken by each country are first compared broadly, then delineated in relation to three policy fields: access (or immigration), integration, and naturalization.

Scandinavia: Similarities and Differences

After World War II, immigration started earlier in Sweden than in the neighboring countries and was far greater in scope. This explains Sweden's position as a pioneer state within the field of integration and its strong influence on the other two states, particularly Norway. After 1980, this pattern became been much less clear, since both Denmark and Norway have gone their separate ways within a number of areas connected to immigration and integration.

In terms of public debate, there have been large differences within Scandinavia. When immigration is publicly discussed, the focus on welfare state issues has been increasing, notably in Denmark and Norway. In the early 1990s, a new concept entered this discourse in Norway—"kindism," or being kind to a fault.[29] A growing number of people used the concept of kindism to criticize the welfare state's rights policy for going too far: the wish to help weak groups in society was outpacing the need to make demands on newcomers. It took about a decade until this rhetoric had a serious impact on policymaking, although the 1990s can be characterized as a period of "preparations for change," when general retrenchments occurred in all three countries. The "work line" approach was reinvigorated by all the states despite political opposition.

In fact, the question "Is the welfare state too kind to immigrants—or is it not kind enough?" sums up the basic structure of the Nordic immigration debate and policy-making since the 1990s, and it is a reminder of the key position welfare policy holds among the Nordics. Over the past years, the tone of the Danish debate has hardened, with more immigration-critical voices making themselves heard. Danish policy has also become more restrictive in terms of both immigration control and social policies. A similar development has been seen in Norway, although not to the same extent. As in Denmark, a critical searchlight has been focused on family immigration policy in the wake of debates about forced marriages and suppression of women. In addition, the Norwegian authorities have signaled a tightening of the requirements for granting asylum, including possible cuts in support for asylum seekers. Changes to immigration legislation and the social rights of new arrivals have not, however, been as marked in Norway as they are in Denmark. Sweden has been the exception among the Nordic countries, more cautious about implementing a comprehensive tightening of immigration policy and with a more subdued public debate. This is so despite the fact that the country underwent considerable general welfare retrenchment measures in the early 1990s as the result of a serious economic crisis. So on a "kindness" continuum Sweden has often been at one extreme, with Denmark at the other and Norway in between. Much of this changed with the 2015 refugee crisis. That crisis disturbed the public consensus to the degree that Swedish public debate today is more similar to that seen in Denmark and Norway than it was before. The refugee inflow in the summer and fall of 2015 resulted in significant changes in all three countries in order to inhibit asylum migration. The most pronounced change was in Sweden, as we will see.

The EU has a significant and increasingly important role in policy to control migrant flow. Since the 1990s, internationalization in general and the development of EU politics more specifically have contributed to reducing the room individual member countries have to make their own immigration control policies. All EU countries have come to depend on each other in terms of external control of migration as a result of the gradual establishment of institutions and harmonization among member states. The welfare state is still the domain of the member states, but coordination of social security rights and harmonization within other areas produce important constraints on national freedom of action within the field of social policy.[30] Especially after the expansion eastward in 2004 and 2007, the EU/EEA membership has implied considerable labor immigration.[31]

The Scandinavian states have chosen different forms of affiliation to European cooperation. Sweden has full EU membership (with the exception of the currency union). Denmark has been a member the longest, yet has negotiated an opt-out position for itself in regard to common immigration policy, and it too remains outside the currency union. Norway has decided to stay outside the EU, but it is fully incorporated in the single-market regime through its EEA membership, and it is part of the Schengen area.[32] Ironically, Norway—the only one of the three that is not a member of the EU system proper—is the most strongly affected by labor immigration from the new member countries that joined in 2004 and 2007.

Access Policy

All three states initially had, as we have seen, the same basic structure in their interconnections between external control and integration policy: a restrictive front and an inclusive inside, in order to protect the welfare/labor market model. Until the early 2000s, the concrete policies were also by and large similar, although with some differences in terms of details.

After the immigration stops of the 1970s, implemented because of challenging labor conditions and the costs of the welfare system, ideally very few people should have been able to have access to any of the three countries. Nevertheless, humanitarian principles resulted in fairly liberal access policies in relation to refugees/asylum seekers and family migrants (in line with the liberal paradox), thus creating self-reinforcing mechanisms that spurred further humanitarian immigration. However, it was not until the late 1980s that the governments in the region started discussing (to different degrees) how to restrict even these channels of access. The legitimacy discourse as it related to asylum seekers became a tool in this respect. Since not all these immigrants could claim a need for protection according to the UN Refugee Convention, restrictions were seen as legitimate. The impact of the more meticulous review of asylum applications is hard to estimate, but regardless, the number of asylum seekers continued to increase, although with some fluctuations during the 1990s. Sweden continued to be the grand magnet in the region.

The problems attached to the productive incorporation of newcomers into the labor market (and the concomitantly growing burdens on the welfare system) gradually developed into a great worry during the same decade, and led to a push for better control. The nature of refugee immigration, however, made it a difficult target for restrictions. Family immigration thus materialized as a better object for retrenchment. This kind of immigration had not been a topic of public discourse nearly to the same extent as asylum seekers had, and the incorporation of family migrants into work and civil society was not widely investigated, despite the magnitude of the inflow. But during the 1990s this category of immigrants came to the fore through a focus on transnational marriages much more than family reunification proper. Issues such as forced and arranged marriages and honor-based violence in the family became targets for heated discussions in the public, and revealed a complicated interplay between immigration control, integration endeavors, human rights, and family relations.

Denmark reformed large parts of its immigration policy as a result of the change of government in 2001. The incoming center-right coalition implemented new control and access policies, including eliminating the category of "de facto refugee" (that is, it would only give protection to refugees qualifying under the 1951 Geneva Convention). In addition, to be able to marry a any foreigner, both partners had to be at least twenty-four years of age and their combined attachment to Denmark had to be stronger than to the country of origin (Green-Pedersen and Odmalm 2008). The reforms also added requirements for the applicants' economic capacity to support themselves with a decent standard of housing, as well as a bank guarantee of Dkr 50,000 to cover any public assistance needed for the foreign spouse. Sweden and Norway did not follow Denmark in these specific reforms, although the general tendency has been more restrictive in both countries, though less so in Sweden. In recent years both Sweden and Norway have required a person seeking to bring over family members to document their ability to economically support the incoming family members. All three countries have stepped up their policy for return of asylum seekers whose petitions have been declined.

These major retrenchments concerning "unwanted" immigrants came around the turn of the twenty-first century—at the same time as a shift in paradigm related to "wanted" immigration. As was the case in several other European states, shortages of skilled labor prompted a more liberal approach to high-skilled immigration. During a short period of time the focus on immigrants as consumers of welfare changed into a new emphasis on the need for more producers from the outside, in order to stem the demographic tide, to compensate for declining birth rates, boost the dependency ratio, and to maintain economic growth and the level of welfare. The result was a mixed approach, where further restrictions were imposed on the humanitarian categories of immigrants, even as regulations were relaxed for attractive immigrants. In one aspect of this Sweden acted unilaterally: in 2008 the state introduced a liberalized labor immigration policy for the entire world. It is driven by demand, and employers are the ones to decide the need. By contrast, Denmark and Norway have judged that the EU extension eastward provides a sufficient supply base for years to come.

Of all the events that have taken place since the initiation of the immigration regulation policy in Scandinavia, the refugee crisis in 2015 is the most significant turning point. The intense pressure (real and imagined) of refugee flows on the three countries' absorption capacity and the fear of further uncontrolled increase led all three states to introduce severe restrictions on influx as well as major retrenchments in the extension of rights to asylum seekers. The changes were by far most striking in the Swedish case. After having received a record number of refugees in 2015 (just over 160,000 by the end of the year), the government was forced to introduce national border controls as an exception to the Schengen agreement.[33] Denmark and Norway, too, accepted far more asylum seekers than normal (approximately 30,000 in Norway and 20,000 in Denmark). Temporary protection for asylum seekers was taking over as the standard approach in all three places. Even if most of the restrictions came about because of the exceptional situation in 2015, five years later none of the states had gone back to the pre-2015 regime, although Swedish and Norwegian authorities have moderated some of the crisis-generated restrictions because of opposition in parliament. Denmark, on the other hand, has reinforced the retrenchments and deepened the transformation of its approach to integration. In a sense, political path dependencies kicked in once the intensity of the crisis had faded. And even though the three countries' immigration policies resemble each other more now than they did before the crisis, there are still significant differences.

Integration Policy

Sweden was the pioneer in the region (and in Europe as a whole) in formulating an integration approach: newcomers should have access to equal rights, at the same time retaining freedom of choice regarding cultural adjustment. In other words, social citizenship should be possible without the newcomers being obliged to identify with the majority nation. Sweden went even further, committing itself to protect minority cultures from being eroded.[34] Freedom of choice had not been a prominent characteristic of the social democratic welfare state in Scandinavia during its "golden age" (1945–1970), and Sweden probably occupied the extreme end of the scale with regard to central planning and governmental zeal.[35] High-quality solutions had become a distinguishing characteristic of the Swedish welfare state, made possible because the country's citizens gave massive support to centrally prescribed models, based on the belief that only a strong and centralized state could provide guarantees of the equality and fairness desired, through universal solutions financed by taxation. This project to establish equality concerned not only rights and economic redistribution; the governing ardor of the Swedish state touched even the private sphere, going far beyond what was perceived as legitimate or desirable in other western European states.

Sweden became world-famous for its social engineering. Norway and Denmark were somewhat less zealous than Sweden in this respect, although control through social policies was a prominent feature in these countries as well. What is notable in this context is that Sweden, where social engineering had proceeded the furthest, also became a pioneer country with regard to multicultural liberalism, in that immigrants could choose to retain their culture and keep their private sphere undisturbed (Gür 1996).

How this has turned out in practice is a recurring topic for debate in all three countries, but early on Sweden was definitely the ideological trendsetter in Nordic integration policymaking. In the early 1970s, when the "new immigration" was starting to make itself felt in Denmark and Norway, Sweden had already had multicultural immigration for several years.

In this historical context, integration policy, through its cultural freedom-of-choice concept, inevitably established the character of exception for a distinctive group—the immigrants. Thus, even if it was argued along equality lines that newcomers should be provided with real opportunities to preserve their language and culture in the same manner as the majority population did, it was hard to escape the implication of deviance. That is, freedom of choice was seen as a concession to people who were so different that they could not be expected to adapt to Sweden's universal solutions, thus emphasizing their position as outsiders.[36]

This apparent oxymoron was accepted as a formative premise by the two other states as well, and it still (although less dogmatically) constitutes the nerve center of integration policy: how should the welfare state's requirements of universal solutions and equal treatment be reconciled with minority rights and cultural diversity?

Since the initial phase of the integration approach (in the 1970s and early 1980s) all three states have adjusted their inclusion policies, and since the late 1990s the differences between the countries have become more marked. For quite some time, internal variation in Scandinavia appeared as a "difference in degree" over the same basic ground concepts. Looking back from the vantage point of 2019, however, it is nevertheless possible to trace early signs of present-day distinctions. Even though all three countries have been influenced by multicultural thinking, the Danish national approach was significantly present already in the 1970s (Jønsson and Petersen 2010). Partly following from this, Denmark has emphasized the duties of newcomers more clearly from an early stage, whereas for quite some time both Sweden and Norway were more inclined to let rights dominate the equation. Even so, the duty side in terms of work-line policies has nevertheless been accentuated more energetically in all three states, particularly after the turn of the century. Denmark has again been in the forefront in reforming important parts of its active labor market policies and more strikingly it introduced a two-tier policy for social security, in order to spur employment among immigrants. Permanent residency will only be given after seven years (a change from the previous three-year requirement), conditioned upon knowledge of Danish and a clean police record. In terms of social assistance, full rights will not be given before seven years of residency. This striking breach of the universalistic Nordic welfare approach was rolled back when the Social Democratic Thorning-Schmidt government took over in 2011, but when the liberal Løkke Rasmussen government took over in 2015, "start help" was reintroduced. Sweden and Norway have so far refrained from similar adjustments in social assistance, but Norway has introduced new conditions (years of residency) for some of its social transfers. Among the three states, Sweden has most strongly retained the "freedom of choice" line in its integration policy, whereas Denmark has taken over the lead when it comes to restriction-oriented social engineering. In early 2019 the Danish Liberal government introduced what it labeled a "shift of paradigm"—a significant move in the sense that temporary protection of refugees and their families is established as the baseline.[37] Social benefits (at reduced rates) to newcomers are relabeled "self-support and return transfer" (to emphasize individual responsibilities and duties), in contrast to the previous "integration benefit" (more social or collective in nature). A cap on the total number of family members who can be brought in under reunification was part of the new policy. Integration is hardly part of the endeavor anymore. Denmark has, with this move, marked a drastic reorientation of its immigration policy, detaching itself from the traditional Scandinavian approach.

As concerns integration rhetoric, differences between the three countries were clear at least up to 2015. In Denmark (in particular) and in Norway there is more open (some would call it "brutal") talk about immigrant "problems" than is the case in Sweden, and the duty to adjust has been increasingly highlighted since the turn of the century. What is called "obligation" in Denmark is generally called "rights," "motivation," or "facilitation" in Sweden. In Norway, rights and duties have become more merged. This contrast may reflect different analyses of integration problems in the three countries. Swedish authorities have targeted structural discrimination and anti-immigrant attitudes among the majority population. Danish authorities have pointed to weak labor incentives for immigrants due to the (overly) generous welfare provisions, while Norway has stressed limitations on the quality of public assistance (Brochmann and Hagelund 2012). In all three countries, the Social Democrats have taken a defensive position in this area, leaving the front line to other protagonists, who have had varying degrees of impact. For quite some time, the hegemony of the Swedish Social Democrats allowed them to keep immigration out of the public debate. In Sweden immigration issues were not politicized to the same degree as in the neighboring countries until the Sweden Democrats managed to mobilize on the question, particularly after 2010.[38]

Naturalization

The welfare state has, as we have seen, been the prime motor of integration among the Nordics, through social engineering and the extension of rights. As concerns the social cohesion issue—that is, the "normative consensus" on a set of shared values needed to sustain the welfare model—the instruments have been less clear-cut. States have a limited number of policy options to deal with this complicated and nebulous challenge. Naturalization policies have since the 1990s been revitalized as one of the instruments in this domain, being located in the intersection between the cultural field (nationhood) and the socio-political field (the right to vote and the full range of social citizenship rights). Although the connection between citizenship legislation and cohesion, identity, and belonging is indistinct and controversial— "identity cannot be legislated" (Joppke 2008, 536)—a number of states in practice act as if it is worth giving that sort of legislation a try. A perceptible dividing line among the policy approaches to this legislation is the relationship between citizenship and integration: whether citizenship for newcomers should serve as a tool in the inclusion process or as a reward for the effort. The three Scandinavian states lie along a scale characterized by the traditional ideal-typical *ethnos/demos* division, both in terms of what it takes to become a national and regarding conceptions of national identity.

Naturalization policies have developed along strikingly different paths among the three states over the last decades. This is even more interesting considering the very close cooperation that existed among the three countries in forging their national citizenship legislation from 1880 up to 1979.[39]

Swedish authorities aim at using access to citizenship as a means for integration, although not a very significant one (Brochmann and Midtbøen 2021). The dual-citizenship policy, in which immigrants can add Swedish citizenship to their original citizenship after five years' legal residence, with no language or skills requirement, is seen as a part of this thinking. Denmark, on the other hand, with its much more demanding naturalization requirements, sees citizenship as a final stage in the integration process—something that immigrants can earn through active efforts to adjust. In 2002 a nine-year residency requirement replaced the former seven-year one, and the government has introduced a demanding language and skills test to qualify. This legislation should contribute to a process in which it becomes more attractive (or absolutely necessary) to attain the needed qualities to become a citizen. Norway has retained its requirement of seven years of residency and a (milder) language and skills rule. On the other hand, a 2005 act served to liberalize naturalization to a certain extent: Norwegian citizenship is now obtained solely by law (that is, an applicant meeting certain criteria has a right to Norwegian citizenship).

Both Denmark and Norway have gradually introduced further reforms to citizenship legislation during the last decade, emphasizing a more demanding attitude that is much in line with what the literature labels the "civic turn" (Jensen et al. 2017; Mouritsen 2013). Sweden, on the other hand, has not (yet) changed its strongly entrenched liberal rights thinking in the realm of citizenship.

It seems correct to interpret the move away from coordinated policymaking among the Nordic countries as an upgrading of the citizenship laws. National interests are apparently conceived as so important that no country wants any longer to be subordinated to a possible Nordic norm. The weight of national sovereignty has been reinforced; national vested interests have increased in line with a more differentiated Scandinavian immigration policy over the last decades. And this divergence most likely reflects basically different viewpoints when it comes to conceptions of the nation, which for a while were subdued in the spirit of postwar cooperation, as well as in response to economic interests in stimulating intra-Nordic migration.

Denmark has, as we have seen, parted from the neighboring countries in formulating a more restrictive immigration policy in terms of both access control and welfare policy. For Denmark to have to adapt to a liberal Swedish citizenship model would simply not match its overall approach to the immigration challenge. Sweden, on the other hand, having pushed the humanitarian ideology some steps further than most other nations, would have problems harmonizing its citizenship law in the Danish direction. Instead, Denmark has served as a negative example in the Swedish public discourse on immigration and plural society. Norway, on its side, wants to reinforce nationhood as well as retain a humanitarian image. Since 2013, with the immigration-critical Progress Party in government, this balance has tipped in favor of a more restrictive line, inspired by Denmark.

Overall, Denmark, Sweden, and Norway want to integrate their accepted immigrant population in functional terms: they want their immigrants to work, to be good parents, and to be participating members of society. To different degrees, they also want them to become citizens, although what is required to become a citizen differs significantly from country to country. The rationale for the policy instruments chosen varies as well. Social cohesion is (at least implicitly) a concern in all three countries, but it is spelled out differently in each. Which tools related to citizenship law are needed to forge "societal glue" and "generalized trust"? Trust is built through slow and complex processes. As long as the institution of denizenship takes care of most substantial social rights for legal newcomers, formal citizenship will have primarily political and symbolic significance. In their respective ways, the three Scandinavian states want their naturalization policies to forge trust and cohesion, although their understandings of the basic mechanisms differ. All three states' policies have elements of a quite liberal, if paternalistic, approach, but they are rooted in strikingly different conceptions of who should be the target for disciplining efforts. In Sweden the majority is the target. They are seen as potentially critical or hostile, therefore they need—in the traditional Swedish way—to be trained and molded into endorsing the multicultural society (see Wickström 2013). Denmark, in contrast, sees the immigrant population as the target: they are required to learn liberal values to be able to function well in a modern *and* plural Denmark. For its part, Norway has taken an ambivalent and somewhat unclear position in this terrain, without a clear message beyond a general statement about integration as a mutual learning process.

The concept of the "Danish nation" has had a much more central position in both discourse and policymaking in Denmark than equivalent concepts have held in Sweden and in Norway. Whereas introductory programs for newcomers in Denmark aim to give immigrants an understanding of "Danish values and norms," the Swedish equivalents underline respect for democratic values, not specifically Swedish ones. And whereas Swedish and Norwegian public statements communicate a positive attitude toward diversity of culture, religion, and values, such signals have disappeared from the Danish official discourse (Holm 2007). On the other hand, Danish policymakers have a tendency to consider *demos* values as part of the Danish *ethnos*; these are values that are held by the Danish majority, in contrast to minority groups—first and foremost Muslims (Mouritsen 2006). Consequently, pressuring newcomers to acquire these "Danish" liberal, democratic values is a necessity to protect the polity for future generations. Regardless of possible dialectical twists in the *ethnos/demos* landscape, substantial differences remain in all three policy areas (see Table 9.1).

The relative importance of legal citizenship may increase in the years to come if rights attached to denizenship are rolled back. At the same time, access to citizenship is (apart from Sweden) becoming harder to get and easier to lose. Both Denmark and Norway are increasingly using naturalization as an extended control mechanism (Jensen et al. 2017).

Concluding Remarks

Roughly fifty years have passed since the initiation of multicultural immigration to Scandinavia. Sweden was the pioneer in formulating a multicultural integration policy in the early 1970s and has stayed with this basic approach. Swedish ideology and

TABLE 9.1. Naturalization Requirements in Scandinavia

Central Stipulations	Sweden	Norway	Denmark
Waiting time	5 years	7 years	9 years
Acceptance of dual citizenship	Yes	yes	yes
Language requirement	No	yes	Yes
Knowledge of society requirement	No	yes	Yes
Economic self-sufficiency requirement	No	Indirectly	Yes
Citizenship ceremony	Voluntary	Voluntary	Voluntary
Oath of allegiance	No	Compulsory if participating in ceremony	Compulsory
Right to citizenship when conditions are fulfilled	Several groups but not all	Yes	Only second-generation Nordic citizens

SOURCE: Midtbøen et al 2018.

policymaking served as beacons for the neighboring countries, and in particular for Norway. The Danish state had a stronger stand on nationhood from early on and was more hesitant to adopt multiculturalism. Identifying the roots of the initial Swedish position would require additional study, yet there are suggestions that point in the direction of the ideological and political sphere.[40] The role of "humanitarian superpower" that Sweden energetically established for itself internationally after World War II (Borevi 2010) provided premises for the handling of immigrants at home. Immigration from Finland dominated the inflow to Sweden prior to the 1970s, and this group of "equals" had a strong impact on the way other immigrants would be handled later.

Much of the difference in policy in Scandinavia after the initial phase is most likely explained by constellations in party politics. The parties to the right have been differently composed and have had diverse positions on immigration. The Danish Progress Party (Fremskridspartiet), to the right of the Conservatives, played a role as early as the 1970s with its immigration-critical line. Its successor, the Danish People's Party, was very important as a supporter for the center-right coalition government, particularly after the 2001 election. It has strongly influenced the reform policy that the coalition government introduced. Moreover, the Danish Social Democrats have been split on the issue, contributing to a stronger politicization of the matter at an earlier stage than occurred in Sweden and Norway. In Norway, the Progress Party, or Fremskrittspartiet (Frp), inspired by the Danish equivalent, was established in the 1970s, but it did not take a formal anti-immigration line until the late 1980s. The

Frp has been extremely important in helping to shape the public discourse since the 1980s, as none of the other parties have considered immigration a winning theme. The Frp has, because of an increased following (since 2000 it has usually figured as the third-biggest party), been able to pressure the major parties toward a more restrictive line.

Sweden has also faced a notable opposition to immigration among parts of the population, yet for a long time there was no significant party represented in parliament that capitalized on anti-immigration sentiments. This changed, however, in the 2010 election when the Sweden Democrats (Sverigedemokraterna) gained 5.7 percent of the vote and twenty representatives in parliament. After this election the party has seen remarkable growth, winning more than 17 percent of the vote in the 2018 parliamentary election. The 2015 refugee crisis contributed significantly to its success.

Immigrants, particularly the ones from the global South, have brought a new low-skilled (sometimes extremely so) element to the Scandinavian "middle-class societies."[41] The reintroduction of enduring low-income groups, marginalized both economically, residentially, and socially, to societies that had largely eliminated such segments from their populations has been a systemic challenge in all three states. Politically, maybe more than economically, this has triggered an increased concern over the sustainability of the welfare model in all three countries, yet—at least till recently—markedly more so in Denmark and Norway than in Sweden. This political discrepancy reveals a variable gap between basis and superstructure in the three countries, to use a classic dichotomy: even though the systemic impact of immigration is quite similar in the three economies, the way it has been handled has been increasingly different. This is particularly so in public discourse, but it holds also in actual policymaking. The cultural dimension (that is, the value conflicts introduced through diversity, especially diversity in terms of religion) has been the touchiest and most contentious element in policymaking in all three contexts. The present success of the populist right in all three countries can partly be explained by their ownership of identity-based opposition, which has manifested itself as anti-immigration mobilization (Kuhnle and Alestalo 2018).

Since the 1990s we have witnessed the emergence of three national policy regimes, still with some basic common features, yet with increasingly distinct approaches on central parameters. The year 2015 represented a watershed in Scandinavia regarding immigration, as was the case in other European receiving states. Yet while the acute crisis measures that were installed in all three contexts may initially have looked like a trigger for convergence, they may prove to be less significant in this regard than envisaged. Despite its reinstalled border controls, Sweden is still the great magnet in the region, and despite the electoral success of the Sweden Democrats, the other parties have managed to keep them at the margins of influence in parliament. The immediate retrenchments in Norway have to some extent been moderated, and due to a strongly reduced inflow after the 2015 crisis, public pressure has largely waned. Denmark, on the other hand, has emerged as an entrenched hard-liner, now taking off in a qualitatively new direction with its dualized welfare state and diluted integration endeavors.

Notes

1. In this connection I am using "Nordic" and "Scandinavian" as synonyms, even if "Nordic" formally also includes Finland and Iceland. It is the three Scandinavian countries that have the greatest number of common features regarding the organization of their societies and historical development relevant to immigration.

2. There is internal variation within Scandinavia. Sweden was the first to recruit foreign labor. It was not occupied by the German Nazi regime, as Denmark and Norway were, and its economy expanded more quickly in the immediate postwar years.

3. "Immigration stops" were introduced in Denmark in 1973 and Norway in 1975. In Sweden stricter regulation developed gradually beginning in the late 1960s.

4. Norway had an opposite business cycle compared to the rest of Western Europe at the time. The main reason for curtailing immigration of low-skilled labor in the early 1970s elsewhere was the substantial increase in oil prices.

5. See, among others, Kauto et al. 1999; Kildahl and Kuhnle 2005.

6. Esping-Andersen and Korpi 1987.

7. Sejersted 2005.

8. Barth, Moene, and Wallerstein 2003.

9. See Esping-Andersen 1990: Kautto et al 1999; Kangas and Palme 2005.

10. Qualification periods are necessary for some of the other benefits, however.

11. Petersen 2007.

12. Esping-Andersen 1996, 2.

13. The politics of "Norwegianization," as it was called in Norway, included cultural, linguistic, educational and religious "normalization" of minorities, in particular the Sami.

14. Loefgren 1999, 54.

15. This theme is further developed in Brochmann and Hagelund 2012.

16. Stråth 2005, 35.

17. Trägårdh 2018, 85.

18. Trägårdh 2018, 85.

19. Lundberg and Åmark 2001, 176.

20. Palme 1999, 41.

21. Again there is internal variation over the years between the three countries as to the strictness of access control, Sweden generally being the most liberal country.

22. See Brochmann and Kjeldstadli 2008) for the historical account and Brochmann and Hagelund 2012) for more details.

23. The welfare state, the most advanced stage of a long historical process, is viewed by Marshall as a fundamental integration project for all of society. Via governmental means, solidarity and loyalty were to be created in the population by incorporating all classes of society into a national community. T. H. Marshall has become the prime reference for modern citizenry (Marshall 1965).

24. See Brochmann and Hagelund 2012; Trägårdh 2018.

25. Both Denmark and Norway used to be high on the Mipex scale as well, but lately their scores have fallen (Norway is now at 69 points, Denmark at 49).

26. In Norway in 2003, the likelihood of a non-Western immigrant receiving social assistance was five times higher than for the population at large. Adding housing support, the likelihood was eight times higher.

27. Langvasbråten 2008; Brochmann and Hagelund 2012.

28. See Brochmann 2007 for a more elaborate discussion of the Norwegian approach.

29. Gerhardsen 1991.

30. Regulation 1408/71.

31. The European Economic Area (EEA) covers all the EU countries as well as Norway, Iceland, and Lichtenstein, and implies access to the internal market but no position in the EU political structures.

32. The only areas of exemption are agriculture and fisheries.

33. The Schengen area represents the border-free zone of the EU, and all three countries have signed the accord defining this area.

34. There are several examples of concerns, particularly in Swedish and Norwegian public records, that encounters with majority institutions would threaten minority cultures. See Brochmann 2003; Brochmann and Hagelund 2010; Björkman et al. 2005.

35. Esping-Andersen 1990.

36. Gür 1996; Borevi 2002.

37. The new law was passed in March 2019. See https://www.fm.dk/publikationer/2019/finansloven-for-2019.

38. In the 2010 election, the radical right-wing party Sweden Democrats received 5.7 percent of the vote; in 2014 their share more than doubled, rising to 12.9 percent. The 2018 election gave them 17.5 percent—a result that was clearly related to their hard line on immigration (Rydgren and van der Meiden 2018).

39. See Brochmann and Seland 2010 for closer scrutiny of citizenship policies in Scandinavia.

40. See Borevi 2010; Björkman et al. 2005.

41. Term used in Kuhnle and Alestalo 2018, 18.

References

Alesina, Alberto, and Edward L. Glaeser. 2004. *Fighting Poverty in the US and Europe: A World of Difference.* Oxford: Oxford University Press.

Banting, Keith, and Will Kymlicka, eds. 2006. *Multiculturalism and the Welfare State: Recognition and Redistribution in Contemporary Democracies.* Oxford: Oxford University Press.

Barth, E., K. Moene, and M. Wallerstein. 2003. *Likhet under press: Utfordringer for den skandinaviske fordelingsmodellen.* Oslo: Gyldendal Norsk Forlag.

Benhabib, Seyla. 2002. "Transformations of Citizenship: The Case of Contemporary Europe." *Government and Opposition* 37, no. 4: 439–465.

Björkman, Ingrid, et al. 2005. *Exit Folkhemssverige. En samhällsmodells sönderfall.* Torsby: Förlag Cruz del Sur.

Borevi, Karin. 2002. *Välfärdsstaten i det mångkulturella samhället.* Skrifter utgivna av Statsvetenskapliga föreningen i Uppsala no. 151. Uppsala: Acta Universitatis Upsaliensis.

Borevi, Karin. 2010. "Sverige: Mångkulturalismens flaggskepp i Norden." In *Velferdens grenser*, edited by Grete Brochmann and A. Hagelund, 41–131. Oslo: Universitetsforlaget.

Borevi, Karin. 2014. "Multiculturalism and Welfare State Integration: Swedish Model Path Dependency." *Identities: Global Studies in Culture and Power.* 21/6: 708-723.

Brandal, N, Ø. Bratberg, and D. Thorsen. 2013. *The Nordic Model of Social Democracy.* London: Palgrave Macmillan.

Brochmann, Grete, editor. 2003. *The Multicultural Challenge.* Amsterdam: Elsevier/JAI.

Brochmann, Grete. 2007. "Til Dovre faller. A bli norsk—å være norsk—troskapsløfte og statsborgerskap i den foranderlige nasjonen." In *Migration och tillhörighet. Inklusions- och exklusionsprocesser i Skandinavieni*, edited by Gunnar Alsmark, Tina Kallehave, and Bolette Moldenhawer. Göteborg: Makadam Förlag, pp. 99–126.

Brochmann, Grete, and Anniken Hagelund. 2005. *Innvandringens velferdspolitiske konsekvenser—Nordisk kunnskapsstatus.* Copenhagen: Nordisk Ministerråd.

Brochmann, Grete and Anniken Hagelund, eds. 2010. *Velferdens grenser.* Oslo: Universitetsforlaget.

Brochmann, Grete, and Anniken Hagelund. 2012. *The Boundaries of Welfare: Immigration Policy and the Welfare State in Scandinavia 1945–2010.* London: Palgrave.

Brochmann, Grete, and Knut Kjeldstadli. 2008. *A History of Immigration: The Case of Norway 900–2000.* Oslo: Universitetsforlaget.

Brochmann, Grete, and Arnfinn H. Midtbøen. 2021. "Philosophies of Integration? Elite Views on Citizenship Policies in Scandinavia." *Ethnicities* 21, no. 1: 146–164.

Brochmann, Grete, and Idunn Seland. 2010. "Citizenship Policies and Ideas of Nationhood in Scandinavia." *Citizenship Studies* 14, no. 4: 429–445.

Brochmann, Grete and Anne Skevik Grødem. 2019. "Absorption Capacity as Means for Assessing Sustainable Immigration." European Migration Network Norway Occasional Paper Series. Oslo: Norwegian Ministry of Public Justice and Security, UDI.

Collier Paul. 2013. *Exodus: How Migration Is Changing Our World.* Oxford, Oxford: Oxford University Press.

Crepaz, Markus M. 2008. *Trust Beyond Borders: Immigration, the Welfare State, and Identity in Modern Societies.* Ann Arbor: University of Michigan Press.

Dølvik, Jon Erik (2008) The Negotiated Nordic Labour Markets: From Bust to Boom. Background/working paper for the conference "The Nordic Models: Solutions to Continental Europe's Problems?" Center for European Studies at Harvard, 9-10 May 2008.

Esping-Andersen, Gösta. 1990. *The Three Worlds of Welfare Capitalism.* Cambridge: Polity Press.

Esping-Andersen, Gösta. 1996. "After the Golden Age? Welfare State Dilemmas in a Global Economy." In *Welfare States in Transition: National Adaptations in Global Economies*, edited by Gösta Esping-Andersen. London: Sage, pp. 1-31.

Esping-Andersen, Gösta, and Walter Korpi. 1987. "From Poor Relief to Institutional Welfare States: The Development of Scandinavian Social Policy." *International Journal of Sociology* 16, nos. 3–4: 39–74.

Freeman, Gary. 1986. "Migration and the Political Economy of the Welfare State." *The Annals* 485: 51–63.

Gerhardsen, Rune. 1991. *Snillisme på norsk*. Oslo: Schibsted.

Goodhart, David. 2004. "Too Diverse? Is Britain Becoming Too Diverse to Sustain the Mutual Obligations Behind Good Society and the Welfare State?" *Prospect*, February.

Gür, Thomas. 1996. *Staten och nykomlingarna. En studie av den svenska invandrarpolitikens ideer*. Stockholm: City University Press.

Hansen, Lars-Erik. 2001. *Jämlikhet och valfrihet. En studie av den svenska invandrarpolitikens framväxt*. Acta Universitatis Stockholmensis. Stockholm: Almqvist och Wiksell International.

Holm, Lærke. 2007. *Folketinget Og Udlændingepolitikken – Diskurser Om Naturaliserede, Indvandrere Og Flygtninge 1973-2002*. Aalborg: Institut for Statskundksbab, Aalborg Universitet.

Jensen, K. K., C. Fernández, and G. Brochmann. 2017. "Nationhood and Scandinavian Naturalization Politics: Varieties of the Civic Turn." *Citizenship Studies*. 21/5: 606-624.

Joppke, Christian. 1999. *Immigration and the Nation-State*. Oxford: Oxford University Press.

Joppke, Christian. 2008. "Immigration and the Identity of Citizenship: The Paradox of Universalism." *Citizenship Studies* 12, no. 6: 533–546.

Jønsson, Heidi Vad, and K. Petersen. 2010. "Danmark: Den nationale velfærdsstat møder verden." In *Velferdens grenser*, edited by Grete Brochmann and A. Hagelund, 131–211. Oslo: Universitetsforlaget.

Kauto, Mikko, Matti Heikkilä, Bjørn Hvinden, Staffan Marklund, and Niels Ploug. 1999. "Introduction: The Nordic Welfare States in the 1990s." In *Nordic Social Policy: Changing Welfare States*, edited by Mikko Kauto, Matti Heikkilä, Bjørn Hvinden, Staffan Marklund, and Niels Ploug. London: Routledge, pp. 1-18.

Kildal, Nanna, and Stein Kuhnle, eds. 2005. *Normative Foundations of the Welfare State: The Nordic Perspective*. London: Routledge.

Koopmans, Ruud. 2010. "Trade-offs Between Equality and Difference: Immigrant Integration, Multiculturalism and the Welfare State in Cross-National Perspective." *Journal of Ethnic and Migration Studies* 36, no. 1: 1–26.

Kuhnle, S. and M. Alestalo. 2018. "The Modern Scandinavian Welfare State." In *The Routledge Handbook of Scandinavian Politics*, edited by P. Nedergaard and A. Wivel, pp. 13-25. London: Routledge.

Langvasbråten, Trude. 2008. "A Scandinavian Model? Gender Equality Discourses on Multiculturalism." *Social Politics: International Studies in Gender, State and Society* 15, no. 1: 32–52.

Lundberg, Urban, and Klas Åmark. 2001. "Social Rights and Social Security: The Swedish Welfare State 1900–2000." *Scandinavian Journal of History* 26, no. 3: 157–176.

Löfgren, Orvar. 1999. "Nationella arenor I." In *Försvenskningen av Sverige*, edited by Billy Ehn, Jonas Frykman, and Orvar Löfgren, pp. 21-117. Stockholm: Natur och kultur.

Marshall, T. H. 1965. *Class, Citizenship and Social Development*. New York: Anchor.

Mouritsen, Per. 2006. "Fælles værdier, statsreligion og islam i dansk politisk kultur. Det nordiske medborgerskabs specifikke universalitet." In *Bortom stereotyperna? Innvandrare och intergration i Danmark och Sverige*, edited by Ulf Hedetoft, Bo Petterson, and Lina Sturfelt, 109–148. Göteborg: Makadam Förlag.

Mouritsen, P. 2013. "Civic Integration in Germany, Great Britain and Denmark." *Ethnicities*. 13/1: 86-109.

OECD. 2018. *International Migration Outlook 2018*. Paris: OECD.

Palme, Joakim. 1999. *The Nordic Model and the Modernisation of Social Protection in Europe*. Copenhagen: Nordic Council of Ministers.

Petersen, Klaus. 2007. "(U)rettfærdigt! Og hvad det så kommer velfærdsstaten ved?" In *13 værdier bag den danske velfærdsstat*, edited by Jørn Henrik Petersen, Lis Holm Petersen, and Klaus Petersen. Odense: Syddansk Universitetsforlag.

Rydgren, J. and S. van der Meiden. 2018. "The Radical Right and the End of Swedish Exceptionalism." *European Journal of Political Science*. 18: 439-455.

Sejersted, Francis. 2005. *Sosialdemokratiets tidsalder. Norge og Sverige i det 20. århundre*. Oslo: Pax.

Stråth, Bo. 2005. "The Normative Foundations of the Scandinavian Welfare States in Historical Perspective." In *Normative Foundations of the Welfare State: The Nordic Perspective*, edited by Nanna Kildal and Stein Kuhnle, pp. 33-51. London: Routledge.

Walzer, Michael. 1983. *Spheres of Justice: A Defense of Pluralism and Equality*. New York: Basic Books.

Wickström M. 2013. "The Difference White Ethnics Made: The Multiculturalist Turn of Sweden in Comparison to the Cases of Canada and Denmark." In *Migrations and Welfare States: Policies, Discourses and Institutions*, edited by Vad Jonsson, H., E. Onasch E., S. Pellander, and M. Wickström, pp. 25-58. Helsinki: University of Helsinki Press.

COMMENTARY

How Do Welfare States Control Migration?

Kristof Tamas

There are several central features that interconnect welfare states and immigration policies. The chapter by Grete Brochmann in this volume highlights some of these. It aims to describe and analyze the contradictory institutional and political impacts of immigration on Denmark, Norway, and Sweden while maintaining an overall focus on the Nordic welfare state model. A main point is that migration control is intrinsically linked to the welfare state. However, as the chapter title indicates, it is more about governance than about control policies. This reinforces the overall impression that the chapter is more about the welfare state, and to some extent about general immigration and integration regulation, rather than about migration control policy.

Brochmann's chapter evokes the related question of why the Nordic welfare state is so important for Scandinavian control policies, compared to the role of the welfare state in migration control elsewhere—for example, other European welfare states such as the Netherlands, Austria, and Germany. I argue that the Nordic welfare state model on its own cannot explain the large differences between Danish and Swedish migration control and related attitudes toward immigration (as Norway is in between, we can mostly leave it aside). Securitization might be one of several additional factors that also need to be taken into account.

The editors of this volume present a model with four aspects, arguing that security, culture, economy, and rights are the four factors that drive immigration control policy. In comparing a large number of liberal states, it is important to assess how the welfare state fits within such an analytical scheme. My suggestion is that welfare states are constrained by both security/culture (securitization) and economy/rights (the liberal paradox).

Defining Control Policy and Its Relevance for the Welfare State

In comparison with the four concepts of security, culture, economy, and rights, Hampshire identifies four facets of liberal states that are relevant to migration control: the democratic state, the constitutional state, the nation-state, and the capitalist state (Hampshire 2013). Guiraudon and Joppke (2001, 2) refer to migration control as dealing with "migration that is happening despite and against the opposite intentions of states." Helbling et al. (2013, 9) argue that control includes "measures set up to make sure that . . . [the] regulations are upheld."

Migration control thus aims to cater to both risks and demands relating to security/culture (securitization) and economy/rights (the liberal paradox). Understood in this way, control is highly relevant for the welfare state, as measures to make sure that regulations are being followed will often be crucial when controlling external territorial access, as well as determining access and claims to welfare provisions (integration control).

Immigration, Social Trust, and Redistribution

Brochmann describes the welfare state as not only for economic redistribution but also a moral construct having to do with institutionalized solidarity, equal treatment, and nation-building. Social rights are key for all citizens, and legal residence enables access to income security and a decent standard of living. Welfare state policies in this way should cater to the whole population, but that population cannot be overstretched. A similar argument is made by Mau and Burkhardt when suggesting that welfare states are built on providing benefits for homogeneous insiders, thereby excluding outsiders, and for this reason large-scale immigration may challenge social security institutions (Mau and Burkhardt 2009).

It can be questioned whether this ideal welfare state still exists and why welfare states would not be able to cope with differentiation and exclusion of residents. After all, like all European welfare states, the Nordic welfare state model encountered substantial challenges in the 1990s, leading to some divergence between Sweden and Finland, on the one hand, and Denmark and Norway, on the other (Eitrheim and Kuhnle 2000). This has resulted in cuts in welfare provisions in Scandinavia since the early 1990s compared to the 1950s and 1960s, cuts that also exclude some insiders. In addition, the 2008 financial crisis led Denmark to focus on employment-centered reforms coupled with more pressure on those who receive social benefits (Greve 2016) and Sweden to emphasize welfare-to-work programs due to demographic challenges (Hort, Kings, and Kravchenko, 2016). Such reforms also raise the issue of how natives react to immigration in defense of their welfare state system.

Securitization and Policy Effectiveness

Calls for reinforced controls in general or to protect the welfare state often have a nationalistic and security-oriented flavor linked to ethnic diversity. Public opinion and discourse on immigration and welfare are also strongly linked to party politics and the politics of securitization. The view of the Copenhagen school was that "for a state, survival is about sovereignty, and for a nation it is about identity" (Buzan and Waever 2009, 255). The defense of cultural identity and the nation (including the welfare state) is therefore very much linked to traditional notions of nationalism. Securitization often involves elements of "strategic social construction" by governments and non-governmental actors and the exaggeration of threat perceptions (Friman 2008, 131; Doty 1999). Huysmans has argued that the "securitization" of societal issues implies that if immigrants cause disharmony, there was harmony and stability before they came, but that this is not always the case. Analyzing immigration, multiculturalism, or societal identity through a security discourse is thus not a neutral practice (Huysmans 1995).

Securitization has become counterproductive and visibly lacking in effectiveness. One aspect in this regard is that it creates higher transaction costs and risks for the migrants, and that restrictive external controls are being circumvented by migrants anyway through the help of smugglers and via irregular routes (Zapata-Barrero 2013, 20). So even if natives try to defend their welfare systems by calling for reinforced controls, those control measures might have unanticipated consequences.

Public Discourse and the Role of Right-Wing Populism

How do these processes of securitization play out in public discourses across the Scandinavian countries? One way this could be explored is by looking at which migration-related terminology is accepted and made mainstream (e.g., the notion of "kindism"). There is a difference between Denmark and Norway compared to Sweden in terms of the role of right-wing populists. While in the former they are more generally accepted, such as in mainstream media, a shift in this direction has only been going on in the past six or seven years in Sweden.

There has been an extensive debate in Sweden since the 2014 elections regarding whether media and public debate shied away from criticizing the generous immigration policy. On this issue, the mainstream media are to an extent self-critical. Former prime minister Fredrik Reinfeldt disapproved of his migration minister Tobias Billström's use of the word "volumes" in regard to how much immigration was conceivable. But Billström mainly responded to restrictive pressures from local and regional Conservative Party members. The official line was still that no ceiling could be imagined. Reinfeldt's reelection campaign in the summer of 2014 confirmed this line, using the phrase "open your hearts" in relation to the Syrian influx, but this led to a great loss for the Conservatives and large gains for Sweden Democrats in the subsequent elections.

Several Swedish mainstream parties use restrictive discourses similar to those used by the populist right parties in Denmark and Norway. Some research shows that despite such copying of restrictive policies and discourses, the populist right usually gains. Moreover, copying the stance of right-wing populists does not necessarily mean cooperation with them. Green-Pedersen and Odmalm (2008) have highlighted the role of center-right parties for such cooperation when comparing Denmark and Sweden. They argue that the Danish shift in position followed upon a change of sides by the party Radical Left (RV). The RV took part in a new government coalition, which led to a marked change in how center-right parties regarded immigration. This shift facilitated the success of the center-right in subsequent elections,. The center-right coalition, in 2001, formed a government with the help of the far-right Danske Folkeparti (DF) as a supporting party.

The success of DF in this cooperation has also been linked to the socio-cultural conflict dimension (Rydgren 2010; Green-Pedersen and Krogstrup 2008). Denmark has, compared to Sweden, a much longer tradition of discussing value issues and lifestyle policies, while Swedish politics has long had a stronger dimension of socio-economic conflict. The center-right parties in Sweden did not arrive at positions as restrictive as those of their equivalent parties in Denmark (Green-Pedersen and Odmalm 2008; Bale 2003). The conservative-liberal Alliance in Sweden aimed to stand as a strong alternative to the Social Democrats and therefore played on the immigration issue to reach agreement on other issues up until the 2014 election. In addition, the background of the Sweden Democrats in neo-fascist and neo-Nazi subcultures led the Alliance parties to isolate it (Erlingsson et al. 2014; Rydgren 2010).

The Welfare State and the Migration Crisis

The challenges to the welfare state related to immigration, increasing politicization, and an inability to achieve effective control are also closely intertwined with a crisis mentality. It has been argued that in 2015 "a series of migratory crises led to simultaneous calls for 'more Europe' on the one hand and increased national discretion vis-à-vis the EU on the other" (Jabko and Luhman 2017, 24). The crisis could lead to more communitarianism within the EU (of relevance mainly for Sweden, less so for Denmark with its opt-out provisions) as well as to externalization of control measures, thereby rendering them more effective.

But others suggest that the crisis runs much deeper. It has been argued that what were regarded as temporary situations of crisis in the Western world after the end of the Cold War now have turned into a "permanent state of crisis" (Zaiotti 2016, 3) or a "permanent state of emergency" (Balibar 2015). The permanent migration crisis for European actors is also linked to the crisis of the sovereign state: "the 'sovereign state' is currently in crisis and its demise is daily becoming more apparent, as globalization undermines the state from within and without" (Hobson 2000 , 164). It could also be argued that the Nordic welfare state is in crisis (Huber and Stephens 2001). It is unclear, however, what role immigration might play in this.

The Control Impact of Welfare Is Twofold

The impact of the Nordic welfare state model on migration control policies, according to Brochmann, has been twofold, affecting both entry control and integration control. Welfare states had to "balance the volume and composition of the inflow, on the one hand, with the institutional and economic integration capacities of the receiving nation-state, on the other." Protecting and preserving the welfare state, Brochmann argues, needs to be linked to a state's absorption capacity, both economic and cultural.

Let us look at these two aspects, entry control and integration control. First, entry control is regarded as necessary in order to uphold the welfare state system. For there to be a generous welfare state for everyone inside the territorial state, generosity has to be curtailed toward the outside and outsiders. External control thus needs to be selective and restrictive. This precondition does not seem to be valid for the case of Sweden, with its relatively high immigration rate. It is also somewhat of a puzzle to explain why Sweden did not try earlier to reduce the volume of immigration by using more effective external migration control, or more restrictive internal regulation on integration or access to citizenship.

Second, for welfare states, social rights are a central element, as Brochmann highlights. Therefore, equality and welfare rights are also of key importance to integration policies. Welfare states are now differentiating between various migrant categories. There is a range of different residence statuses, with different linked rights, depending on the motives for immigration. Again, the case of Sweden is an outlier, with the country's generous rules on access to welfare state provisions for immigrants. It is, however, not certain whether more restrictive policies in Sweden could deter migration in a simple and straightforward way, especially in regard to asylum seekers.

Research on concrete examples of tightening control, both in relation to entry and regarding access to welfare, is inconclusive. Some studies show that restrictive asylum and visa policies are often ineffective (Czaika and Hobolth 2016). Overall, it is hard to explain why "countries implementing policies designed to decrease immigration do not necessarily see a reduction in immigration flows." It is possible that inflows may decrease only gradually after more restrictive policies are introduced, as noted by the OECD (2017, 137–138). While Hatton (2009, 2016) demonstrates a deterrence effect of more restrictive border control and of a more selective assessment in the asylum process, he does not find any effect from differences in welfare policy. Thielemann (2006) and Brekke et al. (2016), on the other hand, find that rules related to physical entry into a state have only a minor effect on asylum flows compared to the welfare that can be offered. Historical, economic, and reputational factors appear to be stronger factors when migrants are deciding on a destination country (Thielemann 2006, 2013)—something that might explain Sweden's profile as a magnet (cf. Jakubiak 2019; Allard and Danziger 2000 ; Peridy 2006).

Consequently, while careful integration of migrants is a prerequisite for a Nordic welfare state, this objective has not been fully achieved. Instead, a large public sector and high taxes are in practice combined with tolerated exclusion of some parts of immigrant communities. While the welfare state is still supported in general, its legitimacy is increasingly being questioned in regard to the costs incurred by the lack of integration of those admitted as immigrants. Some research looks into the link between immigration and the size and maintenance of the welfare state, but the results have not been conclusive. Integration control thus should be further explored.

The Nordic Welfare States and Exclusion

Nordic welfare states de facto accept marginalization, exclusion, and the non-applicability of welfare provisions to certain segments of people living in their territories. For instance, although the Swedish Social Democrats have traditionally had a relatively restrictive view on immigration policy (Hinnfors et al. 2012), the party has for years accepted the presence in the streets of thousands of beggars from some EU member states, notably Romania and Bulgaria. The main argument has been that you cannot forbid poverty. Meanwhile, Sweden to some extent tries to put pressure on the source countries to create better conditions at home.

Also, there is a relatively large number of so-called paperless—people who have no legal rights to stay or work (including failed asylum seekers who await expulsion orders), without much being done about them. To circumvent control measures focusing on these groups, "foggy social structures" have been established by irregular migrants, employers and unofficial agencies, NGOs, and even local authorities, operating without proper authority. States may either informally tolerate or accept these populations (as in the 1970s–1990s in the Netherlands) or attempt to "break open" these foggy structures (as in the Nordic welfare states currently) (Bommes and Sciortino 2011; Broeders and Engbersen 2011, 170–171).

The editors write about the Brochmann chapter that "guaranteeing basic welfare of all citizens and legal residents is fundamental to the Nordic model of government, and for this reason it is difficult to talk about immigrant policies outside of the context of the welfare state." In light of the aspects of policy just described, this seems to be an exaggeration. In addition, Scandinavian countries also have much higher unemployment rates among immigrants than many liberal states with less prominent welfare systems; furthermore, such figures vary across the Nordic welfare state countries (OECD 2020). Although this might confirm Milton Friedman's (1999) famous statement that "you cannot simultaneously have free [or generous] immigration and a welfare state" (see Caplan 2008), it also clearly shows that economically, at least, a large proportion of immigrants are not integrated. They are living on the edges of society, often in segregated, poor-quality housing on the outskirts of cities and municipalities, a number of them in areas that the Swedish police have classified as having especially high crime rates and instability.

As unemployment and lack of labor market incorporation of newcomers have raised concerns in all three Scandinavian countries about added burdens to the welfare states, there have been several initiatives to reinforce control measures, both internally and externally. They have targeted family reunification as well as citizenship. However, such restrictions have been implemented in parallel with the liberalization of economic immigration due to labor shortages and aging populations (Helbling and Kalkum 2017; de Haas et al. 2018, 2).

Conclusions

The threats and risks associated with immigration and the welfare state are often portrayed in a securitizing way. The Nordic welfare states are in a crisis situation, where rollbacks have resulted in exclusion and marginalization. This trend may pose a challenge to the legitimacy of their systems by weakening social trust in light of large-scale immigration over the past decades. In order to regard the Nordic welfare state model as a special case among liberal welfare states, we need further research that could explain the notable differences that have evolved in comparison between the Danish and the Swedish cases. A key aspect might be that these two countries have followed different dynamics in relation to security/culture (securitization) and economy/rights (the liberal paradox).

References

Allard, S. W., and S. Danziger. 2000 "Welfare Magnets: Myth or Reality?" *Journal of Politics* 62, no. 2: 350–368.

Bale, T. 2003. "Cinderella and Her Ugly Sisters: The Mainstream and Extreme Right in Europe's Bipolarising Party Systems." *West European Politics* 26, no. 3: 67–90.

Balibar, E. 2015. "Borderland Europe and the Challenge of Migration." Open Democracy. https://www.opendemocracy.net/can-europe-make-it/etienne-balibar/borderland-europe-and-challenge-of-migration.

Bommes, M., and G. Sciortino, eds. 2011. *Foggy Social Structures: Irregular Migration, European Labour Markets and the Welfare State.* Amsterdam: Amsterdam University Press.

Brekke, J.-P., M. Røed, and P. Schøne. 2016. "Reduction or Deflection? The Effect of Asylum Policy on Interconnected Asylum Flows." *Migration Studies* 5, no. 1: 65–96.

Broeders, D., and G. Engbersen. 2011. "Immigration Control and Strategies of Irregular Immigrants: From Light to thick Fog." In *Foggy Social Structures: Irregular Migration, European Labour Markets and the Welfare State,* edited by M. Bommes and G. Sciortino, pp. 169-188. Amsterdam: Amsterdam University Press.

Buzan, B., and O. Waever. 2009. "Macrosecuritisation and Security Constellations: Reconsidering Scale in Securitisation Theory." *Review of International Studies* 35, no. 2: 253–276.

Caplan, Brian. 2008. https://www.econlib.org/archives/2008/06/milton_friedman_10.html

Czaika, M., and M. Hobolth. 2016. "Do Restrictive Asylum and Visa Policies Increase Irregular Migration into Europe?" *European Union Politics* 17, no. 3: 345–365.

de Haas, H., M. Czaika, M.-L. Flahaux, E. Mahendra, K. Natter, S. Vezzoli, and M. Villares-Varela. 2018. "International Migration: Trends, Determinants and Policy Effects." Working Paper no. 142, DEMIG paper no. 33, International Migration Institute.

Doty, R. L. 1999. "Immigration and the Politics of Security." In *The Origins of National Interests,* edited by G. Chafetz, B. Frankel, and M. Spirtaz, pp. 71-93. London: Frank Cass.

Eitrheim, P., and S. Kuhnle. 2000. "Nordic Welfare States in the 1990s: Institutional Stability, Signs of Divergence." In *The Survival of the European Welfare State,* edited by S. Kuhnle, pp. 39-57. London: Routledge.

Erlingsson, G. O., K. Vernby, and R. Öhrvall. 2014. "The Single-Issue Party Thesis and the Sweden Democrats." *Acta Politica* 49, no. 2: 196–216.

Friman, H. R. 2008. "Migration and Security: Crime, Terror and the Politics of Order." In *Immigration, Integration, and Security: America and Europe in Comparative Perspective,* edited by A. Chebel d'Appollonia and S. Reich, pp. 130–144. Pittsburgh: University of Pittsburgh Press.

Green-Pedersen, C., and J. Krogstrup. 2008. "Immigration as a Political Issue in Denmark and Sweden." *European Journal of Political Research* 47, no. 5: 610–634.

Green-Pedersen, C., and P. Odmalm. 2008. "Going Different Ways? Right-Wing Parties and the Immigrant Issue in Denmark and Sweden." *Journal of European Public Policy* 15, no. 3: 367–381.

Greve, B. 2016. "Denmark: Still a Nordic Welfare State After the Changes of Recent Years?" In *Challenges to European Welfare Systems*, edited by K. Schubert, P. de Villota, and J. Kuhlmann, 159-176. Cham: Springer.

Guiraudon, V., and C. Joppke, eds. 2001. *Controlling a New Migration World*. London: Routledge.

Hampshire, J. 2013. *The Politics of Immigration: Contradictions of the Liberal State*. Cambridge: Polity.

Hatton, T. J. 2009. "The Rise and Fall of Asylum: What Happened and Why?" *Economic Journal* 119, no. 535: 183–213.

Hatton, T. J. 2016. "Refugees, Asylum Seekers, and Policy in OECD Countries." *American Economic Review* 106, no. 5: 441–445.

Helbling, M., L. Bjerre, F. Römer, and M. Zobel. 2013. "The Immigration Policies in Comparison (IMPIC) Index: The Importance of a Sound Conceptualization." *Migration and Citizenship* 1, no. 2: 22-29.

Helbling, M., and D. Kalkum. 2017. "Migration Policy Trends in OECD Countries." SSRN. https://ssrn.com/abstract=2985960.

Hinnfors, J., A. Spehar, and G. Bucken-Knapp. 2012. "The Missing Factor: Why Social Democracy Can Lead to Restrictive Immigration Policy." *Journal of European Public Policy* 19, no. 4: 585–603.

Hobson, John M. 2000. *The State and International Relations*. Cambridge: Cambridge University Press.

Hort, S., L. Kings, and Z. Kravchenko. 2016. "Still Awaiting the Storm? The Swedish Welfare State After the Latest Crisis." In *Challenges to European Welfare Systems*, edited by K. Schubert, P. de Villota, and J. Kuhlmann, pp. 671-691. Cham: Springer.

Huber, E., and J. D. Stephens. 2001. *Development and Crisis of the Welfare State: Parties and Policies in Global Markets*. Chicago: University of Chicago Press.

Huysmans, J. 1995. "Migrants as a Security Problem: Dangers of 'Securitizing' Societal Issues." In *Migration and European Integration: The Dynamics of Inclusion and Exclusion*, edited by R. Miles and D. Thränhardt, pp. 53-72. London: Pinter.

Jabko, N., and M. Luhman. 2017. "Reconstituting Sovereignty in the European Union: A Comparison of the Eurozone Crisis and the Migration Crisis." Paper prepared for the EUSA Fifteenth Biennial Conference, Miami, May 4–6, 2017.

Jakubiak, I. J. 2019. "Does Welfare Drive International Migration? A European Experience." *International Journal of Manpower* 40, no. 2: 246–264.

Mau, S., and C. Burkhardt. 2009. "Migration and Welfare State Solidarity in Europe." *Journal of European Social Policy* 19, no. 3: 213–229.

OECD. 2017. *Perspectives on Global Development: International Migration in a Shifting World.* Paris: OECD.

OECD. 2020. *International Migration Outlook 2020.* Paris: OECD.

Peridy, N. J. 2006. "Welfare Magnets, Border Effects or Policy Regulations: What Determinants Drive Migration Flows into the EU?" *Global Economy Journal* 6, no. 4, pp. 1-29.

Rydgren, J. 2010. "Radical Right-Wing Populism in Denmark and Sweden: Explaining Party System Change and Stability." *SAIS Review* 30, no. 1: 57–71.

Thielemann, E. R. 2006. "The Effectiveness of Governments' Attempts to Control Unwanted Migration." In *Immigration and the Transformation of Europe*, edited by Craig A. Parsons and T. A. Smeeding, pp. 442-472. Cambridge: Cambridge University Press.

Zapata-Barrero, R. 2013. "The External Dimension of Migration Policy in the Mediterranean Region: Premises for Normative Debate." *Revista del Instituto Español de Estudios Estratégicos* no. 2/2013, pp.1-36.

Zaiotti, R. 2016. "Mapping Remote Control: The Externalization of Migration Management in the 21st Century." In *Externalizing Migration Management: Europe, North America and the Spread of "Remote Control" Practices*, edited by R. Zaiotti, pp. 3-30. Milton Park: Routledge.

Clashing Solidarity Logics:
Comments on Grete Brochmann

Lars Trägårdh

As Grete Brochmann notes in her incisive chapter on governing immigration in Scandinavia, the politics of social justice has long constituted an important aspect of Scandinavian identity. This moral and political imperative has been not only expressed at the national level but also projected onto the world stage. Thus, the Scandinavian countries have, especially after World War II, become famous both for their domestic welfare states and for being, in a global context, "moral superpowers."

This dual commitment to expansive social investments at home and human rights and ambitious development projects across the globe were long seen as two aspects of a single, unified commitment to a basic egalitarian, universal ideal of equal opportunity, fairness, and social solidarity. However, in recent years we have, as Brochmann points out, witnessed an increasing tension in the Scandinavian countries between the politics of solidarity, grounded in the national welfare state, and international and even post-national ambitions. This tension, I will argue, is not primarily about sheer cost or conflicts rooted in xenophobia. Rather, the crucial factor involves a shift in focus from development aid directed at states and/or civil society organizations in the faraway developing world to reacting to increasing migration to the Scandinavian countries themselves. This has exposed a fundamental contradiction between two logics of solidarity.

The Scandinavian Social Contract: Social Trust and the Moral Economy of Reciprocity

Scandinavian societies are often portrayed as based on ideals such as altruism, collectivism, and selfless solidarity. In this vein, some scholars have stressed the politics of altruistic solidarity and advanced the notion of a "social democratic regime" characterized by "decommodification," redistribution (equality of outcome), and a logic of pitting "politics against markets" (Esping-Andersen 1990). But what stands out far more than "socialism" in the Scandinavian countries is what at first may appear to be a paradox—namely, that strong social values, expressed in a combination of social trust and a positive view of the state, coexist with a strong emphasis on individual freedom and autonomy.

Given the common misconception about the Scandinavian countries being, in some sense, socialist or social democratic, it becomes all the more important to stress that altruism in the sense of unconditional charity is in fact not the central moral principle of the modern Scandinavian social contract. Nor is it about "welfare" as that word is understood commonly in the Anglo-Saxon countries, where welfare often connotes charitable—and stigmatizing—handouts to the needy. Rather, the social contract is based on a far more demanding moral logic: the figure of the "wholesome worker" (Ambjörnsson 1988) and the idea that each member of society contributes their share (Trägårdh and Svedberg 2013). There are no free lunches in the Scandinavian countries.

At heart, it is a social contract based on a moral economy whose core principle is that of *reciprocity* rather than *charity*, an emancipatory logic that connects citizenship, work, and taxes to social rights (Trägårdh 2018). The citizens generally perceive taxes to be part of a legitimate social contract, where tax revenue is ultimately returned to the citizens in the form of investments in collective infrastructure and social rights (schooling, health care, elderly care, etc.). The most obvious expression of a high-trust society is thus the willingness of its citizens to pay taxes, and the Scandinavian societies stand out both for their high taxes and for the absence of political parties seriously questioning such high taxes.

This strict morality is linked to trust and trustworthiness, and even those who at first seem to be subject to pure altruism—children and the elderly—are in fact viewed as deserving because they either have worked (the elderly) or are expected to eventually work (children). This is true even for those groups that are especially vulnerable in terms of the work ethic: the disabled and the sick. While it is true that these groups are provided assistance based on unconditional solidarity within the nation, much effort is nonetheless devoted to enabling autonomy and discouraging dependency by maximizing the disabled's access to work and minimizing incentives for the sick to remain on sick leave for extended periods of time. Scandinavian societies can thus be thought of in terms of two ideas central to the logic of reciprocity: *investment* and *insurance*. The taxes enable social investments in both individual human capital and in collective infrastructure. They also allow for pooling, or collectivizing, if you will, risk in the form of social insurance.

The result is a state-based social contract, where the state serves both as a giant insurance company and as a social investment scheme. As I have described in more detail elsewhere (Berggren and Trägårdh 2015), this social contract has served to maximize the room for individual autonomy while at the same time liberating those in weaker positions of power—women, children, the elderly, the sick, the disabled—from patriarchal and unequal power relations in the traditional family and civil society. The feature that sets the Scandinavian countries apart is this combination of statism and individualism, a logic that I have termed *statist individualism*: a highly institutionalized alliance between the state and individual citizens, based on trust in institutions and confidence in the state, while enabling an extreme form of individualism linked to a high degree of equality (Berggren and Trägårdh 2015; Trägårdh 1997).

The Scandinavian social contract is thus primarily about scaled-up reciprocity in the context of a modern, highly individualistic market society. The focus has been on creating social mobility and equal opportunity, thus replacing the need for philanthropy and charity with earned income, taxes, and social rights. For this very reason, within the broader framework of the globalized market society, the Scandinavian countries have proved to be winners at the level of the individual as well as those of company, association, society, and state. The Scandinavian states are thus less "welfare states" than "social investment states" (Morel et al. 2012); less "socialist" states protecting themselves from the harshness of capitalism than highly successful "competition states" within a global market economy (Pedersen 2011).

Development Aid, Scandinavian Identity, and the Revival of the Charity Logic

While the postwar decades now appear to have been the heyday of social democracy and the charity-hostile welfare state, charity did manage to survive and even thrive, not only at the margins of the welfare state but even more so on the international scene. Indeed, after World War II, UN-inspired internationalism became increasingly important to Scandinavian international politics and national identity.

If we take Sweden as the prime example, it was Dag Hammarskjöld, the second secretary-general of the UN, and the prominent Social Democratic prime minister Olof Palme who came to symbolize Sweden's (perceived) special role in this regard. As the commitment to foreign aid and the political support of "Third World" countries grew, the idea emerged that Sweden was a country especially devoted to peace and international solidarity. Whereas the United States was the ultimate military power and world police, Sweden projected itself as the "moral superpower." While the United States became known for its military-industrial complex, Sweden could boast a development-aid industrial complex. From Prime Ministers Dag Hammarskjöld and Folke Bernadotte to Olof Palme, and then to Carl Bildt and Margot Wallström in more recent days, the "Swedish way" has been one of whole-hearted support for binding international law, expressed in a language steeped in a deeply moralist vision of a new world order, fashioned according to the logic of human rights and global solidarity.

Thus, by the early 1960s Swedish intellectuals were seriously promoting the rather self-satisfied notion that Sweden was the "world's conscience." The well-known author Lars Gustafsson argued that Swedish "Third Worldism" should be understood as a new and central aspect of Swedish national identity. Indeed, he argued, "if Swedish patriotism exists nowadays, it consists of our desire to make ourselves heard in the connection with which this new solidarity confronts us" (Ruth 1984, 71) As Arne Ruth, a prominent Swedish public intellectual, summarized it, internationalism acquired the status of national ideology: "Equality at home and justice abroad have come to be regarded as complementary and mutually supporting values" (Ruth 1984, 71).

This internationalist turn involved the revival of charity abroad even as the logic of reciprocity and social rights dominated at home. Philanthropy and charity survived in two ways: by offering alms to the truly disadvantaged in Sweden and, most prominently, by providing aid to needy foreigners abroad. Yet the contradictions of the two solidarity logics remained largely invisible. In the case of charity at home, it was concerned with only a small number of citizens and legal residents at the edges of society, largely hidden from view and with little impact on the majority. In the case of development aid, the problematic charity dynamic, so unacceptable at home, remained out of sight, since the act of giving had been divorced from that of receiving. The giving occurred in the safety of one's own home, hiding the problematic inequality inherent in a face-to-face charity-based relationship.

Notably, during this period immigration was not a divisive issue even though immigration, especially in Sweden, was significant. The dominant form was labor immigration, a type of immigration that dovetailed nicely with the Swedish social contract and its stress on work and reciprocity. Labor migrants essentially went to work from day one and thus immediately began to pay taxes and contribute. Even refugees were effectively treated as labor immigrants, and given the huge demand for labor until the oil crisis of 1973, integration through work was largely unproblematic.

Thus, the Swedish development-aid industrial complex proceeded to build on a track parallel to that of the domestic welfare state. (I focus here on Sweden, but similar developments occurred in the other Scandinavian countries to a greater or lesser extent.) While the state continued its project of trying to eliminate the very need for charity at home, organizations like the Red Cross and Save the Children survived and flourished as charities by investing in this basic division of labor: collecting money in the Scandinavian countries and spending it in the global South. For many decades, this oddly schizoid modus vivendi proceeded without anyone paying too much attention to the basic conflict in solidarity logic.

However, this all changed when the empire struck back, Scandinavian style. As immigration from countries plagued by war and poverty increased, the focus of the debate in Sweden shifted from development projects in faraway places to the politics of refugee reception and integration in Sweden itself. And by now, immigration policy had been divorced from labor market policy, thus increasingly placing migrants outside of the social contract based on work and reciprocity. No longer arriving in Sweden through the pull of market demand but instead thanks to a humanitarian impulse to help, they became subject to a charity logic, initially deprived even of the right to work and instead reduced to being dependent on social assistance in various forms.

Finally, then, the inherent contradictions between the two solidarity logics began to become clearer, and the ensuing social tensions were gradually weaponized politically by the immigration-critical Sweden Democrats. As the traditional center-left and center-right parties turned toward an embrace of post-national visions, either of a right-wing, neo-liberal type that envisioned a global market society or through a left-wing, no-borders, cosmopolitan idealism in the name of human rights and a global civil society liberated from xenophobic nation-states, characterized by an odious "welfare chauvinism," the Sweden Democrats increasingly became the sole defenders of citizenship and nation-state.

Sweden as an Outlier: Rights Versus Duties, the National Versus the Global, Pride Versus Guilt

As Brochmann concludes, while there is much that unites the Scandinavian countries, both when it comes to their social contracts and in regard to their policies on immigration and integration, it is also true that they differ in significant ways, with Sweden as an outlier. To invoke Brochmann's analysis, in Sweden the stress has been more on (human) rights than on (citizenship) duties. If in Denmark and Norway the nation-state is embraced, then in Sweden "nationalism" is something of a dirty word. If Danes and Norwegians are comfortable speaking about Danish and Norwegian values, then Swedes tend to prefer a more universal language of liberal democracy and democratic values. If many Danes are forthright about proudly celebrating "Danishness" and thus unafraid of placing demands on immigrants to assimilate on rather strict terms, Swedes more commonly tend to see native Swedes as the true targets of necessary reeducation, since they are seen as guilty of xenophobia and racism, just as Sweden as a whole is complicit in a broader "colonial" project, and Swedish "universalism" is critically viewed as a disguise for a discriminatory "racial regime" (Mulinari and Neergaard 2017).

Thus, in replying to Brochmann's pointed and central question, "How should the welfare state's requirements of universal solutions and equal treatment be reconciled with minority rights and cultural diversity?," we see two distinct tendencies afoot in the Scandinavian countries. Whereas Denmark appears committed to a rejection of multiculturalism in favor of assimilation into the Danish nation, the Swedes—and to a lesser extent the Norwegians—appear more torn between the two competing moral logics.

The central problem regarding immigration in the Scandinavian countries, I would argue, is neither cost nor xenophobia and racism. There is little evidence that the Scandinavian countries are, in comparative perspective, particularly xenophobic. Indeed, Sweden in particular sticks out internationally by only to an extremely low degree associating national identity with ethnicity (Stokes 2017). Rather, what appears to be most important are civic virtues such as following laws and rules. This suggests a potential openness to immigrants becoming Swedes, but, significantly, there is also a demanding side to this stress on laws and rules—namely, that they are in themselves expressions of what I described earlier as the moral logic of the Swedish social contract. While ethnic origin may constitute a relatively low barrier to integration, compliance with the dictates of work-based reciprocity appears to be non-negotiable. And this is in turn linked to culture in the anthropological sense—that is, including not just abstract "values" but also concrete institutions and social practices. Indeed, at a certain point what appears to be a strict emphasis on a civic universalism merges with a more particular conception that obscures the boundary between an ethnic understanding of Swedish national identity and a civic one (Barker 2017).

Thus, since the obligation to work is essentially non-negotiable and linked to radical Swedish individualism, this also implies adherence to gender equality, children's rights, and general individual autonomy, all of which demote family values and religious and ethnic communitarianism in favor of statist individualism. This in practice tends to exclude immigrant cultures that bring a different view on the role of the state, family values, gender relations, sexuality, and the place of religion. At the same time, this uncompromising demand to adopt Swedish culture is partly hidden by the fashionable, state-sponsored dogma of multiculturalism, which appears to celebrate cultural difference, minority group rights, and diversity. This normative take on diversity as always good has, in the dominant discourse, gone hand in hand with a denigration of the nation-state and a devaluation of citizenship in favor of human rights. In this context, integration policy has become a muddle, torn between demands to integrate through work and an official policy that demonizes the very assimilation that the Swedish social contract in fact requires.

References

Ambjörnsson, R. 1988. *Den skötsamme arbetaren*. Stockholm: Carlsson.

Barker, V. 2017. *Nordic Nationalism and Penal Order: Walling the Welfare State*. Abingdon, UK: Routledge.

Berggren, H., and L. Trägårdh. 2015. *Är svensken människa? Gemenskap och oberoende i det moderna Sverige*, 2nd ed. Stockholm: Norstedts.

Esping-Andersen, G. 1990. *The Three Worlds of Welfare Capitalism*. Cambridge: Polity.

Mulinari, D., and A. Neergaard. 2017. "Theorising Racism: Exploring the Swedish Racial Regime." *Nordic Journal of Migration Research* 7, no. 2: 88–96.

Morel, N., B. Palier, and J. Palme, eds. 2012. *Towards a Social Investment Welfare State? Ideas, Policies and Challenges*. Bristol: Policy Press.

Pedersen, O. K. 2011. *Konkurrencestaten*. Copenhagen: Hans Rietzels Forlag.

Ruth, A. 1984. "The Second New Nation: The Mythology of Modern Sweden." *Dædalus* 113, no. 1: 53-96.

Stokes, B. 2017. "What It Takes to Truly Be 'One of Us.'" Pew Research Center. https://assets.pewresearch.org/wp-content/uploads/sites/2/2017/04/14094140/Pew-Research-Center-National-Identity-Report-FINAL-February-1-2017.pdf.

Trägårdh, L. 1997. "Statist Individualism: On the Culturality of the Nordic Welfare State." In *The Cultural Construction of Norden*, edited by B. Stråth and Ø. Sørensen, pp. 143-161. Oslo: Scandinavian University Press.

Trägårdh, Lars. 2018. "Scaling up Solidarity from the National to the Global: Sweden as Welfare State and Moral Superpower." In *Sustainable Modernity: The Nordic Model and Beyond*, edited by Nina Witoszek and Atle Midttun pp. 79-101. London: Routledge.

Trägårdh, L., and L. Svedberg. 2013. "The Iron Law of Rights: Citizenship and Individual Empowerment in Modern Sweden." In *Social Policy and Citizenship: The Changing Landscape*, edited by A. Evers and A. Guillemard, pp. 222-256. Oxford: Oxford University Press.

10 Immigration and Integration in Switzerland

Shifting Evolutions in a Multicultural Republic

Gianni D'Amato

Introduction

As a small country located at the crossroads of northern and southern Europe, Switzerland is widely known for its neutrality and peaceful attitudes, its ethnic and linguistic diversity—German, French, Italian, and Reto-Romansch are all national languages[1]—and a decentralized government that makes most of its laws at the canton (or state) level.[2] There is a good reason that control and integration policies figure so prominently in a federalist country that was challenged since its birth—in the aftermath of the successful liberal revolution of 1848—by centrifugal forces on the religious, regional, political, social, and ideological levels. Certain foreign scholars, puzzled by Switzerland's apparent enduring stability (and overlooking the history of violent and disruptive conflicts from the civil war of 1847 until the social unrest of the 1930s), detect the source of this solidity in the clever management of a multicultural country through its federal institutions (Schnapper 1997). Others see Switzerland as a "paradigmatic case of political integration" as a result of the subsidiary structure of the Swiss state, which supports both strong municipal autonomy and the comparatively high participation rate of the (male—note that women in certain cantons could not vote in federal elections until 1971) constituency in the polity (Deutsch 1976). Still others see the source of the country's stability in the successful creation of a strong national identity, which helped overcome the social distrust that arose during rapid industrialization and which was based on the country's small size and the idea that it was under permanent threat from strong neighboring countries (*Über-fremdung*) (Kohler 1994; Tanner 1998).

Notwithstanding this fear of being demographically and culturally overrun by foreigners, Switzerland had one of the highest immigration rates on the continent during the twentieth century. According to Swiss Statistics in 2019, 37.7 percent of the total population of 8.6 million had a migration background[3]; 25.3 percent, or nearly 2.1 million, were foreign (defined here as persons with a foreign nationality), with the rest naturalized or holders of Swiss nationality in a second or third generation.[4] In relative numbers this is twice as high as the number of foreigners in the United States and considerably higher than the number of foreigners in Canada—both of which are classic countries of immigration. In contrast to its internal pluralistic character, however, Switzerland for a long time did not consider itself a country of immigration—in fact, federal governments denied the existence of an immigration policy at the federal level until the 1990s (Kurt and D'Amato 2021). This long-enduring policy of denial influenced the country's decision not to admit any Jewish refugees after 1933, and it affected the implementation of a "guest worker" rotation model after the oil crisis of 1973. Only recently, after signing a bilateral agreement on the free movement of persons with the European Union in 2002, did Switzerland start to develop a differentiated immigration policy favoring European citizens and revising its Act on Foreign Nationals several times, introducing a path to settlement for long-term residents in 2019.

Another historically influential paradox concerns the handling of admission and integration issues at the political level. For the whole of the twentieth century, even before World War I, Switzerland was a popular destination for guest workers from France, Germany, and Italy. In the second half of the twentieth century, however, it became home to Eastern European dissidents, Yugoslavian refugees, and asylum seekers from the Middle East, Asia, and Africa. During the entire century, and in the complete absence of the social hardships encountered in neighboring countries (high unemployment rates among migrants, ethnic and social segregation, social unrest, etc.), the immigration issue grew contentious. Especially after the 1960s, it frequently appeared on the Swiss political agenda.

This inconsistent situation must be explained by a careful analysis of how immigration and integration policies evolved in Switzerland. In the next section, I describe immigration and integration during the twentieth century by way of a brief historical overview, and present some demographic data. In the following section, I emphasize the importance of various stakeholders who influence migration policies at the different state levels, and I devote attention to external factors that may have had an effect on the creation of these policies. I show that the political opportunity structures in Switzerland—influenced by its federalism, municipal autonomy, and a consensus-oriented political culture—had an impact on the formulation of immigration policy as well, just as much as various external challenges (foreign governments, the European Union) did. In the conclusion, I discuss the factors that may have influenced Switzerland's particular immigration and integration policy outcomes.

Immigration and Immigrant Policies in Historical Perspective

Switzerland's reputation as an ideal place for exiles dates back to the sixteenth century, when the Huguenots of France were welcomed as religious refugees and found their place in the Swiss cultural, political, and entrepreneurial elite. But the modern transformation of Switzerland into a country of immigration—as that term is understood today—took place during its accelerated industrial takeoff in the second half of the nineteenth century (Holmes 1988; Romano 1996). In contrast to its rural image, the Swiss Confederation was a European forerunner in various modern mechanical and chemical industries and has had an enormous need to invest in knowledge and infrastructure. While many rural inhabitants were leaving the country to make their living farming in the New World, many German intellectuals fleeing the failed liberal revolutions of 1848–1849 found a place in Switzerland's universities. Italian craftsmen and workers also were recruited at the end of the nineteenth century and the early twentieth century, mainly in construction and the railroad sector.

During the late nineteenth and early twentieth centuries, the size of the foreign population in Swiss cities increased: 41 percent of Geneva's population was foreign-born, as was 28 percent in Basel and 29 percent in Zurich. Nationwide, the Germans outnumbered the Italians and French (Efionayi-Mäder, Niederberger, and Wanner 2005). Moreover, the proportion of foreigners increased from 3 percent of the total population in 1850 to 14.7 percent on the eve of World War I, with most of them coming from neighboring countries. During the two world wars, however, Switzerland's foreign population decreased significantly. By 1941, it had dropped to 5.2 percent (Arlettaz 1985).

In the liberal period preceding World War I, immigration was largely the responsibility of the cantons, whose laws had to conform to bilateral agreements signed between Switzerland and other European states. Like other agreements from this period concerning free circulation in Europe, these were open toward immigrants because they needed to ensure that Swiss citizens could easily emigrate if they needed to find work. However, after a first campaign against aliens during World War I, a new article was added to the constitution in 1925 (Senn et al. 2017) giving the federal government the power to address immigration issues at the national level, which provided the constitutional basis for the federal aliens police (*Fremdenpolizei*), created by an executive order during the war, and for the enactment of the Law on Residence and Settlement of Foreigners, which came into force in 1931 (Garrido 1990). This law allowed the new federal aliens police to implement immigration policy at their discretion, although at the time their aim was to maintain national identity rather than to regulate migration. Essentially, the authorities had to consider the country's moral and economic interests and the degree of "over-foreignization" (*Grad der Überfremdung*) in making their decisions. The nationwide political consensus on ensuring cultural purity prevented the drafting of any consistent immigrant policy until very recently. Foreigners, in principle, had to leave the country when their visas or residence permits expired, and were not allowed to settle permanently.

Postwar Labor Migration

Shortly after World War II, the economic demands of neighboring countries engaged in industrial recovery stimulated the rapid growth of the Swiss economy. In the context of the postwar economic boom, Switzerland signed an agreement with the Italian government in 1948 to recruit Italian guest workers. These workers were employed mainly in the construction sector but also in textile and machine factories. Afterward, a steady flow of foreign workers immigrated to Switzerland. Their number increased from 285,000 in 1950 (6.1 percent of the total population) to 585,000 (10.8 percent) in 1960 and to 1,080,000 (17.2 percent) in 1970. Predominantly Italian during the 1950s, the group of foreign workers diversified in the 1960s: while over 50 percent were still Italians in 1970, about 20 percent were German, French, or Austrian; 10 percent were Spaniards; and 4 percent were Yugoslavs, Portuguese, or Turks (Mahnig and Piguet 2003). Initially, they were entitled to stay for one year, although their contracts could be prolonged, which frequently happened. A similar agreement with Spain was signed in 1961.

To ensure that the workers did not settle permanently and could be sent home, the period required for obtaining a permanent residence permit was increased from five to ten years, and restrictive conditions on family reunion were adopted. This policy was called the "rotation model" because it meant that new workers could be brought in as others returned home. As the economic boom continued throughout the 1960s, the Swiss government's guest worker system became less tightly controlled. The country faced increasing pressure from Italy to introduce more generous family reunification laws, and the number of Italian workers willing to come to Switzerland decreased as other destinations, such as Germany, became more attractive after the signing of the Treaty of Rome in 1957. Also, Italy's internal economic boom and development started a wave of internal migration, particularly to destinations in northern Italy.

It was also at this time that the Organization for European Economic Cooperation (OEEC) introduced standards for family reunification. Other international regulatory bodies, such as the International Labour Organization (ILO), recommended that the Swiss government make its family reunification policies more "humane." In response, the government started to replace its rotation system with an integration-oriented scheme that facilitated family reunification, made foreign workers more eligible for promotions, and attempted to end labor market segmentation (Niederberger 2004).

Following the oil crisis in 1973, many workers became unneeded and had to leave the country because they did not have adequate unemployment insurance. This allowed Switzerland to "export" its unemployed guest workers without renewing their residence permits (Katzenstein 1987). The total proportion of the population that was foreign fell from 17.2 percent in 1970 to 14.8 percent in 1980. But as the economy recovered, new workers arrived not only from Italy but also from Spain, Portugal, and Turkey. Their percentage of the population increased from 14.8 percent (945,000) in 1980 to 18.1 percent (just under 1.25 million) in 1990, 22.4 percent (nearly 1.50 million) in 2000, and 25.3 percent in 2019 (2.10 million) (Mahnig and Piguet 2003; Swiss Statistics 2021, n. 3).

In the late 1970s, the government gave seasonal workers many of the same rights as guest workers who came on longer contracts—namely, the ability to transform their seasonal permits into permanent residence permits and to bring their families. Since the number of issued seasonal permits did not decrease—they numbered on average 130,000 per year between 1985 and 1995—they became a gateway for permanent immigration and a means for supplying cheap labor to sectors of the economy that otherwise would not have been able to survive given Switzerland's high wages. In 1982, a reform of the aliens law was meant to regulate the transformation of permits heuristically and give permanent residents a firm incentive to stay in the country. But a successful referendum promoted by a radical right-wing fringe party, the Swiss Democrats, which received a slight majority of the vote, put an end to the reform of all immigration and migrant settlement laws. Therefore, seasonal permits were still available until 2008, until the new aliens law entered into force.

The Swiss political process is complex. It is primarily through the institutions of federalism that Switzerland succeeded in accommodating its cultural and religious diversity. The country is a confederation of twenty-three cantons, which have a large measure of autonomy in making policy on education, public safety, and taxation. According to this principle, the Swiss Parliament functions on two levels: the National

Council (Nationalrat, which represents the people) and the State Council (Ständerat, which represents the cantons). New laws have to pass both chambers but can be immediately vetoed by a popular referendum.

By the time the worldwide recession of the early 1990s reached Switzerland, unskilled and aging guest workers were suffering high rates of unemployment and found it very difficult to locate new jobs. This situation led to unprecedented structural unemployment and poverty, which Switzerland had not experienced in recent decades. The larger cities, which, according to the subsidiary logic of the Swiss federal system, had to cover welfare expenses, urged the federal government to act, and they supported expanded integration requirements for immigrant workers (D'Amato and Gerber 2005). A new admission policy was supposed to be defined, which would have the task of combining the evolving needs of a new, more flexible post-industrial economy with those of migration control. Before we turn our attention to the policy-making process, however, the most important actors in Swiss migration policy must be discussed.

Asylum Policy

After World War II, the Swiss government recognized that its authorities had been responsible for denying admission to many Jewish refugees. The government stressed its willingness to uphold the humanitarian tradition of the country and in 1955 signed the 1951 Geneva Convention Relating to the Status of Refugees. During the next two decades, the country adopted a liberal policy, offering asylum to refugees from communist countries in eastern Europe. In 1956, 14,000 Hungarians were allowed to settle permanently after the uprising in their country against Soviet troops, and in 1968, 12,000 Czechoslovakian nationals arrived (Efionayi-Mäder 2003).

These people, who were often well educated, had little difficulty in obtaining refugee status. The government and the public gave them a warm welcome, which is not surprising given the strong anti-communist sentiments at the time. In the mid-1970s, the arrival of a few hundred Chilean dissidents fleeing Pinochet's regime ignited controversial debates about their asylum eligibility. Between 1979 and 1982, Switzerland offered protection to approximately 8,000 Vietnamese and Cambodian boat people, who were accepted on the basis of yearly quotas. The subsequent integration of these refugees was more difficult than for any previous refugee group (Parini and Gianni 1997, 2005).

All these events prompted the creation of a new federal asylum policy in 1981, which codified the country's relatively generous practices. It defined the rules of the refugee status determination procedure and gave the Confederation policymaking power, while clearly giving the cantons the responsibility of policy implementation.

In domains such as welfare, education, and repatriation, the power of the cantons in making refugee-related decisions was significant. As a result, there were major policy differences between cantons (D'Amato and Skenderovic 2009).

After 1981, two trends emerged. First, the number of applications for asylum, which had been steady at about 1,000 per year during the 1970s, increased exponentially. Second, most refugees—except for a large number of Polish refugees in 1982—came from other parts of the world besides Europe: Turkey, Sri Lanka, and other countries in the Middle East, Africa, and Asia. Unlike the anti-communist dissidents, they were not always professionals or university graduates. Some came from rural areas, some had not even finished primary school, and others had university degrees that were not recognized in Europe. In addition, a weak economy made it difficult for these non-Europeans to find work.

As more people from outside Europe filed applications, asylum became a sensitive subject, particularly in the mid-1980s. In public debates, refugees were called "asylum seekers" or even the derogatory "asylants" to indicate that they did not deserve refugee status. After the 1981 law's revisions created stricter procedures, the government gradually started granting a decreasing number of asylum requests, even from people fleeing civil wars and violence. As a rough indicator of this trend, the share of accepted applications averaged 86 percent between 1975 and 1979. This number dropped to an average of 47 percent between 1980 and 1984 and fell again to an average of 6 percent between 1985 and 1990 (Efionayi-Mäder, Niederberger, and Wanner 2005).

Immigration Policies and Policymaking

Because immigration and integration policies in Switzerland are intrinsically bound, this section first presents the main actors in policymaking and then discusses the recent changes in admission, asylum, integration, and naturalization policies.

The Actors in Policymaking

Once separated in two distinct offices within the Federal Department of Justice and Police, the Federal Office for Refugees (FOR) and the Federal Office for Immigration, Integration, and Emigration (IMES) were merged into one entity, the Federal Office for Migration (FOM), on January 1, 2005. Ten years later, with the increasing domestic and international importance of migration, the Swiss government upgraded the office to the new State Secretariat for Migration (SEM) without changing the organization and the structure of the body. One of SEM's branches continues to be responsible for implementing Swiss asylum policy. Another continues to administer admission policy as FOM did, including enforcing laws governing residence in Switzerland (the immigration and residence section); it also assesses labor market needs (the labor market section). The changes in the organization of the federal office reflect the desire to implement a coherent policy dealing with the admission, stay, and integration of foreigners (see Efionayi-Mäder 2018).

The State Secretariat for Economic Affairs (SECO), which is a part of the Federal Department of Economic Affairs (DEA), is the agency responsible for economics and labor issues. SECO has influenced Swiss labor migration policy since 1945 by determining the qualitative and quantitative needs of the country's labor market.

At the federal level, there are two important permanent commissions: the Federal Commission for Foreigners (FCF) and the Federal Commission against Racism (FCR). Established in 1970, the FCF is made up of experts from the Federal Council; it reports directly to the Federal Department of Justice and Police. The Federal Commission Against Racism (FCR) is an extra-parliamentary, independent commission. It was established by the Federal Council in 1995 after the ratification of the International Convention on the Elimination of All Forms of Racial Discrimination (CEDAW) and the adoption of the penal provision on racism, Article 261bis of the Penal Code. It comprises fifteen members expert in the field of racism and a secretariat affiliated to the General Secretariat of the Federal Department of Home Affairs.

The central concern of the FCF is the integration of foreigners. Since 2001, its funds have been available for projects that promote integration. At present, the FCF is made up of thirty members, two of whom have the status of observers. Members are representatives of various foreigners' organizations, municipalities, communities, cantons, employers and employees, and churches, or they have a professional background in integration policy. The FCF assists in the creation of educational and vocational opportunities for foreigners and in the recognition of professional training in cooperation with the relevant cantonal authorities; participates in the international exchange of views and experience; mediates between organizations that are active in the field and federal authorities; publishes opinions and recommendations regarding general issues of migration; and consults on migration questions during legislative proceedings.

The Federal Commission on Foreigners and the Federal Commission against Racism hold meetings on a quarterly basis, and they may organize joint events when it comes to the revision of laws. The FCR is part of the Federal Department of Home Affairs (DHA). Within the DHA, there is a branch that coordinates the various actors participating in the fight against racism. Among other activities, the DHA administers a fund for anti-racism projects. The FCF advises the government and relevant ministries also on refugee issues.

All of these bodies form an important interest group in the promulgation of new laws, insofar as a significant part of decision-making in Switzerland is left to the institutions of direct democracy. Particularly in migration policy, political processes and policymaking are dominated by pre-parliamentarian negotiations and direct democracy, with parliament not necessarily playing a primary role (Mahnig 1996). Significantly, the two levels of policymaking and the political process are characterized by different political styles (Neidhart 1970). In pre-parliamentarian negotiations compromise is the final objective of the consultation process, in which expert commissions play a decisive role; the arena of direct democracy is mainly characterized by confrontational attitudes and divisive outcomes.

At the federal level, the most important political parties in Switzerland are the centrist bloc, composed of the Christian Democrats (CVP), the Conservative Democratic Party (BDP, a moderate spin-off of the radicalized Swiss People's Party), and the Radical Liberal Party (FDP). (In 2021 the CVP and the BDP merged to form the Center Party.) The populist right consists of the Swiss People's Party (SVP). And the left-wing bloc comprises the Social Democratic Party (SPS) and the Green Party (GP). With the exception of the GP, all mentioned parties are members of the government. The SVP is an important stakeholder in debates on migration and asylum policy. Formerly the party of artisans and peasants, it became a modern radical populist party when Christoph Blocher, a charismatic lawyer and entrepreneur, took over its Zurich branch in the late 1970s and transformed it beginning in the 1990s into a campaigning organization. The SVP supported a popular initiative aiming to reduce the number of illegal residents in Switzerland and was in charge of an initiative "against asylum abuse." In Zurich, the party has launched an initiative demanding that all requests for naturalization be subject to popular referendum. Municipalities play a major role in the naturalization process, as discussed below.

Trade unions and employers also play a role in the formulation of immigration policy. Historically, they exerted their influence both in a formal manner (in the consultation procedure) and in an informal manner (in negotiating the quota of non-EU foreigners allowed into Switzerland). Because of the federal structure of the Swiss state, the cantons are also very influential in the formulation of governmental policies. Their sphere of authority includes the aliens police and determination of labor market needs. Furthermore, the cantons are responsible for the implementation of integration measures according to the Cantonal Integration Programs (discussed at length below), a program promoted by the federal level. The cantons are also responsible for maintaining public order and enforcing decisions involving repatriation. Thus, it is through their competence and experience in implementing asylum measures that they contribute significantly to policymaking in this area. The Conference of Cantonal Ministers of Justice and Police (CCMJP) has become increasingly vocal on questions of asylum and interior security (i.e., crimes committed by foreigners).

Cooperation with municipalities in tripartite conferences (joined by the federal and cantonal levels) is important because the municipalities are responsible for accommodating asylum seekers and refugees and must pay the costs of providing social service for regular immigrants. Their standard point of view is that their concerns are not sufficiently taken into consideration in asylum and immigration policymaking and implementation. Larger cities, especially Zurich and Berne, have launched spontaneous initiatives on asylum that have sparked major debates (Kurt and D'Amato 2021). Smaller municipalities have also been in the headlines: recently one refused to accommodate the requested number of asylum seekers, and others have banned them from public areas such as schools, playgrounds, and soccer fields.

NGOs play a part in the implementation of Swiss asylum policy. They offer social counseling and legal advice to asylum seekers. For example, the Swiss Refugee Council, an umbrella organization for Swiss aid groups, seeks to exert influence on political decision-making by publishing position papers on various asylum-related topics. Other NGOs in the asylum field include the charity organizations Caritas and HEKS and the Swiss Red Cross.

Recent Changes in Immigration Policies
The ways in which different interest groups consult with the federal administration, consult with parliament during the policymaking process, and, not least, act through direct democracy are the subject of the following paragraphs.

Regarding regular immigration, there have been two major changes in the last two decades. First, in June 2002 the Bilateral Agreement on the Free Movement of Persons between Switzerland and the EU member states was enacted, as previously noted. Second, since then the admission policy applicable to third-country nationals has become more restrictive "Only urgently required qualified workers" will be admitted from outside the EU/EFTA (European Free Trade Agreement) area. Work permits are issued to executives, specialists, and other highly qualified workers from outside this area only if no Swiss or EU national meets these requirements. Further, when issuing residence permits, the authorities will take into consideration candidates' professional qualifications, ability to adapt to professional requirements, language skills, and age. If a person meets the criteria, she or he should be able to achieve sustainable integration into the Swiss labor market and society (Efionayi-Mäder 2018).

However, the overall revision of the Foreign Nationals Act gave rise to much debate until the regulations were adopted and entered into force in 2008. The draft of a new immigration law was under discussion in 2005 in both chambers of parliament and was passed at the end of 2006 despite the introduction of a referendum to prevent a "two-class" admission system of EU and non-EU immigrants. During hearings, it became evident that this bill would cause sharp and polarized campaigns, not to mention that the last attempt to reform the aliens law in 1982 had been doomed to failure. The reform proposal was supported only by the Christian Democrats and the Radical Liberal Party; the Swiss People's Party did not want any improvements for non-EU nationals, thus denying them the opportunity for family reunification. The political left, particularly the Social Democratic Party, the Green Party, and the unions, criticized the discriminatory partitioning of foreigners into two categories, which for them strongly evoked the memory of old initiatives that had been rejected by voters. When the bill finally was presented at parliament, it was challenged by the left and the right for different reasons: the left asked for equal treatment of all foreigners, the right for a more effective means of combating abuse of foreigners laws and the removal of family reunification provisions.

A few representatives of the political right were especially irritated that the National Council had passed a special regulation concerning the *sans-papiers* (migrants without papers who have resided illegally in the country for more than four years), giving them, for humanitarian reasons, the right to request authorization for legal residence in the near future. Curiously enough, there was no protest over the motion made by an SVP member of parliament, submitted at the same time (but not passed in the final parliamentarian vote), that would have allowed the hiring of unqualified third-country nationals as seasonal workers in farming, tourism, and construction. From then on, the allocation of residence permits would be connected to the completion of integration courses subsidized (against the will of the SVP) by the federal government. The National Chamber also passed articles against migrants marrying for convenience as well as against smugglers and illegal migrants. It also introduced carrier sanctions at Swiss airports for all airlines responsible for the transport of passengers without valid papers.

This bill was ratified by the National Chamber with the support of the Christian Democrats and the Radical Party. The Social Democrats also approved it, largely in order not to hinder further negotiations and to prevent a more restrictive interpretation. The Green Party and the SVP refused to support the law for opposite reasons: the former because of human rights concerns, the latter because the bill was not strict enough against abuse by foreigners. The bill was resubmitted together with the revised asylum law in a referendum that was won by the government in September 2006.

The new Foreign Nationals Act (FNA) of 2008 regulates the principles of residence more clearly than before, improves the legal status of migrants with regard to their geographical and occupational mobility as well as the integration and promotion of integration on the part of the host society, strengthens the fight against abuse, and anchors the so-called dual admission system: the agreement on the free movement of persons now primarily applies to all EU/EFTA nationals, while stricter rules according to the Foreign Nationals Act (FNA) are mainly in force for third-country nationals. This means that the admission and settlement of EU/EFTA citizens are greatly simplified, while immigration from other countries is limited and administratively controlled (Efionayi 2018).

In quantitative terms, the new bill (like the old law) lays the foundation for authorities to pursue a more permissive or a more restrictive admission policy as necessary. For the authorities, the decisive factors in determining the number of people to be admitted from outside the EU/EFTA are the economic situation in Switzerland and the needs of certain segments of the labor market. They will continue to have the right to adopt quotas for nationals of non-EU/EFTA countries (*Kontingentierung*).

The basic policy principle in the current law is that admissions must be in the interest of the entire economy and not just particular segments of it; professional qualifications and the ability to integrate should play a decisive part. In addition, admission has to take the social and demographic needs of Switzerland into consideration.

On the one hand, the new immigration law constructs a higher barrier to admission for nationals of non-EU/EFTA states. On the other hand, the situation for foreigners who lawfully and permanently reside in Switzerland is improved through more opportunities to change their occupation, job, and canton. The immigration of families of short-term residents and students is also permitted, provided that residential and financial requirements are satisfied. These measures facilitate integration, simplify procedures for employers and authorities, and ensure a uniform application of the law. In the areas just mentioned, the law aims to harmonize the rules applicable to EU/EFTA nationals and those applicable to nationals of other countries (Efionayi-Mäder 2018).

While the prevention of immigration is principally focused on non-European nationals, the free movement of persons within the EU represents a remarkable turning point in Swiss migration policy, one that has contributed significantly to the acceptance and normalization of migration—at least from the EU—and has shaped notions of (un)desired immigrants (D'Amato 2008). At the same time, the popular initiative against "mass immigration," which called for the reintroduction of quotas on immigrants from the EU and was adopted by a narrow majority on February 9, 2014, underlines how abruptly opening and closing tendencies can alternate in this policy field: parliament had to implement the result of the voting in such a way as to maintain compatibility with the Bilateral Agreement. This situation also makes clear that it is not as easy to divide up immigration issues into the legal categories of "foreigners," "refugees," and "European" as the broader public might think. On the one hand, there may be confusion between the different categories—for example, between quotas for non-EU/EFTA nationals and the admission of refugees. On the other hand, the supposed confusion may also derive from a critical perception of existing delimitations, which make little sense to the uninitiated. This applies in particular to measures that are difficult to understand or to confusing designations in the refugee system such as "provisional admission" (Efionayi 2018).

Recent Changes in Asylum Policy

As elsewhere in Western Europe, asylum migration gained in importance during the 1980s. It overtook labor migration as an issue for public discourse in Switzerland because of its manifold moral, political, and judicial implications. Although asylum recognition rates decreased in the 1990s, many asylum seekers were able to remain in Switzerland under subsidiary protection or for humanitarian reasons. Although their rights were restricted for a period of time regulated by the cantons—for example, their access to the labor market and to welfare was limited and family reunification was forbidden—most of those who were granted protection were later able to settle permanently.

In the 1990s, war in the former Yugoslavia prompted a massive influx of asylum seekers from Bosnia and Kosovo, many of whom had family ties in Switzerland because of the labor migration that started in the 1960s. Between 1990 and 2002, Switzerland received a total of 146,587 asylum applications from the war-torn Balkans. According to the State Secretariat for Migration, about 10,000 people were granted asylum and 62,000 received temporary or subsidiary protection over the course of several years (Kaya 2005).

The three peaks in asylum applications coincide with the wars in the former Yugoslavia (1991), the Kosovo conflict (1999) and the European refugee crisis of 2015 due to the ongoing Middle East conflict. The fact that Switzerland was more affected during the first two disasters is largely explained by the fact that the former Yugoslavia was a major recruiting country for seasonal workers between 1960 and 1990, many of whom later settled in Switzerland, while migration from the Near and Middle East was hardly established, unlike in Sweden and Germany.

Over the years, the Swiss public had become concerned about the increasing number of asylum applications, largely because the economy was in recession and unemployment was rising. The federal government adopted administrative and legal measures to speed up application processing and decision implementation. But after numerous partial revisions, a completely revised asylum law came into force in

1999. Among the many changes that made it more restrictive, the law introduced new grounds for non-admission to the regular asylum application procedure. This means that applicants who stayed in the country illegally prior to their request or who did not submit travel or identity documents are generally refused asylum. Nevertheless, as a concession to humanitarian arguments, the law now allows for the collective temporary protection of war refugees. Although the government has never used this provision, Kosovars and Bosnians were given temporary admission.

Most of the asylum seekers from Bosnia and Kosovo had to leave Switzerland after the conflicts ended (in 1995 and 1999, respectively). Those who returned home, including those who had waited several years to do so, benefited from a return program offering financial support, construction materials, and support for their home communities. An estimated 40,000 to 60,000 people from Bosnia and Serbia-Montenegro returned home, with or without aid from the Swiss government, while approximately 10,000 with refugee status from the former Yugoslavia stayed. There are no reliable figures for how many asylum seekers from Bosnia and Kosovo remained in the country illegally (Efionayi-Mäder, Niederberger, and Wanner 2005).

Despite the continuing decrease in asylum requests—in 2003, the number fell by around 20 percent (to 20,806) as compared with the year before—the SVP continued its battle to restrict asylum inflows. Because its initiative against asylum abuses did not pass in 2002, the party searched for new fields of operation. Having won what it considered to be a moral victory, it demanded a new asylum initiative in June 2003 because it did not expect any revolutionary improvements from the parliamentarian revisions. Provoked by SVP chairman Christoph Blocher's demand (Blocher was still a member of parliament at this time), the other parties condemned it as a form of "blackmailing" and as pure electioneering, and they reacted with a revision of the asylum law. Although the exact wording was still incomplete at this time, control over asylum matters would be completely transferred to the federal level at a future date. Another idea was to block uncooperative and false asylum seekers, as well as those who were in the country illegally, from beginning the asylum application procedure. Instead, they would face prison or expulsion.[5]

In reaction to the unexpected success of the SVP with its initiative against abuses, the National Council's standing committee on political institutions decided not to revise the foreigners law first and the asylum law second, as had been originally intended, but to take both revisions to a vote simultaneously. Meanwhile, the SVP's plans to bring forward its own revision of the law had no success.[6]

Contrasting tendencies of inclusion and exclusion were expressed in these amendments to the law: although almost all political leaders repeatedly spoke out in favor of the humanitarian tradition or the protection of persecuted persons, two points of contention caused constant disputes. On the one hand, there was disagreement over the unavoidable question of where to draw the line between "genuine" refugees (those in need of a protected status and those to be turned away. On the other hand, what asylum seekers should be allowed to do while their cases were being considered—the procedures often lasted for years—was also highly controversial. Should they be allowed to work as early as possible and to continue their education beyond compulsory schooling? Or was it more sensible, in the interest of so-called returnability as well as for deterrence reasons (to minimize the "attractiveness" of Switzerland), to restrict both possibilities until an asylum decision had been made?

These questions were answered differently in different cantons, depending on the number and profile of asylum seekers and the needs of the labor market (Efionayi 2018). In contrast to countries such as Germany and France, since the 1950s Switzerland did not have a general ban on employment for asylum seekers, apart from exclusion from the labor market for a period of three to six months after entry. In practice, however, the cantons are responsible for issuing work permits; they limit asylum seekers to jobs in so-called shortage occupations, where a particular demand has been indicated by employers. Studies show that the labor force participation of asylum seekers varies greatly from canton to canton but has generally declined over the past twenty years. The extent to which the differences are due to administrative reasons, labor market structure, or context is still disputed (Spadarotto et al. 2014).

The government realistically interpreted the population's skeptical attitude toward its asylum policy, even though the decreasing number of asylum requests no longer supported this interpretation. Its hopes to regain support from the people thus had to be realized through a new asylum law. Asylum seekers whose requests could not be accommodated in the future would now be treated as illegal foreigners without any rights to social welfare benefits. They were left with the less attractive (but still constitutionally protected) emergency aid, which provides a minimum level of accommodation and basic necessities and is subject to administrative controls. Together with the foreigners law, the asylum law was submitted to a popular referendum and passed by a margin of three to one in September 2006.

This modification of 2006 implies the exclusion of rejected asylum seekers who remain in Switzerland (for example, because they cannot be sent back) from social assistance. They will only be entitled to emergency aid. Asylum seekers who can be shown to have transited through a country considered "safe" will also be excluded from asylum. The period of detention prior to forced removal is also increased to a maximum of twenty-four months for people who refuse to leave Switzerland on their own (Piguet 2019).

The newspaper *Neue Zürcher Zeitung* noted with astonishment how unanimously all the center-right parties stood behind Blocher, and expressed its surprise that no further suggestions were introduced in the formulation of future migration policy. This seemed to prove

> how much the mood had changed after Christoph Blocher had taken over the justice department. Today bills are passed with large majorities whereas a few years ago they would have caused even doubt and refusal in the political center-right camp. The left, the charitable organizations, and the churches have not reacted to these changes and, furthermore, practically oppose all changes in the whole country instead of focusing on some really problematic reinforcement of the law.[7]

During this period, certain judicial decisions were made that went in the opposite direction from this policy of hardening. In 2006, the Asylum Appeals Commission (CRA)—which was replaced by the Federal Administrative Tribunal (TAF) in 2007—recognized the status of refugee for victims of non-state persecution if their government did not provide adequate protection. This is an important extension of the definition of who is entitled to asylum. It concerns, for example, people caught between insurgent movements and the authorities, as is the case in Sri Lanka (where the government is battling the Tamil Tigers) or in Turkey (with the PKK insurgency in the Kurdish regions). The CRA also considers that refusal to serve in the military or desertion in Eritrea has disproportionately severe and politically motivated consequences that justify the granting of asylum to the persons concerned. This decision has for once made Switzerland a particularly "progressive" country in comparison with others (see Piguet 2019).

Since 2008 and despite the efforts of legal restrictions and the Dublin agreements, Switzerland has seen an increase in the number of asylum requests made on its territory (from 10,840 in 2007 to 28,631 in 2012). These applications come mainly from nationals of Eritrea, Nigeria, Tunisia, Serbia/Kosovo, Afghanistan, and Syria. This growth is primarily due to the deterioration of the security and political situation in the countries of origin, but also, in the case of Tunisia, to the hopes raised by the Arab Spring.

The great diversity in the countries of origin of these asylum seekers makes the processing of asylum applications complex, insofar as the State Secretariat on Migration needs a thorough knowledge of the situation in each country of origin in order to make its decisions. The processing times are therefore often long, which further increases the difficulty of enforcing removals in the case of negative decisions. The public is chronically dissatisfied with the asylum system, and this dissatisfaction leads to more attempts at adjustment.

Even before the revision of the Asylum Act (accepted by popular vote in 2013), Socialist federal councilor Simonetta Sommaruga, who took over the Federal Department of Justice and Police in 2010, had initiated a major project to reform the processing of asylum applications. This project was widely supported in 2016 (receiving approval from 66.8 percent of voters), and after a test phase, the new model came into force in 2019 (Piguet 2019).

The central objective of this latest reform is the acceleration of the asylum review procedures—something sought constantly since 1979. The scope of this reform, however, gives it a better chance of success than previous reforms, particularly because the entire procedure must now take place in one location. The test phase in Zurich showed that the length of the asylum review process could be reduced by 39 percent. Several federal centers for asylum seekers have been set up for this purpose, with a total of 5,000 accommodation places. The main ones are located in Boudry, Zurich, Altstätten, Balerna, Basel, and Lyss. Asylum seekers will stay there for a maximum of 140 days, and their applications will be processed on site (Thränhardt 2019).

It is expected that 60 percent of all asylum applications will receive a final decision within this period. The remaining cases will be assigned to the cantons, as in the past. Moreover, the reform is flanked by an important innovation in terms of guaranteeing rights, since an independent legal advisor will now be assigned to each asylum seeker. This replaces the current system of representation by aid organizations. The advisor will take part in hearings and possible appeals.

Recent Changes in Integration Policies
When the Swiss government dropped its rotation policy in the early 1960s, it recognized that the alternative could only be a policy of integration. The belief—both then and now—is that integration takes place naturally in the labor market and in schools, as well as in associations, labor unions, clubs, churches, neighborhoods, and other informal networks (Niederberger 2004). Since the 1970s, the Confederation's main integration policy has been to improve the legal status of immigrants, reuniting families more quickly and granting immigrants a more secure status. To facilitate integration and to respond to public concerns about foreigners, the government established the Federal Commission for Foreigners in 1970 (discussed previously), the purpose of which is to promote the coexistence of foreign and native populations and to bring together municipalities, communities, cantons, foreigners' organizations, employers and employees, and churches. The FCF cooperates with cantonal and communal authorities, immigrant services, and immigration actors such as charities and economic associations. It also publishes opinions and recommendations on migration issues and gives testimony in migration-related political policy debates.

After strong lobbying by cities during the economic crisis of the 1990s, Swiss policy on foreigners adapted to the new reality, considering the integration of foreigners a prerequisite for achieving politically and socially sustainable immigration. "Integration" refers to the participation of foreigners in Swiss economic, social, and cultural life. The integration article in the old aliens law, passed in 1999, paved the way for a more proactive federal integration policy; it also strengthened the FCF's role. Since 2001, the government has spent between 10 and 12 million Swiss francs (between €6 million and €7 million) yearly to support integration projects, including language and integration courses and training for integration leaders. Cantons and larger municipalities have their own committees and offices for integration and intercultural cooperation, which also offer courses in language and integration. In many communities foreigners are members of school boards, and in some cases they participate in municipal government. With the support of consulates and local education departments, larger communities offer courses in immigrant children's native languages and cultures. Churches were early promoters of the coexistence of the Swiss and the foreign population. Other nongovernmental organizations have also become more interested in coexistence.

The immigration law of 2008 (the FNA) foresees that immigration candidates will have to fulfill certain criteria to facilitate their integration. On the one hand, the state should provide integration instruments; on the other hand, migrants should contribute to their own integration into Switzerland. This core principle of "promoting and requiring" (*encourager et exiger*; *Fördern und Fordern*) integration is still shaping the Swiss discourse on integration today. The restrictive component corresponds to the criterion of "qualitatively high-standard immigration." An immigrant's level of education and professional qualifications should improve their social integration and guarantee their vocational reintegration if they become unemployed. The restriction aims at avoiding the errors that were committed in the past involving the granting of temporary work permits to low-skilled seasonal workers. As a corrective, the new immigration law abolishes the status of seasonal workers. Furthermore, it explicitly states that it is the immigrant's duty to make every effort to facilitate their integration. Permanent residents and their families are required to integrate on both the professional and social levels (Kurt and D'Amato 2021).

In 2009, the Tripartite Conference, a political platform in which the federal, cantonal and municipal level coordinate their efforts, presented a report on the future development of the Swiss integration policy (TAK 2009). The Tripartite Conference demanded, among other measures, stronger legal regulation of integration measures. The Federal Council responded by suggesting the implementation of cantonal integration policies that could benefit from federal financial support. Moreover, the federal government recommended revising the current integration regulations in the FNA as well as strengthening protections against discrimination (Federal Council 2010). Soon afterward (in 2014), Cantonal Integration Programs (CIPs) were initiated, with their legal provisions embedded in the partially revised FNA.

Another important shift toward a Swiss rationale on integration was the favorable vote on the popular initiative Against Mass Immigration, put to a vote on February 9, 2014, and promoted by the SVP, the biggest rightwing, populist party The article stipulates that the ability to integrate should be a decisive criterion for granting residence permits (now enshrined in Article 121a, paragraph 3 of the Swiss constitution). For the first time an article of the Swiss constitution mentions the term "integration" in connection with migration issues. This voting influenced also the ongoing partial revision of the FNA. Finally, the outcome of this process was a new law, the Federal Act on Foreign Nationals and Integration (FNIA), which entered into force on January 1, 2019. It implements the so-called integration stage model, which promotes the incremental upgrading of an immigrant's legal status in combination with integration exams, a combination of language and civics tests (Kurt and D'Amato 2021). Recently, the Swiss Confederation and the cantons decided to incorporate a supplementary Integration Agenda into the already existing Cantonal Integration Programs. The intent is to strengthen and harmonize integration measures for refugees and temporarily admitted persons and to synchronize these measures with the acceleration of the asylum review procedure. However, because the number of asylum claims decreased (from 39,523 in 2015 to 18,088 in 2017) and because the asylum review process was accelerated, the focus is currently more on labor market integration of asylum claimants who have a high probability of remaining in the country, though they may currently have a different legal status (Eidgenössisches Justiz- und Polizeidepartement. 2018). Additionally, NGO engagement may gain more importance, since the restructuring and acceleration of the asylum review procedure opens to them a new field of action in implementing integration measures among formerly excluded groups (Efionayi-Mäder, Truong, and D'Amato 2015). Nevertheless, specific research on this topic is missing, particularly at the local level.

Recent Changes in Naturalization Policies
The new Federal Law on Swiss Citizenship (nBüG), in force since January 1, 2018, aims to clarify and, where possible, standardize legal provisions relating to naturalization. In some areas, the cantons and municipalities retain a certain degree of discretion, particularly with regard to the requirements that applicants must meet in order to obtain Swiss citizenship (for example, a certain level of language proficiency or knowledge of civics). The nBüG sets the required maximum period of

residence at the cantonal level at five years and at the federal level at ten years instead of twelve. The new Ordinance on Swiss Citizenship (BüV), introduced at the same time, regulates the minimum requirements, which cantons are allowed to tighten by setting stricter conditions (von Rütte 2018). Thus, cantons that were more accommodating under the old legal system are now obliged to adapt their legislation to the nBüG—one of the reasons this law is likely to lead to a tightening of the naturalization requirements.

Usually, the procedure is the following: People who have resided in Switzerland for ten years (the years spent in country between the ages of eight and eighteen are counted double for this purpose) may apply for naturalization. The State Secretariat on Migration examines whether applicants are adequately integrated into the Swiss way of life, whether they are familiar with Swiss customs and traditions, and whether they comply with Swiss laws and do not endanger internal or external security. In particular, this examination is based on cantonal and communal reports. If the requirements of the federal law are satisfied, applicants are entitled to obtain a federal naturalization permit from the Federal Aliens Office (Probst et al. 2019).

Because naturalization proceeds in three stages, the federal naturalization permit constitutes only the green light for acquiring Swiss nationality. The cantons and communities have their own, additional residence requirements that applicants have to satisfy after the federal preconditions are met. Once they have obtained the federal naturalization permit, only those applicants who have also been naturalized by their communities and cantons become Swiss citizens. As a general rule, there is no legally protected right to naturalization by a community and a canton. The cantons' criteria vary greatly, as do the ways in which they decide who gets citizenship. For example, in certain cantons applicants must have spent their entire ten years of residence there. In Geneva, two years of residence are sufficient as long as candidates fulfill the federal preconditions. The requirements at the communal level can vary greatly as well.

In 1992, it was decided to allow dual citizenship. Between 1991 and 2001, the number of naturalizations rose from 8,757 to 37,070 per annum. Nationals from the former Yugoslavia, mostly from Kosovo and Bosnia, have been the quickest to naturalize—they have little interest in returning to their country of origin because of the unstable political situation there. Also, having Swiss citizenship means that they can never be forced to return. Citizenship is not always necessary for voting in local elections, however. In several cantons in the French-speaking part of Switzerland, foreigners who have lived in the area for many years have the right to vote at the municipal level and, in a few cantons, even on cantonal matters. The introduction of such a legal innovation in 2004 led to controversy over the significance of citizenship.

In three referendums that were held over the last forty years (1983, 1994, and 2004), Swiss voters have rejected laws that would have made it easier for the children of immigrants to become naturalized. For example, the 2004 referendum would have allowed the Swiss-born children and grandchildren of a foreign resident to automatically gain Swiss citizenship at birth on Swiss soil. Surprisingly, the logic of the arguments on either side has hardly varied over that period. However, there was a major shift in 2018, when a referendum against an amendment of the constitution that aimed at introducing a facilitated naturalization for foreigners of the third generation failed for the first time.

The birthright citizenship provision in the 2004 referendum would have created a process for "automatic" naturalization that would have eliminated the community's decision-making role, which many Swiss want to retain because they consider it an important step in the political process. These debates notwithstanding, over the last forty to sixty years, naturalization rates have been lower than desired by federal authorities because many immigrants decide to return to their home countries after working in Switzerland.

As already mentioned, in 2002 the Swiss parliament debated the revision of the citizenship law for a third time. In the detailed consultation process, suggestions for shortening the minimum residence requirements presented by the Federal Council and the Christian Democrats were strongly criticized by the SVP, which opposed facilitated naturalization, expressing the opinion that only those born in the country should profit from easier access to citizenship, as opposed to young people who were born in other countries and spent only part of their school years in Switzerland. The National Council rejected the proposal to liberalize the naturalization process. The Social Democratic Party, the liberal FDP, the Christian Democrats, and the Green Party all supported facilitated naturalization; only the SVP rejected it.

However, when the discussion shifted to whether citizenship should automatically be given to the third generation (introducing the principle of *jus soli*), the debate became heavily polarized. This legal innovation was categorically rejected by the SVP. On the other hand, the CVP and the FDP were reluctant to limit the rights of the parents to decide whether they wished their child to have Swiss citizenship; the FDP wanted to make the right of naturalization dependent on the parents' request. In the end, the CVP's proposal found a lot of support with the argument that parents could renounce the citizenship of their child at birth, and that the child was free to revoke his or her decision at the age of majority. Against the acrimonious resistance of the SVP, the National Council also approved the right to file a formal complaint by those whose naturalization request was rejected by a municipality without stating the cause for denial At the end of the consultations, the SVP announced that it wished to initiate a referendum against this revision.[8]

Shortly after this debate, the discussion about granting easier access to citizenship was influenced by a decision of the Federal Supreme Court in Lausanne. The judges decided that refusing to grant citizenship on the basis of an applicant's country origin or religion was unconstitutional because it violated the principle of non-discrimination. The judges ordered that municipalities adopt a procedure that did not offend the constitution, and in their written opinion they declared that while no immigrant had an automatic right to be naturalized, in certain municipalities voting on applicants was an administrative function, since it entailed a decision on the status of inhabitants, and thus required the municipal authorities and the population to respect the prohibition against discrimination.

Many experts as well as the political left voiced support for this judgment. The political center reacted with consternation at such a verdict coming only a few weeks before the general elections. The SVP protested vociferously against the limitation of sovereignty and municipal autonomy, which in their eyes gave the impression of a partisan political decision. With that decision, courts and judges who acted against what was seen as the will of the people became one of the major topics the SVP campaigned on. In the SVP's opinion, naturalizations are political acts, not administrative ones.

On September 26, 2004, the referendum took place. With a rather high voter turnout (54 percent), the majority of the people and the cantons refused to reform the citizenship law. Facilitated naturalization was rejected by a majority of 57 percent; the automatic naturalization of the third generation at birth was also rejected, by a majority of 51.6 percent. The breakdown of the vote on the rollback was very interesting in comparison to that in the referendum of 1994: with the exception of the Canton of Basel City, all other Swiss-German cantons that had approved a more liberal application of the naturalization law ten years earlier had now switched to the other camp.[9]

In the aftermath of the 2004 referendum, the priority of rule of law with regard to applicants who seek access to Swiss nationality (as mentioned, confirmed by a decision of the Federal Court in 2003) was attacked the Swiss People's Party, which in 2008 tried to abolish this rule and eliminate constitutional guarantees for citizenship candidates through a popular initiative (D'Amato 2018). This effort was turned back by the Swiss voting population in 2008. Another initiative that wanted to abolish human rights guarantees—the initiative "Swiss Law Instead of Foreign Judges (Initiative for Self-Determination)"—followed a similar strategy, attempting to reverse the philosophy of the new Swiss constitution, approved in 1999, to secure fundamental rights and human rights protection for all residents. The result of the vote was clearer than some observers had predicted. The Initiative on Self-Determination had been promoted by its backers as saving direct democracy, but direct democracy itself clearly rebuffed that argument: on November 25, 2018, about two-thirds of the voters rejected the self-determination initiative, and in all cantons the promoters did not achieve a majority. At just below 34 percent nationwide, approval was only slightly higher than the SVP's 29 percent voter turnout in the previous parliamentary elections, in 2015.

In the same wave of change, in 2016 both chambers in parliament approved a constitutional amendment to introduce facilitated naturalization for third-generation foreigners, supporting the submission of a parliamentary initiative entitled "Switzerland Must Recognize Its Children," written by the Italian-born Social democratic MP Ada Marra. The cantonal differences in naturalization policies for young people born in Switzerland should be eliminated, the initiative held, and the competence in this matter should be transferred to the Confederation. With the possibility of a facilitated naturalization, young people of the third generation should be recognized as "children" of Switzerland and thus as citizens with full political rights. The two federal chambers agreed on the details and approved the amendment to the Nationality Act (nBüG) and the federal constitution on September 28, 2016. However, there was still a big hurdle to overcome—a constitutional amendment requires the approval of the people and the cantons. The date for the vote was set for February 12, 2017, and the SVP tried to mobilize against it using the rhetoric it had employed before. But this time the SVP failed: 60.4 percent of the Swiss voting population were now in favor of politically including the third generation.

Interests and Orientations

As discussed in the previous section, integration has been the object of political contention in Switzerland. In this respect, different comparative studies have confirmed the perseverance of interests and orientations in discourses on migration politics since the 1990s (Brubaker 1992; Hollifield 1992; Ireland 1994). In the case of Switzerland, it has been shown that migration politics is shaped by three major arguments (see Mahnig 1996). The liberal position argues that the free market is the ideal regime for migration regulation. According to this position, migration is not to be prevented or restricted but handled in a fashion similar to the handling of the free trade of capital and goods. Any state intervention is seen, economically, as highly ineffective unless it is meant to reduce immigration control or adapt immigration rates to business demands.

The internationalist position also takes a critical stand toward national immigration control, but for different reasons. The argument here is based on the proliferation of international human rights calls for global standardization of legal and social equality for individuals. In this view, migration policy is seen as an instrument of social compensation between rich and poor countries.

Finally, the nationalist position seeks to defend Swiss national interests against the interests of immigrants. These interests have economic and labor market dimensions (e.g., protection of certain economic sectors and the local workforce), and they are oriented toward defense of a national identity that seems constantly threatened.

It appears that at the beginning of the 1990s—because of both internal factors (comprehensive citizenship reform, prolonged economic crisis) and external factors (the end of the Cold War, the integration process, changes in naturalization laws all over Europe) factors—government policymakers were forced to redirect their orientation from nationalist-liberal to more liberal-internationalist (Jacobson 1996; Soysal 1994). Adjustments in the EU, acceptance of dual citizenship, attempts to reform citizenship laws, and protection of cultural rights through the recently created Federal Commission Against Racism are all indications of this process of adjustment to the new political environment. The clear shift in matters of immigration, citizenship, and cultural rights also represents new challenges for actors that were always present on the Swiss political scene—the right-wing populist parties, which are discussed in the next section—and it opens for them a new space of contention.

The way in which interests and orientations contend on social cohesion and, in particular, the outcomes of these contests can only be understood if the Swiss institutional context of policymaking is considered. Three areas are relevant for the study of Switzerland: its federalism and its consociational and direct democracy.

The Swiss Policymaking Process

In order to understand Swiss policymaking, three distinct features of the national polity have to be taken into consideration: the federal structure of the state, the financial and political autonomy of the municipalities, and the tool of intervention employed in the consociational negotiations of interest groups and in the participation of the people through direct democracy.

Federalism

The mechanisms of decision-making in Switzerland are complex. The Swiss population does not elect members of the Federal Council directly. That is the prerogative of Parliament, which elects the seven members of the Federal Council for four-year terms. In the Swiss political system, Parliament cannot vote confidence or no confidence on actions of the Federal Council, which gives the Federal Council a certain amount of autonomy. However, this autonomy is restricted by the two instruments of Swiss direct democracy: the referendum and the popular initiative. The popular initiative gives citizens the right to seek a decision on an amendment they want to integrate into the constitution. For such an initiative to be organized, the signatures of 100,000 voters must be collected within a period of eighteen months. Federal laws are subject to an optional referendum: in this case, a popular ballot is held if the signatures of 50,000 citizens are obtained within 100 days of the publication of a decree. The referendum is similar to a veto. For such a plebiscite to pass, it must receive both a majority of the popular vote and a majority of the vote in at least nine cantons. At the cantonal and municipal levels, voters can also launch an initiative. Cantonal laws are subject to the optional referendum.

With regard to the admission and integration of migrants, Switzerland is confronted with the challenges of multi-level governance. Certain centralizing mechanisms, which in Germany and the United States are enforced by each country's Supreme Court, are less successful in Switzerland. Centralizing legal approaches are counteracted by Parliament and the people. As Wolf Linder has stated, one important limitation of the central government institutions in Switzerland is the constrained possibilities for coercive implementation of federal policies (Linder 2021, 22). In this sense, federal political authorities are often compelled to induce cooperation with the cantons by offering financial subsidies (e.g., Cantonal Integration Programs and the Integration Agenda). This federal structure may have an advantage, since knowledge of local interests can lead to quicker, more appropriate decisions, ensuring greater recognition of particular interests (e.g., minorities). While the Federation has legislative power in most areas, responsibility for implementing federal policies resides largely with the cantons. For the Federation, this has the advantage of reducing its workload; for the cantons, the advantage lies in controlling their own program priorities and being able to adapt federal policies to local contexts. These aspects of the Swiss federal state also affect integration policies. In this case, the central actors are the cantons and the municipalities (Cattacin and Chimienti 2009). In particular, cantons have room for maneuver when it comes to the promotion and implementation of integration provisions recommended by federal institutions (D'Amato and Gerber 2005). In many cantons, the Cantonal Office for Migration decides how the law is interpreted and implemented regarding to integration aspects connected to a legal status. Additionally, integration offices develop measures intended to help migrants to integrate in areas such as education, the workplace, and health care (Wichmann and D'Amato 2010). In terms of implementation, this executive federalism is decisive: it is one of the cornerstones of the Swiss political system. Although the legislative authority lies with the federal government, its implementation is entrusted to the cantons. For the cantons to fulfill this role, they need some latitude in the application of federal laws. This allows the adaptation of the implementations to local conditions, which leads to greater legitimacy of the decisions. This is the case for the Cantonal Integration Programs and the newly adopted Integration Agenda, which provide material resources and information about the process that would otherwise not be locally available.

Other characteristics of the Swiss political system are its municipal autonomy, direct democracy, and consociationalism, which above all favor strong organizations that can win a referendum. These peculiarities have consequences for the design of migration policy in Switzerland (for details, see Cattacin and Kaya 2005): there is a risk that federalist regulations at the cantonal level will foster a patchwork of measures that are exposed to continuous populist instrumentalization.

Municipal Autonomy

Strong trade ties among cities and political fragmentation explain why Switzerland has a relatively solid urban network. Moreover, municipal autonomy is a key factor when it comes to citizenship and, paradoxically, nationhood. As already mentioned, there are three stages in the naturalization process: citizenship in the municipality, then citizenship in the canton, and finally citizenship in the nation.

There is much variety in naturalization at the local level, particularly between the German- and French-speaking cantons. While the French cantons have more formalized procedures, many German cantons hold to the romantic principle of adherence to the civic culture as a first step in the naturalization process. The question of who is allowed to apply for citizenship can easily be turned into accusations of preferential treatment and prejudice. Newspaper stories have reported that in several small towns in the German part of Switzerland, applicants for naturalization have been denied because of their eastern European or Asian origins (Ehrenzeller and Good 2003; Leuthold and Aeberhard 2002). Therefore, even if the country was founded on the idea of political contract, naturalization is to a large extent based on local ethnicity. This tendency has been confirmed by more recent studies (Probst et al. 2019).

Furthermore, since the decision by the Federal Supreme Court on July 9, 2003 (1P.228-2000) that declared public votes on naturalization in certain municipalities to be unconstitutional, a new debate has emerged on the role of judicial authority in naturalization matters. This is largely a debate between those who favor the rule of law and those who interpret the granting of access to citizenship as a political and sovereign right of the citizenry. The Ständerat's Political Institutions Committee took a public stand in favor of the right of municipalities to hold votes on individual naturalization applications; nevertheless, it asked localities to provide a justification for refusing a particular application, even if the decision was made by ballot. For this reason, the Court's decision of 9 July 2003 is an indicator of the tension between the Court and conservative parts of the parliament and, at an ideological level, between the opportunities and limits of the rule of law and those of direct democracy.

Consociational and Direct Democracy

Consociationalism and direct democracy are important for understanding Switzerland's outcome and output in integration policies. But, as Mahnig and Wimmer (2003) state in their lucid article, these two characteristics of the Swiss political system are responsible for the country's intense politicization of migration issues and the exclusion of migrants from political participation. Consociationalism includes reaching compromise between political forces that goes beyond the search for simple majorities (Linder 2021). A permanent process of compromise-building between these groups characterizes Swiss politics. Another important means to influence the political decision-making process is the consultation procedure, the phase in legislative preparation when draft bills produced by the Confederation are evaluated by the cantons, the parties, associations, and sometimes other interested circles throughout Switzerland, in order to ascertain the likelihood of their acceptance and implementation. Persons not invited to take part in the consultation procedure can also state their views on a proposal. All views and possible objections are evaluated with a view to the veto power of those who might seek to reject a reform by means of a referendum. The federal government then passes the main points of its proposal on to Parliament and debates the draft bill in light of the outcomes of this consultation.

Direct democracy gives social groups some opportunities to participate directly in the political process through the aforementioned popular initiative and referendum. These are in place at the federal as well as local levels. According to some observers, it is the instruments of direct democracy that allowed the consociational system to emerge, because all laws approved by a vote in parliament can be submitted to a referendum and therefore need the support of large alliances within the political elite (Neidhart 1970). These two main characteristics of the political system provoke major politicization of the migrant issue and the exclusion of immigrants from political participation. Since the interests in the political field of migration are highly divergent, it is difficult for the parties to come to an agreement easily. Second, the instruments of direct democracy have forced the political elite to negotiate anti-immigration attitudes with populist challengers. Prior immigration policies that had permitted the various actors to agree to accommodate the economic needs of the country became one of the most contested and controversial issues since the 1960s, when radical right-wing populist parties started to gain public support by claiming that Switzerland was becoming "over-foreignized" by ever-increasing numbers of immigrants. Using the tools of direct democracy, these xenophobic movements succeeded in vetoing liberal government reforms and put the mainstream political parties under pressure through the launching of eleven popular initiatives and several referendums to curb the presence of foreigners. Although until the 2009 initiative to ban the construction of minarets associated with mosques none of these initiatives passed, since the 1970s they consistently influenced the migration policy agenda and possibly public opinion on immigration issues urging the Swiss government to adopt more restrictive admission policies (Niederberger 2004), as manifested with the approval of the mass immigration initiative in 2014. Other European countries may be able to adopt policies "behind closed doors" (Guiraudon 2000) to extend political and social rights to migrants, but this is nearly impossible in Switzerland.

Concluding Remarks

For a long time—from World War II until the late 1990s—the economic needs of the labor market influenced Switzerland's immigrant admission policy without taking integration into account. Admissions during this time were based on a rotation model that fueled the economy with labor without necessarily introducing any integration provisions for the migrants who came to stay. This was because immigrants were not conceived as a potential part of the population. A utilitarian policy seemed to fit best with the need to keep the country free of foreign cultural influences, as was laid down in the aliens law of 1931—a law that reflected the xenophobic spirit of the 1920s.

Since the 1970s, immigrants' length of stay, changing attitudes, and changing expectations, as well as the evolving needs of the economy and the school system, have made a more inclusive Swiss migration policy inevitable. But the alliance between the government, regional economies, and supranational human rights interests (that labored for inclusion of foreign workers through legislative reforms) was continuously forced to deal with a radical, xenophobic movement that, while politically isolated, seized the opportunity to leverage the government's decision-making through a referendum. This type of policy referendum was generally favored by a minimal welfare state that, until the 1970s, excluded migrants from solidarity networks and thus exposed them to the social risks of returning home.

A paradigm shift occurred in the 1980s, after the oil crisis, when it became clear that many migrants were not returning to their home country and staying in Switzerland. The introduction of unemployment insurance and the inauguration of a larger welfare system also gave protection to labor migrants and introduced them to social citizenship. However, the 1980s were also when the asylum issue emerged as a metaphor for unwanted immigration. The government reacted to this new challenge with a two-tiered approach—first, a new severity on the asylum issue and the enforcement of a policy deterring illegitimate immigration; second, legislative reforms that favored the integration of wanted labor migrants.

The paradigm shift seems to have culminated in the new aliens and asylum laws as well as in the new citizenship law. All three were always contested by radical right-wing challengers and thus had to go through the referendum process.

Federalism, municipal autonomy, and consociational and direct democracy offer a framework within which many actors and stakeholders attempt to influence policymaking. This is a form of multilevel governance that for a long time has prevented Switzerland from matching its immigration policy to European standards of inclusive social rights (and to its new economic needs). Still, in recent years Switzerland's guiding principles have been converging with those of its important European partners. The obvious points of similarity in immigration and migration policy between Switzerland and the EU since the signing of the Bilateral Agreement have no doubt become more numerous. Still, the specter of "over-foreignization" and "Europeanization" will probably prevent Switzerland (at least at the federal level) from adopting a liberal migration policy within a larger legal framework. The question of how a direct democracy like Switzerland should deal in the future with a constantly growing international legal regulation will continue to occupy public opinion. The tug-of-war surrounding the EU Framework Agreement and the UN Migration Compact give a foretaste of the next debates. Switzerland's cultural inhibitions are too strong for it to open its symbolically highly valued citizenship institutions to "undeserving" immigrants.

The discussion about the effects of international law has therefore not come to an end. And the SVP has announced that it will continue its anti-immigration and anti-immigrant campaign.[10] The SVP seeks to use direct democracy, understood as unfiltered majority rule, to reconfigure and reshape the federal state and Swiss society. The objective is to roll the country back to where it was before the despised "1968"—the metaphor for the expansion of rights that is seen as inflicting harm on communitarian beliefs. This will not be an easy task, considering the complexities of a plural society like Switzerland. But the SVP's series of proposed new amendments to limit the division of powers based on the constitution has permanently changed the way political agendas are set. As a side effect, the SVP's actions are conditioning other parties to react to the permanent politicization of issues, and the SVP's efforts to slowly move the political focus to the right have succeeded in influencing the other parties' stands, particularly when it comes to EU and immigrants. Particularly astonishing are the concessions parties have been willing to make. The orientation that has led other parties to allow the SVP's arguments to influence their own positions is all the more remarkable since migration, globalization, and its attendant legal consequences cannot be wished out of the world. As a result, migration issues can always be used, if not misused, for the purpose of political mobilization.

However, one should also not fall prey to the illusion that it is possible to have a direct democracy without populist aspects. Rather, democrats should be ready to commit themselves to open discussions, as was the case during the campaign before the referendum on the new citizenship law and the Initiative for Self-Determination. They also will have to engage in a political culture of debate, opposition, and conflict, which at a fundamental level is about the practice of pluralism and liberal democracy. The opposition attempts to misuse direct democracy through initiatives, like the one on self-determination, has been fierce, and has seen some success. The victory on the self-determination initiative demonstrates one of the strategies that civil society has drawn on to oppose such attempts. This was an important moment, since in good democracies, as we know, the game is never over. And who is to say that in the evolution of politics and society, latecomers to the European debate will not one day become forerunners, especially in the volatile field of migration and citizenship?

Notes

1. The cultural minority who speak different dialects of Reto-Romansch, which is a Romance language, consists of around 50,000 people who live in the canton of Graubünden in the eastern part of Switzerland.

2. Indeed, migration and integration policies are matters of cantonal sovereignty to a certain degree.

3. https://www.swissinfo.ch/eng/a-third-of-swiss-residents-have-migrant-background-/46093696

4. Federal Statistical Office, "Population by Migration Status," https://www.bfs.admin.ch/bfs/en/home/statistics/population/migration-integration/by-migration-status.html, accessed March 31, 2021.

5. *Neue Zürcher Zeitung*, June 11 and September 15, 2003.

6. *Neue Zürcher Zeitung*, January 10, 2003.

7. *Neue Zürcher Zeitung*, September 28, 2005.

8. *Neue Zürcher Zeitung*, September 17, 2002.

9. *Neue Zürcher Zeitung*, September 27, 2004.

10. Christoph Blocher, quoted in *Tages-Anzeiger* November 26, 2018.

References

Arlettaz, Gérald. 1985. "Démographie et identité nationale (1850–1914): La Suisse et 'La question des étrangers.'" *Etudes et Sources* 11: 83–174.

Brubaker, Rogers. 1992. *Citizenship and Nationhood in France and Germany.* Cambridge, MA: Harvard University Press.

Bundesrat (Federal Council). 2010. *Bericht zur Weiterentwicklung der Integrationspolitik des Bundes.* Report Schiesser. Bern: Swiss Confederation.

Cattacin, Sandro, and Milena Chimienti. 2009. "Lokale Politik der Eingliederung der Migrationsbevölkerung in der Schweiz - Zwischen Pragmatismus und Populismus." In *Lokale Integrationspolitik in der Einwanderungsgesellschaft,* edited by Frank Gesemann and Roland Roth, 655–671. Wiesbaden: Springer.

Cattacin, Sandro, and Bülent Kaya. 2005. "Le développement des mesures d'intégration de la population migrante sur le plan local en Suisse." In *Histoire de la politique de migration, d'asile et d'intégration en Suisse depuis 1948,* edited by Hans Mahnig, 288–320. Zurich: Seismo.

D'Amato, Gianni. 2008. "Erwünscht, aber nicht immer Willkommen: Die Geschichte der Einwanderungspolitik." In *Die neue Zuwanderung: Die Schweiz zwischen Brain-Gain und Überfremdungsangst,* edited by Daniel Müller-Jentsch, 27–44. Zurich: Neue Zürcher Zeitung.

D'Amato, Gianni. 2018. "The Migration Challenge: The Swiss Left in the Arena of Direct Democracy." In *The Politics of Migration and the Future of the European Left,* edited by Christoph P. Mohr and Michael Bröning, 133–155. Bonn: Dietz.

D'Amato, Gianni, and Brigitta Gerber, eds. 2005. *Herausforderung Integration: Städtische Migrationspolitik in der Schweiz und in Europa.* Zurich: Seismo.

D'Amato, Gianni, and Damir Skenderovic. 2009. "From Outsider to Playmakers: Radical Right-Wing Populist Parties and Swiss Migration Policy." In *Right-Wing Extremism in Switzerland: National and International Perspectives,* edited by Marcel A. Nigglil, 78–91. Baden-Baden: Nomos.

Deutsch, Karl W. 1976. *Die Schweiz als ein paradigmatischer Fall politischer Integration.* Bern: Haupt.

Efionayi-Mäder, Denise. 2003. "Asylpolitik der Schweiz 1950–2000." *Asyl* 18, no. 3: 3–9.

Efionayi-Mäder, Denise. 2018. "Von Fremdarbeitern und Vorzeigemigrantinnen: Hinweise auf die Migrationsgeschichte der Schweiz." In *Migration und Berufsbildung in der Schweiz,* edited by Sonja Engelage, 19–49. Zurich: Seismo.

Efionayi-Mäder, Denise, Josef Martin Niederberger, and Philippe Wanner. 2005. "Switzerland Faces Common European Challenges." Migration Policy Institute.

Efionayi-Mäder, Denise, Jasmine Truong, and Gianni D'Amato. 2015. *"Wir können uns ein Abseitstehen der Zivilgesellschaft nicht leisten." Zivilgesellschaftliches Engagement im Flüchtlingswesen.* Neuchâtel: SFM Report.

Ehrenzeller, Bernhard, and Paul-Lukas Good. 2003. "Rechtsgutachten zu Handen des Gemeinderates von Emmen betreffend das Einbürgerungsverfahren in der Gemeinde Emmen." *Jusletter,* October 6, 2003.

Eidgenössisches Justiz- und Polizeidepartement. 2018. *Integrationsagenda Schweiz. Bericht der Koordinationsgruppe vom 1. März 2018.* Bern: EJPD.

Garrido, Angela. 1990. "Les années vingt et la première initiative xénophobe en Suisse." In *Racisme et xénophobies: Colloque à l'Université de Lausanne, 24–25 novembre 1988*, edited by Hans Ulrich Jost, 37–45. Lausanne: Université de Lausanne.

Guiraudon, Virginie. 2000. *Les politiques d'immigration en Europe: Allemagne, France, Pays-Bas.* Paris: Harmattan.Hollifield, James F. 1992. *Immigrants, Markets, and States: The Political Economy of Postwar Europe.* Cambridge, MA: Harvard University Press.

Holmes, Madelyn. 1988. *Forgotten Migrants: Foreign Workers in Switzerland Before World War I.* Rutherford, NJ: Fairleigh Dickinson University Press.

Ireland, Patrick. 1994. *The Policy Challenge of Ethnic Diversity: Immigrant Politics in France and Switzerland.* Cambridge, MA: Harvard University Press.

Jacobson, David. 1996. *Rights Across Borders: Immigration and the Decline of Citizenship.* Baltimore: Johns Hopkins University Press.

Katzenstein, Peter J. 1987. *Corporatism and Change: Austria, Switzerland and the Politics of Industry.* Ithaca, NY: Cornell University Press.

Kaya, Bülent. 2005. "Switzerland." In *Current Immigration Debates in Europe: A Publication of the European Migration Dialogue*, edited by Jan Niessen, Yongmi Schibel, and Cressida Thompson, 383–398. Brussels: Migration Policy Group.

Kohler, Georg. 1994. "Demokratie, Integration, Gemeinschaft: Thesen im Vorfeld einer Einwanderungsgesetzdiskussion." In *Migration: Und wo bleibt das Ethische?*, 17–34. Zurich: Schweizerischer Arbeitskreis für ethische Forschung.

Kurt, Stefanie, and Gianni D'Amato. 2021. "The Swiss Rationale of Integration Policies: Balancing Federalism, Consociationalism and Direct Democracy." In *Local Integration of Migrants Policy: European Experiences and Challenges*, edited by Jochen Franzke and José M Ruano de la Fuente, pp. 73-85. Cham: Palgrave Macmillan.

Leuthold, Ruedi, and Christian Aeberhard. 2002. "Der Fall Emmen." *Das Magazin* 20: 18–31.

Linder, Wolf. 2021. *Swiss Democracy: Possible Solutions to Conflict in Multicultural Societies*, 4th ed. Cham: Palgrave.

Mahnig, Hans. 1996. "Das migrationspolitische Feld der Schweiz: Eine politikwissenschaftliche Analyse der Vernehmlassung zum Arbenzbericht." Forum Suisse pour l'étude des migrations, Neuchâtel.

Mahnig, Hans, and Etienne Piguet. 2003. "La politique suisse d'immigration de 1948 à 1998: Évolution et effets." In *Les migrations et la Suisse: Résultats du Programme national de recherche "Migrations et relations interculturelles,"* edited by Hans-Rudolf Wicker, Rosita Fibbi, and Werner Haug, 63–103. Zurich: Seismo.

Mahnig, Hans, and Andreas Wimmer. 2003. "Integration Without Immigrant Policy: The Case of Switzerland." In *The Integration of Immigrants in European Societies: National Differences and Trends of Convergence*, edited by Friedrich Heckmann and Dominique Schnapper, 135–164. Stuttgart: Lucius & Lucius.

Neidhart, Leonhard. 1970. *Plebiszit und pluralitäre Demokratie: Eine Analyse der Funktion des schweizerischen Gesetzesreferendums.* Bern: Francke.

Niederberger, Josef Martin. 2004. *Ausgrenzen, Assimilieren, Integrieren: Die Entwicklung einer schweizerischen Integrationspolitik.* Zurich: Seismo.

Parini, Lorena, and Matteo Gianni. 1997. "La tension entre précarité et intégration: Politique à l'égard des migrants en Suisse." In *Politiques publiques et droit*, edited by Françoise Lorcerie, pp. 1-21. Paris: Ed. LGDJ.

Parini, Lorena, and Matteo Gianni. 2005. "Enjeux et modifications de la politique d'asile en Suisse de 1956 à nos jours." In *Histoire de la politique de migration, d'asile et d'intégration en Suisse depuis 1948*, edited by Hans Mahnig, 189–252. Zurich: Seismo.

Piguet, Étienne. 2019. *Asile et réfugiés: Repenser la protection*. Lausanne: Presses Polytechniques et Universitaires Romandes.

Probst, Johanna, et al. 2019. *Kantonale Spielräume im Wandel: Migrationspolitik in der Schweiz*. Neuchâtel: SFM.

Romano, Gaetano. 1996. "Zeit der Krise—Krise der Zeit: Identität, Überfremdung und verschlüsselte Zeitstrukturen." In *Die neue Schweiz? Eine Gesellschaft zwischen Integration und Polarisierung (1910–1930)*, edited by Andreas Ernst and Erich Wigger, 41–77. Zurich: Chronos.

Schnapper, Dominique. 1997. "Citoyenneté et reconnaissance des hommes et des cultures." In *Dire les autres: Réflexions et pratiques ethnologiques: Textes offerts à Pierre Centlivres*, edited by Jacques Hainard and Roland Kaehr, 139–148. Lausanne: Payot.

Senn, Tobias. 2017. *Hochkonjunktur, "Überfremdung" und Föderalismus: kantonalisierte Schweizer Arbeitsmigrationspolitik am Beispiel Basel-Landschaft 1945–1975*. Zurich: Chronos Verlag.

Soysal, Yasemin N. 1994. *Limits of Citizenship: Migrants and Postnational Membership in Europe*. Chicago: University of Chicago Press.

Spadarotto, Claudio, Maria Bieberschulte, Katharina Walker, Michael Morlok, and Andrea Oswald. 2014. *Erwerbsbeteiligung von anerkannten Flüchtlingen und vorläufig Aufgenommenen auf dem Schweizer Arbeitsmarkt*. Basel: BSS, KEK.

TAK. 2009. *Weiterentwicklung der schweizerischen Integrationspolitik, Bericht und Empfehlungen der TAK vom 29. Juni 2009*. Tripartite Agglomerationskonferenz, Bern.

Tanner, Jakob. 1998. "Nationalmythos, Überfremdungsängste und Minderheitenpolitik in der Schweiz." In *Blickwechsel: Die multikulturelle Schweiz an der Schwelle zum 21. Jahrhundert*, edited by Simone Prodolliet, 83–94. Lucerne: Caritas-Verlag.

Thränhardt, Dietrich. 2019. *Ein funktionierendes Asylverfahrenssystem schafft Vertrauen. Was Deutschland von der Schweiz für die Lösung der Qualitätsprobleme beim Asyl lernen kann*. Berlin: Heinrich Böll Stiftung.

Von Rütte, Barbara. 2018. "Das neue Bürgerrechtsgesetz und dessen Umsetzung in den Kantonen." In *Annuaire du droit des migrations*, edited by Alberto Achermann et al., 67–95. Bern: Stämpfli.

Wichmann, Nicole, and Gianni D'Amato. 2010. *Migration und Integration in Basel-Stadt: ein "Pionierkanton" unter der Lupe*. Neuchâtel: SFM.

COMMENTARY

Rule of Law Versus Sovereignty: On Swiss Immigration Policy

Christian Joppke

Switzerland is a land of paradoxes. It is a land of "apparent enduring stability," as Gianni D'Amato writes, despite an extraordinarily high level of internal diversity, particularly with respect to language (there are four official languages) and religion (sectarian Protestant and Catholic), which finds expression in a unique consociational political system that restricts plain majority power. A leading textbook on Swiss democracy (Linder 2010) is subtitled *Possible Solutions to Conflict in Multicultural Societies*, whereby the adjective "multicultural" stands for Switzerland's historically accumulated internal diversity, not the diversity that is the result of immigration. At the same time, throughout the twentieth century Switzerland has had one of the highest immigration rates in Europe. Currently over 20 percent of the total population is foreign-born, which is twice as much as in the United States. One might think that their positive experience with managing internal diversity has made the Swiss ready for managing immigrant diversity too. Not so, as we learn in D'Amato's chapter; the "fear of being . . . overrun by foreigners" has been a central motive in domestic policy seemingly forever, perhaps dating back to the mythologized thirteenth-century origins of the *Eidgenossenschaft* (Helvetic Confederation) in the *Rütlischwur* (oath taken by the founding cantons) against the House of Habsburg, retold in Friedrich Schiller's Wilhelm Tell saga. One might argue that the Swiss investment in managing their internal diversity has absorbed the country's quantum of acceptable multiculturalism, leaving nothing for the management of external immigrant diversity.

In the past ten years alone, on three occasions the Swiss have used their fabled sovereign instruments of direct democracy to vote on immigrant and minority matters, and each time the result has been disastrous for the rule of law and for immigrants alike. One must know that successful referenda are directly inscribed into the Swiss constitution, whereby the sovereign right of the citizenry trumps the rule of law; after such a referendum, there routinely follows a complex and often protracted process of rendering the vote compatible with domestic and international law.

The first and most infamous of these recent immigrant and minority initiatives, the initiative "Against the Construction of Minarets," held in late November 2009, was supported by 57.5 percent of Swiss voters. Interestingly, and in a pattern that was sustained in similar initiatives later on, German-speaking Switzerland came out strongly in favor of the initiative, particularly in the rural hinterlands, where there was a low immigration rate, while the more cosmopolitan and urban French-speaking part came out strongly against. As all recent immigrant and minority initiatives, the minaret initiative also was instigated by the Swiss People's Party (SVP), the majority German-dominated party in Switzerland since the early years of the twenty-first century, and arguably the most successful right-wing populist party in all of Europe for almost two decades now. In the view of those who supported the initiative, minarets were above all a political symbol, not a religious one, expressing the expansionist power interest of Islam. Therefore, to forbid the construction of minarets was not taken to impair the religious rights of Muslims, as the building and operation of mosques were not affected by the vote. Tellingly, a campaign poster showed a niqab-wearing woman sitting on a Swiss flag, from which scores of black minarets were shooting up like rockets.

Just one year later, in late November 2010, the initiative "For the Deportation of Criminal Foreigners," again organized by the SVP, was successful, with 52.9 percent of the national vote. It called for the automatic deportation, without individual case examination or the possibility of appeal, of all foreigners who are found guilty of physical assault, burglary, drug trafficking, or—most controversially of all—welfare cheating (*Sozialhilfemissbrauch*). Already the new foreigners law of 2005, which had mainly restricted new non-EU migration to the high-skilled and which tied the granting of permanent residence permits to successful integration efforts on the part of immigrants, had provisions for the deportation of criminal foreigners, but according to this law the deportation power was still subject to the discretion of public authorities. The automatic nature of deportation, without any discretion in individual cases, was new. And it was problematic from a legal point of view: as critics pointed out, it potentially violated the non-refoulement norm of the international refugee regime, which is part of the obligatory hard core of international law (*jus cogens*), but it also violated EU law, to which Switzerland has been subjected since the signing of the

Bilateral Treaty in 2002, because the EU free-movement regime allows deportation only in the case of severe public order violations while interdicting any automatism in this respect. The SVP campaign poster, prominently exhibited in train stations and public squares throughout the country, stirred international attention and was criticized by a UN special rapporteur as racist: it showed a group of white sheep grazing on a Swiss flag, kicking out a black sheep. Again, the German-speaking Swiss voters were overwhelmingly in favor, while the majority of French-speaking Swiss voted against.

Finally, a third recent SVP-led initiative, "Against Mass Immigration," was supported by a small majority of 50.3 percent in early February 2014. This initiative targeted primarily EU migrants, who tend to take high-level jobs in Switzerland (for instance, five of nine professors in the Department of Social Sciences at the University of Berne are German, including myself). The (German-speaking) Swiss, one must know, sport two separate xenophobias, one against Muslims, at the low end of the social scale, and one against Germans, at the opposite end (see Helbling 2011). The successful referendum text stipulates annual quotas for migrants (notionally including non-EU migrants, even asylum seekers, which isn't legally possible), and this entails a revocation of the free-movement clause in the Bilateral Treaty. More than the other migration and minority referenda, this one sent shock waves throughout Switzerland, particularly the banking and pharma industries and the academic sector—like Brexit, this act of "taking back control" outcome would cause serious economic harm. The EU immediately retaliated, cancelling Switzerland's participation in the Horizon 2020 research program and in the tremendously successful Erasmus student exchange program. As in previous referenda, the federal government (the Bundesrat) tried hard to soften the illegal-cum-illiberal edges of this populist vote. After years of complicated negotiations, which still need to be formally ratified, a kind of yellow, precautionary light seems to prevail, according to which fixed quotas—the red flag for the European Commission—are avoided, while firms are nominally obliged to report all vacancies and consider Swiss applicants first.

Giovanni Sartori once argued that direct democracy "would quickly and disastrously founder on the reefs of cognitive incompetence" (quoted in Linder 2010, 121). In reality, research on Switzerland has shown that "in their majority, voters decide on a systematic evaluation of arguments" (Linder 2010, 121); even on immediate pocketbook issues of taxing and spending, Swiss voters have generally decided prudently and public-mindedly. However, with respect to the immigrant- and minority-related votes, only one conclusion is possible: democracy is bad for immigrants. D'Amato hints at this when concluding that a "behind closed doors" approach to immigration issues—that is, relegating such matter to bureaucratic venues, which has generally led to liberal outcomes in western Europe (see Guiraudon 1998)—is "nearly impossible" in Switzerland. The restrictionist bent of a democratic membership policy is not limited to the immigration function. As we also learn in D'Amato's chapter, three times between the early 1980s and the first decade of the new millennium Swiss voters rejected propositions to facilitate the naturalization of the children of immigrants or to introduce conditional *jus soli*, thus consolidating the most restrictive nationality law regime in Europe, in which to become Swiss is about as difficult as converting to Judaism through the Orthodox route.

However, it would be erroneous to conclude that the Swiss qua Swiss are more restriction-minded and xenophobic than other European publics. The *differentia specifica* is the democratic mechanism to lend expression to anti-immigrant and anti-minority dispositions that, in shades of gray, are fairly evenly distributed across rich societies (with the possible exception of Canada). Note that after the minaret referendum in 2009, the French public were asked how they felt about a similar restriction in their own country: just 19 percent "favored" the construction of minarets, whereas 41 percent were "against" and 36 percent were "indifferent." These figures suggest that the majority of French also might come out against minarets, the only difference being that they—like their fellow Europeans—are not given the opportunity to do so.[1]

Switzerland's seeming archaism on immigration and citizenship gives an inkling of what a "democratic" immigration and citizenship policy without "liberal" decorum would look like. Contemporary liberals are so infused by a cosmopolitan ideal that they have lost any sense for the ultimately political, boundary-setting function of membership policy that can never be completely caged by liberal law principles. As Stefano Bartolini (2017, 106) reflected on the nature of the "political" (as distinct from the nature of the "legal"), "The integrity of the membership or territorial group and the physical security of its members are constantly at stake. The field of constitutive predicaments of community life is the area in which 'politics' is most clearly foreign and irreducible to law." Henry Sidgwick, a prominent nineteenth-century liberal, had a keen sense for this: he deemed the "cosmopolitan ideal" as "perhaps the ideal of the future," but found that at present the "national ideal[] of political organization prevailed" (1891, 295). Only on the basis of the "national ideal" was it possible to achieve "internal cohesion" and to "raise the standard of living among the poorer classes" (1891, 296). Accordingly, the nature of immigration policy, which he interestingly discussed within a chapter on the "principles of international duty," involved "the right [of the state] to admit aliens on its own terms, imposing any conditions on entrance or any tolls on transit, and subjecting them to any legal restrictions or disabilities that it may deem expedient" (1891, 235). This followed for him from the international law principle of "mutual non-interference," the only restriction on which was to give foreigners "due warning . . . and due time . . . for withdrawal" (1891, 235). The Swiss are modern-day Sidgwickians, and, interestingly, it is now the cause of right-wing populists to defend the "national ideal" that for the nineteenth-century liberal had been the undisputed ideal of the day.

Note

1. IFOP and Le Figaro, "Les Français et la construction des mosquées et des minarets en France," December 2, 2009, https://www.lefigaro.fr/assets/pdf/Sondage-minaret.pdf.

References

Bartolini, Stefano. 2017. *The Political.* Colchester: ECPR Press.

Guiraudon, Virginie. 1998. "Citizenship Rights for Non-Citizens." In *Challenge to the Nation-State: Immigration in Western Europe and the United States*, edited by C. Joppke, pp. 272–318. Oxford: Oxford University Press.

Helbling, Marc. 2011. "Why Swiss-Germans Dislike Germans: Opposition to Culturally Similar and Highly Skilled Immigrants." *European Societies* 13, no. 1: 5–27.

Linder, Wolf. 2010. *Swiss Democracy: Possible Solutions to Conflict in Multicultural Societies.* Basingstoke: Palgrave Macmillan.

Sidgwick, Henry. 1891. *The Elements of Politics.* London: Macmillan.

4   LATECOMERS TO IMMIGRATION

11 Italy

Immigration Policy and Partisanship

Ted Perlmutter

Italy is one of the western European countries where immigration has most recently emerged as an issue and where it has been increasingly politicized. It was not until 1990 that the first effort at comprehensive immigration legislation, the Martelli Law (Law 39/90), was passed. In the intervening decades, there have been dramatic changes in Italian immigration legislation and the party system as well as a regional refugee crisis that made the European Union a critical actor in Italian migration policy. The analytic elements this chapter emphasizes include the effects of political parties on immigration policy regarding the contested issues of planned entry, amnesties, enforcement policies, immigrant naturalization, and the refugee crisis.[1]

We will distinguish three historical moments, each roughly a decade, which will be described in terms of the tenor of the legislation passed and the ways in which immigration policy was politicized.

The first period, which extended from passage of the Martelli Law in 1990 until the passage of the Turco-Napolitano Law in 1998, was characterized by expansionist legislation. It was a followed by a decade of restriction, epitomized by the Bossi-Fini Law of 2002 and the security decrees of 2008–2009. The final period, which has no comparable piece of systematic legislation, commenced with the Arab Spring in 2011 and the attendant refugee crisis and continued until 2018. It was characterized by an inability to move forward on long-standing labor market issues, the increasingly salient issue of *jus soli* (birthright citizenship) for second-generation immigrants, and refugee policies driven by European Union initiatives. This periodization of policy initiatives will be framed in terms of the literature on politicization, which focuses on the ways that issues became salient. In theory, this increased salience should decrease the gap between public opinion and policy outcomes, although as van der Brug et al. argue, there are a multitude of factors (and actors) that can block this result (van der Brug et al. 2015; van der Nagel and Frith 2015; Cf. Urso 2018).

This chapter will argue that from 1990 to 2010 the political salience of immigration was driven by party conflicts and, at a deeper level, the transformations of the party system that occurred simultaneously with the politicization of the issue. From 2011 to 2018, politicization was increasingly driven by European Union policy in the context of a region-wide refugee crisis.

The Italian political system was characterized from 1990 to 2011 by political alternation between weak coalition governments, from 2011 to 2013 by a technocratic (non-partisan) government, and then from 2013 through 2017 by weak, center-left-dominated cross-party coalitions.

The arrival of immigration as a salient political issue mapped with the disintegration of the Italian First Republic in the early 1990s. The Martelli Law would be the last immigration act of the First Republic, which had been characterized by the domination of a center-right Christian Democratic coalition. The political reforms that created the Second Republic in 1994 were intended to produce alternating center-right and center-left political coalitions, and this characterized the political system for two decades. However, this system has lacked stability and produced fragmented alliances, particularly on the right, that have struggled to create coherent and effective immigration policies.

The critical components of Italy's immigration experience are as follows:

- A substantial acceleration in the twenty-first century in the rate of immigration (which stabilized in the mid-twenty thousand range in 2013-2017), and an ongoing demographic and labor market need for high levels of immigration
- Difficulty in elaborating and developing a labor market policy, particularly as regarding planned labor supply (see next section on Labor Markets and Demography, and Table 1 for work-related entry quotas), resulting in frequent recourse to regularization (legalization) of unauthorized immigrants already present
- Contested efforts to produce an effective removal policy for unauthorized immigrants and refugees
- A naturalization policy that was restrictive in nature and difficult to update but which eventually provided citizenship to a large number of immigrants,

even as it was not well suited to accommodate demands for integrating the children of the second generation

- A refugee policy, driven by a recent regional refugee crisis and the failures of the European Union, that politicized migration and made Italian society less welcoming and immigration policy less inclusive

This chapter begins with a description of the labor market, demography, and patterns of immigrant naturalization in Italy before it turns to a three-phase analysis of immigration.

Labor Markets and Demography

The most striking characteristics of Italian economic development are the differences between north and south and the large underground or shadow economy.

Since the founding of the country in 1861, there has been a profound difference between the industrial north and the agricultural south. The resulting "southern question" has preoccupied economic planners in Italy ever since. Indeed, Italy was the only country in Europe that industrialized during the 1960s and 1970s by drawing on its own internal labor reserves. The factories of the industrial triangle of the North—Turin, Milan, and Genoa—drew on rural workers, first from the northeast of the country and subsequently, and to much greater effect, from the south. Italy continues to have the largest regional difference in income in the European Union.

The other striking characteristic of the Italian economy is the large underground or unregulated sector, which encompasses about 13 percent of the workforce. It is also estimated that about 18 percent of Italian income escapes taxation. This underground economy pre-dates the rise of unauthorized migration and has been widely condoned by the Italian polity. The economy facilitates unauthorized migration by providing accessible employment opportunities for low-skilled workers lacking documentation.[2]

Unauthorized migration has permeated the low-skill sectors of the Italian economy, including manufacturing. However, it is particularly noticeable in "domestic services, agriculture, cleaning services, social and personal services, retail and wholesale trade, hotels and catering, [and] construction" (Reyneri 2007, 3–4).

Italy's population has been trending toward zero growth for a number of years. The country has one of the lowest birth rates in Europe—at present an average of 1.32 children per mother, which is well below the 2.1-child replacement level but above its nadir of 1.14 children per mother in 1995. Since 2015, the population has been in absolute decline: between 2015 and the end of 2018, the Italian population declined by 400,000, with a drop of 124,000 occurring in 2018 alone.

Growth in migration had been counteracting this tendency toward population decline for the last two decades. According to recent calculations by the Istituto Nazionale di Statistica (ISTAT), as of January 1, 2018, there were 6,108,000 foreigners in Italy, just over 10 percent of the total population of 60,484,000.

The recent declines in annual migration, as the refugee inflows have diminished, come after a remarkable increase (at least in European terms) of migration into Italy. In 1998 the foreign resident population was under 1 million, but by 2015 it had quintupled, showing the fastest growth in western Europe.[3] In 2018, the percentage of foreign-born in Italy was greater than in France, similar to the percentage in the United Kingdom, and less than in Germany, Belgium, Ireland, and Austria (Pannia, Federico, and D'Amato 2018). These numbers were driven first by labor migration and subsequently by asylum seekers. The category of migration that has attracted the greatest attention and been the most politically polarizing, family reunification, has become the most consistent source of immigrants. Between 2011 and 2016, it represented 40 to 45 percent of all visas granted.

Naturalization

As the number of immigrants increased, the questions of naturalization became increasingly pressing. And the Italian case presents a paradox: the number of naturalizations has increased dramatically in the last decade despite restrictive rules for obtaining citizenship, an inefficient and cumbersome bureaucracy, and the country's inability to develop new integration policies.

While Italian nationality law (Act 91/1992) makes it difficult for immigrants to obtain citizenship based on residence (Zincone 2009), the number of those being naturalized has increased enormously in recent years—from 10,000 in 2002 to 212,000 in 2016. In fact, Italy was the country with the highest numbers of naturalizations in 2015 in all of the European Union, accounting for 20 percent of the total that year (followed by Spain and the United Kingdom with 15 percent of the total each, France with 12 percent, and Germany with 11 percent). While it has lost the top spot in that list in recent years, Italy is still well above the average naturalization rate of foreign citizens in the EU (Eurostat 2019). (EU countries in terms of naturalizations.)

Citizenship Trends in Italy
Figure 11.1 shows that beginning in 2011, there was a dramatic increase in residence-based citizenship applications.

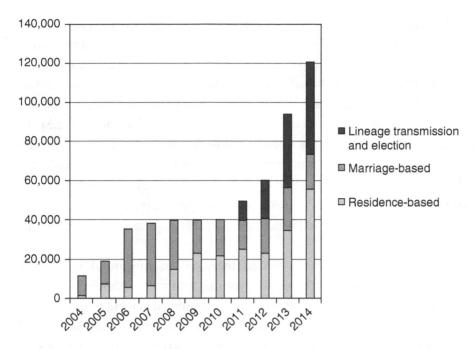

FIGURE 11.1. Citizenship Acquisition Trends in Italy, 2004–2014

SOURCE: Ministry of Interior (2004–2010); ISTAT (2011–2014).

For the period 2011–2014, figures on lineage transmission are estimated on the basis of the age of naturalized migrants, while residence-based naturalizations only include individuals who have already taken the oath of the Italian Constitution.

The most immediate cause for this increase is the number of those who reached the ten years of residency required before an application can be submitted. (Most of these applicants were originally granted residency permits as a result of large-scale legalizations.) Other contributing factors include publicity campaigns that made potential second-generation applicants aware of their rights; more expeditious administrative procedures; an increasing openness to immigration among bureaucratic officials when exercising their discretionary power; and as a response among potential applicants to the increasingly hostile political environment (Tintori 2018).

Immigration Legislation Regimes

By using the original Martelli Law (1990) as the starting point, we get a sense of the relation between political coalitions and immigration politics at the time of the law's passage and the challenges that this posed for a comprehensive immigration policy.

On planned entry and enforcement, the original Martelli legislation was underdeveloped—and dealing with the lacuna in policy would be one of the challenges for subsequent legislation. The Martelli Law's efforts at regularization were partially successful but did not encourage as many immigrants to apply as had been hoped for. The 1992 citizenship law, which regulated naturalization, was more concerned with Italians living abroad than with the new wave of migrants, and in fact made it more difficult for recent immigrants to Italy to become naturalized.

By the late 1980s, the need for new immigration legislation had become clear to all parties concerned. Italy had been a country of net immigration since at least the late 1970s. The immigrant population, both documented and undocumented, was estimated at between 750,000 and 1,250,000, approximately 2 percent of Italy's population. Immigrants entering in the late 1980s were faced with a regulatory system that had only recently been amended and which inadequately addressed many of the immigration issues of the time.

Before 1986, when Law 943/1986 was passed, there was no substantial body of law covering immigration, which left the rules governing entry to the fascist decrees of June 18, 1931, and May 6, 1940. The 1986 legislation regulated the entry of migrants seeking work and provided regularization for those already living in Italy who could prove they had a job. The regularization provisions turned out to be less than successful, as a disappointing percentage of immigrants legalized their status. The legislation also suffered from a limitation in that it did not apply to the self-employed, a category that encompassed a substantial number of immigrants.

As political actors became aware of the limited scope and efficacy of the 1986 law and the costs of the having no comprehensive legislation, recognition of the need for a new law grew. In addition, there was pressure from the European Commission to bring Italian immigration and refugee provisions into accord with the Schengen Agreement.

Immigration Politics in the First Republic

The First Republic party system was characterized by political fragmentation among the ruling parties and polarization between left and right. In the 1980s and early 1990s, when the first immigration legislation was passed, Italy was governed by five-party (*pentapartito*) coalitions dominated by the Christian Democrats, a highly factionalized mass party with a substantial working-class constituency in addition to its traditional Catholic base.

Of the four minor parties in the alliance, the Republican Party and the Socialist Party were the most visible and powerful, and they took the most outspoken stands in the immigration debates. The other two small parties, The small parties more clearly staked out public claims than the mass parties— the Christian Democrats and the Communists. The latter supported moderately open immigration policies but primarily did so in ways that did not increase the issues salience or visibility. Even though these parties provided crucial support for the Martelli legislation in parliament but they were rarely heard from during the critical months of public discussion.

Claudio Martelli, a Socialist leader who was the vice president of the Council of Ministers, proposed new legislation that would have opened immigration much more widely. He sought out the support of the left, including the unions and the Catholic voluntary sector, and dismissed the concerns of conservatives within his own government who were much more concerned with the Schengen Agreement and the need for restrictionist policies.

By all accounts, there was a substantial gap between the law's intention and its accomplishments in three critical areas. One, the planned inflows (*programmazioni dei flussi*), did not hit their targets. The bureaucratic challenges to hiring through this channel were so great as to discourage employers from using it. In addition, the quotas set were too low, not based on a realistic assessment of the Italian labor market. Two, the regularization provisions of the law legalized 235,000 immigrants, but this was far less than the estimated number of those illegally in Italy at the time. Three, the expulsion procedures were deeply problematic:

Act 39/90 helped however to strengthen the control apparatus. . . . The number of expulsions started slowly to increase though enforced expulsions remained a small percentage of the overall expulsion orders. The difficulty to enforce them was partly due to the absence of detention centres for irregular immigrants who had to be expelled. Police forces, moreover, often did not have the administrative resources needed to carry out successfully the implementation of expulsion orders. In addition, the expulsion procedure was too long and bureaucratic, because expulsions could not be enforced without the *nihil obstat* of the competent judge. (Finotelli and Sciortino 2009, 13)

If during the next five years little was done to transform the legislative landscape, it was not because the issue was not politically salient. Indeed, it seemed as though this would be a propitious period for restrictive immigration legislation. From 1991 to 1995, overall Italian employment dropped considerably (Reyneri 2004, 73) and unemployment rose from 8.6 percent in 1991 to 11.2 percent in 1995—nearly the highest levels of unemployment since World War II. This period also saw the rise of the Lega Nord (LN, Northern League), a xenophobic party that often played on anti-immigrant themes, although it opted not to mobilize around immigration issues during this period as much as it would in the 2000s.

Party Transformations and the Immigration Policy Debates, 1992–1995

Absent a strong xenophobic popular or party mobilization, the policy debates in 1992 and 1993 were framed by the conflicts between the left and the center, and the issue was contested in parliament, largely outside the scope of public debate. The gaps in the 1990 Martelli legislation and the problems with its enforcement would provide the terrain for subsequent legislative conflicts. Although the legislation had provided for broad regularization, many immigrants could not or would not legalize their status. The accompanying legislation originally envisioned as necessary to complete the process, particularly to regulate seasonal labor, never passed. A further gap in the legislation was the difficulty of deporting those in the country illegally, and consequently there remained a sizable population of unauthorized foreigners, primarily in the south, whom Italy could neither legalize nor expel.

As the political class came under greater assault, the two governments of the eleventh legislature became increasingly technical, and the direct control that parties had maintained over the governments became more attenuated. Civil society organizations, primarily lawyers' groups and advocacy groups, filled this void, as they would in subsequent periods of party decline and technical governments after 2011. It was progressive civil society organizations, most notably an alliance called the Anti-Racist Pact, that shaped the legislative battles during the immediate aftermath, pressuring the government on a range of fronts with a diversity of tactics. It organized public demonstrations to defeat deportation decrees that it deemed too restrictive, and it proposed measures to increase the rights and opportunities of seasonal and permanent immigrants, putting the government on the defensive.

The electoral reforms of the early 1990s were intended to produce a system that would guarantee strong parties and alternation between left and right. While alternation was achieved, a low (4 percent) threshold of votes cast was required for election to parliament allowed small parties to continue to have a role in the broader center-right and center-left coalitions.[4] It produced a system described by Ilvo Diamanti "as a fragmented and unstable bipolarism, which works for winning elections, but becomes a setback when governing or organizing the opposition in parliament" (2007, p. 740).

The center-right coalition would prove to be a dominant force in Italian politics (in power in 1994, from 2001 to 2006, and from 2008 to 2011). The parties making up this coalition, however, did not have a shared ideology on immigration. The Northern League was aligned with the interests of the northern regions, particularly

Lombardy and the Venetian region. It sought to loosen the central government's hold on the regions, sometimes by making separatist claims, at other times pursuing federalist claims. League members were often xenophobic and extremist in their rhetoric, even if, as will be seen, they were willing to compromise. The National Alliance (AN, Aleanza Nationale) was largely a party of the south and center of the country, building from its neo-Fascist roots to encompass a broader range of support as the Christian Democratic party dissolved. Its members tended to favor a strong national identity and were often at odds with the anti-state components of the Northern League's ideology.

The leading party, Forza Italia (FI, Forward Italy), represented business interests and was opposed to the most restrictive policies favored by the Northern League and the National Alliance. In subsequent administrations, Forward Italy would be joined by groupings of small Catholic parties that were more sympathetic to immigrants and equally opposed to the more conservative members of the coalition.

The likelihood of restrictive legislation appeared to increase substantially after the national elections in March 1994, when a coalition of the center right, led by Silvio Berlusconi of Forward Italy, won by constructing an alliance in the north with the Northern League and in the south with the National Alliance. However, the government was internally divided, with the Northern League not buying into a fully restrictionist agenda; it never demonstrated a sense of urgency, and eventually failed to produce a policy before it came to a premature end.[5]

The center-right coalition would be replaced by a technical government under the leadership of Lamberto Dini. In the fall of 1995, when the Dini government sought to develop a legislative agenda on immigration, the Northern League was willing to cooperate. In exchange for policies that would facilitate expulsions, the Northern League made concessions on a wide range of more integrative policies. Most important was a new regularization that would eventually encompass 256,000 applicants, of whom 238,000 were accepted.

In terms of policy polarization, the lessons of this interim period of party weakness and system evolution were that the Northern League could be both more flexible and less consequential on immigration than its critics had anticipated. In the 1992–1993 period, in which political parties were reshaping themselves and a viable coalition was difficult to form, it was interest groups that were most effective in making claims to the government on immigration. In 1994, the sharp divisions within the center-right coalition, resulting in an inability to pass legislation, were quite clear. In terms of policy, the cost of this phase of weak and divided party coalitions was that the obvious lacunae in the Martelli legislation could not be resolved. An organic effort to put forward comprehensive legislation would have to await the arrival of a center-left government in 1996 that would develop and pass comprehensive legislation two years later.

1998 Turco-Napolitano Act (Center Left)

When the center left came to power, it began a decade of systematic immigration policy. Its underlying approach to immigration policy was to draw on solidaristic and multicultural ideas that emphasized the need to make immigrant rights as equivalent as possible to Italians' rights. In terms of labor inflows, a high priority was the development of more rigorous and effective procedures that would go beyond this need for regularizations of unauthorized immigrants. Secretary of the Interior Giorgio Napolitano said:

> There is no doubt that we share the need to get beyond "emergency" approaches, whose effects are difficult to see and to pin down, and inevitably create diffuse situations of illegality. As a result, there are the amnesties regarding which there are justly many concerns; we want to put an end to this practice. (Einaudi 2007: 244)

Planning for employment quotas was made mandatory and was based on a three-year planning document, the product of an extraordinarily wide-ranging consultation process that involved local associations concerned with integration, employer associations, organizations of regional and provincial governments, and national ministries and parliamentary committees. The slots available under the employment quotas grew from 20,000 in 1997 to 58,000 in 1998, and eventually to 89,400 in 2002—an increase of almost 450 percent in five years. A striking example of policy innovation was the expansion of who could sponsor immigrants. Previously only employers with a job to offer could be sponsors, but this proposed legislation added Italian citizens and resident foreigners, regions, local authorities, professional associations and unions, and voluntary organizations.[6]

This rigorous approach to planning labor flows would eventually give way to pressures from others within Prime Minister Romano Prodi's own coalition and from civil society, and there would be a substantial regularization (for those who could show that they had an opportunity to work, housing, and a clean criminal record). This regularization effort would receive 308,000 applications, of which 192,300 would be approved.

Another significant cause for the passage of the Turco-Napolitano Act was to ensure Italy's entry into the Schengen Agreement, itself a measure of Italy living up to European standards and requirements (Zincone 2006a, 26). Interior minister Giorgio

Napolitano captured this partisan satisfaction with his country's success: "It put the lie to many forecasts that had been made, such as those that say Italy is a sieve, that it is the soft underbelly of Europe, and so forth, continuing that national self-defeating attitude, promoted by the intemperate statements of the opposition."

To live up to European immigration standards required a more effective expulsion regime. The main proposal to accomplish this involved the creation of temporary detention centers (*centri di permanenza temporanea*, or CPTs), in which foreigners who had illegally entered or were without documents could be held to determine their identity and facilitate their expulsion.

In addition to the CPTs, there were other enhancements to the control regime. The new law would permit forced expulsion for reasons of public order; allow police to treat immigrants found within six months of illegal entry like those who had been refused entry; and increase penalties for smuggling.

Also, Italy would sign bilateral accords with various countries, granting higher inflows for workers in exchange for facilitated deportations, an issue that will be addressed at greater length in the discussion of the refugee crisis that began after the Arab Spring.

The rationalization of the work-based quota system, as well as the increase in applications allowed, would be a lasting achievement of this government. It would also mark a triumph of the center-left party leadership against the left's internal opposition to the detention centers.

2002 Bossi-Fini (Center-Right) Response

If the 1990s can be viewed as the effort to fulfill the promises of the Martelli Law, culminating in the Turco-Napolitano Law, the first decade of the twenty-first century can be seen as the fight to reverse those efforts.

During the early 2000s migration would become increasingly politicized and seen as a security threat (Urso 2018). There was a high level of polarization around migration that mapped clearly to the left-right divide in the country. The right, which dominated the government during this period, was seen as being more in accord with public opinion and more capable of enacting its agenda. Around the elections of 2001 and 2008, fully 25 percent of those polled said that the center right was more capable of dealing with migration than the center left (Massetti 2015).

Following its success after a long electoral season, from 1999 to 2001, in which immigration was a critical and explosive issue, the center right immediately set out to implement immigration policies that would mark a profound rupture from the past. As Giovanna Zincone described it, the campaign had produced an "electoral bill of exchange that centrist parties were obliged to honour" (2006a, 30). The issues advanced during the election campaign included:

- Greater severity in combating illegal immigration, particularly when it involved human smuggling, fraud, and other criminal activity
- Reduction of long-stay visas based on the inflow planning process
- A return to earlier policies emphasizing the use of guest workers, by limiting the possibilities for migrants to become citizens and by reducing the emphasis on integration (Einaudi 2007, 308)

Pressing forward on immigration would unify the coalition by pushing on an issue that both the Alleanza Nazionale (National Alliance) and the Northern League, often at odds, could agree on.[7] The legislation would draw on two proposals, written while the center right was in opposition. One was the Bossi-Berlusconi bill, which emphasized work as the only legitimate motive for migration and would have made citizenship more difficult to obtain. The other was the National Alliance's Landi-Fini bill, which would have criminalized illegal migration, calling for immediate arrest and trial of migrants found to have entered illegally, and deportation for those found guilty.

These proposals would most effectively be resisted from within the coalition by two small Catholic parties, the Centro Cristiano Democratico (Christian Democratic Centre) and the Cristiani Democratici Uniti (United Christian Democrats), which would merge into the Unione dei Democratici Cristiani e Democratici di Centro (UDC, Union of Christian Democrats and Center Democrats) in 2002. The Catholic parties pushed for regularization and resisted the more radically repressive proposals of the National Alliance and the Northern League to criminalize illegal entry or undocumented presence.

Some policies that increased the penalties for crimes committed by unauthorized immigrants passed (see Bossi-Fini Law), but the Constitutional Court of Italy turned a skeptical eye toward a number of these new policies. In 2003, fully 56.3 percent of the cases that arrived on the docket of the constitutional court concerned immigration law (Einaudi 2007, 322), and two of the more far-reaching and controversial provisions of the Bossi-Fini Law 189/2002 were ruled unconstitutional.

After failing in its initial efforts to abolish the three-year planning process for determining employment quotas, the conservative members of the governing coalition sought to reduce the number of long-term permits for immigrant workers, which were seen as leading to settlement, and replace them with seasonal permits. The 2002 decree, the first after the Bossi-Fini Law took effect, decreased the overall number of employment quota positions (with long-stay visas) by almost 10,000, from 89,400 to 79,500 and dramatically increased the number of seasonal permits. In 2001, there were 50,000 long-term permits, approximately 54 percent of the overall pool of applicants. In 2002, there were only 19,500, or 20 percent of the pool, and by 2003 that number had fallen to 11,000, or 12 percent of the pool, representing the lowest number of long-term permits since the three-year planning process had begun in 1991 (see Table 11.1).

However, the number of long-term permits would subsequently rebound, to the point that by 2006 they were around 90,000, which had been the level under the earlier center-left government. Indeed, the effective quota for legal work visas was even higher, because the number of long-term permits would be supplemented by the visas allocated to the countries in southeastern Europe that had become members of the EU in the latest round of expansion and were included in the EU's "transitional quotas." Those quotas would be 36,000 in 2004, 79,500 in 2005, and 170,000 in 2006.[8]

This reversal was caused by a range of factors, both external and internal. Externally, the enlargement of the EU (and Germany's open visa policy) increased the flows to all EU member states, including Italy. And EU as well as Italian sentiment was opposed to mass regularization or amnesty for undocumented migrants. Internally, Italy needed to maintain relations with sending countries. Finally, it had to accept the increasing role of foreign labor in the country (Finotelli and Sciortino 2008, 8).

In many ways, the most surprising result of the center right's policy initiative was the large number of regularizations. The process by which this came about is indicative of the forces in play. The Catholic parties made a great effort to change the immigration law to introduce regularization. Originally, their efforts were rejected, but over time their demands were accepted incrementally, over the opposition of the Northern League and the more restrictionist element of the National Alliance. First, there was an acceptance of a new category, care providers (*badanti*). Acceptance was then extended to all domestic service workers and, after complaints by employers that they were being discriminated against, finally all workers.

It would be far and away the largest regularization in Italian history—634,700 of the 700,000 who applied were accepted. Of these 700,000 applications, 372,000 were "general" employees, 190,000 were domestic workers, and 140,000 were care providers.

The failure of the center right to implement its campaign promises on immigration despite its domination of the political process is reflective of a gap between the campaign promises and the policies enacted and a limit on the effects of the more conservative element of the center right to benefit from politicizing the issue.

TABLE 11.1. Summary of Legal Entries for Work in Italy, 1991–2006

Year	Entry Authorization for Work	Work Authorization	Entry Authorization for Non-Seasonal Work	Entry Authorization for Seasonal Work	Entry Authorization for Domestic Work	Quota for New EU Community Members	Demand from New EU Community Members
1991	6,000	—	6,000	—	—		
1992	31,630	—	29,971	1,659	21,828		
1993	23,088	—	20,300	2,788	14,555		
1994	22,474	—	16,697	5,777	12,420		
1995	25,000	25,000	17,413	7,587	6,183		
1996	23,000	23,000	14,120	8,880	6,795		
1997	20,000	20,000	11,551	8,449	—		
1998	27,303	58,000	10,743	16,560	—		
1999	36,454	58,000	16,074	20,380	—		
2000	83,000	83,000	41,944	41,056	—		
2001	89,400	89,400	50,000	39,400	—		
2002	79,500	79,500	19,500	60,000	—	Transitional Period	
2003	79,500	79,500	11,000	68,500	—		
2004	79,500	79,500	29,500	50,000	—	36,000	26,000
2005	99,500	99,500	54,500	45,000	—	79,500	57,000
2006	170,000	550,000	120,000	50,000	—	170,000	79,500

SOURCE: Ministero dell'Interno (2007).

[a]Since 1996, quotas from inflow decrees, including seasonal and nonseasonal work.

2007 Amato-Ferrero Proposal (Center Left)

When the center left returned to power in 2006 with the election of Romano Prodi as prime minister, it put forward a series of wide-ranging proposals known collectively as the Amato-Ferrero Law. Because of the government's thin parliamentary majority, ongoing internal conflicts between the center and left elements of the coalition, and the coalition's short lifespan, it was unable to pass these reforms, which would have favored more open policies toward entrance and more solidaristic policies toward immigrants, oriented toward facilitating long-term settlement.[9]

The quota requests under this legislation were reported to be 200,000, a figure substantially higher than in previous years. There was also a provision that would have allowed domestic service workers and care providers, two of the largest groups, to be excluded from these ceilings (Reyneri 2007, 26). In addition, there would have been a reversion to the Turco-Napolitano provisions allowing a variety of entities to sponsor immigrants, provisions that had been struck down by the center-right government. Finally, the work permits for foreigners seeking jobs would be greatly extended and made easier to access, thereby making it more likely that immigrants would find and keep jobs.

The one element of this group of proposals that was enacted, largely because it could be done by decree and did not require an extended legislative process, was the regularization decree, which granted visas to 350,000 formerly undocumented immigrants.

On immigration control, the proposals were nuanced, but largely in favor of reducing the weight of the more repressive control mechanisms. On the one hand, the government wanted to close down or at least radically reduce the role of detention centers, which had been a cornerstone of Italian expulsion strategies since the Turco-Napolitano Law in 1998. On the other hand, in 2007 the government proposed allowing the police to deport EU citizens and their family members from Italy if they were considered a threat to public order.

Security Package, 2008–2009 (Center Right)

In the 2008 elections, won overwhelmingly by the center-right coalition, the Northern League successfully mobilized around issues of criminality and illegal immigration. The candidate of the center left also emphasized the need for public order. The center-right coalition, with core members Forward Italy, the National Alliance, and the Northern League, won so convincingly that it did not need the support of the UDC, the small Catholic party that had played a critical role in constraining previous administrations.

The center right quickly sought to redeem its electoral promise to deal with immigration as a security issue (Finotelli and Sciortino 2008) by passing a security package (Laws 125/2008 and 94/2009).[10] The package increased the control powers of the state and included a series of measures criminalizing immigrants. It defined unauthorized presence as a crime, establishing a fine of €5,000–10,000 for those convicted. It included provisions that allowed unauthorized status to be seen as an aggravating factor to be considered in criminal sentencing, though these were later annulled by the Constitutional Court (Ambrosini and Triandafyllidou 2011, 267). It impinged on the social rights of immigrants by cracking down on landlords who rented to undocumented immigrants and requiring public officials, except for health care workers, to report on the legal status of their tenants. This law also amended the penal code to enable deportation of a foreigner or removal of an EU citizen if convicted of a crime carrying a sentence greater than two years.[11]

On the questions of worker immigration, the center-right coalition proposed quotas that were substantially lower than the demand. In 2005, employers made 210,000 applications for visas in this category; in 2006, 480,000; and in 2007, over 700,000. The government adopted a ceiling of 150,000 in 2008 and in 2009 decided to provide entrance only to temporary workers, citing the economic recession.

On the question of regularization, the government offered it only to domestic workers and care providers in 2009 (Law 102/2009) with a ceiling of 300,000. By September 30, 180,408 domestic workers and 114,336 care providers had applied.

Policy Stalemate, Weak Parties, and the EU: 2011–2018

The interest in developing major immigration policies lagged after 2008 as the economic crisis deepened and the Berlusconi government, unable to respond effectively, was replaced by a technical government led by Marco Monti in 2011. This caretaker government, which had a mandate to deal with the economic crisis, would last until the elections of 2013, when Enrico Letta of the Partito Democratico (Democratic Party) would be elected as the leader of a center-left coalition.

The issues that had defined the immigration policy agenda through the previous two decades and had been increasingly shaped by left-right partisan conflict would have substantially less purchase on the immigration agenda after 2011. The ensuing decade would be characterized by a stepping away from any consideration of a labor market policy; an extended (if episodic and eventually failed) effort to reform *jus soli*, particularly the unresolved naturalization issues regarding the children of foreigners; and an increasing preoccupation with refugee issues.

The major reasons for these changes would be the weak and divided governments led by the left and the increasing EU involvement in a dramatic refugee crisis. The

2013 election would produce a series of weak center-left governments that would last until 2018. These governments were headed by a series of Democratic Party prime ministers (Enrico Letta, Matteo Renzi, and Paolo Gentiloni) but lacked a governing majority in the upper house and so were dependent on opposition members to pass legislation (Chiaramonte et al. 2018). The European Union would fail to live up to its promise to share the burdens of the surge in refugees among the member states, as it required Italy to take on a greater role than other countries in accepting refugees and allowing them to apply for asylum status in Italy (Pastore 2014).

Labor Market Policy

The Great Recession in 2008 did not lead to a major change in Italian labor market policy from its center-right-driven tradition of harsh rhetoric, low and inadequate quotas, and mass regularizations (Pastore 2014). However, the political salience of labor migration would markedly decrease in the decade that followed As Bonizzoni argues, "First the economic crisis and then the growth of asylum seekers have contributed to pushing labour migration—and, especially, the management of low-skill labour market needs—off the political agenda" (Bonizzoni 2018, 57). One can see the effects of the change in numbers in the quotas themselves. Non-seasonal quotas declined from 150,000 in 2008 to 17,850 by 2012, a level that they would not exceed through 2017 (See Table 11.2).

Regularizations continued to play a role, with substantial numbers both in 2009 under the Berlusconi government and in 2012 under the Monti government. These regularizations, however, were primarily restricted to domestic work, which accounted for the entire quota in 2009 and 85 percent of the quota in 2012. As Ester Salis (2012) points out, there were 294,744 applications in 2009, 61 percent of which were for domestic workers and 39 percent for care providers. In 2012, there were 134,576 applications, of which 115,969 were for domestic work.[12] Caregiving employment has expanded, largely responding to deficiencies in care for the elderly within the Italian welfare state. As Salis argues, "Care work provided by migrant women has been an effective and low-priced response to the structural deficiencies of the Italian elderly care system, which has allowed the State to recurrently postpone the necessary and highly expensive reforms that demographic ageing would have imposed" (Salis 2014, 537). Estimates by the Ministry of Labor in 2012 show that over half of all migrant women active in the Italian labour market are employed as domestic and care workers.

The openness and growth of this component of the economy can obscure the lack of dynamism and planning within the immigrant job market. As Paola Bonizzoni put it in 2018 (p. 58), "Since 2011, the system has been almost (both quantitatively

TABLE 11.2. Italy, Entry Quotas Allowed Each Year, 2007–2017

Year	Non-Seasonal	Seasonal	Total
2007	170,000	80,000	250,000
2008	150,000	80,000	230,000
2009	Not allowed	80,000	80,000
2010	86,600	11,400	98,000
2011	Not allowed	60,000	60,000
2012	17,850	35,000	52,850
2013	17,850	30,000	47,850
2014	17,850	15,000	32,850
2015	17,850	13,000	30,850
2016	17,850	13,000	30,850
2017	13,850	17,000	30,850

SOURCE: Decrees of the President of the Council of the Ministers (2007–2017).

TABLE 11.3. Residence permits for non-EU citizens, 2007–2017

Year	Work	Family	Study	Asylum/request for asylum	Elective residence	All (total)
2007	150098	86468	11523	9971	9540	267600
2008	145091	101613	12426	18345	8767	286242
2009	250883	111145	15628	7300	8075	393031
2010	358870	178797	26343	10336	24221	598567
2011	124544	140846	31295	42672	22333	361690
2012	70892	116891	31005	22916	22264	263968
2013	84540	105266	27321	19146	19373	255646
2014	57040	101422	24477	47873	17511	248323
2015	21728	107096	23030	67271	19811	238936
2016	12873	102351	17130	77927	16653	226934
2017	12200	113549	18323	101065	17633	262770

and qualitatively) closed. While the numbers have returned to those of the pre-2000 period, its highly selective nature—with all the places left to seasonal workers, workers with stay permits for e.g. study converted to work purposes, and self-employed workers—makes applying for long-term jobs basically impossible."

The center-left government that followed the center-right and technical governments in 2013 made no effort to raise the quotas. A primary reason for that would be the arrival on Italian shores of an increasing number of economic migrants and refugees, precipitated by the Arab Spring.

The decline in labor migration in the decade following the Great Recession of 2008 would be accompanied by a dramatic rise in asylum seekers. The data on residence permits (*permesso di soggiorno*) demonstrates this dramatic change (Table 11.3). While employment-related permits went from 150,000 in 2007 to a peak of 360,000 in 2010 and then down to 12,000 in 2017, asylum applicants rose from approximately 10,000 to 100,000 over that period.

Refugees and the European Union

The refugee crisis in Italy began in the aftermath of the Arab Spring when the regimes in Tunisia and Libya fell and along with them the carefully crafted arrangements that had regulated immigration between Italy and its North African neighbors (Tsourapas 2017; Cetin 2015; Cuttitta 2018). The cornerstone to these arrangements was the Treaty of Friendship, Partnership, and Cooperation signed in August, 2008 between Italy and Libya. This treaty promised Italian financial support to Libyan efforts to curtail the migration that flowed to Italy from Central and East Africa. This arrangement reduced the numbers from 50,000 in 2008 to under 10,000 in 2009 and 2010. After the Libyan government fell in the Arab Spring, the number of migrants returned to its previous level, 50,000, by the end of 2011.

While Italian politicians, left and right, treated this resurgence both as a humanitarian emergency and as a security threat (McMahon and Sigona 2018), the initial Italian policy response was largely accommodating, viewing it through a humanitarian lens. The Italian government would, for example, grant humanitarian visas to all Tunisian migrants who arrived in the period in 2011 when Tunisia lacked a functioning government (Cetin 2015). Parties of all persuasions agreed on the need for greater EU support, particularly regarding the need to share among all the EU states the burden of the refugees landing on Italian shores.

EU policy significantly impacted the Italian response to the post-2011 refugee crisis, requiring the legal acceptance processes to become "more rigorous" and challenging the humanitarian tendencies of the Italian center-left governments to present an open, if not lax, response to asylum application management and hosting arrangements. Ignoring EU regulations, Italy had allowed migrants crossing the Mediterranean to enter Italy without proper registration, assuming that Italy was not their final destination (Caponio and Cappiali 2018, 125).

The EU's instruments for responding to the refugee crisis, particularly regarding burden sharing, proved inadequate. EU policies exacerbated the difficulties Italy faced concerning refugees, weakened the support for other progressive immigration policies, and contributed to the rise of the right as a governing coalition. A system built on Dublin rules requiring that refugees file their applications in the country of first entry placed the burden on the countries of southern Europe. To enforce these priorities, the European Agenda on Migration was adopted in May 2015 and mandated the creation of "hot spots" at refugee camps in Italy and Greece. These hot spots were intended to register and fingerprint migrants, with an eye toward establishing who would be eligible for refugee status either in Italy or as part of a planned Europe-wide burden-sharing arrangement. As Florian Trauner wrote, "To put it more bluntly, the frontline member states may no longer have the liberty to ignore the EU rules on fingerprinting and registration . . . if they want to benefit from the relocation scheme" (Trauner 2016, 320).

The policy increased the number of immigrants registered and enforced the Dublin rules mandating that Italy assume responsibility for registering refugees and allow them to apply for asylum. At its peak, the new system was registering 2,000 individuals per day (Beirens 2018), and in the end the system would register 92 percent of potential applicants (European Court of Auditors 2017).

The burden that this placed on southern European countries was enormous and one that the EU sought to ameliorate in September 2015, when the European Council passed an emergency two-year plan to transfer 160,000 asylum claimants arriving in Italy and Greece to other member states. The numbers to be transferred would subsequently be reduced to 40,000, and even the transfer of this reduced number would not be accomplished in a timely fashion. The number of relocations from Italy would not reach the level of 1,000 per month until May 2017. In the period between October 15, 2016, and November 2017, only 10,842 relocations occurred (Ekinci 2018).

One can see a similar resistance to burden-sharing by the European Union on issues related to naval patrols of the Mediterranean. In response to the rise of asylum-seekers coming to Italy, the Italian navy increased its presence in the Mediterranean, first by expanding the Constant Vigilance campaign, which long pre-dated the 2011 crisis, and then, in response to increasing numbers of migrants and deaths at sea, by initiating the Mare Nostrum operation in October 2013. That operation, which lasted until October 2014, rescued and brought to Italy 150,000 migrants. The European Union turned down Italy's request to financially support Mare Nostrum, replacing it with its own naval patrols, called Triton and Poseidon, which had a significantly lower budget. Only after mass drownings in April 2015 did the European Union increase the budget to the level of Mare Nostrum.

Another European policy that would have effects, both short- and long-term, on Italian immigration and refugee policy was the April 2016 EU-Turkey agreement that required Turkey to accept returned migrants from Greece in exchange for financial compensation, visa liberalization, and easing Turkey's accession into the EU. This arrangement, seen as outside the normal order for treaties (Lavenex 2018) and as threatening to undermine human rights standards, would become a template for a similar arrangement that that Italy would make with Libya in 2017.

As the Aegean route into Europe was closed as a consequence of this treaty, the importance of the central Mediterranean route increased (Geddes 2018 and Geddes and Hadj-Abdou in this volume). According to the Frontex Annual Risk analysis (2017), the number of migrants crossing through the central Mediterranean increased to

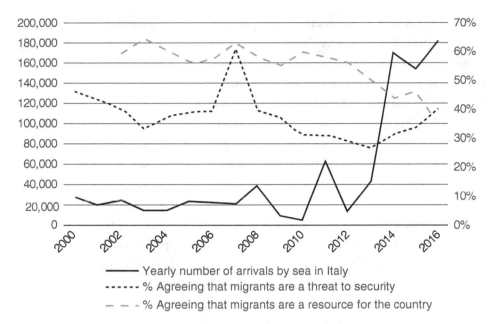

FIGURE 11.2. Arrivals by Sea and Evolution of Public Opinion on Migration in Italy, 2008–2017
SOURCES: UNHCR; DemosΠ SWG.

181,459 in 2016, 18 percent higher than 2015 and the highest level ever recorded. Even more troubling, data from the International Organization for Migration showed that deaths and missing persons increased by 42 percent in one year, from 3,175 in 2015 to 4,500 in 2016. "While these policies were implemented, arrivals in Italy increased in 2016, with more than 180,000 new arrivals by sea, compared with 150,000 in 2015 (UNHCR 2016b, 2018a). . . . Although this figure fell to around 120,000 in 2017, Italy received more than 65% of asylum seekers and refugees who arrived in Europe by sea (UNHCR 2018a)."

The increase in refugees contributed to declining support for immigration overall. Public opinion shifted during this time from seeing migrants as an asset to seeing them as a security threat (see Figure 11.2).

Libya Accord.   The measure that was most effective at limiting sea arrivals reconstructed the arrangements with Libya that had historically served to limit migration into Italy. The diplomatic process to restrict the flows across the Mediterranean could only begin once there was a UN-recognized Libyan government with which Italy could negotiate. This occurred in April 2016 with the establishment of a Government of National Accord. In February 2017, Italy signed a new treaty with

Libya and provided ten patrol boats to the Libyan coast guard (Cuttitta 2018 , 17). At the same time, Italy became more deeply involved in Libyan internal politics, seeking to limit sub-Saharan African migration into the country (Palm 2018).

This closing of the sea route to Italy passed on costs to others—both the asylum seekers forced to remain in Libya in circumstances substantially beneath international human rights standards and to the countries of the western Mediterranean (Ekinci 2018; Amnesty International 2017). By 2018, the central Mediterranean had been eclipsed by the western Mediterranean as a route of passage. In that year only 23,400 migrants arrived on Italian shores, compared with 65,400 in Spain and 50,500 in Greece.

While the Libya policy eventually resolved the central Mediterranean passage issue, the two years of substantial increases without any appreciable burden sharing took its toll on the Italian polity. The increasing pressure of absorbing asylum seekers who could no longer migrate through Italy and apply in other countries contributed both to the rising numbers of those illegally present and to the political backlash against all forms of immigration. The estimates of those illegally present, which had declined from 422,000 in the years following the 2009 amnesty to 294,000 in 2013, rose to 435,000 in 2017, with expectations that the number would reach 533,000 by 2020. While these numbers included unauthorized workers overstaying their visas (Sciortino 2014), the number of failed asylum seekers increasingly became a contributing factor starting in 2014 (see Figure 11.3).

The challenges posed by the rising number of failed asylum seekers were exacerbated by the weakness of Italian repatriation policy. Italy lacked agreements with countries to which it wanted to repatriate migrants, and it did not have the

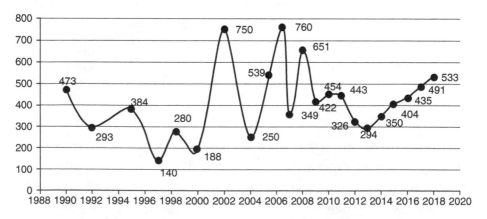

FIGURE 11.3. Estimate of Irregular Immigrants Present, 1990–2018
SOURCE: "Ventiquattresimo Rapporto sulle Migrazioni," 2018, Fondazione ISMU.

administrative capacity to repatriate those who had received deportation orders. Between 2013 and 2017, 145,155 orders for repatriation were issued, but only 28,600 (or 19.7 percent) were carried out. As McMahon and Sigona put it, "Measures designed to deter secondary migration toward the north of Europe in practice created a large undocumented and yet non-deportable population in Italy with fewer rights" (2018, 504). This phenomenon helped bring about a change in public opinion that would have an effect on constraining progressive measures on citizenship law reform.

Jus Soli and Naturalization of the Second Generation

The other issue that became dramatically politicized during this post-2011 period was *jus soli*. These debates took place during a period when there was a substantial increase in the overall naturalization rates in Italy, despite a legislative and bureaucratic environment that was among the most restrictive in Europe. This section will discuss the campaigns to modify and modernize the 1992 citizenship law, particularly regarding children born in Italy of parents without residency permits. The explanation for the trajectory of these policy debates will emphasize the long-standing inability of political parties to reach an agreement on this issue and the increased importance of civil society actors at moments when political polarization was at its peak and the stalemate between parties was the greatest. It will argue that the failure in 2017 to reform the law was a result of political fragmentation, a weakening of civil society groups, and a decreased tolerance for any open immigration policy as a result of the refugee crisis. While there was broad agreement among progressive policymakers on the need to modify and modernize the 1992 citizenship law, there has been no legislative progress despite initiatives beginning in 2000. Particularly striking was the inability of new legislation to be passed in the period starting in 2012 but before the refugee crisis, a time when there was broad public support for such measures.

The fundamental impetus for reforming nationality law was the situation of second-generation foreigners born in Italy who could not obtain citizenship through parents who were non-nationals. This was a group that was growing in number, organizational capacity, and political consciousness in the 2000s as the number of children increased and they as a group became more visible (Zinn 2011). The percentage of children born of two foreign parents as a share of all children born in Italy increased from 1 percent of the total in 1992 to 6.2 percent in 2002, and eventually stabilized at 15 percent in 2012 (Tintori 2018).

These numbers were supplemented by the increase of foreign-born children who migrated to Italy with their parents. As Figure 11.4 indicates, the number of

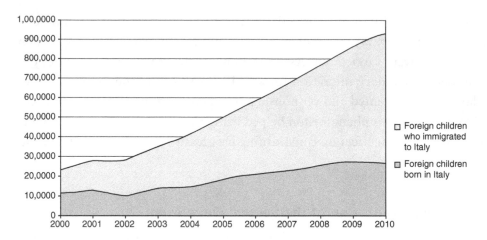

FIGURE 11.4. Foreign Minors Residing in Italy, 2000–2010
SOURCE: Citalia, from ISTAT data.

foreign-born children equaled the number of children born in Italy to at least one foreign parent in 2000, but by 2012 the number of foreign-born children was more than twice the number of Italian-born children of immigrants.

These heated debates were in part the result of internal divisions within the center-right coalition, the result of efforts of Gianfranco Fini to burnish his image on these issues and move his party to the center, away from its Fascist past (Urso 2018, 374). There would be continued opposition to these reforms from other elements within the center-right coalition, particularly the Northern League, which led to the failure on this front.

Only with the fall of the Berlusconi government and its replacement by a technical government run by Monti in 2011 were circumstances again ripe for a move forward on these issues. As in the early 1990s, when there was a technical government, civil society actors played a more prominent role in immigration issues during this period. In this case, it was a mobilization campaign called "L'Italia sono anch'io" (I am Italy too) involving twenty-two civil society organizations, including the major immigration organizations and particularly those representing immigrant youth, such as G2. These groups collected 150,000 signatures on a citizens' initiative, which they presented directly as a legislative proposal to parliament. The initiatives regarded both *jus soli* and foreigners' rights to vote in local elections. This initiative obtained substantial public and progressive elite support, including from Italian president Giorgio Napolitano (Sredanovic and Farina 2015).

Center-Left, 2013–2017. When a new government of the left came to power in 2013, there was optimism that progress might be made on second-generation naturalization, even though this issue was not a part of any party's electoral platform in 2013. While there was a wide range of proposals, they shared two characteristics: a conditional *jus soli* at birth, dependent on parental long-term residence or birth in the country, and the adoption of *jus culturae*, which provided access to citizenship to children born abroad after the completion of a school cycle in Italy.

The primary reason for the failure of these proposals was not disunity on the left but firm opposition from the right, which had sufficient influence to block the initiative. Indeed, Forward Italy threatened to withdraw its support from the government if the left insisted on their passage (Bianchi 2014).

When the Letta government fell and was replaced by the Renzi government, the issue was taken up again. In 2015, the Chamber of Deputies overwhelmingly passed legislation (310 to 66, with 83 abstentions) that authorized *jus soli temperato* (that is, granting citizenship to a child born in Italy when at least one of the child's parents had a long-term residence permit) and to those children, regardless of place of birth, who could show five years of attendance in Italian schools (*jus culturae*). The legislation was supported by the left in government, with opposition from the Northern League, Forward Italy, and other minor parties, and abstentions by the Movimento Cinque Stelle (M5S, Five Star Movement, a right-wing party). This legislation was never brought up for a vote in the Senate, where the governing coalition depended on opposition support.

Even at the end of the legislative session in 2017, the reforms' supporters in government opposed voting on the issue. Public opinion had become increasingly hostile, and, the government turned its attention to other issues. A 2017 *Corriere della Sera* poll points to diminished public support for the measures and politically polarized attitudes on the issue. If in 2011 71 percent of the population supported the principle of *jus soli temperato*, by 2017 that figure had dropped to 44 percent. The partisan division was equally striking. In 2017, 78 percent of center-left Democratic Party voters supported the issue, with only 22 percent opposed. For supporters of parties of the right like Forward Italy and the Northern League, 86 percent were opposed. The Five Star Movement was divided, with 42 percent of its supporters favoring the legislation and 58 percent opposed.

In the summer of 2017, as the legislative session was concluding and the political will to move forward was flagging, civil society groups became increasingly active, staging public demonstrations and keeping the issue on the public agenda in ways that were reminiscent of 2011. Backed by the left-liberal mainstream newspaper *La Repubblica*, they organized a series of public actions to exert pressure on parliament to expedite the approval of the law. These campaigns managed to reinvigorate the debate on *jus soli* in the public sphere but were in the end unable to convince the government to vote.

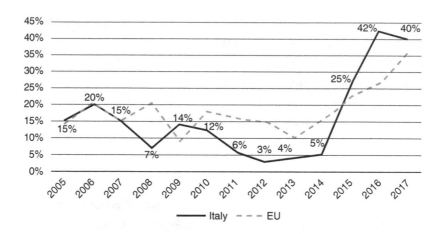

FIGURE 11.5. Share of People Considering Immigration the Most
Important Problem in Their Country, 2005–2017
SOURCE: Standard Eurobarometer, 2005–2017.

The reasons for this failure were multiple, including the divisions in public opinion and the deeply partisan nature of those divisions. With an impending election on
the horizon, parties were not willing to press forward. This decline in public support
mirrors a deepening concern within Italian public opinion on refugees.

As Eurobarometer data indicates, concern with immigration accelerated at a
rapid rate in 2015 throughout Europe, with the advent of refugees fleeing the Syrian
conflict. If the salience of immigration averaged about 5 percent in the period of the
first refugee crisis as migrants arrived from Libya and Tunisia (2011–2014), by 2015
the level of concern increased to 25 percent, and in 2016 it was 42 percent. This was a
much steeper rise than in the rest of the EU, where the numbers were higher in the
2011–2014 period and rose more slowly in the period 2014–2016 (see Figure 11.5).

Popular opinion turned against immigration in part because of the way the
Northern League sought to tie all immigrants with refugees, as a way of tarnishing
their reputation. As Tintori put it:

Matteo Salvini, leader of the [Northern League], exploited the so-called "refugee
crisis" that since 2013 had involved the central Mediterranean, with thousands of
arrivals each month on Italian shores. He ably turned *ius soli* reform into a political
liability for the [Democratic Party] and its allies. Salvini conflated legally residing
immigrants, including second generation foreigners, and migrants disembarking at
southern Italian harbors into a single indistinct threat. (Tintori 2018)

Electing the First Conte Government
Increasing polarization on migration matters politically, as can be seen in its contribution to the right-populist coalition elected in 2018 (Figure 11.6). The Italian results

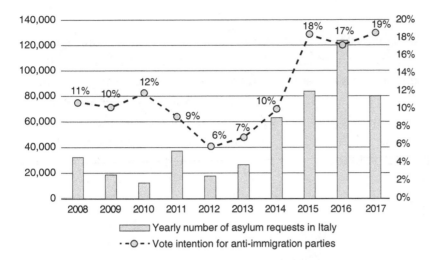

FIGURE 11.6. Asylum Requests and Support for Anti-Immigration Parties, 2008–2017

followed on a series of elections in 2017 in France, Austria, Germany and the Netherlands where the salience of immigration contributed to the growing voter share of anti-immigration parties (Geddes 2018).

The Italian election of 2018 produced the first right-wing populist government in western Europe. It replaced a government elected in 2013 that had been evenly divided between the traditional center-left and center-right coalitions, with a 25 percent share gained by the Five Star Movement, which ran on an anti-system platform centered around the idea of a guaranteed basic income for citizens. The results highlighted a resurgent Northern League, which ran primarily on immigration and security issues and gained enough votes to construct a coalition government with the Five Star Movement (Garzia 2019). The losers were the traditional center right and the center left.

Between the elections of 2013 and 2018, the number of voters who mentioned immigration as the most important issue rose from 5 percent to 33 percent.

Security Decrees of 2018

The most important elements of the first Conte governments were the two security decrees: Law 132, of December 1, 2018, and Law 53, of June 14, 2019. The most critical component of the first was the abolition of the humanitarian protection for asylum applicants, an increase in the severity of the regulations regarding deportation, and an increase in the resources available for these deportations. The list of crimes for which refugees could be deported was broadened, as the length of time that refugees could be detained in anticipation of deportation was extended.

Given the challenges surrounding deportation, the abolition of the humanitarian protection provisions risked further increasing the number of asylum applicants that Italy could neither legalize or deport. The second decree was concerned with increasing the penalties for NGOs that were engaged with rescuing immigrants at sea, particularly those seeking to cross from Libya. The law held them responsible for encouraging illegal migration. It prevented ships that had rescued migrants at sea from landing in Italian ports. It increased the fines for violating these provisions, allowed for the arrest of ship captains, and called for the seizure and potential destruction of the vessels engaged in these practices (Passini e Regalia 2018 ; Cesareo 2019).

Conclusion

With political polarization remaining strong, the post-2011 environment would not produce substantial policy innovations, largely as a result of three factors. One was the refugee crisis, which vitiated the possibilities of developing a more proactive labor market policy. Another was the weakness in the center-left coalitions that governed between 2011 and 2018, and which failed to move on *jus soli* modernization. A third factor was the increasing authority of the EU regarding refugee matters, which decreased the Italian government's autonomy and forced the left to take its internal asylum and refugee obligations more seriously. The EU's hot spot policy, which required Italy to live up to its Dublin obligations and eliminated the "safety valve" of allowing those who crossed the Mediterranean to seek asylum in northern Europe, contributed to the politicization of immigration in Italy and the impression that Italian migration politics were out of control.

Any discussion today about the trajectory of Italian immigration policy is a substantially different enterprise than it would have been a decade ago as the Berlusconi-led center-right coalition was winding down. At that point, one would have focused on the end of a tumultuous decade of comprehensive immigration policy, starting with the center-left Turco-Napolitano Law in 1998, followed by sustained efforts at policy reversal, first with the Bossi-Fini Law in 2002 and then with the security package in 2008 and 2009. While the center-right reluctantly agreed to regularization legislation, one would have been hard pressed to ignore the sharp political polarization around a range of other issues.

In judging the coherence of Italy's immigration policies, one needs to pay attention to the internal coherence of the coalitions, particularly given the electoral system, which tends to privilege disparate, fragmented party groupings and give substantial weight to the small parties within them. This has been particularly true for the center right, which in 1994 developed out of a marriage of convenience between three political traditions. Even though it had a larger number of parties and less identifiable and powerful leadership, the center-left coalition was more ideologically compact. This difference was accentuated when it came to immigration, where there was much more of a governance-based approach on the left and much more of an electorally driven one on the right (Zincone 2006a).

In the last decade, as the issues have changed and the political alternation between left and right has become less meaningful as the coalitions have weakened and refugee policy has become more dependent on the European Union, this policy polarization has become less determinant and the likelihood of dramatic policy oscillations has decreased. Labor market planning has been an Italian policy aspiration. Unlike most countries in Europe, Italy has, in both law and self-conception, accepted the need for labor recruitment from outside its borders and in particular from outside the EU. That said, it has not developed the policy instruments that would keep up with labor demand and channel immigration in an effective manner. As argued by Christian Joppke (2002), there is a considerable difference between regulating existing flows ("stemming") and actively seeking new ones ("soliciting"). The Italian employment quota policy in 2010 in principle accepted the possibility of actively "soliciting" but was in reality more comfortable with "stemming"—that is, regularizing the flows of those already in the country illegally.[13] As Francesco Ciafaloni has noted, the practice was often to legalize those who were already present in Italian territory:

It has been noted, but must be remembered, that to understand the mechanisms and the conflicts, that the only immigration policy that has really been followed by Italian governments—of the old five party system, technical government, or those of the Right or the Left . . . , has been to tolerate unregulated entry and the presence of those without adequate documents and to give them amnesty every four or five years. (Ciafaloni 2004, 138)

Indeed, the five regularizations that occurred from 1986 onward affected 1,419,600 people plus the 300,000 applicants from the 2009 process whose applications were pending (see Table 11.4).

Every major change in Italian immigration law was accompanied by a regularization. Particularly in the more recent episodes, regularizations tended to start with a narrow category of applicants and then expand. They were increasingly regarded as a necessary evil, with each government stressing that they were not an amnesty since they were a "one off" and involved only one-time regularizations.

There has always been considerable dispute between left and right over labor market policy. The center left generally supported larger quotas with an easier path to long-term residency, while the center right, at least since the early years of the second Berlusconi regime in 2001, favored programs closer to guest worker policies. With

TABLE 11.4. Numbers of Migrants Regularized in Italy, 1986–2009

Year	Applicants	Regularized
1986–1987	Not known	118,700
1990	Not known	235,000
1995–1996	256,000	238,000
1998–1999	308,000	193,200
2002	700,000	634,700
2009	300,000	Not known

the influx of refugees, the number of labor market applicants has dropped to histori-cally low levels.

An active labor market policy requires taking on a degree of risk. Sciortino (2009, 15) acknowledges the challenges:

> The government is then called to assume responsibility for uncertainties linked to the process of establishing a quota and the future impact of the flows. In other words, governments undertaking an active immigration policy must define as certain what is unknown, knowing perfectly well that this will imply both a restriction of the future room for maneuver and the assumption of responsibility for the policy outcomes.

The question of regularization, however, remains very much on the table, particu-larly as the number of asylum seekers who have neither been granted a stable status nor been deported has continued to grow.

The fate of *jus soli* reform is difficult to foresee. The center-left government that took power in 2019 pushed for it, but at this writing the outcome is far from certain, and it is likely to be determined both by the coalition in power and by the public's acceptance of migrants, which was substantially weakened during the refugee crisis and has yet to fully rebound. But clearly the impacts of the Libyan and then the Syr-ian refugee crises have had an enduring impact on Italian openness to migration, willingness to support other policies such as *jus soli*, and support for anti-immigrant parties. Public opinion did not recognize an end to the crisis, even as the numbers of refugees dropped from their peak in 2017.

Relevance of the Literatures on the Gap Hypothesis and Politicization

Both the literature on politicization and the gap hypothesis theorize the relation be-tween public opinion, political party behavior, and policy outcomes. It is beyond the scope of this chapter to disentangle the theoretical complexities of these debates; instead, our consideration of these issues will focus on the role of political parties and subsequently the European Union's handling of the refugee crisis in mediating the relationship between public opinion and immigration policy (Morales, Pilet, and Ruedin 2015).

Politicization of immigration could be seen as positive in terms of a gap hypothesis, to the extent that it minimizes the distance between public opinion and policy. In one early version of this gap hypothesis originally argued by Gary Freeman, a small mobilized minority of interest groups took advantage of issues of low general political salience to work toward expansionist objectives that he claimed were not in the general/public interest (Freeman 1995). Others have elaborated the centrality of interest groups but sought to broaden the number of actors and institutions involved and develop more refined historical analyses (Lahav and Guiraudon 2006; Caponio and Cappiali 2018). My interpretation of the role of interest groups has them playing a critical role in Italian immigration politics only in moments of transition when political parties are weak

This chapter has highlighted three aspects of the politicized relationship between public opinion and public policy. First, it has emphasized party polarization as a cause of a lack of policy continuity, with there being a rapid oscillation between left and right. It has argued that the defects in the party system have contributed to this, particularly as the low thresholds for party representation in the legislature undermined governing coherence. This was particularly true in the decade from 1998 to 2008, when critical comprehensive policy decisions were made. The dramatic oscillations in policy during the first decade of the twenty-first century resulted in continuities on amnesties but constant disputes on a range of other issues (Massetti 2015).

The second party-related issue affecting the relationship between public opinion and immigration policy involves the solidity and stability of party governance. The 1996–2008 era was preceded and succeeded by extended periods when there was not a government with a solid enough majority or a long enough tenure to pass systematic legislation. In these periods, which were often characterized by technical governments, interest groups tended to make the most effective political claims on the government. The 2013–2018 period was characterized by the type of weak coalition governments and the lack of clear alternations in power that the Second Republic system of governance was constructed to avoid. Recent efforts to reform this system have failed.

While European Union considerations and external shocks to the political environment have always circumscribed Italian immigration policy, these factors became increasingly central after 2011. During this period, starting with the Arab Spring, the locus of dynamics shifted away from internal nation-state politics and toward the EU. By the middle of the decade, one can see the full effects of rising numbers of migrants and ineffective burden-sharing arrangements on public opinion, which paid more attention to and was more hostile toward immigrants as the refugee crisis deepened. Subsequently, and partially as a consequence, voter support for right-wing, xenophobic parties increased, and the first right-wing populist government in western Europe was elected in Italy in 2018. As the voluminous literature on politicization of immigration indicates (Morales, Pilet, and Ruedin 2015 ; Grande, Schwarzb☐zl, and Fatke 2018; van der Brug et al. 2015; Giuseppe 2015), Italy is not alone among its western European counterparts in this matter. As the inability of the United States to pass any meaningful immigration legislation since the 1990s shows, political stalemate is also not a uniquely Italian outcome. Italy has often been a forerunner in terms of political party crisis and the politicization of immigration, but rarely has it lacked followers.

Notes

1. This choice of issues tends to emphasize the contrast between political parties. If one were to choose social rights of immigrants, one would find less contestation between center-left and center-right parties on access to health and educational services. Focusing on temporary protection issues would likely be a middle case, with little apparent difference between the coalitions in 2009 when the Berlusconi government's treatment of potential asylum seekers from Libya, along with other issues, aroused the ire of the European Commission and the United Nations High Commission for Refugees.

2. For a description of sources regarding illegal migration, see Fasani 2009.

3. These trends have long been noted by immigration scholars. Castiglioni and Dalla Zuanna (2009, 25) illustrate how immigration shapes these dynamics. They point out that while the native population declined by 700,000 between 1999 and 2006, overall population for those eight years showed a growth rate of 2.1 million; the difference is immigrants and their children.

4. This quota would, in subsequent changes to the electoral law, be lowered to 2 percent.

5. This section draws heavily on Perlmutter (2002).

6. This sponsorship would consist of assisting the applicant in gaining access to the labor market and housing and medical services.

7. This account draws primarily on Einaudi 2007. For a comprehensive version in English that focuses on party dynamics, see Geddes 2008.

8. The number of those who actually came was substantially lower.

9. This interpretation was reconstructed from three sources: Pastore 2007, Einaudi 2007, and EMN 2008.

10. One cannot but be struck by the convergence here with the efforts of American states over the past five years, and particularly recent legislative initiatives, such as SB 1070 in Arizona. If this trend continues, it would mark a fundamental change with previous policy by center-right governments, which had generally refrained from restricting the social rights of illegal immigrants.

11. Zincone (2006a, 2006b) tends to emphasize convergence, as does Geddes (2008), whereas Einaudi (2007), who gives greater weight to the specifics of the quota-planning debates, sees greater distance between the center right and the center left. Finotelli and Sciortino (2008) occupy a position somewhere in the middle.

12. Critical analyses of the regularization process suggest that a portion of these domestic applications were for non-domestic labor. The domestic work application qualifications were easier to fulfill and the process less bureaucratically burdensome than the other categories.

13. The idea was associated with Ray Marshall, labor secretary in the Carter administration (*Los Angeles Times*, March 29, 2009), and elaborated in AFL-CIO and Change to Win 2009, although similar ideas had been articulated in discussions held by the Migration Policy Institute.

References

Adinolfi, Adelina. 1992. *I lavoratori extracomunitari: Norme interne e internazionali*. Bologna: Il Mulino.

AFL-CIO and Change to Win. 2009. "The Labor Movement's Framework for Comprehensive Immigration Reform." April.

Ambrosini, M., and A. Triandafyllidou.,2011. "Irregular Immigration Control in Italy and Greece: Strong Fencing and Weak Gate-Keeping Serving the Labour Market." *European Journal of Migration and Law* 13, no. 3: 251–273.

Amnesty International. 2017. "Libya's Dark Web of Collusion," December 11, 2017. https://www.amnesty.org/en/documents/mde19/7561/2017/en/.

Beirens, H. 2018. "Cracked Foundation, Uncertain Future: Structural Weaknesses in the Common European Asylum System." Migration Policy Institute Europe.

Bianchi, G. 2014. "Italiani Anche Noi: Minister Kyenge, Children of Immigrants, and the Pathway to Citizenship Reform." *Italian Politics* 29, no. 1: 257–272.

Bonifazi, Corrado. 2007. *L'immigrazione straniera in Italia*. Bologna: Il Mulino.

Bonizzoni, P. 2018. "Looking for the Best and Brightest? Deservingness Regimes in Italian Labour Migration Management." *International Migration* 56, no. 4: 47–62.

Caponio, T., and T. M. Cappiali. 2018. "Italian Migration Policies in Times of Crisis: The Policy Gap Reconsidered." *South European Society and Politics* 23, no. 1: 115–132.

Castelli Gattinara, P. 2017. "The 'Refugee Crisis' in Italy as a Crisis of Legitimacy." *Contemporary Italian Politics* 9, no. 3: 318–331.

Castiglioni, Maria, and Gianperra dalla Zuanna. 2009. "La bassa fecondità italiana: Cause, consequenze e politiche." In *La fatica da cambiare: Rapporto sulla società italiana*, edited by Rainaldo Catanzaro and Giuseppe Sciortino, 17–32. Bologna: Il Mulino.

Cesareo, Vincenzo, ed. 2019. *The Twenty-Fifth Italian Report on Migrations 2019*. Rome: Fonadazione ISMU.

Cetin, Elif. 2015. "The Italian Left and Italy's (Evolving) Foreign Policy of Immigration Controls." *Journal of Modern Italian Studies*. 20/3: 377-397.

Chiaramonte, A., et al. 2018. "Populist Success in a Hung Parliament: The 2018 General Election in Italy." *South European Society and Politics* 23, no. 4: 479–501.

Ciafaloni, Francesco. 2004. "I meccanismi dell'emergenza." In *I sommersi e i sanati: Le regolarizzazioni degli immigrati in Italia*, edited by Marzio Barbagli, Asher Colombo, and Giuseppe Sciortino, 187–200. Bologna: Il Mulino.

Cuttitta, Paolo. 2018. "Repoliticization Through Search and Rescue? Humanitarian NGOs and Migration Management in the Central Mediterranean." *Geopolitics*. 23/3: 632-660.

Diamanti, Ilvo. 2007. "The Italian Center-Right and Center-Left: Between Parties and 'the Party.'" *West European Politics* 30 (, no. 4): 733–762.

Einaudi, Luca. 2007. *Le politiche dell'immigrazione in Italia dall'unità a oggi*. Bari: Laterza.

Ekinci, M. 2018. "Italy's Migration Conundrum Continues in 2018." *Al Sharq Strategic Research*. February 06, 2018: 1-10.

EMN (European Migration Network). 2008. *ITALIA: Rapporto annuale sulle politiche 2007*. Rome: Idos.

European Court of Auditors. 2017. "EU Response to the Refugee Crisis: The 'Hotspot' Approach." Report no. 06. https://www.eca.europa.eu/Lists/ECADocuments/SR17_6/SR_MIGRATION_HOTSPOTS_EN.pdf.

Eurostat. 2019. *Migration Integration Statistics*. Brussels: European Commission.

Fasani, Francesco. 2009. "Undocumented Migration: Counting the Uncountable. Data and Trends Across Europe." Clandestino Country Report.

Finotelli, Claudia, and Giuseppe Sciortino. 2008. "New Trends in Italian Immigration Policies: 'To Change Everything in Order to Keep Everything the Same.'" ARI 161/2008, Real Instituto Elanco, September 12, 2008.

Finotelli, Claudia, and Giuseppe Sciortino. 2009. "The Importance of Being Southern: The Making of Policies of Immigration Control in Italy." *European Journal of Migration and Law* 11: 119–38.

Freeman, Gary. 1995. "Modes of Immigration Politics in Liberal Democratic States." *International Migration Review* 29, no. 4: 881–913.

Frontex. 2017. *Frontex Risk Analysis*. Frontex: Warsaw.

Garzia, D. 2019. "The Italian Election of 2018 and the First Populist Government of Western Europe." *West European Politics* 42, no. 3: 670–680.

Geddes, A. 2018. "The Politics of European Union Migration Governance." *Journal of Common Market Studies* 56: 120–130.

Geddes, Andrew. 2008. "Il Rombo dei Cannoni? Immigration and the Centre-Right in Italy." *Journal of European Public Policy* 15, no. 3: 349–366.

Giuseppe, S. 2015. "Immigration." In *The Oxford Handbook of Italian Politics*, edited by Erik Jones and Gianfranco Pasquino. Oxford: Oxford University Press, pp. 633-644.

Golini, Antonio. 2001. *L'emigrazione italiana all'estero e la demografia dell'immigrazione straniera in Italia*. Bologna: Il Mulino.

Grande, E., T. Schwarzb□zl, and M. Fatke. 2018. "Politicizing Immigration in Western Europe." *Journal of European Public Policy* 26, no. 10: 1–20.

Joppke, Christian. 2002. "European Immigration Policies at the Crossroads." In *Developments in West European Politics*, edited by Paul Heywod, Erik Jones, and Martin Rhodes, 259–276. New York: Palgrave.

Lahav, G., and V. Guiraudon. 2006. "Actors and Venues in Immigration Control: Closing the Gap Between Political Demands and Policy Outcomes." *West European Politics* 29, no. 2: 201–223.

Lavenex, S. 2018. "Failing Forward: Towards Which Europe? Organized Hypocrisy in the Common European Asylum System." *Journal of Common Market Studies* 56, no. 5: 1195–1212.

Massetti, E. 2015. "Mainstream Parties and the Politics of Immigration in Italy: A Structural Advantage for the Right or a Missed Opportunity for the Left?" *Acta Politica* 50, no. 4: 486–505.

Morales, L., J.-B. Pilet, and D. Ruedin. 2015. "The Gap Between Public Preferences and Policies on Immigration: A Comparative Examination of the Effect of Politicisation on Policy Congruence." *Journal of Ethnic and Migration Studies* 41, no. 9: 1495–1516.

Palm, A. 2017. "The Italy-Libya Memorandum of Understanding: The Baseline of a Policy Approach Aimed at Closing All Doors to Europe?" EU Immigration and Asylum Law and Policy, October 2, 2017. https://eumigrationlawblog.eu/the-italy-libya-memorandum-of-understanding-the-baseline-of-a-policy-approach-aimed-at-closing-all-doors-to-europe/.

Palm, A. 2018. "Leading the Way? Italy's External Migration Policies and the 2018 Elections: An Uncertain Future." *The International Spectator.* January 03, 2018.

Pannia, P., V. Federico, and S. D'Amato. 2018. "Italy—Country Report: Legal and Policy Framework of Migration Governance." http://www.diva-portal.org/smash/record.jsf?pid=diva2%3A1248410&dswid=-825

Passini, Nicola and Marta Regalia. 2018. "The European Elections." In *The Twenty-Fifth Italian Report on Migrations 2019*, edited by Vincenzo Cesareo. Rome: Fonadazione ISMU.

Pastore, F. 2014. "The Governance of Migrant Labour Supply in Europe, Before and During the Crisis." *Comparative Migration Studies* 2, no. 4: 385–415.

Pastore, Ferruccio. 2007. "La politica migratoria italiana a una svolta: ostacoli immediati e dilemmi strategici." http://www.cespi.it/PDF/Pastore-POL-MIG-IT-07.pdf.

Perlmutter, Ted. 1996b. "Bringing Parties Back In: Comments on 'Modes of Immigration Politics in Liberal Democratic Societies.'" *International Migration Review* 30: 375–388.

Perlmutter, Ted. 2002. "The Politics of Restriction: The Effect of Xenophobic Parties on Italian Immigration Policy and German Asylum Policy." In *Shadows over Europe: The Development and Impact of the Extreme Right in Western Europe*, edited by Martin Schain, Aristide Zolberg, and Patrick Hossay, 269–298. London: Palgrave.

Reyneri, Emilio. 2004. "Immigrants in a Segmented and Often Undeclared Labour Market." *Journal of Modern Italian Studies* 9, no. 1: 71–93.

Reyneri, Emilio. 2007. "Immigration in Italy: Trends and Perspectives." International Organization for Migration, Argo.

Salis, E. 2012. "Labour Migration Governance in Contemporary Europe: The Case of Italy." Country Report for the LAB-MIG-GOV Project "Which Labour Migration Governance for a More Dynamic and Inclusive Europe?"

Salis, E. 2014. "A Crucial Testing Ground: The Governance of Labour Migration in the Long-Term Care Sector." *Comparative Migration Studies* 2, no. 4: 519–545.

Sartori, Giovanni. 1976. *Parties and Party Systems: A Framework for Analysis*. Cambridge: Cambridge University Press.

Sciortino, Giuseppe. 2009. "Fortunes and Miseries of Italian Labour Migration Policy." Politiche Migratorie e Modelli di Società, Centro Studi di Politica Internazionale, Rome.

Sciortino, Giuseppe. 2014. "Commentary." In *Controlling Immigration: A Global Perspective*, edited by James F. Hollifield, Pia M. Orrenius, and Philip L. Martin. Stanford: Stanford University Press: 366-370.

Sredanovic, D., and F. G. Farina. 2015. "Can Youth with a Migrant Background Speak? Representation, Citizenship and Voice in Italian TV and Press Journalism." *Journal of Intercultural Studies* 36, no. 6: 693–709.

Tintori, G. 2018. "Ius Soli the Italian Way: The Long and Winding Road to Reform the Citizenship Law." *Contemporary Italian Politics* 10, no. 4: 434–450.

Trauner, F. 2016. "Asylum Policy: The EU's 'Crises' and the Looming Policy Regime Failure." *Journal of European Integration* 38, no. 3: 311–325.

Tsourapas, G., 2017. "Migration Diplomacy in the Global South: Cooperation, Coercion and Issue Linkage in Gaddafi's Libya." *Third World Quarterly* 38, no. 10: 2367–2385.

Urso, O. 2018. "The Politicization of Immigration in Italy: Who Frames the Issue, When and How." *Italian Political Science Review/Rivista Italiana di Scienza Politica* 48, no. 3: 365–381.

van der Brug, W., et al. 2015. "A Framework for Studying the Politicisation of Immigration." In *The Politicisation of Migration*, edited by W. van der Brug et al., 17–34. London: Routledge.

van der Nagel, E., and J. Frith. 2015. "Anonymity, Pseudonymity, and the Agency of Online Identity: Examining the Social Practices of r/Gonewild." *First Monday* 20, no. 3. https://firstmonday.org/article/view/5615/4346

Zincone, Giovanna. 2006a. "The Making of Policies. Immigration and Immigrants in Italy." *Journal of Ethnic and Migration Studies* 32, no. 3: 347–375.

Zincone, Giovanna. 2006b. "Italian Immigrants and Immigration Policy Making: Structures, Actors, Practices." Paper presented at the IMISCOE Conference on the Making of Migratory Policies in Europe, University of Turin, Turin, May 19–20.

Zincone, Giovanna. 2009. "Citizenship Policy Making in Mediterranean EU States: Italy." European University Institute, Florence Robert Schuman Centre for Advanced Studies, and EUDO Citizenship Observatory.

Zinn, D. L. 2011. "'Loud and Clear': The G2 Second Generations Network in Italy." *Journal of Modern Italian Studies* 16, no. 3: 373–385.

COMMENTARY

A Method to the Madness

Giuseppe Sciortino

For many foreign observers, and for some native ones, any attempt to understand Italy's migratory situation quickly encounters two main stumbling blocks. The first is the enduring, entrenched, pervasive perception of the country as a former "emigration country" and a "new country of immigration." The second is the fascination with the extraordinary intricacies of the Italian political system: its ever-changing party politics, the strangeness of its political coalitions, the impermanence of any governing majority. Regarding the first obstacle, many features of Italian migration policy are often prematurely explained away as a matter of inexperience. As a consequence of the second, superficial shifts are often magnified as tremendous structural changes, while substantial policy continuities remain latent.

Italy's migratory balance turned positive long ago. True, emigration looms large in Italian history. Still, today an astonishing number of emigrants and their descendants are (somewhat) members of the Italian polity. Thanks to an extraordinarily generous (for them) citizenship law, many descendants may still claim a right of abode, an EU passport, and even access to certain social allowances. They can even elect their own representatives to the houses of parliament. These "diaspora" representatives are well known for their uncanny ability to wreak havoc on Italian governments.

Italy, however, has never been only an emigration country: immigration, mobility, and emigration have always coexisted. Its postwar history, for example, has been marked by the management of hundreds of thousands of internally displaced people, by the massive "return" of settlers from former African colonies and from the territories along the Adriatic (Ballinger 2020), and by the massive internal migration from southern (and northeastern) Italy to the industrial triangle in the northwest (Gallo 2012). Long before the migratory balance turned positive, Italian authorities had already faced the challenges posed by the regulation of territorial mobility (Einaudi 2007).

Nor should it be forgotten that the inflow of foreign-born workers started approximately a half century ago. The first settlements of foreign-born workers can be traced back to the late 1960s (Colombo and Sciortino 2004; Colucci 2018). In contrast to many other western European countries, Italy has never experienced a latency phase. Immigration has never been an ignored, marginalized, or denied issue. Its causes and consequences have been avidly interrogated, socially debated, and politically contested for decades. The first documentary on Africans in Italy was actually shot in 1969. The first main character in Italian film who was a "foreign" immigrant appeared one year later. The first countrywide opinion poll on the topic was carried out in 1977 (a sizable percentage of the interviewees stated even then that there were "too many" foreign-born workers). The first front-page column dealing with immigration in the mainstream press appeared in the same year. The first "systematic" immigration law, heralded as the solution to all of migration's evils, was approved in 1986. The first governmental collapse over immigration issues took place in 1990. In short, both the phenomenon and its discursive representation are actually older than the (fairly advanced) median age of the Italian population. If the proper time frame is adopted, many features of Italian migration policy can be explained more adequately.

A long-term view is, in fact, necessary to understand the context and outcomes of Italian immigration policymaking. Many Italian migration policies appear as rushed and often ill-conceived attempts to deal with unexpected emergencies. Approved legislative provisions are constantly amended, struck down in the courts, or simply never implemented. When asked, many policymakers candidly acknowledge that legislative proposals are often brought forward without considering if they can ever be actually implemented. The shifts in political attitudes can also be extraordinarily rapid: European directives that never previously received significant public attention may suddenly be perceived as hallmarks of civilization one moment and as illegitimate authoritarian orders the next.

Unsurprisingly, when covering Italian migration policy, the international press nearly always adopts an elegant, simple, scheme: immigration is a complex, difficult challenge, and Italian gatekeepers, policymakers, bureaucrats, and experts, unfortunately, are too busy quarreling, infighting, and squandering time and resources to deal effectively with it. Nothing is ever accomplished, and the problem grows worse and worse. As the Romans would say, *Dum Romae consulitur, Saguntum expugnatur*—roughly, "while they discuss in Rome, Sagunto is being conquered." The main responsibility for such a dismal state of affairs is always attributed to Italian party politics, the arcane world where even angels fear to tread.

Ted Perlmutter has in fact done a superb job of summarizing the many (shifting) differences between the numerous parties, sub-parties, and sub-sub-parties that exist along the entire Italian political spectrum. He is also right in characterizing the main actors involved. First, there are the "Goods"—the traditional center-left and left parties. They are inconsistent and weak-willed. They never do enough. They sometimes try to do the right thing, but they always become frightened by the backlash and back off. Then there are the "Bads"—the traditional center-right actors. They behave cynically and unscrupulously. They sometimes espouse xenophobic sentiments, while occasionally giving in to the demands of the business world for new manual laborers. Until 2011, the conflicts between the Bads and the Goods represented a carefully choreographed dance, a balancing act in which each coalition tried to appease its constituencies without excessively antagonizing the opposition. Such a dynamic, according to Perlmutter, has broken down in recent years under the pressure of two new realities. The first is that the geopolitical context has been radically modified by the Arab Spring: migration pressures from the South have dramatically increased, while many government of the southern Mediterranean rim have reduced their willingness to prevent transit migration to the EU. Italy has suddenly rediscovered that it is located at the center of the Mediterranean and is the natural target of these unwanted flows. At the same time, European constraints on its control policies have become increasingly tight, sharply reducing the previously existing room for maneuver. Unable to provide a minimally consistent model of migration policy, the annoying skirmishes between the Good and the Bad have paved the way for the success of the "Ugly": the new populist actors, who openly endorse a politics of exclusion, if not downright cruelty.

With his focus on party politics, Perlmutter has surely identified an important feature of the Italian immigration situation. Actually, his analyses apply well beyond Italy. In many European countries, immigration politics in recent years has quickly "Italianized." The naive Good, the cynical Bad, and above all the vociferous Ugly are now present in nearly all European political systems. Social polarization and a growing electoralization/politicization of migration issues have become endemic. We do not yet know if the Ugly will be more effective than the Good and the Bad of yesterday. We may safely bet, however, that their actions will be explicitly directed toward exclusionary, rights-curbing goals.

Perlmutter's narrative is elegant but also incomplete. It cannot adequately explain two important features of the Italian migration situation: the actual effectiveness of its control measures and the actual consistency of its migration strategy (as far as migration controls are concerned). There is, in fact, a method to the madness.

There is no need to remind the readers of *Controlling Migration* about the difference between the perception of immigration controls in the public mind and their reality. Public opinion in Italy (like anywhere in western Europe) is highly unsatisfied with the country's immigration controls. Such dissatisfaction, however, is not necessarily proof of actual poor performance. It may well be the outcome of unrealistic expectations. In fact, whenever *reliable* indicators are available, the actual outcomes of the Italian system of migration controls are not as disastrous as Italian public opinion tends to believe (Colombo 2012). The weaknesses of Italian controls are shared by many other European countries (for example, the low effectiveness of deportation orders). In some important policy areas, such as visa policy, Italian authorities are actually stricter than many other EU member states. Even the size of its irregular population is actually smaller than in other western European countries of comparable size and, thanks to the economic crisis, has been shrinking (as the diminishing success of the last regularization programs seems to also point out).

The "failure" of Italian migration controls is usually documented with images of crowded boats landing, if not sinking, along Italian shores. The connection between these sea landings and Italy's irregular population, however, is vague at best. The incoming boats are crowded with sub-Saharan African asylum seekers, disproportionately young and male, and with limited access to already established social networks in Italy. Those networks, by contrast, are mostly composed of visa overstayers, very often young or even middle-aged white women. Very often they already have some family connection within the territory. For many asylum seekers, moreover, Italy remain above all a transit country, to be left as soon as possible (Belloni 2019). The contribution of boat landings to the 5.5-million-strong foreign-born population in the country has, consequently, always been limited.

Italian authorities, moreover, have been quite successful in dealing with unwanted flows across the country's maritime borders. Since the end of the 1990s, in fact, sea landings are increasingly composed of refugees. Their entry is made possible not by ineffective controls—actually, all boats are identified long before they land—but rather by the legal protection guaranteed by the non-refoulement principle of international refugee law. The containment of such flows takes place not at the border but rather through the externalization of controls in sending and transit countries. This is precisely what Italy had achieved along the Adriatic at the end of the 1990s and with the reduction of migration from Tunisia in 2011. There has been a heated debate on the 2017 Italian agreement with a long string of Libyan actors (some of them of doubtful humanitarian credentials) to provide aid in exchange for increased controls over the departures of boats. The 2017 Libyan agreement is surely muddled, controversial, and morally problematic. It is not a novelty, however.

Contrary to expectations, moreover, Italian migration control strategy has always been very consistent. Since its very beginning, it has always been more a variant of the European pattern than an exotic anomaly. Italy has been an early adopter of a restrictive attitude toward migration regulation. The few delusionary visions of the country as the cultural and humanitarian bridge between "Europe" and the "Third World" have quickly dissipated (or been confined to cultural studies circles). Already in 1990, when the number of international migrants in Italy was extremely small, Law 39/90 introduced systematic visa requirements. In order to become a loyal member of the Schengen club, moreover, the country removed any geographical limitation to its responsibilities under the Geneva Convention, thus transforming itself into the ideal "first safe country." For many years, gaining membership in the Schengen club has been the leading goal of most immigration policymaking (Paoli 2018). After much cajoling, Italy became a full-fledged Schengen member in 1998. Since very early on, in other words, Italian migration policy has been inspired by what I call the EU's "gentle monster" (Sciortino 2017). On one hand, EU policy has accepted, even nurtured, a rights-based understanding of international migration (including a "full and inclusive application of the Geneva Convention") *within* EU borders (the "gentle" part). On the other, it has made it increasingly difficult for potential asylum seekers to cross such borders, tightening its visa policy, increasing the monitoring of its physical borders, introducing carrier sanctions, and involving actual and potential transit countries in the prevention of unwanted flows, in short, sharply reducing the numbers of those who can claim the rights granted (the "monster" part).

For the last three decades, this logic has been so widely accepted that it has become self-evident. In fact, it may be even argued that the main weakness of the Italian migration regime has been precisely its extreme loyalty to such a restrictive program. Until 2010–2011, immigration to Italy had been nearly exclusively a labor migration, driven by basic demographic and labor market factors (Colombo and Dalla-Zuanna 2019). For decades, the number of refugees and asylum seekers has been quite small. In other words, Italy has had to manage classical labor migration within a "European" policy framework inspired, nearly exclusively, by the goal of preventing the arrival of asylum seekers. The difficulties of such a position are particularly evident in the few attempts to design some kind of active labor migration policy. Such attempts, besides being timid, have always being pursued only as long as they could be justified as functional to the overall restrictive aim. Yearly recruitment quotas and contingencies, far from being related to choices of economic policy, were defined as possible bargaining chips that could be used to persuade sending countries to sign readmission agreements.

From 1986 to 2009, labor migration had been managed through the development of a (relatively reasonable) back-door policy. Prospective foreign-born workers would enter the country (usually with a tourist visa), find a job, overstay, and wait for the next regularization program. Once regularized, they would move to the areas where the demand for unskilled workers was greater, apply for family reunification, and start the arduous work of settling down for good. Today, immigrants represent more than one-third of the Italian working class. They have a very high activity rate and millions of them have satisfied year by year all the requirements for renewing their papers. Until 2009–2010, the Italian migration regime had been largely dualistic: a "European" restrictive regime (mostly targeted to prevent the unwanted arrival of potential asylum-seekers) coexisted with a (less visible) back-door policy providing much-needed unskilled workers to the Italian economy. The much-maligned amnesties taking places every four years or so, far from being epiphanies of mistaken policies, were actually a key tool for managing and stabilizing a migratory inflow that, before the economic crisis, was very intense.

The dualistic migration regime has, however, tumbled over the past decade. Immigration in Italy has indeed changed profoundly, making the slowly and painfully developed back-door policy irredeemably obsolete. The roots of such change can be found in Italy's deep economic crisis, starting in 2009–2011 and not yet concluded (even before the COVID-19 pandemic, Italian GDP was lower than it had been two decades before). The crisis has hit particularly hard the labor-intensive, innovation-scarce sectors of the Italian economy—agriculture, tourism, construction—that represent the traditional employers of foreign labor. The demand for foreign-born workers for care work and household services has remained strong, but salaries and working conditions have worsened (Cvajner 2019). New arrivals, both official and irregular, have significantly slowed, the unemployment rate among the foreign-born workforce has increased, and many of the gains achieved by the foreign-born population in previous years have been eroded. Labor migration to Italy has basically halted, and it is likely that substantial return and secondary migration has occurred (ISTAT 2019). A second important change was the Libyan civil war in 2011, which opened a key passage through the Mediterranean arc of potential transit countries involved in the EU's externalized controls. While the traditional labor migration has disappeared, Italians have experienced a crash course in unwanted humanitarian migration. Although the number of arrivals through the Libyan route has never been substantial in comparison to previous flows, the fact that they are mostly young Black males (not to mention that they are perceived to be Muslim) has had a strong impact on public opinion. The refugee crisis of 2015–2016 dismantled the last surviving element of traditional Italian attitudes toward immigration. It must be remembered that "Europe" has always been perceived in Italy as an important constraint that could force Italian politicians to behave better. In 2010, the Transatlantic Trends survey had revealed that Italy was the only country in which a majority of interviewees would have been more than happy to transfer all the key immigration decisions to Brussels (as long as it implied distance from their own government). The mix of indecisiveness, hypocrisy, and shortsightedness revealed by the refugee "crisis" of 2015 has radically modified the idea that "Europe" necessarily means "good." Italy has started to see itself rather as a victim of European regulations. The substantial costs imposed on the countries with external borders by the Dublin rules—well known to the experts but studiously ignored in the public debate until then—have become suddenly visible. The outcome has been the strengthening of an (already widespread) negative view of immigration and immigrants, and the increasing popularity of openly xenophobic policies. In fact, if attitudes were geography, Italy in recent years would be a leading member of the Visegrad group. On the verge of the country's historic 2018 general elections, Italian public opinion was the most hostile to immigrants in the entire EU, east and west. There has been nothing that the Goods and the Bads, no matter how hard they tried, could do to prevent the Ugly from gaining electorally from it.

Will the emergence of these new populist actors, boosted by an ever more sluggish economy, really usher a new era of consistent restrictionist policies? Perlmutter's detailed analysis of party politics surely provides an important piece of the puzzle. To understand the real space for substantial innovation, however, the analysis of changes in party politics is not enough. The other key mechanisms identified—not least by *Controlling Migration*—through decades of research on immigration policy in democratic states must be brought into the picture. What are migratory consequences of a largely unreformed economy? There is a myriad of small enterprises that require—even to barely survive—a large supply of cheap, unskilled labor. How would such a new restrictionist stance interact with the aging of the Italian population? An increasing number among the Italian elderly can be cared for—given the slowly but substantially rising employment rate of Italian women—only through the rapid marketization of care. The household services sector, in fact, provides employment to a little less than 1 million foreign-born workers (Sciortino 2013). These tendencies may coexist with systematic restrictionist attitudes, leading to the slow reproduction of a sizable unauthorized population as the only acceptable solution.

Another important dimension to be considered is Italy's high level of embedded liberalism. Whatever the restrictive preferences of Italian citizens (and the rhetoric of its rulers), the main stumbling block in the past has hardly ever been the opposition of parties or social movements. The actual obstacle to the adoption of highly restrictionist stances has always been Italy's highly independent judiciary. Hundreds of restrictive measures approved by center-right cabinets (and quite a few approved by center-left ones) have been struck down by the courts. Some of the measures of the first, short-lived populist government in 2018–2019 have already encountered the same fate.

Last but not least, it is important to remember the existence of a wide and ramified humanitarian infrastructure, committed to an ethic of principles rather than of consequences. Such an infrastructure, often linked to the Catholic Church, enjoys a high level of prestige and provides immigrants, regardless of their legal status, with a key set of resources.

Until now, these constraints—the structure of the economic system, the activism of an independent judiciary, and the strength of a humanitarian infrastructure—have seriously limited the restrictive practices of the Italian state. Will the new Ugly succeed in breaking through these constraints? Such a change would be felt well beyond the southern rim of the Union.

References

Ballinger, P. 2020. *The World Refugees Made: Decolonization and the Foundation of Postwar Italy*. Ithaca, NY: Cornell University Press.

Belloni, M. 2019. *The Big Gamble: The Migration of Eritreans to Europe*. Berkeley: University of California Press.

Colombo, A. 2012. *Fuori controllo? Miti e realtà dell'immigrazione in Italia*. Bologna: Il Mulino.

Colombo, A., and G. Dalla-Zuanna. 2019. "Immigration Italian Style, 1977–2018." *Population and Development Review* 45, no. 3: 585–615.

Colombo, A., and G. Sciortino. 2004. "Italian Immigration: The Origins, Nature and Evolution of Italy's Migratory Systems." *Journal of Modern Italian Studies* 9, no. 1: 49–70.

Colucci, M. 2018. *Storia dell'immigrazione straniera in Italia*. Rome: Carocci.

Cvajner, M. 2019. *Soviet Signoras: Personal and Collective Transformations in Migration Processes*. Chicago: University of Chicago Press.

Einaudi, L. 2007. *Le politiche dell'immigrazione in Italia dall'unità a oggi*. Bari: Laterza.

Gallo, S. 2012. *Senza attraversare le frontiere: le migrazioni interne dall'unità a oggi*. Gius: Laterza & Figli.

ISTAT. 2019. "Cittadini non comunitari in Italia, 2018–19." Istituto Nazionale di Statistica, Rome.

Paoli, S. 2018. *Frontiera Sud. L'Italia e la nascita dell'Europa di Schengen*. Milan: Mondadori.

Sciortino, G. 2013. "Immigration in Italy: Subverting the Logic of Welfare Reform?" In *Europe's Immigration Challenge: Reconciling Work, Welfare and Mobility*, edited by G. Brochmann and T. Jurado, 77–94. London: I. B. Tauris.

Sciortino, G. 2017. *Rebus immigrazione*. Bologna: Il Mulino.

COMMENTARY

Change and Continuity in Migration Control

Camille Schmoll

Italy at the Forefront of EU Policy

It is probably unfair to describe Italy as a latecomer immigration country, as many studies show that immigration dates back to the 1960s.[1] However, Italy has undergone dramatic changes over the past two decades, both in terms of migration trends and in terms of political and economic context. The early twenty-first century has been punctuated by several crises: an economic crisis, a refugee crisis, a political crisis. My commentary sheds light on change and continuity in the Italian migration context and policies in the last two decades, focusing particularly on the last ten years and the aftermath of the Arab spring. In order to fully comprehend migration control, one needs not only to puzzle out the roles of immigrants, labor market dynamics, and national migration policy but also to bring in European policies, the workings of local and transnational activists, and the input of local actors, such as mayors.

Changing Features of (Ir)regular Migration, Continuities in the Labor Market

As Ted Perlmutter observes, the nature and status of immigration to Italy have dramatically changed since the beginning of the 2000s. Two factors have led to an increase in regular migration during the last twenty years: the EU enlargement to eastern European countries has brought migrants in through free circulation (mostly from Bulgaria, Poland, and Romania), while family reunion has allowed non-European foreigners to come and settle in Italy. Yet some specific groups of immigrants have increasingly been denied access to visas, while a series of crises as well as the harshening of authoritarianism and civil wars in Africa and the Middle East has triggered mass departures. This partly explains the increase of irregular entries and in particular the rise in sea landings observed since the beginning of the 2010s. During these years, large numbers of immigrants have lost their lives taking the central Mediterranean route. More than 22,000 people have died since 2011 crossing the Strait of Sicily.

These circumstances have been overwhelmingly tagged as part of the "refugee crisis." The media and public opinion, in participating in this "crisis" narrative, have brought sea arrivals into focus, even as the ordinary business of Italian immigration was in part happening elsewhere. I want here to reiterate a critical point: while there has been a substantial increase in sea landings from 2011 to 2017, the immigration situation taken as a whole is far from unusual. Unauthorized migrants have been present in substantial numbers in Italy in the 1990s and 2000s. In most cases, though, they had reached the country regularly and then slipped into irregularity afterward, thus contributing to what Giuseppe Sciortino calls in his comment a "dualistic immigration regime." During the 2010s, unauthorized migration did not increase suddenly. Simply, a huge proportion of African and Middle Eastern nationals were left with no other option but to enter irregularly and use asylum procedures in the hope of obtaining a residence permit. At the same time, issues of race came to the fore of societal debates, as Black immigrants were increasingly stereotyped as irregular immigrants sailing to Italy.

Sea arrivals call into question European solidarity and the very principles of European integration. Member states struggle to find common responses to this challenge. Although a European pact on immigration and asylum was signed in September 2020, EU states failed to reach an agreement to manage sea arrivals and reform the Dublin system. Southern European countries are still holding the front line of migration control and emergency reception in a silent war against immigrants. This actually means that southern European countries bear the burden of everyday logistical operations to identify incoming migrants, such as fingerprinting and screening, and to process asylum requests. They are also in charge of reception and provision of first relief including temporary shelter and emergency sanitary and health care.

Moreover, while Ted Perlmutter suggests that the decade of the 2010s was "characterized by a stepping away from any consideration of a labor market policy," I would argue that migration remains central to the shadow economy and that informal employment is part and parcel of Italian socio-economic dynamics. Italy suffered a major recession in the late 2000s, and this had a negative impact on immigrants' employment. However, some authors observe a "refugeezation" of Italy's labor market: asylum seekers also enter the workforce.[2] Both intra-European and extra-European immigrants with varying legal statuses are seen in the manufacturing and agricultural sectors. Employers largely depend upon the migrant and refugee labor force, and their position is worth investigating: at first glance, their interests do not seem overly threatened by the government's repressive policies. Immigrants keep coming despite increased controls, but legal precarity forces them to accept lower wages and exploitative practices. Lastly, given Italy's rapidly aging population, families and private individuals often employ migrant workers for household and care services. The importance of micro-sociological dynamics linking care work and migration control should not be underestimated.[3]

Migration Policy in the 2010's: Polarization or Lukewarm Centrism?

Broad governing coalitions are the main feature of Italy's successive governments since 2011: neither truly right-wing nor left-wing, these governments were in any case supported by forces drawn from both sides of the political spectrum, as in the cases of prime ministers Mario Monti, Enrico Letta, Matteo Renzi, Paolo Gentiloni, Giuseppe Conte, Mario Draghi. Governmental inertia in immigration policy is also largely explained by the institutional and political instability inherent in the Italian proportional system: the Italian "perfect bicameralism" creates considerable uncertainty and grants disproportionate power to smaller parties. The fragility of coalition governments supported by a wide range of small parties partly explains institutional challenges in migration and citizenship policies, such as that of the failed reform of *jus soli* in 2015. This lukewarm centrism not only blurred the distinction between progressive and conservative policies but also played a central part in the emergence of new political parties. In Italy, as in Hungary and the United Kingdom, lukewarm centrist coalitions or governments have contributed to shift voters toward "alternative" or "extreme" parties that were more explicit in their political messaging and where (anti)-migration discourses play a central role.

Electoral outcomes and political bargaining—what one might expect given the theoretical framework of a "liberal paradox"—are often seen as the main explanatory factors for restrictive immigration policies. In the case of Italy, the main political changes in the 2010s consist in the rise of populism and the consolidation of two major political actors, the new Five Star Movement and the Northern League, both of which have a strong anti-immigration platform. These parties have joined in the coalition of the first Conte government, with Matteo Salvini (Northern League) as a deputy prime minister and minister of the interior from June 2018 to September 2019. Yet is it accurate to talk of a "Salvinian" repressive turn in migration control? In other words, did the Northern League's rise to power—in alliance with the Five Star Movement—fundamentally redefine Italy's immigration policy? Conversely, how do current migration and asylum policies build upon past ones?

Continuity in Border Control and External Migration Policy

At first glance, the populist and xenophobic politicians taking office across Europe seem to explain the backlash against migrants' human rights described in the introduction of this book.

However, Italian external migration and border control policies lead one to reflect critically upon this hypothesis. The Italy-Libya agreement on migration management notably illustrates a form of continuity in migration control.[4] In February 2017 the Gentiloni government, a center-left government, signed a memorandum of understanding with Fayez al-Serraj, head of the UN-backed Libyan Government of National Accord, to "curb migration flows to Europe."[5] This agreement aimed at "closing" the central Mediterranean route and "all doors to Europe" by providing the UN-backed Libyan government with equipment, funding, and training for its inland border control and coast guard fleet.[6] This agreement kept up a long-standing history of cooperation between Italy and Libya since the 2000s and a series of bilateral externalization agreements.

In these circumstances, the Salvini offensive in 2018 intensified a process that was already entrenched: the first Conte government closed all ports to NGO rescue ships and issued two decrees designed to tighten up its repressive policies against irregular migrants and asylum seekers. These involved the suspension of humanitarian permits (provisions quashed by the courts in 2021), the extended detention of irregular migrants, and the criminalization of humanitarian assistance. Care workers, humanitarian professionals, and volunteers could, under these new decrees, be put on trial for allegedly aiding and abetting illegal immigration.

Mare Nostrum: A Humanitarian Parenthesis

To put it in a nutshell, the cooperation policy with Libya reveals patterns of continuity in anti-immigrant policies and counters the idea of a Salvinian turn. Salvini has, to some extent, prolonged and strengthened policies that were already in place. The Mare Nostrum search-and-rescue operations (2013–2014), which took place long before Giuseppe Conte and Matteo Salvini came to power, demonstrate an exception in the overall trends of policy making. As the Mediterranean migration context turned into a protracted humanitarian crisis in the early 2010s, the short-lived Letta government adopted a quite radical and disruptive policy option between October 2013 and November 2014. This center-left government, bolstered by the right-wing party People of Freedom (Il Popolo della Libertá), whose Angelino Alfano acted as minister of interior, designed and launched the Mare Nostrum operation. This naval and air operation organized ambitious search-and-rescue activities around Italy and down to the Libyan coast. It was launched in the aftermath of a shipwreck that killed 366 migrants off the island of Lampedusa in October 2013. The operation was discontinued a few months after the fall of the Letta government. Yet its collapse is mainly attributed to the pressure exerted by European governments, as Ted Perlmutter observed. Internal criticism from the Italian right and notably by a member of the Letta government, Angelino Alfano, was only ancillary to the collapse of the initiative. The episode was convincingly captured by Gianfranco Rosi in his film *Fuocammare*. During Mare Nostrum, the country's political identity was in the balance in the media: the operation was simultaneously framed as a humanitarian duty, an expression of national pride, and a security measure. At the time, Italian public opinion seemed to swing toward solidarity policies, but shortly afterward it demonstrated a dramatic anti-immigrant shift afterward, which translated into electoral outcomes. The lack of financial and political support for Mare Nostrum from the EU and other member states seemed to have negatively impacted trust in EU institutions and bolstered Euroskepticism in Italy. The replacement program, Triton—managed by Frontex, the EU agency for border protection—only offered an extremely limited range of search-and-rescue activity. Mare Nostrum was not a "magnet" for irregular migration, as some claimed, but it did rescued around 150,000 people in one year, and its end in 2014 did precipitate a rise in the number of deaths among border crossers in the Mediterranean.

The Mare Nostrum case indicates how migrants' sea crossings have become a pivotal issue in Italian migration policies and civil society activism around them in the 2010s. Advocacy campaigns against extended detention of migrants were partly superseded by campaigns against the death and abuses migrants suffered at sea. Activism also become increasingly transnational, both for pro-immigrant NGOs and civil society organizations involved in sea rescue and cross-border solidarity, on one hand, and among far-right groups, such as Generation Identity in France, on the other. Borders in general and the Mediterranean in particular have thus become loci of both migration control and activism, while the European Union, through Frontex, has come to be a key player in the political arena. Sea rescue has progressively moved from a solely public concern, regulated by international public law, to a private preserve, as Marta Esperti observed.[7] As a result, search-and-rescue operations that were initially framed as technical, humanitarian, and legal issues became increasingly repoliticized.[8] Concurrently, scholars interested in border and migration politics increasingly came to investigate the role of migrants[9] and particularly of migrants' deaths in the making of maritime borders.[10]

The Local Politics of Migration Control and Its Discontent

Since the 1990s, Italian migration politics has been increasingly defined by border externalization, migrant illegalization, securitization, transnational activism, privatization of migration, border management, and recurring emergencies.[11] These international and transnational dynamics, however, are combined with local initiatives and endeavors. At the local level, both left- and right-wing politicians and organizations have played a pivotal role in defining policies. Local actors have been tremendously empowered for the past twenty years. Such a power shift is partly explained by the 1992 reform that boosted the role of mayors and municipalities. Migration issues polarized debates and affected outcomes of local elections, generating alignments and realignments. Mayors and local politicians have increasingly harnessed the media and social networks to publicize their positions, especially regarding solidarity and migrants' integration. The local politicization of migration issues has created occasional discrepancies between municipal migration policies and national or European ones. A number of Italian mayors have either championed alternative migration policies at the city level or openly defied governmental decisions. The movement evolved toward what some have called a "new municipalism," which is tied not only to local dynamics but also to transnational coalitions of cities and local political actors.[12] These processes are epitomized by transnational alliances between cities across Europe, such as the initiative "We the Cities of Europe," launched by the mayors of Barcelona, Lesbos, Paris, and Lampedusa in 2015, and the first international Fearless Cities summit in 2017.

In 2018 a coalition of Italian mayors took a public stand against the governmental crackdowns on refugees—for instance, refusing to implement Matteo Salvini's hardline measures against asylum seekers. Contemporary challenges of migration control and asylum politics have thus brought about a variety of dynamics that operate at different scales and are sometimes contradictory.[13] Far from scaling down migration control, these trends illustrate the role of migration politics and its discontent in producing new, complex and political processes.

The Blind Side: Rising Emigration

Emigration politics in advanced democracies are often overlooked in migration studies, as scholars tend to focus on immigration control and integration policies.[14] Yet emigration has become—again—a key feature of Italian contemporary history, and migration rates have been consistently negative since the beginning of the twenty-first century.

On the one hand, Italy has become a springboard for secondary migration of non-European immigrants and/or of their families toward other European countries. Moroccans and sub-Saharan Africans are largely moving to France; Bangladeshi and Pakistani residents are leaving for the United Kingdom. In recent years, these outflows have had a major impact on Italy's net migration. These flows are connected to the lack of job opportunities in Italy and to the lack of political integration of second-generation immigrants in Italian society. Yet these flows hardly feature in public debates and public policies.

On the other hand, a more classical trend of Italian emigration has become resurgent in the past decades: the outmigration of skilled and unskilled workers. This is largely driven by economic factors and directed not only to the United Kingdom, Germany, Switzerland, and France but also to the United States, Brazil, and Spain.[15] Emigration jumped after the 2008 recession, from 36,000 in 2007 to around 130,000 annual departures in the following decades. Yet the 2008 crisis only potentiated the impact of a long-term structural economic crisis that started in the 1980s. Italian are leaving today at a pace quite similar to the one recorded after World War II.

The resurgence of Italian emigration features prominently in public debates and is often presented as an issue of brain drain: in 2013 one-third of Italian emigrants had received tertiary education, compared to less than 15 percent of the working-age resident population.[16] The loss in human capital can also be tied to a loss in political capital that is weighing on electoral outcomes and public choices. In 2010, the Berlusconi government adopted Law 238, which fostered the (re)migration of skilled Europeans to Italy, but policies also sought to leverage the Italian diaspora for resources and prestige. Such concerns had notably driven the 1992 acceptance of dual citizenship and the 2000–2001 reform on external voting that created a representative channel for citizens abroad. Overall, since 2008, both the national and regional administrations passed legislative acts targeting "Italians abroad."[17] But emigration has not been fully addressed as part and parcel of a multidimensional migration politics.

Notes

1. Sciortino and Colombo 2004.
2. Dines and Rigo 2015.
3. Artero, Hajer, and Ambrosini 2021.
4. Pastore and Roman 2020.
5. Euronews 2017.
6. Palm 2017.
7. Esperti 2020.
8. Cuttitta 2018.
9. Schmoll 2020.
10. Heller and Pezzani 2017.
11. Campesi 2018.
12. Russell 2019.
13. Caponio 2018.
14. Thiollet 2020.
15. Dubucs et al. 2015.
16. Eurostat 2021.
17. Tintori 2017.

References

Artero, Maurizio, Minke Hajer, and Maurizio Ambrosini. 2021. "Working with a Family: The Role of Migrant Care Workers in a Family-Oriented Welfare System." *Revue Européenne des Migrations Internationales* 37, nos. 1–2.

Campesi, Giuseppe. 2018. "Crisis, Migration and the Consolidation of the EU Border Control Regime." *International Journal of Migration and Border Studies* 4, no. 3: 196–221.

Caponio, Tiziana. 2018. "Immigrant Integration Beyond National Policies? Italian Cities' Participation in European City Networks." *Journal of Ethnic and Migration Studies* 44, no. 12: 2053–2069.

Cuttitta, Paolo. 2018. "Repoliticization Through Search and Rescue? Humanitarian NGOs and Migration Management in the Central Mediterranean." *Geopolitics* 23, no. 3: 632–660. https://doi.org/10.1080/14650045.2017.1344834.

Cvajner, Martina. 2019. *Sociologia delle migrazioni femminili.* Bologna: Il Mulino.

Dines, Nick, and Enrico Rigo. 2015. "Postcolonial Citizenships and the Refugeeization of the Workforce: Migrant Agricultural Labour in the Italian Mezzogiorno." In *Postcolonial Transitions in Europe: Contexts, Practices and Politics*, edited by Sandra Ponzanesi and Guido Colpani, 153–174. Lanham, MD: Rowman and Littlefield.

Dubucs, Hadrien, Ettore Recchi, Thomas Pifrsch, and Camille Schmoll. 2015. "Je Suis un Italien de Paris: Italian Migrants Incorporation in a European Capital City." *Journal of Ethnic and Migration Studies* 43, no. 4: 578–595.

Esperti, Marta. 2020. "Rescuing Migrants in the Central Mediterranean: The Emergence of a New Civil Humanitarianism at the Maritime Border." *American Behavioral Scientist* 64, no. 4: 436–455.

Euronews. 2017. "Italy-Libya Sign Agreement to Curb Flow of Migrants to Europe." Euronews, February 2, 2017. https://www.euronews.com/2017/02/02/italy-libya-sign-agreement-to-curb-flow-of-migrants-to-europe.

Eurostat. 2021. https://ec.europa.eu/eurostat/statistics-explained/index.php?title=Migration_and_migrant_population_statistic.

Heller, Charles, and Lorenzo Pezzani. 2017. "Liquid Traces: Investigating the Deaths of Migrants at the EU's Maritime Frontier." In *The Borders of "Europe,"* edited by Nicholas De Genova, 95–119. Durham, NC: Duke University Press, 2017. https://doi.org/10.1215/9780822372660-004.

Pastore, Ferruccio, and Emanuela Roman. 2020. "Migration Policies and Threat-Based Extraversion: Analysing the Impact of European Externalisation Policies on African Polities." *Revue Européenne des Migrations Internationales* 36, no. 1: 133–152.

Pécoud, Antoine. 2010. "Death at the Border: Revisiting the Debate in Light of the Euro-Mediterranean Migration Crisis." *American Behavioral Scientist* 64, no. 4: 379–388.

Russell, Bertie. 2019. "Beyond the Local Trap: New Municipalism and the Rise of the Fearless Cities." *Antipode* 51, no. 3: 989–1010. https://doi.org/10.1111/anti.12520.

Sciortino, Giuseppe, and Asher Colombo. 2004. "The Flows and the Flood: The Public Discourse on Immigration in Italy, 1969–2001." *Journal of Modern Italian Studies* 9, no. 1: 94–113.

Schmoll, Camille. 2020. *Les damnées de la mer: Femmes et frontières en Méditerranée.* Cahiers Libres. Paris: La Découverte.

Thiollet, Hélène. 2020. "Unlocking Migration Politics: Researching Beyond Biases and Gaps in Migration Studies and Comparative Politics." In *Renewing the Migration Debate: Building Disciplinary and Geographical Bridges to Explain Global Migration*, 115–125. Amsterdam: International Migration Institute. http://spire.sciencespo.fr/hdl:/2441/2g9h37uqer8n3abt5ko21qec94.

Tintori, Guido, and Valentina Romei. 2017. "Emigration from Italy After the Crisis: The Shortcomings of the Brain Drain Narrative." In *South-North Migration of EU Citizens in Times of Crisis*, edited by Jean-Michel Lafleur and Mikolaj Stanek, 49–64. IMISCOE Research Series. Cham: Springer International. https://doi.org/10.1007/978-3-319-39763-4_4.

12 Spain

The Uneasy Transition from Labor Exporter to Labor Importer and the New Challenges Ahead

Miryam Hazán[1] and Rut Bermejo Casado

Introduction

By the end of 2020 the foreign population residing in Spain amounted to 5.4 million people and represented 11.4 percent of the total population (Table 12.1).[2] While this number was slightly higher than the previous year (a 0.7 percent increase), the reality was that the percentage of foreigners, as a share of the total population, had not shown much change in recent years, remaining at around 11 percent for almost a decade, and dropping to 9.8 percent in 2017 after having reached a peak in 2010 and 2011 at 12.2 percent, the highest level in modern Spanish history (Table 12.1).

This lack of growth in the number of immigrants as a share of the total population seemed to be behind the severe decline in the growth of the Spanish population at the beginning of the second decade of the twenty-first century and very limited growth thereafter. For instance, a 2020 press release by the Instituto Nacional de Estadística noted that in 2019 the country's population grew by 392,921, reaching 47,329,981 million people, and that this growth was the result of a net positive immigration balance of 451,391 people, compensating for the total negative net growth of the total population, which showed a decrease of 57,146 people.[3] This report is consistent with demographic data showing that the population growth Spain experienced in the past two decades was in great part the result of rapid and intense growth in the number of international migrants who arrived in Spain, especially from 1996 to 2008—a trend that waned as the number of newcomers diminished in the context

TABLE 12.1. *Immigration Trends in Spain Since the 1980s*

Year	Foreigners registered	Percentage of total population
1981	198,042	0.52
1986	241,971	0.63
1991	360,655	0.91
1996	542,314	1.37
1998	637,085	1.60
2000	923,879	2.28
2001	1,370,657	3.33
2002	1,977,946	4.73
2003	2,664,168	6.24
2004	3,034,326	7.02
2005	3,730,610	8.46
2006	4,144,166	9.27
2007	4,519,554	10.0
2008	5,220,600	11.3
2009	5,648,671	12.1
2010	5,747,734	12.2
2011	5,751,487	12.2
2012	5,736,258	12.1
2013	5,546,238	11.8
2014	5,023,487	10.7
2015	4,729,644	10.1
2016	4,618,581	9.9
2017	4,572,807	9.8
2018	4,734,691	10.1
2019	5,036,878	10.7
2020	5,434,153	11.4

SOURCE: Instituto Nacional de Estadística.

of the economic crisis that Spain confronted in 2008. Only as immigration gradually resumed did the total population begin to grow as well. However, this new immigration was different from the migratory dynamics observed prior to the 2008 economic crisis.

If we analyze changes in the major nationalities of origin among immigrants in recent years (2011–2020, totaling about 100,000 people), the immigrant group that has shown the most significant growth, as can be seen in Table 12.2, is Venezuelans

TABLE 12.2. *Ranking of Immigrant Nationalities in Spain by Selected Years*

Rank	Country	2001	2006	2011	2018	2019	2020	Percent Change 2011–2020
1	Romania	31,641	407,159	**865.707**	676,005	671,985	**667,378**	−22,1
2	Morocco	233,415	563,012	**773.995**	770,523	813,587	**865,945**	11,9
3	U. Kingdom	107,326	274,722	**391.194**	242,837	250,392	**262,885**	−32,8
4	Ecuador	139,022	461,310	**360.710**	135,275	131,814	**130,919**	−63,7
5	Colombia	87,209	265,141	**273.176**	165,918	206,719	**273,050**	0
6	Bolivia	6,619	139,802	**199.080**	99,441	95,717	92,630	−53,5
7	Germany	99,217	150,490	**195.987**	111,495	111,911	**111,937**	−42,9
8	Italy	34,689	115,791	**187.993**	206,524	228,283	**252,008**	34,1
9	Bulgaria	12,035	101,617	**172.926**	124,404	122,813	**122,375**	−29,2
10	China	27,574	104,681	**167.132**	215,970	224,559	**232,807**	39,3
11	Portugal	47,064	80,635	**140.824**	89,616	93,440	97,628	−30,7
12	Peru	30,574	124,681	**132.552**	70,980	84,179	**106,712**	−19,5
13	France	51,582	90,021	**122.503**	99,013	103,517	**108,275**	−11,6
14	Argentina	32,429	150,252	**120.738**	72,401	77,649	89,029	−26,3
15	Brazil	17,078	72,441	**107.596**	81,712	90,304	98,655	−8,3
16	Dominican R.	31,153	61,071	91.148	71,826	73,623	75,261	−17,4
17	Paraguay	928	28,587	87.906	75,718	80,218	87,045	−1
18	Ukraine	10,318	69,893	86.316	106,987	111,736	**115,186**	33,4
19	Poland	13,469	45,797	85.956	52,446	53,003	53,418	−37,9
20	Pakistan	8,274	42,138	70.165	82,874	88,935	97,705	39,3
21	Senegal	10,627	35,079	63.601	66,203	71,020	76,973	21
22	Algeria	18,265	47,079	60.912	60,942	63,182	66,893	9,8
23	Venezuela	16,549	51,261	59.805	95,633	137,776	**189,110**	216,2
24	Netherlands	23,146	39,484	54.493	44,458	45,931	46,891	−14
25	Cuba	24,534	44,739	54.680	49,257	55,906	64,634	18,2
26	Russia	10,047	39,904	53.166	73,930	77,715	82,788	55,7
27	Nigeria	7,598	31,588	45.132	39,439	39,306	39,345	−12,8
28	Uruguay	6,828	45,508	42.828	25,521	26,406	28,166	−34,2
29	Chile	11,674	39,704	41.939	25,523	26,406	28,153	−32,9
30	Belgium	19,869	29,526	35.892	31,068	32,893	34,352	−4,3

SOURCE: Instituto Nacional de Estadística..

(increasing by 216.2 percent). This situation could be understood not as a reanimation of the migratory dynamics that the country had experienced in previous years (which resulted from the economic boom of the late 1990s and the first few years of this century) but as an exception derived from the dramatic humanitarian crisis in Venezuela in recent years that has produced massive migratory flows to other countries, including Spain. Spain had been a destination place for Venezuelan emigrants in the past, but it is interesting to note that when Venezuelans left their country in massive numbers between 2015 and 2020, Spain was not a major destination for them compared to other countries, especially in South America. The number of Venezuelans in Spain has increased, but not as much as the number of Venezuelans in other countries. Venezuelans who have arrived in Spain in recent years are relatively well-off or highly educated migrants with the capacity to make a living even in a context of continuing high unemployment in Spain (13.78 percent in 2019 prior to the COVID-19 pandemic)[4] and an uncertain economic recovery, even though the economy had been growing in recent years after a severe decline.[5] Three other immigrant groups in Spain that have shown a major increase in their total numbers, according to data from 2011 to 2020, are Russians (55.7 percent), Pakistanis (39.3 percent), and Chinese (39.3 percent) (see Table 12.2). In contrast, immigration from other countries of origin that were relevant during the late 1990s and the first decade of the twenty-first century, such as Ecuador and Bolivia, actually showed a dramatic decrease during the period 2011–2020, as can be seen in Table 12.2, suggesting that Latin American immigration will not be as prominent as it was once. In addition, Moroccans, which in 2001 were the largest immigrant group in Spain, did not experience much change in the period 2011–2018, though their numbers began to grow again in 2019 and 2020.

At the same time, Spain faced a new reality, albeit one that had once been familiar: it had again become an exporter of labor, as it had been from the mid-1950s until the early 1970s, when close to 1.5 million Spaniards left to work in other western European countries. This time around, however, the problem was not so much the number of emigrants, which nonetheless had become significant, as the fact that most of them were of working age (63 percent were between the ages of sixteen and sixty-four) and educated, according to data from the Instituto Nacional de Estadística (INE). For instance, over the course of a little less than a decade more than 1 million Spaniards left the country: in 2009 the total number of Spaniards residing abroad was 1,471,691, compared with 2,545,729 in 2018 (according to the INE). Spain was losing the very people it needed to restructure its economy from one highly dependent on construction and services to one more diversified and more dependent on research and development and industrial innovation in fields in which Spain already had a competitive advantage (e.g., renewable energy, biotechnology, and transportation).

Even while emigration rates were diminishing thanks to the economic recovery, the emigration phenomenon Spain experienced in recent years, along with the relative stagnation of immigration, demonstrated the particular population dynamics the country was facing as well as its specific realities and dilemmas with regard to international migration and human mobility dynamics overall (international migration and refugee movements). The most specific reality, visible in the trends just described, is that Spain was not getting the sustained immigration rates it would need if it wanted to address, at least partially, the demographic problems it was confronting. These include one of the lowest fertility rates in all of Europe (1.24 children per woman),[6] the stagnant and even negative population growth of the native population, and the depopulation of significant parts of its territory—a trend that evidently would be very hard to reverse without renewed immigration and serious policies aimed at discouraging youth emigration to bigger urban areas or abroad, as well as creating incentives for Spaniards to have more children. Instead, in some regions of the country, depopulation had been sharp enough to make economic recovery really unsustainable in the medium and long terms without further policy measures.

Thus while immigration has shown some growth after a long period of negative growth or stagnation, Spain still faces the question of how it will eventually fill, from the ranks of its prospective highly educated young workforce, the low-skilled positions that formerly were held by now-aging Spaniards.[7] Clearly there is still a need for immigrants to fill these low-skilled jobs; what the country has faced instead has been a shortage of low-skilled workers and emigration among those trained for better jobs. Even if emigration might be stopping (and this trend is not even clear), the country still needs higher rates of immigration to supply its labor market and demographic needs in the medium and long terms.

Spain's Dilemmas

Spain's transformation from major exporter to major importer of low-skilled labor was effected over a relatively short time. It started in the 1980s, when the country's economic prospects were improving via consolidation of its young democratic system and entry into the European Community; it accelerated in the late 1990s as a result of an economic expansion generated by membership in the EU monetary union and the associated real estate boom. When the country entered a new economic decline in 2008, that transformation was perhaps complete. Since then the country has been dealing with the challenge of integrating the immigrant population that settled in the country during the period of economic expansion, while at the same time discouraging the emigration of at least part of its young population. It has done so, however, in a very de facto way, as no serious policies related to international migration, including emigration and immigration, have been adopted in recent years apart from partially taking away access to welfare benefits and health services for the undocumented population during the administration of People's Party prime minister Mariano Rajoy, policies that were rolled back when Pedro Sánchez from the Socialist Party took power during the summer of 2018.[8]

While notably sharp in the Spanish case, the dilemmas originally presented by Spain's transformation from an emigration to an immigration country were not unique to it. Like other economically advanced countries, Spain faced both an imperative to expand its immigrant population and an imperative to restrict it. The need to expand its labor supply and the size of its domestic market, to finance its welfare system, and to address its demographic imbalances pushed Spain to implement proactive policies that facilitated the arrival of newcomers. At the same time, the need to protect its native population from job displacement and wage depression and its welfare system from a fiscal burden; to avoid the emergence of xenophobic sentiment; to maintain the balance of its national and cultural composition; and to fulfill its commitments to the EU on immigration control compelled the country to restrict newcomers, especially during the Rajoy administration but even during the present Sánchez administration.

All of these competing factors led the government to enact a series of immigration reforms starting in the mid-1980s that were more or less restrictive depending on evolving political and economic dynamics. These reforms included periodic regularizations to incorporate newcomers into the formal economy and make them contributors to the welfare system, but they also included policies to order and control migratory flows, such as guest worker agreements, visa requirements, and greater collaboration with African countries to contain irregular migration.

Today Spain faces similar dilemmas, but in a more complex context, as major political cleavages such as nationalism have been reignited, expressed in a growing tension between the national government and the regional Catalonian government. This in turn has awakened Spanish nationalism, which during the last few decades had been more moderate, and opened up a space for right-wing political parties with an anti-immigrant predisposition, such as Vox, which previously represented an irrelevant political force but now is more prominent.[9] While the percentage of Spaniards who express negative feelings toward immigrants, especially non-EU ones, is considerably smaller than in other EU countries,[10] and while Spain does not really have a strong anti-immigrant political party, since even Vox's main agenda is to guarantee the territorial integrity of Spain and less so to drastically contain immigration, the reigniting of nationalism and the electoral strengthening of parties like

Vox further complicate the policy responses available for Spain to address its policy dilemmas related to international migration. How is Spain able to reconsider having a more proactive immigration policy to attract new immigrants to address its demographic and economic needs when at the same time the legitimacy of the political community as it is today is widely questioned by possibly around half of Catalonians, who want their autonomous community to defect from Spain? Answers to these and similar questions will certainly determine the developmental path of this country in years to come.

At the same time, at the continental level, the EU has moved to the right in the immigration arena after the large refugee flows Europe experienced in 2015 and 2016 strengthened the political positions of right-wing political parties by turning immigration into a more salient topic.[11] Compared to other countries, Spain was not the recipient of significant flows of refugees, and it certainly did not face the political anger that the arrival of refugees generated in other parts of Europe, even when in 2018 a small proportion of the flows was diverted into continental Spain as other routes into the continent were closed to them, while it kept receiving small flows of sub-Saharan migrants through the Canary Islands, a trend that continued during 2019 and 2020 even in the context of the COVID-19 pandemic.[12] However, the EU's shift toward further restrictive measures on immigration reduces the policy options of countries like Spain, where public opinion is not as anti-immigrant as in other EU countries, making it more difficult to act in the immigration policy arena in a way that could address, at least partially, the country's demographic and economic imbalances.[13]

The basic dilemmas today faced by Spain transcend a narrow definition of immigration policy as the questions of how many and whom to allow to enter or to stay. These dilemmas also appear in the field of citizenship and integration policies: how to accelerate the integration of those newcomers who arrived during the economic boom without altering too much of the country's cultural and national balances in a polity already facing major challenges as a result of the reigniting of the nationalist cleavage reflected in the current Catalonian nationalist movement and the pro-Spain neo-nationalistic trend. During the first decade of the twenty-first century, this question led to a variety of policy responses at the national and subnational levels. On the one hand, the national government maintained citizenship policies derived from its authoritarian past that primarily benefited immigrant groups perceived as closer to the idea of a cultural Iberoamerican nation—specifically, those from Latin America—and made entrance into the polity more difficult for all other national groups. Somewhat in contrast to this policy, Spain also embraced the ethnic and cultural diversity brought by new immigrant groups and followed an "intercultural" approach toward integration. As described by Spanish officials at the time, interculturalism had the goal of encouraging a mutual exchange between natives and newcomers in a way that was supposed to transform both groups into a new and better national whole. This policy was supposed to be different from other European models (French assimilationism and Dutch multiculturalism), which Spanish elites portrayed as failing to acknowledge the value of difference or as promoting political fragmentation.[14] In practice, however, the Spanish model amounted to the implementation of social and educational policies that attempted to facilitate the coexistence of natives and newcomers and to smooth the assimilation of immigrant groups deemed to have values different from Spaniards', especially those immigrants of Muslim/African origin. With respect to this last group, elite and institutional responses were clearly ambiguous.

On the one hand, they emphasized the value of cultural and religious diversity and tolerance. On the other, they argued that immigrants should share Spain's democratic values, including those of gender equality and avoidance of non-Western practices such as female genital mutilation. This discourse reached its climax in 2008 when the People's Party candidate for prime minister, Mariano Rajoy, proposed that immigrants sign an "integration contract" after one year in Spain that would commit them to respect the country's laws.[15] This proposal copied a French law implemented by President Nicolas Sarkozy in 2004.

In addition, in the context of an expansionary economic period, Spain put in place an ambitious experimental policy to link newcomers to the development of their country of origin as a way to facilitate their integration into Spanish society. This policy was termed "co-development." Although it did not survive the economic downturn, it helped create an entire institutional infrastructure that engaged local and regional institutions with immigrants and with the realities of their places of origin, which Spain could draw upon in the future if it chooses to pursue again a proactive immigration policy to attract new migratory flows.

Today, integration policies present an even more complex challenge, as the re-igniting of the nationalistic cleavage makes it hard to even define which values and what notion of the political community immigrants are supposed to assimilate to, and what aspects of their culture should be acknowledged in a way that does not ignite additional political fragmentation over cultural values and heritage. Furthermore, from a territorial perspective, are there different expectations today regarding the ways immigrants should integrate in different communities?

In this chapter, we discuss Spain's evolution from an emigration country to an immigration country, analyzing the different dilemmas it confronted as a result, and the policy responses it has pursued at the national and subnational levels. We also analyze the implications of the Spanish turn into a new emigration country (even as this trend appears to have waned for now) and the new dynamics in the immigration arena in the context of the reawakening of the nationalist cleavage in Spain and the EU's rightward shift on immigration matters.

We argue that Spain's rapid evolution from an emigration country to an immigration country was a product of a combination of demographic deficits and the development model the country pursued in recent times, both of which encouraged the arrival of massive numbers of low-skilled migrants. The prospect of Spain becoming an exporter of high-skilled labor in the context of a deep economic crisis is also a consequence of the economic model pursued for the past few decades. On the one hand, economic growth became highly dependent on sectors of the economy that required low-skilled rather than high-skilled, formally trained labor. On the other hand, the existence of a labor market that protects seniority made it difficult for young and educated Spaniards to integrate themselves into the labor force. Today Spain may be entering a new stage in which immigration is mostly stagnant or showing a small rate of growth compared to previous years and emigration may have finally diminished, but the country remains unable to address even in a minimal way its demographic and territorial imbalances—a situation that may inhibit sustainable rates of economic growth. This situation became even more challenging in the context of the COVID-19 pandemic, which produced a virtual stop to the growth of immigration, though it is still unclear what migratory dynamics we will identify in the pandemic's aftermath.

We also want to understand how Spain has chosen its immigration and integration policy responses to its basic dilemmas. The Spanish state's policies in these areas, we argue, are the result of three factors. First are the country's historical legacies, including (1) its experiences as an emigration country and (2) its national, cultural, and linguistic diversity, which has forced its elites and state institutions to try to deal with the problem of difference more proactively and to become more tolerant than other European countries toward the presence of "others" for the sake of maintaining the territorial integrity of the country. Second are its corporatist institutional arrangements, which have granted a predominant voice in the immigration field to three main actors at different stages (the government, with its varying perspectives depending on the governing party coalition; the unions; and the business community), and its highly decentralized political system, which has allowed subnational governments to have significant leverage in defining the integration of newcomers. Third is its membership in the EU, which at different times has exerted pressure on Spanish elites to become more proactive in securing the country's borders as Europe's southernmost point, the consequence of which makes it very hard for the country to attract newcomers who could help ameliorate its demographic and economic dilemmas.

From an Emigration Country to an Immigration Country

When Spain Was an Emigration Country

From the mid-1850s until 1979, Spain was primarily a country of emigration. Through the 1920s, Spaniards emigrated mostly to Latin America, a region with which Spain had had continuous and very intense contact since the time of Columbus and which resulted in the colonization by Spaniards of a large part of the Americas. Although migration flows to this region were briefly arrested by the region's movements for national independence, emigration from Spain reemerged at midcentury, when restrictions on immigration in most of Latin America were lifted. Migrants went primarily to Argentina, Cuba, Brazil, and, to a lesser extent, Uruguay and Mexico. Like most migrants from Europe to the Americas at the time, Spaniards were looking for economic opportunities promised by the newly created countries' low population density, abundant natural resources, and general sense of infinite possibility. The common language, common religion, and cultural similarities made Latin America the almost exclusive destination of Spanish emigration during this period. It is estimated that between 3 million and 4 million Spaniards emigrated to Latin America between 1882 and 1930.[16] The late nineteenth century also witnessed Spanish emigration to North Africa (Morocco, Algeria) and less to Equatorial Guinea.

Emigration for economic reasons ground to a halt around 1930, as Latin American countries introduced immigration controls, following the example of the US Immigration Act of 1924, which dramatically reduced immigration from southern and eastern Europe. Spanish emigration reemerged quickly, however, driven now by the flight of socialist, communist, and other republican exiles from General Franco's regime as his control of the country reached its peak in 1939. Around half a million Spaniards left for France and Mexico, but significant numbers headed for the Soviet Union, Algeria, and other countries in the Americas and Europe. Many among the exiles were highly educated, producing a brain drain for Spain and a brain gain for receiving countries—most notably, perhaps, Mexico, which took in many public intellectuals, scientists, and artists during this time.

Although emigration of political exiles eventually abated, in part because of exit controls instituted by Franco's regime, a new wave of emigration arose in the mid-1950s, when these controls were lifted. This wave, which lasted into the early 1970s, landed largely in western Europe, with particularly large numbers received by France, Germany, Switzerland, and the United Kingdom. These most recent immigrants resembled the standard migrants of today, moving from developing to developed countries. Economic modernization in Spain, after the failure of an autarkic economic model originally implemented by Franco's regime, produced major economic and regional imbalances. In the countryside, mechanization of agriculture during the 1950s generated worker displacements in the poorest areas of the country, especially in Extremadura, Andalucía, and Castilla–La Mancha. Workers migrated to big cities such as Barcelona and Madrid and to the Basque country as industrial production in these places gradually expanded with some government support. National industry, however, did not provide jobs to all of these internally displaced workers, or to the growing urban labor force more generally; conditions thus favored emigration to other European countries, and it was facilitated and actually encouraged by the Franco regime, which, in a full policy reversal, eliminated the previously imposed emigration restrictions and created the National Institute for Emigration (NIE) in 1956. The NIE was in charge of channeling migratory flows in a way that would be most profitable for the country. With that goal in mind, it negotiated guest worker agreements with Belgium (1956), Germany (1960), France, Switzerland, the Netherlands (all in 1961), and Austria (1966).[17] The NIE monopolized information on job offers coming from these countries, and it was also responsible for recruiting suitable workers for these positions. Generally, poorly educated workers from areas of the country with high unemployment rates were the ones selected. Emigration was thus explicitly used as a safety valve in easing the country's economic adjustment and modernization and in containing social instability.[18] A new economic stabilization plan implemented in 1959 also liberalized the economy, produced additional economic displacement due to salary freezes, reduced investment and consumption, and generated higher unemployment rates—all of which created additional incentives to emigrate. Because of the many bureaucratic hurdles that would-be emigrants had to clear in order to qualify for positions offered abroad, around 50 percent of them left the country without authorization. It is estimated that around 1.5 million Spaniards went to work abroad from 1960 to the early 1970s, although many of them repatriated themselves thereafter.[19]

Becoming an Immigration Country

Restrictions on immigration imposed by receiving countries as a result of the economic crisis of the 1970s, along with improving economic conditions in Spain, finally brought the midcentury migratory wave to a halt. A few years later, in the 1980s, the country gradually started to become a country of immigration. By the mid-1980s, Spain was receiving substantial numbers of immigrants attracted by the beginnings of the economic boom that coincided with its entry into the European Community (see Table 12.1).

Through the 1990s, however, the immigrant population grew at a relatively slow pace. In 1981, there were 233,000 immigrants, representing 0.6 percent of the population. As Table 12.1 shows, in 1998 there were 637,085 immigrants, 1.6 percent of the population. Immigration accelerated dramatically as the 1990s came to a close, and that acceleration continued into the 2000s. As is reflected in Table 12.1, between 1998 and 2008 Spain received around 500,000 immigrants each year.[20] In the peak year of 2008 alone, it received 701,046.[21]

Although this rate of growth diminished in the ensuing years as a result of the acute economic crisis in Spain, by 2011, when the growth of the immigrant population finally stabilized,[22] there were 5.7 million foreigners registered,[23] representing, as mentioned previously, 12.2 percent of the total population (see Table 12.1). As a result of this growth, which was exceptional in the European context, Spain became the third-largest recipient of immigrants in the world in absolute numbers after the United States and the Russian Federation. Apart from Europeans and other immigrants who qualify for admission under the "communitarian regime," Spain received a large number of migrants from many other parts of the world.[24] These migrants are of particular interest for this chapter, because while communitarian migrants can enter, work in, and reside on Spanish territory with few restrictions, which limits the capacity of the Spanish government to do anything about them, non-communitarian immigrants face many restrictions and are the natural targets of new policy initiatives, even while their numbers may not be growing anymore.[25]

The 1980s and 1990s witnessed a surge of immigrants from North Africa and eastern Europe. In the boom years of this century, Spain also attracted large numbers of immigrants from Latin American countries that at the time were confronting major economic crises. These included Ecuador, Colombia, Peru, and the Dominican Republic (which together surpassed Morocco as providing the largest immigrant contingent after 2000), and to a lesser extent Argentina, then Bolivia and Paraguay. Still, Moroccans remained the largest non-communitarian national immigrant group, followed by the Romanians, who since 2007 have qualified for the communitarian regime following Romania's accession to EU membership (see Table 12.2).

By the beginning of this century migratory dynamics had begun to show some changes. It is worth noticing, for example, that immigration from Bolivia and Paraguay showed striking growth during the first decade of this century. As a result, the number of immigrants from those countries approached the number of immigrants that had come during the 1990s from other Latin American countries, including Ecuador, the Dominican Republic, and Colombia. In addition, the number of immigrants from Romania grew by 2,036 percent, from Ukraine by 937 percent, from Bulgaria by 934 percent, and from Pakistan by 902 percent. However, between 2011 and 2020, most immigrant groups have not grown or have decreased their number, except in the case of some non-EU nationalities such as Moroccans, Ukrainians, Chinese, Venezuelans, Cubans, Pakistanis, Russians, Senegalese, and Algerians.

Most immigrants who have arrived in Spain in the last few decades have done so as tourists or in other legal ways, generally reaching Spanish territory by air or land and never leaving; very few have arrived clandestinely by sea, even though such arrivals get so much attention.[26] Their arrival as tourists who can move freely across the EU has forced Spain to begin requiring visas of visitors from countries that have been the source of large numbers of immigrants, such as Morocco and more recently Ecuador, Colombia, Peru, and Bolivia (though in December 2015 Colombians and Peruvians were once again exempted from this obligation).[27] In addition, some migrants have arrived as dual nationals, qualifying as such by different citizenship policies adopted by Spain at different times

Even though most immigrants have arrived legally, in recent years the total number of people who crossed Spain's borders irregularly has increased, reaching 63,298 in 2018, 131 percent more than in 2017, when the total was 27,834. This was expected after the closure of routes in the central Mediterranean that year. Today, nearly all irregular arrivals come by sea (40,106 of 41,861), predominantly arriving in the Canary Islands (23,023), with the rest coming to mainland Spain or the Balearic Islands (16,610), according to 2020 official data.[28] In this regard, the United Nations High Commissioner for Refugees has been calling attention to the increase in the number of deaths in the Mediterranean Sea and particularly in the Strait of Gibraltar. It is worth noticing that after becoming prime minister, Sánchez began his mandate by opening Spanish ports to the arrival of migrants and refugees rejected in other parts of the Mediterranean. In June 2018, for example, the port of Valencia welcomed the *Aquarius* "flotilla," composed of three rescue boats carrying 629 people. Italy and Malta had refused to accept the migrants, but Spain offered protection and allowed them to land.[29] This action led to reproach by some European nations, which argued that Spain had breached international law, since the ships should be accepted at the nearest safe port,[30] in this case in Malta and Italy. The next controversial boat was *Nuestra Madre Loreto*, which rescued twelve people in December 2018.[31] In this case the ship was of Spanish flag, but Spain notified Malta that the nearest safe port was Malta. Malta agreed to accept the newcomers on the condition that they be transferred to Spain. Another controversial ship was the *Open Arms*, with 311 people, which was refused by Malta and unsuccessfully requested support from France, Italy, and Greece before finally docking in Algeciras, in southern Spain.[32]

The rapid growth of the immigrant population has been tightly linked to economic developments. After a recessionary economic period during the early 1990s,

Spain entered a period of economic expansion that lasted from 1994 to 2007, during which the economy grew at an average of 3.5 percent a year. This growth encouraged a notable rate of expansion of the money supply. The standard policy response would have been to raise interest rates, with the goal of lowering inflation, forcing people and companies to save, and discouraging new debt facilitated by cheap credit. In Spain, however, this response proved impossible. Complying with the 1992 Maastricht Agreement establishing the EU monetary and economic union, Spain *lowered* interest rates in pursuit of equalization with the more sluggish economies of the EU, most notably France and Germany. Interest rates fell even further when the peseta stopped circulating in 2002, with foreign investors showing great trust in Spain as a eurozone economy. With greater access to credit for the Spanish population and investment coming from abroad, the economy grew even more. Most of this growth stemmed from investments in real estate and in tourism-related industries, which in turn spurred the expansion of the construction sector to build the new properties and tourist infrastructure.

Construction and tourism had already become important sectors of the Spanish economy starting in the 1960s, when the country urbanized and opened up to the world. These sectors, however, acquired even greater relevance when the country entered a period of deindustrialization, especially after having joined the EU. Thus, the high unemployment rates Spain experienced during the 1990s were related to employment losses in the industrial sector,[33] and Spain's employment and growth prospects thereafter became more dependent on construction, tourism, and finance.[34] Construction and tourism generated strong demand for low-skilled workers. Stagnant population growth due to low birth rates, combined with ever higher average education levels of the native-born population, ensured that only immigration could provide a stable labor pool adequate to meet demand in these fields.[35] Immigrants certainly responded to, or validated, these demand-side incentives, with immigration peaking alongside the real estate bubble in 1998. From this perspective, immigration can be seen as both a cause and a consequence of Spain's bubble era of economic expansion.

However, immigrants were not only employed in construction and similar industries linked to the real estate bubble. They also responded to Spain's broader demographic and economic dynamics. As the economy grew and unemployment decreased, more women joined the labor force. As a result, many immigrants, especially women, were employed in domestic services. They were also employed in care jobs, which have gained in importance as Spanish society ages. Finally, immigrants also worked in intensive agriculture and other areas of the primary sector (see Table 12.3 for a breakdown of immigrant employment by economic sector).

TABLE 12.3. *Distribution of Legal Immigrant Workers in Spain by Sector, First Trimester 2009 and First Trimester 2019 (thousands of persons)*

Sector	Number of workers 2009	Number of workers 2019
Agriculture	213,4	225,5
Industry	367,5	231,6
Construc-tion	671,7	255,7
Services	2,050,7	1,932,5
Total	3,303,3	2,645,3

SOURCE: EPA, Instituto Nacional de Estadística.

Of the close to 7 million jobs that the Spanish economy created between 1998 and 2007, half were filled by immigrants. The developmental model pursued during those years—highly dependent on construction and services along with demographic factors, including a declining fertility rate and the growing participation of women in the labor market—helps explain Spain's transformation into a country that imported low-income labor, primarily low-skilled workers.[36] The crisis in the construction sector and the impact of the economic crisis in the service industry destroyed many of the jobs that immigrants had filled and encouraged many of them to leave (Table 12.3). Others stayed despite unemployment or underemployment, while still others were able to keep their jobs but remained in precarious conditions.[37] While the economic model has not changed much today, the number of foreigners employed in the construction sector is less than half of those employed ten years before (Table 12.3). The problem is that the rest of the sectors have not absorbed the number of foreigners that worked in the construction sector; thus, in 2012 there was a negative migratory balance (more people leaving than entering Spain) of 162,000 (out) migrants of which 83 percent were foreign-born.[38]

The Demographic and Economic Transformation

Immigration is undoubtedly behind the extraordinary population growth that Spain experienced in little more than a decade, with the number of inhabitants rising from 39.8 million in 1998 to 46.8 million in 2012.[39] Since then the size of the Spanish population has stabilized at around 46 million, though in recent years it showed moderate growth, reaching 47.4 million in 2020.[40] Apart from the large number of newcomers, immigrants also contributed to this growth because they have been overrepresented in the young adult population, especially the cohort of those thirty to thirty-four years of age, and because of the high fertility rates of immigrant women compared to those of native women (though over time the fertility rate of immigrant women tends to diminish as immigrant women adopt the same behavioral patterns related to childbearing as native women, with 1.33 children per native woman versus 1.67 children per immigrant woman in 2009 and 1.17 versus 1.59 respectively in 2019).[41] Immigrants have thus been playing an increasingly important role in population replacement. In 2017, 76,060 of the children born in Spain had a foreign mother and 317,121 had a Spanish mother.[42]

During the economic boom, immigrants contributed significantly to the country's economic development. Newcomers played an important role in reinvigorating the labor market by helping to reduce imbalances between demand and supply and by providing flexibility and geographical mobility. According to the Spanish government, more than 50 percent of GDP growth from 2000 to 2005 can be attributed to the arrival of foreign workers. Without them, GDP would have shown a 0.6 percent annual average drop instead of the 2.6 percent increase during those years. Furthermore, immigration helped reduce structural unemployment between 1996 and 2005 because of the flexibility it introduced to the labor market (which, for example, allowed more women to enter the workforce) and because it helped increase national demand for goods and services. Finally, immigrants helped expand the tax base and, because of their underrepresentation in the population of those over fifty years of age, were net contributors to, rather than claimants on, the social security system. Today, considering the increasing number of aged and retired people with pensions, and the consequent fiscal crisis of the social security system, Spain needs to increase the base of its population pyramid to sustain the public pension system even in the short term, and a new expansion of immigration appears to be the only viable option to solve this structural problem.[43]

Spain's Immigration and Integration Dilemmas: The Policy Responses

The rapid and somewhat unexpected growth of the immigrant population starting in the 1980s and accelerating during the late 1990s forced the Spanish government to implement a variety of immigration and integration policies to balance the country's demographic and economic needs with its political imperatives. These policies have been guided primarily by the country's historical legacies; by the evolving dynamics among the government, unions, and the private sector; and by the influence of the EU on the country's decision-making.

Historical Legacies

Spain's experience as an emigration country, the persistence of strong internal divisions along linguistic/cultural lines, and its experience as an empire and as a nation that forged itself in the fight against Islam have been important factors in shaping the country's responses to immigration.

Although Spain experienced minimal immigration for close to five centuries following unification under its Catholic kings after the conquest of Granada in 1492, it has a long and rich history of linguistic and cultural differences that at times have challenged its very survival as an integral political entity. During Franco's regime, such cultural and linguistic differences were repressed through political and cultural constraints, although the regime finally interpreted this diversity as an expression of the "richness and diversity of a single Spanish nation." However, conflicts reemerged under democratic rule. The constitution of 1978 tried to address the differences by allowing regional decentralization of state functions and recognizing the different regional languages. It also granted autonomy to several different nationalities in political and territorial entities known as autonomous communities. Still, conflict remained over issues related to fiscal solidarity and the competencies that autonomous communities should have. The need to deal continually with political difference and the presence of "others" means, at least in theory, that elites and institutions are more practiced in and comfortable with the arrival and integration of newcomers than their long isolation from international immigration should have made them. A similar effect can perhaps be attributed to Spain's experience as an emigration country. Spanish elites continually refer to the Spanish emigration experience as a reason for accepting and integrating newcomers and regularly refer to it as an antidote to racism and xenophobia.[44] On an abstract level, Spaniards seem to have more positive views on immigration than other Europeans, linking the immigrants among them with stories of ancestors forced to emigrate. In a 2010 national poll,[45] for example, when the country was in a recessionary period after the economic boom years, 59 percent of respondents stated that when they think about immigration they think about the "need to come and find a job," "an analogy to the Spanish emigration experience," "poverty and inequality," "feelings of empathy and solidarity," and the "*pateras.*"[46] In contrast, only 20 percent associated immigration with negative factors such as "excessive increase of immigrants," "illegality and irregularity," "social privileges vis-à-vis Spaniards," "crime and insecurity," "negative impact in the labor market," and "problems of integration and coexistence." More recent data suggests that these perspectives have remained roughly the same. A comparison with other EU countries demonstrates that among Spaniards negative feelings against both EU immigrants and non-EU immigrants have been consistently diminishing to levels comparable to those in Sweden, but while in Sweden antipathy toward non-EU immigrants has grown in recent years, in Spain it has actually been diminishing.[47] This situation may be related to the fact that Spain was not directly affected by the recent refugee crisis that impacted Europe from 2014 to 2016. But this would not be a sufficient explanation, since negative attitudes toward immigrants, both EU and non-EU, are increasingly less common in Spain than in other EU member states, even though more negative attitudes are typical of the EU as a whole.[48]

At the same time, however, prevailing notions of nationhood based on Spain's imperial past have created a dual system of access to membership in the polity, which means that the country has been more welcoming toward some immigrant groups than toward others. Immigrants from former Spanish colonies or from countries linked to Spain through certain types of historical connections (identified as belonging to an Iberoamerican cultural idea) are granted citizenship in only two years. These include newcomers from Latin America (including Brazil), Portugal, the Philippines, Andorra, and Equatorial Guinea. Other immigrants must have been residents for ten years before being eligible for citizenship. For this reason, immigrants from Latin America, who arrived in massive numbers during the economic boom, were the primary recipients of most citizenship concessions Spain granted, even while immigrants from Morocco, for example, may have been in the country for a longer time. Figure 12.1 shows trends in nationality acquisition due to residence in the last six years.

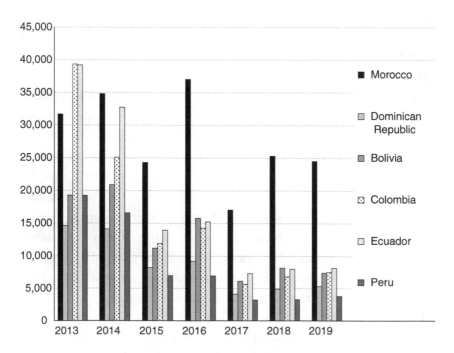

FIGURE 12.1. Acquisition of Nationality by Residence
SOURCE: INE.

In 1982, the Spanish government modified Article 22 of its civil code to extend citizenship to Sephardic Jews after only two years of residence. This legal change was an official recognition that Jews had been unfairly expelled from Spain in 1492, over 500 years ago. Similarly, in 2015, the Spanish government passed a new law that during a three-year window (later extended by one additional year) granted access to citizenship to Sephardic-origin Jews who met certain requirements.[49] Immigrants from Morocco have expressed dissatisfaction with the fact that they did not obtain similar benefits, claiming that they too have had a historical connection to Spain after many centuries of Moorish presence.[50] The national perception of Moroccans and other immigrants from Africa, however, is more ambiguous. While it is still politically incorrect in Spain to warn darkly of Europe's impending "Islamization" or "Africanization," there also has been skepticism about the country's capacity to absorb large numbers of Muslim and African migrants.

In 2010, when asked in the national poll mentioned earlier, "How important is it for you that immigrants to Spain come from countries with a Christian tradition?," only 7.7 percent of respondents answered that it was very important. This was in contrast to the 33.9 percent who declared it very important that those who come to the country have labor qualifications the country needs, the 20.9 percent who answered that immigrants should have a good educational level, and the 23 percent who said that immigrants should speak Spanish or the language of the autonomous community where they reside.[51] In 2017, those questions were again asked in a similar survey, and in this case only 4.7 percent considered origin from a Christian-tradition country very important; 14.7 percent said that labor qualifications were very important, 12.7 percent said that a good education level was very important, and 13 percent considered it very important that immigrants speak Spanish or the language of the autonomous community where they reside. And 36.1 percent agreed on the idea that is very important that immigrants should be willing to accept the way of life of the country.

Furthermore, though Spaniards tend to express a preference for Latin American and European immigrants over other groups, the most disliked are not Moroccans or others from Africa but Roma, formerly referred to as Gypsies (and by extension Romanians, notwithstanding differences between Romanian and Roma), who are popularly associated with high levels of criminality.[52] Around 750,000 Gypsies live in Spain,[53] and they are the most frequent targets of racism, although there have been incidents of racist hostility directed against Muslims[54] and other groups.[55] As noted earlier, the standard position taken on Muslims is that they should be welcomed, provided they accept Western values, including those related to gender equality and the rejection of practices such as female genital mutilation. As we have seen, this view was dramatically advanced by Mariano Rajoy in 2008 when he proposed during his unsuccessful bid to become prime minister that immigrants should sign an "integration contract" like that employed in France, a proposal clearly targeted toward Muslim immigrants. Though it went nowhere at the time, probably because Latin Americans were taking over as a larger immigrant contingent, the proposal reflected Spain's complex relationship with Islam. The country's identity was forged in its great victory for Christendom, but the long history of Muslim settlement (between two and eight centuries prior to the Reconquista, depending on the region, and with many Muslims remaining after Muslim dominion had been broken) and the sheer proximity to North Africa have meant a richness of exchange unparalleled elsewhere in the West.

The lack of fast-track access to citizenship for immigrants from African and other non-EU countries outside Latin America has meant that these immigrants are more likely to fall into irregularity. During the late 1990s and the first few years of this century, Spain implemented a number of regularizations, but they were for legal temporary, not permanent, long-term residence. This is not a minor issue. Spain has a complex system of short-term labor contracts, work permits, and residence permits, all mutually contingent. An immigrant can obtain a residence permit lasting anywhere from ninety days to a maximum of five years. To obtain permanent residence, immigrants must have lived legally in the country for at least five years. This means that an immigrant who benefited from regularization and now has a permit that lasts less than five years cannot renew it, and if he does not have access to citizenship in two years, he can fall back into irregularity very easily. The impact of this situation obviously increases during an economic downturn, when many immigrants are not able to renew their work permits, which are necessary to maintain legal status. Although the number of irregular migrants arriving in Spain decreased as a result of the economic crisis that started in 2008, estimates based on government data show that by the third trimester of 2009, 500,000 immigrants who had once enjoyed legal residency had fallen back into illegality.[56] In 2017 the government estimated that a total of 44,625 immigrants were irregular, but other sources estimated their number at 825,000 that same year.[57] A recent study estimated that around 430,000 immigrants in Spain were undocumented in 2019.[58] It is worth noting in this regard that estimates about irregular migrants are still fairly inaccurate.

National Institutional Arrangements

Spain's responses to immigration and integration policies have also been shaped by the country's institutional arrangements. Particularly important in this respect is the high degree of decentralization that has granted a very important role to regional and municipal institutions in the integration of newcomers.

The Role of Socioeconomic Actors.   In Spain, two main unions, the General Workers Union (Union General de Trabajadores, UGT) and the Workers Commissions (Comisiones Obreras, CCOO), represent most of the working class, and one business association, the Spanish Confederation of Business Organizations (Confederación Española de Organizaciones Empresariales, CEOE), represents most of the business class. This grouping of interests has been institutionalized over the years by national legislation that has granted a privileged role in decision-making to institutions considered the most representative of the population, making it possible to argue that in terms of policymaking on social and economic issues, Spain operates in a corporatist fashion. This has certainly been the case in the immigration and integration arenas, where the majority of decisions have been made by one or the other of these competing interests, especially during the first decade of this century, when immigration to the country accelerated dramatically and these actors had greater stakes in influencing the national immigration debate. The capacity of such corporate actors to exercise influence, however, has been greatly determined by their level of access to a political party or a political coalition in power or their ability to challenge the dominant power structure. In general, unions have shown a greater capacity to influence immigration decision-making when the Socialists (Partido Socialista Obrero Español, PSOE) have been in power, while the business community has had more influence during People's Party (Partido Popular, PP) administrations.

Decentralization.   Regional and municipal authorities have played a very important role in the integration of newcomers over the past twenty years. Municipal governments are the first institutions with which immigrants come into contact once they arrive and settle in Spain. To receive any kind of services, including health care and education, they are required by law to register with the municipalities where they reside regardless of their legal status. Some services are provided by autonomous communities, including health care and education, while municipal governments provide social aid and housing subsidies, among other services. All such points of interaction help define the integration path immigrants can pursue. In 2005, the government implemented for the first time an integration program known as the Strategic Plan for Citizenship and Integration 2007–2010,[59] followed by a second plan implemented in 2010–2014; at this writing (2020) the Ministry of Labor, Migrations, and Social Security was working on a new plan. The first plan included the creation of a national fund to supplement the costs associated with the integration of newcomers (Asylum, Migration, and Integration Fund, AMIF).[60] The fund reached a peak of €200 million in 2008. However, as a result of the economic crisis, it fell to €100 million in 2009, €70 million in 2010, and €66.6 million in 2011, even as the number of immigrants as a percentage of the total population reached its highest point during those years. Operation of the fund was suspended in 2012. In December 2018, however, the new Spanish Socialist government announced the new Strategic Plan for Citizenship and Integration, allocating €318 million to fund its activities.[61]

Even with reduced resources, all regional and local entities that receive large numbers of immigrants currently have in place specific integration policies with different priorities. In places where a language other than Castilian Spanish predominates, such as Catalonia, the main priority has been to facilitate the cultural and linguistic immersion of newcomers. Here the goal is not only to facilitate their adaptation but also, though less explicitly, to diminish the challenge that newcomers may represent to local power arrangements. Evidently, the influx of residents more likely to speak Spanish than Catalan, as is overwhelmingly the case for Latin American immigrants, may imply the political marginalization of Catalan-speakers. Thus, in Catalonia there has been more pressure to require immigrants to "integrate" by forcing them to sign an "integration contract" that commits them to having at least a working knowledge of Spanish and Catalan, as well as an "adequate knowledge of Catalan civil life."[62]

Probably because of the political challenge newcomers represent to local power arrangements, anti-immigrant and xenophobic sentiment has been prominent only in specific places where immigrants concentrate. A prominent example was in the municipality of Vic, in Catalonia, which underwent a significant shift in its population structure during the first decade of this century after the arrival of large numbers of immigrants primarily from Morocco. In 2010, Vic authorities announced that they would not register any more newcomers unable to prove legal residence, thus denying them basic services such as health care and education.[63] Similar challenges and incidents have taken place in rural areas such as Almeria province and the Murcia region, where large numbers of temporary labor migrants concentrate.[64] In those regions there have been confrontations between migrants and the native population after incidents in which migrants were accused of committing crimes or other offenses. In more recent years, there have been some xenophobic incidents against foster homes that shelter unaccompanied minors, fueled by extreme right-wing politicians. In one occasion, in November 2019, during a televised electoral debate, the extreme right-wing national leader of the political party Vox, Santiago Abascal, associated unaccompanied minors with crimes in different localities of Spain, stating that "out of the 100 rapist bands in the country, 70% are foreigners."[65]

The Role of the European Union

Since Spain joined the EU, its responses to immigration have been very much determined by EU immigration prerogatives, even as Spain has occasionally defied these
prerogatives to address its own needs. Faced with immigration challenges from the
east and south, the EU's main priority has been to control its borders by imposing
restrictions on immigration; these restrictions have increased in recent years in the
context of the refugee crisis that impacted the continent especially from 2014 to 2016.
Spain has been crucial in this regard because of its strategic location as Europe's
southernmost country. Spain's preferred strategy from the very beginning has been
to avoid being cast in the role of "police officer of southern Europe," keeping the
Third World hordes at bay. Instead, it has attempted to persuade its fellow EU members to step up development assistance to the labor-exporting countries of North
Africa. However, Spain's capacity for persuasion has been dependent on its influence
vis-à-vis other countries, which in turn has depended on its economic situation and
its position in the changing geopolitical dynamics within the continent. As we will
see, in the beginning Spain had no choice but to follow the dictates of the European
Community, which were reflected in its first immigration law enacted under democratic rule. During the economic boom of the late 1990s and early 2000s, the country
acquired a greater capacity to decide its own policies, as seen in a 2005 regularization
that was implemented despite strong opposition from other EU member countries,
which then pushed to impose the requirement that EU member states consult each
other before implementing any massive regularization.[66]

By this time, the pendulum was swinging again, helped by a widely held perception that immigrant numbers had surpassed the point at which liberal accommoda-
tionist policies no longer made sense, and Spain was forced to step up its immigration
control efforts through the gradual imposition of visa requirements and more control
at the borders. An additional mechanism of immigration control has been Plan Africa (now in its third version, which started in March 2019 with no specific end point,
unlike the previous versions of this plan [2006–2008, 2009–2012]). At the discourse
level this plan identifies Spain's preferred strategy of providing development assistance to sending African countries. This new plan's argument is that demographic
growth in Africa, which in the next thirty years will bring the population of the continent to 2.4 billion people from the current level of 1.2 billion, will become a challenge for Europe, especially considering that the European population will dwindle
to below 600 million inhabitants over this same period.[67] Therefore, the Spanish government maintains, if Africans do not have access to dignified life conditions, it is
possible to foresee an increase in political conflict, fundamentalism, and irregular
migration, whereas if Africans are able to have access to sustainable opportunities,

Africa may become a space of accelerating economic growth, which may contribute to the strengthening of economic growth in Europe as well.[68] In practice, however, a significant part of the aid under Plan Africa has been devoted to projects intended to manage migratory flows rather than to generate development, as reflected in a thorough analysis of the destination of assistance funds in the plan's 2009–2012 version.[69] Interestingly, the new version of the plan does not allocate additional funds for investment in African countries beyond the resources that Spain has already devoted to the continent as part of its policies of international cooperation. Instead, it aims at introducing a new approach to Spanish policies toward Africa, commanding all sectors of government, the private sector, and society to contribute to the development of the continent, focusing efforts strategically in countries that could serve as engines of growth for the whole continent, such as Nigeria, South Africa, and Ethiopia, but also where Spain may have significant interests.[70] In this regard it expands the scope of Spanish policy toward sub-Saharan Africa, which has been highly focused on security concerns and less so on investment and economic opportunity.[71]

Despite this new policy approach, which considers the African continent from a developmental perspective in addition to a security one, Spain's policies of recent years have focused on strengthening its borders further in order to contain immigration pressures from that continent—an approach very much in alignment with the EU policy imperatives on immigration. For instance, this new developmental perspective toward Africa is coherent with a new European trend, led by Germany at the G20 Hamburg summit in 2017, to support investment projects in Africa, which is seen as a place of economic opportunity for European companies.

Nonetheless, it is also worth remarking that on occasion Spain has pursued an approach toward immigration that has defied the EU, in a context of great division within that institution about that subject. One example was when Spain "sought to give the world a lesson" by granting safe harbor to the migrants aboard the rescue ship *Aquarius* in June 2018.[72] This position, however, did not last long, as flows into Spain increased considerably thereafter, in the absence of an EU policy response to address immigration in a coherent and sustainable way. This situation has helped strengthen political parties such as Vox, which, though not originally anti-immigrant, has in recent years advocated for a crackdown on immigration.

Stages in Spanish Immigration

Considering the factors that have shaped Spanish immigration and integration policies, we can identify three distinct stages of immigration.[73]

In the first stage, which lasted roughly from 1985 to 2005, the guiding factors were to satisfy the immigration imperatives of the EU as well as the needs of the business sector. During the early 1980s, the main national goal was to modernize the country and to become part of the European Community. In this context, the administration of prime minister Felipe González produced in 1985 the first law on the rights and liberties of foreigners in Spain, which attempted to satisfy the security requirements of the European Community. Popularly known as the Ley de Extranjería (Law on Foreigners), it focused more on restrictions than on defending the rights of immigrants, even though it was implemented by the Labor Ministry rather than the Interior Ministry. This is interesting because over the years these two ministries have competed intensely over control of the immigration agenda.

The main goal of the Law on Foreigners was to control immigrant access to the labor market, which made stable residency very difficult. Newcomers could obtain residency permits only once they had a job offer, and they could only renew those permits after meeting numerous requirements.

Because of these limitations, many immigrants ended up with an irregular status. Furthermore, in contrast to the United States, where family reunification had been the guiding principle of immigration law since 1965, Spanish law made family reunification very difficult, a situation that was corrected only in 1996 when an amendment to the law was introduced that acknowledged immigration as a structural phenomenon and recognized that newcomers' rights included the right to reunify their families.

As compensation for the many limitations it imposed, the Law on Foreigners considered the possibility of regularization but, as noted previously, only under temporary conditions. Immigrants could attain regular status by applying on an individual basis or through their employers; they had three months to present the necessary documents. Because the foreign population in Spain was still relatively small, regularization was not significant in terms of numbers—only 38,131 benefited from it—and it did not require the involvement of major societal actors such as the unions and the business community.

Because of the harsh immigration policies introduced in 1985, many immigrants were left without the possibility of securing the documentation necessary to attain legal status. This situation left the door open for further regularizations, in 1991 and 1996, still under the government of Felipe González, although the 1996 regularization was designed but not implemented by the Socialists because the PP took control of the national government that year.

In 2000 and 2001, the PP was forced to implement yet two more amnesties because the flaws in the 1985 law, despite the 1996 reforms, were still making it very difficult for foreigners to acquire legal status. As the migratory flows into the country were becoming larger, however, so were the numbers of those affected by the regularizations.

This, in turn, magnified political and social tensions. Labor unions began to perceive these amnesties as counter to their interests—as a means of expanding the pool of legal workers and thus pushing wages down. In contrast, the business sector not only did not suffer real sanctions for hiring unauthorized immigrants but also was not forced to register workers in the social security system. Because the amnesties only required immigrants to have a job *offer* (and on many occasions even this was not necessary) rather than an employment *contract*, in many cases they had offers but maintained their irregular status in the labor market.

The tensions created by the amnesties were reflected in a conflict between the PP government of José María Aznar and the opposition when a new foreigner law was being negotiated. In January 1998, the opposition—including the Catalan nationalist party Convergencia I Unió (IU) and Grupo Mixto—introduced an initiative to create a new foreigner law, which was finally approved on January 12, 2000, with a broad political consensus; all political parties voted in favor, including the PSOE and the PP. However, the PP did so only because it did not have an absolute majority in Parliament; indeed, the new law was against its interests.

The Law on the Rights and Freedoms of Foreigners in Spain and Their Integration—technically Organic Law 4/2000—marked a drastic shift in Spanish immigration policy that would have repercussions in the future, especially in 2005. Until 2000, the main function of Spanish immigration law had been immigration control rather than promoting integration. The new law would grant more rights to immigrants regardless of their legal status, including the right to associate, to rally, and to unionize. (The right to unionize was a triumph for UGT and CCOO, the main Spanish unions.) It also recognized the immigration phenomenon as global and permanent and accordingly emphasized the importance of incorporating newcomers into the labor market. In addition, it introduced for the first time in Spanish legislation the notion of co-development—the idea that to control its migratory flows Spain had a responsibility to help in the economic and social development of sending areas. This policy was supported by local and regional governments, some of which were already implementing pioneering policies in this field, drawing on their previous support of cooperation in development of the Third World and inspired by the work of Sami Nair, a French political scientist and official of Algerian origin who first articulated the potential benefits of such cooperation.

After the March 2000 elections, the PP recovered its absolute majority in Parliament and just a few months later passed Organic Law 8/2000 to amend the previous legislation. This law was less generous than Organic Law 4/2000. Among other things, it granted the rights of association, rallying, and unionizing only to legal immigrants.[74] Nonetheless, it kept integration as a key to Spanish immigration policy.

Organic Law 8//2000 was the basis for what became known as Plan GRECO—a program for presenting immigration as a desirable phenomenon, with foreigners seen as active contributors to Spain's economic development. However, the PP argued that Spain should follow the principles of the EU, including the emphasis on security. On those grounds, the regulatory functions concerning immigration were transferred from the Labor Ministry, where they had been until passage of Organic Law 8/2000, to the Interior Ministry.

An important contribution of Plan GRECO was its recognition of the vital role of regional governments in the integration of newcomers; this recognition would become very important in government integration policies implemented thereafter. In addition, as part of a broad policy on immigration designed by the PP, Spain concluded guest worker agreements with sending countries. After the first such agreement was signed with Morocco in 1997, Spain concluded similar agreements with Romania and Bulgaria. These countries had not yet joined the EU and so sent many undocumented immigrants to Spain. A few years later, Spain also signed similar agreements with Senegal, Ecuador, Colombia, and Peru. An interesting aspect of these programs is that they provided workers access to Spanish citizenship after a certain period of time if they returned to their countries of origin when their work contracts ended. If a worker duly returned to his/her home country, he/she was allowed to come back to Spain the following year, subject to agreement with her Spanish employer.

The guest worker programs were important because they offered the business sector a pool of workers it could hire without running afoul of the law. This facilitated the support of the business sector in 2005 for an ambitious regularization system that would be in stark contrast to previous ones. It would be implemented by the incoming Socialist government after Zapatero's victory in the 2004 elections.

While previous regularizations had been carried out on an individual basis and, for the most part, without regard to the immigrant's job prospects, the 2005 regularization was clearly undertaken with labor market needs in mind. Only immigrants who had a work contract could be regularized, and the onus of regularization was not on immigrants but on employers, who became responsible for regularizing their workforce within a specified period of time to avoid sanctions. Immigrants benefited from this because they were directly integrated into the welfare system, becoming beneficiaries of it as well as net contributors to it. The 2005 regularization marked a second stage in Spain's immigration history, one characterized by a broad consensus among business and labor at a time when large migrant contingents were arriving in the country and immigration was being recast as necessary to address labor shortages and demographic needs. It benefited 577,923 people and was enacted with little public debate and in closed-door meetings between the government, the UGT and CCOO, and the CEOE.

Parallel to the 2005 regularization, two extraordinary amnesties were created to facilitate the regularization of those who did not qualify for legal status and those who arrived after the regularization was implemented. The first is known as social attachment, or *arraigo social*, whereby an immigrant could qualify for legal residency if he/she had been in the country for a period of at least three years (a fact that could be confirmed simply by registering on arrival with the municipality in which he/she was settling), did not have a criminal record in Spain or in his/her country of origin, had a work contract of at least one year, and could prove some social links to the community where he/she would be residing in Spain.

The second mechanism is known as labor attachment, or *arraigo laboral*, whereby an immigrant could attain legal permanent residency if he/she could prove that he/she had been in Spain for a period of at least three years, had a labor relation with an employer (proved by bringing the employer into court), and had no criminal record in Spain or in his/her country of origin.

The new amnesties were implemented in an atmosphere uncommonly favorable to immigration experimentation: after eight years in opposition, the Socialists had just assumed power, with high legitimacy and public support. Also, Spain's strong economic growth underpinned arguments for amnesty based on the demand for immigrant labor. Furthermore, Socialist governments were less interested in following the dictates of the EU than they had been in the past because Spain was by then sufficiently powerful and institutionalized, and had been accepted as a member of the EU, which had confidence in its independent political judgment.

The new Socialist president, José Luis Rodríguez Zapatero, had won the 2004 legislative elections against Mariano Rajoy, who had been selected by outgoing president José María Aznar to replace him as PP leader. The dramatic events immediately preceding the 2004 elections are worth recalling. Aznar blamed the separatist ETA (Euskadi Ta Askatusuna) for the terrorist attacks that took place in Madrid three days before the election, even though the ETA denied responsibility. These attacks killed 191 people—almost a third of them recent immigrants to Spain on their way to work—when a series of bombs exploded in trains approaching Madrid's Atocha Central Train Station. The public was angered by Aznar's hasty, unfounded, and false accusation of ETA and punished the PP by giving an unexpected victory to the PSOE. In fact, investigations already becoming public suggested that Muslim extremists from Morocco were the authors of the attacks. Thus, disgust with the PP government's cynical handling of the nation's trauma fed into preexisting public animosity over its support of the US war in Iraq, producing a sharp electoral repudiation.[75]

Zapatero responded by immediately setting out to govern from the left, in pointed contrast to the markedly right-wing Aznar administration.

The Iraq War, the Madrid bombings, and the politics of immigration came together as the Zapatero government quickly began to distance itself from xenophobic stances toward Muslims and immigrants. This position-taking was reinforced by the government's transferring of most immigration policy jurisdiction from Interior back to Labor and Social Affairs. In both rhetorical and practical terms, transferral reframed immigration as an economic and labor issue. As part of this process, Zapatero created a new secretariat in the Labor Ministry focused on immigration and emigration. Four years later, right after the legislative elections of March 2008 confirmed the results of 2004, a further emboldened Zapatero changed the name of the Ministry of Labor to the Ministry of Labor and Immigration, thus consolidating the perception of immigration as a matter of labor and welfare.

In line with these administrative changes, immigrant integration became a major goal of the Spanish state. Starting in 1994, during the González administration, the Council of Ministers approved the Plan for the Social Integration of Immigrants, the goal of which was to aid the settlement of newcomers. Although many of the plan's objectives were never fully realized, two major instruments that emerged from it not only survived but actually set the parameters of future integration policy. These were the Forum for the Integration of New Immigrants and the Permanent Observatory of Immigration to Spain. The first had the goal of promoting immigrants' civic participation and representation by allowing them to elect representatives to the forum, which plays an advisory role. The second produced research on immigration and integration for use in policymaking. Both were emulated at the subnational level in most Spanish autonomies and cities where large numbers of immigrants had settled, including those controlled by the PP, which, as noted earlier, in Plan GRECO also emphasized the important role of local governments in immigrant integration. In 2007, a year before the transformation of the Labor Ministry, the Zapatero administration presented the Strategic Plan on Citizenship and Integration, the goal of which was the promotion of social cohesion in the country through policies granting equal rights to newcomers. Working with this same logic, in July 2008 the Socialist government proposed to grant the right to vote to non-EU citizens in local elections, conditioned on the principle of reciprocity established by the Spanish constitution. By this time, however, the country was immersed in a major economic crisis, signaling a new stage in Spanish immigration history.

This third stage, which started in 2008, has been characterized by greater alignment with the restrictive policies of the EU, including those that emphasize return migration and, at the same time, immigrant integration. Also in 2008, the Zapatero government restricted access to family reunification by excluding parents and in-laws of naturalized immigrants and immigrants with permanent residence on the grounds that they would burden the welfare system as likely dependents of productive laborers. The administration also increased inspections of employment sites and offered incentives for legal residents without employment to return to their countries of origin.[76] These incentives included initially paying them right away 40 percent of their unemployment benefits and 60 percent on their return to their home countries, in exchange for forfeiting residence rights and promising not to return to Spain for at least three years. This program had little success, but migrants nonetheless started to leave the country as the economic crisis deepened, and there was a drop in incoming flows. Together, these phenomena reduced the size of the immigrant population as a share of the total population to below its peak of 2012—a trend that has continued until today, even as particular events, such as the welcoming of the *Aquarius,* had a temporary effect of increasing the flows into Spain.

Since immigration policy has been aligned with labor market needs, the government has also followed a policy of banning direct recruitment of foreign workers in the countries of origin. The result has been a freeze on new immigration from non-EU countries for the most part. On the integration front, however, the government introduced a new process to regularize newcomers who were settling in the country, even as many others were joining the ranks of the undocumented as they lost their jobs and with them the work permits allowing them to be in the country legally. This new process, called *arraigo familiar* (family attachment), had the goal of regularizing the parents of Spanish-born minor children to avoid them being effectively orphaned by their parents' deportation. Women able to prove domestic abuse were also allowed to obtain residence on their own account.

These measures, together with the *arraigo laboral* and the *arraigo social* introduced earlier, helped address the situation of many immigrants who had fallen into illegality during the economic crisis. The ascension of Mariano Rajoy to the post of prime minister in 2011, however, changed the immigration power structure once again. Just a month after Rajoy took office, his government announced that it would tighten immigration law by allowing entrance only to those immigrants who had obtained a work contract and deporting all those who had lost their jobs. In addition, the Rajoy government eliminated the social attachment mechanism that was widely used to regularize newcomers and which had helped to keep the numbers of irregular migrants down since its implementation.[77] At the same time, its administration took away the right for undocumented immigrants to have access to public health services except emergency rooms. These measures were repealed when Sánchez took office in 2018, though his government is far from proactively facilitating the reception and integration of newcomers (as was the case with the Zapatero administration) in a context in which the EU has moved to the right in the immigration arena. This is reflected in the fact that in 2020 his government chose not to embrace a regularization proposed by second deputy prime minister Pablo Iglesias in the parliament.[78] At the same time, the Sánchez government announced a reform of the asylum system.[79] The intention of this reform was to deal with deficiencies related to asylum resolutions and to the living conditions of asylum seekers in Spain while they wait for the resolution of their cases.[80] So far this reform has not been implemented.

The Emigration Trend

In 2011 a new trend emerged in Spain: the emigration of its young and educated. With youth unemployment rates nearing 50 percent, Spain saw emigration levels increase considerably even if they did not reach the levels of the past.[81] At the end of 2018 2,545,729 Spaniards lived abroad, though it is important to point out that not all of them were emigrants, as this number also includes those who were not born in Spain but still had Spanish citizenship.[82] While this emigration trend seemed to be waning during 2019 and 2020, it has represented a significant loss of human capital for this country at a time when the restructuring of its economy into one that is more diversified and dependent on technological advances through research and development is crucial to guarantee sustainable economic growth. Furthermore, we do not know yet if emigration will resume in the aftermath of the COVID-19 pandemic and the economic downturn it produced in the country. While some of those who left may have returned or may return, Spain still faces the challenge of generating enough job opportunities for its young and educated population to avoid the prospects of future emigration trends that will certainly imply the depletion of a very valuable segment of the population in the context of a low fertility rate and stalled immigration flows.

International Migration Dilemmas for Spain: Similar Concerns, Less Room for Action

By the end of 2020, after having navigated the transformation from an emigration country to an immigration country, Spain still faces some of the same dilemmas and concerns it had a few decades ago with respect to international migration, but this time in a considerably more complex domestic and international scenario. As was the case a few decades ago, today Spain again needs to deal with the prospect of population decline. It also needs to expand its labor supply, grow the size of its domestic market, and guarantee the feasibility of its welfare system by bringing in new contributors, all important factors in its current developmental phase. These needs point toward the necessity of attracting new and sustained international migration flows.

However, it also faces the need to maintain a balanced national and cultural composition under its intercultural premise, as well as to address security concerns. In this regards there are two questions still without a clear answer: (1) how many immigrants Spain needs to receive to address its demographic and economic needs without the inflow being too many, and (2) what groups, if any, should be favored, in order to maintain prevailing notions of nationhood. The answers to these questions are not easy. If Spain wants to address its demographic imbalances, for example, it may have to accept many new immigrants. This, however implies a challenge to its current and future leaders because few of them would be willing to pay the political price of justifying a new increase in the size of the immigrant population as a share of the total population, even though Spaniards do not have generally a negative perspective on immigration overall compared to other EU countries. With respect to what groups to favor, the answer might not be straightforward either. During the 1990s and the early years of this century, when it received steady migratory flows, Spain dealt with this problem by maintaining a dual system of access to membership in the polity through old and new citizenship policies that incorporated a prevailing notion of nationhood derived from its imperial past, thus favoring immigrants from former Spanish colonies, and especially from Latin America, rather than from other places of the world (outside of the EU). This situation allowed the country to build a "nation by design" to a certain extent. However, this time around, trying to attract new immigration from Latin America might not be as feasible, since many countries that previously had been steady sources of newcomers are themselves facing the prospect of slow population growth and even population shrinkage, as family sizes are increasingly smaller and birth rates decreasing.[83] While some Latin American countries may become a more relevant immigrant source, as is the case of Venezuela due to its economic crisis or Colombia, Honduras, Nicaragua, Peru, and El Salvador via people seeking international protection, it is also not clear that Spain will be able to attract many more migrants from that region.[84] In this regard, immigration might have to come from other parts of the world, possibly from Africa—a situation that may pose new political challenges, as up until now Spain has shown a preference for immigrants from countries with linguistic, religious, and cultural similarities.

In addition to those factors, Spain faces today complex domestic and international challenges that may make it difficult to take a more proactive role in attracting new migratory flows. Domestically, it still has to address the need to create new and sustainable jobs for those who lost their employment during the economic recession and for its young population entering the labor market, so that new immigration can be justified—even though it still might be true that immigrants tend to occupy positions in the labor market that are not generally filled by the native population. This will certainly become even more challenging in the next few years considering the economic downturn that Spain confronted as a result of the policies adopted by the government to address the effects of the COVID-19 pandemic, which increased the number of unemployed and underemployed in the country.[85] It also will have to find some workable solutions to its current nationalist conflict, which has been re-awakened in recent years, before facilitating the entrance of immigrants that may help deepen its nationalistic cleavage. Internationally, Spain faces the challenge that the EU has moved in recent years further to the right in the immigration arena, a fact that may make it hard for this country to justify more proactive steps to increase current immigration levels.

Nevertheless, Spain does not face major challenges like those encountered in other countries, such as Italy or Greece, that also need new immigration to address their population imbalances. The political environments in Italy and Greece make it harder for those governments to be more proactive in attracting new flows of immigrants. In contrast to those countries, Spain has a population that has more favorable views toward immigration overall. Also, the country does not seem to have a strong right-wing anti-immigrant party that would seek to mobilize the population against immigrants the way anti-immigrant parties in other European countries do, although this is probably very much conditioned on the type of immigrant groups that Spain has been receiving in recent years. Where most migrants come from Africa or from Muslim countries, for example, reactions might be different. It is also true that Vox, a political party that does have an anti-immigrant view, has gained more importance in recent years in Spain. But Vox's success seems to be less the direct result of its anti-immigrant positions beyond specific contexts than the product of its neo-nationalistic position in view of the current conflict between the autonomous community of Catalonia and the central government. In this regard, Spain may have more room to maneuver in addressing its immigration dilemmas in the near future. What road it will pursue is still an open question, but clearly at some point it will have to deal with its demographic imbalances by taking more proactive views with respect to international migration if it does not want to compromise its prospects for economic growth in the medium and long terms, and, in fact, wishes to enhance such prospects.

Notes

1. Dr. Miryam Hazán is an employee of the InterAmerican Commission for Human Rights and the Organization for American States, and the perspectives presented in these

chapters do not necessarily represent the views of the General Secretariat of the OAS, the OAS, or the IACHR as institutions. They are her personal views.

2. The term "foreign-registered" or "foreign nationals" excludes those who have naturalized but includes children born to immigrants who retain their parents' nationality. Hein de Haas, Stephen Castles, and Mark J. Miller, *The Age of Migration*, 6th ed. (New York: Guilford Press, 2020), xv. The category "foreign-born" or "overseas-born" includes persons who have become naturalized but would exclude children born to immigrants in the receiving country (second generation) if they are citizens of the receiving country. In this latter case, in 2020 the total foreign-born population was 7,231,195, 15.2 percent of the total population (Instituto Nacional de Estadística).

3. Instituto Nacional de Estadística, "Cifras de población (CP) a 1 de enero de 2020; estadística de migraciones (EM), Año 2019: datos provisionales," press release, June 8, 2020, https://www.ine.es/prensa/cp_e2020_p.pdf.

4. This is the lowest level since 2008. EPA, Active Population Survey.

5. After several years of severe drops in GDP (2019–2013, except 2010, which had a 0.01 percent increase), the situation stabilized in 2014 (with a 1.4 percent increase), and the GDP increased again in 2015 (3.6 percent), 2016 (3.2 percent), 2017 (3.0 percent), and 2018 (2.6 percent). Instituto Nacional de Estadística, "Producto interior bruto (PIB), crecimiento en volumen (revisión estadística 2019)," https://www.ine.es/prensa/pib_tabla_cne.htm.

6. The 2019 data disaggregated the information between Spanish women (1.17 children per woman) and foreign women (1.59 children per woman). They are very similar, as foreigners' fertility rates quickly converge with those of natives. Instituto Nacional de Estadística, "Birth-Rate Indicators: National Results: Global Fertility Rate by Nationality (Spanish/Foreign) of the Mother," https://www.ine.es/jaxiT3/Tabla.htm?t=1409&L=1.

7. In 2009 there were estimates of nearly 2 million positions in the labor market that would possibly be left vacant by retiring Spaniards and needed to be filled by immigrants, since it was not likely that Spanish entrants into the labor market would be sufficient or willing. While this scenario might have changed somewhat because of the recession Spain confronted in recent years, the demographic challenges in the country suggest that immigrant low-skilled labor will still be needed to make up for those who retire. See Florentino Felgueroso and Pablo Vázquez, "Immigración y crisis: Aciertos, desaciertos y políticas complementarias," in *La crisis de la economía española: Lecciones y propuestas* (Madrid: Sociedad Abierta & FEDEA, 2009), http://www.crisis09.es/ebook/inmigracion-y-crisis.html.

8. E. De Benito, "Sánchez devolverá la sanidad a los inmigrantes irregulares," *El País*, June 16, 2018, https://elpais.com/politica/2018/06/15/actualidad/1529059447_733412.html. They passed the Real Decreto–Ley 7/2018, July 27, on universal access to the health system.

9. Founded in December 2013, Vox went to the 2014 European Parliament elections, taking 245,000 votes. In the following elections in Andalusia in 2015 the party won 0.45 percent of the votes (18,017). In comparison, in December 2018 it got 395,978 votes, which gave it representation and input in the regional government of Andalusia. Between 2015 and 2018 Vox had twenty-two councilors and two mayors in thirteen municipalities. In the general election of December 2015 Vox gained 0.23 percent of the votes (57,733), and in the June 2016 it got 0.2 per cent (46,781). "Vox: ¿Cuándo se fundó, cuáles han sido sus resultados en

las elecciones, cuál es su programa?," Europa Press, December 5, 2018, https://www.europress.es/nacional/noticia-vox-cuando-fundo-cuales-sido-resultados-elecciones-cual-programa-20181205144555.html. In the general election of April 2019, Vox entered the Chamber of Deputies for the first time, with twenty-four members, and it ranks as the fifth-mostpowerful force, with more than 2.6 million votes. Ana Martín Plaza, "Elecciones generales 2019: Vox irrumpe en el Congreso con 24 diputados y se sitúa como quinta fuerza con más de 2,6 millones de votos," RTVE, April 29, 2019, http://www.rtve.es/noticias/20190429/elecciones-resultados-vox/1929067.shtml. In the 2017 Catalonian elections, Vox obtained 243,640 votes and two seats in the Catalonian parliament for the first time in its short existence.

10. See J. Dennison and A. Geddes, "A Rising Tide? The Salience of Immigration and the Rise of Anti-Immigration Political Parties in Western Europe," *Political Quarterly* 90, no. 1 (2019): 112.

11. Dennison and Geddes, "A Rising Tide?," 112.

12. It is also worth noticing that arrivals of irregular vessels through the Canary Islands brought 59,000 people during 2018, 26,168 in 2019, and 41,000 in 2020, even in the context of the COVID-19 pandemic. See Joaquín Arango et al., "Introducción: inmigración y movilidad humana en tiempos de coronavirus," *Anuario CIDOB de la Inmigración*, 2020, 22. The official report on 2020 irregular immigration shows that nearly all the irregular arrivals come by sea (40,106 of 41,861).

13. The scope to design their own immigration policy is very limited. See L. Abellán, "With No EU Policy Forthcoming, Spain Gets Tougher on Immigration," *El País*, January 28, 2019, https://clpais.com/clpais/2019/01/28/incnglish/1548672833_325170.html.

14. The minister of immigration said publicly in 2002 that multiculturalism is "unacceptable" for Spain. At most, he argued, Spain might become a "multi-ethnic society." Quoted in Amnesty International, "Spain: Crisis of Identity," www.amnesty.org, April 16, 2002, 6.

15. See Tomás Bárbulo and Josep Garriga, "Rajoy quiere obligar a los inmigrantes a firmar 'un contrato de integración,'" *El País*, February 7, 2008, http://elpais.com/diario/2008/02/07/espana/1202338806_850215.html.

16. See Alicia Alted, ed., *De la España que emigra a la España que acoge* [catalog for the exhibition "Madrid, Círculo de Bellas Artes"] (Madrid: Fundación F. Largo Caballero y Obra Social Caja Duero, 2006), 33.

17. Alted, *De la España que emigra*, 33.

18. See Gobierno de España, Ministerio de Educación, Cultura y Deporte, "Cúales fueron las causas de la emigración," auce.pntic.mec.es/jotero/Emigra3/causas.htm.

19. Until early 1992, the immigration office in the Ministry of Labor was anachronistically called the Spanish Institute of Emigration. For the number of emigrants during that period, see Valeriano Gómez, "Crisis, inmigración y política de empleo: Una visión de conjunto," in *Inmigración y crisis económica, impactos y perspectivas de futuro*, edited by Eliseo Aja, Joaquín Arango, and Josep Oliver Alonso (Barcelona: CIDOB, Diputació Barcelona, Fundación Acsar, Centro de Estuidos Andaluces & Unicaja, 2010), 112.

20. See Secretaria de Estado de Inmigración y Emigración, "II Plan Estratégico de Ciudadanía e Integración," 2014, 26–27.

21. See Joaquín Arango, "Después del gran boom: La inmigración en la bisagra del cambio," in *La inmigración en tiempos de crisis: Anuario de la inmigración en España*, edited by Eliseo Aja, Joaquín Arango, and Josep Oliver Alonso (Barcelona: Fundación CIDOB & Diputació Barcelona, 2009), 54.

22. During 2008, immigration flows were not directly affected by the economic crisis, as immigrants still retained their jobs at even higher rates than the native population. By mid-2009, however, these flows had finally slowed down as unemployment among the immigrant population increased. See Eliseo Aja, Joaquín Arango, and Josep Oliver Alonso, "Bajo el influjo de la crisis," in *La inmigración en tiempos de crisis: Anuario de la inmigración en España*, edited by Eliseo Aja, Joaquín Arango, and Josep Oliver Alonso (Barcelona: Fundación CIDOB & Diputació Barcelona, 2009), 11.

23. These numbers come from the Instituto Nacional de Estadística, which totals all of the immigrants registered by Spanish local governments. It includes the unauthorized population, since to receive health and education services immigrants have to register with local authorities regardless of their status. It is important to point out, however, that there can be unauthorized migrants who have not registered, which may add to the size of the total immigrant population. The number used by the INE differs from the number used by the Labor Minister for Immigration and Emigration, which counts only legal immigration.

24. The "communitarian regime," or *régimen comunitario*, is the legal framework that regulates the entrance of citizens from EU countries and those from countries in the European Free Trade Association (EFTA). It grants entrance to family members of EU citizens and family members of Spanish citizens regardless of their nationality. The legal framework that oversees entrance of all other nationalities is the "general regime," or *régimen general*.

25. Romanian immigrants, and especially the Roma, also known as Gypsies, present a more complex situation, however, since they do shape many perceptions about immigration and have been a major concern of the Spanish state both before and after they became communitarian immigrants. The complexity of their case deserves a more profound analysis. For this reason, it is not considered here.

26. Ministry of Interior, "Immigración irregular: informe quincenal," December 2018, http://www.interior.gob.es/documents/10180/9654434/24_informe_quincenal_acumu lado_01-01_al_31-12-2018.pdf/d1621a2a-0684-4aae-a9c5-a086e969480f.

27. As of November 28, 2018, visas were required for citizens of 102 countries. "Lista de terceros países cuyos nacionales están sometidos a la obligación de visado para cruzar las fronteras exteriores y de aquellos cuyos nacionales están exentos de dicha obligación," Ministry of Foreign Affairs, http://www.exteriores.gob.es/Portal/es/ServiciosAlCiudadano/InformacionParaExtranjeros/Documents/listapaisesvisado.pdf.

28. See Ministry of Interior, "Immigración irregular: informe quincenal," 2021, http://www.interior.gob.es/documents/10180/11389243/Informe+Quincenal+sobre+Inmigraci%C3%B3n+Irregular+-+Datos+acumulados+desde+el+1+de+enero+al+31+de+diciembre+de+2020.pdf/e5553964-675a-40d7-9361-5dbf4dfd3524. An increase in arrivals to the Canary Islands was perceived as a major issue during the last quarter of 2020. There was talk of a new crisis similar to 2006, "crisis de los cayucos," while the United Nations High Commissioner

for Refugees and the International Organization for Migration got involved in the management of the situation. The Arguineguín dock, where many immigrants were arriving, was identified as a particular "hot spot" by authorities in October and November of that year. "La llegada de migrantes a Canarias por mar crece un 1.019% en lo que va de año y supera al resto de España," RTVE, November 17, 2020, https://www.rtve.es/noticias/20201117/crisis-migratoria-canarias-datos/2056893.shtml.

29. http://www.rtve.es/noticias/20180617/llegan-puerto-valencia-migrantes-rescatados-aquarius/1751740.shtml; https://elpais.com/politica/2018/08/14/actualidad/1534250252_962443.html; https://www.europapress.es/epsocial/migracion/noticia-donde-estan-migrantes-aquarius-espana-pacto-ue-acoger-20181015175652.html; https://www.elmundo.es/espana/2018/08/14/5b72c2e7268e3ee5048b4644.html.

30. https://elpais.com/politica/2018/08/23/actualidad/1535027726_131749.html; https://es.euronews.com/2018/09/23/el-aquarius-exige-a-los-gobiernos-europeos-que-se-le-permita-seguir-su-mision; https://es.euronews.com/2018/09/25/aquarius-sin-pabellon-pide-atracar-en-francia; https://www.europapress.es/epsocial/migracion/noticia-paises-ue-no-tienen-obligacion-legal-acoger-aquarius-20180814191032.html; http://euroefe.euractiv.es/1311_actualidad/5440832_discrepancias-en-la-ue-con-la-crisis-del-aquarius.html.

31. https://www.eldiario.es/desalambre/Gobierno-politica-Aquarius-Libia-rescatados_0_840266232.html; https://elpais.com/politica/2018/12/01/actualidad/1543667213_477165.html.

32. https://www.eldiario.es/desalambre/Gobierno-aguas-Proactiva-Open-Arms_0_849015423.html; https://www.lasexta.com/noticias/sociedad/barco-open-arms-regresa-barcelona-prepararse-proxima-mision-rescate-mediterraneo_201812295c277c3f0cf24fd75739d563.html.

33. Gómez, "Crisis, inmigración y política de empleo," CIDOB, March, 2011, page 109. https://www.cidob.org/es/articulos/anuario_cidob_de_la_inmigracion/2010/crisis_inmigracion_y_politica_de_empleo_una_vision_de_conjunto

34. Although there are various explanations for the Spanish real estate boom, experts now agree on its fundamental reliance on expansionary monetary policy. See Juan Ramón Rallo, "Los precios de la vivienda y la burbuja inmobiliairia en España," Observatorio de Coyuntura Económica, Instituto Juan de Mariana, Madrid, 2008, http://www.juandemariana.org/pdf/080304burbuja.pdf.

35. As Valeriano Gómez demonstrates, of the five largest European economies (Germany, France, Spain, Italy, and the United Kingdom), Spain had become the largest employer in the construction industry by 2007. This situation was abnormal given that, being the smallest economy of the five, it should have been the one that employed the fewest workers. For this very reason, 50 percent of job losses during the economic crisis that officially began in January 2008 have been in this sector. See Gómez, "Crisis, inmigración y política de empleo," 109–110.

36. See Ruth Ferrero Turión, "Migration and Migrants in Spain: After the Bust," in *Migration and Immigration Two Years After the Financial Collapse: Where Do We Stand?*, edited by Demetrios Papademetriou, Madeleaine Sumption, and Aaron Terrazas (Washington, DC: Migration Policy Institute and BBC World Service, 2011), 105.

37. A recent and comprehensive study assesses that the crisis years (2008–2013) particularly affected migrants in terms of "unemployment and family adjustment" and that during the recovery years (2014–2018) there has been a wage devaluation and a slow awakening of immigrant employment. "In fact, in relative terms, immigrant employment grew above the native one, and its unemployment rate decreased more than the native one." See Juan Iglesias, Antonio Rúa, and Alberto Ares, *Un arraigo sobre el alambre: La integración social de la población de origen inmigrante en España* (Madrid: FOESSA, 2020), 129.

38. A. González Ferrer, "La nueva emigración Española. Lo que sabemos y lo que no," Fundación Alternativas, 2013.

39. Trading Economics, "Spain Population," https://tradingeconomics.com/spain/population.

40. Instituto Nacional de Estadística, "España en cifras 2020," 2020, https://www.ine.es/ss/Satellite?L=es_ES&c=INEPublicacion_C&cid=1259924856416&p=12547 35110672&pagename=ProductosYServicios%2FPYSLayout&param1=PYSDetalleGratuitas.

41. Instituto Nacional de Estadística.

42. Instituto Nacional de Estadística.

43. In June 2019, the Spanish government had to use debt to finance the summer double payroll of retired people (there are two double payrolls in June and December), with the Reserve Fund for Pensions almost exhausted. Susana Alcelay, "El Gobierno tira de crédito para pagar más de 19.200 millones en pensiones," ABC, June 12, 2019, https://www.abc.es/econo mia/abci-gobierno-tira-credito-para-pagar-mas-19200-millones-pensiones-201906112149 _noticia.html.

44. Interestingly, the current institution in charge of newcomer integration, the State Secretary of Immigration and Emigration, in the Ministry of Labor and Immigration, evolved from the former Spanish Institute of Emigration. This secretariat has assumed a very active role in newcomer integration in the same way that the Institute of Emigration once assumed an active role in regulating emigration and protecting emigrants.

45. See Centro de Investigaciones Sociológicas, "Distribuciones marginales, actitudes hacia la inmigración (IV)," Estudio 2.846, September–October 2010, http://www.cis.es/cis/export/ sites/default/Archivos/Marginales/2840_2859/2846/Es2846.pdf. The center has conducted polls over the years that show the prevalence of similar perceptions.

46. *Pateras* are the boats in which immigrants from Africa cross the Mediterranean into Spain; they are generally associated with the suffering that the immigration experience entails.

47. Dennison and Geddes, "A Rising Tide?," 112.

48. Dennison and Geddes, "A Rising Tide?," 112.

49. Law 2/2015, of June 24, 2015. However, the law has been criticized for an excess of bureaucracy and for the way it obliges requesters to travel to Spain to sign in front of a Spanish notary an "Act of Notoriety" that could easily be done at the Spanish consulates.

50. This, for example, was expressed in interviews with leaders of immigrant organizations from Morocco in 2007.

51. Centro de Investigaciones Sociológicas, "Distribuciones marginales," 10.

52. Centro de Investigaciones Sociológicas, "Distribuciones marginales," 10.

53. https://elpais.com/cultura/2018/10/10/television/1539170508_189986.html.

54. One of the most publicized cases was that of a Muslim student forbidden to attend school wearing a veil. See "El Ayuntamiento contra el velo de Najwa," ABC.es, April 18, 2010, http://www.abc.es/20100418/madrid-madrid/ayuntamiento-contra-velo-najwa-20100418 .html.

55. See Amnesty International, "España: Entre la desgana y la invisibilidad, políticas del estado español en la lucha contra el racismo," April 10, 2008, http://www.es.amnesty.org/ uploads/media/Datos_y_Cifras_Racismo_Espana.pdf. The 2018 RAXEN report states that the number of racist incidents and assaults is around 4,000.

56. Cristina Manzanedo and Raúl Gonzáez Fabre, "Impacto de la crisis económica sobre los inmigrantes irregulares en España," contribución de Pueblos Unidos a PICUM como parte del input para un reporte del Committee on Migration, Refugees and Population de la Asamblea Parlamentaria del Consejo de Europa.

57. This number of foreigners in an irregular situation comes from the difference between the 2,938,720 foreigners from countries without free movement who were registered in Spanish municipal records (*Padrón*) and the 2,113,120 who present labor documentation. Ana Luisa Pombo, "¿Cuántos inmigrantes irregulares hay realmente en España?," COPE, October 29, 2018, https://www.cope.es/actualidad/espana/noticias/ gobierno-dice-que-sabe-cadena-cope-hace-numeros-20181029_283978.

58. This study estimated that irregular migrants could represent 12.5 percent of the total number of immigrants. Ismael Gálvez Iniesta, "The Size, Socio-economic Composition and Fiscal Implications of the Irregular Immigration in Spain," UC3M working paper, 2000.

59. See http://extranjeros.mitramiss.gob.es/es/Programas_Integracion/index.html.

60. "El gobierno dota al Fondo de Integración de Inmigrantes con 66 millones de euros, un mínimo histórico," *El Día*, April 29, 2011, http://www.eldia.es/2011-03-11/sociedad/23-Go bierno-dota-Fondo-Integracion-Inmigrantes-millones-euros-minimo-historico.htm.

61. https://www.europapress.es/epsocial/migracion/noticia-gobierno-destinara-318-mil lones-euros-migrantes-refugiados-2018-millones-mas-2017-20180403173352.html.

62. "Cataluña: Partido de derecha exige el contrato de integración a los inmigrantes," *LibreRed*, April 26, 2011, http://www.librered.net/?p=6760.

63. To understand the demographic transformations that Vic has undergone as a result of immigration, see Lucía González Rodríguez, "El impacto sociodemográfico de la inmigración extranjera en Vic," *Cuadernos Geográficos* 36, no. 1 (2005): 451–463, http://www.ugr .es/~cuadgeo/docs/articulos/036/036-027.pdf.

64. Some of the first and most relevant problems took place in El Egido back in 2000. Some recent publications about those events include: https://www.publico.es/sociedad/ despues-ocho-20-anos-del.html;

https://www.publico.es/sociedad/racismo-veinte-anos-despues-ataque-xenofobo-ejido -causas-persisten.html;

https://es.euronews.com/2018/12/03/la-paradoja-de-el-ejido-vox-se-convierte-en -primera-fuerza-en-un-municipio-con-un-30-de-mi.

65. Incidents against shelters for unaccompanied minors in 2019 occurred in Hortaleza (Madrid), Canet de Mar, Castelldefels, Masnou (Catalonia), and Alhama de Murcia. The

UN Committee on the Rights of the Child and UNICE reproached Spain. Enes Bayrakli and Farid Hafez, eds., *European Islamophobia Report 2019* (Ankara: SETA/Foundation for Political, Economic and Social Research, 2020), 744–746.

66. See "UE analiza sistema para informar sobre regularización," *El Universo*, February 25, 2005, http://www.eluniverso.com/2005/02/21/0001/626/4C96D296076D4474A6C 6FAAAFD827F50.html.

67. "UE analiza sistema para informar sobre regularización."

68. "UE analiza sistema para informar sobre regularización."

69. See Nerea Azkona, *Políticas de control migratorio y de cooperación al desarollo entre España y Africa Occidental durante la ejecución del primer Plan Africa* (Bilbao: Alboan & Entreculturas, 2011), http://www.entreculturas.org/files/documentos/estudios_e_informes/In formeControlMigratorioyAOD_2011.pdf?download.

70. https://www.europapress.es/nacional/noticia-gobierno-aprueba-plan-africa-de fiende-continente-oportunidad-no-amenaza-20190301172758.html.

71. Marín Egoscozbal Ainhoa, "Africa Subsahariana en 2019: desafíos para la Política Exterior Española," Real Instituto Elcano, January 31, 2019.

72. Lucía Abellán, "With No EU Policy Forthcoming, Spain Gets Tougher on Immigration," *El País in English*, January 28, 2019.

73. This section is partly based on Miryam Hazán, "Políticas de inmigración y regularización en los Estados Unidos y España: Una perspectiva comparada," in *Estudios sobre la integración de los inmigrantes*, edited by Enrique Alvarez Conde and Ana M. Salazar de la Guerra, 107–136 (Madrid: URJC & Consejería de Inmigración y Cooperación, Comunidad de Madrid, 2010).

74. In 2007, the Constitutional Court declared that the limits introduced by Organic Law 8/2000 on the rights of association, rallying, and unionizing were unconstitutional.

75. According to polls, more than 95 percent of the Spanish population was against Spain's involvement in the war. Even most right-wingers were against the official policy of the Spanish government on Iraq.

76. Tomás Bárbulo, "El cambiazo en inmigración," *El País*, July 20, 2008, http://elpais. com/diario/2008/07/20/espana/1216504803_850215.html.

77. "El gobierno de Rajoy exigirá contrato a los inmigrantes," *Periodista Latino*, January 29, 2012.

78. https://elpais.com/espana/2020-06-26/unidas-podemos-pide-al-gobierno-la-regular izacion-urgente-de-todos-los-inmigrantes.html;

https://www.elsaltodiario.com/migracion/resumen-2020-migracion-estado-espanol;

https://www.publico.es/sociedad/regularizacion-migrantes-covid-19-espana-no-regular izar-migrantes-italia-portugal.html.

79. Joaquín Arango, Blanca Garcés, Ramón Mahía, and David Moya, "Introducción: inmigración y movilidad humana en tiempos del coronavirus," *Anuario CIDOB de la Inmigración 2020* (Barcelona: CIDOB, 2021), 25, DOI: doi.org/10.24241/AnuarioCIDOBInmi.2020.14.

80. For a comprenhensive analysis of its deficiencies, see J. Iglesias, G. Urrutia Asua, and J. Buades Fuster, "¿Acoger sin integrar? El sistema de asilo y las condiciones de integración de personas solicitantes y beneficiarias de protección internacional en España," Asociación Claver, 2018.

81. "Los jóvenes emigran de España en busca de empleo," *La Voz de Rusia*, February 6, 2012, http://spanish.ruvr.ru/2012/02/06/65432018.html.

82. See Instituto Nacional de Estadística, "Estadística del Padrón de Españoles Residentes en el Extranjero (PERE) a 1 de enero de 2018," March 20, 2018, https://www.ine.es/prensa/pere_2018.pdf.

83. Stef W. Kight, "Where Populations Are Booming and Shrinking," Axios, May 26, 2019.

84. The 2019 data shows that the highest number of applications for international protection came from Venezuela, with 40,886 applications, followed by Central American countries: Honduras (6,803), Nicaragua (5,935) and El Salvador (4,784). The numbers of Syrians and Ukrainians are between 2,000 and 2,500 applications. In 2020 data, two groups stand out in terms of the number of applications: 28,365 applications for protection were made by Venezuelans and 27,576 by Colombians. These groups are followed by Hondurans (5,536), Peruvians (5,162) and Nicaraguans (3,750). See Ministerio del Interior, "Asilo en Cifras 2019," 2020,

85. Spain lost 622,600 jobs and the unemployment rate rose to 16.13 percent in 2020, the first year of the coronavirus pandemic. However, during the fourth quarter of 2020, a slow recovery began, and the number of those employed increased by 167,400. Manuel V. Gómez, "España destruyó 622.600 empleos y la tasa de paro aumentó hasta el 16,13% en el año de la pandemia de coronavirus," *El País*, January 28, 2021, https://elpais.com/economia/2021-01-28/espana-destruyo-622600-empleos-y-la-tasa-de-paro-aumento-hasta-el-1613-en-el-ano-de-la-pandemia-de-coronavirus.html.

COMMENTARY

Spain and the Liberal Paradox

Blanca Garcés-Mascareñas

How can countries be simultaneously open and closed to immigration? As the question is posed by Hazán and Bermejo's chapter, how did Spain resolve the dilemma between the imperative to expand its immigrant population and the imperative to restrict immigration? In this commentary I will give an answer to this question and argue that what in the European context was seen as a clear policy gap (with non-functioning entry policies and periodic regularization programs) should be seen as a policy in itself, as a way to reconcile in practice these contradictory demands.

If we look at numbers, Spain seems to have been rather open to immigration during the 2000s. As Hazán and Bermejo's chapter shows, the percentage of registered foreigners rose from 2 percent in 2000 to 12 percent in 2012. At first sight, this seems to suggest that in the Spanish case demands for openness were given priority over demands for closure. However, when we look at Spanish immigration policies in more detail, including different policy measures as well as policy implementation and outcomes, two nuances should be introduced. First, entry policies worked in a rather restrictive way. In fact, it was regularization programs that turned Spain into a rather open immigration country. Second, while access to "papers" granting temporary status was relatively easy, permanent residence permits have been made dependent on integration into the labor market during the first five years. This is in fact how demands for closure were responded to as well.

Openness

Throughout the 1990s and particularly from 2000 to 2007, Spain had an insatiable hunger for immigrant workers. As explained by Hazán and Bermejo, this had to do with changes in the Spanish labor market and the coexistence of sectors of high and low productivity. Though Spanish economic growth depended on migrant labor, entry policies were rather restrictive: the first law on foreigners (1985) was promulgated to block entry to immigrants en route to western European countries via Spain and, even more important, entry policies were restrictive in actual practice, with long and very complex procedures. These restrictions did not mean, however, that low numbers of immigrants were entering Spain. Most arrived with a tourist visa, found work, and subsequently legalized their situation. This mismatch between legality and reality—between a particularly restrictive policy and a reality notable for the large numbers of people entering the country—made it possible to comply with contradictory demands: on the one hand, demands for closure by the EU but also by the trade unions, who did not look kindly on the entry of new workers into a job market characterized by high unemployment figures, and on the other, demands for openness by employers but also by an increasing middle class who rapidly became dependent on female migrants for care work.

While regularizations have frequently been interpreted as the best illustration of the "failure" of immigration policies and, more generally, the state's loss of control, regularizations in the Spanish case should be understood primarily as a de facto entry policy, basically because the end result was deferred entry—deferred, since the condition for every regularization is a period of illegal status—of however many immigrant workers were required by employers. As González-Enríquez (2009) noted, this is nothing more than a cheap recruitment model—cheap because the costs and risks of the migratory process were shouldered by the immigrant, and cheap because in political terms it was possible to have a high-numbers policy without putting it in writing and thus without needing to justify it.

Closure

Demands for closure brought about restriction of legal entry, thereby making illegal entry (or, rather, legal entry and illegal stay) the only alternative. Furthermore, the demands for closure also explain conditional residence. Indeed, renewal of work and residence permits (at the end of the first, third, and fifth years) depends on effective and formal integration into the labor market. Without formal employment, immigrants can lose their status (and hence their social and residence rights) during the first five years. Relapse into illegality of those unable to renew their documents is, in fact, a decisive feature that explains much about the Spanish model of illegal immigration. This leads one to conclude that the demands for closure have not only limited entry but also restricted access to membership in the early years after arrival.

These limitations are defined (almost exclusively) on the basis of employment. It is employment that distinguishes the deserving from the undeserving. As the key question is not employability but actual employment, deservingness may change over time. It is the job offer (and therefore the employer behind the job offer) that ultimately decides: it decides who enters (though, again, entry policies did not really work), who regularizes, and who remains after renewing the residence permit. This situation is not so far from European guest worker programs: migrant workers are invited and expected to remain as long as they are needed by employers. The dominance of employment in determining who is in and who is out means that immigration policies in Spain are not open or closed per se; rather, they function in a more or less restrictive manner depending on the economic conjuncture (Garcés-Mascareñas 2012).

The key role played by the job offer explains and is explained by the influence of the corporate actors (employers and trade unions) in immigration policymaking. While there has always been disagreement vis-à-vis entry policies (with employers in favor of easy procedures and trade unions against), regularization programs have always been supported by both parties. It could even be said that regularization programs are paramount examples of the classic corporatist decision-making process that characterizes the Spanish case, as described by Hazán and Bermejo. With regularizations, the government sought to gain greater capacity for control—particularly in the early 2000s, with an estimated 1 million irregular immigrants—and to ensure that more people would be making social security contributions. The employers saw in regularizations a recognition of their demands for migrant workers, as a way of having foreign workers within the law and therefore on more stable terms. Trade unions pushed for regularizations with the aim of clamping down on the informal economy and thereby imposing minimum wage and working conditions. This tripartite structure of unions, employers, and government has also been fundamental in the actual implementation of regularization programs, with employers requesting the regularization of migrants and unions selecting, filtering, and approving applications in the name of both workers and employers (Chauvin, Garcés-Mascareñas, and Kraler 2013).

But it would be only partially correct to conclude that the market (through the job offer) is what decides. Rights have also played a fundamental role. First, they introduced a time constraint: even while the rights of immigrants were curtailed in the early years (because of the immigrants' illegality and, subsequently, their conditional legality), they could not remain so in the long term. Over the years, the majority of long-term immigrants managed to obtain permanent resident status and, in the end, Spanish citizenship. In other words, they stayed on and were finally recognized as fully fledged citizens with all the rights that such a status entails. Second, rights constraints have introduced a geographic factor that also affects policy: the inability to completely exclude the irregular immigrant once he or she has entered the country. In Spain the irregular immigrant is documented at the local level and has access to basic social services (health care and education) along with regularization after three years (through the *arraigo social*). This explains why immigration control has taken place and been reinforced at the border and beyond, in origin and transit countries. If Europe exerted an influence on Spanish immigration policy early on, in terms of border control (and its externalization) Spain seems to have led European thinking.

(Thick and Thin) Borders

In parallel to the dominance of the job offer as a pathway to residence, Spain's immigration policies since the 1990s can be summed up as strengthening its southern border. On the one hand, changes in Spain's visa policy with regard to African countries contributed to reducing the chances for legal migration. On the other hand, the "fight against irregular migration," as it was called by the Ministry of Interior, developed fast with the building up of barrier technology at land borders (particularly at the two African enclaves of Ceuta and Melilla); the expansion of surveillance, detection, and interception at maritime borders (Strait of Gibraltar and Alboran Sea); the detection of (potential) departures from transit countries, particularly along the African coast; and the identification and return of migrants intercepted in Spain, including (first illegal and later legalized) pushbacks at the border (López-Sala 2015). On the basis of bilateral agreements with African countries and Plan Africa (now in its third version), a plan that links development, security, and migration, Spain was a pioneer in the externalization of migration control and the construction of a thick border with Africa.

In contrast, visa policies toward Latin America have been more lenient. Though Spain's becoming a signatory to the convention implementing the Schengen Agreement in 1993 imposed the need for a common visa policy, the fact that the visa requirement did not come into force for most Latin American citizens until long after it did for nationals of other countries and that several countries (such as Argentina,

Chile, Colombia, and Venezuela) are exempted partially explains the Latin Americanization of immigration. As shown by Hazán and Bermejo, this thinner border toward Latin America is also evident in the citizenship law, which concedes citizenship after two years of legal residence to people from Latin America and the Philippines and to Sephardic Jews, and after ten years of legal residence for the rest. This dual system of access to membership is justified by an alleged need to cultivate relations with the former colonies and to respond to a historical debt Spain incurred with countries receiving Spanish immigrants for decades. Of course, these are not objective categories: Morocco is not among the privileged nations despite strong historical, cultural, and social ties. This makes clear how the construction of borders and the perceptions of security behind are inseparable from prevailing notions of nationhood and cultural identity.

Asylum

Hazán and Bermejo's chapter explains in great detail Spain's "uneasy transition" from an emigration country to an immigration country, combined with the emigration of its young and educated since 2011. But if we look at recent years, we cannot avoid mentioning as well the increase in the number of asylum applications: from 2,588 requests in 2012 and 5,947 in 2014 to 14,881 in 2015, 31,120 in 2017, 55,668 in 2018, and 118,264 in 2019 (CEAR 2020). After being at the bottom among EU member states in the number of asylum seekers, Spain has now become one of the first destination countries. Numerically speaking, though, these are low figures if we recall the annual average increase of 600,000 foreign residents from 2001 to 2006. But it has a highly significant implication, as Spain has become for the first time a country of asylum.

Beyond the global context, with the wars in Syria and Ukraine as major triggers and later with the situations in Venezuela, Colombia, and Central America, two major changes in Spain explain this shift: with the new Asylum Law of 2009 the number of false asylum claims decreased substantially, while job offers, which had been the key to entry before the economic crisis, became harder to get. Those who previously might have entered the country via a job offer now have the option of doing so by means of requesting asylum. Becoming a country of asylum means that for the first time not all depends on the job offer. Deservingness frames have thus slightly changed: where previously the deserving migrant was a worker with a formal and long-term job (performance frame), now that category includes the refugee escaping war and violence back home (humanitarian frame). However, as most asylum seekers (between 60 and 80 percent depending on the year) will not receive any kind of protection, in the medium and long term their chances to be recognized as legal residents will depend again on regularization, and thus again on the availability of the job offer.

Conclusion

The Spanish case does not change much regarding the convergence and gap hypotheses. It shows clear convergence in terms of migration policies, and obviously this is to a great extent due to European integration. While European principles and standards have shaped Spanish migration and asylum policies from the very beginning, Spanish border control policies functioned as a laboratory for later European policy developments. But convergence is much more limited with regard to access to membership (either residence or nationality), which continues to be shaped by very specific notions of nationhood based either on economic performance (access to the job offer) or on perceived historical and cultural proximity (specifically, with Latin American countries).

With regard to the gap hypothesis, Spain is indeed the best illustration of a policy gap. However, when taking into account both policy implementation and outcomes, what might be seen as a chaotic and ad hoc policy could also be interpreted as a way to respond simultaneously to demands for openness and demands for closure. This is in fact what Spain (intendedly or unintendedly) did. But this had a price in terms of immigrants' rights: when it all depends on markets, immigrants' basic rights are not guaranteed; the same policy that included them may exclude them again; and, more broadly, access to membership is the result of a long and probationary period of hardship (for some more than others), which at the end is subject to the changing needs of the labor market.

References

CEAR. 2020. "Informe 2020: Las personas refugiadas en España y Europa." Comisión Española de Ayuda al Refugiado, Madrid.

Chauvin, S., B. Garcés-Mascareñas, and A. Kraler. 2013. "Working for Legality: Employment and Migrant Regularization in Europe." *International Migration* 51, no. 6: 118–131.

Garcés-Mascareñas, B. 2012. *Labour Migration in Malaysia and Spain: Markets, Citizenship and Rights.* Amsterdam: Amsterdam University Press.

González-Enríquez, C. 2009. "Spain, the Cheap Model: Irregularity and Regularisation as Immigration Management Policies." *European Journal of Migration and Law* 11, no. 2: 139–157.

López-Sala, A. 2015. "Exploring Dissuasion as a (Geo) Political Instrument in Irregular Migration Control at the Southern Spanish Maritime Border." *Geopolitics* 20, no. 3: 513–534.

13 Greece and Turkey

From State-Building and Developmentalism to Immigration and Crisis Management

Fiona B. Adamson and Gerasimos Tsourapas

Introduction

Since the European "migration crisis" of the mid-2010s, Greece and Turkey have been bound together in the management of irregular migrant flows through their respective roles in the so-called EU-Turkey Deal. The arrangement provided Turkey with economic assistance from the European Union in return for strengthening its external border controls and accepting the return of irregular migrants from Greece. The agreement also provided for an emergency relocation mechanism for refugees in Greece, and led to the geographic concentration of migrants and refugees in Greece with the establishment of EU "hot spots" on Moria and other Greek islands.[1] This highly interdependent relationship is facilitated by the EU but managed largely by Greece and Turkey. It is indicative of the extent to which the two states are affected by common migration management and border control dilemmas in ways that put the "convergence hypothesis" to the test, as well as how their geographical position on the periphery of Europe affects the two states' internal politics of migration control.

Greece and Turkey share similar trajectories in the evolution of their migration management regimes, which include the use of cross-border mobility as a tool in nation-building during the post-independence periods, the emergence of emigration and labor export policies during the 1960s and 1970s, and their transition to countries of return migration in the post-1973 era. Since the end of the Cold War, both Greece and Turkey have managed increasing numbers of migrant inflows, as latecomer immigration states. Finally, both countries are currently playing a front-line role in the management of irregular migration flows from the Middle East, Asia, and Africa.[2] Despite these shared trajectories and common border, there are also some striking differences between the two: while Greece and Turkey are both full NATO member states, their size and geopolitical positions are sharply different, and subject to different regional "push" and "pull" factors that affect their migration management strategies. Importantly, Greece became an EU member in 1981, whereas Turkey has been an official candidate since 1999. Thus, since 1981 the border separating Greece from Turkey is also an external EU border—a fact that impacts on the migration management of both states. This border was accentuated in 2005 with the establishment of the European Border and Coast Guard Agency (Frontex) in 2004 and the commencement in 2006 of a joint operation, Poseidon, which focused on Greek sea and land borders.

In this chapter, we take a *longue durée* perspective on migration management in Greece and Turkey. Although they are often viewed as migration latecomers due to the prominence of labor emigration from both countries mainly to Western Europe in the mid-twentieth century, in this chapter we also attempt to show the complexity of types of migration flows, migration management, and bilateral relations over time. This allows us to show how shifts in migration management regimes in the two states are linked to changes in the broader structural context, as well as larger state interests of nation-building, economic development, and the maintenance of national sovereignty (Adamson and Tsourapas 2020). As we demonstrate, both states have used the cross-border flow of people for strategic and instrumental purposes and as a means of asserting state sovereignty, with factors such as security, culture, economic interests, and rights taking more or less prominent positions in the two states' migration management regimes over time.

The order of the rest of the chapter is as follows. First, we provide a brief historical overview of the role that cross-border mobility played in Greek and Turkish state formation—including a discussion of the role that population exchanges between the two countries played in the 1920s and beyond. Second, we discuss the emergence of developmental emigration in the two states, in which Greece and Turkey both participated in bilateral temporary migration programs established by Western European states in the aftermath of World War II. Third, we discuss the transition of Greece and Turkey from countries of emigration to countries of return migration, immigration, and transit migration from the 2000s onward, including the role that both have played as "front-line" transit states during the European "migration crisis." Finally, we discuss some future directions for migration management policy in both states, including the increasing prominence of neoliberal forms of migration management, such as "golden visa" and "citizenship-by-investment" programs, as well as the monetization of migration in light of restrictive pressures emanating from Europe.

State-Building, Migration, and the "Unmixing of Peoples"

State formation processes across the wider Mediterranean basin involved mass population movements and expulsions throughout the nineteenth and twentieth centuries.[3] The formation of modern Greece and Turkey, both of which emerged out of the remnants of the Ottoman Empire in 1830 and 1923, respectively, were no different in this regard. At the time, the "unmixing" of populations was viewed "as a legitimate, internationally sanctioned form of state building" by many international actors (Robson 2017, 74; see also Brubaker 1998; Iğsız 2018).

Initially, modern Greece contained fewer than a third of the Greek inhabitants of the region, with the rest scattered across other parts of the Ottoman Empire (Clogg 2021, 46). Efforts to incorporate Greek populations residing outside the state's borders materialized in the "Megali Idea," the irredentist vision of a greater Greece encompassing much of the Balkan Peninsula and Asia Minor. This placed the Greek state at odds with the Ottoman Empire, which remained in control of these territories, as well as with Serbia and Bulgaria, which had developed similar irredentist claims over Macedonia (Yosmaoğlu 2013). At the same time, following four centuries of Ottoman rule, the newly independent state contained within its borders numerous communities that were not ethnic Greeks, primarily Muslims. Between 1831 and 1923, the Greek state included cross-border mobility in its nation-building processes via three ways: the dislocation and disenfranchisement of population groups both within its borders as well as in territories it sought to acquire; the implementation of population transfer agreements; and, finally, population resettlement strategies.

The lack of official data prevents an exact analysis of the Muslim population of post-1831 Greece. The War of Independence (1821–1830) involved numerous atrocities and mass killings of Muslim populations, which partly explains the exodus of these communities toward other parts of the Ottoman Empire (McCarthy 1995). Intermittent acts of violence continued after independence, although it is dubious whether these constituted state policy; that said, a long process of state-led Hellenization of Greek Muslims, intensifying in the post-1923 period, aimed at the assimilation of minority communities. This involved the replacement of geographical and topographical names of non-Greek origin with Greek names, as well as the use of educational policies promoting a Hellenic national identity. The state also encouraged Muslims to convert to the Orthodox Christian religion by offering economic incentives to each *neofytos* (newly planted): by 1857, 5,843,915 acres of land had been distributed to Muslim converts (Katsikas 2012). It is indicative that a number of bilateral treaties between Greece and the Ottomans, including the 1881 Convention of Constantinople that ceded Epirus and Thessaly to Greece, included clauses on respect for local Muslims' autonomy.

At the same time, the Greek state also developed strategies of targeted dispossession toward population groups residing in territories outside its borders—namely, Ottoman Macedonia. The decline of the Ottoman Empire following the 1877–1878 Russian-Ottoman War and expectations of its eventual collapse led Greece into an intense competition with Bulgaria and Serbia over the future fate of Ottoman Macedonia (Veremis 2010, 47–50; Triandafyllidou 1998). As part of the "Macedonian Struggle," the Greek and Bulgarian states engaged in proselytizing activities aimed at supporting their ethnonationalist claims on the region, based primarily on religion and language. The use of population transfer agreements emerged as a novel strategy toward nation-building in the region: the 1913 Treaty of Constantinople between Bulgaria and the Ottoman Empire included the voluntary exchange of populations over a period of four years, and as a result, some 47,000 Bulgarians and 49,000 Turks relocated between the two countries (İçduygu and Sert 2015). Similarly, the 1919 Treaty of Neuilly between Greece and Bulgaria and the 1924 Politis-Kalvov Protocol, under the auspices of the League of Nations, led to the exodus of approximately 50,000 Greeks from Bulgaria (Karakasidou 1997).

The transition from the Ottoman Empire to the modern nation-state of Turkey also included population exchanges, expulsions, and ethnic cleansing. During this period populations of the old Ottoman Empire were ethnicized and nationalized, which was achieved both by internal nation-building processes that homogenized diverse populations and by the removal or exchange of populations (Mylonas 2012; Kasaba 2011; Clark 2007; Şeker 2013). In the late nineteenth and early twentieth centuries, the shrinking Ottoman Empire already had developed a structured migration and refugee settlement policy, to deal with the turbulent effects of large-scale population movements from the Balkans, Russia, and elsewhere (Kale 2014; Chatty 2013). And there were expulsions toward the end of the Ottoman Empire, most famously the Armenian expulsions between 1915 and 1917, which were followed by smaller population transfers of Armenians to Syria and Lebanon in 1921–1922 (Robson 2017, 78). The founding of the new Turkish Republic saw rounds of deportations in the form of the Greek-Turkish population exchange of 1923, in which 1.2 million Christian "Greeks" in Anatolia were denationalized and exchanged for 350,000 Muslim "Turks" from Greece (Yildirim 2007; Robson 2017, 74; Hirschon 2003;Triadafilopoulos 2008; Clark 2007). For Greece, this provided another opportunity for nation-building via targeted resettlement; as Clogg argues, "Greeks who had been in a minority in Greek Macedonia in the immediate aftermath of the Balkan wars now became a clear majority," with the 1928 census recording almost half its inhabitants as being of refugee origin (Clogg 2021, 103). Similarly, Greeks would constitute over 60 percent of all Western Thrace inhabitants by the end of the exchange, as opposed to fewer than 20 percent at the end of World War I. At the conclusion of the bilateral population transfer, Greece would become "one of the most ethnically homogenous countries in the Balkans" (Clogg 2021, 104).

The period of Turkish nation-building under a secular Kemalist ideology between 1923 and 1959 saw a simultaneous attempt to homogenize an identity within the territorial borders of the newly created Turkish state, undertaking widespread processes of "Turkification," including in the southeastern Kurdish-dominated regions (Yildiz 2010). It also included a general rejection of irredentism or pan-Turkism (which had been an important political ideology in the late Ottoman period). At the same time, the Turkish state used immigration policies during the 1923–1939 period to promote the development of an ethno-religiously defined Turkish identity, encouraging the migration of over 700,000 Muslims from a variety of states in the Balkans, including Greece, Romania, Yugoslavia, and Bulgaria (Akgündüz 1998; Kirişci 2000). Despite the move toward secularization and "Turkification" in the early Republican period, the role of religious identity was still significant in state migration management policy, as is evidenced by the state's rejection of Christian Gagauz Turks and Shi'a Azeris, whereas non-Turkish Bosnians, Albanians, Pomaks, and other Muslim groups were allowed to migrate and settle (Kirişci 2000, 6; Ülker 2008). The use of nationalizing practices continued into the 1960s and beyond, with the exodus of thousands of Greeks from Istanbul in 1964, as well as the approximately 30,000 people—many of them of Kurdish origin—who were forced out of the country in the wake of the 1980 military coup (Kaliber 2019; Eligür 2020; McLaren and Cop 2011, 501; Yavuz 2001).

Emigration, Developmentalism, and Diaspora

Emigration has been part and parcel of Greek life since the late nineteenth century. Between 1880 and 1920, approximately one-seventh of the country's population (370,000 Greeks) emigrated to the United States (Kalyvas 2015; Roucek and Saloutos 1956). In the 1945–1974 period, roughly one in six Greeks relocated abroad (Fakiolas and King 1996, 172). A number of factors contributed to Greeks' decision to emigrate. Many sought to escape political persecution in the context of the 1946–1949 civil war and the vehemently anti-communist political situation that ensued by emigrating to the USSR and other Warsaw Pact countries. The 1967 military coup d'état and the installation of a military junta (1967–1974) propelled a second wave of politically driven emigration. At the same time, the harsh living conditions in the Greek countryside and high underemployment among farmers (as well as among those who were self-employed in towns and cities) constituted another "push" factor. And host states such as Germany were able to offer wages that were three to five times higher than those in Greece. Two emigration peaks occurred in the second half of the twentieth century, 1962–1966 and 1969–1970 (on either side of the West German recession), with approximately 100,000 Greeks emigrating annually.

The emergence of the Greek developmental migration state occurred in the mid-1950s, as elites recognized the potential of exporting labor abroad. This is demonstrated, first, by the decision to commence an accurate collection of emigration statistics from 1955 onward, and second, by the signing of a number of bilateral migration agreement with host countries: France in 1954 ("On Migration," ratified in 1955), Belgium on July 12, 1957 ("On Greek Workers' Migration to Belgium for Employment in Mines"), and West Germany on March 30, 1960 ("Convention on the Selection and Placement of Greek Workers in German Businesses"). In terms of Greek-German cooperation, in particular, a high degree of administrative facilitation existed on both ends: German employers recruited new laborers across Greece, facilitated by social networks across towns and villages that spread information about life abroad; as a result, it was not uncommon for Greeks from a specific island to emigrate to a specific destination. Neither side doubted that this emigration was temporary: on the one hand, Greek emigrants saw this as a short-term opportunity to save money in order to gain a better socio-economic position upon their return to their home country; on the other hand, Germany incorporated Greek workers into its *Konjunkturpuffer* (shock absorbers for the ups and downs of the business cycle) mentality (Papademetriou 1985), mostly employing them at harsh, low-skill jobs in factories.

The successive emigration flows since the establishment of the Greek state contributed to the creation of large diaspora communities across the world. Centers of the Greek diaspora include major cities across the United States, Canada, and Australia. Many of these diaspora groups have mobilized at various times in Greece's modern history, and they continue to play an important role in host countries' domestic and foreign policymaking—notably in the United States. While there is no precise estimate of the Greek diaspora, the World Council of Hellenes Abroad, an institution that was created in 1995 and tasked with connecting Greeks abroad to the home state, argues that there are approximately 7 million worldwide, although other estimates are much more conservative (Tziovas 2016).

In Turkey, there was also substantial outmigration historically in the late nineteenth and early twentieth centuries (during the late Ottoman period), meaning that there is a significant "Ottoman" diaspora throughout the world (see, e.g., (Fahr-enthold 2019; Mirak 1983; Gutman 2019). Most of the contemporary Turkish "dia-sporam," however, stems from labor migration to Europe and elsewhere that oc-curred during the 1960s and 1970s (Adamson 2019). This period saw the emergence of a developmental state in Turkey, which relied on the use of import substitution industrialization (ISI) strategies. As part of these strategies, labor emigration was promoted as a means of reducing unemployment, alleviating the strain on the infra-structure that had resulted from massive internal rural-to-urban migration, and in-creasing foreign exchange reserves through remittances. Remittances were also used to keep the value of the Turkish lira artificially high (Martin 1991). The state-driven economic policy of ISI provided an incentive for labor exports by creating domestic unemployment through the focus on capital investment and technology as opposed to labor, while producing goods primarily for an internal market rather than ex-port, thereby eliminating trade-based sources of foreign revenue. Centers of urban industrialization grew at the expense of impoverished peripheral areas, which faced declining agricultural production and were thereby reduced to areas populated by excess pools of unharnessed labor (Keyder and Aksu-Koc 1988).

Like Greece, Turkey began to send migrant labor to Germany and other states in western Europe in the 1960s, responding to their postwar economic need for la-bor, and relying on a network of private recruiters from Europe as well as the social and network ties that led to regional patterns of chain migration (Abadan-Unat 2011; Hollifield 1992). Representatives of German employers established a recruitment bu-reau in Istanbul in July 1960 in order to channel workers to West Germany. Ger-many and Turkey signed a bilateral labor agreement in 1961, in which the German Bundesanstalt für Arbeit was made responsible for setting up recruiting agencies in Turkey. The agency linked German employers with potential labor recruits in Tur-key. The bilateral agreement created an official framework for workers' migration, regulating issues such as migration levels, worker benefits, and the responsibilities of sending and receiving countries. It was revised in 1964, and similar agreements were signed with Austria, Belgium, and the Netherlands (1964) followed by agreements with France (1965) and Australia and Sweden (1967) (Akgündüz 1993, 155). Turkey en-tered into multiple labor agreements in order to fall "back on other countries if one showed signs of saturation and diminished absorption ability" (Bahadir 1979, 105). Indeed, following the 1973 oil embargo, which led to a decline in the need for labor migrants, Turkey signed additional agreements with Libya (1975), Jordan (1982), and Qatar (1986) (İçduygu and Sert 2011; Seccombe and Lawless 1986).

By the early 1970s, remittances represented 70 percent of Turkey's foreign cur-rency earnings, 84 percent of export earnings, and 5 percent of the gross national product (Sayari 1986, 92–93). As part of its state policy of migration management, Turkey attempted to direct the flow of remittances through official channels, such as state banks, although many transfers continued to occur through informal and unofficial channels (Richards and Waterbury 1990, 389; Choucri 1986). Worker remittances in the form of foreign currency or consumer goods were important in driving much of the underground economy of Turkey, helping to pay for about $1.5 billion worth of smuggled imports, many of which "consisted of badly needed equipment and primary inputs, without which Turkish industry would have probably collapsed" (Hale 1981, 232). In addition to the desire to ease unemployment and urban migration and to attract remittances, Turkish migration policy was also viewed as a way of ensuring that rural migrant workers would acquire new skills and training that could be tapped later upon their return, when they would also bring with them foreign capital to invest in their local communities (Sayari 1986, 92–93). Additionally, labor migration was treated as a safety valve for easing social and political discontent (Akgündüz 1993, 171).

The years following 1973 brought a change in the type of migration to Germany. With German employers no longer recruiting workers, migration now took different forms: family reunification, politically motivated migration such as asylum seekers (particularly in the years following the military coup in Turkey in September 1980), irregular migration, and a small amount of legal migration of specialized persons (including Turkish state employees such as government teachers or religious personnel) (Akgunduz 1993). Indeed, the early 1980s were defined by the institutionalization of state engagement policies with its diaspora in Europe, which included the establishment of the Turkish Islamic Union of the State Office of Religious Affairs (DITIB) in Cologne, Germany, which was organized under Turkey's Ministry of Religious Affairs (Diyanet), and which sent imams and other religious figures to Germany. This supplemented the Turkish consular functions, which had been the main source of Turkish émigrés' engagement in Turkey by providing legal and administrative services to its citizens abroad, such as registering births, marriages, and deaths and providing advice on pensions (Aydin 2018). In 1981 Turkey also for the first time passed a law allowing dual citizenship, and in 1982 it included Turkish citizens abroad within the constitution, as well as establishing the Higher Coordination Council for Workers, which included the Social Affairs and Economic Affairs Committees, designed to foster the attachments of citizens abroad to Turkey (Aksel 2014, 203–204).

The labor emigrants who left for Europe in the 1960s and 1970s formed the basis for a large Turkish diaspora, which Turkey has steadily engaged with over time (Adamson 2019; Sayari 1986; Miller 1981; Østergaard-Nielsen 2003; Kastoryano 2002)—first by providing services and then increasingly, like many other countries, by formalizing its diaspora engagement policy in the 2000s (Gamlen 2014; Délano and Gamlen 2014; Ragazzi 2009, 2014), viewing it as an extension of Turkish soft power and as a valuable economic and political resource. A formal Office for the Turks Abroad and Related Communities (YTB) was established in 2010. The office combined elements of earlier policies that had been aimed at Turkish citizens abroad in Europe as well as managing international students on government scholarships (Öktem 2014, 13–16). Part of this strategy included leveraging the diaspora as a resource that could be utilized as a tool of state economic and lobbying power in ways that could ensure that Turkey would have a global presence and influence (Adamson 2019; Aksel 2014, 205; Arkilic 2021; Mügge 2012).

Return Migration and Diversification

The Greek state shifted from a net emigration state to an immigration state in the 1980s, defined by two phenomena: the steady inflow of return migration of Greeks from the late 1960s until the late 1970s, and the immigration of foreign-born laborers and asylum seekers from the 1980s onward. In terms of the former, the Greek state experienced two types of return migration flows. One consisted of returning economic migrants. Official numbers indicate that there were 238,000 Greek returnees in the decade 1968–1977, of whom 161,000 returned from western Europe (primarily Germany). The number of returnees first exceeded that of emigrants in 1966–1967, during the economic recession in West Germany, and continued to do so from 1974 onward. From 1974 until the late 1980s, another 250,000 Greeks returned—again, primarily from European host states. Structural and political economic factors account for this wave of return migration: the end of the German *Wirtschaftswunder* (the economic miracle), within a broader context of economic stagnation across the Western world, led to high unemployment across traditional countries of destination for Greek workers abroad. In Germany, the switch in immigration policy from recruitment of foreign labor to family reunification schemes, coupled with the lack of sufficient integration of Greek workers, became a factor in Greeks' decision to return to the homeland. The conditions in western Europe were not mirrored in Greece, which had transitioned into multiparty, parliamentary democracy after the end of the military dictatorship in 1974. Political optimism was coupled with economic development: unlike other European states, Greece continued to enjoy economic development and low rates of unemployment throughout the 1970s.

A second wave of return migration was distinctly political—namely, political refugees who had fled to the USSR and other socialist countries during the 1946–1949 Greek civil war and its immediate aftermath. Some 120,000 Soviet Greeks (known as *homogenis*, "of Greek descent") had returned by 1993 (Voutira 2004). And beginning in 1988, approximately 50,000 Pontic Greeks, who had moved from Pontos in Asia Minor to the USSR in 1922, also returned to the homeland. The 2001 census numbered 152,204 Soviet Greeks, of which approximately 80,000 had arrived from Georgia, 31,000 from Kazakhstan, 23,000 from Russia, and 9,000 from Armenia.[4]

The influx of economic refugees, immigrants, and ethnic Greeks from Albania following the collapse of communism in the country demonstrates the blurred lines between return migration and immigration: the absence of sufficient border controls between Greece and Albania in the early 1990s—ostensibly to encourage the repatriation of ethnic Greeks who resided in southern Albania (or northern Epirus, according to Greece)—allowed the immigration of thousands of Greek and non-Greek Albanians in two waves, in 1991–1992 (with 200,000 arriving in 1991 alone) and in 1997. The 2011 census registered 480,804 Albanian migrants—of them, only approximately 189,000 are ethnic Greeks (or northern Epirotes, known as Vorioipirotes).

Immigrant communities in Greece existed well before the 1980s: it is estimated that some 15,000 to 20,000 African and Turkish migrants were working in the tourism and shipyard industries as early as 1972. From the mid-1970s onward, the number of EU citizens in Greece has increased exponentially, but non-EU citizens (primarily from Asia) have come to constitute the majority of immigrants. It is worth noting that irregular migrants are not captured in official data. To the diversification of migration in recent decades, the Greek state has also added a "Golden Visa" program that, since 2013, offers a residency permit to anyone investing €400,000 in the Greek stock or real estate market.[5] The scheme has been popular with Chinese, Turkish, and Russian investors seeking visa-free entry into the EU. Forty-two visas were granted in 2013, with that number rising to 6,200 in 2017 and to over 10,000 in 2018.[6]

Although return migration was not as significant a factor in Turkey as in Greece, nevertheless there was also a move in Turkey from the 1980s onward away from emigration and toward return migration. Germany halted recruitment of foreign labor in the mid-1970s and in the 1980s began to offer incentives for the return of Turkish laborers to Turkey at the rate of DM 10,500 per adult and DM 1,500 per child, leading to an increase of Turkish emigration from Germany (Martin 1991, 39). With regard to the latter, migration between Turkey and Germany today is now more circular, with more migration from Germany to Turkey every year than in the opposite direction (Diehl and Liebau 2015; Aydın 2016; Abadan-Unat and Bilecen 2020).

As in Greece, the end of the Cold War and the collapse of the Soviet Union in 1991, as well as conflicts in Iraq and the Balkans, precipitated new migration flows to Turkey. Migration increased from countries from the former Soviet Union, including Russia, the Caucasus, and Central Asia. Some of this included high-skilled migration, but much of it also included irregular migration, including a significant amount of human trafficking from Russia and eastern European states (Kaya and Erez 2018; Korfalı and Acar 2018). Georgia, which borders Turkey on the northeast, has been a significant source of migration to Turkey. On top of a historically large Georgian diaspora within Turkey (approximately 2.5 million people), there have also been several waves of migration from Georgia to Turkey since the early 1990s. Since the establishment of a visa-free regime with Georgia in 2006, there has been a significant circular migration in the agricultural sectors for seasonal work, as well as the construction industry and domestic service sector (Kalça and Ari 2016). Turkey also took in significant numbers of refugees from Iran and Iraq in the late 1980s, as well as almost half a million Kurdish refugees from Iraq in 1988 and 1991, many of whom later returned. In addition, significant numbers of Albanians, Bosnian Muslims, Pomaks (Bulgarian-speaking Muslims), and Turks arrived in Turkey in 1989, 1992–1995, and 1999 (Kirişci 2007; Parla 2007, 2019; Düvell 2020).

In the 2000s, Turkey continued to have restrictive immigration laws, but increasingly became a transit and destination state for irregular mixed migrants, including asylum seekers, trafficked migrants, irregular labor, and transit migrants (Kaya 2008; İçduygu and Yükseker 2012). Turkey also has large numbers of female domestic workers from a number of neighboring countries, as well as from countries farther afield, such as the Philippines (Toksöz 2020). In addition, Turkey is increasingly encouraging immigration of high-wealth individuals via its citizenship-by-investment schemes. Foreigners who buy real estate in Turkey for $250,000 or more are immediately eligible for Turkish citizenship, whereas individuals who deposit $500,000 in a Turkish bank account are eligible for Turkish citizenship after a period of five years.[7]

Forced Migration and "Crisis Management" in the Eastern Mediterranean

Greece and Turkey's geographical position on the southeastern periphery of Europe has had a strong impact on their migration management regimes. Greece has been a full member of the European Union since 1981, whereas Turkey has been an official candidate since 1999. Thus, since 1999 both Greece and Turkey's internal migration management regimes have been shaped in part by pressures from the European Union, albeit in different ways. In Greece, national immigration policy was traditionally characterized as "reactive" and "piecemeal," suffering from excessive red tape and structural weaknesses (Triandafyllidou 2009). The major test for the country's migration management came in the aftermath of the 2011 Arab uprisings and the Syrian civil war, which contributed to a broader phenomenon of irregular migration that has come to be known as the European "migration crisis." The Greek state responded to this challenge in three phases: in the first, broadly occurring between 2011 and 2015, national authorities developed tight policy controls via a combination of measures, including border controls, police monitoring, and repatriation strategies in coordination with the EU and the Common European Asylum System (CEAS) (Karyotis 2012).

In late 2011, Greece initiated the construction of a fence and electronic surveillance system in Evros, along its land border with Turkey. A few months later, in early 2012, the first migrant detention center was created in Amygdaleza. A series of police operations, such as Operation Xenios Zeys in Athens and Operation Aspis in Evros, also attempted to seal the Greek-Turkish border and arrest irregular migrants within the country. From September 2012 onward, Operation Aspis was expanded to key Aegean islands—Chios, Samos, Lesbos, and the Dodecanese—that were frequent destinations of Syrian refugees smuggled from the Turkish coast. At the same time, Greece engaged in close cooperation with European and international agencies and organizations, including the International Organization for Migration. In coordination with the latter, Greek authorities launched assisted voluntary return and reintegration programs for thousands of migrants (Lazaridis and Skleparis 2016).

The second phase of Greece's management of the European migration crisis coincided with the rise to power of a new coalition government in January 2015. The Syriza-ANEL coalition, under Prime Minister Alexis Tsipras, sought to shift away from securitization toward a more humane refugee policy. Having campaigned on an anti-austerity platform that rejected the harsh economic measures implemented in the context of the post-2009 Greek government debt crisis, Tsipras was also keen to distance his government from the country's traditional European partners. For Syriza-ANEL, the European "migration crisis" was an opportunity to demonstrate how Europe was in dire need of a reevaluation of its policymaking in terms of values of solidarity and respect for human rights (Stivas 2021).

This led to a vast transformation of Greek refugee policy, both discursively and substantively. Greek authorities ended cooperation with the International Organization for Migration, while Operation Aspis in Evros was abandoned in June 2015. As border controls relaxed, the country witnessed an unprecedented influx of asylum seekers that strained governmental resources (Micinski 2019). Between January and July 2015, Frontex documented an astonishing 663 percent increase in irregular border crossings into the western Balkans compared to the previous year; illegal border crossings into Greece increased from 24,800 in 2013 to 885,400 in 2015 (Tsourapas and Zartaloudis 2021). Greece would serve as the initial point of the so-called Balkan Corridor, which led asylum seekers transiting through Greece and the western

Balkans to central and western European countries. The fact that transfers of asylum seekers to Greece under the Dublin Regulation had been suspended since 2011, as a result of the country's poor record of migration management, was also key: Greece remained responsible for processing applications of asylum seekers arriving in is territory, but a key pillar of the Dublin Regulation, aimed at preventing "asylum shopping," was suspended.[8] EU member states no longer had the right to transfer back to Greece those asylum seekers who had applied for asylum in that country, or for whom Greece was the first country of entry to the EU. This implied that Greece theoretically received carte blanche to wave asylum seekers through its territory.

The Syriza-ANEL government's management of the European "migration crisis" created significant friction between Greece and European states. Greek policymakers did not hesitate to employ particularly belligerent rhetoric, as they sought to link the government's management of the "migration crisis" to the ongoing negotiations among Greece, the European Commission, the European Central Bank, and the International Monetary Fund on a third economic bailout agreement. Tsipras did not hesitate to target specific European leaders in his speeches, asserting that "if the Europeans want us to kill or carry the bodies of refugees then they should say so openly" (Tsourapas and Zartaloudis 2021).

By mid-2016 it had become evident that the Greek government's issue-linkage strategy was not paying off. Three particular events contributed to this realization: first, on March 9, 2016, Slovenia, Serbia, Croatia, and Macedonia closed their borders to new migrants, effectively sealing off the Balkan Corridor. Vesna Gyorkos Znidar, Slovenia's interior minister, declared that "there will be no more migration on the Western Balkan route as it took place so far." Describing the rationale behind the policy, Croatian prime minister Tihomir Oreskovic referred to transit migration through Greece: "In what way can we destroy this business model? . . . The message is clear. Illegal migrants will no longer pass along this route."[9] Second, in April 2016, the European Commission found that the country "has significantly increased its overall reception capacity" and that "significant progress had been achieved by Greece in putting in place the essential institutional and legal structures for a properly functioning asylum system."[10] As a result, asylum transfers from other EU states to Greece under the Dublin Regulation would gradually resume. Third, European leaders agreed to the EU-Turkey Statement in March 2016, which, as will be discussed later, drastically reduced the number of asylum seekers entering Greece.

This led to the third phase of Greece's management of the European "migration crisis." Significant economic aid began flowing into Greece beginning in March 2016, as Greek policymakers abandoned their coercive rhetoric and sought closer cooperation with European partners.. In May 2016, Greek authorities began relocating asylum seekers from the infamous Idomeni camp on the border with North Macedonia (the camp subsequently closed operations). The aggressive government rhetoric of 2015 and early 2016 also disappeared for the remainder of the coalition government's term. Since 2016, the Syriza-ANEL government agreed to abide by EU rules and detain asylum seekers in five hot spots across islands neighboring Turkey (Lesvos, Samos, Chios, Leros, and Kos) with a total capacity of 6,178 places; by the end of 2019, they contained 38,423 persons.[11] In the absence of the conditions necessary for stronger leverage, Greece effectively complied with demands for externalization control through immigration detention in the European periphery.

In Turkey, the pressures coming from Europe are multiple and at times contradictory. On the one hand, Turkey has faced pressure from the European Union to liberalize its migration and asylum policies in order to bring it into line with EU asylum laws as part of the overall process of accession, and in the broader context of EU harmonization of its asylum laws (Kirişçi 1996). Following Turkey's acceptance as an official candidate for membership in the European Union, it began the process of negotiation and accession, which included the adoption of sets of laws and constitutional amendments to bring it into line with the requirements for EU membership, known as the *acquis communautaire*. In 2005 Turkey produced a plan to modernize and update its migration and asylum laws to bring them into harmony with EU requirements and in 2008 established an asylum and migration bureau, which precipitated a period in which Turkey undertook a series of legal and policy reforms that eventually led to the 2013 Law on Foreigners and International Protection (LFIP), which was officially adopted in 2014 and which replaced the earlier Law on Settlement (İçduygu and Üstübici 2014; Elitok 2013; Kilberg 2014). It also, for the first time, provided a domestic legal basis for asylum governance in Turkey (Aydin and Kirişci 2013). Turkey established the Directorate General of Migration Management (DGMM) in 2014, which brought migration and asylum management under civilian control for the first time and provided a bureaucratic framework for policy formulation and coordination with migration-related international and non-governmental organizations (Norman 2019, 2020a).

While Turkey is a member of the 1951 United Nations Convention Relating to the Status of Refugees (and adopted the Convention's 1967 Protocol), its original instrument of accession applied only to refugees coming from Europe (Güler 2020). In a strict legal sense, Turkey can only accept European asylum seekers as "refugees," treating others as "guests" (Abdelaaty 2019). Nevertheless, Turkey has allowed the United Nations High Commissioner for Refugees (UNHCR) to operate within its boundaries and conduct refugee status determinations with the understanding that those who are given such status will be resettled in a third country. For refugees within its boundaries, Turkey offers temporary protection rather than permanent resettlement.

Since the start of the Syrian conflict in 2011, Turkey has largely had an open-door policy when it comes to admitting Syrians. As of 2020, Turkey is home to the largest refugee population in the world, with approximately 3.6 million Syrians and approximately 370,000 refugees and asylum seekers of other nationalities.[12] Turkey hosts the largest number of Syrians in the region—about 45 percent of the total, followed by Lebanon and Jordan. Most Syrians in Turkey have been provided with temporary protection status. Under the LFIP, non-European refugees can be given a "conditional refugee status, humanitarian residence permit or temporary protection" until they are processed by the UNHCR. Due to the high volume of refugees in Turkey, such processing can take years. Syrians as a group, however, have been granted special protection under the Temporary Protection Regulation of 2014. Subsequently a small number have also received work permits or access to Turkish citizenship, although the vast majority exist in a precarious state, often surviving by work in the gray economy, which is widespread in Turkey (Norman 2020b). Only 2 percent of Syrian refugees live in temporary accommodation centers or Turkish government-run camps, most of which are found close to the Syrian border in southeastern Turkey. The vast majority of Syrians live among the general population, in southeastern cities such as Gaziantep, Urfa, and Kilis or in major urban areas such as Istanbul, Ankara, and Izmir (Abdelaaty 2019; Norman 2020b).[13]

In addition to the effect of the EU on the internal migration policies of Greece and Turkey, European migration governance has also had an effect on their border control policies. Since 1981 the border separating Greece from Turkey is also an external border of the European Union. This border was accentuated with the establishment of the European Border and Coast Guard Agency (Frontex) in 2005 and with the commencement of Joint Operation Poseidon in 2006, which focused on Greek sea and land borders. In the early 2000s, the Greek-Turkish border had become one of the main routes of irregular migration into the European Union, along with the central Mediterranean and Balkan routes.

The creation of the European External Action Service (EEAS) in 2010 built on earlier efforts that linked migration, development, and security, such as the Union for the Mediterranean, and was set up to "develop capacity-building measures and migration management activities" for third parties (Carrera et al. 2013 , 5). At the same time, Turkey has faced equally strong pressure from Europe to control its borders and limit migration flows—the EU has often treated Turkey as a buffer zone between Europe and migration source countries to the south and east, especially the war-torn states of Syria and Iraq. This has occurred both within the overall accession process of strengthening the external borders of the European Union and within the larger policy of the externalization of EU migration control and its delegation of border control responsibilities to third-party states. These contradictory policies from Europe—simultaneously encouraging the liberalization and restriction of migration flows—are neither new nor limited to Turkey. The EU had similarly contradictory policies toward eastern European states in the 1990s via pre-accession programs such as TACIS (Technical Assistance to the Commonwealth of Independent States) and toward Mediterranean states in the 2000s via the Barcelona process.

Turkey's role in managing the Syrian refugee crisis has brought to the fore the ways in which cross-border migration flows affect not just the internal context of states but also their relations with one another (Adamson and Tsourapas 2019; Özerim 2018). In particular, the role Turkey plays as a host for Syrian refugees and as a major transit state for migrants trying to reach Europe has emerged as a key factor in Turkey-EU relations over the past several years (İçduygu and Üstübici 2014). Europe's interests in preventing the flow of migrants and refugees to the continent have raised the importance of Turkey as a buffer and transit state and in some ways increased Turkey's bargaining power vis-à-vis Europe. In combination with Erdogan's heated rhetoric toward Europe, this has created tensions in the relationship, but it has also allowed Turkey to use its leverage to extract significant concessions and financial resources from the EU (Greenhill 2016).

In November 2015, Turkey signed a Joint Action Plan with the European Union in which the EU committed both to giving Turkey €3 billion to assist with managing the refugee crisis and to enacting EU visa liberalization for Turkish citizens. In return, Turkey committed to using sea patrols and border restrictions to prevent the exit of migrants and refugees to Europe, as well as to crack down on passport forgeries and human trafficking and return those who failed to meet refugee determination criteria to their countries of origin. The Joint Action Plan was supplemented by the March 2016 EU-Turkey deal, in which Europe agreed to take one registered Syrian refugee in Turkey for every Syrian asylum seeker crossing the Turkish border into Greece who was subsequently returned—the "one-in, one-out" deal. In exchange, Europe committed to speeding up the liberalization of visas for Turkish citizens and committed an additional €3 billion in assistance to Turkey—bringing the total assistance package to €6 billion.

The "deal" received heavy criticism from human rights organizations, and also raised the issue of whether "Turkey used the refugees and management issues on irregular migration as a bargaining chip in its relations with the EU in order to accelerate negotiations and visa liberalization" (Özerim 2018; see also Kale 2016). The migration deals struck with Turkey to control its borders can be understood as a larger effort by Europe to manage what it perceives as a "migration crisis" by pushing the border of Europe deeper into Europe's periphery and beyond. This includes enhanced border control and screening measures by states in the Maghreb, the Middle East, and sub-Saharan Africa (Andersson 2014). The relationship between Turkey and Europe in many ways embodies larger North-South dynamics in terms of pressures for migration control and border enforcement coming from "Northern" states at the same time that pressures for outmigration are increasing from "Southern" states. In Turkey's case, this dynamic is replicated on its own borders, and compounded with the outpouring of refugees from Syria and elsewhere, such as Afghanistan (Sert and Yildiz 2016; Özden 2013; İçduygu 2015).

Turkey has spent approximately $8 billion domestically to address the Syrian refugee crisis, and as of 2020 there was little prospect of large numbers of Syrian refugees returning to Syria. In 2019 a survey showed that the vast majority of Syrians in Turkey reported feeling relatively integrated into Turkey, although very few have Turkish citizenship and there is widespread anti-Syrian sentiment within Turkey. Nevertheless, the impacts of the COVID-19 crisis have been especially felt by refugees in Turkey, with many of them losing employment. Furthermore, the refugee issue in Turkey continues to intersect with other foreign policy issues and with ongoing tensions with Greece and other EU countries in the eastern Mediterranean, including triggering a February 2020 humanitarian border crisis with Greece (Muftuler-Bac 2020; Kirisci and Yavcan 2020; Kirişci 2021).

Conclusions

This chapter has demonstrated the ways in which Greece and Turkey have faced similar dynamics with regard to cross-border migration movements throughout their modern history. Linked via a shared history and a common border, the two countries' migration management practices share a number of commonalities: both states engaged in targeted migration for purposes of state-building and regime consolidation, culminating in the 1923 Greek-Turkish population exchange agreement. They developed similar ways of employing labor emigration for developmental purposes, particularly toward western Europe in the aftermath of World War II. In the post-1973 era, emigration gave way to other types of cross-border mobility across Greece and Turkey, including return and transit migration, as well as immigration.

In the last few decades, both states have witnessed large influxes of foreign populations, seeking either employment or refuge. Their geographical position on the periphery of Europe, in which the boundary between Greece and Turkey has also become an increasingly fortified external European Union boundary, means that both states have also been heavily affected by broader South-North migration dynamics. On the one hand, both Greece and Turkey have become countries of transit and destination for a range of migrants who are crossing borders in search of economic opportunity or safety. In the latter case, millions of refugees escaping the Syrian conflict have crossed into Turkey, and a significant portion of those also continued farther on to Greece. These have been part of mixed migration flows in the region that also include refugees and asylum seekers from Afghanistan, Iran, Iraq and Pakistan, as well as—increasingly—irregular migrants and asylum seekers from a range of African and Asian countries. Both countries have built fences on their southern and eastern borders as a means of controlling migration and have sought financial compensation from the European Union for their roles in hosting disproportionate numbers of refugees and restricting migration outflows to the rest of Europe.

Thus, there has been a degree of convergence of immigration control policy between Greece and Turkey that has included formalization, and to some extent liberalization, of asylum laws, combined with an increasing focus on border control and restriction. At the same time, with regard to how Greece and Turkey fit into broader global patterns of immigration control, there are also identifiable trends that are significant for understanding transformations in global migration control policy. These include the intensification of the externalization of migration control from "Northern" to "Southern" states (FitzGerald 2019) and the use of forms of "migration diplomacy" between states, in which migration management and control intersect with state foreign policy interests and geopolitics (Tsourapas 2019; Adamson and Tsourapas 2020; Thiollet 2011).

Notes

1. See Karakoulaki 2018.

2. Migration issues have also been a key factor in the Greek-Turkish relationship with respect to the island of Cyprus. However, discussion of this is beyond the scope of this paper.

3. In this sense, they also resembled state-building processes in eastern Europe and elsewhere (Zolberg 1983).

4. See Hellenic Republic 2001.

5. See In.gr. 2019.

6. See To Vima 2019.

7. Hurriyet 2019. See also www.invest.gov.tr and www.goldenvisas.com/turkey.

8. See Voguel 2011..

9. See Chan 2016.

10. See European Commission 2016.

11. See Hellenic Republic 2019.

12. UNHCR 2020.

13. UNHCR 2020.

References

Abadan-Unat, Nermin. 2011. *Turks in Europe: From Guest Worker to Transnational Citizen.* New York: Berghahn Books.

Abadan-Unat, Nermin, and Başak Bilecen. 2020. "The Turkey-Germany Migration Corridor." In *Routledge Handbook of Migration and Development,* edited by Tanja Bastia and Ronald Skeldon, pp. 458-463. London: Routledge.

Abdelaaty, Lamis. 2019. "Refugees and Guesthood in Turkey." *Journal of Refugee Studies* 34, no. 3: 3837–2848. https://doi.org/10.1093/jrs/fez097.

Adamson, Fiona B. 2019. "Sending States and the Making of Intra-Diasporic Politics: Turkey and Its Diaspora(s)." *International Migration Review* 53, no. 1: 210–236.

Adamson, Fiona B., and Gerasimos Tsourapas. 2019. "Migration Diplomacy in World Politics." *International Studies Perspectives* 20, no. 2: 113–128.

Adamson, Fiona B., and Gerasimos Tsourapas. 2020. "The Migration State in the Global South: Nationalizing, Developmental, and Neoliberal Models of Migration Management." *International Migration Review* 54, no. 3: 853–882.

Akgündüz, Ahmet. 1993. "Labour Migration from Turkey to Western Europe (1960–1974): An Analytical Review." *Capital and Class* 17, no. 3: 153–194.

Akgündüz, Ahmet. 1998. "Migration to and from Turkey, 1783–1960: Types, Numbers and Ethno-religious Dimensions." *Journal of Ethnic and Migration Studies* 24, no. 1: 97–120.

Aksel, Damla B. 2014. "Kins, Distant Workers, Diasporas: Constructing Turkey's Transnational Members Abroad." *Turkish Studies* 15, no. 2: 195–219.

Andersson, Ruben. 2014. *Illegality, Inc.: Clandestine Migration and the Business of Bordering Europe.* Berkeley: University of California Press.

Arkilic, Ayca. 2021. "Explaining the Evolution of Turkey's Diaspora Engagement Policy: A Holistic Approach." *Diaspora Studies* 14, no. 1: 1–21.

Aydin, Umut, and Kemal Kirişci. 2013. "With or Without the EU: Europeanisation of Asylum and Competition Policies in Turkey." *South European Society and Politics* 18, no. 3: 375–395.

Aydin, Yaşar. 2018. "The New Turkish Diaspora Policy." *Stiftung Wissenschaft und Politik.* Pp. 1-28.

Aydın, Yaşar. 2016. *The Germany-Turkey Migration Corridor: Refitting Policies for a Transnational Age.* Washington, DC: Migration Policy Institute.

Bahadir, Sefik Alp. 1979. "Turkey and the Turks in Germany." *Aussenpolitik* 30, no. 1: 100–114.

Brubaker, Rogers. 1998. "Migrations of Ethnic Unmixing in the 'New Europe.'" *International Migration Review* 32, no. 4: 1047–1065.

Carrera, Sergio and Guild, Elspeth and Hernanz, Nicholas. 2013. "Europe's Most Wanted? Recalibrating Trust in the European Arrest Warrant System." CEPS Paper Liberty and Security in Europe 55/21 March 2013: 1-34.

Chan, Sewell. 2016. "Balkan Nations Shut Down March of Migrants." *New York Times*, March 10, 2016. https://www.nytimes.com/2016/03/10/world/europe/europe-refugee-crisis.html.

Chatty, Dawn. 2013. "Refugees, Exiles, and Other Forced Migrants in the Late Ottoman Empire." *Refugee Survey Quarterly* 32, no. 2: 35–52.

Choucri, Nazli. 1986. "The Hidden Economy: A New View of Remittances in the Arab World." *World Development* 14, no. 6: 697–712.

Clark, Bruce. 2007. *Twice a Stranger: How Mass Expulsion Forged Modern Greece and Turkey.* London: Granta.

Clogg, Richard. 2021. *A Concise History of Greece.* Cambridge: Cambridge University Press.

Délano, Alexandra, and Alan Gamlen. 2014. "Comparing and Theorizing State-Diaspora Relations." *Political Geography* 41, no. 7: 43–53.

Diehl, Claudia, and Elisabeth Liebau. 2015. "Turning Back to Turkey—or Turning the Back on Germany? Remigration Intentions and Behavior of Turkish Immigrants in Germany Between 1984 and 2011." *Zeitschrift für Soziologie* 44, no. 1: 22–41.

Düvell, Franck. 2020. "Shifts in the Global Migration Order and Migration Transitions in Europe: The Cases of Turkey and Russia." *Comparative Migration Studies* 8, no. 1: 1–22.

Eligür, Banu. 2020. "The 1964 Expulsion of Greek Citizens from Turkey: Economic and Demographic Turkification Under Ethnocultural Nationalism." *Journal of the Middle East and Africa* 11, no. 4: 319–340.

Elitok, Secil Paçacı. 2013. "Turkish Migration Policy over the Last Decade: A Gradual Shift Towards Better Management and Good Governance." *Turkish Policy Quarterly* 12, no. 1: 161–172.

European Commission. 2016. "Questions and Answers: Recommendation on the Conditions for Resuming Dublin Transfers of Asylum Seekers to Greece." https://ec.europa.eu/commission/presscorner/detail/en/MEMO_16_4253.

Fahrenthold, Stacy D. 2019. *Between the Ottomans and the Entente: The First World War in the Syrian and Lebanese Diaspora, 1908–1925.* New York: Oxford University Press.

Fakiolas, Rossetos, and Russell King. 1996. "Emigration, Return, Immigration: A Review and Evaluation of Greece's Postwar Experience of International Migration." *International Journal of Population Geography* 2, no. 2: 171–190.

FitzGerald, David Scott. 2019. *Refuge Beyond Reach: How Rich Democracies Repel Asylum Seekers.* New York: Oxford University Press.

Gamlen, Alan. 2014. "Diaspora Institutions and Diaspora Governance." *International Migration Review* 48 (September): S180–S217.

Greenhill, Kelly M. 2016. "Open Arms Behind Barred Doors: Fear, Hypocrisy and Policy Schizophrenia in the European Migration Crisis." *European Law Journal* 22, no. 3: 317–332.

Güler, Arzu. 2020. "Turkey's Geographical Limitation: The Legal Implications of an Eventual Lifting." *International Migration* 58, no. 5: 3–17.

Gutman, David. 2019. *The Politics of Armenian Migration to North America, 1885–1915.* Edinburgh: Edinburgh University Press.

Hale, William M. 1981. *The Political and Economic Development of Modern Turkey.* London: Taylor & Francis.

Hellenic Republic. 2001. "Population and Housing Census of March 18th, 2001." http://www.e-demography.gr/ElstatPublications/censuses/docs/eDemography_Metadata_Censuses_Doc_000002_gr.pdf.

Hellenic Republic. 2019. "Reflection of the National Situation on the Refugee/Migrant Issue, 31/12/19." https://infocrisis.gov.gr/7344/apotyposi-tis-ethnikis-ikonas-katastasis-gia-to-prosfygiko-metanasteftiko-zitima-tin-31-12-2019/.

Hirschon, Renée. 2003. *Crossing the Aegean: An Appraisal of the 1923 Compulsory Population Exchange Between Greece and Turkey.* New York: Berghahn Books.

Hollifield, J. F. 1992. *Immigrants, Markets, and States: The Political Economy of Postwar Europe.* Cambridge, MA: Harvard University Press.

Hurriyet. 2019. "250 Apply for Turkish Citizenship Through Investment." *Hurriyet Daily News,* January 2, 2019. https://www.hurriyetdailynews.com/250-apply-for-turkish-citizenship-through-investment-140193.

İçduygu, Ahmet. 2015. *Syrian Refugees in Turkey: The Long Road Ahead.* Vol. 3. Washington, DC: Migration Policy Institute.

İçduygu, Ahmet, and Deniz Sert. 2011. "Project-Tied Labor Migration from Turkey to the MENA Region: Past, Present, and Future." *International Labor and Working-Class History* 79: 62–80.

İçduygu, Ahmet, and Deniz Sert. 2015. "The Changing Waves of Migration from the Balkans to Turkey: A Historical Account." In *Migration in the Southern Balkans: From Ottoman Territory to Globalized Nation States,* edited by Martin Baldwin-Edwards and Riki van Boeschoten Hans Vermeulen, 85–104. IMISCOE Research Series. Cham: Springer.

İçduygu, Ahmet, and Ayşen Üstübici. 2014. "Negotiating Mobility, Debating Borders: Migration Diplomacy in Turkey-EU Relations." In *New Border and Citizenship Politics,* edited by Helen Schwenken and Sabine Ruß-Sattar, 44–59. London: Palgrave Macmillan.

İçduygu, Ahmet, and Deniz Yükseker. 2012. "Rethinking Transit Migration in Turkey: Reality and Re-Presentation in the Creation of a Migratory Phenomenon." *Population, Space and Place* 18, no. 4: 441–456.

Iğsız, Aslı. 2018. *Humanism in Ruins: Entangled Legacies of the Greek-Turkish Population Exchange.* Stanford, CA: Stanford University Press.

In.gr. 2019. "Changes to the 'Golden Visa': Who and How Much Can They Invest" [in Greek]. In.gr, March 8, 2019. https://www.in.gr/2019/03/08/economy/allages-sti-xrysi-viza-poioi-kai-posa-mporoun-na-ependyoun/.

Kalça, Adem, and Yılmaz Onur Ari. 2016. "Circular Migration Between Georgia and Turkey: Is Triple Win a Solution for Illegal Employment?" In *International Conference on Eurasian Economies,* edited by Selahattin Sarı and Alp H. Gencer, 14–19. Istanbul: Beykent Ünivertesi.

Kale, Başak. 2014. "Transforming an Empire: The Ottoman Empire's Immigration and Settlement Policies in the Nineteenth and Early Twentieth Centuries." *Middle Eastern Studies* 50, no. 2: 252–271.

Kale, Başak. 2016. "The EU-Turkey Action Plan Is Imperfect, but Also Pragmatic, and Maybe Even Strategic." German Marshall Fund of the United States. https://www.academia

.edu/download/56398589/KALE_Basak_GMF_On_Turkey_EU-Turkey_Plan_Imperfect-Pragmatic_Feb_2016.pdf.

Kaliber, Alper. 2019. "Re-Engaging the Self/Other Problematic in Post-Positivist International Relations: The 1964 Expulsion of Greeks from Istanbul Revisited." *Southeast European and Black Sea Studies* 19, no. 3: 365–386.

Kalyvas, Stathis. 2015. *Modern Greece: What Everyone Needs to Know.* New York: Oxford University Press.

Karakasidou, Anastasia N. 1997. *Fields of Wheat, Hills of Blood: Passages of Nationhood in Greek Macedonia, 1870–1990.* Chicago: University of Chicago Press.

Karakoulaki, Marianna. 2018. "EU-Turkey Deal: The Burden on Refugees in Greece." Open Migration. https://openmigration.org/en/analyses/eu-turkey-deal-the-burden-on-refugees-in-greece/.

Karyotis, Georgios. 2012. "Securitization of Migration in Greece: Process, Motives, and Implications." *International Political Sociology* 6, no. 4: 390–408.

Kasaba, Resat. 2011. *A Moveable Empire: Ottoman Nomads, Migrants, and Refugees.* Seattle: University of Washington Press.

Kastoryano, Riva. 2002. *Negotiating Identities: States and Immigrants in France and Germany.* Princeton, NJ: Princeton University Press.

Katsikas, Stefanos. 2012. "Millet Legacies in a National Environment: Political Elites and Muslim Communities in Greece (1830s–1923)." In *State-Nationalisms in the Ottoman Empire, Greece and Turkey: Orthodox and Muslims, 1830–1945*, edited by Benjamin C. Fortna, Stefanos Katsikas, Dimitris Kamouzis, and Paraskevas Konortas, 60–84. London: Routledge.

Kaya, Ibrahim. 2008. *Legal Aspects of Irregular Migration in Turkey.* Irregular Migration Series, vol. 73. Legal Module. Fiesole: European University Institute.

Kaya, Omur, and Edna Erez. 2018. "Migration, Agency, and the Sex Industry: Practitioners' Perspectives on Foreign Sex Workers in Turkey." *International Journal of Offender Therapy and Comparative Criminology* 62, no. 10: 2954–2981.

Keyder, Caglar, and Ayhan Aksu-Koc. 1988. *External Labour Migration from Turkey and Its Impact: An Evaluation of the Literature.* Ottawa: International Development Research Center.

Kilberg, Rebecca. 2014. "Turkey's Evolving Migration Identity." *Migration Information Source* 24. https://www.migrationpolicy.org/article/turkeys-evolving-migration-identity.

Kirişçi, Kemal. 1996. "Is Turkey Lifting the 'Geographical Limitation'? The November 1994 Regulation on Asylum in Turkey." *International Journal of Refugee Law* 8, no. 3: 293–318.

Kirişci, Kemal. 2000. "Disaggregating Turkish Citizenship and Immigration Practices." *Middle Eastern Studies* 36, no. 3: 1–22.

Kirişci, Kemal. 2007. "Turkey: A Country of Transition from Emigration to Immigration." *Mediterranean Politics* 12, no. 1: 91–97.

Kirişci, Kemal. 2021. "As EU-Turkey Migration Agreement Reaches the Five Year Mark, Add a Job Creation Element." Brookings Institution, March 17, 2021. https://www.brookings.edu/blog/order-from-chaos/2021/03/17/as-eu-turkey-migration-agreement-reaches-the-five-year-mark-add-a-job-creation-element/.

Kirisci, Kemal, and Basak Yavcan. 2020. "As COVID-19 Worsens Precarity for Refugees, Turkey and the EU Must Work Together." Brookings Institution, June 11, 2020. https://www.brookings.edu/blog/order-from-chaos/2020/06/11/as-covid-19-worsens-precarity-for-refugees-turkey-and-the-eu-must-work-together/.

Korfalı, Deniz Karcı, and Tuğba Acar. 2018. "Migration from Central and Eastern Europe to Turkey." In *Between Mobility and Migration*, edited by Peter Scholten and Mark Van Ostaijen, 227–248. Cham: Springer.

Lazaridis G. and D. Skleparis. 2016. "Securitization of Migration and the Far Right: The Case of Greek Security Professionals." *International Migration.* 54/2: 176-192.

Martin, Philip L. 1991. *The Unfinished Story: Turkish Labour Migration to Western Europe: With Special Reference to the Federal Republic of Germany.* Geneva: International Labor Organization.

McCarthy, Justin. 1995. *Death and Exile: The Ethnic Cleansing of Ottoman Muslims, 1821–1922.* Princeton, NJ: Darwin Press.

McLaren, Lauren, and Burak Cop. 2011. "The Failure of Democracy in Turkey: A Comparative Analysis." *Government and Opposition* 46, no. 4: 485–516.

Micinski, Nicholas R. 2019. "Everyday Coordination in EU Migration Management: Civil Society Responses in Greece." *International Studies Perspectives* 20, no. 2: 129–148.

Miller, Mark J. 1981. *Foreign Workers in Western Europe: An Emerging Political Force.* New York: Praeger.

Mirak, Robert. 1983. *Torn Between Two Lands: Armenians in America, 1890 to World War I.* Cambridge, MA: Harvard University Press.

Muftuler-Bac, Meltem. 2020. "Turkey and the European Union Refugee Deal: Assessing Turkish Migration Policies and the External Protection of European Borders." MAGYC Project, University of Liège. http://www.magyc.uliege.be/wp-content/uploads/2020/06/D2.2-v1June2020.pdf.

Mügge, Liza. 2012. "Ideologies of Nationhood in Sending-State Transnationalism: Comparing Surinam and Turkey." *Ethnicities* 13, no. 3: 338–358.

Mylonas, Harris. 2012. *The Politics of Nation-Building: Making Co-Nationals, Refugees, and Minorities.* Cambridge: Cambridge University Press.

Norman, Kelsey P. 2019. "Inclusion, Exclusion or Indifference? Redefining Migrant and Refugee Host State Engagement Options in Mediterranean 'transit' countries." *Journal of Ethnic and Migration Studies* 45, no. 1: 42–60.

Norman, Kelsey P. 2020a. "Migration Diplomacy and Policy Liberalization in Morocco and Turkey." *International Migration Review* 54, no. 4: 115–1183. https://doi.org/10.1177/0197918319895271.

Norman, Kelsey P. 2020b. *Reluctant Reception: Refugees, Migration and Governance in the Middle East and North Africa.* Cambridge: Cambridge University Press.

Öktem, Kerem. 2014. *Turkey's New Diaspora Policy: The Challenge of Inclusivity, Outreach and Capacity.* Stiftung Mercator Initiative. Istanbul: Istanbul Policy Center, Sabanci University.

Østergaard-Nielsen, Eva. 2003. *Transnational Politics: The Case of Turks and Kurds in Germany.* London: Routledge.

Özden, Senay. 2013. *Syrian Refugees in Turkey*. Vol. 5. MPC Research Report. Fiesole: European University Institute, Migration Policy Centre.

Özerim, Mehmet Gökay. 2018. "Stretching, Opening or Sealing the Borders: Turkish Foreign Policy Conceptions and Their Impact on Migration, Asylum and Visa Policies." *Journal of Balkan and Near Eastern Studies* 20, no. 2: 165–182.

Papademetriou, Demetrios G. 1985. "Emigration and Return in the Mediterranean Littoral." *Comparative Politics* 18, no. 1: 21–39.

Parla, Ayse. 2007. "Irregular Workers or Ethnic Kin? Post-1990s Labour Migration from Bulgaria to Turkey." *International Migration* 45, no. 3: 157–181.

Parla, Ayse. 2019. *Precarious Hope: Migration and the Limits of Belonging in Turkey*. Stanford, CA: Stanford University Press.

Ragazzi, Francesco. 2009. "Governing Diasporas." *International Political Sociology* 3, no. 4: 378–397.

Ragazzi, Francesco. 2014. "A Comparative Analysis of Diaspora Policies." *Political Geography* 41, no. 7: 74–89.

Richards, Alan, and John Waterbury. 1990. *A Political Economy of the Middle East: State, Class, and Economic Development*. Boulder, CO: Westview Press.

Robson, Laura. 2017. *States of Separation: Transfer, Partition, and the Making of the Modern Middle East*. Berkeley: University of California Press.

Roucek, Joseph S., and Theodore Saloutos. 1956. *They Remember America: The Story of the Repatriated Greek-Americans*. Berkeley: University of California Press.

Sayari, Sabri. 1986. "Migration Policies of Sending Countries: Perspectives on the Turkish Experience." *Annals of the American Academy of Political and Social Science* 485, no. 1: 87–97.

Seccombe, Ian J., and Richard I. Lawless. 1986. "Between Western Europe and the Middle East: Changing Patterns of Turkish Labour Migration." *Revue Européenne des Migrations Internationales* 2, no. 1: 37–58.

Şeker, Nesim. 2013. "Forced Population Movements in the Ottoman Empire and the Early Turkish Republic: An Attempt at Reassessment Through Demographic Engineering." *European Journal of Turkish Studies* 16: 1–15.

Sert, Deniz, and Ugur Yildiz. 2016. "Governing Without Control: Turkey's 'Struggle' with International Migration." In *The Making of Neoliberal Turkey*, edited by Cenk Ozbay, Maral Erol, Aysecan Terzioglu, and Z. Umut Turem, 53–72. Farnham, Surrey: Ashgate.

Stivas, Dionysios. 2021. "Greece's Response to the European Refugee Crisis: A Tale of Two Securitizations." *Mediterranean Politics*, published online March 30, 2021. https://doi.org/10.1080/13629395.2021.1902198.

Thiollet, Helene. 2011. "Migration as Diplomacy: Labor Migrants, Refugees, and Arab Regional Politics in the Oil-Rich Countries." *International Labor and Working-Class History* 79, no. 1: 103–121.

Toksöz, Gülay. 2020. "The Gendered Impacts of Migration and Welfare Regimes: Migrant Women Workers in Turkey." In *Women, Migration and Asylum in Turkey: Developing Gender-Sensitivity in Migration Research, Policy and Practice*, edited by Lucy Williams, Emel Coşkun, and Selmin Kaşka, 69–92. Cham: Springer.

To Vima. 2019. "Government Trick with the 'Golden Visa'" [in Greek]. To Vima, March 19, 2019. https://www.tovima.gr/2019/03/19/inbox/handelsblatt-kolpo-tis-kyvernisis-me-ti-xrysi-viza/.

Triadafilopoulos, Triadafilos. 2008. "The 1923 Greek-Turkish Exchange of Populations and the Reformulation of Greek National Identity." Paper presented at the conference on *Exchange of Populations Between Greece and Turkey: An Assessment of the Consequences of the Treaty of Lausanne*. Refugee Studies Centre, University of Oxford.

Triandafyllidou, Anna. 1998. "National Identity and the 'Other.'" *Ethnic and Racial Studies* 21, no. 4: 593–612.

Triandafyllidou, Anna. 2009. "Greek Immigration Policy at the Turn of the 21st Century: Lack of Political Will or Purposeful Mismanagement?" *European Journal of Migration and Law* 11, no. 2: 159–177.

Tsourapas, Gerasimos. 2019. "The Syrian Refugee Crisis and Foreign Policy Decision-Making in Jordan, Lebanon, and Turkey." *Journal of Global Security Studies* 4, no. 4: 464–481.

Tsourapas, Gerasimos, and Sotirios Zartaloudis. 2021. "Leveraging the European Refugee Crisis: Forced Displacement and Bargaining in Greece's Bailout Negotiations." *Journal of Common Market Studies*, published online June 8, 2021.

Tziovas, Dimitris. 2016. *Greek Diaspora and Migration Since 1700: Society, Politics and Culture.* London: Routledge.

Ülker, Erol. 2008. "Assimilation of the Muslim Communities in the First Decade of the Turkish Republic (1923–1934)." *European Journal of Turkish Studies* (online). http://ejts.revues.orgwww.ejtsn.revues.org/822.

UNHCR. 2020. "UNHCR Turkey—Fact Sheet September 2020." https://data2.unhcr.org/en/documents/details/79121.

Veremis, Thanos. 2010. "The Making of Modern Greece." *Southeast European and Black Sea Studies* 10, no. 2: 259–260.

Vogel, Toby. 2011. "Greek Asylum System in Disarray." *Politico*, January 26, 2011. https://www.politico.eu/article/greek-asylum-system-in-disarray/.

Voutira, Eftihia. 2004. "Ethnic Greeks from the Former Soviet Union as "Privileged Return Migrants." *Espaces, Populations, Sociétés.* Pp. 533-544.

Yavuz, M. Hakan. 2001. "Five Stages of the Construction of Kurdish Nationalism in Turkey." *Nationalism and Ethnic Politics* 7, no. 3: 1–24.

Yildirim, Onur. 2007. *Diplomacy and Displacement: Reconsidering the Turco-Greek Exchange of Populations, 1922–1934.* London: Routledge.

Yildiz, Ahmet. 2010. *Ne Mutlu Türküm Diyebilene: Turk Ulusal Kimliginin Etno-Sekuler Sinarlari 1919–1938.* Istanbul: Iletisim Yayinlari.

Yosmaoğlu, İpek. 2013. *Blood Ties: Religion, Violence and the Politics of Nationhood in Ottoman Macedonia, 1878–1908.* Ithaca, NY: Cornell University Press.

Zolberg, Aristide R. 1983. "The Formation of New States as a Refugee-Generating Process." *Annals of the American Academy of Political and Social Science* 467, no. 1: 24–38.

COMMENTARY

Forced Migration and Nation-State Building

Riva Kastoryano

Greece and Turkey have a common border at the gate of the European Union. From within and without, they are affected, in different ways, by the "migration crises" of the 2020s. Turkey is a buffer state between the Middle East and the European Union, and as a result it has to control its borders from the East (Syria, Iraq, Iran, Afghanistan, Pakistan) and it has to filter departures to the West—to the European Union. Greece, a gateway to the Schengen space, has to manage its internal migration policy and its cooperation with member states of the European Union and with Turkey. Adamson's and Tsourapas's paper shows chronologically how these two neighboring countries have had historically converging and diverging dynamics with regard to forced migration, nationhood, border control, and sovereignty. However, other factors must be taken into account in these dynamics, such as integration/assimilation; citizenship/nationhood; diaspora formations and transfer of norms and values; and state and non-state actors. All these factors help to redefine the limits of policy with regard to the management of migration and the paradox of free movement in the European Union.

Greece and Turkey share history and geography. Their empires succeeded each other on the same territory. Their respective nation-state building with a common border occurred in the nineteenth and twentieth centuries. From empires to nation-states, border changes and international treaties led to displacement and to the forced migration of individuals between the two countries, creating "new diasporas" in every turn of their history. The agreed exchange of populations between

Greece and the new Turkish Republic in 1923, per the Treaty of Lausanne, concerned the expulsion of Orthodox Christians from Turkey to Greece and of Muslims from Greece to Turkey. The Treaty confirmed the ethno-religious origins of each nation. In Turkey, the "politics of population" at the core of a nationalist project has been translated to mean "eliminating the Other" with forced migration or deportation and/or expulsion.[1] Despite the adoption of state secularism as the foundation for the new Turkish Republic, "Islamic affiliation is seen a fundamental requirement for Turkishness."[2] Muslims from territories in the Balkans conquered or invaded by the Ottomans, categorized as "non-Turkish speaking Muslims," migrated to Turkey in the aftermath of the Balkan wars and the War of Independence, and melted into the Turkish identity.[3] Turkey thus became a "country of immigration" and settlement as a result of the collapse of the Ottoman Empire and loss of territories. The diversity of a multi-ethnic and multi-religious Ottoman Empire gave way to a new diversity still based in part on territorial identities and a "unified," nominally secular (Kemalist) nation, but with religion (Islam) as a cultural cornerstone of the new state (Turkey). Muslim identity thus became the leverage for assimilation of different peoples to the Turkish nation.

Different times, different empires, similar ambitions: Greeks, one of the oldest diaspora of human history, had dispersed all over the world long before and after the Byzantine Empire, all the while maintaining their ambition to "re-create a new Hellenic entity."[4] The historical emigration of Greeks was followed by the "repatriation" of the Greeks expelled from Turkey at the beginning of the twentieth century and again in 1966 and 1973, following the wars in Cyprus. At the end of the twentieth century, we saw the return of one part of the old diaspora, with the arrival in Greece of large numbers of people with Greek ancestry who had settled in different parts of the Soviet Union. This return migration is reminiscent of the arrival of *Aussiedler* (ethnic Germans) in Germany after the fall of the Berlin Wall in the same period.[5] The question that comes to mind is: Does Greek ancestry give the right to Greek citizenship in the same way that *Aussiedler* are de facto and de jure German citizens? Obviously, economic opportunities in modern Greece, its membership in the European Union, and the possibility of free circulation within the European space are important incentives for such return migration to Greece. It would be interesting to know, however, how many of these immigrants remained in Greece, and how many moved to another European country—all part of the story of the long and troubled relationship between Greece and Turkey.

Greeks and Turks: From *Gastarbeiter* (Guest workers) to Diaspora and Active Citizenship in the EU

A common ethno-religious understanding of nationhood made Greece and Turkey countries of immigration and settlement at different stages in their history. In the twentieth century both countries experienced military regimes, and refugees from Greece and Turkey flowed to Western Europe, the last big wave coming as the consequence of the 1980 coup in Turkey. In the 1960s, both countries responded to the call of Western Europe for cheap labor, with the objective of economic reconstruction in war-ravaged countries after World War II. Bilateral agreements brought migrants from Greece and Turkey, as well as from other Eastern Mediterranean countries, to Western Europe. While the emigration from Greece added to an old, existing diaspora in Western Europe, emigration from Turkey was a relatively new experience, yet both migrations were pushed mainly by economic incentives, with the persistent idea of return. This was true for Greek as well as Turkish migrants to Western Europe.

More than 4 million people who migrated from Turkey currently live in Europe. For Turkey, they constitute a new social category: Turks abroad. Circulating among different family, commercial, and voluntary associations, they link European private and public spaces as well as economic and political spaces to places in Turkey.[6] Turkey, like many other countries of emigration, has developed what is called "diaspora politics" and created in 2010 the Presidency for Turks Abroad and Related Communities (YTB). Despite their long experience as a diaspora, Greek expatriates created the World Council of Hellenes Abroad in 1995. While the declared objective of this organization is to "connect Greeks abroad to the home state," the Turkish state promotes the development of its diaspora with the aims of maintaining the loyalty of its citizens abroad and extending the home state's power *beyond* the national territory. The Turkish state expects Turks abroad to lobby for Turkey's full membership in the European Union. This implies the mobilization of business organizations and voluntary associations sometimes collaborating with the Turkish state and sometimes independently lobbying supranational institutions to put pressure on Turkey to democratize in order to respond to the Copenhagen criteria.

Adamson and Tsourapas's article attributes relations between migrants and home countries to the state's institutions and national strategy. Obviously, diaspora politics affects migrants' identification with home countries and orients their social, cultural, and political activities abroad. Even more important, however, are the activities, organizations, and mobilizations outside official diaspora channels and their effects on the home country.

It is important to note that Turks abroad are not homogeneous: they are Kurds, Alevîs, Sunni Muslims, secular Kemalists, and/or religious conservatives, all represented in diasporic associations, and they are active in the countries of destination. Yet despite their ethnic, religious, and ideological heterogeneity, Turks abroad refer to the Turkish nation-state as a source of national identity and of political conflict. Some diasporic organizations aim to influence the policies of host countries, lobbying governments on issues of integration, citizenship, and equality, promoting human and minority rights. Other groups push against the official ideology of Turkey as a unitary state. Together pro- and anti-Turkish diaspora link home and host country politics. The organization, mobilization, and participation of these diaspora reflect multiple belongings and competing identities, as migrants to western Europe and citizens of Turkey. Their political activities bring Turkey and Europe closer together, allowing expatriates to air their grievances in the courts and legislatures of west European democratic states and in the supranational institutions of the EU.

Political activities of the diaspora led Turkey to legalize dual citizenship and voting rights for Turks living abroad. Maintaining loyalty and a sense of belonging to the home country is a way to fight for their rights in the host countries, and their rights and recognition in the country of origin. New Turkish political actors have emerged in voluntary associations supported by European institutions, and some of these groups work against Turkish foreign policy. Such is the case of the Kurds, who found recognition and legitimacy through European institutions and political freedom that has allowed them to make claims based on their national, regional, and ethnic belonging as well as on divisions of identity in Turkey. As for religious representation, the brotherhoods (*tarikat*) correspond to interest groups that play the political game in Europe and in Turkey. They gain recognition with the AKP in power, as with Millî Görüs which competes with Diyanet (DITIB) to represent Turkish Islamic groups that also have gained legitimacy through the AKP. The Alevis, on the other hand, thanks to their mobilization in associations have sensitized European public opinion and governments to the historical, sociological, and political realities in Turkey. It is not just the state using the diaspora to shape migration and settlement. We also must take into account the struggle for rights of Turks abroad and at home that are the products of emerging non-state transnational actors and their growing influence.

The key difference between the Greek diaspora and the transnational mobilization of Turkish migrants stems from the relationship of Greece and Turkey to the European Union and other supranational institutions. How are Greeks abroad organized? What is their strategy with regard to home-state politics, but most important toward European politics, mainly when Greece was going through the euro crisis? As a gateway to the European Union at the border of Schengen, what is the role of the

Greek diaspora in the management of migration? And what are the terms of lobbying if any, by the European branch of Greeks abroad before the European Commission, or in the courts? It is obvious that Turks abroad have a lot of issues to present and negotiate with European institutions: in working for EU membership, the opponents of the Turkish regime express their claim on human and minority rights, as well as freedom of speech.

Migration Crises at the Gate of the European Union: Internal and External Borders

Both Greece and Turkey have become countries of immigration in many ways:

1. Through return migration from Western Europe—Greeks from the former Soviet Union migrating to Greece and non–Turkish speaking Muslims from the Balkans migrating to Turkey. Together these flows confirm the nature of the *ethno-religious nationhood* of both countries, going back to the beginning of the twentieth century.
2. Both countries attract migrants via economic liberalism and golden passports in exchange for investment. These policies grant access to the citizenship of the European Union through Greece and, for Turkey, the incentives to migrate are big for Iranians, Qataris, and Egyptians, among others, eager to flee stifling autocratic regimes, spurred on by religious affinity and economic opportunities in strong emerging markets in neighboring countries.
3. Flows of asylum seekers to Turkey from its southeastern border because of the wars in Iraq and Syria have made Turkey an important country of destination; many of these migrants travel through Turkey and Greece on their way to Western Europe, raising the stakes of border control during migration crises..

Migration management in times of crisis brings the importance of border control to the fore, and this ties directly into the internal and external policies of the European Union. Greece (as a member state) and Turkey (as a country bound by European Union neighborhood policies) have had to cope with the arrival of large numbers of asylum seekers following the onset of the Syrian civil war. Studies show that many of the millions of asylum seekers planned to stay in Turkey, and in the region, waiting for the end of the war; while some hoped to move on from Turkey to Europe and other destinations.[7]

The so-called migration crises generated by these flows from Syria has revealed the contradictions of European Union principles and discourses on human rights. The contradictions are exacerbated by the extensive Greek coastline, which has been the scene of illegal entries to the European space, challenging EU policies on migration, asylum, and protection of human rights. The management of asylum seekers has been a challenge to the unity of the European Union, revealing the lack of a common migration policy, difficulties in cooperation in migration control among member states, and the prioritization of narrow national interests over broader EU migration and refugee policies. Another contradiction in the policies stems from the difficulty of rebuffing asylum seekers at countries of first arrival or transit,[8] especially Turkey, which has been criticized for its unwillingness to abide by European principles with respect to human rights.

In response to EU pressures, Turkey had to introduce legal and institutional changes with regard to laws concerning the status of asylum seekers and refugees.[9] Turkey reformed its asylum policies, to consider asylum seekers not just as temporary but as permanent and to ensure their protection. At the same time, the presence of 3.5 million refugees settling on its territory gave Turkey leverage to negotiate with the European Union. In order to prevent the transit of asylum seekers and migrants to Europe, the European Union has externalized border control to Turkey. Six million Euros were allocated to build decent refugee camps and increase protections for refugees in Turkey. As a quid pro quo, Turkey negotiated a new visa waiver policy with the EU to allow greater freedom of movement for Turkish nationals in the EU.[10] The liberalization of Turkish visa policy has implications for immigration control as does the decision by Turkey to grant Turkish citizenship to Syrian refugees.[11] At the same time, political and economic instability in Turkey constitutes another push factor for migration to Europe.

The convergent and divergent dynamics of migration policy in these two neighboring countries show that migration is more than ever inscribed within the process of globalization. The chapter by Adamson and Tsourapas opens new theoretical perspectives such as the question of territory and border in globalization, the importance and the limits of extra-territoriality and the political power of diasporas. Many unanswered questions arise from the relationships between Turkey, Greece, and the EU, including questions about migration interdependence—a new and not very well understood dynamic in international relations,[12] and questions about human rights discourse and the rights of ethnic and immigrant groups, which are hotly debated in the European Union and beyond.

Notes

1. Ahmet Icduygu, Sule Toktas and B. Ali Soner, "The Politics of Population in a Nation-Building Process: Emigration of Non-Muslims from Turkey," *Ethnic and Racial Studies* 31, no. 2 (2008): 358–389.

2. Aron Rodrigue, "Reflections on Millets and Minorities: Ottoman Legacies," in Riva Kastoryano (ed.), *Turkey Between Nationalism and Globalization* (London: Routledge, 2013), 36–46.

3. Erol Ülker, "Assimilation of the Muslim Communities in the First Decade of the Turkish Republic," *European Journal of Turkish Studies* 7 (2007): 1-26.

4. Rodrigue, "Reflections on Millets."

5. Triadafilos Triadafilopoulos, "The Political Consequences of Forced Population Transfers: Refugee Incorporation in Greece and West Germany," in *European Encounters: Migrants, Migration and European Societies Since 1945*, ed. Rainer Ohliger, Karen Schönwälder and Triadafilos Triadafilopoulos (London: Routledge, 2017), https://doi.org/10.4324/9781315255972.

6. Stéphane de Tapia, "L'Émigration turque: circulation migratoire et diaspora," *L'Espace Géographique* 23, no. 1 (1994): 19–28.

7. Bill Frelick, I.M. Kysel, J. Podkul, "The Impact of Externalization of Migration Controls on the Rights of Asylum Seekers and Other Migrants," *Journal on Migration and Human Security* 4, no. 4 (2007): 190–220.

8. Ibid.

9. A. Içduygu, *Syrian Refugees in Turkey, The Long Road Ahead* (Washington, D.C.: Migration Policy Institute, 2015).

10. L. Laube, "The Relational Dimension of Externalizing Border Control: Selective Visa Policies in Migration and Border Diplomacy," *Comparative Migration Studies* 7, no. 29 (2019).

11. S. K.Akcapar and D.Simsek, "The Politics of Syrian Refugees in Turkey: A Question of Inclusion and Exclusion through Citizenship," *Social Inclusion* 6, no. 1 (2018): 176–187.

12. On the question of migration interdependence, see James F. Hollifield and Neil Foley, eds., *Understanding Global Migration* (Stanford, CA: Stanford University Press, 2022).

COMMENTARY

Migration Control as State-Making:
Toward an *Illiberal* Convergence Hypothesis?

Hélène Thiollet

Fiona Adamson and Gerasimos Tsourapas's chapter offers a historical comparison of migration policies in Greece and Turkey, covering mainly the period from the early twentieth century to the present. It provides a moving picture of migration trends—immigration, displacement, asylum, emigration—and examines the various and changing citizenship and integration policies that have been devised and implemented over time in both countries. Much of the scholarship tends to focus on the study of immigration control and integration policies in OECD countries, thus overlooking emigration politics. In contrast, Adamson and Tsourapas's careful analysis of the modern history of Greece and Turkey shows that neither country fits into the neat categories of "immigration/asylum" and "emigration/exile." This is a theoretically and empirically rich text, but three lines of inquiry stand out: first, and most importantly, the chapter shows that migration control has been, and remains, central to state formation; second, it sheds light on the entwined role of state and non-state actors in migration control; finally, it calls into question core theoretical assumptions discussed elsewhere in this volume—the liberal paradox and the liberal convergence hypothesis.

Migration Control as State-Making

Turning the approach taken in this volume—migration control as an output of state politics (see the Introduction)—on its head, Adamson and Tsourapas argue that emigration and immigration control, forced displacement, discriminatory policies, and even mass killings have been integral to Turkish and Greek state-making. To borrow from Charles Tilly's famous aphorism, migration control made the modern state.[1]

Historians of imperialism have emphasized the pivotal role that violent demographic and migration engineering played in the emergence of independent India,[2] as well as in African post-colonial states.[3] The Ottoman, as well as Greek, Hellenistic, and Byzantine, imperial roots of modern population and migration control are not, however, just "imperial debris," as Ann Laura Stoler has observed.[4] Critically examining such histories also implies, Ranabir Samaddar suggests, locating the colonial and imperial forces at work in contemporary migration governance.[5] At the domestic level, state-making operated through the forced displacement of targeted minority groups and, concomitantly, the resettlement of majority groups in areas that constituted an "internal frontier." It took the shape of discriminatory laws and assimilationist policies targeting specific ethnic groups as well as cultural and religious minorities. At the international level, through diplomacy and conflict, such state-making was bound up with long-distance population control, as evidenced by the long history of international population exchange, deportation, and repatriation, all of which was designed to create or consolidate demographic boundaries along state borders.

Extreme cases of such demographic engineering led to mass murder and ethnic cleansing in Greece and Turkey: from April 1915 to 1923, republican elites in the decaying Ottoman Empire organized the displacement, deportation, and massacre of some 2 million Armenians. Hans-Lukas Kieser's comparative study shows that the removal of the American Indians from Georgia and the Carolinas in the 1830s was seen as central to the birth of the American Republic and, likewise, the decimation of the Armenian population in Asia Minor was deemed necessary to the formation of the Turkish Republic.[6] Such a comparative perspective helps us understand violent migration and racial politics as an integral part of the *longue durée* history of state-making and nation-building.

Historical considerations on migration control as state-building draw our attention to the unequal, brutal, and murderous process that the transition from empire to modern state actually was, leading us to reconsider the merits of republican or democratic regimes in terms of migration politics. Indeed, this chapter makes an important contribution to ongoing debates on cosmopolitanism as well as on the limits of democratic inclusion.

As regards cosmopolitanism, both ancient Greece and Ottoman Turkey are held as examples of the ways in which multicultural empires, based as they were on local mechanisms of coexistence, accommodated super-diversity and fostered transnational circulation. It was only in the nineteenth century—early in it for Greece and later in it for Turkey—that modern states sought to homogenize their cosmopolitan subjects to forge them into a nation, a process fraught with conflict, as illustrated by the case of late nineteenth-century Ottoman cities.[7] Ottoman cosmopolitanism was, however, intrinsically hierarchical, as it was governed by the imperial *millet* system, whereby distinct ethnic and religious minorities were granted different rights and duties. Recent scholarship has shown that these post-colonial legacies pervade contemporary management of transnational migration and diversity.[8] Today, even in liberal contexts, the management of immigration and integration is underpinned by differentiated policies and racialized practices.[9] The 2015 refugee crisis in the European Union was a case in point. Depending on the categories of migrants and on their countries of origin, European migration and asylum policies have fluctuated between hospitality and refoulement, between integration and encampment, thus establishing, again, a hierarchical management system.

Regarding democratic inclusion, it should be noted that the democratic culture of Greek city-states was actually based on a myth, that of the autochthony of the *demos*. Civic integration was strictly limited, creating a mass of "perpetual immigrants."[10] Contemporary Gulf monarchies, with their throngs of eternal "guest workers," could be described as the latest iteration of this restrictive system. Such a comparison between illiberal and liberal systems may seem surprising since, unlike ancient Greece, Gulf states are often characterized as highly exclusionary contexts.[11] But in fact, in the classical *polis*, a very small number of male citizens were granted differentiated rights, while foreigners or *metoikoi* (as well as women and slaves) were excluded from the *demos*. A nativist definition of citizens as "sons of the soil" or autochthones underpinned this exclusionary democracy. The beliefs underlying the politics of internal migration and ethnic conflict in modern and contemporary India are also reminiscent of the Greek myth of an autochthonous citizenry: as Myron Weiner demonstrated in his seminal *Sons of the Soil*, political rights and mobility in the world's largest democracy were tied to ethnicity.[12] There are echoes of such representations and practices limiting democratic inclusion in today's nativist discourses and anti-immigrant politics in OECD countries: anthropologist Michel Agier sees, indeed, the rise of the idea of "national autochthonies" as a key aspect of, and a decisive factor in, contemporary migration management.[13]

Who Controls Migration?

Greek and Turkish histories exemplify the complex array of social, economic and political dynamics, both public and private, that combine to generate migration. In the fifteenth and sixteenth centuries, Greek-speaking Ottoman subjects traveled far and wide and, relying on Orthodox and Jewish social networks and devotional confraternities, settled throughout the Mediterranean, especially in the Italian port cities of Ancona, Genoa, and Venice.[14] They served as a means of commercial expansion and as a channel of private diplomacy for the Ottoman Empire. From 1805 to 1848, Muhammad Ali, the Ottoman ruler of Egypt, encouraged Europeans, notably Greeks and Italians, to move to Egypt with a view to fostering trade relations across the Mediterranean. The Greek community of Egypt (Aigyptiotes) grew in size and influence as a result of the cotton boom in the 1860s, and over time it came to constitute an ethnic minority operating migration and commercial networks, which, in turn, attracted more immigrants in the wake of the 1893 economic crisis in Greece. After Egypt gained independence in 1922, the Egyptian Greeks, however, ended up losing their legal and trade privileges and tax exemptions, first as a result of the Montreux Convention Regarding the Abolition of the Capitulations in Egypt (1937) and later following Nasser's sweeping nationalization of the economy in the late 1950s and early 1960s. Although they had Egyptian nationality, a majority of them reemigrated to Australia, North America, or Europe, using the new diasporic networks that had been established by emigrants during the Greek civil war (1946–1949) and in the early days of the Regime of the Colonels (1967–1974).

From the 1960s onward, emigration from Greece and Turkey was channeled through social networks for labor recruitment and family reunification, and was, moreover, facilitated by formal agreements between sending and receiving countries across Europe. Greek and Turkish diasporas grew accordingly to encompass hundreds of thousands of workers and, later on, their families as well. The Greek and Turkish states would, however, only formalize their relations with their respective diaspora communities much later, in the 1980s, for financial purposes and with an eye to political mobilization. The increasing role of the state notwithstanding, private networks and institutions remained influential actors weighing in from abroad, sometimes supporting their government's policies, sometimes opposing them. One such example of a powerful, albeit ultimately unstable, public-private partnership is the Gülen movement, a transnational religious network also known as the Cemaat (community). In the lead-up to the 2002 general elections, the Gülen movement was active in mustering support in the diaspora for the Justice and Development Party's (AKP) bid for power, and it was instrumental in consolidating President Recep Tayyip Erdoğan's rule thereafter. The ruling party relied on the Cemaat to further Turkey's diplomatic objectives abroad, especially in Iraqi Kurdistan, where it promoted Turkification policies through schools and charity organizations. This public-private partnership between the AKP and the Cemaat lasted until 2013, when their relations irretrievably broke down in the context of a series of corruption investigations. In 2016, after a failed coup attempt, which the ruling party blamed on Fethullah Gülen, the government retaliated with a massive crackdown on the movement and classified it as a terrorist organization.

Recognizing that migration control is an integral part of state formation does not mean overstating the role of the state and thus disregarding non-state actors. Rather, state and non-state actors, as well as social, economic, and cultural dynamics, combine in various ways, determining migration flows and shaping the lives of immigrants in the process. As states constantly push for greater migration control, social intermediaries and institutions fostering population movements as well as promoting migrant integration policies have been either turned into state partners or criminalized. On the one hand, scholars have shown that public-private partnerships in migration management, involving employers, labor recruiters, and other service providers, have fueled the privatization of migration control.[15] While such forms of hybrid governance have sometimes been praised for their efficiency, they have also been denounced for their lack of democratic accountability and legitimacy in instances where private security companies operate border control,[16] run detention centers, and carry out deportation orders.[17] On the other hand, smugglers have been consistently portrayed in political discourse as the main culprits in the abuse and exploitation that migrants suffer and, moreover, as the driving force behind unwanted immigration flows.

Governmental policies both create and are based on a strict moral distinction between those deemed legitimate managers of "orderly" migration (where such migration is invariably tied to a Weberian definition of the state) and those vilified as unruly social actors and harbingers of disorder. Yet in both host and origin countries, the public image of intermediaries is, in fact, more ambivalent, oscillating as it does between greedy villains and good Samaritans.[18] Beyond the politicization of the figure of the intermediary and the resulting contest of moral imaginations, several scholars have identified policies aimed at stemming migration flows as the major factor behind the boom in the illegal migration industry:[19] as greater restrictions have been placed on the legal channels for labor migration and asylum, irregular routes have attracted growing numbers of migrants, and the smuggling business has prospered as a result. To borrow again from Charles Tilly, states have sought to distinguish their legitimate migration control and integration policies, especially those assuming violent forms (deportation, detention, death at the border, forced settlement, encampment, etc.), "from violence delivered by anyone else."[20] But, as Adamson and Tsourapas point out in relation to the particularly violent "migration politics" that marked the Greek war of independence (1821–1830), it is "dubious whether [acts of violence against Muslim Greeks] constituted state policy." State-sponsored legitimizing discourses oversimplify complex realities, thus obfuscating the actual, sometimes messy, processes taking place on the ground, in which political intentions, contingencies, and structures are inextricably intertwined.

The Illiberal Paradox and Illiberal Convergence

The idea that regime type makes a difference in governance outcomes is central to a number of theoretical assumptions discussed in this volume, notably the liberal paradox in migration policymaking[21] and the liberal convergence hypothesis.[22] A comparative analysis of Greece and Turkey, such as that offered here by Adamson and Tsourapas, calls into question the difference supposed to exist between "liberal" migration control in the West and "illiberal" migration policies in the rest.[23] Moreover, it challenges the belief that Western liberal democracies contribute to the diffusion of norm-abiding and rights-based migration governance in non-Western contexts.

Greece joined the EU in 1981; Turkey was officially recognized as a candidate for full membership in 1999, but EU accession negotiations were effectively frozen in 2018 due to "backsliding in areas of democracy, rule of law and fundamental rights."[24] Yet Adamson and Tsourapas's study reveals that convergence between countries might not, in fact, be dependent on regime type, but rather determined by perceived political interests and international power politics: following the 2015 refugee crisis, the Greek-Turkish border was significantly strengthened and increasingly politicized, de facto becoming a front line. In 2016, Serbia and Hungary erected walls and deployed troops to close the Balkan route, thus isolating Greece and turning it into the latest battlefield of an ever more securitized asylum and migration management system. In keeping with similar regional agreements with countries in the Maghreb, the Horn of Africa, and the Sahel, the 2016 EU-Turkey declaration was designed to drastically restrict the influx of Syrian, Afghan, Iraqi, and Eritrean asylum seekers into Europe.[25] While Turkish borders had previously been liberally open to both labor migrants and asylum seekers from the Middle East, EU external migration governance led to greater closure and more control, reaching into Turkey itself. Surely this represents some sort of *illiberal* paradox: an illiberal regime, Turkey, has implemented liberal migration and asylum policies, whereas European liberal democracies, including Greece, have restricted migrant rights and mobility.

Furthermore, in contrast to the liberal promise, the foreign policy of European immigration control can hardly be described as an attempt to export liberal norms.[26] EU externalization policies—Eurocentric in nature and by design—have created buffer zones around the Schengen area to contain migrants and asylum seekers within neighboring countries, collectively transformed into a "transit" space as a result.[27] The EU's migration control agenda trumps the principles of the liberal paradox in member states and, moreover, promotes *illiberal* convergence abroad: offshoring (and funding) refugee refoulement and migration policing allows liberal EU states to escape the many constraints placed on policymaking at the European and national level.

While this type of migration management is particularly prevalent in times of crisis, it has been a structural feature of EU migration policies since the 1990s. Greece and Turkey are, moreover, part of the trend toward the global commodification of citizenship and the expansion of visa policies giving the rich and "talented" differentiated access to mobility at the expense of low-skilled and poorer migrants.[28] Class- and nationality-based inequalities are the "new normal," or so we are told, but they are often combined with other intersectional hierarchies in terms of access to citizenship and mobility, such as gender, age, and race. Such openly discriminatory practices and policies have created a global mobility divide.[29] These structural developments in migration management suggest new avenues of inquiry and open up scholarly discussions on what may be called the global *illiberal* convergence hypothesis.

Notes

1. Charles Tilly, "War Making and State Making as Organized Crime," in *Bringing the State Back In*, ed. Peter B. Evans, Dietrich Rueschemeyer, and Theda Skocpol, 1st ed. (Cambridge: Cambridge University Press, 1985), 170, https://doi.org/10.1017/CBO9780511628283.008.

2. Radhika Viyas Mongia, *Indian Migration and Empire: A Colonial Genealogy of the Modern State* (Durham, NC: Duke University Press, 2018).

3. Frederick Cooper, *Citizenship, Inequality, and Difference: Historical Perspectives*, The Lawrence Stone Lectures (Princeton; NJ; Oxford: Princeton University Press, 2018).

4. Ann Laura Stoler, "'The Rot Remains': From Ruins to Ruination," in *Imperial Debris: On Ruins and Ruination*, ed. Ann Laura Stoler (Durham, NC ; London: Duke University Press, 2013), 1–37.

5. Ranabir Samaddar, *The Postcolonial Age of Migration* (London: Routledge India, 2020).

6. Hans-Lukas Kieser, "Removal of American Indians, Destruction of Ottoman Armenians. American Missionaries and Demographic Engineering," *European Journal of Turkish Studies*, no. 7 (23 September 2008), https://doi.org/10.4000/ejts.2873.

7. Ulrike Freitag and Nora Lafi, eds., *Urban Governance under the Ottomans: Between Cosmopolitanism and Conflict*, First issued in paperback, SOAS Routledge Studies on the Middle East 21 (Abingdon; New York; London: Routledge, 2017).

8. Sheldon Pollock et al., "Cosmopolitanisms," in *Cosmopolitanism*, ed. Sheldon Pollock et al. (Durham, NC; London: Duke University Press, 2002), 1–14, https://doi.org/10.2307/j.ctv11smfp5.3.

9. Catherine Lejeune et al., "Migration, Urbanity and Cosmopolitanism in a Globalized World: An Introduction," in *Migration, Urbanity and Cosmopolitanism in a Globalized World*, ed. Catherine Lejeune et al., IMISCOE Research Series (Cham: Springer International Publishing, 2021), 1–13, https://doi.org/10.1007/978-3-030-67365-9_1.

10. Demetra Kasimis, *The Perpetual Immigrant and the Limits of Athenian Democracy*, 2018.

11. Hélène Thiollet and Laure Assaf, "Cosmopolitanism in Exclusionary Contexts," *Population, Space and Place*, 2021, e2358, https://doi.org/10.1002/psp.2358.

12. Myron Weiner, *Sons of the Soil: Migration and Ethnic Conflict in India* (Princeton, N.J: Princeton University Press, 1978).

13. Michel Agier, *La Condition Cosmopolite: L'anthropologie à l'épreuve Du Piège Identitaire* (Paris: La Découverte, 2013).

14. Niccolò Fattori, *Migration and Community in the Early Modern Mediterranean: The Greeks of Ancona, 1510-1595*, Palgrave Studies in Migration History (Palgrave Pivot, 2019), https://doi.org/10.1007/978-3-030-16904-6.

15. Gallya Lahav, "Immigration and the State: The Devolution and Privatisation of Immigration Control in the EU," *Journal of Ethnic and Migration Studies* 24, no. 4 (October 1998): 675–94, https://doi.org/10.1080/1369183X.1998.9976660; Thomas Gammeltoft-Hansen and Ninna Nyberg Sørensen, eds., *The Migration Industry and the Commercialization of International Migration*, Routledge Global Institutions Series (London ; New York: Routledge, 2013).

16. Lemberg-Martin Lamberg Pedersen, "Private Security Companies and the European Borderscapes," in *The Migration Industry and the Commercialization of International Migration*, ed. Thomas Gammeltoft-Hansen and Ninna Nyberg Sørensen, Routledge Global Institutions Series (London; New York: Routledge, 2013), 152–72.

17. Nicholas De Genova and Nathalie Mae Peutz, eds., *The Deportation Regime: Sovereignty, Space, and the Freedom of Movement* (Durham, NC; London: Duke University Press, 2010).

18. Anna Triandafyllidou, "Migrant Smuggling: Novel Insights and Implications for Migration Control Policies," *The ANNALS of the American Academy of Political and Social Science* 676, no. 1 (March 2018): 212–21, https://doi.org/10.1177/0002716217752330.

19. Koser, "Why Migrant Smuggling Pays"; Gathmann, "Effects of Enforcement on Illegal Markets: Evidence from Migrant Smuggling along the Southwestern Border."

20. Tilly, "War Making and State Making as Organized Crime," 172.

21. James Hollifield, *Immigrants, Markets, and States: The Political Economy of Postwar Europe* (Cambridge, Mass: Harvard University Press, 1992).

22. Marc R. Rosenblum and Wayne A. Cornelius, "Dimensions of Immigration Policy," in *Oxford Handbook of the Politics of International Migration*, ed. Daniel J. Tichenor and Marc R. Rosenblum (New York: Oxford University Press, 2012), 245–73, https://doi.org/10.1093/oxfordhb/9780195337228.013.0011.

23. Research on immigration control still focuses mainly, if not overwhelmingly, on the study of immigration politics in (Western) liberal democracies, thus making any promise of providing a "global perspective" on immigration control ring hollow.

24. Source: https://ec.europa.eu/neighbourhood-enlargement/countries/detailed-country-information/turkey_en; Council of the European Union, "Enlargement and Stabilisation and Association Process," 12.

25. European Commission, "EU-Turkey Statement," institutional, Europa.eu, 2016, https://www.consilium.europa.eu/en/press/press-releases/2016/03/18/eu-turkey-statement/.

26. Sandra Lavenex, "Shifting Up and Out: The Foreign Policy of European Immigration Control," *West European Politics* 29, no. 2 (March 2006): 329–50, https://doi.org/10.1080/01402380500512684.

27. Michael Collyer, Franck Düvell, and Hein de Haas, "Critical Approaches to Transit Migration," *Population, Space and Place* 18, no. 4 (July 2012): 407–14, https://doi.org/10.1002/psp.630.

28. Ayelet Shachar and Ran Hirschl, "On Citizenship, States, and Markets," *Journal of Political Philosophy* 22, no. 2 (June 2014): 231–57, https://doi.org/10.1111/jopp.12034.

29. Steffen Mau et al., "The Global Mobility Divide: How Visa Policies Have Evolved Over Time," *Journal of Ethnic and Migration Studies* 41, no. 8 (3 July 2015): 1192–1213, https://doi.org/10.1080/1369183X.2015.1005007.

14 Immigration and Citizenship in Japan and South Korea

Erin Aeran Chung

Introduction

Japan and South Korea (hereafter "Korea") are among the few liberal democracies where immigration does not occupy center stage in politics today. Often described as negative cases in comparative studies of immigration and citizenship (Bartram 2000; Seol and Skrentny 2009; Chung and Hosoki 2018), the two East Asian democracies have maintained consistently low levels of immigration despite labor shortages beginning in the 1980s and impending demographic crises. Both countries' working-age populations are projected to fall to a little over 50 percent of their total population by 2050, similar to the rapidly aging societies of Italy and Spain. The United Nations Population Division issued a report two decades ago that suggested that replacement migration would be necessary to meet the challenges of declining populations. According to the 2001 report, Japan would have to admit approximately 647,000 immigrants and Korea 129,000 immigrants annually in order to meet their demographic challenges.[1] Although the number of foreign nationals in both countries has grown at a rapid pace in recent years—over threefold in Japan, from about 850,000 in 1985 to over 2.9 million in 2019, and almost twelvefold in Korea, from about 210,000 in 2000 to almost 2.5 million in 2019 (see Figure 14.1)—foreign residents made up only about 2 percent of the total population in Japan and approximately 5 percent in Korea as of 2019, which is especially stark given the record pace at which both countries' total populations are shrinking (Chung 2019b).

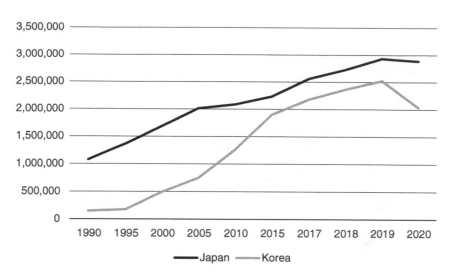

FIGURE 14.1. Foreign Residents in Japan and Korea, 1990–2020
SOURCES: Ministry of Justice, Japan; Korea Immigration Service.

As traditional migrant-sending countries, Japan and Korea have seen their emigrant populations far outnumber their immigrant populations until recently. The net migration rate as of 2020 was 0.75 per 1,000 persons in Japan and 2.65 for Korea.[2] It was only in the late 1980s that both countries began to receive relatively large numbers of immigrants, mostly from other parts of Asia, and their immigration policies have consistently restricted entry, employment, and settlement rights to select categories of migrants, mostly high-skilled professionals, dependents, and co-ethnic immigrants (see Tables 14.1 and 14.2). Unskilled migrant workers were prohibited from entry through official channels until 2004 in Korea and 2019 in Japan and continue to face significant barriers to settlement (due to the length of their visas) and family formation (because they do not have family reunification rights). And citizenship policies in both countries extend descent indefinitely such that native-born generations of immigrant descendants must undergo the formal process of naturalization in order to gain citizenship status, regardless of generation or co-ethnicity.

To explain why East Asian countries have resisted large-scale importation of foreign labor, the dominant scholarship has tended to focus on cultural determinants, particularly claims of ethnocultural homogeneity, characterizing Japan and Korea as "laggards" (Sellek 2001; Tsuda 2006; Seol and Skrentny 2009; Castles et al. 2014; Sharpe 2014). Are Japan and Korea fundamentally "latecomers" to immigration that will eventually liberalize their immigration and citizenship policies like other recent countries of immigration?

TABLE 14.1. Registered Foreign Residents in Japan by Nationality, 1985–2019

Year	Korea (N&S)	China	Philippines	U.S.A.	Brazil	Peru	Vietnam	Bangladesh	Othera	Total	%b
1985	683,313	74,924	12,261	29,044	1,955	N/A	4,126	684	44,305	850,612	0.7
1990	687,940	150,339	49,092	38,364	56,429	10,279	6,233	2,109	76,532	1,075,317	0.9
1995	666,376	222,991	74,297	43,198	176,440	36,269	9,099	4,935	128,766	1,362,371	1.1
2000	635,269	335,575	144,871	44,856	254,394	46,171	16,908	7,176	201,224	1,686,444	1.3
2005	598,687	519,561	163,890	49,390	298,382	52,217	28,932	11,015	289,481	2,011,555	1.6
2010	560,799	687,156	200,208	50,667	228,702	52,385	41,354	10,175	255,815	2,087,261	1.7
2015	491,711	665,847	229,595	52,271	173,437	47,721	146,956	10,835	413,816	2,232,189	1.8
2019	481,522	813,675	260,553	55,713	191,362	47,972	262,405	14,144	517,287	2,561,848	2.0

SOURCES: Ministry of Justice; Japan Statistical Yearbook.

aThe "other" category includes nationals of more than 200 countries in every continent. Among the largest numbers of foreign residents in this category include nationals of Nepal, India, Thailand, Indonesia, the United Kingdom, Canada, and Australia.

bThis column refers to the percentage of the total Japanese population.

TABLE 14.2. Foreign Residents in Korea by Nationality, 2000-2017

Year	China (Korean Chinese)	Vietnam	Philippines	U.S.A.	Thailand	Indonesia	Taiwan	Myanmar	Mongolia	Other[a]	Total[b]	%[c]
2000	58,984 (32,443)	15,624	15,961	22,778	3,240	16,700	23,026		769	53,167	491,324	1.1
2005	282,030 (167,589)	38,902	38,057	103,029	34,188	25,599	25,121	3,374	22,475	172,692	747,467	1.5
2010	608,881 (409,079)	103,306	47,241	127,140	44,250	31,728	24,760	4,565	29,920	239,624	1,261,415	2.5
2015	955,871 (626,655)	136,758	54,977	138,660	93,348	46,538	30,002	19,209	30,527	393,629	1,899,519	3.7
2016	1,016,607 (627,004)	149,384	56,980	140,222	100,860	47,606	34,003	22,455	35,206	446,118	2,049,441	4.0
2017	1,018,074 (679,729)	169,738	58,480	143,568	153,259	45,328	36,168	24,902	45,744	485,237	2,180,498	4.2

SOURCES: Korea Immigration Service; Korean Statistical Information Service.

a"Other" includes nationals of more than 200 countries on every continent. Among the largest numbers of foreign residents in this category are nationals of Japan, Uzbekistan, Sri Lanka, Cambodia, Pakistan, Canada, Bangladesh, and India.

bThe numbers include unauthorized foreigners in Korea. In 2017, they numbered 251,041, making up 11.5% of the total foreign population.

cPercentage of total Korean population.

This chapter examines how Japan and Korea maintained low levels of immigration while securing necessary foreign labor through "side door" immigration policies that eventually generated divergent patterns of immigrant incorporation in each country. While international norms and domestic political elites such as political parties, bureaucrats, and activist courts have played central roles in expanding immigrant rights and services in North America and Europe (Soysal 1994; Guiraudon 1998; Joppke 1999; Matias 2016; Ellermann 2021), liberal reforms in East Asian democracies were implemented only after considerable pressure was applied from internal grassroots movements (Gurowitz 1999; Kim 2003; Lim 2003; Chung 2010a, 2020b, 2020b). Liberal reforms have, moreover, been applied unevenly to different categories of foreign nationals within Japan and Korea and have not resulted in the liberalization of immigration policies themselves (Kim 2008; Surak 2008). In areas such as social welfare in Japan and local voting rights in Korea, non-citizen rights surpass those prescribed in international human rights treaties (Chung 2020b). But Japan and Korea have remained immune to international pressure in other areas such as refugee policies, where they hold among the worst records in the industrialized world for accepting refugees (Flowers 2009; Wolman 2013).

The dominant English-language scholarship on citizenship and immigration based on case studies of liberal democracies in North America and Europe has offered insights into migration policies across a wide array of countries. At the same time, they are often inadequate for explaining patterns among countries that have resisted large-scale importation of foreign labor through a set of relatively restrictive immigration and citizenship policies, which not only prohibit the permanent settlement of migrant populations but also may not acknowledge their presence or permit their entry at the formal level. In these cases, the expansion of one area, such as migrant worker quotas, does not necessarily imply the liberalization of another, such as pathways to citizenship for migrant workers. And the expansion of institutionalized rights for one subcategory of migrants in a single national context does not make those rights universal, or even accessible, for others.

The following section surveys the overlapping immigration histories and policies of Japan and Korea through the late 1990s, focusing on how bureaucrats in both countries formulated unofficial "side door" policies and practices to meet domestic demands for labor while maintaining closed borders to unskilled foreign labor. The next section examines the areas where immigrant policies have diverged, focusing on each country's first comprehensive proposals for immigrant incorporation and rates of naturalization and permanent residency. Finally, I discuss the prospects and challenges for immigrant incorporation in East Asia. This chapter defines "immigrant incorporation" as the process by which immigrants and their descendants become permanent members of their receiving societies, including political participants (see Messina 2007, 233). Although I use the term "immigrants" to refer primarily to the first generation, "immigrant incorporation" can refer to policies and practices pertaining to multiple generations of foreign residents (Chung 2020b). Incorporation, as understood this way, is equivalent neither to full legal membership as national citizens nor to socio-cultural assimilation (see Chung 2010b, 677).

Immigration Control Through Closed Borders and Side Doors

Japan and Korea's overlapping immigration policies are, in part, the product of their intertwined migration histories. Until 2006, Koreans made up the largest foreign community in Japan. While some within the community were recently arrived South Korean immigrants, the vast majority were colonial-era migrants and their descendants. Japan's colonization of Korea (1910–1945) set in motion mass emigration from the Korean peninsula to the Japanese archipelago, Manchuria, maritime Russia, and the Americas. By the end of the Pacific War in 1945, approximately 15 percent of the total Korean population had migrated from the Korean peninsula, including more than 4 million to Japan and Manchuria, approximately 170,000 to Russia/USSR, and over 10,000 to the Americas (J. Kim 2016). Unlike European imperial powers, Japan colonized neighboring territories, which allowed for large numbers of colonial migrants to enter the metropole in the early stages of colonization and facilitated the forced recruitment of colonial subjects in the later stages as laborers and soldiers. Korea was an especially important source of industrial labor and military manpower.

On the eve of Japan's defeat in the Pacific War, over 2 million Korean and Formosan (Taiwanese) colonial subjects had migrated to the Japanese metropole as laborers, soldiers, and students (Chung 2020b). About two-thirds of this population repatriated to the Korean peninsula and Taiwan during the early postwar years; the some 700,000 who remained were reclassified from Japanese nationals to aliens. The Alien Registration Law (first enacted in 1947 and revised in 1952 in conjunction with the San Francisco Peace Treaty that formally declared colonial subjects aliens) required non-Japanese nationals to register with their local authorities, submit their fingerprints, and carry their alien registration card with them at all time, thereby allowing government authorities to closely monitor their whereabouts (Chung 2010a).[3] In 1950, the Diet passed the Nationality Act (modeled after Germany's citizenship policies), which affirmed the principle of patrilineal *jus sanguinis* from the 1899 Meiji law. This law was subsequently amended in 1985 to allow individuals to acquire nationality through either their mother or their father following Japan's ratification of the Convention on the Elimination of All Forms of Discrimination Against Women.

Postwar Japan's immigration and border control laws, which were modeled after the 1924 US Johnson-Reed Immigration Act, which set specific quotas based on country of origin, fortified what had been the porous borders of the Japanese Empire. Not only did these new policies aim to curb new immigration—primarily from Japan's former colonies—but they also sought to prevent return migration by Korean colonial-era migrants who had recently repatriated to the Korean peninsula but, upon encountering politically and socially volatile conditions there, sought reentry into Japan. Korean return migrants, thus, became postwar Japan's first "illegal" immigrants, subject to deportation in a newly fortified Japanese nation-state with closed borders (Morris-Suzuki 2010).

South Korea, meanwhile, did not establish its Immigration Control Act until 1963, following the tumultuous years of the Korean War (1950–1953), the toppling of Syngman Rhee's dictatorial regime (1948–1960) by a student-led mass movement, and two years of martial law that followed a military coup led by Park Chung Hee in 1961. Like many of the policies enacted during his presidency, Park modeled Korea's immigration laws after those of Japan with strict border controls. But Korea was not an attractive migration destination until the late 1980s following the country's democratic transition in 1987 and two decades of rapid economic growth, when per capita GDP grew from approximately $100 in 1965 to over $5,700 in 1989.

Until the 1980s, Japan and Korea responded to intermittent labor shortages by recruiting domestic sources of underutilized labor, such as rural workers and women. Following decades of urbanization and the expansion of educational and employment opportunities for women, these sources were largely depleted by the time that both countries faced another labor shortage beginning in the late 1980s. Rather than open their borders to foreign labor, however, Japan and Korea instituted almost identical de facto guest worker policies through the reorganization and expansion of visa categories that included (1) short-term visas for "trainees" and "interns" under the guise of a skills training program and (2) favorable visa policies for co-ethnic migrants (immigrants of "native" ethnicity with foreign nationality), the majority of whom were ethnic Japanese immigrants from Brazil and Peru coming to Japan and ethnic Koreans from China coming to Korea (Chung 2010b; Surak 2018; Chung and Tian 2018).

Japan

Japan's immigration history can be divided broadly into three categories: (1) colonial migration from the early twentieth century to the immediate post–World War II period; (2) relatively small numbers of refugee and "skilled" migration from the late 1970s to the early 1980s; and (3) large-scale unskilled labor migration from Asia and

Latin America from the late 1980s to the present (Chung 2020b). Although Japanese employers and officials played important roles in recruiting immigrants—forcibly for a subsection of colonial migrants starting in 1939—Japan's borders were, until 2019, officially open only for the first wave of migration, when Japan was a colonial power with territories that included Formosa, Korea, southern Sakhalin Island, the Kwantung Leased Territory on the Liaotung peninsula, and Japanese mandate islands of Micronesia (Chen 1984, 241). In addition, over 2 million emigrants from the Japanese archipelago settled in the Americas and in Japan's former colonies in Asia by the 1960s.

Postwar Japan's disincorporation of former colonial subjects from Japanese citizenship resulted in the formation of a legal "limbo" status (see Lori 2019) that would have path-dependent effects on how this population of mostly Korean colonial-era migrants and their descendants in Japan would negotiate the terms of their incorporation. While colonial-era migrants and their descendants could petition for naturalization in order to recover their Japanese nationality, only a small minority chose this option and even fewer succeeded because of high rejection rates. Between 1952 and 1955, there were fewer than 10,000 naturalizations in Japan (Kim 1990). Choosing neither repatriation nor naturalization, the overwhelming majority of Koreans occupied an undetermined legal status in Japan until the 1965 Japan–South Korea Normalization Treaty established "treaty-based permanent residency" (*kyotei eijyū*), which provided South Korean nationals with expanded foreign travel rights and protection from arbitrary deportation (Iwasawa 1986; Chung 2010a). Reforms in 1982 conferred greater residential security to Chōsen (de facto North Korean) nationals, who were designated "exceptional" permanent residents (*tokurei eijū*). The two categories (*kyotei eijyū* and *tokurei eijū*) were unified with the 1990 revisions to the Immigration Control and Refugee Recognition Act, which established the legal category of "special permanent resident" (*tokubetsu eijūsha*) to cover all former colonial subjects and their descendants. As second-generation Korean residents came of age at the height of Japan's new social movements of the 1960s, Korean nationality came to be associated less with the homeland governments and more with Korean ethnocultural identity, on the one hand, and permanent residency in Japan as non-citizen members of their local communities, on the other. Without fear of deportation, the second generation in particular focused their political movements on their positions as permanent members of their local communities deserving of equal rights. From the 1970s to 1980s, they made dramatic gains in claims to social welfare benefits, public sector jobs, and civil rights protections through the courts and local-level reforms that followed years of lawsuits, public campaigns, and protests (see Chung 2010a). The first wave of migration by colonial-era migrants thus shaped postwar Japan's immigrant incorporation patterns well before Japan encountered another wave of large-scale immigration starting in the late 1980s.

Like other industrialized countries, Japan experienced labor shortages in the 1960s. Instead of importing foreign labor as their North American and European counterparts did, Japanese officials and corporations opted instead to automate production, shift production abroad, and tap into alternative sources of domestic labor such as women, students, the elderly, and rural migrants (Chung 2010a, 149; cf Hollifield and Sharpe 2017). Japan's high-growth period in the 1960s coincided with the country's greatest rural-urban exodus, as 4 million farmers migrated to urban areas annually (Mori 1997, 55–57; Lie 2001, 9).

The second wave of immigration, from the 1970s to the early 1980s, did not represent responses to labor shortages. Rather, this wave was made up largely of four unrelated groups. The first and largest group consisted of "skilled" workers, most of whom were white-collar professionals, many of them from the United States and Europe. By 1985, US citizens made up the third-largest population of registered foreign residents after Koreans and Chinese. Others who were classified as "skilled" workers residing in Japan during this period were women from the Philippines, Thailand, South Korea, and Taiwan who were recruited to Japan to fill the demand in the so-called entertainment industry. By 1987, the number of immigrants from Asian countries with "entertainer" visas reached over 40,000 (Ministry of Justice 1989). During this period, most "entertainers" were recruited to work as hostesses in the industry known in Japan as *mizu shōbai* ("water trade," in reference to bars, cabarets, restaurants, and so forth) and in the sex industries (Sellek 2001, 37–38, 160–161).[4] The third-largest migrant group during this period were the children and grandchildren of Japanese nationals who had remained in Japan's former colonies, mostly China, after the war. Although ethnically Japanese, and recognized as Japanese nationals, this relatively small group, known as "returnees," encountered significant problems of adjustment and discrimination as they resettled in Japan, similar to non-Japanese immigrants (see Dower 1999, 48–64; Goodman 2003). Finally, asylum seekers from Indochina made up the fourth group, with more than 10,000 entering Japan on temporary visas between 1979 and 1999 (Ministry of Foreign Affairs 2014). It should be noted, however, that the Ministry of Justice recognized only a total of 315 refugees out of 3,118 applications between 1981, when Japan ratified the UN refugee convention, and 2004 (Flowers 2008, 340).

Beginning in the mid-1980s, Japan confronted a second labor shortage. This time, internal sources of labor were depleted and rising land prices in urban centers triggered a reverse migration to surrounding areas (Mori 1997, 56). Furthermore, the expansion of private brokers and intermediaries in Japan and various sending countries expedited labor migration to Japan. Immigration policies that prohibited the import of unskilled foreign labor remained unchanged, however, and starting in the late 1980s, growing numbers of foreign workers entered Japan with tourist visas and overstayed their three-month limit, thus establishing a formidable undocumented immigrant population that reached a high of 300,000 in 1993 (SOPEMI 2007).

In an effort to combat unauthorized immigration and, at the same time, meet labor demands, the government revised the Immigration Control and Refugee Recognition Act in 1990, setting the foundation for Japan's next wave of immigration. In addition to imposing criminal penalties on employers knowingly hiring undocumented workers, the revision reorganized visa categories and expanded them from eighteen to twenty-seven.[5] In particular, Japan responded to domestic demands for migrant labor through two key legal loopholes: (1) preferential policies for co-ethnic immigrants and (2) "industrial trainee" programs. Together, these legal loopholes gave employers "side doors" for importing cheap labor that did not violate official closed-door policies. The revision further allowed pre-college and college students to work for a limited amount of time.

First, the establishment of visas and programs specifically for co-ethnic immigrants provided loopholes for recruiting unskilled workers who, based on their shared ethnicity, would presumably be invisible foreigners in each society. Among the expanded visa categories created by the 1990 revision is the long-term resident (*teijūsha*) visa, providing unrestricted entrance and employment rights in Japan, for which ethnic Japanese immigrants (popularly called Nikkei) and their descendants (up until the third generation) qualified. This visa status is one of only four that permit unrestricted economic activities—the others are visas for special permanent residents (*tokubetsu eijūsha*, created specifically for colonial-era migrants and their descendants), ordinary permanent residents (*ippan eijūsha*), and spouse or child of a Japanese national and spouse or child of a permanent resident (Tsuda and Cornelius 2004, 439; Chung 2010a). The long-term resident visa thus allowed for permanent settlement, unlike the industrial trainee visa, which restricted employment and residence and was contingent on continued employment by the sponsoring company (Chung 2019a; Tian 2019). While the stated purpose of the visa was to invite Nikkei to learn the Japanese language, explore their cultural heritage, and visit their relatives, the vast majority of long-term resident visa holders were Brazilian and Peruvian nationals recruited to work in the construction and manufacturing sectors (Tsuda 2003). Only a year after the creation of this visa, the Brazilian population (the vast majority of whom were Nikkei) became the third-largest foreign population in Japan, following Koreans and Chinese.

Second, the industrial trainee program, first established first in Japan in 1981 (and adopted in toto by Korea in 1991), served as a de facto guest worker program whereby foreign workers were initially granted one-year visas to acquire technical skills. The Immigration Control and Refugee Recognition Act defines "trainees" broadly as those who undertake activities to learn and acquire technology, skills, or knowledge at public and private organizations in Japan. But because "trainees" were not officially recognized as workers, they received only "trainee allowances" and were not protected by labor laws in either country, making them vulnerable to industrial accidents, unpaid wages, and employer abuse. Despite several revisions to better regulate these programs—including extensions to trainee visas, government guidelines prohibiting employers from engaging in abusive practices, and landmark court decisions from 1993 affirming foreign workers' rights to industrial accident compensation, back wages, and severance pay—trainees continued to be subjected to poor working conditions, overstayed their visas, and/or sought employment in higher-paying jobs. In response to reports of endemic abuse, the Japan International Training Cooperation Organization (JITCO) established the Technical Intern Training Program (TITP) in 1993, which allowed trainees to apply to have their residence status changed to "designated activities," which after 1997 made them eligible to work in Japan for up to three years and protected them from exploitative practices, at least on paper. The Diet passed revisions to the TITP in 2009 (effective in 2010) to streamline the two-step trainee–technical intern program structure so that employers could recruit technical interns from the beginning, ensuring that these individuals entering into employer-employee relationships are protected under the Labor Standards Law. Further revisions were passed in 2016 that would, among other things, increase protections for trainees and technical interns and increase the maximum stay from three to five years combined.[6]

On November 27, 2018, Japan's parliament passed an unprecedented bill to open the country's borders to up to 345,000 semi-skilled workers in agriculture, construction, shipbuilding, hospitality, and nursing over a five-year period. The bill, which was introduced by the ruling Liberal Democratic Party (LDP), generated considerable controversy for two central reasons. First, it represents the first time in postwar Japan's history that the country's borders were officially open to unskilled foreign labor. Although Japan had instituted de facto guest worker policies to fill labor shortages since the 1980s, the government has neither recognized these groups formally as migrant workers nor acknowledged the existence of a guest worker program. Second, the Abe administration made clear that the proposed revision is not equivalent to a full-fledged immigration policy, whereby immigrants and their families would be admitted to Japan without restrictions. While the new plan will allow some foreign workers to reside in Japan for up to ten years, it also periodically compels them to return to their home countries so that they will not be able to meet the continuous residency requirements for permanent residency and naturalization. In other words, migrant workers are not *immigrants*. Some have speculated that this move represents a radical shift away from Japan's restrictive immigration policies; however, the parameters of the proposed guest worker system are consistent with the incremental steps employed by Japan to satisfy labor demand with de facto low-skilled migrant labor schemes.

Korea

Korea's immigration history can also be divided into three stages: (1) intraregional trade-related immigration in the nineteenth century; (2) refugee flows from northern Korea before and after the Korean War to the present day, and (3) large-scale unskilled labor migration from South and Southeast Asia and China starting in the late 1980s, especially around the 1988 Seoul Summer Olympics. The first immigration wave dates back to 1882, when Korea and China signed a trade agreement permitting Chinese merchants to own and lease land in Korea's treaty ports, which eventually resulted in the permanent settlement of Chinese residents (who eventually became Taiwanese nationals), known as Hwagyo (or Huaqiao in Chinese) (Lee 2002). While the Hwagyo are the oldest foreign community in Korea, with a population of over 42,000 in 2019—spanning six generations—their history in Korea is marked by residential segregation in ghettoized Chinatowns, social discrimination, and, until recently, political exclusion.

Refugees from northern Korea (popularly called *t'albukja* or *bukan-italjumin* in contemporary South Korea), in contrast, have historically been welcomed as fellow Koreans in South Korea.[7] Between 1945 to 1950, when the Korean War broke out, an estimated 740,000 *wŏllamin* ([border] crossers to the South) migrants fled from northern Korea to the south, and by the end of the Korean War in 1953, approximately 650,000 *p'inanmin* (war refugees) had settled in South Korea (Chung 2008, 6). Until the early 1990s, the South Korean government heralded the handful of North Korean political exiles as *kwisun yongsa*, or "defecting heroes," and provided generous economic support, including cash payments, and political recognition (Lee 2015, 2688–2689). Although the number of refugees grew significantly in the post–Cold War period, from fewer than ten annually during the Cold War to an average of sixty per year between 1994 to 1998, the numbers skyrocketed in the early 2000s, years after the 1995 North Korean famine, from 148 in 1999 to a high of over 2,900 in 2009.[8]

Upon their arrival, North Korean migrants are placed in a resettlement facility (*hanawŏn*, or "unity institute") for a mandatory twelve-week resettlement program where they are introduced to South Korean history, culture, and law and receive vocational training (see Park 2016). It is during this period that they are registered as residents of South Korea and gain legal status as South Korean nationals. They are subsequently placed in government-subsidized housing throughout the country and are assigned officers to help them with their integration into their local communities; additionally, North Korean migrants receive resettlement funds and are eligible for social welfare benefits, tuition assistance for college, vocational training, and counseling programs (N. Kim 2016b). Korea's Ministry of Unification estimates that over 30,000 individuals have settled in South Korea from the North between 1948 and 2019. Since North Koreans are automatically granted South Korean nationality, they are not viewed as immigrants in South Korean law.

Until the 1980s, South Korea was among the largest exporters of foreign labor, with an annual emigration rate of approximately 30,000 throughout the 1980s, according to the Korea Ministry of Foreign Affairs and Trade. Although there was no official South Korean emigration policy, thousands of Koreans emigrated to North America, Australia, Germany, and the Middle East from the 1960s to the late 1980s as students and guest workers, including nurses and miners to Germany and construction workers to the Middle East (Oh et al. 2011, 32–33, 61–64; Chung and Kim 2012, 207). It was during this same period that Korea also began to experience its most significant labor shortages following two decades of rapid economic growth. In order to meet short-term demands for labor, especially in the manufacturing, production, and service industries, Korean government officials turned a blind eye to companies that recruited migrant workers who entered the country with tourist visas and overstayed their visas in what Lim (2003) calls a "wink-and-nod" approach. What began as an unofficial practice of importing migrant labor on an as-needed basis quickly became a de facto guest worker program that generated growing numbers of unauthorized migrant workers.

In response, Korea instituted the Industrial and Technical Training System (ITTP) in 1991 and the Industrial Trainee Program in 1993, which was intended to provide a government-administered system for overseeing and controlling the migration of unskilled foreign labor (Seol 2000, 6; Oh et al. 2011, 72). Similar to their Japanese counterparts, the two programs left "trainees" vulnerable to exploitation since they were not recognized as workers and thus not protected by labor laws. By imposing a one-year limit on the period of sojourn, moreover, they contributed to the growth of unauthorized migrant workers in Korea. Following intense lobbying by immigrant advocacy groups—made up of a cross section of civil society that had been central to

Korea's own recent democratization movement—and a series of high-profile protests from 1994 to 1995 by migrant workers themselves, the government introduced the Employment Permit System (EPS) in 2004 and phased out the industrial trainee program in 2007 (Chung 2020b). Through the EPS, the Korean government grants basic labor rights to migrant workers, including pensions and health insurance, a standard that is on par with those granted to Korean workers as stipulated in the Labor Standard Act.[9] The significance of this system was that it far exceeded the rights extended to foreign residents and workers in other industrialized countries.

A second strategy employed by the government was preferential treatment for ethnic Koreans in immigration policy within the industrial trainee system and, later, the EPS (Skrentny et al. 2007, 799). Both systems allocated the largest quotas to ethnic Koreans from China (commonly referred to as Joseonjok; hereafter "Korean Chinese"). Following the normalization of diplomatic relations between South Korea and mainland China in 1992, Korean Chinese formed the largest foreign resident community in Korea by far, growing more than twentyfold from 32,443 in 2000 to over 700,000 in 2019 (see Table 14.2).

In 1999, the National Assembly passed the Overseas Korean Act ("Act on the Immigration and Legal Status of Overseas Koreans"; hereafter "OKA") with the stated purpose of creating a "global" Korean community. Defining "overseas Koreans" as "Koreans citizens residing abroad" and "Koreans with foreign citizenship" (Article 2-2), the OKA created an "Overseas Korean" (F-4) visa category that gave eligible co-ethnic immigrants quasi-dual-citizenship rights (Park and Chang 2005). Ethnic Koreans from China and the former Soviet Union were initially excluded based on the definition of overseas Koreans as those who had previously held South Korean nationality and their descendants. This provision thus limited eligibility to those who left the Korean peninsula after the founding of the Republic of Korea (ROK) in 1948, accounting for less than half of all Korean diasporic populations. In particular, the vast majority of ethnic Koreans in China and the former Soviet Union are colonial-era migrants and their descendants; the largest communities of post-1948 emigrants reside in the United States and Japan.

Barely two weeks after the National Assembly passed the OKA bill, three Korean Chinese residents filed a complaint with the Constitutional Court claiming that the OKA violated the principle of equality in the constitution. Their constitutional complaint was supported by sixty NGOs (Lee 2010). In 2001, the Constitutional Court ruled that the provision excluding pre-1948 emigrants and their descendants in the OKA did not conform to the principle of equality (Article 11) in the constitution because it discriminated against those who had emigrated from Korea before the establishment of the ROK (Lee 2012).[10] In response to this ruling and pressure from civil society groups, a 2004 amendment to the OKA made some pre-1948 emigrants and their descendants eligible for the overseas Korean visa by replacing the prior South Korean nationality requirement with documentary evidence of household registration (*hojeok*) in Korea. Nevertheless, not a single F-4 visa was issued to an ethnic Korean migrant from China or the former Soviet Union for the first three years after the amendment (Lee 2012, 94–95). Since then, the number of Korean Chinese with overseas Korean visas has grown to 72 percent of all overseas Korean visa holders (Lee and Chien 2017 , 2201). In 2007, the Ministry of Justice also created the H-2 working visit visa exclusively for ethnic Koreans from China and the former Soviet Union (up to the third generation) to work in the labor-starved service and construction industries.

Prospects for Permanent Settlement

By the mid-2000s, Korean and Japanese government officials could no longer turn a blind eye to the swelling ranks of immigrants within their borders and announced comprehensive proposals for immigrant incorporation: the Basic Act on the Treatment of Foreigners in Korea (Chaehan oegugin ch'ŏu kibonpŏp; hereafter "Basic Act") and the Ministry of Internal Affairs and Communications (MIC) Plan for "Multicultural Coexistence Promotion in Local Communities" (Tabunka kyōsei suisin puroguramu; hereafter "MIC Plan") in Japan. Unlike previous legislation that focused on immigration and border control, these plans not only acknowledged the need to manage foreigners settled within each country's borders but also represent the first attempts by each state to establish an overarching framework for their incorporation. At the same time, they diverge dramatically in their degree of centralization, the scope of reforms, and target populations.

Korea's Basic Act

Korea's National Assembly passed the 2007 Basic Act after years of debate, research, and negotiations between policymakers and civil society organizations. Following a 2006 meeting of representatives from the major government ministries, migrant advocacy organizations, and the scholarly community, the government announced plans to enact the Basic Act with the stated purpose of promoting immigrant social integration and mutual respect between foreigners and Korean nationals. This act calls for the implementation of a Basic Plan for Immigration Policy every five years that entails the cooperation of the national, municipal, and local governments and the designation of a Foreigner Policy Committee to coordinate all policies regarding foreign residents. The First Basic Plan for Immigration Policy (2008–2012; hereafter

"First Basic Plan"), which included a total budget of 612.7 billion Korean won, set the basis for designing and funding programs and assigning specific ministries with tasks related to the following four goals: "1) enhancing national competitiveness with a proactive openness policy; 2) pursuing quality social integration; 3) enforcing immigration laws; and 4) protecting human rights of foreigners" (Korea Immigration Service 2009).

Although the Basic Act is meant to serve as a general guide for drafting the five-year Basic Plan for Immigration Policy, it is notable for its explicit provision to safeguard the human rights of foreign residents in Korea (Article 10). As mentioned previously, this provision was adopted as one of the four stated goals of the First Basic Plan with the explanation that, as minorities in Korean society who are vulnerable to "human rights abuse," foreigners require "national-level protection against discrimination" (paragraph 13). In addition to outlining broad plans for reviewing and reforming discriminatory practices and institutions, the First Basic Plan offers specific provisions for protecting migrant women, foreigners in detention facilities, and refugees.

Migrant women, especially marriage migrants, are also central to the First Basic Plan's second goal of "pursuing quality social integration." Among the four major tasks assigned to this objective are two that are devoted solely to marriage migrants and their children: "helping immigrants through marriage get settled" and "creating a sound environment for multicultural children." In a similar vein, the last task in this section concerns the social integration of co-ethnic immigrants or the "Korean diaspora," while the first section that discusses reforms to immigration policies makes clear that co-ethnic immigrants have priority over other foreign nationals in entry and employment rights. This section additionally includes a framework for equalizing working conditions for foreign and Korean workers as well as reducing industrial accidents and protecting foreign workers from workplace abuse. Accordingly, the Basic Act and the First Basic Plan set distinct guidelines for incorporating specific immigrant populations: social integration for marriage migrants, preferential entry and employment rights for co-ethnic immigrants, and human rights protection for migrant workers

Japan's MIC Plan

Although the Immigration Bureau within the Ministry of Justice is responsible for immigration policies, there is no single agency in Japan that manages *immigrant* policies, akin to the KIS. Instead, immigrant integration programs and services in Japan were, until recently, spearheaded by civil society organizations and local governments. In 2001, a network of twenty-one cities and one town established the

Convention for Cities and Towns with Concentrations of Foreign Residents (Gaikokujin shuju toshi kaigi). Local government officials within the network declared that they had exhausted their resources in their attempts to incorporate foreign residents in their communities and called for national-level legislation to coordinate local immigrant incorporation programs and services. In 2005, the MIC established the Committee for the Promotion of Multicultural Community Building, which conducted a nationwide survey of local governmental programs and policies and, in 2006, announced an unprecedented proposal that called for all of Japan's prefectures and major cities to devise plans for "multicultural community building" (Yamawaki 2008).

Similar to Korea's Basic Act, Japan's MIC Plan provides general guidelines for implementing policies and programs; however, whereas Korea's Basic Act gives the task of policy and program design, implementation, and assessment to the central ministries, Japan's MIC Plan is explicitly designed for adoption by local governments with the stipulation that authorities should make adjustments according to local needs and characteristics. The guidelines for implementing the MIC Plan are divided broadly into four tasks: (1) intercultural communication support, (2) assistance in everyday life, (3) the development of a "multicultural coexistence" (*tabunka kyōsei*) community, and (4) the development of a system to promote "multicultural coexistence" policies. While the focus on social integration and coexistence with foreigners is largely similar to the goals of Korea's Basic Act, the methods for achieving these goals vary considerably. Whereas Korea's First Basic Plan concentrates on providing *support* and *protection* for foreigners through centralized, top-down policies and programs, the MIC Plan rests on the pillars of *support* and foreign resident *participation* in the local community through decentralized coordination between local governments, civil society organizations, and foreign residents themselves. Unlike Korea's Basic Plan, the MIC Plan neither targets specific groups of foreigners nor offers any specific guidelines for protecting foreign residents' "human rights."

What is striking about the MIC Plan is the inclusion of foreign residents not only as the beneficiaries of incorporation policies and programs but also as active participants of "multicultural coexistence" community building. An entire section is devoted to encouraging foreign resident participation through support of key foreign resident leaders, the formation of foreign resident advisory bodies, the promotion of foreign resident participation in local civic associations, and public acknowledgment of foreign residents' contributions to their local communities. This framework contrasts strikingly with the comparatively thin proposals for "encouraging foreigners' participation in local communities" found in Korea's First Basic Plan. Aside from a brief reference to future research on the living conditions of foreigners in Korea, the only proposals outlined in this section of the Basic Plan refer to "multicultural festivals," cultural events, and the establishment of a "Together Day" and "Together Week" every May, according to Article 19 of the Basic Act.

Naturalization and Permanent Residency

The divergent approaches to immigrant incorporation in Japan and Korea are evident in the general patterns of naturalization and permanent residency. Naturalization rates in Japan remain among the lowest of all liberal democracies and have continually fallen behind those of Korea since 2008. Although Zainichi Korean residents (those Korean migrants who stayed in Japan) are naturalizing at higher rates than ever before—at an annual average rate of about 8,000 since 1995—and Chinese residents are naturalizing at an annual average rate of about 4,000, overall, naturalization rates in Japan remain at less than 1 percent of the total foreign population annually.

In contrast, the number of naturalizations in Korea went up by more than twenty-three times, from 538 in 1991 to 12,357 in 2019 (KIS 2020). At its peak in 2009, 26,756 individuals, or 3 percent of the total foreign resident population, naturalized in Korea, compared to 14,785, or 0.7 percent, in Japan.[11] Between 2010 and 2019, annual naturalizations in Korea have ranged from a high of 18,355 (1.9 percent) in 2011 to a low of 12,357 (0.5 percent of the total foreign resident population) in 2019; the comparable figures in Japan were 13,072 (0.6 percent) in 2010 and 8,453 (0.4 percent) in 2019 (see Figure 14.2).

The informal practices associated with naturalization in Japan have, until recently, posed considerable hurdles for individuals seeking to naturalize. Until 1985, local officials typically required naturalization applicants to adopt a Japanese name (family name and surname) and conducted painstaking evaluations of applicants' cultural assimilation to determine eligibility under the "good behavior and conduct" requirement. While naturalization applicants are no longer required to adopt a Japanese name, the pressure to do so remains, especially for applicants with Chinese-character surnames that are not listed in the official *jōyōkanji* (characters in common use) or *jinmeiyō kanji* (name characters) lists, such as the common Korean surnames "Choi," "Kang," and "Yoon." In some cases, local officials may offer unsolicited advice about the convenience of having a Japanese name over a "foreign" name or the benefits of adopting a Japanese name for the sake of the applicant's children (see Chung 2010a).

Low naturalization rates in Japan contrast strikingly with the rapid growth of permanent residents among registered foreign residents, from approximately 63,500 in 1995 to more than 1 million in 2019 (KIS, 2020). In 2019, permanent

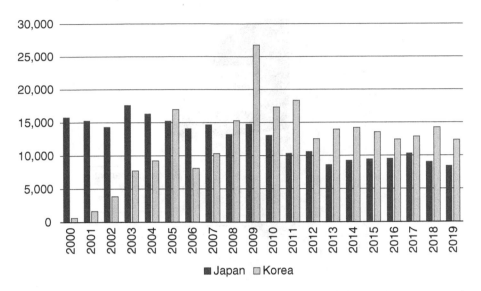

FIGURE 14.2. Annual Naturalizations in Japan and Korea, 2000–2019
SOURCES: Ministry of Justice, Japan; Korea Immigration Service. Naturalization figures for Korea include "Reinstatement of Nationality."

residents—including both "general permanent residents" (*ippan eijūsha*, 27 percent) and "special permanent residents" (*tokubetsu eijūsha*, 11 percent)—accounted for al most 40 percent of the total foreign resident population in Japan. Among the remaining categories of registered foreign residents include some whose visas allow for unrestricted employment and multiple visa renewals, making them de facto permanent residents. When combined, permanent residents and quasi permanent residents made up over half of registered foreign residents in Japan in 2019 (see Figure 14.3).

Unlike Japan, the Korean government actively encourages specific categories of foreigners—particularly migrant spouses—to naturalize through government-run support centers, the KIS "E-Government for Foreigners" website, and simplified naturalization procedures. Although the naturalization process in Korea is not easy, immigrant advocacy organizations in Korea, such as the Ansan Migrant Center, routinely help foreign residents with their naturalization applications, and government-sponsored multicultural family centers provide preparatory citizenship exam courses and "Korea immigration and integration programs" that eligible applicants can take in lieu of the written exam (personal interviews with Ryu Sung-hwan of the Ansan Migrant Center, May 25, 2010, Ansan, Korea, and Shin Sang-rok of Pocheon Multicultural Family Support Center, May 24, 2010, Pocheon, Korea). With a few exceptions, pro-immigrant advocacy groups in Japan rarely encourage foreign residents to naturalize as a means of political empowerment.

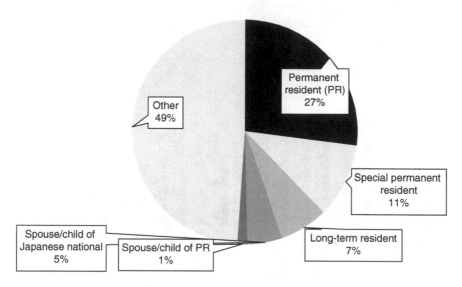

FIGURE 14.3. Registered Foreign Residents in Japan, 2019
SOURCE: Japanese Ministry of Justice, 2019.

At the same time, incorporation policies and programs that target migrant women and co-ethnic immigrants conspicuously exclude the largest category of foreign nationals in Korea from permanent settlement: migrant workers. Spouses of Korean nationals (including those with F-2 long-term resident and F-6 marriage migrant visas), accompanying spouses (F-3 visa), and co-ethnic immigrants with overseas Korean (F-4) visas made up a relatively small percentage of the total foreign population in Korea, at 26 percent combined in 2019 (KIS 2018). Permanent foreign residents (with F-5 visas), moreover, were among the smallest group of foreign residents, at slightly over 6 percent. In contrast to Japan, permanent residents and quasi permanent residents combined constituted only 32 percent of the total foreign population in Korea in 2019. Consequently, immigrants with temporary visas that make them ineligible for naturalization or permanent residency constitute almost 70 percent of foreign residents in Korea. Korea, therefore, appear to be heading toward a type of bifurcated immigrant incorporation pattern that embraces some immigrants as potential citizens and excludes others from permanent settlement.

Immigrant Incorporation Without Immigrants

Do the trajectories of other reluctant countries of immigration in Europe provide a road map for East Asia's immigration future (Hollifield and Sharpe 2017)? Similar to the situation in Europe in the 1960s and 1970s, migrant workers in East Asia are not acknowledged as potential citizens or permanent settlers by either the state or the public. Japan and Korea's reluctance to open their borders at the level necessary to alleviate labor shortages and demographic deficits underscores that they are willing to give up the significant economic gains from migration to avoid the long-term costs of social integration, or more specifically, what policymakers view as the long-term costs of social instability arising from the permanent settlement of migrants largely from the global South. Perhaps Japan and Korea are, in fact, "undeclared" countries of immigration, as Thränhardt (1995) characterized Germany over two decades ago.

Based on their recent implementation of guest worker programs, it may appear that both countries are converging toward greater openness in their immigration policies as they slowly open their borders to meet labor demands and gradually expand immigrant incorporation programs and services (Hollifield 2004, 2017). Both countries have additionally expanded institutionalized rights for non-citizens over the past several decades. Today, Japan makes almost no distinction between Japanese nationals and foreign residents with long-term visas in the area of social welfare benefits. In Korea, spouses of Korean nationals are eligible for dual nationality, for which not all Korean nationals qualify. And political rights for qualified foreign residents in both countries surpass those of many other democracies with more liberal immigration and citizenship policies, including in the areas of local voting rights in Korea and foreign resident assemblies in Japan.

While the expansion of non-citizen rights in Korea and Japan may be consistent with a general convergence trend among liberal democracies, the drivers of liberalization (and their barriers) are closely tied to the subcategories of targeted migrants, on the one hand, and the timing and sequencing of their incorporation in the context of closed border policies, on the other. In Japan, immigrant incorporation *preceded* immigration policy reform. The largest category of foreign residents in Japan until the late 2000s—colonial-era migrants and their descendants, most of them Korean—had already gained hard-fought institutionalized rights before the arrival of the most recent of wave of immigrants from the late 1980s and well before Japan partially opened its borders to foreign labor in 2019. In Korea, the expansion of migrant rights has been circumscribed to specific visa statuses: that is, the expansion of rights for one migrant group has not made them universal, or even accessible, to others. While a powerful migrant workers' movement successfully pressured Korea to implement a formal guest worker program that guaranteed rights protections for foreign labor in 2004, it did not lead to the liberalization of Korea's admission and settlement policies for them. And while Korea stands out as the only Northeast Asian country to extend local voting rights to foreign residents and recognize dual nationality, only a small percentage of foreign residents with specific visa statuses in the country are eligible in practice.

The gaps between subcategories of migrants in each country are compounded by the multiple generations that separate them. Despite their categorization as "recent countries of immigration," Japan and Korea have long migration histories and established foreign communities that extend across multiple generations. As a formal imperial power to which the largest flows of immigration occurred before 1945, Japan has been grappling with the challenge of immigrant incorporation well before its European counterparts encountered large-scale immigration (Hollifield and Sharpe 2017). While post-colonial South Korea remains one of the major migrant-sending countries, with almost 2.9 million overseas South Korean citizens making up part of the 7.5-million-member Korean diasporic population throughout every region in the world, it also is home to generations of Chinese descendants who settled in Korea well before the ROK was established. Having maintained citizenship policies based almost entirely on descent and entrenched ideologies of racial, ethnic, and cultural homogeneity, foreign residents within Japan and Korea's borders remain foreigners regardless of nativity, leading to the growth of six generations of foreign residents as of 2020.

Japan and Korea's long immigration histories and long-established foreign resident communities combined with borders that remained closed to unskilled immigration until recently contributed to the development of immigration and immigrant policies that are internally inconsistent. Rather than open their borders, both countries met labor market demands using "side doors" that provided informal labor channels through the proliferation of visa categories. While some visas, such as those for "industrial trainees," did not allow for permanent settlement (or recognize foreign labor as "workers," for that matter), others extend quasi-dual-citizenship rights on the basis of kinship ties (for co-ethnic immigrants and "marriage migrants"). And, in Japan's case, claims to institutionalized rights by highly assimilated, often native-born, but legally foreign descendants of colonial-era migrants made their "special permanent residence" status closer to that of Japanese nationals than other foreign residents. While various migrant rights movements based on appeals to democratic principles and international norms have led to the expansion of rights *within* individual visa categories, they have not resulted in the liberalization of either country's migration regime. On the contrary, the expansion of rights for select subcategories of migrants has led to the institutionalization of non-citizen hierarchies in each country, widening the gap between those eligible for select visa statuses that come with quasi-dual-citizenship rights and those with temporary visas that strictly limit their employment and residence rights (Chung 2020a).

The COVID-19 pandemic exacerbated these hierarchies and brought into stark relief the distinct ways that migrant populations are incorporated, or not incorporated, as actual or potential citizens, as permanently settled residents, or as temporary, disposable workers. In Japan, the pandemic highlighted the wide chasm between long-term foreign residents, who benefited from the government's one-time stimulus payment to all residents, and migrant workers, who were among the first to be laid off with the pandemic-induced economic downturn. Although the Japanese government approved limited visa extensions for migrant workers unable to return home, the Ministry of Justice retained its discretionary power to withdraw visas from those who remained unemployed for more than three months (Human Rights Now 2020). The only foreign residents who were eligible for COVID-19 economic relief in Korea were permanent residents and migrant spouses of Korean nationals. Even after the National Human Rights Commission of Korea concluded that excluding foreign nationals from pandemic-related assistance was discriminatory, only a limited number of local governments reversed course. And all foreign nationals caught violating quarantine measures have been subject to stringent deportation regulations (Im 2020).

Migration governance in Japan and Korea thus reflects not liberal convergence but, rather, multi-tier migration regimes that extend generous institutionalized rights for some categories of migrants and treat others as permanently deportable populations (Lori 2019). Rather than "laggards" that are decades behind on a single pathway toward becoming a liberal migration state, the two East Asian democracies have been on a different trajectory altogether that increasingly resembles the Singaporean and Gulf State models rather than what we would expect to find in a mature democracy. But as so-called traditional countries of immigration such as the United States enact increasingly restrictive measures to curb both unauthorized and legal immigration, we may soon find that the East Asian model of immigration control is the norm.

Notes

This chapter is a revised, expanded, and updated version of Chung 2010b and 2014. It also draws heavily on Chung 2020a. The author thanks Jim Hollifield, Phil Martin, Pia Orrenius, François Héran, Midori Okabe, Michael Sharpe, and other participants at the 2019 conference "Immigration Policy in an Era of Globalization and Crisis" at the Collège de France for their insightful comments and suggestions. Funding for the research was provided by the Laboratory Program for Korean Studies through the Ministry of Education of the Republic of Korea and Korean Studies Promotion Service of the Academy of Korean Studies (AKS-2018-LAB-2250001) and a grant from the Abe Fellowship Program administered by the Social Science Research Council and the American Council of Learned Societies in cooperation with and with funds provided by the Japan Foundation Center for Global Partnership (CGP).

1. See United Nations, Department of Economic and Social Affairs, Population Division, "Replacement Migration: Is It a Solution to Declining and Ageing Populations?," U.N. Doc. ST/ESA/SER.A/20, https://www.un.org/en/development/desa/population/publications/age ing/replacement-migration.asp.

2. The CIA World Factbook calculates the net migration rate based on the number of persons entering and leaving a country during the year per 1,000 persons. In 2020, South Korea was ranked fortieth and Japan sixty-fourth. See https://www.cia.gov/the-world-factbook/field/net-migration-rate/country-comparison.

3. The 1947 law effectively made Koreans in Japan stateless since their designated status as Chōsen nationals (designating their origin in the colony Chōsen) preceded the establishment of the Republic of Korea and the Democratic People's Republic of Korea in 1948. North Korea retained Chōsen (Chosŏn in Korean) as its official name, but because Japan does not recognize North Korea, those with Chōsen nationality remain stateless.

4. In 1988, the Ministry of Justice revised the application procedures for "entertainer" visas to prevent the entry of "entertainers" whose actual work was in the *mizu shōbai* and sex industries (see Komai 1995, 74–75).

5. The revision, modeled after US immigration laws, made employers who hired undocumented workers and brokers who facilitated their employment subject to a maximum of three years imprisonment and fines up to 2 million yen. See Komai 1995, 5–6.

6. See Ministry of Justice, http://www.moj.go.jp/nyuukokukanri/kouhou/nyuukoku-kanrio5_00011.html; Ministry of Health, Labor, and Welfare, http://www.mhlw.go.jp/stf/houdou/0000149333.html.

7. For discussion of the politics of "naming" North Korean migrants, see Yoon 2012; N. Kim 2016a.

8. The number of North Korean refugees decreased by half after 2011 due to tightened border controls. See South Korea Ministry of Unification website, www.unikorea.go.kr.

9. See the Employment Permit System website, "Legal Rights," http://www.eps.go.kr/en/duty/duty_01.jsp.

10. The proceedings are summarized in "Decisions of the Korean Constitutional Court (2001)," www.ccourt.go.kr.

11. In Korea, this number includes both naturalizations and "reinstatement of nationality" for eligible co-ethnics.

References

Bartram, David. 2000. "Japan and Labor Migration: Theoretical and Methodological Implications of Negative Cases." *International Migration Review* 34, no. 1: 5–32.

Castles, Stephen, Hein de Haas, and Mark J. Miller. 2014. *The Age of Migration: International Population Movements in the Modern World.* 5th ed. New York: Guilford.

Chen, Edward I-te. 1984. "The Attempt to Integrate the Empire: Legal Perspectives." In *The Japanese Colonial Empire, 1895–1945*, edited by Ramon H. Myers and Mark R. Peattie, pp. 240-274. Princeton: Princeton University Press.

Chung, Byung-Ho. 2008. "Between Defector and Migrant: Identities and Strategies of North Koreans in South Korea." *Korean Studies* 32: 1–27.

Chung, Erin Aeran. 2010a. *Immigration and Citizenship in Japan*. New York: Cambridge University Press.

Chung, Erin Aeran. 2010b. "Workers or Residents? Diverging Patterns of Immigrant Incorporation in Korea and Japan." *Pacific Affairs* 83, no. 4: 675–696.

Chung, Erin Aeran. 2014. "Japan and South Korea: Immigration Control and Immigrant Incorporation." In *Controlling Immigration: A Global Perspective*, edited by James F. Hollifield, Philip L. Martin, and Pia M. Orrenius, pp.399-421. Stanford: Stanford University Press.

Chung, Erin Aeran. 2019a. "Ethnic Return Migration and Noncitizen Hierarchies in South Korea and Japan." In *Diasporic Returns to the Ethnic Homeland the Korean Diaspora in Comparative Perspective*, edited by Takeyuki Tsuda and Changzoo Song, 179–197. London: Palgrave Macmillan.

Chung, Erin Aeran. 2019b. "Japan's Model of Immigration Without Immigrants." *Current History* 118, no. 809: 215–221.

Chung, Erin Aeran. 2020a. "Creating Hierarchies of Noncitizens: Race, Gender, and Visa Categories in South Korea." *Journal of Ethnic and Migration Studies* 46, no. 12: 2497–2514. doi: https://doi.org/10.1080/1369183X.2018.1561061.

Chung, Erin Aeran. 2020b. *Immigrant Incorporation in East Asian Democracies*. New York: Cambridge University Press.

Chung, Erin Aeran, and Ralph I. Hosoki. 2018. "Disaggregating Labor Migration Policies to Understand Aggregate Migration Realities: Insights from South Korea and Japan as Negative Cases of Immigration." *Comparative Labor Law and Policy Journal* 39, no. 1: 83–110.

Chung, Erin Aeran, and Daisy Kim. 2012. "Citizenship and Marriage in a Globalizing World: Multicultural Families and Monocultural Nationality Laws in Korea and Japan." *Indiana Journal of Global Legal Studies* 19, no. 1: 195–219.

Chung, Erin Aeran, and Yunchen Tian. 2018. Is Japan Becoming a Country of Immigration? *Foreign Affairs*.

Dower, John. 1999. *Embracing Defeat: Japan in the Wake of World War II*. New York: W. W. Norton/New Press.

Ellermann, Antje. 2021. *The Comparative Politics of Immigration: Policy Choices in Germany, Canada, Switzerland, and the United States*. Cambridge Studies in Comparative Politics. Cambridge: Cambridge University Press.

Flowers, Petrice R. 2008. "Failure to Protect Refugees?: Domestic Institutions, International Organizations, and Civil Society in Japan." *Journal of Japanese Studies* 34, no. 2: 333–361.

Flowers, Petrice R. 2009. *Refugees, Women, and Weapons: International Norm Adoption and Compliance in Japan*. Stanford, CA: Stanford University Press.

Goodman, Roger. 2003. "The Changing Perception and Status of Japan's Returnee Children (Kikokushijo)." In *Global Japan: The Experience of Japan's New Immigrant and Overseas Communities*, edited by Roger Goodman, Ceri Peach, Ayumi Takenaka, and Paul White, 177–194. London: Routledge Curzon.

Guiraudon, Virginie. 1998. "Citizenship Rights for Non-Citizens." In *Challenge to the Nation-State: Immigration in Western Europe and the United States*, edited by Christian Joppke, 272–318. Oxford: Oxford University Press.

Gurowitz, Amy. 1999. "Mobilizing International Norms: Domestic Actors, Immigrants, and the Japanese State." *World Politics* 51, no. 3: 413–445.

Hollifield, James F. 2004. "The Emerging Migration State." *International Migration Review* 38, no. 3: 885–912. doi:10.1111/j.1747–7379.2004.tb00223.x.

Hollifield, James F., and Michael O. Sharpe. 2017. "Japan as an 'Emerging Migration State'." *International Relations of the Asia-Pacific* 17, no. 3: 371–400. doi: 10.1093/irap/lcx013.

Human Rights Now. 2020. "HRN Releases Statement Concerning the Effects of Covid-19 on Migrant Workers in Japan." Human Rights Now, Tokyo.

Im, Esther S. 2020. "How Multiculturalism Has Fared in South Korea Amid the Pandemic." In *Carnegie Compendium on "The Case for South Korean Soft Power,"* edited by Chung Min Lee and Kathryn Botto. Washington, DC: Carnegie Endowment for International Peace. https://carnegieendowment.org/2020/12/15/how-multiculturalism-has-fared-in-south-korea-amid-pandemic-pub-83410.

Iwasawa, Yuji. 1986. "Legal Treatment of Koreans in Japan: The Impact of International Human Rights Law on Japanese Law." *Human Rights Quarterly* 8, no. 2: 131–179.

Joppke, Christian. 1999. *Immigration and the Nation-State: The United States, Germany, and Great Britain.* Oxford: Oxford University Press.

Kim, Jaeeun. 2016. *Contested Embrace: Transborder Membership Politics in Twentieth-Century Korea.* Stanford, CA: Stanford University Press.

Kim, Joon. 2003. "Insurgency and Advocacy: Unauthorized Foreign Workers and Civil Society in South Korea." *Asian and Pacific Migration Journal* 12, no. 3: 237–269.

Kim, Nora Hui-Jung. 2008. "Korean Immigration Policy Changes and the Political Liberals' Dilemma." *International Migration Review* 42, no. 3: 576–596.

Kim, Nora Hui-Jung. 2016a. "Co-Ethnics, Refuges, or Immigrants? Multiple Identities of North Koreans in 'Multicultural' South Korea." *Asian Ethnicity* 17, no. 2: 167–170. doi: 10.1080/14631369.2016.1151238.

Kim, Nora Hui-Jung. 2016b. "Naturalizing Korean Ethnicity and Making 'Ethnic' Difference: A Comparison of North Korean Settlement and Foreign Bride Incorporation Policies in South Korea." *Asian Ethnicity* 17, no. 2: 185–198. doi: 10.1080/14631369.2016.1151234.

Kim, Y.D. 1990. *Zainichi Chōsenjin no kika.* Tokyo: Akasi Shoten.

Komai, Hiroshi. 1995. *Migrant Workers in Japan.* London: Kegan Paul International.

Korea Immigration Service. 2009. "First Basic Plan for Immigration Policy, 2008–2012." Korea Immigration Service, Ministry of Justice, Gwacheon.

Korea Immigration Service (KIS), Ministry of Justice. 2018. K.I.S. Statistics 2017 (2018 Chulipguk Oegukin Tong'gye Yonbo).

Korea Immigration Service (KIS), Ministry of Justice. 2020. K.I.S. Statistics 2019 (2019 Chulipguk Oegukin Tong'gye Yonbo).

Lee, C. 2010. "South Korea: The Transformation of Citizenship and the State-Nation Nexus." *Journal of Contemporary Asia* 40, no. 2: 230–251. doi:10.1080/00472331003597562.

Lee, Chulwoo. 2002. "'Us' and 'Them' in Korean Law: The Creation, Accommodation, and Exclusion of Outsiders in Korean Law." In *East Asian Law: Universal Norms and Local Cultures,* edited by Arthur Rosett, Lucie Cheng, and Margaret Woo, 105–134. London: Routledge Curzon.

Lee, Chulwoo. 2012. "How Can You Say You're Korean? Law, Governmentality and National Membership in South Korea." *Citizenship Studies* 16, no. 1: 85–102. doi: 10.1080/13621025.2012.651405.

Lee, Jung-eun. 2015. "Disciplinary Citizenship in South Korean Ngos' Narratives of Resettlement for North Korean Refugees." *Ethnic and Racial Studies* 38, no. 15: 2688–2704.

Lee, Sohoon, Yi-Chun Chien. 2017. "The Making of 'Skilled' Overseas Koreans: Transformation of Visa Policies for Co-ethnic Migrants in South Korea," *Journal of Ethnic and Migration Studies.* 43/13: 2193-2210.

Lie, John. 2001. *Multiethnic Japan.* Cambridge, MA: Harvard University Press.

Lim, Timothy C. 2003. "Racing from the Bottom in South Korea? The Nexus Between Civil Society and Transnational Migrants." *Asian Survey* 43, no. 3: 423–442.

Lori, Noora. 2019. *Offshore Citizens: Permanent Temporary Status in the Gulf.* Cambridge: Cambridge University Press.

Matias, Gonçalo Saraiva. 2016. *Citizenship as a Human Right: The Fundamental Right to a Specific Citizenship.* London: Palgrave Macmillan.

Messina, Anthony M. 2007. *The Logics and Politics of Post-Wwii Migration to Western Europe.* New York: Cambridge University Press.

Ministry of Foreign Affairs, Japan. 2014. "Refugees." Accessed August 26, 2014. http://www .mofa.go.jp/policy/refugee/japan.html.

Ministry of Justice, Japan. 1989. "Zairyu gaikokujin tokei" [Statistics for foreign residents in Japan].

Mori, Hiromi. 1997. *Immigration Policy and Foreign Workers in Japan.* New York: St. Martin's Press.

Morris-Suzuki, Teresa. 2010. *Borderline Japan: Foreigners and Frontier Controls in the Postwar Era.* Cambridge: Cambridge University Press.

Oh, Jung-Eun, Dong Kwan Kang, Julia Jiwon Shin, Sang-lim Lee, Seung Bok Lee, and Kiseon Chung. 2011. "Migration Profile of the Republic of Korea." IOM MRTC Research Report Series. IOM Migration Research and Training Centre, Goyang-si, Korea.

Park, Jung-Sun, and Paul Y. Chang. 2005. "Contention in the Construction of a Global Korean Community: The Case of the Overseas Korean Act." *Journal of Korean Studies* 10, no. 1: 1–27.

Park, Seo Yeon. 2016. "Street-Level Bureaucracy and Depoliticized North Korean Subjectivity in the Service Provision of Hana Center." *Asian Ethnicity* 17, no. 2: 199–213. doi: 10.1080/14631369.2016.1151231.

Sellek, Yoko. 2001. *Migrant Labour in Japan.* New York: Palgrave.

Seol, Dong-Hoon. 2000. "Past and Present of Foreign Workers in Korea 1987–2000." *Asia Solidarity Quarterly* 2: 1–17.

Seol, Dong-Hoon, and John D. Skrentny. 2009. "Why Is There So Little Migrant Settlement in East Asia?" *International Migration Review* 43, no. 3: 578–620.

Sharpe, Michael O. 2014. *Postcolonial Citizens and Ethnic Migration: The Netherlands and Japan in the Age of Globalization, Palgrave Studies in International Relations.* Houndmills, Basingstoke: Palgrave Macmillan.

Skrentny, John D., Stephanie Chan, Jon Fox, and Denis Kim. 2007. "Defining Nations in Asia and Europe: A Comparative Analysis of Ethnic Return Migration Policy." *International Migration Review* 41, no. 4: 793–825.

SOPEMI. 2007. International Migration Outlook: Annual Report. Paris: Organisation for Economic Co-operation and Development.

Soysal, Yasemin Nuhoglu. 1994. *Limits of Citizenship: Migrants and Postnational Membership in Europe.* Chicago: University of Chicago Press.

Surak, Kristin. 2008. "Convergence in Foreigners' Rights and Citizenship Policies? A Look at Japan." *International Migration Review* 42, no. 3: 550–575. doi: 10.1111/j.1747-7379.2008.00137.x.

Surak, Kristin. 2018. "Migration Industries and the State: Guestwork Programs in East Asia." *International Migration Review* 52, no. 2: 487–523. doi: 10.1111/imre.12308.

Thränhardt, Dietrich. 1995. "Germany: An Undeclared Immigration Country." *New Community* 21, no. 1: 19-36.

Tian, Yunchen. 2019. "Workers by Any Other Name: Comparing Co-Ethnics and 'Interns' as Labour Migrants to Japan." *Journal of Ethnic and Migration Studies* 45, no. 9: 1496–1514. doi: 10.1080/1369183X.2018.1466696.

Tsuda, Takeyuki. 2003. *Strangers in the Ethnic Homeland.* New York: Columbia University Press.

Tsuda, Takeyuki, ed. 2006. *Local Citizenship in Recent Countries of Immigration: Japan in Comparative Perspective.* Lanham, MD: Lexington Books.

Tsuda, Takeyuki, and Wayne A. Cornelius. 2004. "Japan: Government Policy, Immigrant Reality." In *Controlling Immigration: A Global Perspective*, edited by Wayne A. Cornelius, Takeyuki Tsuda, Philip L. Martin, and James Frank Hollifield. Stanford, CA: Stanford University Press, pp. 439-477.

Wolman, Andrew. 2013. "Korea's Refugee Act: A Critical Evaluation Under International Law." *Journal of East Asia & International Law* 6, no. 2: 479–496.

Yamawaki, Keizo. 2008. "The Challenges for Japanese Immigrant Integration Policy." *Around the Globe* 4, no. 2: 42–44.

Yoon, In Jin. 2012. "Circumstantial Citizens: North Korean 'Migrants' in South Korea." In *Contested Citizenship in East Asia: Developmental Politics, National Unity, and Globalization*, edited by Kyung-Sup Chang and Bryan S. Turner, 218–239. London: Routledge.

COMMENTARY

On Japanese and Korean Immigration Legislation, Global Responsibility Sharing, and the EU Leadership

Midori Okabe

Erin A. Chung's article insightfully takes up the Japan and South Korean cases and raises questions about why international norms regarding protection of migrants do not produce effective migration management.

This commentary will briefly discuss postwar Japanese and Korean immigration legislation, reflecting on how the global migration regime could develop through effective collaboration with Asian countries.

A Convergent Path to Follow Liberal Democracies: The Emergence of Japanese and Korean Immigration Regimes in the Post–World War II Period

Legislation on immigration control was indispensable in the immediate post–World War II era both in Japan and on the Korean peninsula. For Japan, it was part of the process of postwar reconstruction. The postwar Japanese authorities had to manage the mass migration of people in numerous regions within the areas in Asia the Japanese Imperial Army had occupied. The main targets were Koreans (from both the northern and southern parts of the peninsula), "Formosans" (persons from Taiwan), and repatriated Japanese citizens (mainly from Taiwan and Manchuria), though there was also a significant number of American-Japanese dual nationals.

On the other hand, even after independence, Korea was still tossed around by the dynamics of the international environment, featuring the nascent bipolar international structure of the Cold War. It indeed makes sense that the Korean War (1950–1953) and the subsequent decade of dictatorship were factors in the delay of democratic legislation on immigration control, as Chung describes. On one hand, it shows how a country had to acquiesce in underdevelopment due to military occupation by another country. On the other hand, a weak country can become the victim of power games in the international arena.

Indeed, this kind of "weakness" is shared by Japan as well. The Japanese Immigration Act of 1951, which took effect when Japan's sovereignty was restored in 1952, was not "modeled" after US legislation, as Chung argues, but rather was "ordered" by the United States. On the one hand, it was a necessary element of moving the Japanese regime from imperialism toward liberal democracy, something postwar Japan appreciated. On the other hand, however, it reflected pressing demand by the United States to fortify Japan as a buffer zone against the Soviet (and communist Chinese) alliance. The Supreme Commander of the Allied Powers initially requested that the Japanese legislative body bestow fundamental (political) rights to every resident on a non-discriminatory basis. It then altered its policy to limit those rights to Japanese nationality holders, allowing Japan to oust Korean citizens, especially those who were communist activists with Chongryon, or the Association of (North) Korean residents in Japan.[1] That policy produced undocumented migrants, which entailed human security problems as a consequence. However, it was not the policymakers' intention to leave Koreans exposed to social discrimination. Nor did Japan officially introduce quotas for particular categories of non-nationals. Postwar Japanese immigration legislation was heavily influenced by US leadership during the postwar period, when the United States removed its own discriminatory quota system, which had aimed at limiting the number of immigrants with Asian ethnic backgrounds, including Japanese. In this regard, I would claim that the legal base of Japanese immigration control in the postwar era is the 1952 US Immigration and Naturalization Act, not the 1924 Johnson-Reed Immigration Act, as Chung argues (the 1924 legislation was intended to exclude Japanese residents from the US society and to securitize Asian ethnic minorities, often referred to as the "yellow peril").[2]

However, the issues of human rights and human security remained problematic in both Japan and Korea. Both issues were "untouchable" in part because of social taboos. A Cold War confrontation occurred inside the respective territories, with non-nationals and nationals as invisible (or pretended to be unseen) security actors.

Compliance with the international norms for human rights protection has been practiced on an ad hoc basis. Japanese immigration policy before 2018, for example, did result in problems of labor exploitation, often in combination with a severe violation of human rights, most notably when it came to the Technical Intern Training

Program. The initial reaction by the Japanese government was a non-policy—that is, the central government's negligence of its responsibility to tackle such issues. However, reform began after the government faced strong criticism from the United States for its lack of response to human trafficking. South Korea also faced the necessity of reform when international society highlighted the country's discriminatory policy against non-national laborers.[3]

As Chung aptly observes, the transition of these two countries toward a liberal integration scheme interestingly coincided with their commitment to international norms on human rights. One can argue that what was seen as discrimination against non-national ethnic groups was, in fact, discrimination against many other (social) categories within its own national groups, such as women and the working class. To put it another way, both Japan and Korea have yet to experience a full-fledged endogenous political development as liberal democracies.

How about partially, then? The answer may be yes. The 2018 Japanese reform introducing an open labor migration scheme can be seen as a typical case of "interest-group politics" in a liberal democratic country, as Freeman argues.[4] The business association Keidanren, in combination with the Ministry of Economy, Trade and Industry (METI) and its Small and Medium Enterprise Agency, became a powerful interest group that had a massive influence on the Abe administration's pro-neoliberal policies. In addition, the labor union confederation, Rengo, was relatively weak, which facilitated this tendency. In sum, Japan has followed the liberal democratic trend to improve its macroeconomic performance, as may also be the case with Korea. The other significant aspect of liberal democracy—namely, the embracing of human dignity—is still waiting to find a place on the political agenda.

On Global Migration Governance and the Relevance of (European) Liberal Democracies

While Chung correctly observes that comprehensive reform on immigration policy, particularly to meet the global standard of human rights protection, is not expected in the current Japanese and Korean domestic political environments, can academic theories offer any guidance? Chung mentions the reluctance of the Japanese and Korean government to accept refugees as problematic. This remark is accurate, but it should not be taken to imply that the two countries do not abide by the refugee convention they signed, because they do. On the other hand, it is true they are not keen on rescuing other countries, particularly in Europe, that have a heavier burden in terms of forced migration problems. If we take the perspective of a realistic and feasible solution rather than a dogmatic one, we may have a viewpoint from which to understand the actions by these Asian states in terms of bounded rationality. I suggest that the Asian states (including Japan and Korea) have been marginalized by the decision-making process of international mechanisms for migrant protection since their launch.

While the universal aspect of the international refugee regime stands out in the context of global migration governance, little has been said about the historical background for the two refugee conventions— the 1951 Convention Relating to the Status of Refugees and the 1967 Protocol. It has often been noted that the primary objective for the international legal system for refugee protection in the early post–World War II period was to solve the problem of European refugees in an emergent international structure of East-West confrontation in the initial stage of the Cold War.[5] In contrast, the hesitancy of many Asian states to join the legal regime is often considered a sign of their unpreparedness. It is not. Rather, it results from their explicit rejection of the regime because they were deliberately excluded from the legal circle for essential decision-making.[6] The structural change in world politics did not bring Asian countries to the fore (in contrast to African countries).[7] And the structure that was established remained unchanged even after Japan and Korea signed the two treaties. As a result, Asian states' motivation was either to get credit in the international community or to achieve more benefit from international assistance through functions of the United Nations.

Another factor is that until recently the policy on the management of migration (often of the irregular kind), both from an economic angle and from the human rights/humanitarian protection angle, has largely been a matter of trade-offs. Even the international cooperation on the Rohingya refugee crisis entails a geo-economic element given the fact that that their home area, Rakhine state in Myanmar/Burma, has plentiful natural energy resources. The principle of non-interference has largely justified migration governance in Asia.

Meanwhile, the contemporary global environment poses the question of whether an international regime is possible without a hegemon. The problem when it comes to sharing responsibility for refugees in the global arena at present is not one of cooperation but one of commitment. On this point, I entirely agree with Thielemann's claim that the Dublin system works more as a mechanism of burden-shifting rather than burden-sharing.[8] If Europe is willing to spread its burden-shifting system to the world, then the question of legitimacy (in addition to feasibility) needs to be examined.

What we witness at present—in the political turmoil in European countries, in the intensified confrontation between the United States and China, and in expansionist attempts to form an alliance—shows that the existing international structure, characterized by a liberal international order, has been destabilized. When democracies undermine international goodwill and cooperation, we need to rethink global migration governance and find new ways to ensure the protection of migrants.

Notes

1. Details are in Morris-Suzuki 2006. Also see Takenaka 2015.

2. The law is also called "a law to exclude Japanese residents" (*hainichi imin hou*). A relevant argument is found, for instance, in Minohara 1996.

3. Such as Human Rights Watch 2019.

4. Mainly I refer to his argument in Freeman 2006.

5. For instance, Loescher 2003; Betts et al. 2013.

6. Davies 2006, 2007.

7. A detailed argument is found in Okabe 2021.

8. Thielemann 2018.

References

Betts, Alexander, James Milner, and Gil Loescher, eds. 2013. *UNHCR: The Politics and Practice of Refugee Protection*. Global Institutions Series. Florence: Taylor & Francis.

Davies, Sara E. 2006. "The Asian Rejection? International Refugee Law in Asia," *Australian Journal of Politics and History* 52, no. 4: 562-575.

Davies, Sara E. 2007 *Legitimizing Rejection: International Refugee Law in Southeast Asia*. Refugees and Human Rights Series. The Hague: Martinus Nijhoff.

Freeman, G. 2006. "National Models, Policy Types, and the Politics of Immigration in Liberal Democracies." *West European Politics* 29, no. 2: 227-247.

Human Rights Watch. 2019. "Report 2019: South Korea." https://www.hrw.org/world-report/2019/country-chapters/south korea.

Loescher, G. 2003. *The UNHCR and World Politics: A Perilous Path*. Oxford: Oxford University Press.

Minohara, T. 1996. "The Road to Exclusion: The 1920 California Alien Land Law and U.S.-Japan Relations." *Kobe University Law Review* 30: 39-73.

Morris-Suzuki, T. 2006. "Invisible Immigrants: Undocumented Migration and Border Controls in Early Postwar Japan." *Journal of Japanese Studies* 32, no. 1: 1-28.

Okabe, M. 2021. "How States React to the International Regime Complexities on Migration: A Study of Cases in South East Asia and Beyond." International Relations of the Asia-Pacific 21, no. 1: 65-90.

Takenaka, R. 2015. "Sengo Nihon ni okeru gaikokujin seisaku to zainichi Korean no shakai undou" [Immigration policy of postwar Japan and social movement by ethnic Koreans]. *Kawasaki Iryo Hukushi gaku Zasshi* 24, no. 2.

Thielemann E. 2018. "Why Refugee Burden-Sharing Initiatives Fail: Public Goods, Free-Riding and Symbolic Solidarity in the EU." *Journal of Common Market Studies* 56, no. 1: 63-82.

COMMENTARY

Two Sides of a Coin: A New Norm of Constrained Rights or Latecomers to Immigration in East Asia?

Michael Orlando Sharpe

Japan and South Korea have a shared history of colonialism (with one the perpetrator and the other the victim), emigration, authoritarian legacies, equivalent conceptions of homogenous ethno-cultural identity, nationality and citizenship, contemporary problems of demographic crisis, and remedial immigration policies. Until the 2000s, South Korea mimicked Japan's closed door and exclusionary immigration policy with "side doors" for unskilled migrant workers, including preferential policies for co-ethnics and an Industrial Training System that mirrored Japan's Technical Intern Training Program, including a tendency for exploitation (Chung, 2014, 405). By 2004, South Korea had ceased to follow Japan's lead and opened to unskilled foreigners with its Employment Permit System (EPS) and the discontinuation of its Industrial Training System. Only in 2019 did Japan, paradoxically, announce that it was not adopting an immigration policy but opened to unskilled foreign labor by implementing a scheme for the importation of hundreds of thousands of such workers by 2025, with a high bar for permanent residence and naturalization. Chung's chapter argues that closed borders have produced alternative entry points for immigration in Japan and South Korea that suggest an East Asian pattern of immigration with constrained rights akin to that seen in Singapore and the Gulf States. While I concur with Chung on Japan's and South Korea's intertwined histories and their side door remedies for immigration, I argue that these two countries may look less like the illiberal regimes of Singapore and the Gulf States and more like liberal democratic latecomers to immigration reluctantly accommodating old and new diversity.

The extension of rights are a function of the liberal state, civil society, and international norms. Japan (and South Korea) are in fact making incremental moves as emerging migration states (Hollifield and Sharpe 2017) where migrants acquire legal rights and protections under liberal constitutions and statutory law that may include basic civil rights and a package of social or welfare rights and even political or voting rights. (Hollifield 1986, 1992,1998). Chung notes that foreign residents in Japan and South Korea have gained rights that go beyond those specified by international human rights treaties and even beyond those seen in some "more liberal" industrial democracies. (Chung, 2020, 8). I contend that the exercise of rights in the liberal democracies of Japan and South Korea is dependent on civil society groups that go beyond their ethnic, religious, or other self-interest working in collaboration with others, the state, and international society to push for enforcement. Japan and South Korea have much to offer each other in the interactions between "new immigration" and their "existing institutions," the empowerment of migrants, and the broadening of their conceptions of membership.

Identity Politics Versus Ideology

Japan and South Korea trend much more in the direction of their Western liberal democratic counterparts than toward the political regimes of Singapore and the Gulf States. Freedom House's measure of political rights and civil liberties in 2019/2020 ranked Japan 96/100, South Korea 83/100, the United States 86/100, and Germany 94/100, all giving them the identifier of "free."[1] They stand in contrast to Singapore, with a score of 50/100,[2] and the United Arab Emirates, with a score of 17/100,[3] classified respectively as "partly free" and "not free." That said, in the absence of national directives in Japan and South Korea, civil society actors and local government had to accommodate the challenges faced by new immigrants and their local communities. South Korea's first national attempt at immigrant incorporation was its 2006 "multicultural coexistence" plan in coordination with previously existing local government programs (Chung 2014, 401). Japan's first national measure to support recent immigrants was in response to the 2008 financial crisis, and it included children's education, employment and training supports, housing, and (in a rather ironic twist) paid voluntary return for Latin American residents of Japanese descent, known as Nikkeijin (Milly 2014, 174; Sharpe 2014; Takenoshita 2015). Chung (2020) argues that civil society and preexisting legacies explain how South Korea has changed more than Japan. In both countries, civil society and local governments urged the national government to initiate immigrant incorporation policies and programs. Chung (2014) brings out this distinction and argues that unlike South Korea's pro-immigrant advocacy, which emerges from within the country's democratization movement, Japan lacks "mass mobilization" and "the leadership of a vanguard group from previous rights movements." For Chung, immigrants in Japan benefited from welfare benefits, legal protections, and incorporation won by the historically marginalized but well assimilated Zainichi Korean community, but this was not necessarily adequate for recent migrants. In sum, while South Korea's movement that encompassed migrants was centered around the country's ideological commitment to democratic reform, Japan's lack of mass movement remains grounded in ethnic identity politics, meaning that the older rights movements of mostly non-citizen Zainichi Koreans and Chinese seek to advance each group's own interests. Whether identity politics or ideology, the strategies in the two countries reveal a mobilization of ideas and interests within a liberal democratic framework.

Vanguard Groups, Civil Rights, and Universal Human Rights

Chung refers to the Zainichi Korean rights movement as a "noncitizen civil rights movement" (Chung 2010), and the lessons of coalition-building that can be taken from the US civil rights movement, which was rooted in the African American community but worked across groups, should not be lost. One wonders about the potential collaborative efforts between the Zainichi Korean community, with its 600,0000-plus members, and the ethnically Japanese but long discriminated-against Buraku community (Japan's largest minority group, with 3 million people, and a liberation movement that began in the 1920s) as well as the indigenous Ainu community (about 25,000 individuals). Tsutsui (2018) makes a very compelling argument about the more recent recognition and concessions that these three minority groups have won in Japan through using the language of international human rights. Since 1993, the Buraku liberation movement maintains an international NGO called the International Movement Against All Forms of Discrimination and Racism (IMADR), with offices in Tokyo and Geneva, that lobbies with other discriminated groups around issues of descent-based caste and racial discrimination at the level of the United Nations (Tsutsui 2018). What about the religious alliance of some Japanese citizens and Zainichi Koreans and the many bills to propose local voting rights for permanent foreign residents introduced by the Komeito party, which has an affiliated Buddhist religious organization, Soka Gakkai, of which many Zainichi Koreans are members (Sharpe 2014; McLaughlin 2019)? What about the marginalized Okinawan community (1 million)? How to bridge the divide between long-established Zainichi Korean foreign residents and "newcomer" Korean immigrants, and between older invisible post-colonial minorities (Zainichi Koreans, Chinese, and others) and newer visible communities of migrants and their descendants? How do these various older and newer identities manage belonging in an ethno-nationalist society (Liu-Farrer 2020; Strausz 2019)? Older minority communities can play a role as a vanguard linking interests that can push beyond identity politics across groups, including recent migrants, using the language of rights to leverage enforcement for themselves and others as important constituents in Japan's liberal democracy.

Moreover, Japan has long wanted to be respected as part of the international liberal order (Gurowitz 2006, 155, 156; Surak 2008; Tsutsui 2018), and South Korea, since its 1980s transition from authoritarianism, is no different. The acceptance of a limited number of refugees during the 1970s compelled the Japanese government to accede to several international conventions. This consequentially required that foreigners be treated equally in the areas of social security and welfare; effectively removed Japanese nationality restrictions in the national pension system, public housing, health insurance, and civil service jobs; and even changed nationality derivation from a patrilineal system to a bilineal system. In 2017, the Japanese government released the results of its first national survey on racial and ethnic discrimination, featuring reports of employment discrimination, racist taunts, discriminatory speech, Japanese-only recruitment, and denial of rental applications. UN special rapporteur Doudou Diene's scathing 2006 special report on racism and discrimination in Japan was largely ignored by the Japanese media and faced harsh criticism from Japan's right wing. The UN Human Rights Commission recommended that Japan prohibit hate speech, particularly regarding racial discrimination, citing increasingly serious vitriol from groups such as Zaitokukai (Association of Citizens Against the Special Privileges of Zainichi) against Koreans and Chinese. Japan's Diet passed the Hate Speech Elimination Law in 2016, but the law has no penalties and thus is viewed by many as ineffectual.

Like Japan, Korea grants no family reunification rights to migrant laborers, but, as Chung notes, Korea is the only Asian country to extend local voting rights to foreign residents in 2006, and the option of dual nationality became available in some circumstances in 2010. However, again, possession of a right does not ensure its fulfillment. There are news reports of the rights of foreigners in Korea being violated by electoral authorities not providing candidate information in other languages and a statute disallowing foreign citizens from participating in other political activities.[4] Others speculate the move for local voting rights in Korea was really intended to apply diplomatic pressure to add to the previously mentioned long-standing demand for local voting rights for non-citizen Zainichi Koreans in Japan.[5] Again, like in

Japan, there is no comprehensive law against discrimination in South Korea, though it has been admonished by the UN.[6] There are some reports in South Korea of discrimination against visible foreigners, including not being allowed in some public facilities. The South Korea National Human Rights Commission notes that seven out of ten foreign residents report discrimination.[7] In addition to Chung's civil society and movement-politics-oriented analysis, what is the impact of the global human rights regime on the incorporation of foreign migrants and the protection and enforcement of their rights?

The Lives of "Others" and Their Rights

Japan's reticence notwithstanding, evidence of migrants and their descendants in daily life abound in Japan. Migrants are visible as servers in the restaurants of Narita and Haneda airports, as clerks in convenience stores, in family restaurants, on farms harvesting vegetables sold in Tokyo supermarkets, in food processing plants, at construction sites, and as high-skilled foreign workers in the IT, finance, and education sectors. Their presence is evident in popular culture as well, from sumo wrestlers, J-pop and traditional Enka singers, TV personalities, and the fashion industry to the recent crowning of a biracial Miss Universe and Miss Japan (Hollifield and Sharpe 2017). In politics, Marutei Tsurunen, from Finland (Japan's first foreign-born naturalized politician), Shikun Haku, a Japan-born naturalized Korean Japanese descendant, and Renho Murata, a Taiwanese Japanese descendant, have served in Japan's national parliament (Sharpe, 2014). Two foreign-born naturalized politicians, Puranik Yogendra from India and Noemi Inoue of Bolivia, won seats in the April 2019 Tokyo local assembly elections. In business, in addition to entrepreneurs running small and medium-sized companies, Mayoshi Son, a Zainichi Korean—Japan-born and a naturalized Japanese citizen—is founder and chief executive officer of the telecommunications giant Softbank and allegedly the richest person in Japan. Despite this, education is not compulsory for foreigners in Japan, so there are many problems around the schooling and integration of foreign children (Sharpe 2014). The number of mixed-race Japanese, also known as *hafu*, is expanding, but they face varying degrees of discrimination. There has been racist language on the internet against the biracial Miss Universe and Miss Japan, and others arguing that they are aberrations and do not represent the country. The biracial Japanese Haitian tennis star Naomi Osaka has been depicted as an essentially white or Caucasian anime character by her corporate sponsor, prompting controversy and apologies. The same predictable scenario occurred in summer 2020 when Japan's public broadcaster, NHK, released an animated video that attempted to explain the Black Lives Matter protests with stereotypical and racist depictions of African Americans, with no mention of police brutality or the killings of unarmed individuals. Zaitokukai has been identified by the national police agency as a hate speech organization. Osaka was the first city in Japan to enact a hate speech ordinance. Indeed, rights have accrued in Japan's liberal democracy, but these are halting steps toward their overall realization.

In South Korea, the introduction of the Employment Permit System (EPS) has accelerated the number of unskilled foreign workers, with some 480,000 arriving in the country since 2004 from Vietnam, Cambodia, Thailand, the Philippines, Indonesia, and some eleven other countries through bilateral agreements. Among these are some 220,000 ethnic Koreans from China or other foreign nationals of Korean heritage who have the advantage of speaking Korean[8] (though North Koreans face discrimination and integration problems). The presence of these non-nationals, along with the Support for Multicultural Families program in 2008, purportedly gives Korea an advantage over Japan in attracting foreign workers. Still, children of foreigners continue to suffer discrimination, including in education and health care systems.[9] The number of Kosians (children of a Korean parent and a parent from another Asian country) is increasing, and these individuals are subject to prejudice and bullying. Hines Ward, the Korean-born biracial African American and Korean NFL player, has become a celebrated advocate of biracial Koreans in Korea.[10] In Japan, dual nationality past the age of twenty-one is generally not possible; in South Korea it is limited but gaining in popularity. South Korea has invisible older (though still more recent than in Japan) communities of Chinese, ethnic Koreans of Chinese citizenship, and North Koreans as well as newer visible foreign residents and their children. An official rhetoric of multiculturalism exists to varying degrees in both countries. As is the case in Japan, there is a possibility of collaboration beyond ethnicity and religion, using the language of rights, to gain enforcement in South Korea's liberal democracy.

Conclusion

Both Japan and Korea will likely become increasingly diverse in terms of population and the claiming of rights. One concern in these two countries that share so much is the establishment and modification of foreign or "othered" hierarchies based on length of residence, proximity to a Japanese or Korean somatic norm, color of skin, and country of origin. These notions of racial and ethnic hierarchy, likely introduced by the West and internalized in both societies, could prove an impediment to bridging divisions. Civil society groups must work beyond their ethnic or other self-interest in collaboration with others, the state, and international society to push for enforcement of rights. One promising development is that the Black Lives Matter movement triggered protests in the summer of 2020 in Japan and South Korea in which young people demonstrated in solidarity with the movement in the United States and used it to highlight the realities of racism in their own countries. Both Japan and Korea can learn from the other in terms of the strengths and limitations of ethnic politics, the rhetoric and realization of rights and democratic inclusion, the mechanisms of international human rights, and the expansion of the meaning of Japanese and Korean nationality and citizenship. Hopefully, an East Asian model of "constrained rights," nearly equivalent to that seen in Singapore or the Gulf States, is not the new norm. Despite an East Asian pattern, Japan and South Korea are making incremental steps toward converging with other liberal democratic countries of immigration. The ways in which visible foreigners and their descendants and invisible older historically marginalized groups are accommodated and can exercise their rights are litmus tests for these two countries as liberal democracies.

Notes

1. Freedom House, "Freedom in the World 2019: Japan," https://freedomhouse.org/country/japan/freedom-world/2019; Freedom House, "Freedom in the World 2020: Korea," https://freedomhouse.org/country/south-korea/freedom-world/2020; Freedom House, "Freedom in the World 2020: United States," https://freedomhouse.org/country/united-states/freedom-world/2020; Freedom House, "Freedom in the World 2020: Germany," https://freedomhouse.org/country/germany/freedom-world/2020.

2. Freedom House, "Freedom in the World 2020: Singapore," https://freedomhouse.org/country/singapore/freedom-world/2020.

3. Freedom House, "Freedom in the World 2020: United Arab Emirates," https://freedomhouse.org/country/united-arab-emirates/freedom-world/2020.

4. Park 2018.

5. Cho 2006.

6. Lee 2021.

7. UNHCR 2018.

8. Nikkei Asia 2017.

9. Freedom House, "Freedom in the World 2020: South Korea," https://freedomhouse.org/country/south-korea/freedom-world/2020.

10. Branch 2009.

References

Branch, John. 2009. "Ward Helps Biracial Children in Journey Towards Acceptance." *New York Times*, November 9, 2009. https://www.nytimes.com/2009/11/09/sports/football/09ward.html

Cho, Chun-un. 2006. "Elections Expand Voting Rights for Foreigners, Younger Citizens." *Digital Korea Herald*, June 16, 2006. https://yaleglobal.yale.edu/content/elections-expand-voting-rights-foreigners-younger-citizens.

Chung, Erin. A. 2010. *Immigration and Citizenship in Japan*. New York: Cambridge University Press.

Chung, Erin. A. 2014. "Japan and Korea: Immigration Control and Immigrant Incorporation." In *Controlling Immigration: A Global Perspective*, 3rd ed., edited by James F. Hollifield, Philip L. Martin, and Pia Orrenius, pp. 399-421. Stanford, CA: Stanford University Press.

Chung, Erin. A. 2020. Immigrant Incorporation in East Asian Democracies. Cambridge: Cambridge University Press.

Gurowitz, Amy. 2006. "Looking Outward: International Legal Norms and Foreigner Rights in Japan." In *Local Citizenship in Recent Countries of Immigration: Japan in Comparative Perspective*, edited by Takeyuki Tsuda, pp. 153-171. Lanham, MD: Lexington Books.

Hollifield, James F. 1986. "Immigration Policy in France and Germany: Outputs vs. Outcomes." *Annals* 485 (May): 113–128.

Hollifield, James. 1992. *Immigrants, Markets, and Rights: The Political Economy of Postwar Europe*. Cambridge, MA: Harvard University Press.

Hollifield, James F. 1998. "Migration, Trade and the Nation-State: The Myth of Globalization." *UCLA Journal of International Law and Foreign Affairs* 3(2): 595–636.

Hollifield, James F. and Michael O. Sharpe. September 2017. "Japan as an Emerging Migration State", *International Relations of the Asia-Pacific*, Volume 17, Issue 3, pp. 371–400.

Hollifield, James F., and Michael O. Sharpe. 2017. "Japan as an Emerging Migration State." *International Relations of the Asia-Pacific* 17, no. 3: 371–400.

Hollifield, James. 1992. *Immigrants, Markets, and Rights: The Political Economy of Postwar Europe*. Cambridge: Harvard University Press.

Lee Ji-hye. 2021. "Anti-Discrimination Legislation Would Have Kept Forcibly Discharged Transgender Soldier Alive." *Hankyoreh*, March 5, 2021. http://english.hani.co.kr/arti/english_edition/e_national/985629.html.

Liu-Farrer, Gracia. 2020. *Immigrant Japan: Mobility and Belonging in an Ethno-nationalist Society*. Ithaca, NY: Cornell University Press.

McLaughlin, Levi. 2019. *Sokka Gakkai's Human Revolution: The Rise of a Mimetic Nation in Modern Japan*. Honolulu: University of Hawaii Press.

Milly, Deborah J. 2014. *New Policies for New Residents: Immigrants, Advocacy, and Governance in Japan and Beyond*. Ithaca, NY: Cornell University Press.

Nikkei Asia. 2017. "South Korea's Permit Program Swell Ranks of Foreign Workers." *Nikkei Asia*, March 22, 2017. https://asia.nikkei.com/Economy/South-Korea-s-permit-program-swells-ranks-of-foreign-workers2.

Park Ji-won. 2018. "Foreigners with Voting Rights Being Ignored." *Korea Times*. http://www.koreatimes.co.kr/www/nation/2018/04/356_247360.html.

Sharpe, Michael O. 2014. *Postcolonial Citizens and Ethnic Migration: the Netherlands and Japan in the Age of Globalization*. Houndmills, Basingstoke: Palgrave Macmillan.

Strausz, Michael. 2019. *Help (Not) Wanted: Immigrant Politics in Japan*. Albany: SUNY Press.

Surak, Kristin. 2008. "Convergence in Foreigners' Rights and Citizenship Policy? A Look at Japan." *International Migration Review* 42, no. 3: 550–575.

Takenoshita, Hirohisa. 2015. "Labor Market Structure. Welfare Policy, and Integration: Brazilian Immigrants During the Economic Downturn." In *International Migrants in Japan: Contributions in an Era of Population Decline*, edited by Yoshitaka Ishikawa, pp. 563-585. Melbourne: Trans Pacific Press.

Tsutsui, Kiyoteru. 2018. *Rights Make Might: Global Human Rights and Minority Social Movements in Japan*. New York: Oxford University Press.

UNHCR. 2018. "Committee on the Elimination of Racial Discrimination: The Report of the Republic of Korea." United Nations Office of the High Commissioner, December 4, 2018. https://www.ohchr.org/en/NewsEvents/Pages/DisplayNews.aspx?NewsID=23972&LangID=E.

5 THE EUROPEAN UNION AND REGIONAL MIGRATION GOVERNANCE

15 The European Union

From Politics to Politicization

Andrew Geddes and Leila Hadj-Abdou

Introduction

In early 2021 human rights lawyers filed a preliminary action against the European Border and Coast Guard Agency (Frontex) in which they accused the agency of taking part in "pushbacks" of asylum seekers in the Mediterranean toward the Libyan coast that violated the non-refoulement principle enshrined in international human rights law (Brito 2021). A similar case had been filed in 2019 with the International Criminal Court (ICC) accusing the European Union and its member states of being knowingly responsible for migrants drowning in the Mediterranean. EU officials, it was argued, exhibited "a clear consciousness and willingness" to let many migrants die in order to deter immigration to the EU (Stierl 2019). The EU also found itself the subject of strong criticism on the migration issue, including from some of its own member states. The Hungarian prime minister, Viktor Orbán, threatened to take legal action against the EU for being "pro-immigration" and trying to undermine his country's ability to defend its borders (Mischke 2018). Just a few days before the action by human rights lawyers against Frontex, the EU agency had ceased operations in Hungary following a European Court of Justice (ECJ) ruling that the country's government was unlawfully detaining migrants in "transit zones." In response to Frontex's withdrawal, the Hungarian government emphasized that it would not give in to what it called "pro-migration pressures," and would continue to "defend the Hungarian people and the country's—and EU's—borders" (Cook and Spike 2021). These contrasting perspectives indicate the ways in which migration and asylum, as common EU concerns, have become politicized and salient, with the debate seeming to be increasingly polarized.

This chapter picks up on this book's two major themes—convergence and the gap hypothesis—by focusing on recent trends, dynamics, and fault lines within the EU that have become more manifest in the past years. We develop two arguments. First, that underlying political dynamics shape the scope for and extent of convergence. Intensified politicization makes "vertical," top-down, EU-driven convergence less likely to occur. More likely is "horizontal convergence" between coalitions of EU member states that share similar perspectives. These are not stable coalitions, but they can provide a base for practice-based learning among the like-minded about the management and implementation of policy. This changes the dynamics: not only are states trying to "upload" preferences to the EU level or "download" agreed-upon EU decisions into national systems, but there are also situations of "cross-loading," where groups of like-minded states work together (Aggestam and Bicchi 2019).

Second, the gap between the rhetoric of control and the reality of continued immigration that has been an observable characteristic of European and EU migration policy and politics since the early 1970s has become more difficult to manage when levels of politicization are high and when, importantly, this politicization extends to include the EU itself. As "Europe" becomes politicized, the tendency to search for external solutions beyond the EU's borders has been reinforced. This was evident in September 2020 when the European Commission presented proposals for a *New* Pact on Migration and Asylum (emphasis added) (CEC 2020). This proposal is another attempt to address ongoing migration conflicts and resolve long-standing challenges centered on asylum seeking and irregular migration, and with ever greater efforts to work with non-EU member states and externalize the EU response (Hadj Abdou 2021).

The Constraining Dissensus

It is tempting to search for dramatic changes or critical junctures. The 2015 "migration crisis" that led to more than 1 million people moving to Europe via Mediterranean Sea crossings could seem an ideal candidate. As has been shown, however, the crisis actually amplified existing tendencies in European and EU migration policy and politics rather than inducing some kind of new path or decisive break with previous approaches (Guiraudon 2018; Trauner and Servent 2016). While there has been significant institutional change, with vastly increased resources and also increased political attention, the EU's "policy core" on immigration and asylum and the ideas that animate it were established in the 1990s. Priorities established more than thirty years ago—combatting irregular flows, reducing asylum seeking—have remained consistent components of EU action.

An underlying justification for this can be found in views about and representations of the underlying dynamics of migration to Europe. Clearly, migration is driven or caused by major structural changes such as economic inequality or conflict, but there are significant uncertainties about how these will affect migration (who moves, where to, in what numbers, for what reason, and for what duration) plus important social and political risks. Uncertainty and risk mean that representations of the causes and effects of migration—whether accurate or not—can have powerful effects on policy (Geddes 2021b). More specifically, there is a long-established view that the EU faces large-scale and sustained pressures on its external frontiers that is likely to persist. Capturing this, in late 2014, an EU official put it to us like this:

> Yesterday at this meeting of the US and the Commission and others . . . [they] were repeatedly mentioning that this will be the new normal. These 250,000–280,000 irregular migrants a year, that's basically what we have to count on in the foreseeable future. Nothing will change in this regard. I tend to agree, because as long as things are going the way they are going on in North Africa, sub-Saharan African countries, Afghanistan, Iraq, what have you, I don't see an end unfortunately to that. (Interview of EU official, December 2014, cited in Geddes 2019, 84)

Around eighteen months later, in June 2016, the Commission published its New Partnership Framework for working with non-EU states, particularly in Africa. This new framework identified external migratory pressures on EU member states as

> the "new normal" both for the EU and for partner countries. Responding to the current situation requires a more coordinated, systematic and structured approach, matching the EU's interests and the interests of our partners. (CEC 2016, 5)

The "new normal" is actually quite similar to the "old normal," as cooperation on migration and asylum by the EU has been driven since the end of the Cold War by concerns about large-scale and potentially uncontrollable migration flows. There has been a long-standing tendency in Europe to view migration itself from a perspective of crises of various types (poverty, conflict, climate) (Geddes 2021a, 30). Moreover, with the end of the Cold War era and EU enlargement, which also implied a continuous increase of labor supply within the EU, the refugee and the migrant worker ceased to be viewed as "economic, political or ideological assets" (Lindstrøm 2005, 589) in European migration-receiving states.

In addition to these underlying continuities, it is important to identify an important change in the underlying structures of European politics and its implications for the politicization of both immigration and European integration. Until the early 1990s, European integration was largely focused on technical issues that were not seen to impinge directly upon state sovereignty ("low politics"). As Hooghe and Marks (2009, 5) note about European integration until the 1990s: "Public opinion was quiescent. These were years of permissive consensus, of deals cut by insulated elites." This insulation appealed to the executive branches of national governments as they began to intensify their cooperation on immigration and asylum at an EU level (Guiraudon 2000). It was, however, the continued development of EU competencies for issues such as immigration but also for economic and monetary policy that meant that national-level and EU leaders would have to look over their shoulders at public opinion on European integration. By the 1990s, public opinion was becoming structured, affecting national voting, and related to the underlying dimensions of political contestation in Europe (Hooghe and Marks 2009, 7). Attitudes toward European integration now form part of a new dividing line or cleavage that has variously been labeled as pro- or anti-globalization or cosmopolitan versus communitarian but has in common that opposition to European integration and immigration has motivated political behavior and new forms of political mobilization (Hutter and Kriesi 2019). These changes pre-dated the migration and refugee crisis of 2015 but were the social and political backdrop against which the crisis became a broader crisis of politics and institutions in Europe and the EU. This is not the same as saying that there has been a growth in anti-immigration sentiment in Europe. In fact, attitudes toward migration are relatively stable and actually became more favorable toward migration from both within and outside the EU, even after 2015—that is, precisely at the peak of the crisis. Rather, the importance that people attribute to the immigration issue—its salience—increased dramatically after 2015 in many European countries, triggering latent anti-immigration dispositions among sections of the European electorate and fueling growth in support for right-wing populist and nationalist political parties (Dennison and Geddes 2018). There are some exceptions to these patterns. The four central European member states that comprise the Visegrád Group (Czech Republic, Hungary, Poland, and Slovakia) have greater levels of public opposition to immigration and political leaders who have expressed strong opposition both to immigration and to common EU measures that might include the redistribution of migrants between EU member states. Prior to the COVID-19 pandemic the salience of migration had been declining, and this tendency became more marked during the pandemic because concerns about health care and the economic reconstruction became more pressing (Geddes 2021a). There were, however, new opportunities for anti-migrant political entrepreneurs to frame migration as a threat and, more broadly, to mobilize against globalization and its effects (Wondreys and Mudde 2020).

The Development of EU Competences

While the EU's "policy core" on immigration and asylum was established in the early 1990s and has remained consistent over more than thirty years, there has been significant institutional development (Hadj Abdou 2016; Geddes et al. 2020). From the outset it should be made clear that while we can speak of a common EU migration and asylum policy, EU competences are limited. The number of migrants to be admitted remains a competence of the member states, as does the integration of immigrants. EU competencies tend to focus on those forms of migration defined as unwanted by states, such as asylum seeking and irregular migration.

Political and economic integration, which can be understood as a process by which states cease to be wholly sovereign, was shaped by both economic and security dynamics (Haas 1970). Economic integration in the form of the common market and, most significantly after 1986, the single market induced cooperation on security issues within what was then known as the European Community. In 1985, the Schengen Agreement was signed in the eponymous Luxembourg town by Belgium, France, Germany, Luxembourg, and the Netherlands to cooperate outside the formal treaty framework on the removal of controls and checks at national borders. The end of the Cold War further impelled cooperation on immigration and asylum by prompting concern in Germany about both the flows of migrants (although many were actually ethnic German returnees) and the potential for continued large-scale flows. Germany sought to Europeanize the response to migration and to develop closer cooperation between member states (Henson and Malhan 1995). The Maastricht Treaty (1992) brought this forward in a form of intergovernmental cooperation, although the limits of such an approach soon became evident, as it was very difficult to reach decisions on the basis of intergovernmental cooperation and a requirement for unanimity. The Amsterdam Treaty (1999) was highly significant because it "communitarized" migration and asylum, which means that it incorporated these issues into the legal framework of the EU, although with continued constraints on decision-making that left member states with the upper hand. The progressive development of the treaty framework by the Nice Treaty (2001) and, more significantly, the Lisbon Treaty (2009) meant that a more fully communitarized treaty framework was created for aspects of migration and asylum. The Council of Ministers and the European Parliament share legislative authority and the Commission is responsible for the management and implementation of policy, while the treaty provisions are justiciable in the EU's Court of Justice.

While there has been an intensification of EU action on policy, massively greater financial commitments plus the creation of European agencies working on border security (Frontex) and asylum (European Asylum Support Office, EASO), it is also the case that the core policy priorities have remained fairly consistent.

Core Policy Priorities

Reducing Irregular Migration.   Strongly driven by a focus on tackling the "root causes" of migration, measures target both countries of origin as well as transit countries, including conflict prevention, development aid, trade relations, and agreements with origin and transit countries to contain international migration and regarding the return of irregular migrants. This policy priority has been strongly focused on migrant smuggling (and trafficking), with an ever-increasing tendency to conceptualize smuggling as organized crime that, as the legal scholar Valsamis Mitsilegas (2019) has framed it, turned policy into a "smuggling crusade."

Management of the EU's External Borders.   Barriers to the free movement of goods, capital, and people have been vanishing as European integration progressed. Since it came into effect in 1995, the Schengen Convention abolished internal border controls between Schengen states, although there was scope for their reimposition in the face of security threats or the COVID-19 pandemic, which has led to arguments that Schengen itself has been "securitized" (Ceccorulli 2019). The creation of the Schengen area led to a stronger collective focus on the management of the member states' external borders. Cooperation on border security was also powerfully impelled by the EU's widening from fifteen to twenty-eight member states between 1995 and 2019 (with a reduction to twenty-seven when the United Kingdom left in January 2020). After 2015, there were largely unsuccessful efforts to develop "solidarity" toward member states such as Greece and Italy that were the particular focus of arrivals via Mediterranean routes. In September 2015, EU member states agreed on a two-year plan to relocate up to 160,000 asylum seeking migrants from Greece and Italy to other member states, according to a distribution key based on population, national income, numbers of asylum applicants, and unemployment rates. Two years later, by the end of 2017, just 34,705 asylum applicants had been relocated. Hungary and Poland did not relocate any migrants, and the United Kingdom and Denmark made use of their opt-out rights under EU law (European Court of Auditors 2019, 21). The creation of "hot spots" in Greece and Italy where initial reception, identification, registration, and fingerprinting of arriving asylum seekers and other migrants were conducted and from where relocation could be organized was initially intended to be an emergency response to the 2015 crisis, in which more than 1 million people arrived via Mediterranean crossings, but these have remained a key component of external border management. Overall external border management has remained a key concern and challenge for the EU, as is also expressed in the 2020 New Pact for

Migration and Asylum proposal. The 2015 crisis induced a reemergence of national border controls that gained further impetus during the COVID-19 pandemic.

The Common European Asylum System.   Strongly interlinked with the management of the external borders has been efforts to develop a common EU asylum system since the late 1990s. The key sticking point in the domain of asylum has been reform of the Dublin regulation, which, named after the city where agreement was initially reached in 1992, determines that an asylum claim must be made in the first EU member state through which an applicant passes.

The Dublin system has now become a key component of the EU's Common European Asylum System (CEAS). In August 2015, German chancellor Angela Merkel announced that all Syrians would be able to make an asylum claim in Germany irrespective of their point of entry to the EU. This led to more than 800,000 people making claims in Germany, but it also meant the reimposition of border controls and fences along the "Balkan route" through southeast Europe. As a direct result of Dublin there was also disproportionate pressure on southern member states, particularly Greece and Italy, that were the first countries of entry for many asylum seekers. "Secondary movements" between one member state and another induced a "reverse domino effect," with new fencing and border controls introduced within the Schengen area to stop onward movement. By April 2016, there was an estimated 1,200 kilometers of border fencing, erected at a cost of €500 million (EPRS 2018). Attempts to renegotiate the Dublin system have been bedeviled by diverging interests. As a result of these failed attempts the 2020 Pact on Asylum and Migration (CEC 2020) officially declared the end of the Dublin regulation. The underlying policy principle of the regulation, however, did not change (discussed later in the section on asylum). It thus remains to be seen whether the EU can solve this issue during the negotiations on the proposals contained in the New Migration and Asylum Pact. Specifically, the pact proposes a scheme for relocation of asylum applicants between member states, but, crucially, it also allows member states to opt out of relocation and, instead, "sponsor" (meaning fund) expulsion of rejected asylum applicants from other member states.

Regular Migration Pathways to the EU.   The weakest component of the priorities that came onto the EU agenda very tentatively in the 2000s involves "regular" migration, for which EU competencies are extremely limited. Member states decide on the numbers of migrants to be admitted, although the EU can legislate for the conditions in which regular migration can take place, including the rights of long-term residents and provisions for seasonal workers, intra-corporate transferees, highly skilled workers, students and researchers, and family migrants. Member states, however, tend to adopt rather different approaches when implementing these directives. For example, as concerns the Blue Card Directive, which regulates conditions for entry and stay for migrants in highly skilled employment, in different states salary thresholds ranged from €13,000 to €68,000 and conditions for labor market testing varied, as did the work permit's duration (ranging from one to four years) (Cerna 2018). The New Pact of 2020 proposes "talent partnerships" and "talent pools" to enhance regular migration pathways into the EU. Such efforts will remain constrained by member states' control over admissions.

Irregular Migration: The Quest for External Solutions

The "fight against irregular migration" has long been a top EU priority and a particular salient type of migration in public debate. Whilst regular migrants actually vastly outnumber irregular ones, a Eurobarometer survey published in 2018 found that 47 percent of respondents thought that there are at least as many irregular migrants in the EU as those that were regular (Eurobarometer 2018, 5).

The EU plays a significant role in this area through regulations, funding, and technical cooperation. While implementation remains a member state responsibility, the EU is effectively steering and coordinating these responses. In terms of laws, the Return Directive of 2008 seeks to harmonize the procedures of expulsion of irregular immigrants across member states. In 2009 a directive (2009/52/EC) was adopted to sanction the employment of workers without a legal residence status, and to establish common minimum standards and measures against employers infringing that prohibition.

Funding is a further crucial element of EU action in this policy domain. The EU has significantly increased the overall financial resources allocated to curb irregular migration over time. For the period 2021 to 2027 the commission proposed to nearly triple funding for migration and border management to €34.9 billion, compared to €13 billion in the previous seven-year period (CEC 2018a).

An important tool of coordination is the European Coast and Border Guard Agency (Frontex). Frontex has been steadily expanding its responsibilities and is one of the fastest-growing agencies in terms of financial and human resources in the EU. In 2021, Frontex became the EU's first uniformed service. The agency is in charge of a variety of tasks, including the coordination of control operations at the EU's external borders, analyzing migration flows, supporting member states with training and technical assistance, conducting interventions to tackle high migration inflows in member states, and executing the return of irregular immigrants. Its staff is projected to grow from around 6,500 in 2020 to around 10,000 by 2027.

In 2016 an EU regulation tasked Frontex with conducting "vulnerability assessments" of each member state's capacity and weaknesses concerning the "protection" of its borders. Two new powers are especially important in the 2016 regulation. First, Frontex is granted a supervisory power it did not previously have. The agency now carries out a yearly assessment of each member state's capacity and border vulnerabilities. An additional element of this "major innovation" (Deleixhe and Duez 2019 , 928) is that if a member state fails to comply with Frontex's vulnerability assessment recommendations, this could trigger an intervention by the agency. The so-called right to intervene (Article 19) gives Frontex the power to deploy border guards to a member state if the functioning of the Schengen area is threatened—subject to a Council decision. This is "unprecedented in the integration process of the EU's external border management" (Deleixhe and Duez 2019 , 922; see also Niemann and Speyer 2018 , 27).

Convergence: Externalization

The twin components of the EU policy agenda addressing irregular migration are border control and the external dimension through which the EU seeks to co-opt non-EU countries into its migration framework.

The external dimension represents a shift of territorial control and legal responsibility to countries outside the EU. Its aims to prevent non-EU "nationals from leaving their countries of origin, but also to ensure that if they manage to do so, they remain as close to their country of origin as possible, or in any case outside EU territory" (Rijpma and Cremona 2007 , 12). It also covers measures ensuring that if immigrants do manage to enter EU territory irregularly, they can be returned to transit countries or countries of origin through agreements with those states. This approach is anything but new; it reaffirms existing policy approaches and fosters ideas that have been floating around for decades. An EU official put it to us like this:

> All those solutions I think had been around for quite a long time. I always remember, for example, my . . . colleague in Brussels, who had been around since the '90s, [told us] what we are discussing, what we consider as new ideas, they've already been discussing that in the early '90s . . . focusing on the external dimension . . . The difference now is, with the crisis . . . now there is the political will to change things and follow up those ideas. I think you could see that the attempts that have been tried in the past don't work. If one member state closes its borders, the problem will not be solved, but will be shifted. Maybe on the European level the good example is Spain. I remember 15 years ago when they were faced with big immigration waves from Northern Africa. They managed to get their own package with their neighboring countries. This has often been cited as a role model how it could be solved, creating some kind of part-

nership that both sides have a vested interest in, so both are interested in keeping the situation stable. . . . I think it's changing geopolitical dynamics and also the realization that in a globalized world, what happens somewhere in the world will, sooner or later, affect us. (Interview of member state official, February 2018)

The 2015 crisis thus served as an opportunity to strengthen this path due to heightened political attention to the issue and the picking up of already existing ideas that affirmed existing policy paths.

A case in point is cooperation on immigration with Libya since the early 2000s. This type of externalization has created "'off-shore' black holes where European norms, standards and regulations simply do not apply" (Bialasiewicz 2012, 862). The near total collapse of Libya's state structures after the fall of Gaddafi has not diminished the EU's focus on Libya as part of its externalization agenda despite public debate in Europe about human rights violations of migrants in Libya. Another major cooperation effort by EU member states was the 2016 EU-Turkey Statement. This intergovernmental agreement was a key EU response to the migration crisis. This deal aimed at stemming of flows of migration through the provision of border control resources to Turkey, and resettling in the EU Syrians registered in Turkey in exchange for the return of irregular migrants from Greece to Turkey. By March 2021, 28,300 Syrians had been resettled in one of twenty EU member states. Considerably greater resources were devoted to funding the Turkish authorities to keep Syrian refugees in Turkey, with an allocation of up to €6 billion (CEC 2021).

The EU has also sought to intensify cooperation with African countries (Carling and Hernández-Carretero 2011; Geddes and Maru 2020; Mouthaan 2019). In June 2016 the New Partnership Framework for working with non-EU member states, particularly in Africa, was proposed by the European Commission to tackle the "root causes of irregular migration and displacement." Prior to this, in 2015 the Emergency Trust Fund for Africa was established to invest €3.9 billion in the Sahel region, the Lake Chad area, the Horn of Africa, and North Africa (CEC 2018b). While these funds have effectively created opportunities for economic development, a major emphasis has been on containment and control of irregular migration (Oxfam 2017).

The fact that external dimension is the pact's component for which there is the most consensus among EU member states highlights that the external approach has become one of the preferred policy solutions to address irregular migration.

EU cooperation on migration matters was initially driven by national policy actors aiming to push through restrictive migration control policies to circumvent domestic constraints by forces pushing for liberalization (Guiraudon 2000). The shift to making policy in new institutions (i.e., venues) was driven by the aspiration to pursue restrictive policies. Restriction-minded policy actors tried Brussels as a venue but were eventually confronted with domestic-level constraints (Bonjour and Vink 2013). New efforts to circumvent these constraints include the creation of new solutions in places such as Agadez, Bamako, Tripoli, and Rabat, where a range of actors—both formal, such as state actors, and more informal, such as people smugglers—participate in and thus structure the external dimension of EU migration governance (Geddes 2021b).

The external approach yielded some success for the EU and its member states. These new arrangements, however, also exhibit considerable constraints, most notably often differing interests such as the different levels of interest in curbing or facilitating migration between destination, origin and transit countries (Frowd 2020). The African Union reacted negatively to EU attempts to establish regional disembarkation platforms, or asylum processing centers, outside of Europe (Boffey 2019).

The EU's negotiation leverage is also severely limited given its legal competences, or lack thereof. In negotiations, there is often talk of "pathways for legal migration," but as noted previously, the EU does not have legal powers in relation to the numbers of migrants to be admitted. The commission's bargaining power in negotiations with third countries is weakened by the reluctance of EU governments to open legal migration pathways. The commission has opted to follow a strategy of integrating other policy sectors, such as development aid, trade, mobility, and energy, in its negotiations in order to broaden its bargaining leverage.

To summarize, notwithstanding its limitations, externalization can be identified as of growing relevance at the EU level. The idea that it is about fighting the "root causes" of migration in destination countries, which has accompanied the externalization agenda, has become a dominant perspective throughout Europe. Externalization of migration control policies is not unique to Europe. When we look at North America, for instance, we can observe very similar dynamics (Hadj Abdou 2019). Both in North America and Europe, security concepts were imported through this agenda to countries to the south. In both regions, perceptions of crises have further perpetuated the path of externalization, and in both cases, we see considerable human rights concerns that have accompanied these processes.

Gap: The Continuation of Irregular Migration.   While we can observe a strong rhetorical commitment to control, we also see a continued reality of irregular migration, and at times contradictory politics. This is not to say that levels of irregular migrants in the EU remain constant or are necessarily growing. While it is impossible to provide exact numbers, in 2019, the EU's statistical office, Eurostat, noted that there were 627,900 non-EU citizens reported to be irregularly present in the EU, with Germany, Greece, and France reporting the largest numbers of irregulars (Eurostat 2020). According to the statistics, this represented an increase of 9.7 percent compared with the previous year (when the total was 572,200), but a significant decrease of 69.9 percent compared with the 2015 migration crisis year peak (Eurostat 2020).

The size of admissions channels for regular migrants, however, has not served to choke off demand for irregular migration, and—despite the stated but largely unfulfilled intention to create more legal pathways—is unlikely to do so in the future. This then raises the question of the factors that shape political responses to irregular migration. A dominant idea across the EU and its member states is that irregular migration is foremost grounded in exploitation by smugglers and traffickers. Irregular migrants are seen as victims of ruthless criminal smuggling and trafficking networks, who are putting migrants' life at risk. Although research evidence suggests a more nuanced picture (Sanchez 2018), this perspective on criminal activity has driven policy developments across the EU and its member states in terms of criminalization of irregular migration and has made the "fight against smuggling" a policy priority. In 2016, the EU's own law enforcement agency, Europol, established a European Migrant Smuggling Centre with a strong focus on organized criminality (Europol 2019).

The "fight against smuggling" can actually be seen as illustrative of how an existing solution attaches itself to a policy problem rather than a solution emerging as a response to a problem. As Kingdon observed (1984), policy problems and solutions are not necessarily always causally or temporally linked; problems do not necessarily initiate policy responses. Instead, it might well be that a stream of solutions is waiting to attach themselves to a particular problem. Solutions favored by policymakers for addressing particular policy problems may have been on the agenda for some time but were not taken up because they did not garner enough support at the time. They might be later picked up when an opportunity arises. Solutions thus may have preceded policy problems, and preferred "solutions" can help determine which problems get attention and how these problems are defined. By focusing on smugglers operating in organized criminal gangs as the main source of the problem, attention is directed away from another potential solution to irregularity: regular pathways. The focus thus remains on the ways in which relatively small numbers of irregular migrants arrive via clandestine border crossing rather than on more common pathways into irregularity in Europe, such as the overstaying of visas, or on the underlying structural socio-economic conditions that generate irregularity, such as reliance on migrant workers in key sectors such as social care. This type of irregularity has been often tolerated by governments in Europe and elsewhere.

This interview with an EU official shows how policy "solutions" can precede the formulation of the problem:

> An essential part of our work is to try to fill the narrative with policy, in a way, because sometimes we get very fancy phrases which our political headmasters say here and there because this is a catchy word where they can look good and look successful. Then we have to fill it with substance. It happens very often. For example, this emphasis on disrupting smuggler networks and trafficking, it came from the top, definitely, as a catchphrase. Then we had to substantiate it with concrete action. There were even some proposals to go as far as developing a rationale/argument for declaring smuggling and trafficking, I think, as crimes against humanity. After substantive analysis by lawyers, by diplomats at expert level, it became evident that this is a no go. We had to think of other specific actions in order to justify this narrative about disrupting smuggler networks. . . . (Interview of EU official, October 2017)

An increased emphasis on external solutions and on combatting smuggling has also been accompanied with opposition to regularization programs by European governments (Kraler 2018). Previously, control measures of control were accompanied by regularizations or amnesties for irregular migrants, especially in the south of Europe (Greece, Italy, Spain). In the post-2015 environment, and as a result of politicization, regularizations have become much less of a viable policy option. The COVID-19 pandemic did prompt initiatives to regularize. In Italy a program for agricultural workers and domestic workers was introduced, although bureaucratic difficulties meant that only around 1,400 of the more than 200,000 applicants had actually received a residence permit by the end of 2020 (Buccini 2021).

Generally, however, there has been an increased policy emphasis on the return of irregular migrants, although the practice is more difficult. This has also driven the attempts to revise the 2008 Return Directive in order to increase return rates. This does not mean that there is a coherent hard-line approach. Tough talk and focus on irregular boat arrivals from African countries and the Middle East coexist with much laxer approaches to irregular migrants from non-EU countries in Europe (Ambrosini 2018 , 15). The largest group of irregular migrants in the EU is in fact Ukrainians, a fact largely absent from public debate (Frontex 2019).

While the EU and national governments stress that they are stepping up their efforts to deport people, there are various factors that limit these efforts and result in a continuous presence of irregular migrants in EU member states. There is indeed a significant gap between return decisions and the number of actual returns. In 2019 EU member states returned 142,300 people to non-EU countries, while having issued a significantly higher number of return orders (491,200) (Eurostat 2020). This gap is rooted in several factors, including the high costs of deportations and the necessity to comply with human rights provisions. A lack of papers can also limit the possibility to return irregulars—for example, officials may not be able to determine where an irregular migrant comes from. The absence of readmission agreements with non-EU countries to readmit their own nationals and other persons found irregularly present in the EU is another factor, since non-EU countries have often little incentive to co-operate. By 2021, the EU had readmission agreements with eighteen states (see CEC 2021); in other cases negotiations have been ongoing for a considerable time or have stalled (see Geddes et al. 2020). Notwithstanding these barriers in reaching agreements, the numerous internal constraints within EU member states on their ability to control irregular migration has put a stronger emphasis on cooperation with non-EU states of transit and origin.

In sum, the major focus by the EU has been on stemming irregular flows through border control measures and preventing them as early as possible through cooperation with third countries. We can also see an ongoing divergence between tough talk and continued migration, despite a tendency toward more policy restriction because of immigration's politicization.

Asylum: The Failure of Top-Down Convergence

In 2015, 1,255,600 first-time asylum seekers applied for international protection in an EU member state, more than double the 2014 numbers (Eurostat 2016). This led to a de facto breakdown of the EU asylum framework. As already noted, a major problem is that asylum applications are very unevenly distributed across Europe. This became very apparent during the migration crisis, in which a small group of member states—either because of their geographic location at the EU's external borders, or because of existing migrant networks and economic attractiveness—were bearing the largest share of the responsibility of dealing with asylum seekers. Compared with their population, Hungary, Sweden, Austria, Finland and Germany received the largest share of asylum applicants (Eurostat 2016).

Many observers have spoken of "fortress Europe" (e.g., FitzGerald 2019, 160) when it comes to asylum seekers. Given that CEAS development was driven by the desire to clamp down on what were perceived as non-genuine refugees, a restrictive policy approach could be expected. In reality, the picture is slightly more complex (Thielemann and Zaun 2017). Restrictive and liberal tendencies actually coexist. The CEAS minimum standards introduced in the early 2000s increased protection for asylum seekers in some member states, especially in newer receiving states, while maintaining standards in others (Zaun 2017). At the same time, incoherent implementation especially in those member states where the standards were raised on paper—that is, countries that previously had weak or non-existent protection systems—made the EU protection standard less strong de facto than it appeared de jure. Second, the externalization agenda described earlier and the tendency to outsource asylum and migration policies not just to non-EU member states but also to private actors such as airlines also weakened the European asylum protection standards. In sum, two competing approaches to asylum have characterized this EU policy domain: a commitment to the protection of vulnerable persons and a defense against and prevention of "unwanted" immigration.

The coexistence of competing approaches is an expression of the different institutional interests at stake in EU asylum policy, the shifting political agendas of national governments, and the varying priorities of non-state actors, such as international organizations and NGOs. In sum, it reflects the complex negotiation architecture of the EU, within which there is a multiplicity of actors, locations, and levels. This means that the outcome of policy processes can differ, depending on the institutional venue or the constellation of interests around a given issue. For this reason, we can often observe what appears to be a pendulum movement between bold, expansive pledges to develop common approaches to asylum and disappointingly slow progress in agreeing on the details of legislation. This can create the impression of EU asylum policy as inconsistent, although it could also be seen as an example of what Hall (1986) refers to as "deliberate malintegration"—the fudging of policy goals and measures so as to provide different signals to appease different set of actors and to manage conflicting and at times contradictory demands. The migration crisis put severe pressure on this "strategy." Asylum became a highly politicized issue, with expectations raised about what the EU could or should do—expectations that, as it has turned out, cannot be met precisely because of the presence of these conflicting demands. This has put the EU's credibility severely into crisis (Lavenex 2018). Moreover, the overall consensus in Europe to grant protection to those in need has come under severe pressure.

In the New Pact of 2020, the commission proposed to keep the responsibility for asylum applications with country of first entry, but it ditched the mandatory relocation of asylum seekers. Instead it has envisaged a variety of support measures, including relocation, capacity-building measures, and other forms of operational support, as well as the possibility of taking over the responsibility to return migrants (the "return sponsorships") (CEC 2020). The proposed changes are, however, consistent with the "policy core" established in the early 2000s rather than disruptive of its rationale, which implies that the harmonization and streamlining of EU asylum policies has remained incomplete. In consequence, countries aim to shift responsibility to other member states and to non-EU member states.

Across the EU we can identify basically three competing visions regarding EU asylum cooperation.

- Traditional asylum-seeker-receiving member states, such as Germany, Austria, and Sweden. These countries have tended to see EU cooperation as a way to adjust imbalances in asylum application numbers between member states. Before the 2015 crisis (which led to the reevaluation of Dublin mentioned earlier), these countries had been keen to maintain the Dublin regulation in order to reduce their own share of applicants. Post-crisis, their objective was to reduce their own, relatively high numbers of asylum applications. During the refugee and migration crisis, these countries preferred EU-level solidarity and burden-sharing, including the introduction of refugee quotas. Given the ongoing policy gridlock, the positions of some of these countries shifted to some extent. Powerful EU states such as Germany, for instance, became more open to the idea of more "flexible" modes of responsibility-sharing (Sundberg Diez, 2020). This shift has also manifested itself in the New Pact, which represents a concession to EU member states that have continuously opposed mandatory relocation (discussed later).

- Member states at the Mediterranean border, such as Greece, Italy, and Spain, which before the crisis had already been challenged by the Dublin regulation. They had little inclination to chip in further. While they seek greater solidarity (via relocation of asylum seekers) to deal with their own high numbers of arrivals (a consequence of their location at the EU's external borders), they also see divergent asylum standards and procedures among member states as beneficial since it would stimulate onward "secondary" movement to other EU countries with better standards.

- The group of EU member states that strongly oppose solidarity measures. Prominent among these have been the Visegrád countries (Czech Republic, Hungary, Poland, and Slovakia). Given the flows of asylum applicants it received after 2015, the most restrictive actor among this group, Hungary would actually have benefited from burden-sharing measures, but such measures clashed with Viktor Orbán's Euroskeptic views, hostility to immigration, and resistance to EU cooperation. In April 2020, the Court of Justice ruled that the Czech Republic, Poland, and Hungary had failed to implement their treaty obligations in refusing to accept any relocated asylum applicants, but even after this negative decision, the Hungarian interior minister, Judit Varga, was able to tweet that the "EU compulsory relocation system of migrants is dead and today's CJEU judgement won't change that. It must be lonesome in the saddle since the horse died" (Zalan 2020).

The Problem of Top-Down Convergence.   Rather than just being political episodes, these conflicts are based on systemic shortcomings of the CEAS. EU integration from the late 1990s onward has been mainly driven by traditional asylum-seeker-receiving countries in western and northern Europe. These countries, with a strong regulatory expertise in the domain of asylum, effectively "uploaded" their domestic protection standards to the EU level (Zaun 2017). Southern European countries such as Italy and Greece, on the other hand, only established asylum systems beginning in the 1990s, as a result of the development of EU measures. Lacking experience with asylum, these countries were not active players in the CEAS negotiations. Instead, they "downloaded" a system devised by member states in western and northern Europe. This downloading was, however, often nothing more than a tick-box exercise and lacked full implementation given that these states lacked capacity for doing so (Zaun 2017, 16). In other words, while a group of stronger regulators was able to create a dense EU regulatory system, the group of weaker regulators was unable to build up the necessary structures to implement this system (Ripoll Servent 2018, 84). Yet, by establishing common regulations, the de facto responsibility for asylum in these countries with weaker capacities actually increased.

These divergent political and administrative approaches and capacities toward refugee protection are mirrored in the significantly varying amount of annual decisions on asylum applications taken and the differing refugee recognition rates across Europe. From the perspective of an asylum seeker, the asylum process thus can resemble a lottery. These are all issues that point toward the incomplete harmonization of EU asylum policy, and which contributed the breakdown of the system during the 2015 crisis, when asylum flows increased significantly.

Increasing Restriction Post-Crisis and a Continuous Gap.   EU member states have used tough talk when stating that that those who are not in need of protection will be returned swiftly, but in practice, rejected asylum seekers often cannot be returned to their countries of origin. There are various practical impediments to returning failed asylum seekers, as discussed previously. This has meant that increased emphasis has been put on efforts to prevent asylum seekers from moving to Europe in the first place. As the issue has become more politicized, the aspirations to outsource protection and even to question the fundamentals of the protection system itself have become more prevalent. This has become especially apparent in countries such as Hungary, led by hard-liner Viktor Orbán, but there has been a more general trend across the EU to tighten asylum legislation in the wake of the crisis in order to decrease the attractiveness of their countries to asylum applicants. In a July 2018 "vision paper" the Austrian and Danish interior ministries argued for a wholly different EU approach to asylum that advocates protection outside the EU in areas close to origin countries of displaced people. In effect, the vision paper proposed to effectively abolish or at least massively reduce the scope for asylum to be secured in Europe (Federal Ministry of the Interior 2018).

In sum, cooperation on asylum policy is—along with irregular migration—one of the most developed areas of EU migration policy. However, the issue of asylum reveals strong power asymmetries between member states, and deep fault lines that account for the weakness of the CEAS.

Conclusion

The direction of EU migration and asylum policy was established in the early 1990s. Priorities identified then have continued to shape EU action. These priorities are informed by the idea that there are large-scale and potentially uncontrollable migration flows and that the EU needs to secure its borders. Whether accurate or not, this understanding has had—and will continue to have—powerful effects. EU actions on asylum and irregular migration have to a great extent been focused on stemming such flows. There has been significant institutional development to the extent that it now makes sense to talk of a common migration and asylum policy, but for some not all aspects of policy. Importantly, admissions and integration are—and are very likely to remain—member state competencies.

While there is little evidence of change in the underlying policy priorities established in the 1990s, there are other important changes. One is EU widening, which has brought new member states, some of which have been strongly opposed to common measures on migration and asylum. There have also been important changes in the social foundations of politics, with the emergence of a new dividing line in European politics to which attitudes toward both immigration and European integration are central.

The 2015 crisis did not change the policy core but did see a highly significant politicization of migration; importantly, this politicization was of migration as a European concern (not a series of national debates). This exposed the limits of vertical or top-down convergence because the political stakes were much higher and the basis for agreement in a wider Europe was much weaker. Most notably, the CEAS as a form of vertical convergence effectively broke down. More likely are forms of "horizontal convergence" between groups of states within the EU that share similar perspectives. These are not stable coalitions, but can provide a base for practice-based learning among the like-minded about the management and implementation of policy rather than the development of new policy directions.

There is likely to be a continued quest for new arrangements to find policy solutions, but the EU is no longer insulated in the way it used to be, as Brussels is now more deeply politicized. If new arrangements are to be found, then it seems likely that they will be sought outside the EU. Externalization has been on the EU agenda since the 1990s, and the quest for these new "external" arrangements will intensify.

Note

This chapter is based upon results of the project "Prospects for International Migration Governance," which has received funding from the European Research Council under the European Union's Seventh Framework Programme (FP7/2007–2013), ERC grant agreement no. 340430.

References

Aggestam, L., and Bicchi, F. 2019. "New Directions in EU Foreign Policy Governance: Cross-Loading, Leadership and Informal Groupings." *Journal of Common Market Studies* 57, no. 3: 515–532.

Ambrosini, M. 2018. *Irregular Immigration in Southern Europe: Actors, Dynamics and Governance.* London: Palgrave Macmillan.

Bialasiewicz, L. 2012. "Off-shoring and Out-sourcing the Borders of Europe: Libya and EU Border Work in the Mediterranean." *Geopolitics* 17, no. 4: 843–866.

Boffey, D. 2019. "African Union Seeks to Kill EU Plan to Process Migrants in Africa." *Guardian*, February 24, 2019. https://www.theguardian.com/world/2019/feb/24/african-union-seeks-to-kill-eu-plan-to-process-migrants-in-africa.

Bonjour, S., and M. Vink. 2013. "When Europeanization Backfires: The Normalization of European Migration Politics." *Acta Politica* 48, no. 4: 389–407.

Brito, R. 2021. "Frontex Accused of Violating Rights of Migrants to Seek Asylum." *Irish News*, February 16, 2021. https://www.irishnews.com/news/worldnews/2021/02/16/news/eu-agency-frontex-accused-of-violating-rights-of-migrants-to-seek-asylum-2226167/.

Buccini, G. 2021. "Sanatoria fallita, così i lavoratori stranieri restano invisibili." *Corriere della Sera*, March 19, 2021. https://www.corriere.it/cronache/21_marzo_19/sanatoria-fallita-cosi-lavoratori-stranieri-restano-invisibili-b920a7aa-88ef-11eb-9214-48facb37773c.shtml?&appunica=true.

Carling, J., and M. Hernández-Carretero. 2011. "Protecting Europe and Protecting Migrants? Strategies for Managing Unauthorised Migration from Africa." *British Journal of Politics and International Relations* 13, no. 1: 42–58.

CEC. 2016. "On Establishing a New Partnership Framework with Third Countries Under the European Agenda on Migration." No. COM(2016) 385 final. Commission of the European Communities, Brussels.

CEC. 2018a. "EU Budget: Commission Proposes Major Funding Increase for Stronger Borders and Migration." Commission of the European Communities, Brussels. June 12, 2018. http://europa.eu/rapid/press-release_IP-18-4106_en.htm.

CEC. 2018b. "EU Emergency Trust Fund for Africa." Commission of the European Communities, Brussels.

CEC. 2020. "A New Pact on Migration and Asylum." No. COM(2020) 609 final. Commission of the European Communities, Brussels. https://eur-lex.europa.eu/resource.html?uri=cellar:85ff8b4f-ff13-11ea-b44f-01aa75ed71a1.0002.02/DOC_3&format=PDF.

CEC. 2021. "State of Play of EU-Turkey Political, Economic and Trade Relations." Commission of the European Communities, Brussels.

Ceccorulli, M. 2019. "Back to Schengen: The Collective Securitization of the EU Free-Border Area." *West European Politics* 42, no. 2: 302–322.

Cerna, L. 2018. "European High-Skilled Migration Policy: Trends and Challenges." In *High-Skilled Migration: Drivers and Policies*, edited by M. Czaika, 87–107. Oxford: Oxford University Press.

Cook, L., and J. Spike. 2021. "EU's Border Agency Exits Hungary, as Bloc Warns Country to Change Migrant Policy." *Sydney Morning Herald*, January 29, 2021. https://www.smh.com.au/world/europe/eu-s-frontex-departs-hungary-as-bloc-warns-country-to-change-its-migrant-policy-20210129-p56xod.html.

Deleixhe, M and Denis Duez. 2019. "The New European Border and Coast Guard Agency: Pooling Sovereignty or Giving It Up?" *Journal of European Integration.* 41/7: 921-936.

Dennison, J., and A. Geddes. 2018. "A Rising Tide? The Salience of Immigration and the Rise of Anti-Immigration Political Parties in Western Europe." *Political Quarterly* 90, no. 1: 107–116.

EPRS, European Parliamentary Research Service. 2018. *The Work of EPRS, The First Five Years: 2014-2018.* Strasbourg: European Parliament.

Eurobarometer. 2018. "Special Eurobarometer 469: Integration of Immigrants in the European Union." https://data.europa.eu/euodp/data/dataset/S2169_88_2_469_ENG.

European Court of Auditors. 2019. "Asylum Relocation and Return of Migrants." Special Report. https://www.eca.europa.eu/Lists/ECADocuments/SR19_24/SR_Migration_management_EN.pdf.

Europol. 2019. "European Migrant Smuggling Centre." https://www.europol.europa.eu/about-europol/european-migrant-smuggling-centre-emsc.

Eurostat. 2016. "Asylum in the EU Member States: Record Number of over 1.2 Million First Time Asylum Seekers Registered in 2015." https://ec.europa.eu/eurostat/documents/2995521/7203832/3-04032016-AP-EN.pdf/790eba01-381c-4163-bcd2-a54959b99ed6.

Eurostat. 2020. "Enforcement of Immigration Legislation Statistics." https://ec.europa.eu/eurostat/statistics-explained/index.php/Enforcement_of_immigration_legislation_statistics#Non-EU_citizens_found_to_be_illegally_present.

Federal Ministry. 2018. "Vision for a Better Protection System in a Globalized World: Mending a Broken System." Austrian Interior Ministry, Vienna, and Danish Ministry of Immigration and Integration, Copenhagen.

FitzGerald, D. S. 2019. *Refugees Beyond Reach*. Oxford: Oxford University Press.

Frontex. 2019. "Risk Analysis for 2019." Frontex, Risk Analysis Unit, Warsaw. https://frontex .europa.eu/assets/Publications/Risk_Analysis/Risk_Analysis/Risk_Analysis_for_2019 .pdf.

Frowd, P. M. 2020. "Producing the 'Transit' Migration State: International Security Intervention in Niger." *Third World Quarterly* 41, no. 2: 340–358.

Geddes, A. 2019. "'Crisis,' 'Normality' and European Regional Migration Governance." In *The Dynamics of Regional Migration Governance*, edited by A. Geddes, M. V. Espinoza, and L. Brumat, pp. 73–90. Cheltenham: Edward Elgar.

Geddes, A. 2021a. "Objective and Subjective Migration Trends in Europe." *Migration Policy Practice* 11, no. 1: 29–31.

Geddes, A. 2021b. *Governing Migration Beyond the State*. Oxford: Oxford University Press.

Geddes, A., L. Hadj Abdou, and L. Brumat. 2020. *Migration and Mobility in the European Union*. London: Macmillan.

Geddes, A., and M. T. Maru. 2020. "Localizing Migration Diplomacy in Africa? Ethiopia in Its Regional and International Setting." Working paper, European University Institute. https://cadmus.eui.eu//handle/1814/68384.

Guiraudon, V. 2000. "European Integration and Migration Policy: Vertical Policy-making as Venue Shopping." *Journal of Common Market Studies* 38, no. 2: 251–271.

Guiraudon, V. 2018. "The 2015 Refugee Crisis Was Not a Turning Point: Explaining Policy Inertia in EU Border Control." *European Political Science* 17, no. 1: 151–160.

Hadj Abdou, L. 2016. "The Europeanization of Immigration Policies." In *An Anthology of Migration and Social Transformation*, edited by Anna Amelina, Kenneth Horvath, Bruno Meeus, 105–120. Heidelberg: Springer.

Hadj Abdou, L. 2019. "North America: Weak Regionalism, Strong Borders." In *The Dynamics of Regional Migration Governance*, edited by Andrew Geddes, Marcia Vera Espinoza, Leila Hadj-Abdou and Leiza Brumat, pp. 146–165. Cheltenham: Edward Elgar.

Hadj Abdou, L. 2021. "From the Migration Crisis to the New Pact on Migration and Asylum: The Status Quo Problem." BRIDGE Network Working Paper 11. Available at SSRN.

Haas, E. B. 1970. "The Study of Regional Integration: Reflections on the Joy and Anguish of Retheorizing." *International Organization* 24, no. 4: 606–646.

Hall, Peter A. 1986. *Governing the Economy: The Politics of State Intervention in Britain and France*. Oxford: Oxford University Press.

Henson, P., and N. Malhan. 1995. "Endeavours to Export a Migration Crisis: Policy Making and Europeanisation in the German Migration Dilemma." *German Politics* 4, no. 3: 128–144.

Hooghe, L., and G. Marks. 2009. "A Postfunctionalist Theory of European Integration: From Permissive Consensus to Constraining Dissensus." *British Journal of Political Science* 39, no. 1: 1–23.

Hutter, S., and H. Kriesi. 2019. *European Party Politics in Times of Crisis*. New York: Cambridge University Press.

Kingdon, J.W. 1984. *Agendas, Alternatives, and Public Policies*. Boston: Little, Brown.

Kraler, A. 2018. "Regularization of Irregular Migrants and Social Policies: Comparative Perspectives." *Journal of Immigrant and Refugee Studies* 17, no. 1: 94–113.

Lavenex, S. 2018. "Regional Migration Governance—Building Block of Global Initiatives?" *Journal of Ethnic and Migration Studies*. 45/8: 1–19.

Lindstrøm, C. 2005. "European Union Policy on Asylum and Immigration. Addressing the Root Causes of Forced Migration." *Social Policy and Administration* 39, no. 6: 587–605.

Mischke, J. 2018. "Orbán Says Hungary Considering Legal Actions Against EU." *Politico*, September 14, 2018. https://www.politico.eu/article/viktor-orban-says-hungary-considering-legal-actions-against-eu-epp-vote-european-parliament/.

Mitsilegas, V. 2019. "Extraterritorial Immigration Control, Preventive Justice and the Rule of Law in Turbulent Times: Lessons from the Anti-Smuggling Crusade." In *Constitutionalising the External Dimensions of EU Migration Policies in Times of Crisis*, edited by Sergio Carrera, Juan Santos Vara, and Tineke Strik. Cheltenham: Edward Elgar, pp. 290-308. doi: https://doi.org/10.4337/9781788972482.0002.

Mouthaan, M. 2019. "Unpacking Domestic Preferences in the Policy-'Receiving' State: The EU's Migration Cooperation with Senegal and Ghana." *Comparative Migration Studies* 7, no. 1: 35: 1-20

Niemann, A. and Speyer, J. 2018. "A Neofunctionalist Perspective on the 'European Refugee Crisis': the Case of the European Border and Coast Guard." *Journal of Common Market Studies*. 56/1: 23-43.

Oxfam. 2017. "An Emergency for Whom? The EU Emergency Trust Fund for Africa—Migratory Routes and Development Aid in Africa." Oxfam, Oxford.

Rijpma, J.J. and M. Cremona. 2007. "The Extra-Territorialisation of EU Migration Policies and the Rule of Law." *EUI LAW Working Paper* No. 2007/01: 1-29.

Ripoll Servent, A. 2018. "A New Form of Delegation in EU Asylum: Agencies as Proxies of Strong Regulators." *Journal of Common Market Studies* 56, no. 1: 83–100.

Sanchez, G. 2018. "Five Misconceptions About Migrant Smuggling." Policy brief, Migration Policy Centre. http://cadmus.eui.eu//handle/1814/54964.

Sundberg Diez, O. 2020. "Discussions on EU Migration and Asylum Policy Ahead of the New Pact." MEDAM Assessment Report. https://www.medam-migration.eu/fileadmin/Dateiverwaltung/MEDAM-Webseite/Publications/Assessment_Reports/2020_MEDAM_Assessment_Report/MEDAM_Assessment_Report_2020_Discussions.pdf.

Stierl, M. 2019. "EU Sued at International Criminal Court Over Mediterranean Migration Policy—as More Die at Sea." The Conversation. http://theconversation.com/eu-sued-at-international-criminal-court-over-mediterranean-migration-policy-as-more-die-at-sea-118223.

Thielemann, E. and N. Zaun. 2017. "Escaping Populism – Safeguarding Minority Rights: Non-majoritarian Dynamics in European Policy-making." *Journal of Common Market Studies*. 56/4:

Trauner, F., and A. Servent. 2016. "The Communitarization of the Area of Freedom, Security and Justice: Why Institutional Change Does Not Translate into Policy Change." *Journal of Common Market Studies* 54, no. 6: 1417–1432.

Wondreys, J., and C. Mudde. 2020. "Victims of the Pandemic? European Far-Right Parties and COVID-19." *Nationalities Papers*, special issue, 1–18. doi:10.1017/nps.2020.93.

Zaun, N. 2017. *EU Asylum Policies: The Power of Strong Regulating States*. New York: Palgrave Macmillan.

Zalan, E. 2020. "Court: Three Countries Broke EU Law on Migrant Relocation." *EU Observer*, April 2, 2020. https://euobserver.com/migration/147971.

COMMENTARY

The European Union: From Politics to Politicization

Virginie Guiraudon

Andrew Geddes and Leila Hadj Abdou's chapter on the European Union first deserves praise for their apt, comprehensive, and didactic description of EU prerogatives in the area of migration, asylum, and external borders and concrete realizations and the evolving historical and geographical context in which this policy domain *emerged*, became *institutionalized*, and is now *politicized*. This is no small feat. First, "EU policy" is not "US policy" or "German policy." This is a case where some competences have been transferred to supranational institutions, while others have not, a case of "incomplete integration," as is very commonly seen when studying the EU yet difficult to grasp analytically. In effect, "immigration policy" in the EU is essentially "border policy" and focused on stemming certain flows; long-term entry and stay remain a national competence. Second, they are studying a moving object, whereby rules over who decides change all the time. Over a thirty-year period, scholars have observed a quintet of northern and western European countries sign an intergovernmental treaty on border management called "Schengen." Free movement is a policy area involving all EU branches of government. The functioning of this policy is relatively arcane, almost thirty countries are involved, including non-EU countries such as Norway or Switzerland.

In brief, as the authors rightly point out, the "policy core"—or, in any case, policy goals and instruments—has been very stable even as nothing else has, since there has been new involvement of EU institutions and new member states involved in decision-making and implementation. Even in a country like France, where immigration law has been revised on average every one and a half years since the early 1980s, at least the constitution and territory of France have remained stable. And in countries such as the United States, where there was a shift in levels of governance from states to the federal level, the centralization of migration policy is a longer process (Neuman 1996).

This is what makes studying the EU as a case all the more interesting but also a challenge—one that the authors take on with analytical finesse and clarity. This commentary is thus not a rebuttal in a debate. I will instead focus on their main arguments about the modes of *policy* convergence in this domain in a context of *political* divergence and polarization. I end with a question relevant to the volume rather than the chapter: does EU policy differ from the national cases studied in this book, or are there similar patterns in policy elaboration and cross-fertilization or horizontal transfers across cases?

Common Patterns in Policy-making: Revisiting the Immigration Trilemma Between Law, Politics, and the Economy

Gary Freeman in his seminal 1995 article "Modes of Immigration Politics in Liberal Democratic States" pointed out that governments wanted to show mass publics that they were controlling immigration while in fact catering to a number of organized interest groups that benefitted from migration. In the European context, scholars such as Christian Joppke (1998) also insisted on the contrast between a restrictionist political discourse on immigration and an expansive legal reality driven in part by court cases whereby a number of unwanted migrants could in fact settle through a system of asylum claims and family reunification. In brief, there was a "gap" between politics and policy, let alone between policy outputs and actual outcomes (the combined numbers of legal or irregular foreign arrivals). That gap is not surprising if one takes into account the contradictory logics of political, legal, and economic actors.

Two decades later, it may be useful to examine the three components of what I once called a "trilemma" between politics, law, and economics (Guiraudon 2000), how EU policies fit in, and whether they converge with other contexts.

Showing Control

As discussed earlier, the need for governments to show that they in fact govern, that they are in control, is as critical as ever, whether they are from the populist right or are pitted against populist oppositions that denounce globalization (the loss of sovereignty through European integration). This is in any case the conclusion of scholars who analyze the evolution of European party systems, electoral behavior and public attitudes, and the emergence of new Rokkanian cleavages. So how do you show control? Many governments of different partisan colors reinstated internal Schengen borders in 2015. Viktor Orbán, the right-wing populist prime minister of Hungary, built a wall; Matteo Salvini, then the interior minister of Italy from the radical right, prevented rescue boats from landing in Sicily and sued NGO personnel. They did so unilaterally, without permission from Brussels or other member states. Therefore, even if border control policy has been de jure delegated to the EU and takes place de facto via EU-level instruments, national politicians want to claim credit for border control. This may lead to some kind of overbidding by EU executive agencies such as Frontex to show muscle or to international organizations such as the IOM asking for more funds, as both have done in the recent past, but clearly national dynamics remain central.

Given that the Council of Ministers, representing governments, is the key legislative body, and EU summits with heads of state and government are rare moments of media attention, the polarization of immigration has moved from the national public sphere to EU venues. Posturing by a range of populist governments in the last years has thus had some impact on EU policy-making by blocking any measure or reform that would entail some countries to accept more refugees and, conversely, has led to few debates or scrutiny on border-reinforcement agencies. Still, this just exacerbates enduring features of EU policy, with its bias against inter-state solidarity and in favor of buffering certain migration flows at the EU external borders.

Sheltering Interest Groups

The second aspect of Gary Freeman's model of "client politics" regards the influence of groups with concentrated interests in hiring immigrants. As the chapter rightly points out, EU member states have retained sovereignty over the granting of residence permits and have not been keen to cooperate with respect to legal immigration policy (as in the case of the Blue Card Directive). There is no incentive to upload the recruitment of "global talent" (or any foreign worker, for that matter) to the EU level, since you want them to come to your territory, and you are competing with other European economies. As Christian Joppke underlines in his commentary on the introduction, European states have not been as successful in soliciting highly skilled migration as older settler nations: both France and Germany failed to fill specific quotas. Still, in some key sectors where demand is not met by domestic labor, there is already a large supply market through the free movement of EU citizens—for instance, in the care and domestic work sector. Moreover, several sectors rely on "posted workers," personnel hired by EU companies. Typically, in 2020, during the

COVID-19 pandemic, when internal and external EU borders were closed, individual member states organized the travel and stay of seasonal workers, whether to pick asparagus in Germany or clementines in Corsica.

I would add that EU immigration, asylum, and border policing has in fact expanded the market for security services and benefited a number of large firms. These include multinationals like Sieens, Indra, and Thales, which provide technological solutions in the form of databases that have proliferated at the EU level (SIS, VIS, EURODAC, PNR, etc.) or hardware such as sensors, radar, and digital border surveillance equipment. We also find companies providing security guards in camps or airports, or visa services such as VFSGlobal. Consultancies such as McKinsey also regularly win contracts put out for bid by the European Commission—recently, for instance, to monitor the situation in Greek camps known as "hot spots." Migration control technologies have become a flourishing business, illustrated by the annual "industry days" organized by the EU border agency Frontex.

Shifting Back the Border to Circumvent Liberal Constraints on Migration Control

In the end, the EU "policy core" remains the same: it focuses on preventing migrants from reaching EU soil. Getting EU-wide support to cooperate with transit and origin countries has been easy in the two main legislative bodies, the Council and Parliament. Pooling resources makes sense, as interdicting migration at the source potentially benefits all member states. It is a "win-win scenario," as opposed to redistributive initiatives like the reallocation of asylum seekers throughout the EU.

As Andrew Geddes and Leila Hadj Abdou's chapter makes clear, the "external dimension" of EU border policy is an old and key feature of immigration control, "theorized" at the 1999 Tampere summit. It is the dark side of policymaking, in contrast with visible bordering and spectacular wall-building, as it is often difficult to even obtain information on the deals struck or trace the allocation of EU funds. It is also considered dark in normative terms by human rights activists, as it has involved legitimizing dictatorships such as Muammar Gaddafi's in Libya. Yet it is precisely these policies that seek to circumvent the aforementioned liberal constraints on immigration policy in Europe itself (Joppke 1998; see also Guiraudon 2000). Since the 1980s, law and order agencies in charge of migration management in northern and western Europe knew that once a migrant was on EU soil, the rule of law and access to a modicum of rights would, inter alia, make it hard to expel that person.

A key development of the so-called 2015 crisis is a joint statement negotiated by the German and Dutch heads of government with the Turkish prime minister and then accepted by other EU leaders and signed on March 22, 2016. This is level "high politics," far from the protracted decades-long negotiations between EU Commission civil servants and Moroccan officials on the readmission of third-country nationals. This diplomatic policy solution was not novel, as it consisted in convincing a transit country to stem flows and readmit foreigners, in his case Syrian nationals in Turkey, with some financial compensation (€6 billion). It was also mostly a matter of political expediency. EU governments were divided in a moment of heightened public attention, unable to agree on reforming key policy instruments (Dublin and Schengen). Turkey appeared as a deus ex machina, and the deal as a quick fix to relieve interstate tension. We should underline that EU institutions supposedly involved in policymaking regarding immigration, asylum, and border policy were bypassed. The Parliament was not even consulted, and the Court ruled that it was not competent to examine what it deemed as a "non-EU" agreement made *at the margin* of a European Council meeting.[1]

In brief, in spite of intense activity at EU level, it is an incomplete process where member states jealously guard their prerogatives (the "low politics" of labor migration) and circumvent the regular inter-institutional decision process when they deem fit (the "high politics" of diplomacy to externalize control).

Conclusion: The EU in Comparative Perspective

In conclusion, I would stress that the EU case bears many similarities with those of the traditional immigration countries discussed in this volume. As Dutch centrist politician Sophia in't Veld argued in a plenary session of the European Parliament, European politicians act horrified by the Trump administration's action at the US southern border while in fact they enact policies that are even more lethal.[2] The EU now features a number of "prison islands" (Malta, Lesbos, Lampedusa) and camps that resemble the so-called Australian model, whose offshore "processing centers" for asylum seekers, such as on Nauru, were an inspiration for a 2018 European Council proposal to create "disembarkation platforms" in Africa.[3] This is not to say that EU policy will work, and African countries condemned the proposal. As David Fitzgerald's latest book (2019) shows, there is a clear convergence across Europe, the United States, Canada, and Australia when it comes to implementing a range of deterrence methods to shut out asylum seekers.

One looming question regards the "gap" between policy goals and outcomes. If the EU focuses on buffering certain flows, is it efficient? If one looks at the number of irregular arrivals before and after the 2016 EU-Turkey deal (Frontex and IOM figures), the drop in number is spectacular. Yet irregular arrivals continue via the central Mediterranean route in 2017 and, after the Italian elections in 2018, with sea voyages from Morocco to Spain. To be more precise, since 2015, data sources point to a decrease in sea crossings and an increase in mortality: fewer people arrive, more die on the way.[4] Clearly, it is very difficult to establish a solid link between a policy measure and its effects. Still, migration scholars have pointed out that EU policies are based on erroneous paradigms. This is the case of the dominant discourse in EU circles on the migration-development nexus and the "root causes of migration" that wrongly posits that more funds for Africa will lead to less outmigration. We cannot expect policies based on the wrong diagnostic about migration dynamics to be efficacious.

Notes

1. Joined Cases C-208/17 P to C-210/17 P.

2. "Sophia in't Veld 15 Jan 2019 Plenary Speech on EU Asylum and Migration Policy," YouTube, posted by Renew Europe, January 15, 2019, https://www.youtube.com/watch?v=TQd7TGaKfDg.

3. "The European Council supports the development of the concept of regional disembarkation platforms in close cooperation with [UN refugee agency] UNHCR and IOM (the International Organisation for Migration) . . . Such platforms should provide for rapid processing to distinguish between economic migrants and those in need of international protection, and reduce the incentive to embark on perilous journeys." "European Council Conclusions, 28 June 2018," Council of the EU press release 421/18, June 29, 2018, https://www.consilium.europa.eu/en/press/press-releases/2018/06/29/20180628-euco-conclusions-final/pdf.

4. "Migrant Deaths and Disappearances," Migration Data Portal, consulted June 22, 2019, https://migrationdataportal.org/themes/migrant-deaths-and-disappearances.

References

Fitzgerald, David. 2019. *Refuge Beyond Reach: How Rich Democracies Repel Asylum Seekers.* Oxford: Oxford University Press.

Freeman, Gary. 1995. "Modes of Immigration Politics in Liberal Democratic States." *International Migration Review* 29, no. 4: 881–902.

Guiraudon, Virginie. 2000. "European Integration and Migration Policy: Vertical Policy-Making as Venue-Shopping." *Journal of Common Market Studies* 38, no. 2: 251–271.

Joppke, Christian. 1998. "Why Liberal States Accept Unwanted Immigration." *World Politics* 50, no. 2: 266–293.

Neuman, Gerald. 1996. *Strangers to the Constitution: Immigrants, Borders, and Fundamental Law.* Princeton, NJ: Princeton University Press.

Postscript

War, Displacement, and Migration in Europe

As we complete the fourth edition of *Controlling Immigration*, Russia's invasion of Ukraine unleashed the largest migration flows in Europe since 1945, so far displacing over 10 million Ukrainians, including 3.5 million who have fled to neighboring countries such as Poland. By some estimates, a prolonged conflict could result in one-fourth of the pre-war population of Ukraine (43.3 million) seeking refuge in other European countries and elsewhere, making the Russia-Ukraine war one of the largest humanitarian disasters since World War II.

The analytical framework outlined in *Controlling Immigration* can help us understand the response of the European Union, marked by the willingness of member states to share responsibility for welcoming Ukrainians. By contrast, during the 2015-16 refugee crisis that involved Syrians and others from the Middle East, member-states could not agree on a common policy and Eastern Europe member states refused to host asylum seekers. Migration policymaking is a multi-dimensional and multi-level game (see Figure 1.1). The Russia-Ukraine conflict generated refugees from another European country, raising the geopolitical stakes for Europe (EU and NATO), and prompting the EU to implement its Temporary Protection Directive, which grants Ukrainians a residence permit, and immediate access to social services and the labor market.

The EU took the lead in welcoming Ukrainian refugees, but the reception and integration of refugees occurs at the state and local levels. Looking at the policymaking diamond (Figure 1.1), which depicts tradeoffs between markets/economics, rights, culture, and security, we can see that security and foreign policy considerations are more important than the other dimensions early in a crisis. There was a notable shift in current public opinion from 2015-16, with polls showing most Europeans in favor of welcoming Ukrainians. Geographical and cultural proximity matters, and even xenophobic politicians of the radical right have been quick to point out that Ukrainians are "civilizationally" compatible with Europeans, a reference to Samuel Huntington's *Clash of Civilizations*. Moreover, a large majority of those fleeing the conflict are women and children; not young, single men traveling alone, as was the case in 2015-16. Gender and family play a role in welcoming the first waves of Ukrainian refugees, as most Ukrainian men are required to stay home to help defend the country.

The Ukrainians are displaced people and asylum seekers, not refugees, until individual adjudication under the 1951 Geneva Convention using the standard of a "well-founded fear of persecution" determines that they are refugees. Refugee status normally is not granted de jure to entire groups of people based on ethnicity or nationality; but many ethnic and national groups have received blanket protection, including Somalis and Sudanese in Kenya and Uganda, Afghans in Pakistan, Rohingya in Bangladesh, Syrians in Lebanon and Jordan, and Venezuelans in Colombia and elsewhere in South America. The justifications for granting temporary protection to such large groups are varied, but there is almost always an ethnic and geographical (neighborhood) component to such decisions. Ukrainians are seen by the EU much in the same light as refugees during the cold war (pre-1989) because they are fleeing an invasion and hence deserving of immediate protection, which prompts granting them a package of rights, including the right to settle.

Finally, it is important to note that most Ukrainians are educated, have skills, often including good knowledge of other languages, and many have deep family ties in Europe, Canada, and the United States. Their socioeconomic profile, human and social capital, increase the chances for quick integration, hence there is a market logic to welcoming them. Many Ukrainians spend only one or two nights in welcome centers and camps in bordering states before moving on to join family in Europe, Canada, and the United States, meaning they are not an immediate and obvious burden, economically or otherwise, for the societies that are hosting them.[1] The Ukrainian diaspora in Europe and North America is organized and lobbying to open "western" societies and economies to their compatriots.[2]

A policy gap could emerge if the conflict persists and makes it impossible for Ukrainians to return. One thing is clear from the research in this volume: respecting the rights of Ukrainians, affording them a chance to get on their feet, put their lives back together, and make a home in their adoptive countries—even if only temporarily—strengthens western solidarity, speeds integration, and prevents nativist and xenophobic backlashes. The movements of people, to echo the language of the United Nations global compact, must be legal and orderly, which places pressure on governments to get their migration policies correct. The EU appears to have risen to the initial challenge with Ukrainians.

The Editors, 28 March 2022

Notes

1. The one exception is Moldova, which because of proximity to the conflict—much like Lebanon in the Middle East—is a first country of refuge. The ferocity of the fighting in southern Ukraine along the Black Sea has resulted in rapid and massive displacement of the Ukrainian population in that region and many (roughly 300,000) have fled to neighboring Moldova, although Poland remains the first (and largest) country of refuge for most Ukrainians, with Germany a close second.

2. As of this writing, the one glaring exception to the blanket welcome is the United Kingdom, where the Tory government of Boris Johnson is dragging its feet in granting visas and residence permits to Ukrainian refugees because of the political overhang of Brexit and fear of the electoral consequences of another wave of East European migrants (see chapter 6, "UK Immigration and Nationality Policy: Radical and Radically Uninformed Change," in this volume). Likewise, Ukrainians desperate to flee to the United States face a complicated application process (red tape), although the Biden administration has pledged to accept up to 100,000 Ukrainian refugees. Canada, on the other hand, has put in a place a fast-track policy for welcoming Ukrainian refugees.

Index

Italic page numbers indicate material in figures and tables.

A8 (Accession 8) countries, *287,* 290
Abbott, Tony, 189, 213
absorption capacity, 417, 419, 427, 444, 604
Accession Treaty (EU), 290
adjustment-of-status immigration: France, 226, 230, 237, 238, 251; US, 74
admissionists: Scandinavia, 420; US, 15, 86–87, 92
Afghanistan: displaced population from, 5; emigration to Australia, 212; emigration to France, *232;* emigration to Germany, 318–319, 333–334, 350; emigration to Greece and Turkey, 614, 615, 623, 635; emigration to Netherlands, *364, 370;* emigration to Switzerland, 472; emigration to US, 74
AFL-CIO, 529
Africa: emigration to Australia, 200; emigration to Canada, 126, *127, 129;* emigration to EU, 53, 54, *54;* emigration to France, 224–230, *228, 232,* 235, 238, 240, 251–252, 254–255, 264, 278–279; emigration to Greece and Turkey, 607, 614, 615, 631; emigration to Italy, 515, 518, 534, 536; emigration to Netherlands, 362, 365, 395, 408; emigration to New Zealand, 191, *193, 194;* emigration to Spain, 556, 558,

560, 562, 569–570, 573–574, 582–583, 595; emigration to Switzerland, 458, 463; involuntary passage to US as enslaved persons, 110–114; migration statistics, 5; refugees in US, 72
African Americans, 96–97, 110–114, 155, 674, 677
Against the Islamicization of our Culture (Fortuyn), 377
Agier, Michel, 632
aging society. *See* birth and fertility rates
agricultural and farm workers: in Australia and New Zealand, 196; in Canada, 138; in France, 229, 272, 273, 274; in Germany, 318, 319, 324, 327, 336; in Greece and Turkey, 604, 608; in Italy, 499, 538, 544, 695; in Japan, 649, 676; in Netherlands, 357, 361; rural-urban migration in Japan, 647; in Spain, 561, 564, *565;* in Switzerland, 467; in UK, 286, 290, 303–304; in US, 17, 77–78, 81, 83–84, 86, 89, 118
AKP (Justice and Development Party; Turkey), 386n30, 626, 633
Alevis, 626
Algerian emigration to France, 223, 226, 228–229, 232, 233, 238–239

CPSIA information can be obtained
at www.ICGtesting.com
Printed in the USA
JSHW011523310722
28696JS00001B/1